Contents

Using this book

This is an in-depth study of Weimar and Nazi Germany. It contains everything you need for examination success and more. It provides all the content you would expect, as well as many features to help both independent and class-based learners. So, before you wade in, make sure you understand the purpose of each of the features.

Focus route

On every topic throughout the book, this feature guides you to produce the written material essential for understanding what you read and, later, for revising the topic (e.g. pages 33, 44). These focus routes are particularly useful for you if you are an independent learner working through this material on your own, but they can also be used for class-based learning.

Activities

The activities offer a range of exercises to enhance your understanding of what you read and to prepare you for examinations. They vary in style and purpose. There are:

- a variety of essays, both AS exam-style structured essays (e.g. pages 32, 57) and more discursive A level essays (e.g. pages 209, 368)
- source investigations (e.g. pages 84, 87)
- examination of historical interpretations which is now central to A level history (e.g. pages 122-3, 156-7)
- decision-making exercises which help you see events from the viewpoint of people at the time (e.g. pages 19, 79, 148)
- exercises to develop Key Skills such as communication (e.g. pages 277, 292), ICT (e.g. page 130), and numeracy (e.g. pages 74–5, 214-5) and much more.

These activities help you to analyse and understand what you are reading. They address the content through the key questions that the examiner will be expecting you to have investigated.

Overviews, summaries and key points

In such a large book on such a massive topic, you need to keep referring to the big picture. Each section and chapter begins with an overview and each chapter ends with a review that includes a key-points summary of the most important content of the chapter.

Learning trouble spots

Experience shows that time and again some topics cause confusion for students. This feature identifies such topics and helps students to avoid common misunderstandings (e.g. pages 27,117). In particular, this feature addresses some of the general problems encountered when studying history, such as assessing sources (e.g. page 177); analysing the provenance, tone and value of sources (e.g. page 60); handling statistics (e.g. page 72); and assessing historians' views (e.g. page 152).

Charts

The charts are our attempts to summarise important information in note or diagrammatic form (e.g. pages 71, 103). There are also several grid charts that present a lot of information in a structured way (e.g. page 297). However, everyone learns differently and the best charts are the ones you draw yourself! Drawing your own charts in your own way to summarise important content can really help understanding (e.g. page 109) as can completing assessment grids (e.g. page 122).

Glossary

We have tried to write in an accessible way but occasionally we have used advanced vocabulary. These words are often explained in brackets in the text but sometimes you may need to use a dictionary. We have also used many general historical terms as well as some that are specific to the study of Weimar and Nazi Germany. You won't find all of these in a dictionary, but they are defined in the Glossary on pages 435–8. The first time a glossary word appears in the text it is in SMALL CAPITALS like this.

You will also find in the Glossary all the acronyms (words formed from the initial letters of other words) used in the text (e.g. NSDAP, KPD, KdF, OKW, SS, ZAG).

Talking points

These are asides from the normal pattern of written exercises. They are discussion questions that invite you to be more reflective and to consider the relevance of this history to your own life. They might ask you to voice your personal judgement (e.g. pages 3, 283, 427); to make links between the past and present (e.g. pages 113, 257, 278); or to highlight aspects of the process of studying history (e.g. pages 76, 158, 331).

The Weimar Republic and the Third Reich are among the most popular A level history topics. The content is deeply relevant to the modern world. But the actual process of studying history is equally relevant to the modern world. Throughout this book you will be problem solving, working with others, and trying to improve your own performance as you engage with deep and complex historical issues. Our hope is that by using this book you will become actively involved in your study of history and that you will see history as a challenging set of skills and ideas to be mastered rather than as an inert body of factual material to be learned.

Introduction

Democracy

SOURCE 1 Friedrich Ebert addressing the first meeting of the National Assembly of the democratic Weimar Republic in February 1919

Fascism

SOURCE 2 Adolf Hitler at the Nuremberg rally of the Nazi Party in 1934

Disaster

SOURCE 3 Berlin in ruins and occupied by Soviet troops in May 1945

In 1918 the German people were shattered by unexpected defeat in the First World War. As the war ended, the German Emperor, the Kaiser, abdicated and early in 1919 Germany's politicians drew up what has often been described as the most democratic constitution in the world. Just fourteen years later that DEMOCRACY was overthrown when Adolf Hitler, the leader of the Nazis, Germany's most popular but anti-democratic party, was appointed CHANCELLOR and so became Germany's leader. He developed a TOTALITARIAN regime, suppressing all opposition, ridding Germany of all those whom he regarded as alien elements and embarking on a campaign to dominate Europe and the world. By 1945, at the end of the Second World War, Germany was devastated, invaded from west and east by Great Britain, the USA and the SOVIET Union.

This book examines these dramatic events, looking both at the years of optimism in the new democratic regime of the 1920s and at the horrors of the Third Reich in the 1930s and 1940s. Our core investigations are shown in Chart A. We will begin in Section 1 by exploring the reasons why a democratic state, known as the Weimar REPUBLIC, was created in Germany in the aftermath of the First World War and why it was able to survive a series of difficult challenges only to be replaced by the Nazi DICTATORSHIP in 1933. Section 2 of the book will investigate the nature of that dictatorship and its impact on the German people. Finally, we will look at how Hitler's foreign policies, after initial success, once again brought Germany to ruin.

■ A Key questions for Weimar and Nazi Germany

Why was a strongly democratic constitution created in Germany in 1919? (pp. 12–30)

How did the Weimar Republic survive the crises of the 1920s but collapse in the 1930s? (pp. 33–88)

Key questions for Weimar and Nazi Germany

Why did Hitler come to power in 1933? (pp. 99–160)

What impact did Nazism have on the German people? (pp. 161–369)

Why did the Nazi dictatorship's foreign policy eventually lead to ruin for Germany? (pp. 370–423)

Two views of German history

Such was the enormity of the Nazi regime and so devastating was it for those involved that it has raised much historical controversy. Some historians have questioned whether Germany was suited to democracy in the post-First World War period and have suggested that Hitler represented profound undemocratic forces in German history. An alternative view maintains that Hitler's regime should be seen as a mistake, an avoidable aberration, and that the democratic Weimar Republic could have survived. These issues have aroused considerable debate and so, to begin this study, we introduce below these two alternative views of German history.

The two views presented here in Chart B are a simplification, but each separate statement would be accepted by some historians. Many would hold a mixture of positions from within the alternatives. Overall, however, they show the different perspectives from which modern German history (and Hitler in particular) can be viewed.

■ B Two views of German history

View 1: 'Hitler, Germany's fate!'

In the eighteenth century, Prussia, the main German state, with its capital in Berlin, developed a strong army and conquered its neighbours.

In 1848 a feeble attempt was made by intellectuals to create a united Germany but it failed.

From 1864 to 1871, Prussia's Chancellor, Otto von Bismarck, used Prussian military and economic might to defeat neighbouring countries, and set up a CONSERVATIVE German Empire. This united Germany, the Second Reich, was thus created by 'blood and iron'.

The Second Reich built up its navy and army in order to dominate Europe and assert itself in the world. Aggressive ideas (MILITARISM, ANTI-SEMITISM and SOCIAL DARWINISM) became widespread. Germany's attempted grab for world power caused the First World War (1914–18).

18th century	1848	1864–71	Second Reich 1871–1918	1914–18 First World War

1918

In the eighteenth and nineteenth centuries, Germans, although politically divided, developed a rich culture, with great poets and composers, such as Goethe and Beethoven.

A brave attempt by LIBERALS, in 1848, to create a united democratic Germany failed, as conservative rulers and foreign powers combined to crush the liberal revolution.

Between 1864 and 1871, Bismarck created a united German state. It had a parliament elected by universal SUFFRAGE.

From 1871 to 1918, this united conservative German state came under increasing threat from liberal and SOCIALIST movements in Germany. Governments saw making minor gains abroad as a way to divert attention from these problems. The British and French empires were jealous of and resented this upstart state, and Europe stumbled into war.

View 2: 'Hitler, Germany's misfortune!'

advanced
history
core texts

advanced
history
core texts

THE SCHOOLS HISTORY PROJECT
S·H·P
THE
SCHOOLS
HISTORY
PROJECT
OFFICIAL TEXT

WEIMAR & NAZI GERMANY

John Hite
with
Chris Hinton

Editor: Ian Dawson

FOR
RENCE ONLY

JOHN MURRAY

In the same series

The Early Tudors: England 1485–1558	Sam Ellsmore, Dave Hudson and Dave Rogerson	ISBN 0 7195 7484 6
The Reign of Elizabeth: England 1558–1603	Barbara Mervyn	ISBN 0 7195 7486 2
Britain 1790–1851	Charlotte Evers and Dave Welbourne	ISBN 0 7195 7482 X
Communist Russia under Lenin and Stalin	Terry Fiehn and Chris Corin	ISBN 0 7195 7488 9
Fascist Italy	John Hite and Chris Hinton	ISBN 0 7195 7341 6

The Schools History Project

This project was set up by the Schools Council in 1972. Its main aim was to suggest suitable objectives for history teachers, and to promote the use of appropriate materials and teaching methods for their realisation. This involved a reconsideration of the nature of history and its relevance in secondary schools, the design of a syllabus framework which shows the uses of history in the education of adolescents, and the setting up of appropriate examinations.

Since 1978 the project has been based at Trinity and All Saints' College, Leeds. It is now self-funding and with the advent of the National Curriculum it has expanded its publications to provide courses for Key Stage 3, and for a range of GCSE and A level syllabuses. The project provides INSET for all aspects of National Curriculum, GCSE and A level history.

Dedication
For our parents

© John Hite, Chris Hinton 2000

First published in 2000
by John Murray (Publishers) Ltd
50 Albemarle Street
London W1X 4BD

Reprinted 2000 (twice)

Layouts by Stephen Rowling/unQualified Design
Artwork by Oxford Illustrators Ltd
Typeset in 10/12pt Walbaum by Wearset, Boldon, Tyne & Wear
Printed and bound by Butler and Tanner, Frome and London

A catalogue entry for this title is available from the British Library

ISBN 0 7195 7343 2

SOURCE 4 A. J. P. Taylor, *The Course of German History*, 1951 (new ed.), p. 7

It was no more a mistake for the German people to end up with Hitler than it is an accident when a river flows into the sea.

SOURCE 5 K. Epstein in *Hitler and Nazi Germany*, ed. R. Holt, 1965, p. 41

A profound and balanced history of Nazi Germany remains to be written … It must seek to understand Nazism in the general context of totalitarianism. It must seek to ascertain [find out] the specific pattern of causation, including national character and historic legacies, but also the concrete circumstances, national and international, which led to the Nazi triumph in 1933 … It should comprehend not only Nazi criminals and accomplices, but also heroic resistance.

ACTIVITY

1 Read the two views in Chart B. What differences are there between them in the following areas:
   a) the possibilities of Liberals unifying Germany in 1848
   b) the reasons for the First World War
   c) the reasons why the Weimar Republic failed
   d) how Hitler came to power
   e) the efficiency of the Nazi regime
   f) the reasons for the Second World War
   g) the nature of the post-war German state?
2 Which view of German history do you think A. J. P. Taylor (Source 4) held?
3 Taylor's book was commissioned by the British government to issue to troops occupying Germany after 1945 to help them understand German history. However, the government eventually decided not to issue it. Can you suggest why?
4 How does Epstein's view of German history (Source 5) differ from Taylor's?

TALKING POINTS

1 Try to describe a period of British history in two contrasting ways. What reasons are there why historians interpret the past in different ways?
2 Is it either possible or desirable to say that a country has national characteristics? How important do you think 'national traditions' are in explaining a country's development?

In 1919, revolutionaries created the Weimar Republic. This democratic regime went totally against Germany's militaristic traditions. It failed to gain support and collapsed in 1933.

The German people voted the anti-semitic Hitler into power. He established a totalitarian, typically efficient German state, and embarked on his plan to annihilate the Jews. He prepared for world war which he launched in 1939. An unnatural alliance of the Soviet Union and the democratic USA eventually forced Germany's defeat.

Germany was divided by the victors to prevent its resurgence. Massive American economic help allowed a parliamentary system to become established in West Germany. East Germany submitted to an AUTHORITARIAN COMMUNIST regime. Despite a massive DENAZIFICATION programme, neo-nazism lurked beneath the surface of post-war Germany. Germans expressed their power in legitimate ways by dominating international football and athletics, hogging deckchairs around hotel swimming pools and by developing their economy. The collapse of communism led to a united Germany, and renewed fears of German domination of Europe. Other states responded by creating a strong European community.

Weimar Republic	Third Reich	East Germany – communist / West Germany – liberal	Liberal united Germany
	1933	1945	1990

In 1918 a popular revolution led to the triumph of democratic forces with the creation of the Weimar Republic, the most democratic regime in the world. It lasted for fourteen years despite major blows. The vindictive Treaty of Versailles and the Great Depression in 1929 caused major problems. In a desperate gamble, the conservative German ELITE appointed the Austrian-born, anti-communist Hitler as ruler to try to save their position. Germany joined the growing number of dictatorial states in Europe.

Hitler skilfully exploited NATIONALIST resentment and conservative fears to establish an impressive-looking regime, which in fact masked a chaos of different interests. Internal problems encouraged Hitler to look abroad for success. The feebleness of the Western democracies encouraged Hitler to revise the unfair Versailles Peace Settlement, but misunderstandings meant his attack on Poland led to war. Europe stumbled into another major world war. The so-called 'Thousand Year Reich' collapsed after just twelve years in power.

The developing COLD WAR meant that the temporary division of Germany between the Allies became solidified. The new FEDERAL Republic developed into a stable, prosperous parliamentary regime. The failings of the imposed communist system in East Germany and the success of West Germany, led to Germany becoming peacefully unified in 1990 after a popular revolution in 1989. Isolated neo-nazi violence provoked general revulsion. The new united German state contributed to creating a more unified Europe to avoid tensions leading to war.

■ **Learning trouble spot**

The German Reich

The Third Reich, the official title the Nazis gave to their regime between 1933 and 1945, is a well-known phrase. You could probably guess, if you did not know already, that Reich means empire. However, why was this the Third Reich?

The First Reich was the Holy Roman Empire whose ruler had usually been a German prince. It lasted from the Middle Ages until 1806 when it was abolished by Napoleon. The Second Reich was proclaimed in 1871 when Prussia united the German states into the German Empire after war with France. This Second Reich lasted until the Kaiser's abdication in 1918. The leaders of both the Second and Third Reichs believed the title to be an important link to Germany's imperial heritage.

■ **Learning trouble spot**

Prussia and Germany

There was no single country called Germany until 1871. Until then, there had been a large number of small, independent states, loosely allied in the German Confederation. The most powerful state was Prussia: you can see Prussia's location on the map on page 11. The creation of Germany was the work of Prussia's chief minister, Otto von Bismarck. The King of Prussia, Wilhelm I, became the first German Kaiser. After 1871 Prussia ceased to be an independent country and in her place Germany became one of the most powerful countries in Europe.

■ **Learning trouble spot**

The Weimar Republic

The democratic regime set up in Germany in 1919 is known by historians as the Weimar Republic, although it was not a phrase commonly used at the time. Contemporaries called the early COALITION governments the 'Weimar Coalition'. This was because the elected assembly and government met initially in the city of Weimar, partly because Berlin was wracked by unrest following the end of the war. A second reason for the choice of Weimar was that it was famous for its culture (as the home of the poets Goethe and Schiller) and so gave the impression of a fresh start for Germany after the militarism of the Second Reich and Prussia.

In September 1919 the government moved back to Berlin, which remained the centre of government throughout the period covered by this book. The term 'Weimar Republic' was only widely used after the regime collapsed in 1933.

Germany 1918–33: Why did Weimar democracy fail?

Section 1 (Chapters 1–9) enables you to understand whether the failure of the **Weimar Republic** was inevitable or whether it could have succeeded. By the end of Section 1 you will understand

- why the Weimar Republic was created and how it survived the early crises of 1919–23

- how successfully the politicians of the Republic governed Germany between 1923 and 1929 and how secure the democratic regime became

- why the Weimar Republic collapsed after 1929. Was Hitler the main cause of the collapse of democracy or were other factors more important?

The purpose of the timeline on page 6 and the Activity on page 7 is to help you develop an outline knowledge of the period covered in Section 1 before you go on to study each issue in detail. They will help you to

- identify the pattern of events
- recognise key names, incidents and issues
- think about the main questions posed in this section.

Friedrich Ebert, chosen to be the first President of the Weimar Republic in February 1919, inspecting the German army in 1922

President Hindenburg greeting Chancellor Hitler at a ceremony of remembrance in Berlin in 1934. Adolf Hitler was the last Chancellor appointed under the Weimar Republic

■ **Timeline of Weimar Germany**

BACKGROUND TO 1918

1864–71	Prussia unifies Germany by defeating Denmark, Austria and France
1871	The German Empire (Second Reich) is proclaimed
1897	Germany embarks on a WELTPOLITIK of trying to create an overseas empire
1914	The First World War breaks out
1916	Army generals dominate the government and virtually run Germany
1917	Growing discontent in Germany

CRISES 1918–23

1918	Mar	Germany defeats Russia and imposes the harsh Treaty of Brest-Litovsk
	29 Sept	German generals propose an ARMISTICE and a new civilian government
	3 Oct	A new civilian government based on support in the REICHSTAG is appointed
	31 Oct	German fleet mutinies at Kiel
	9 Nov	A republic is declared. A socialist government is set up, the first of twenty coalition governments over the next fourteen years
	10 Nov	The new democratic government makes an agreement with the authoritarian army
	11 Nov	The government signs an armistice ending the fighting
1919	Jan	A communist rising is suppressed
	Feb	The newly elected assembly meets at Weimar. Ebert is chosen as President
	June	The government is forced to accept the harsh Treaty of Versailles
	Aug	The new democratic Weimar constitution is finalised
1920	Mar	The right-wing Kapp PUTSCH tries to overthrow the government
	Mar	Workers' unrest is put down by the army
	June	Extremist parties make gains in elections
1921	Mar	Further left-wing unrest
	Apr	Allies fix level of REPARATIONS (compensation paid by Germany for war damage) at £6,600 million
1922	Apr	Germany makes the Rapallo Pact (covering economic and military aid) with the USSR
	June	Foreign Minister Rathenau is assassinated
1923	Jan	French and Belgian troops invade the Ruhr. Massive inflationary crisis
	Aug	The skilful Stresemann becomes Chancellor and Foreign Minister; adopts PRAGMATIC policies to win international support
	Nov	Hitler's Nazis try but fail to seize power in Munich

RECOVERY 1923–9

1923	Nov	New Rentenmark currency ends inflationary crisis, and economic recovery begins
1924	Feb	Hitler sentenced to five years' imprisonment in Landsberg Castle
	Apr	Dawes Plan reorganises German reparation payments to the Allies. Germany gains foreign loans
	Dec	Hitler released early from prison
1925	Feb	President Ebert dies
	Apr	General Hindenburg elected President
	Oct	Germany signs Locarno Pact with France and Belgium, willingly accepting its western borders
1925–6		Economic recovery continues
1926	Apr	Treaty of Berlin with the USSR confirms Rapallo Pact
	Sept	Germany joins the League of Nations
1927	July	Major unemployment insurance law
1928	May	Moderates do well in elections
	June	Socialist leader Müller forms a new coalition government
	Oct–Dec	Major industrial dispute in the Ruhr
1929	June	Young Plan reorganises reparation payments to the Allies

COLLAPSE 1929–33

1929	Oct	Wall Street Crash leads to mass unemployment in Germany. Stresemann dies
1930	Mar	Socialist-led coalition government falls; no later government is able to get reliable parliamentary support for its measures. Brüning becomes Chancellor, relying on the President, not the Reichstag, to support his policies
	June	Allied troops finally withdraw from Germany
	Sept	Nazis do well in elections
1931	Feb	Unemployment reaches 5 million
	July	Reparation payments are suspended
1932	Feb	Unemployment peaks at 6 million
	Apr	Hindenburg beats Hitler in presidential elections
	May	Brüning is replaced as Chancellor by Papen
	July	Reparations ended
		Nazis become the largest party in the Reichstag with 37 per cent of the vote
	Nov	In new elections, the Nazi vote falls to 33 per cent
	Dec	General Schleicher becomes Chancellor
1933	Jan	Hindenburg appoints Hitler as Chancellor

1   Using the timeline, make a list of examples of problems facing the Weimar Republic 1919–33, using these categories:
    a) political
    b) economic
    c) diplomatic.
2   Were these problems greater at some times than at others?
3   Is there any evidence of encouraging signs? When?
4   Do your answers to questions 1–3 suggest that the downfall of the Weimar Republic was inevitable or avoidable?

Why study German history 1918–45?

Three of the major reasons for studying this period of German history are:

- **that it gives you an understanding of the meaning of democracy**

- **that it gives you insight into how easily democracy can be overthrown and**

- **how catastrophic the results of totalitarianism can be.**

To begin thinking about what is involved in democracy try this Activity. Divide up into groups, and draw up your own proposals for a democratic constitution. To be democratic means to give ordinary people control over how their country is governed. Consider the following and other aspects:

a) How would you choose the following and what powers would they have:
    • Head of state
    • Government
    • Parliament?
b) What other offices of state might be elected?
c) Would you include in your constitution a statement of citizens' rights? If so, which rights?
d) Add any other ideas to make your country more democratic.

PART 1.1
Weimar Germany 1918–23: Creation and crises

Was the Weimar Republic doomed from its very beginnings?

CHAPTER OVERVIEW

Although the Weimar Republic did not collapse until 1933, this chapter begins to investigate the causes of its collapse.

One historical interpretation is that the Weimar Republic was doomed to fail from the beginning because of long-term weaknesses. These include a long-established anti-democratic tradition in Germany and the possibility that some of the politicians who created the Republic never meant it to succeed. They were powerful right-wing politicians and generals who hoped the Republic would take the blame for defeat in the First World War. You will need to decide whether you agree that these factors were so important that they undermined the new Republic from the very beginning.

The second strand of investigation in this chapter is the constitution of the new Republic. Did it create a sound structure for post-war government or was the constitution another of the long-term causes of the Republic's downfall?

Therefore, the subsections of this chapter are:

A How strong were the roots of democracy in nineteenth-century Germany? (pp. 8–11)

B The 'revolution from above': why was a democratic regime born out of Germany's defeat? (pp. 12–15)

C The revolution from below: did the 1918 German Revolution provide a strong basis for democracy? (pp. 16–24)

D Did the constitution of the Weimar Republic establish a sound structure for democracy in Germany? (pp. 25–30)

E Review: Was the Weimar Republic doomed from its very beginnings? (pp. 31–2)

A How strong were the roots of democracy in nineteenth-century Germany?

When the democratic Weimar Republic was set up in 1919 it was not created on virgin political territory. If we are to understand the challenges the Republic faced, we need to look at the political and cultural traditions of Germany. On pages 2–3 you saw how German historical traditions have been interpreted in very different ways. Were the roots of democracy in Germany strong enough to sustain the regime or did a hostile authoritarian tradition threaten Weimar from the outset?

FOCUS ROUTE

1 As you study pages 9–11, complete your own copy of the table below about two trends in German history. Note down any evidence that supports either trend. You could use these subheadings in your table:
- Political structure
- Economic and social tensions
- Nationalism and foreign policy.

Democratic aspects of nineteenth-century Germany	Authoritarian, anti-democratic tradition in nineteenth-century Germany

2 Which trend appears to be the strongest?

The political structure of the Second Reich

Germany was a young nation at the turn of the century. Less than 30 years had passed since, between 1864 and 1871, Bismarck had used the economic and military might of Prussia to reorganise the map of central Europe through a series of wars. He expelled Austria, the other main German state, from the German Confederation, and set up a North German Confederation which was dominated by Prussia. Finally, in 1871, Prussia defeated France, and brought the south German states into a united Germany. Amidst the glory of this victory, Bismarck proclaimed the Second German Reich in the Hall of Mirrors at the Palace of Versailles, just outside Paris. This Second German Empire (which was to last until 1918) was thus a product of brilliant military success. It included all the German states, except Austria, in a new federal state. It had a written constitution and an assembly, the Reichstag, elected by universal male suffrage.

■ **IA The political structure of the Second Reich 1871–1918**

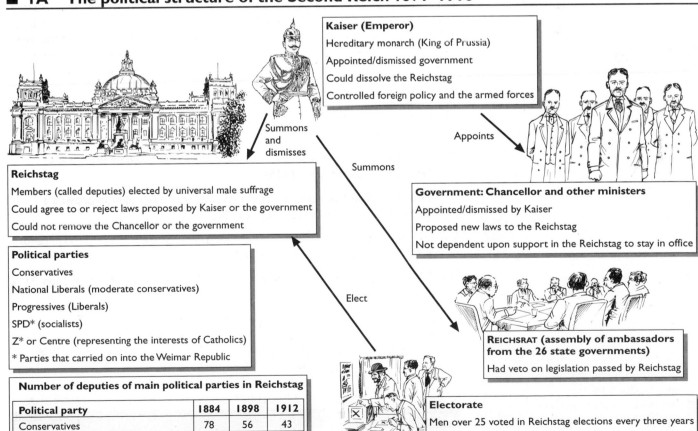

Kaiser (Emperor)
Hereditary monarch (King of Prussia)
Appointed/dismissed government
Could dissolve the Reichstag
Controlled foreign policy and the armed forces

Summons and dismisses

Summons

Appoints

Reichstag
Members (called deputies) elected by universal male suffrage
Could agree to or reject laws proposed by Kaiser or the government
Could not remove the Chancellor or the government

Government: Chancellor and other ministers
Appointed/dismissed by Kaiser
Proposed new laws to the Reichstag
Not dependent upon support in the Reichstag to stay in office

Political parties
Conservatives
National Liberals (moderate conservatives)
Progressives (Liberals)
SPD* (socialists)
Z* or Centre (representing the interests of Catholics)
* Parties that carried on into the Weimar Republic

Elect

REICHSRAT (assembly of ambassadors from the 26 state governments)
Had veto on legislation passed by Reichstag

Electorate
Men over 25 voted in Reichstag elections every three years
Also voted for local state assemblies
Written constitution but no statement of individual rights

Number of deputies of main political parties in Reichstag			
Political party	1884	1898	1912
Conservatives	78	56	43
Progressives	67	41	42
SPD	24	56	110

Otto von Bismarck, 1815–98

- The creator of a united Germany
- Became Chancellor of Prussia in 1862, then of Germany 1871–90
- A realistic conservative, he was prepared to accept some changes to strengthen the existing political system
- Led Prussia/Germany to victory in three wars 1864–71, then declared Germany a satisfied state, and worked to keep peace in Europe
- Argued that German interests lay in Europe and that overseas colonies were not important

Kaiser Wilhelm II

- Born in Berlin in 1859
- King of Prussia (HOHENZOLLERN dynasty) and Emperor of Germany, 1888–1918
- Believed in the DIVINE RIGHT OF KINGS
- An unstable, impulsive character
- Had an inferiority complex, but was determined to assert both himself and German power
- Supported a more assertive *Weltpolitik*
- Abdicated in 1918
- Died in Holland in 1941

Although the Second Reich had an elected parliament, the Reichstag, it did not have a parliamentary government (see page 27). The Reichstag did not control the government. The Chancellor and other ministers were not usually members of the Reichstag and they were appointed by the Kaiser. They could not be removed or replaced by the Reichstag. However, the government had to co-operate with the Reichstag because laws had to be agreed by it. It was really a semi-ABSOLUTIST regime, a form of modernised conservative state.

The success of the conservative Bismarck in creating a united Germany persuaded many middle-class Liberals to support the new authoritarian nation-state above their commitment to genuine parliamentary government. This was to have important effects, as it weakened potential support for full democracy in Germany.

Economic and social tensions

The newly unified Germany soon dominated central Europe. Its economy grew rapidly during the late nineteenth century, and this caused increasing social and political problems. The rapidly expanding industrial and urban working class – the PROLETARIAT – increasingly supported the Socialist Party (the SPD). SPD supporters wanted political reform to accompany Germany's economic growth. Bismarck sought to restrict SPD support by repression, then by introducing social reforms to win the working class from socialism. Both policies were unsuccessful and the SPD continued to grow. This reinforced conservative tendencies within the middle class.

The conservative elite which had created the Second Reich was hostile to reform. Real power remained with the Kaiser and Prussian landowners, the JUNKERS. The Junkers were traditionalist aristocrats, who owned large estates in East Prussia, but they also dominated the new German state by holding most of the key positions as army officers, diplomats, top civil servants and senior judges. They scorned 'politics' and resented the Reichstag, whose members voiced the views of reformers. They were also fearful of revolution led by Socialists.

Nationalism and foreign policy

Germany had a proud cultural tradition that had produced a stream of great thinkers, writers and composers. Its people were one of the most educated in Europe. However, by the 1890s some Germans were being influenced by the theory of social Darwinism. This was the application of Charles Darwin's theory of the survival of the fittest in nature to society and states. A strong state would prosper; a weak one would die! Some Germans became concerned about what they saw as the biological degeneration (decline) of the nation. This was linked to the growth of anti-semitism, both amongst the ruling elite, including Wilhelm II, and amongst the middle and lower classes. This feeling was especially strong amongst those who felt threatened by the influx from Russia of the so-called *Ost-Juden*, mainly orthodox Jews fleeing from Tsarist persecution.

German nationalism was therefore both increasing and fearful for the future. This led to nationalism sometimes taking an aggressive form, with demands for Germany to expand. The German ruling class also saw an aggressive foreign policy as a way to win over working-class support and so reduce the threat of revolution. From the 1890s, Kaiser Wilhelm II and his ministers pursued an ambitious foreign policy of developing an overseas empire. This policy was called *Weltpolitik*, world policy.

ACTIVITY

'The roots of democracy in Germany were weak.' Explain whether you think this statement is true or not.

Geography
● Germany had no clear natural boundaries
● No major mountain ranges
● Rivers (Rhine, Ruhr, Elbe, Oder) cut through German territory

Prussia
Prussia was originally a small kingdom in eastern Germany but formed the basis of the Second Reich. Containing two-thirds of the area of Germany, it was dominated by a powerful conservative Junker class, which controlled both the army and the state

Economy
● Fertile land
● Expanding population
● Extensive mineral resources, especially coal in Ruhr, Saar, Silesia; iron ore in Alsace–Lorraine, Ruhr; potash in Alsace–Lorraine
● Massive industrial development (8 per cent per annum 1890–1914) of old industries (iron, coal) and new (steel, chemicals, electrical)
● Sophisticated banking system; close links with industry
● CARTELS
● Advanced communications, especially rail

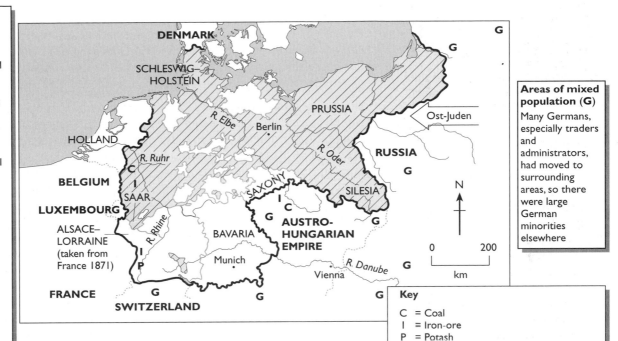

Areas of mixed population (G)
Many Germans, especially traders and administrators, had moved to surrounding areas, so there were large German minorities elsewhere

Key
C = Coal
I = Iron-ore
P = Potash
▨ = Prussia
⌐ = Border of German Empire
G = areas where German minorities existed

German culture: 'the land of poets and thinkers'
● Great composers
  – Beethoven
  – Wagner
  – Richard Strauss
● Great writers
  – Goethe
  – Heine
  – Schiller
● Great thinkers
  – Hegel
  – Marx
  – Kant
  – Nietzsche

Bavaria
The third major German state. It kept its own monarch when it joined the German Empire in 1871. It was a strongly Catholic area, and remained proud of its own identity

Austria
For hundreds of years Austria's rulers, the Habsburgs, had ruled over German-speaking Austria, and lands in Italy and central Europe. Between 1859 and 1867, Austria was expelled from Italy and Germany. In 1867 it reorganised itself into the Austro-Hungarian Empire, a separate state from the new unified Germany

Society
● Most urbanised state in Europe with 60 per cent of people living in towns
● Best elementary education system in world
● Good technical higher education
● Growing number of white-collar workers, civil servants (lower middle class)
● Declining ARTISANS; looking back to golden age
● Poor agricultural population
● Industrial workers with rising wages but poor conditions

WAS THE WEIMAR REPUBLIC DOOMED FROM ITS VERY BEGINNINGS?

Using these questions as a guideline, make notes on pages 12–15.

1 How did the German people and government react to the outbreak of war?
2 How did these reactions change during the war?
3 What were Germany's chances of victory in
   a) March 1918
   b) September 1918?
4 Why did Ludendorff propose the setting up of a new democratic government?

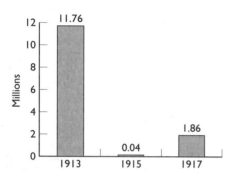

SOURCE 1.1 Working days lost through strikes

1918	The last months of the war
June	German western offensive halted
Aug	Allies advance
Sept	Germany's allies request an armistice
28 Sept	Hindenburg line (major German fortifications in Belgium) breached
29 Sept	German generals support the idea of a new civilian government to seek an armistice. Reichstag calls for a government that has its confidence
3 Oct	Prince Max of Baden becomes Chancellor with support of the Reichstag
4 Oct	German government opens negotiations with President Wilson
9 Nov	The Socialist Friedrich Ebert becomes Chancellor German Republic proclaimed Kaiser abdicates and flees to Holland

TALKING POINT

During the war, the government frequently told the people that they could 'be sure of the thanks of the Fatherland'. How might this cause problems after the war for the new Weimar Republic?

B The 'revolution from above': why was a democratic regime born out of Germany's defeat?

In July 1914 the heir to the Austro-Hungarian Empire was assassinated at Sarajevo by a Slav nationalist. This event, seemingly irrelevant to life in Germany, France, Britain and Russia, released the tensions that had already threatened on several occasions to engulf Europe in war. Within a week of the assassination the First World War had begun. This is not the place to deal with the causes or events of the war, as they are not directly relevant to the theme of this chapter. Instead, this subsection analyses how the German people's reactions to the war and the experience of unexpected defeat led to the creation of the Weimar Republic.

Reactions to war

When war was declared in 1914, the overwhelming majority of Germáns rallied to their nation. A *Burgfrieden* (peace in the fortress) was declared. Even the MARXIST SPD abandoned its INTERNATIONALISM to support the war effort. An SPD newspaper editorial proclaimed in July 1914: 'We Social Democrats in this solemn hour are at one with the whole German nation, without distinction of party or creed, in accepting the fight forced upon us by Russian barbarism, and we are ready to fight till the last drop of blood for Germany's national independence, fame and greatness.' In return, the government acknowledged that trade unions and working-class leaders had an important part to play in helping the war effort. It also promised great rewards, when the war was won, to the German people in return for their efforts.

The German High Command's military plans for a quick victory failed in 1914. Therefore, Germany had to fight a prolonged war on two fronts, a struggle for which it was economically and militarily unprepared. Worse still, the Allies maintained a naval blockade which, by 1917, was causing severe shortages of food and vital raw materials.

By 1917 the *Burgfrieden* was breaking down, as the German people became divided over the war. Many, especially Socialists, questioned why Germany was still fighting. They had initially seen the war as a defensive war, not a war of conquest. In April 1917 RADICALS, opposed to the war, broke with the SPD to form the Independent Socialist Party (USPD). In July the Reichstag voted 212 to 126 for a peace resolution: 'a peace of understanding and permanent reconciliation of peoples. Forced territorial gains and political, economic and financial oppressions are irreconcilable with such a peace.'

Others had different aims. During the war the German government had become increasingly dominated by generals. From 1916 General Ludendorff and Field Marshal Hindenburg exercised a virtual military dictatorship. They dominated not just military but political and economic decisions, and blocked several opportunities for a compromise peace. Assertive German nationalists demanded a *Siegfriede*, a peace through victory, with Germany making major land gains in the west, the east and overseas. In September 1917 the Fatherland Party was founded by Admiral Tirpitz and a right-wing journalist, Wolfgang Kapp, to rally support for an ANNEXATIONIST war. By 1918 their party had over 1 million members.

Military defeat

By the autumn of 1917, Germany faced a growing economic and military crisis. Starvation was near and military supplies were critically short. Worse still, in April 1917 the United States had entered the war against Germany and large numbers of American troops were soon expected in Europe. Then Germany was offered a lifeline when the Communists seized power in Russia and sought peace terms. In March 1918 Russia accepted the humiliating Treaty of Brest-Litovsk where Germany made major gains of territory. Germany also imposed a harsh peace on Romania in the Treaty of Bucharest.

At last, Germany was fighting on just the Western Front. General Ludendorff could have used the troops transferred from the Russian Front to buttress his defences and wait for the war-weary Allies to make peace. Instead, he gambled on

Paul von Hindenburg, 1847–1934

- Recalled from retirement at the outbreak of the First World War and became Commander-in-Chief in the east
- Won battle of Tannenberg over Russia in 1914, establishing his reputation
- Promoted to field marshal
- Put in overall command of German forces in 1916
- Helped restore morale, but unable to break trench system in the west despite ordering massive assaults
- In August 1918 he realised the war was about to be lost, and advised an armistice
- Retired again from the army after the war
- Elected President in 1925 (see page 69)

Field Marshal Hindenburg, Wilhelm II and General Ludendorff

Erich von Ludendorff, 1865–1937

- Hindenburg's subordinate commander at the battle of Tannenberg
- In 1916 promoted to Quartermaster General and in control of Germany's war policy
- Virtual military dictator; hostile to the Reichstag
- Firm supporter of unrestricted submarine warfare
- Victorious in Russia and dictated the terms of the Treaty of Brest-Litovsk
- In charge of 1918 spring offensive
- Dismissed on 26 October 1918 by the new civilian government
- Involved in Kapp Putsch (see pages 42–3)
- Involved in Hitler's Munich Putsch (see pages 53–4)
- From 1924 to 1928 sat as a Nazi Reichstag deputy
- In 1925 he was the Nazi candidate for presidency; he won 1 per cent of the vote

a new offensive, telling his soldiers that within months they would have victory. In March 1918 the German attack nearly broke through the Allied lines. Only the arrival of large numbers of American troops stopped the German advance.

By August 1918 the tide of war had clearly been reversed. The USA had poured in nearly 2 million fresh troops to reinforce the Allies. Germany's allies, Bulgaria, Turkey and Austria–Hungary, were on the verge of collapse and seeking peace. The German generals realised it was only a matter of time before Germany was defeated. Their troops began a gradual retreat towards the German frontier. At home there was growing unrest as economic crisis and war weariness sapped the commitment of many Germans to the war. Civilian and, in places, military morale was disintegrating and there was a danger of revolution.

■ 1C The effects of the First World War on Germany

Economy/finance
- Between 1913 and 1918 the mark lost 75 per cent of its value
- Industry made vast profits, which were increasingly resented by ordinary Germans
- Agricultural production fell
- December 1916 Auxiliary Labour Law gave government harsh powers over labour
- War financed by printing money and borrowing: led to inflation
- Expectations of booty from victory
- Only 16 per cent of cost of war met from taxation

The cost of war	Germany
Killed (millions)	2
Wounded (millions)	6.3
Cost (£ million)	8, 394

Living conditions
- Real earnings fell 20–30 per cent
- Meat consumption fell to 12 per cent of pre-war level
- 1917 winter called 'turnip winter' – the only food to eat
- Major food and fuel shortages
- Disease (thousands dying each day from major flu epidemic), starvation
- Deaths from starvation and hypo-thermia
  1916: 121, 000
  1918: 293, 000

Political developments during war

1914	Most Germans rallied to nation; but by 1917 unity breaking down
1916	Increasing military control of government; growing criticism of the war
1917 April	Radicals opposed to war formed the USPD (Independent Socialist Party)
July	Reichstag voted for peace
Sept	Fatherland Party founded by nationalists who wanted Germany to make a 'peace of victory' with land conquests in west, east and overseas

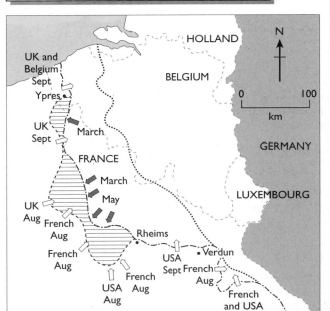

Key
- –·–·– Front line, March 1918
- ·········· Front line, Nov 1918
- ◀ German offensive
- ◁ Allied offensive
- ▤ Area captured by Germans in spring offensive 1918

Terms of the Armistice
- The new German government signed a 30-day armistice on 11 November 1918
- Key terms:
  - Alsace–Lorraine and invaded lands would be evacuated by Germany
  - West bank of Rhine to be occupied by Allies; German troops to evacuate east bank
  - Most of the German fleet, many armaments and transport equipment to be handed over
  - Germany (but not the Allies) to hand over prisoners of war
  - Treaties of Brest-Litovsk and Bucharest to be renounced
  - Allied naval blockade to remain

■ **Learning trouble spot**

'The stab in the back.' Who was responsible for Germany's defeat?

Origins

In the bitter atmosphere in Germany after the defeat, a simple explanation for it quickly spread. It was claimed that the German army had been 'stabbed in the back' by unpatriotic and weak politicians. According to this view the German army had been a formidable fighting force until the end of the war and could have won. Germany had not been defeated on the battlefield but by pacifists and Socialists who had undermined the war effort. Firstly, anti-war agitators had fomented unrest amongst civilians and weakened the morale of the troops. Then the new civilian government from October 1918 failed to support the military. Unrest had then spread throughout Germany. This culminated in the revolution of November 1918 when these same unpatriotic elements, the 'November criminals', seized power and declared a republic. The new government arranged an unnecessary armistice and then accepted the humiliating Versailles peace terms.

Significance

This belief that Germany's brave, undefeated army had been 'stabbed in the back' by unpatriotic Socialists was quickly used to criticise the democratic Weimar Republic. Weimar became associated with Germany's apparently undeserved defeat and the humiliation of the peace treaty. This association weakened the prospects for Weimar democracy.

The evidence suggests that the idea of a 'stab in the back' was a very distorted view of the reasons for Germany's defeat. However, it was widely believed and reinforced the hostility of many Germans to the new Weimar Republic. In explaining the history of the Weimar Republic the real reasons why Germany lost the war are less important than what many people believed were the reasons. History is made by people who act partly in response to their beliefs. Even if later historians show those beliefs to have been unjustified, it is still those beliefs that help explain events.

The creation of a democracy

As Germany faced the threat of invasion and defeat in September 1918 the supreme commander, General Ludendorff, made an extraordinary decision. He persuaded the Kaiser to transform the Second Reich into a virtual parliamentary democracy by handing over power to a civilian government that had the support of the Reichstag. He also urged an immediate armistice. Ludendorff had two motives. Firstly, he hoped this new civilian government would be able to get better peace terms from the Allies. Secondly, he cynically hoped the new civilian government would be blamed for Germany's defeat because it would have to end the war. This in turn would mask the responsibility of the generals for Germany's defeat, preserve their reputations and so help them maintain their positions in the post-war world. As he said to his military staff: 'I have advised His Majesty to bring those groups into government whom we have in the main to thank for the fact that we have reached this mess. We will now therefore see these gentlemen move into the ministries. Let them now conclude the peace that has to be negotiated. Let them eat the broth they have prepared for us.'

Ludendorff's manoeuvre, the development of the myth of the 'stab in the back' and the shock of defeat created the background to the birth of democracy in Germany. It was not a promising beginning.

FOCUS ROUTE

In the 1920s, right-wing critics of the Weimar Republic made great play of what they called 'the stab in the back' to explain Germany's military defeat. Explain

a) the origins of the myth of 'the stab in the back'
b) its validity
c) its significance.

Was the story of the 'stab in the back' valid?

ACTIVITY

1 Referring to events on the eastern and western fronts in spring 1918, and the position of German troops at the time of the Armistice (see map in Chart 1C), explain why Germany's surrender came as a surprise to many Germans in November 1918.
2 Study Sources 1.2–9 to assess the validity of the 'stab in the back' theory.
   a) Whom do Ludendorff and Hindenburg (Sources 1.2 and 1.3) blame for Germany's defeat?
   b) What do Sources 1.3 and 1.4 suggest about why the idea of the 'stab in the back' became so widely held?
   c) What evidence do Sources 1.5–8 provide of Germany's military position in autumn 1918?
   d) Do Ludendorff's views on the state of the German army (Sources 1.2 and 1.5) seem consistent? What explanation for this could be given?
   e) How do Ebert and Scheidemann (Sources 1.8 and 1.9) explain how Germany lost the war?
   f) How valuable are these sources for explaining why Germany lost the war?

SOURCE 1.2 The historian J. Wheeler-Bennett, *Hindenburg, 'The Wooden Titan'*, 1936, p.238

[Ludendorff was complaining that] the High Command had always suffered from lack of support from the civilian Government and [that] the Revolution had betrayed the army ... General Malcolm asked him: 'Do you mean, General, that you were stabbed in the back?' Ludendorff's eyes lit up and he leapt upon the phrase like a dog on a bone. 'Stabbed in the back?' he repeated. 'Yes, that's it, exactly. We were stabbed in the back.'

SOURCE 1.3 Hindenburg's evidence in a report to a government commission investigating the defeat, November 1919. On his way to the commission he was greeted as a hero by vast crowds. He refused to reply to questions but instead read a prepared statement that included this section

Our repeated requests [to the government] for strict discipline and strict laws were never met. Thus our operations were bound to fail and the collapse had to come: the revolution was only the last straw. An English general rightly said, 'The German army was stabbed in the back.' No blame is to be attached to the sound core of the army. Its performances call like that of the officer corps for equal admiration. It is perfectly plain on whom the blame rests.

SOURCE 1.5 General Ludendorff's evidence to a post-war Reichstag committee

The war was now lost ... After the way in which our troops on the Western Front had been used up, we had to count on being beaten back again and again. Our situation could only get worse, never better.

SOURCE 1.6 Erich Ludendorff, *Ludendorff's Own Story*, 1919

Whole bodies of our men had surrendered to single soldiers or small patrols. Retreating troops, meeting a fresh division going bravely into action, shouted at them things like 'Blacklegs' and 'You're prolonging the war.' ... The officers in many places lost their influence and allowed themselves to be swept along with the rest.

SOURCE 1.4 A conservative DNVP election poster from 1924, using the story of 'the stab in the back'

SOURCE 1.7 Prince Rupprecht of Bavaria, Commander of the German army in Flanders, in a report to Chancellor Prince Max of Baden, 18 October 1918

Our troops are exhausted and their numbers have dwindled terribly ... Quantities of machine guns ... and artillery have been lost ... There is also a lack of ammunition ... The morale of the troops has suffered seriously ... They surrender in hordes whenever the enemy attacks. Whatever happens we must obtain peace, before the enemy breaks through into Germany; if he does, woe on us.

SOURCE 1.8 President Ebert's address to the Weimar CONSTITUENT Assembly, February 1919

We have lost the war. This fact is not a consequence of the revolution. Ladies and Gentlemen, it was the Imperial Government of Prince Max of Baden which made arrangements for the armistice which disarmed us. After the collapse of our allies and in view of the military and economic situation there was nothing else it could do. The revolution refused to accept the responsibility for the misery into which the German people were plunged by the mistaken policy of the old regime and the irresponsible over-confidence of the militarists [generals].

SOURCE 1.9 Philipp Scheidemann, Socialist leader and Chancellor February–July 1919, in his *Memoirs of a Social Democrat*, 1929

The guilty consciences of those laden with guilt later invented the 'stab in the back'. The collapse was not the result of revolution; it was the other way about; without the collapse, the revolution that broke out six weeks later would probably not have occurred.

C The revolution from below: did the 1918–19 German Revolution provide a strong basis for democracy?

The First World War left a dangerous legacy for the new democratic regime. It left a heavy financial burden and continuing inflation. Germany's unexpected defeat was blamed on the new regime and when it was forced to accept the harsh peace terms at Versailles the prospects for success weakened further. We now examine the limited nature of the German Revolution of 1918–19 that left so much of the traditional elite intact. How would this affect the prospects for a strong democratic government?

FOCUS ROUTE

Study pages 17–24. Then copy and complete the two tables below. Give each cause and change a mark out of 5 to show how far it applied (0 = not at all, 5 = greatly).

The causes of the German Revolution

In a political revolution, one group of people wanting change take power from the group defending the existing political system. For this to happen there must be some or all of the causes listed in the table below. Note that 1–3 are weaknesses in the status quo; 4–6 are forces likely to bring about change.

Causes	Degree present 0–5	Evidence for choice
1 Severe weaknesses in the existing governing system		
2 Collapse of law and order		
3 A major setback for the government		
4 Mass discontent		
5 Organised revolutionary groups		
6 Determined revolutionary leaders with a clear vision of change		

The effects of the German Revolution

If the revolutionaries succeed in taking power, you might expect the changes shown in the table below.

Changes to	Degree occurred 0–5	Evidence for choice
1 Government structure		
2 Administrative and judicial machinery		
3 Organisation of the army		
4 Ownership and organisation of industry and land		
5 The lives of the mass of the people		

From monarchy to democratic republic in six weeks!

In October 1918 a new government based on the Reichstag was formed. This was 'a revolution from above', as this great change was initiated by the ruling class itself. The new government under Prince Max of Baden passed some reforms, but in these turbulent days they were not sufficient. Economic discontent and war weariness caused growing popular unrest. The German people had been promised, and expected, a great victory. When it was clear that the war was lost, Germany erupted in a wave of unrest, often described as the 'German Revolution' of 1918–19, the 'revolution from below'.

Serious trouble began in late October at the naval bases of Kiel and Wilhelmshaven when sailors refused to obey an order to sail out to salvage German honour in a final battle. They stopped the fleet sailing by putting out the fires in the ships' boilers, raised the red flag and took over Kiel. News of the mutiny encouraged the creation of a series of sailors', soldiers' and workers' COUNCILS throughout Germany. These challenged the authority of *Länder* (state) governments. Desperate to prevent a full-scale revolution, Prince Max announced the Kaiser's abdication and handed over the chancellorship to the moderate socialist leader Friedrich Ebert.

Moderate and radical Socialists were competing for leadership of the revolution. To outmanoeuvre the radicals, Philipp Scheidemann, a moderate SPD leader, declared a republic to cheering crowds in Berlin. Karl Liebknecht, the leader of the communist SPARTACIST movement, declared a soviet republic from another balcony. Ebert was furious that a republic had been declared illegally but had to accept that the monarchy had collapsed. Two days later, on 11 November, the government signed an armistice.

TALKING POINT

The proximity of the beginning of the Republic and the ending of the war was unfortunate for the new Republic. Why do you think it was unfortunate?

■ 1D   Key stages in the German Revolution 1918–19

1 REVOLUTION FROM ABOVE. THE CREATION OF A PARLIAMENTARY MONARCHY		**2 REVOLUTION FROM BELOW. THE CREATION OF A PARLIAMENTARY REPUBLIC**		**3 LIMITED REVOLUTION: THE DEAL WITH THE ARMY**	
29 Sept	Generals recommend a new civilian government and an armistice.	31 Oct	Kiel sailors mutiny. Unrest spreads.	10 Nov	The new socialist government makes an agreement with General Groener to gain the support of the army.
3 Oct	A new civilian government led by Prince Max of Baden, based on Reichstag support and including Liberals and Socialists, is formed.	9 Nov	Prince Max hands over the chancellorship to Socialist leader Ebert. A republic is declared. The Kaiser abdicates and flees to Holland.		

General Groener

The German delegation arrive to sign the Armistice, 1918, in a railway carriage in the Forêt de Compiègne

Spartacist supporters defending their position from behind a barricade of newsprint

4 ARMISTICE		**5 REVOLUTION SUPPRESSED**		**6 FORMAL ESTABLISHMENT OF THE NEW REGIME**	
11 Nov	The new government signs the Armistice.	1919 Jan	A communist rising by the Spartacists is suppressed by the socialist government. (Later, in spring 1919 and spring 1920, further waves of strikes and risings are suppressed.)	1919 Feb	A new elected National Assembly meets at Weimar to draw up a new constitution. This is completed by August 1919.

■ IE Germany's left-wing parties

1. KPD/Spartacists

Aims: to sieze power and enact a soviet revolution, developing a series of local and national councils to create a communist state

- Named after the Roman rebel slave Spartacus
- Formed in 1916 from radical SPD members opposed to the war
- In early 1919 had about 5,000 members
- Led by Karl Liebknecht and Rosa Luxemburg

2. USPD (radical Socialists)

Aims: remove enemies of democracy and create conditions for a secure socialist society

- Formed in 1917 from SPD members hostile to the war
- In 1919 had about 300,000 members
- Led by Hugo Haase and Karl Kautsky

3. SPD (moderate Socialists)

Aims: establish democratic socialist system by democratic means

- Formed in 1875
- After 1890, the largest party in the Reichstag
- In 1919 had about 1 million members
- Led by Friedrich Ebert and Philipp Scheidemann
- In Nov–Dec 1918, the SPD formed a coalition government with the USPD

■ Learning trouble spot

Political terms and Weimar political parties

Here we provide a very simplified summary of the main political groups in 1918–19. As you deepen your knowledge of Weimar Germany, you will modify this simplified picture, but at the moment it will clarify some issues.

Left and right   These terms derive from the French Revolution of 1789. In the new French parliament, representatives wanting greater change with more power for ordinary people sat on seats on the left of the assembly, and those wanting little or no change, preferring greater power for the existing elite and the monarchy, sat on the right. This seating arrangement has led to conservative groups, i.e. those favouring the status quo, being called right wing and those wanting social and political change being called left wing.

Socialism and communism   Normally Communists are more radical Socialists. In Weimar Germany there were two parties that called themselves Socialists (the moderate SPD and the more radical USPD), and the more extreme Communists (KPD). All three groups based their ideas on Karl Marx.

Radical   This term can also cause confusion. It is usually used to describe people on the extreme left, i.e. those who want great changes. But technically it just means extreme, so you will encounter radical right-wing parties as well, such as the Nazis. (Calling the Nazis a right-wing party is, however, another problem. We tackle that one on page 117.)

Conservative   This name comes from to conserve, to keep things as they are. It usually means the same as right wing. Conservatives generally favour more authoritarian government, i.e. one where much power lies with one leader or a few leaders, rather than a more liberal–democratic government where more power is given to ordinary people. The actual position a conservative holds depends on the period and overall context. For example, the British Conservative Party supports democracy as this is well-established in Britain. In 1918, German conservatives hoped to maintain the Second Reich, with a strong monarchy. Conservative groups in Weimar Germany remained at best suspicious of and usually hostile to democracy.

Political Parties

	Left ⟵		⟶ Right
Parties in the Weimar Republic	Communist/socialist	Liberal/democratic	Conservative
	KPD USPD SPD	DDP	DVP DNVP
		Centre Party (Z)	
		The Centre Party was a party that had been created to protect the interests of the Catholic Church. The political views of its supporters covered a broad range, but most were supporters of the new democratic regime.	
Where their main support came from	Working class	Middle class	Upper class

On 9 November 1918 Friedrich Ebert, the former saddler and leader of the SPD, found himself at the head of the newly proclaimed republican government. The future of Germany would be determined by the decisions he and his colleagues took.

You are going to carry out a decision-making exercise to decide **what you would have done in Germany in 1918–19**. As a class, divide into three groups, then:

1 Each group should choose one of the socialist parties (KPD, USPD or SPD). Ensure you understand its political position (see Chart 1E opposite).

2 Look through Ebert's problems shown on the diagram below.

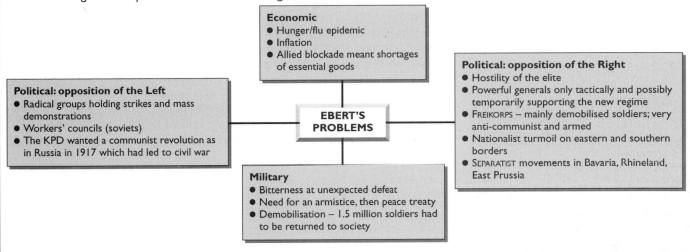

Economic
- Hunger/flu epidemic
- Inflation
- Allied blockade meant shortages of essential goods

Political: opposition of the Left
- Radical groups holding strikes and mass demonstrations
- Workers' councils (soviets)
- The KPD wanted a communist revolution as in Russia in 1917 which had led to civil war

EBERT'S PROBLEMS

Political: opposition of the Right
- Hostility of the elite
- Powerful generals only tactically and possibly temporarily supporting the new regime
- FREIKORPS – mainly demobilised soldiers; very anti-communist and armed
- Nationalist turmoil on eastern and southern borders
- SEPARATIST movements in Bavaria, Rhineland, East Prussia

Military
- Bitterness at unexpected defeat
- Need for an armistice, then peace treaty
- Demobilisation – 1.5 million soldiers had to be returned to society

3 Look through Ebert's options on the five topics below. Decide which option your party should support. In each topic, one option is moderate, one more radical and one even more extreme.

4 You should then explain your party's policies to the class.

5 As a class, decide which party's policies you feel are most likely to succeed in securing effective democracy, given the conditions in Germany.

6 Read pages 20–3. How did your decisions compare with what Ebert did?

Ebert's options

1 POLITICAL
Elections
a) Call an election for a new parliament as soon as possible
b) Take revolutionary measures (without calling elections) immediately as the people have given you power
c) Delay elections for a new parliament until major measures weakening the position of the elites are taken

Councils
a) Give workers' councils extensive powers to negotiate improved working and living conditions
b) Create a new government structure based on workers' councils
c) Allow existing workers' councils to continue only until a newly elected assembly takes over

2 INDUSTRY
a) Pass decrees nationalising major industries, and enabling workers' participation in management
b) Take over all industry and hand it over to workers' control
c) Persuade industrialists to come to agreements with responsible trade union representatives to give workers more say in their working conditions

3 THE CIVIL SERVICE AND JUDICIARY
a) Keep the existing experienced personnel in their jobs
b) Purge the administration of conservative officials
c) Create a new system of elected officials and judges

4 THE ARMY
a) Create a new workers' army, modelled on Russia's Red Army
b) Try to win the support of the existing army by maintaining its basic structure
c) Create workers' militia alongside the existing army, and remove REACTIONARY elements from the military High Command

5 WORKING-CLASS UNREST
a) Organise protests demanding a soviet-style revolution giving power to workers' councils
b) Use army and volunteers to suppress revolutionary communist elements
c) Pass radical reforms benefiting the working class to reduce potential support for a communist rising

Ebert's decisions and deals

Ebert chose the moderate course. He believed the majority of the German people wanted an end to the war and were for moderate change. Even the majority of members of the councils did not have genuine revolutionary feeling and supported the SPD line. He was determined to defend the new democratic system from what he saw as the horrors of BOLSHEVISM (communism). The new government was concerned to maintain order and organise elections for a constituent assembly which would draw up a democratic constitution. Ebert believed the new regime needed the support of the traditional elite and was prepared to co-operate with them.

He was helped in this policy by the support of many of the elite. They too were terrified of a real socialist revolution and were prepared, for the moment, to help the new government. On 10 November General Groener telephoned Ebert and made a secret deal. In return for the government promising to maintain the authority of the existing officers, the army would defend the new government. Ebert also asked the existing civil servants to stay in their positions.

■ 1F   General Groener and Chancellor Ebert make a deal, 10 November 1918

We'll support these Socialists for the moment, then try to get back to a more natural order of things.

You need our support and we need yours. We both agree we've got to crush Bolshevism. We'll help you do this, as long as you don't interfere with the army.

I agree Bolshevism is public enemy number one. We'll need your forces to keep order.

I'd better keep this deal secret. The radicals will accuse me of selling out, but it's a risk I've got to take.

Wilhelm Groener, 1876–1939

- Groener was a career soldier who co-operated with the SPD during the First World War to increase production.
- He succeeded General Ludendorff as senior Quartermaster General in October 1918, and actually advised the Kaiser to abdicate.
- Groener tried to reconcile the differences between army tradition and the new democratic constitution. He held a series of government posts, and from 1928 to 1932 was Minister of Defence.
- He initially made Kurt von Schleicher (see page 133) his protégé, but later broke with him.
- Groener became committed to the Weimar regime, and was critical of the Nazis, even banning the SA in 1932.
- His resignation in May 1932 was a particular blow to the Weimar regime. He took no further part in politics.

Friedrich Ebert, 1871–1925

- Friedrich Ebert was a saddler who rose to become one of the leaders of the SPD.
- In November 1918 he became Chancellor, and in February 1919 he was elected by the new assembly to be President of the republic.
- Ebert steered the Weimar Republic to safety, seeking the support of both workers and the elite. However, this conciliatory approach aroused the hostility of extremists of both the Left and Right.
- His humble origins and socialist beliefs meant that despite his position as President he never won the respect of large numbers of Germans.
- He died of a heart attack in 1925.

Rosa Luxemburg, 1870–1919

- Rosa Luxemburg was a German–Polish Socialist who had been imprisoned for her opposition to the First World War.
- She welcomed the 1917 Bolshevik Revolution in Russia, but criticised Lenin's repressive policies. She argued that a true communist revolution must have popular support.
- With Karl Liebknecht she founded the Spartacist League which became the German Communist Party.
- She thought Germany was not yet ready for communism in 1919, but when a workers' revolt broke out in January she felt she had to side with the workers.
- She was captured by the Freikorps, assaulted, then shot. Her body was dumped in a Berlin canal. Thus ended the brief career of a revolutionary who has won respect for her humane vision of communism, but one who was unable to channel the chaotic socialist movement of 1918–19 into an effective revolution.

FREIKORPS

The Freikorps (Free Corps) was a general name for about 200 PARAMILITARY groups, largely recruited from demobilised soldiers and officers. They were dominated by right-wing nationalists. They saw themselves as the protectors of Germany from Bolshevism and as the kernel of a new German army.

The Freikorps helped the new government forcibly to suppress left-wing revolts even though many of them were hostile to the Weimar regime.

They were similar to the Fascist squads in Italy; many members of the Freikorps later joined Hitler's SA.

Not all decisions were so conservative. Major industrialists thought it wise to make concessions to trade union representatives to ward off workers' unrest. On 15 November industrialists, led by Hugo Stinnes, and trade unionists, led by Karl Legien, agreed to create a *Zentralarbeitsgemeinschaft* (ZAG), or 'central working association'. This established the principle of workers' committees, trade union negotiating rights with binding ARBITRATION on disputes, and an eight-hour day. This was one of the greatest achievements of the German Revolution.

A new compromise caretaker government, the Council of People's COMMISSARS, was set up with three members from both the SPD and USPD. Some of the protesters expected the new government to set up a socialist republic, but it was more moderate than its title suggested. The temporary government gained the support of representatives from the numerous councils throughout Germany. In December 1918 the National Congress of Workers' and Soldiers' Councils voted 344 to 98 to reject a government based on the councils, supporting instead Ebert's preference for electing a constituent assembly. They did, however, favour some more radical changes, for example in the nature of the army and the SOCIALISATION of some industries, than Ebert's government was prepared to endorse.

Ebert's moderate line aroused left-wing opposition. In December 1918 the USPD left the government. In January 1919 mass protests at the dismissal of a radical official turned into a largely spontaneous rising which communist members of the Spartacist League tried to take over in the hope that it would turn into a communist revolution, as in Russia. The SPD government, led by Defence Minister Gustav Noske, ordered the army to suppress the Spartacist rising. The army was supported by the Freikorps, and the Spartacist leaders, Rosa Luxemburg and Karl Liebknecht, were shot. Over a hundred workers were killed. Thus the German Revolution of 1918 ended in the suppression of radical revolutionaries.

The crucial decisions had been taken. The agreements with the army and the industrialists were vital in establishing the Republic, but these short-term measures were destined to have long-term effects on Weimar democracy, as Chart 1G shows.

■ 1G   The effects of Ebert's short-term measures

Short-term measure	Immediate effect	Long-term effect
Deal with Groener and army	Army support for government against Left	Military elite in strong position to undermine democracy later
Deal with industrialists	Workers rally to reforming new government, and do not challenge private ownership of industry	Industrialists came to resent power given to workers, and rejected the Weimar regime

Was Ebert's policy of co-operating with the elite and crushing the Communists justified?

For a long time, the period 1918–19 was not the subject of major historical debate. Most historians in the West accepted that Ebert's actions in suppressing the communist threat and making deals with the old order were vital for the creation of democracy. The Cold War atmosphere of the 1950s, with its exaggerated fear of communism, encouraged acceptance of the view of the German Communists of 1919 as dangerous and of the consequent need for repression. The possibility of other routes to democracy, besides that of Ebert's, was underplayed.

In East Germany, on the other hand, communist historians portrayed Ebert as the servant of the BOURGEOISIE, saving CAPITALISM from the revolutionary threat of the communist-inspired masses. This view was dismissed in the West as mere communist propaganda.

It was only in the 1970s, with a more fluid political and academic atmosphere after the relaxation of the Cold War, that more thorough reassessments of the various options in 1918–19 were made. The creation of councils from November 1918 has been studied more closely and seen as having greater potential. There is now a strong argument that:

- the chances of a Soviet-style communist regime were far lower than Ebert and his worried supporters believed; Ebert overestimated the threat to democracy from the Communists and underestimated the threat from the Right.
- there was, however, a broader movement, within and outside the councils, that desired more radical transformation of the Second Reich, and which might have led to a more secure democratic regime. This third way (broadly represented by the USPD), between Ebert's relative conservatism and radical Soviet-style communism, was a possible alternative route to democracy, which might have strengthened the chances for the Weimar Republic to survive.

Deutschland, haß Du ein Schwein!

SOURCE 1.10 'Germany, you have a pig of a problem.' A communist view of Ebert in *The Red Truncheon* magazine

SOURCE 1.11 Arnold Brecht, an SPD member and civil servant during the Weimar Republic

Ebert and Scheidemann ... were convinced opponents of [a communist system], in the interest of both the working classes and their own ideals of freedom, self-determination, justice and culture. By far the larger section of the working classes were behind them in this and certainly have no reason to maintain that they were betrayed by them. A moderate revolution is far more difficult to carry through than one which is radical, extremist, and determined to apply any means.

SOURCE 1.12 The historian Sir Lewis Namier assesses the Groener–Ebert telephone deal in 'The Nemesis of Power', *The Listener*, 19 November 1963, pp. 853–4

In a few sentences a pact was concluded between a defeated army and a tottering semi-revolutionary regime; and the Weimar Republic was doomed at birth ... When the troops, like victors, [returned] ... they were greeted with the words: 'I salute you, who return unvanquished from the field of battle.' So saying, [Ebert] unwittingly absolved the General Staff and INDICTED the revolution. The legend of the 'stab-in-the-back' was born.

Thus Ebert's unintentional exaggeration of the danger of a Soviet-style revolution and his overreliance on the old elite unwittingly contributed to the eventual failure of the Weimar Republic. Furthermore, the suppression of Communists by a socialist government, helped by conservatives, led to great bitterness on the extreme left. The Communist Party never forgave the SPD. The USPD itself split: some joined the Communists; some rejoined the SPD. The forces of the Left were to remain bitterly divided until they met up in Hitler's concentration camps after 1933!

ACTIVITY

1 What do you think is the message of the cartoon in Source 1.10?
2 How justified do you consider this view of Ebert?
3 In Source 1.11, why do you think Brecht considers a moderate revolution more difficult to carry through than a radical one?
4 Why does Namier in Source 1.12 consider Ebert's greeting to the soldiers unwise?

SOURCE 1.13 M. Hughes, *Nationalism and Society*, 1988, p. 184

There is still dispute among historians as to whether there was a genuine revolution in November 1918. In view of the fact that there was so little real change – the removal of the Kaiser and the other German monarchs was of symbolic rather than real significance – it is more accurate to talk of a potential revolution which ran away into the sand rather than the genuine article. The republic that eventually emerged contained at once too much and too little of the old Germany: powerful institutional centres of the old ruling class remained intact and were not subject to democratic control while many Germans saw the republic as originating in a revolution and therefore illegitimate.

SOURCE 1.14 W. Carr, *A History of Germany 1815–1985*, 1987, p. 249

The achievements of the revolution were undoubtedly limited ... The reign of parliamentary democracy began, but all this had been achieved before the November Revolution which merely confirmed a new political order brought into being by the German High Command ... The Republic was accepted by many Germans not as a superior form of government but a convenient means of filling a void left by the collapse of monarchy. It was widely – but quite erroneously – believed that the alternative to a conservative parliamentary regime was a RED dictatorship which only a tiny minority wanted. The structure of German society was hardly affected by the revolution. The spirit of Imperial Germany lived on in the unreformed civil service, the judiciary and the officer corps. Nor did the powerful industrial barons have much to fear from the revolution. If one believes, as many socialists did in 1918, that democracy is fatally weakened unless the citadels of power and privilege are stormed and subjected to the general will, then the German revolution was certainly a failure for which the three Socialist parties bear much of the responsibility.

FOCUS ROUTE

Look at your completed tables from the Focus Route on page 16. Using the knowledge you have gained and Sources 1.13 and 1.14, answer the following questions.

1 What were the major changes resulting from the German Revolution of 1918–19?
2 Which areas of German society were not changed?
3 How might the events of the German Revolution
   a) help
   b) hinder
   the development of a successful democracy?

TALKING POINT

Do you think that the events in Germany in 1918–19 should be called a revolution?

The German Revolution 1918–19: sources and soundbites

SOURCE 1.15   Chancellor Ebert addressing the leaders of the German states on 25 November 1918

The entire political leadership has been placed in the hands of the Council of People's Commissars. This . . . consists entirely of representatives of the socialist parties . . . But we had to make sure, once we had taken over political power, that the Reich machine did not break down . . . to maintain our food supplies and the economy. We worked with all our strength day and night to prevent collapse and downfall within a few days. The six of us could not do that alone; we needed the experienced co-operation of experts. Had we removed the experienced heads of the Reich Offices, had we replaced them with people who did not possess the necessary knowledge and experience, then we should have faced failure within a few days.

SOURCE 1.16   General Groener recalls his actions of 10 November 1918

In the evening I telephoned the Reich Chancellery and told Ebert that the army put itself at the disposal of the government, that in return for this the Field Marshal and the officer corps expected the support of the government in the maintenance of order and discipline in the army. The officer corps expected the government to fight against Bolshevism and was ready for the struggle. Ebert accepted my offer of an alliance. From then on we discussed the measures which were necessary every evening on a secret telephone line between the Reich Chancellery and the High Command. The alliance proved successful.

We [the High Command] hoped through our actions to gain a share of power in the new state for the army and the officer corps. If we succeeded, then we would have rescued into the new Germany the best and strongest elements of old Prussia, despite the revolution.

At first, of course, we had to make concessions, for developments in the army and in the homeland had taken such a turn as to make the vigorous issuing of commands by the High Command impossible for the time being. The task was to contain and render harmless the revolutionary movement.

■ 1H   Soundbites on the 1918 Revolution

That the German working class movement, disorientated during the war, should have taken over the old state apparatus practically unchanged was its grave historical error.

SPD member in exile 1934

What they want, it sounds laughable I know, is revolution without revolution ... the revolutionary vocabulary of Marxism is maintained with religious fervour, but its meaning has evaporated.

Clara Zetkin to SPD assembly about its leadership

Comrades! Maintain revolutionary discipline. Do not walk on the grass!

A shout during a Berlin demonstration, 1918

We have done all we can to keep the masses on the halter.

SPD leader Philipp Scheidemann

They would not even storm a railway station unless they'd first bought platform tickets.

Lenin on the German revolutionaries

When the house is burning, you may have to put out the fire with water from a cesspool, even if it stinks a bit afterwards.

Industrialist Bosch 1918

Did the constitution of the Weimar Republic establish a sound structure for democracy in Germany?

The fledgling democracy in Germany faced two immediate challenges. One was the signing of a peace treaty, which you will study in Chapter 2. The other was the writing and acceptance of a constitution. This task began in January 1919 when elections were held for the German Constituent Assembly. The elections for the assembly were held on the basis of universal male and female suffrage, and used a proportional representation system similar to the one that would be adopted in the Weimar constitution a few months later.

The moderate Socialists, the SPD, hoped to gain a majority but did not. However, three-quarters of voters chose parties committed to the new republic. The Assembly met in the city of Weimar and set about drawing up a new constitution. A committee headed by the liberal lawyer Hugo Preuss drew up a constitution which was accepted in August by 262 to 75 votes. Then they chose Ebert as President and Scheidemann as Chancellor of a coalition government. The constitution has been described, ironically, both as the most democratic in the world and as a major reason why democracy failed in Germany.

SOURCE 1.17 The Constituent Assembly election results, January 1919

Parties committed to democracy that later voted for the Weimar constitution		
	% of vote	Deputies
SPD	38	163
Z/BVP*	20	91
DDP	19	75

Parties that later voted against the constitution		
	% of vote	Deputies
DNVP	10	44
USPD	7.6	22
DVP	4.4	19

* In Bavaria, there was a separate Catholic party, the Bavarian People's Party.

Notes: The turnout was 83 per cent. The KPD boycotted the election.

ACTIVITY

1 What was encouraging for the survival of democracy in the election results of January 1919?
2 Was this surprising?
3 What do the results suggest about the strength of socialism (both moderate and revolutionary) in Germany?
4 Do they prove that Ebert's fears of radical revolution in 1918 were unjustified?

FOCUS ROUTE

1 a) Read the explanation of the Weimar system of government and the extracts from the constitution, then copy and complete the following table.

Aspects	British system	Second Reich (see pages 9–10)	Clause in Weimar constitution	Weimar
Head of state and how chosen				
Head of government				
How the head of government is chosen				
Law-making body				
How assembly chosen				
Power of assembly over government				
Written constitution				
Constitutional statement of rights				

b) What do you consider were the most significant differences between the constitutions of the Second Reich and the Weimar Republic?
2 Assess the strengths and potential weaknesses of the Weimar constitution in providing a base for democracy in Germany.

ACTIVITY

Develop a basic understanding of the Weimar constitution by answering these questions based on the extracts in Source 1.18.

1 Separate groups of students could each look at one of the four aspects listed below. For the first three, note down how they were chosen and what powers they had.
   a) The President
   b) The Chancellor
   c) The Reichstag
   d) The relationship between the national (federal) government and the local states.

2 Read Part Two of the constitution about fundamental rights. Divide into three groups.
   a) One group should try and identify rights which were probably not very controversial and which most Germans might accept.
   b) The second group should identify those rights that might particularly appeal to German workers/Socialists, and which might worry the conservative Right.
   c) The last group should identify those rights that might reassure industrialists/the Right, and might worry Socialists.

3 How might Article 48 be used to
   a) protect
   b) threaten
   parliamentary democracy?

The Weimar constitution

The Weimar constitution is very important for understanding how the new regime developed, so we have included some major extracts. These cover not just the political structure, but also considerable extracts from Part 2: Fundamental Rights and Duties of Germans, which contains over 60 articles.

SOURCE 1.18 Essential articles from the constitution of the Weimar Republic

Preamble

The German people, united in all their branches, and inspired by determination to renew and strengthen the Commonwealth in liberty and justice, to preserve peace at home and abroad, and to foster social progress, have adopted the following Constitution.

Section One. Federation and States

Art. 1. The German Federation is a republic. Political authority is derived from the people.

Art. 5. Political authority is exercised in national affairs by the national government in accordance with the constitution of the Reich, and in state affairs by the state government in accordance with state constitutions.

Art. 13. Federal law overrides state law.

Section Two. The National Assembly

Art. 22. The delegates are elected by universal, equal, direct and secret suffrage by all men and women over twenty years of age, in accordance with the principles of proportional representation.

Art. 23. The National Assembly is elected for four years.

Art. 25. The President of the Federation may dissolve the Reichstag, but only once for any one reason. The general election shall take place not less than 60 days after the dissolution.

Section Three. The National Presidency and National Cabinet

Art. 41. The National President is chosen by the whole German people.

Art. 43. The term of office of the Reich [National] President is seven years.

Art. 47. The National President has supreme command over all the armed forces of the Federation.

Art. 48. If any state does not perform the duties imposed on it by the Constitution or the national laws, the National President may hold it to the performance thereof by force of arms. If public safety and order in the Federation is materially disturbed or endangered, the National President may take the necessary measures to restore public safety and order. The Reich President is obliged to inform the Reichstag immediately of all measures taken under this article. If the Reichstag demands it, these measures are to be revoked [cancelled].

Art. 53. The National Chancellor and, on his proposals, the National Ministers are appointed and dismissed by the National President.

Art. 54. The National Chancellor and the National Ministers require for the administration of their offices the confidence of the National Assembly. Each of them must resign if the National Assembly by formal resolution withdraws its confidence.

Art. 56. The Chancellor . . . determines the main lines of policy, for which he is responsible to the Reichstag.

Art. 60. A Reichsrat is formed to give the German states representation in the law making and administration of the Reich.

Art. 73. A referendum shall take place if one-tenth of those entitled to the FRANCHISE petition for the submission of a proposed law.

Art. 76. The Constitution may be altered by legislation. But decisions of the Reichstag as to such alterations come into effect only if two-thirds of the legal total of members be present, and if at least two-thirds of those present have given their consent.

Part Two. Fundamental Rights and Duties of Germans

Art. 109. All Germans are equal before the law. Men and women have fundamentally the same rights and duties.

Art.114. Personal liberty is inviolable [cannot be taken away].

Art. 117. Every German has the right, within the limit of the general laws, to express his opinions freely, by word, printed matter or picture, or in any other manner . . . Censorship is forbidden.

Art. 124. All Germans have the right to form unions and societies.

Art. 135. All inhabitants of the Reich enjoy full religious freedom and freedom of conscience.

Art. 137. There is no state church.

Art. 142. Art, science and the teaching thereof are free.

Art. 151. The organisation of economic life must conform to the principles of justice, with the object of assuring humane conditions for all. Within these limits the economic freedom of the individual must be guaranteed.

Art. 153. The right of property is guaranteed by the Constitution.

Art. 156. The Federation may by law . . . [with compensation] . . . transfer to public ownership private business enterprises adapted to socialisation.

Art. 157. Labour is under the special protection of the Federation.

Art. 161. The Reich shall organise a comprehensive system of [social] insurance.

Art. 163. Every German has the moral obligation, his personal freedom not withstanding, to exercise his mental and physical powers in a manner required by the welfare of all.

Every German shall be given the opportunity to earn his living through productive work. If no suitable opportunity can be found, the means necessary for his livelihood will be provided. Further particulars will be given in subsequent legislation.

Art. 164. The independent, agricultural, industrial and commercial middle class shall be fostered by legislation and administration, and shall be protected against oppression and exploitation.

Art. 165. Workers and employees are called upon to co-operate, on an equal footing, with employers in the regulation of wages and of the conditions of labour, as well as in the general development of the productive forces.

TALKING POINT

'A well-balanced statement of rights and duties.' Do you agree with this comment on Part Two of the constitution?

■ Learning trouble spot

What do we mean by a parliamentary government?

The **head of state** is the formal leader of a country. Originally, most countries had a monarch as head of state; now most have an elected president. In Britain, the Queen has a ceremonial role, above party politics. Technically she appoints the Prime Minister, but this is just a formality, as the leader of the party winning a majority in Parliament becomes Prime Minister.

A **parliament** is an assembly elected by the people. This is essential for a democracy. It can have various powers, most notably the power to legislate (make laws). It is thus a legislative body. In the British form of democracy, but not in all systems, some of its members also make up the government.

The **government** is the group of people who actually run the country: that is, make decisions about foreign policy, taxation, expenditure, etc. The government is the executive power. It carries out policy. Government ministers are in charge of the various departments of state: for example, foreign affairs, finance, etc. Before many of their decisions can be enacted, a new law has to be passed by parliament. The **cabinet** consists of the most important members of the government, i.e. heads of important departments. Junior ministers are members of the government, but not the cabinet.

In Britain, the government consists of elected members of the House of Commons and members of the House of Lords. The government is formed from the party that has a majority in the House of Commons. (Our tradition of having two major parties and our first-past-the-post electoral system normally ensure one party has a clear majority of MPs.) The government has to have the support of Parliament. In Britain this is easy as the party in government has a majority of MPs in the House of Commons who will normally pass whatever the government wants. If Parliament passes a vote of no confidence in the government, it has to resign.

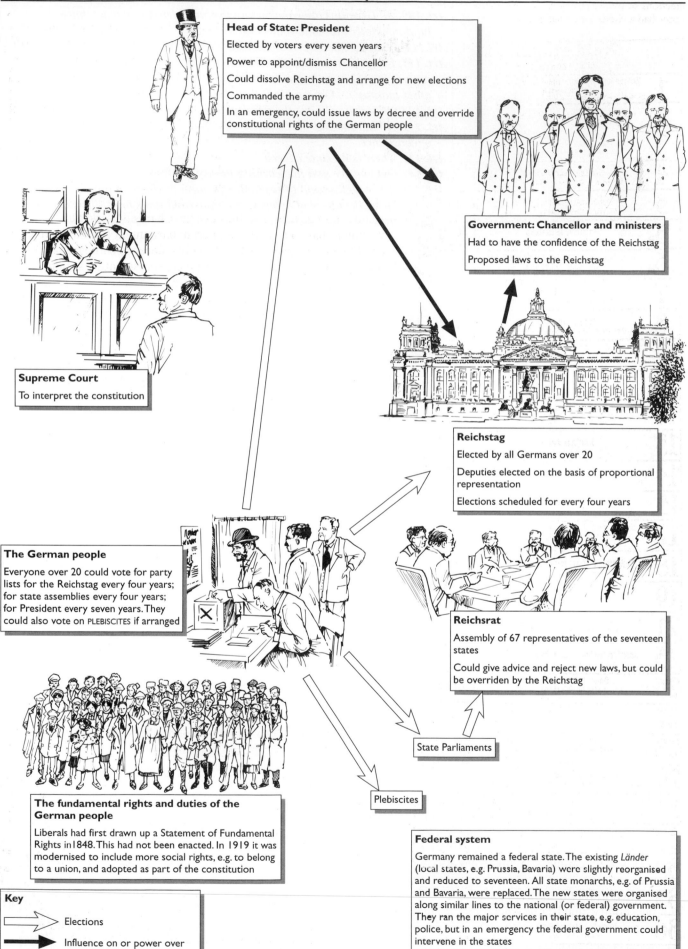

Head of State: President

Elected by voters every seven years

Power to appoint/dismiss Chancellor

Could dissolve Reichstag and arrange for new elections

Commanded the army

In an emergency, could issue laws by decree and override constitutional rights of the German people

Government: Chancellor and ministers

Had to have the confidence of the Reichstag

Proposed laws to the Reichstag

Supreme Court

To interpret the constitution

Reichstag

Elected by all Germans over 20

Deputies elected on the basis of proportional representation

Elections scheduled for every four years

The German people

Everyone over 20 could vote for party lists for the Reichstag every four years; for state assemblies every four years; for President every seven years. They could also vote on PLEBISCITES if arranged

Reichsrat

Assembly of 67 representatives of the seventeen states

Could give advice and reject new laws, but could be overriden by the Reichstag

State Parliaments

Plebiscites

The fundamental rights and duties of the German people

Liberals had first drawn up a Statement of Fundamental Rights in 1848. This had not been enacted. In 1919 it was modernised to include more social rights, e.g. to belong to a union, and adopted as part of the constitution

Federal system

Germany remained a federal state. The existing *Länder* (local states, e.g. Prussia, Bavaria) were slightly reorganised and reduced to seventeen. All state monarchs, e.g. of Prussia and Bavaria, were replaced. The new states were organised along similar lines to the national (or federal) government. They ran the major services in their state, e.g. education, police, but in an emergency the federal government could intervene in the states

Key

➡ Elections

➡ Influence on or power over

SOURCE 1.19 A ballot paper used in the 1920 elections to the Reichstag. In Schleswig-Holstein the voter had a choice of 29 party lists

How did the new voting system in Germany actually work?

Germany was divided up into 35 equal electoral districts. There were 29 million voters (just under a million in each area). Parties drew up a list of candidates, and voters voted for the party list as a whole. Voters thus chose parties not candidates. For every 60,000 votes in each district the party gained one deputy. (Party officials then chose their allocated number of deputies from their party's list of candidates.) If a party did not gain 60,000 votes in any district but won over 30,000 votes in some districts, these votes would be added up and translated into deputies. The number of deputies in the Reichstag was not fixed; it depended upon the total number of votes cast.

The new system of government (but not elections) created in the Weimar Republic was very similar to the one in the UK today. It was a parliamentary government because the Chancellor and his government had to have the support of parliament (unlike under the Second Reich, see pages 9–10). The big difference compared to the British system was that the proportional representation system, together with Germany's multi-party tradition, meant that no party ever had a majority in parliament. This was because no party ever gained a majority of votes in elections during the Weimar Republic. This meant the President, who appointed and could dismiss the Chancellor, had a vital role, since there was often no obvious Chancellor; it was a matter of who might be most able to win majority support in the Reichstag by forming a coalition government. This caused instability. There were frequent changes of Chancellor and of government, not just after elections but between elections.

SOURCE 1.20 A comparison of Weimar election results in 1919 with results from the British election of 1997, showing the different effects of proportional representation and the 'first past the post' system

Germany 1919			UK 1997			
Party (examples only)	Vote (%)	Deputies	Party	Vote (%)	MPs	% of total number of MPs
SPD	38	163	Labour	44	419	64
Centre (Z)	20	91	Conservatives	31	165	25
DNVP	10	44	Liberal Democrats*	17	46	7
Total		421	Total		659	

*The Liberal Democrat vote was actually smaller than the party's 1992 figures when with 1% more of the vote (18%) it actually gained 26 fewer MPs (20).

Verdicts on the constitution

SOURCE 1.21 From a speech by Hugo Preuss, the liberal lawyer who headed the Commission that drew up the constitution, to the Weimar Assembly, April 1919

I have often listened to the debates with real concern, glancing often rather timidly to the gentlemen of the Right, fearful lest they say to me: 'Do you hope to give a parliamentary system to a nation like this, one that resists it with every sinew in its body? Our people do not comprehend at all what such a system implies.' One finds suspicion everywhere; Germans cannot shake off their old political timidity and their deference to the authoritarian state.

SOURCE 1.22 Gustav Stresemann, DVP leader, talking to a German ambassador

The ordinary people have no affection for Ebert. The truth is, the Germans do not want a president in a top hat ... He has to wear a uniform and a fistful of medals.

SOURCE 1.23 During the debates on the constitution, a USPD deputy, Cohn, warned of possible dangers under Article 48

... if some henchman of the Hohenzollerns [the royal family], a general perhaps, were to be at the head of the Reich.

SOURCE 1.24 A. Nicholls, *Weimar and the Rise of Hitler*, 1979, p. 128

Whatever problems faced the Weimar Republic they were not attributable to the democratic nature of the Constitution, which was a brave statement of liberal and democratic principles.

SOURCE 1.25 K. Fischer, *Nazi Germany. A New History*, 1995, pp. 56–9

... The final document ... was in many ways a mirror image of the social dissonances of [lack of harmony in] German society. The Weimar Constitution was a hodge-podge of principles drawn from Socialist and liberal agendas; it represented so much confusion in regard to economic objectives and unresolved class conflicts that German democracy was stymied [impeded] from the beginning ...

[It was] one of the most democratic documents in the world. In 1919, however, it was doubtful whether such a democratic constitution could work in the hands of a people that was neither psychologically nor historically prepared for self-government.

SOURCE 1.26 D. Peukert, *The Weimar Republic*, 1991, p. 50

Despite its imperfections, the Weimar Reich constitution provided an open framework for an experiment in democracy which would have been quite capable of further refinement under more favourable circumstances. It brought different groups into the new order; enduringly so in the case of the old 'enemies of the Reich' in the Social Democratic labour movement and Catholic political groups, temporarily so in the case of sections of the middle class. It offered new CORPORATIST ways of attempting to reconcile basic social divisions, and it laid down the foundations for an expansion of the welfare state. Finally, it was signally successful, by international standards, in helping make possible the transition to a peacetime economy.

ACTIVITY

1 Read the contemporary accounts in Sources 1.21–3.
   What problems for the survival of democracy in Germany do these comments suggest?
2 Read the verdicts of historians in Sources 1.24–6.
   a) What strengths do they identify in the Weimar constitution?
   b) What weaknesses do they identify?
3 Do they think that the constitution itself was a strong basis for democracy or a recipe for chaos?

E Review: Was the Weimar Republic doomed from its very beginnings?

You have now studied how parliamentary democracy came to Germany. You have examined its difficult birth during military defeat, the nature of the revolution that created the Weimar Republic, and the new democratic constitution. You now need to decide whether the background and the events of 1918–19 doomed the new Republic to failure or whether it still had a chance of establishing democracy in Germany.

■ 1J The Weimar constitution: will it survive?

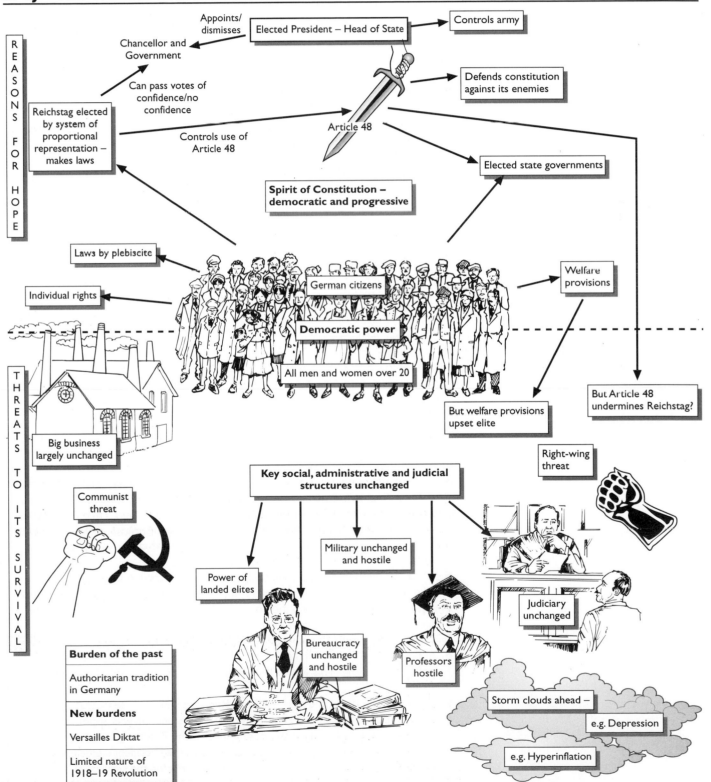

REASONS FOR HOPE

Appoints/dismisses

Elected President – Head of State

Controls army

Chancellor and Government

Defends constitution against its enemies

Can pass votes of confidence/no confidence

Article 48

Reichstag elected by system of proportional representation – makes laws

Controls use of Article 48

Spirit of Constitution – democratic and progressive

Elected state governments

Laws by plebiscite

German citizens

Welfare provisions

Individual rights

Democratic power

All men and women over 20

But Article 48 undermines Reichstag?

THREATS TO ITS SURVIVAL

Big business largely unchanged

But welfare provisions upset elite

Right-wing threat

Communist threat

Key social, administrative and judicial structures unchanged

Military unchanged and hostile

Power of landed elites

Judiciary unchanged

Bureaucracy unchanged and hostile

Professors hostile

Burden of the past

Authoritarian tradition in Germany

New burdens

Versailles Diktat

Limited nature of 1918–19 Revolution

Storm clouds ahead – e.g. Depression

e.g. Hyperinflation

ACTIVITY

1 Study Chart 1J, then list the strengths and weaknesses of the democratic system set up in Germany in 1918–19. Refer to:
   a) Germany's political tradition
   b) the nature of the 1918 Revolution
   c) the Weimar constitution
   d) the overall context of 1918–19, especially Germany's defeat in 1918.

2 Reconstruction Minister Walther Rathenau said in 1919: 'Now we have a Republic, the problem is we have no republicans.' Explain what you think he meant.

3 Debate: 'Fatally flawed'. Discuss this view of Germany's infant democratic system.

4 Structured essay.
   a) Describe how Germany changed from being a semi-absolutist monarchy in 1918 to a parliamentary republic in 1919.
   b) Explain why the prospects for the survival of the new democratic regime were not great.

ACTIVITY

Copy this table and complete columns 2 and 3 from the two lists below. This activity will help you grasp the overall theme that the way the Weimar Republic was created caused problems that reduced its chances of flourishing.

Potential problem	Details of the problem	Significance/possible effects
Legacy of the First World War		
Nature of the German Revolution		
Weimar constitution		

Details of the problems

i) Growth in government debt and inflation
ii) Voting by proportional representation
iii) SPD government's suppression of communist uprising in January 1919
iv) Germany's unexpected defeat and the myth of the 'stab in the back'
v) Article 48
vi) Inclusion of the principles of a welfare state
vii) Treaty of Versailles
viii) Ebert's deal with Groener and the 'unrevolutionary revolution', November 1918

Significance/possible effects

a) The Weimar regime printed too much money to meet its expenditure requirements, causing continued inflation; groups on fixed incomes became discontented.
b) The two main left-wing parties remained bitterly divided.
c) Weimar's 'November criminals', not the army generals, were blamed for Germany's defeat.
d) The President could bypass the Reichstag.
e) Weimar governments were associated with this national humiliation.
f) The elites might later turn against the constitution, considering it too radical.
g) Influential social groups and institutions, potentially hostile to democracy, were not removed from their positions of power.
h) This made coalition governments very likely.

KEY POINTS FROM CHAPTER 1: Was the Weimar Republic doomed from its very beginnings?

1 Until 1918 Germany had been a semi-absolutist state dominated by the Prussian AGRARIAN elite.
2 In 1918 Germany came close to military success in the First World War, but then was forced to seek peace to avoid military disaster.
3 Parliamentary government was created in October 1918 in a 'revolution from above', advocated by the generals as a device to blame others for military defeat.
4 Late in October a 'revolution from below' began when unrest spread from sailors in Kiel throughout Germany.
5 On 9 November, a Socialist-led republic was declared in Berlin.
6 The 'German Revolution' was very limited. Ebert's government made a deal with the army, and gained the co-operation of the old elites. This would be harmful for the future development of full democracy.
7 On 11 November, the new government accepted an armistice.
8 In January 1919 the socialist government used the Freikorps to crush a communist rising. This led to lasting bitterness between Socialists and Communists.
9 The constitution of the new Weimar Republic was very democratic. It established parliamentary government. The Chancellor was appointed by the President, but had to have the confidence of the Reichstag.
10 The system of proportional representation and the President's emergency powers under Article 48 were to create problems for the survival of democracy.

2

Why did the Weimar Republic survive the crises of 1919–23?

CHAPTER OVERVIEW

The Weimar Republic's infancy was just as traumatic and turbulent as its birth. Early in 1919, just as the new state was being created, it faced its first threat, the communist-inspired Spartacist rising. Then, in August 1919, even before the constitution had been formally adopted, the Republic received a hammer blow when the peace terms in the Treaty of Versailles laid full blame for the war on Germany and exacted crushing financial compensation. Within a year, in 1920, came a second attempt to overthrow the Republic, this time in the right-wing Kapp Putsch. A brief period of relative calm followed, only to be disrupted in 1923 by HYPERINFLATION that threatened economic chaos and undermined the government's reputation. Finally, in this period, came another right-wing assault, the Munich Putsch led by Adolf Hitler.

Despite these threats, the Republic survived – but why? Was its survival the result of its own strengths or because of the weaknesses of the challenges? This chapter enables you to answer these questions by looking at the following issues:

A How great a burden for the Weimar Republic was the Treaty of Versailles? (pp. 35–9)

B Did Weimar democracy face a serious challenge from the Left? (pp. 40–1)

C How strong was the challenge from the Right? 1: The Kapp Putsch and assassinations (pp. 42–4)

D Did the hyperinflation crisis of 1923 undermine Weimar democracy? (pp. 44–50)

E How strong was the challenge from the Right? 2: Hitler's Munich Putsch, 1923 (pp. 51–5)

F Review: Why did the Weimar Republic survive the crises of 1919–23? (p. 56)

FOCUS ROUTE

As you read this chapter, you will be asked to copy and complete a table like the one below. It will help you to assess the danger posed by each challenge and to decide why the Weimar Republic survived. Use the table to compile evidence of the reasons why the challenges failed. The Review at the end of the chapter (page 56) refers back to this Focus Route.

	Major challenges to Weimar democracy			
	Radical Left		Radical Right	
	The Spartacist rising 1919	Further unrest 1919–23	The Kapp Putsch 1920	The Munich Putsch 1923
Reasons for challenges				
Possible reasons for failure	Evidence			
1 Lack of support				
2 Lack of firm leadership				
3 Lack of a clear strategy				
4 Internal divisions				
5 Actions by the government				
6 Support for the government				
7 Attitude of elite/powerful people, army and police				
Degree of danger (scale 1–5, with 1 = minimal danger)				

■ 2A   Problems facing the Weimar Republic 1919–23

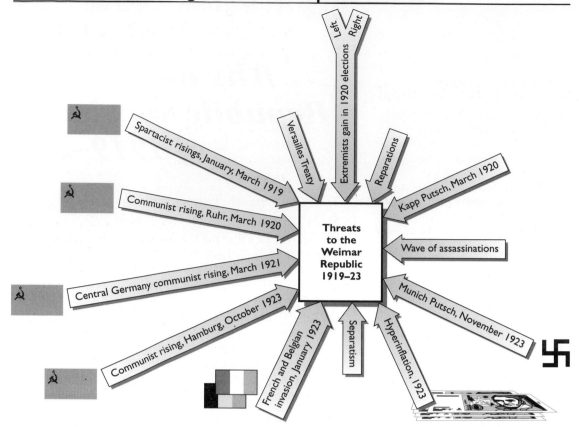

Threats to the Weimar Republic 1919–23

Left Right

Extremists gain in 1920 elections

Versailles Treaty

Reparations

Spartacist risings, January, March 1919

Kapp Putsch, March 1920

Communist rising, Ruhr, March 1920

Wave of assassinations

Central Germany communist rising, March 1921

Munich Putsch, November 1923

Communist rising, Hamburg, October 1923

French and Belgian invasion, January 1923

Separatism

Hyperinflation, 1923

■ 2B   Key events 1919–23

1919	**Jan**	Left-wing Spartacist rising
	Jun	Treaty of Versailles lays blame for war on Germany: Allies demand reparations
1920	**Mar**	Right-wing Kapp Putsch attempts to overthrow the new Republic
1923	**Jan**	French and Belgian troops occupy the Ruhr. Hyperinflation threatens economic chaos
	Nov	Right-wing Munich Putsch led by Adolf Hitler challenges the Weimar regime

TALKING POINT

Using what you have already learned, would you expect the greatest threat to the Weimar Republic to come from the Right or the Left?

TALKING POINT

A lot of words with similar meanings are used in this chapter, such as revolution, COUNTER-REVOLUTION, COUP, putsch, INSURRECTION and revolt. What does each one mean?

■ Learning trouble spot

The Armistice, November 1918, and the Treaty of Versailles, June 1919

Students often confuse these events, not appreciating the time gap between the two. The First World War formally ended at 11 a.m. on 11 November 1918 when Germany and the Allies signed the Armistice. This laid down certain conditions, many of which were then built into the final treaty. The economic blockade and threat of renewed war were used as a lever to pressurise Germany to agree to the eventual terms. It took months of negotiations between the Allies before the actual Versailles Treaty (along with others with Germany's allies) was signed in June 1919.

A How great a burden for the Weimar Republic was the Treaty of Versailles?

FOCUS ROUTE

1. **a)** List the key features of the Versailles settlement.
   b) Give two examples where the principle of self-determination did not apply to Germans.
   c) Give two examples where it was applied, with the effect of harming Germany.
2. Which aspects of the treaty were most likely to
   a) annoy
   b) damage
   Germany?
3. In what ways did the treaty harm the prospects for Weimar democracy?
4. **a)** What arguments are there that in practice Germany was not greatly burdened by the Treaty of Versailles?
   b) Do these arguments mean that the treaty did not undermine the Weimar Republic?

'Death rather than slavery' thundered the nationalist newspaper *Deutsche Zeitung* in response to the Treaty of Versailles. But it was not just the Right that was infuriated by the treaty. Virtually the whole German nation rejected it. Even the government was split over whether to accept it but in the end it had no choice. The threat of the Allies to resume the war and the fear of total German dismemberment led the government reluctantly to urge acceptance. The Constituent Assembly finally did so in June 1919 by 237 votes to 138.

German outrage at the treaty is explained in a number of ways. Most Germans, as late as spring 1918, had expected victory and to make major gains. The sudden collapse of their hopes bred anger as well as frustration. Secondly, Germany hoped that the Fourteen Points (proposed by President Wilson of the USA in 1917 as the basis for a treaty) would lead to a fair peace.

They were in for a major shock. The Fourteen Points were applied selectively so that millions of Germans were denied their national rights. The German government was excluded from the negotiations and was merely asked for comments within 21 days of a final draft. Two minor amendments were made and then the settlement was imposed as a Diktat, a dictated peace. In the hated 'war guilt' clause, Germany was blamed for the war in order to justify making her pay compensation to the Allies in the form of reparations.

Throughout the Weimar Republic's history its opponents laid the blame for Germany's humiliation at Versailles at the door of the new republic and the 'November criminals' who had stabbed the German army in the back. Did the democratic regime's association with the hated Treaty of Versailles severely weaken its prospects for survival? We focus on this issue below.

Demonstration for the Fourteen Points and against the Treaty of Versailles in Berlin in 1919

ACTIVITY

Complete the following statements by matching the phrases in the two columns.

Under the treaty	Intended result
a) *Anschluss* was forbidden	**g)** so reparations could be demanded.
b) Germany was blamed for the war	**h)** to give independent Poland access to the sea.
c) The Rhineland was permanently demilitarised	**i)** to reassure France against German attack.
d) The Rhineland was temporarily occupied	**j)** to stop Germany gaining territory.
e) Germany was split in two	**k)** to weaken Germany militarily.
f) A German air force and U-boats were banned	**l)** to make sure Germany paid reparations.

■ 2C   The key features of the Treaty of Versailles

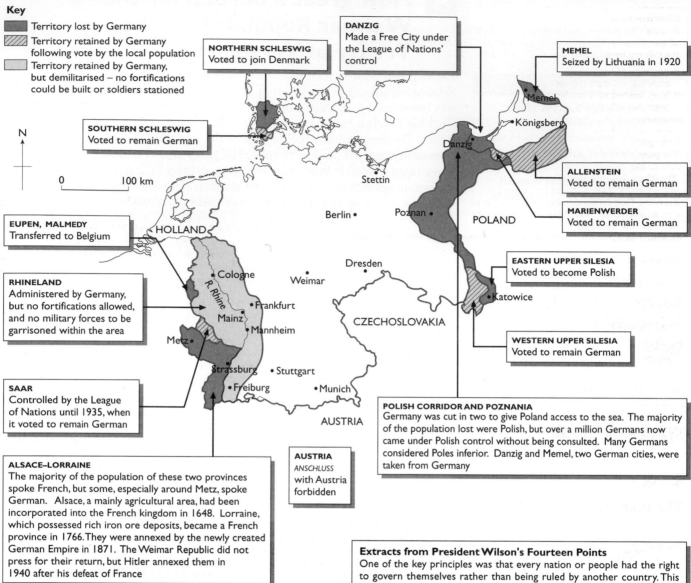

Key

- Territory lost by Germany
- Territory retained by Germany following vote by the local population
- Territory retained by Germany, but demilitarised – no fortifications could be built or soldiers stationed

NORTHERN SCHLESWIG
Voted to join Denmark

DANZIG
Made a Free City under the League of Nations' control

MEMEL
Seized by Lithuania in 1920

SOUTHERN SCHLESWIG
Voted to remain German

ALLENSTEIN
Voted to remain German

EUPEN, MALMEDY
Transferred to Belgium

MARIENWERDER
Voted to remain German

RHINELAND
Administered by Germany, but no fortifications allowed, and no military forces to be garrisoned within the area

EASTERN UPPER SILESIA
Voted to become Polish

SAAR
Controlled by the League of Nations until 1935, when it voted to remain German

WESTERN UPPER SILESIA
Voted to remain German

ALSACE–LORRAINE
The majority of the population of these two provinces spoke French, but some, especially around Metz, spoke German. Alsace, a mainly agricultural area, had been incorporated into the French kingdom in 1648. Lorraine, which possessed rich iron ore deposits, became a French province in 1766. They were annexed by the newly created German Empire in 1871. The Weimar Republic did not press for their return, but Hitler annexed them in 1940 after his defeat of France

AUSTRIA
ANSCHLUSS with Austria forbidden

POLISH CORRIDOR AND POZNANIA
Germany was cut in two to give Poland access to the sea. The majority of the population lost were Polish, but over a million Germans now came under Polish control without being consulted. Many Germans considered Poles inferior. Danzig and Memel, two German cities, were taken from Germany

Map labels: N, 0–100 km, HOLLAND, Cologne, R. Rhine, Frankfurt, Mainz, Mannheim, Metz, Strassburg, Stuttgart, Freiburg, Munich, Weimar, Dresden, Berlin, Stettin, Poznan, Danzig, Königsberg, Memel, Katowice, POLAND, CZECHOSLOVAKIA, AUSTRIA

People and events that influenced the treaty

Most work was done by a council of four government leaders, President Wilson of the USA, French Prime Minister Clemenceau, British Prime Minister David Lloyd George and the Italian Prime Minister Orlando.

The experience of total war raised great passions amongst the Allied populations. In December 1918 Lloyd George won the 'khaki election' on a fiercely patriotic, anti-German platform. The French were determined to exact revenge and to remove German power from the Rhineland so that the threat of a further German invasion was ended. The 'hawks' in Britain and France pointed out that the Treaty of Brest-Litovsk with Russia in March 1918 showed German harshness in peacemaking and their assumption that a defeated enemy paid the cost of the war. An Allied economic naval blockade of Germany continued until the permanent peace treaty was signed. Another significant factor was the fear of communism spreading from Bolshevik Russia

Extracts from President Wilson's Fourteen Points

One of the key principles was that every nation or people had the right to govern themselves rather than being ruled by another country. This was known as the right to self-determination. Other points included:

- 4 'Armaments would be reduced to the lowest point consistent with domestic safety'
- 7 Evacuation and restoration of Belgium
- 8 Evacuation and restoration of French territory and the return of Alsace–Lorraine to France
- 10 AUTONOMY for the peoples of Austria–Hungary
- 13 'Creation of an independent Poland ... and this state to have secure access to the sea'

Effects on Germany

- Lost 13 per cent of its territory
- Lost 12 per cent of its population (6.5 million); half of whom were ethnic Germans. One and a half million Germans became part of new Polish state
- Lost 48 per cent of its iron ore; 16 per cent of its coal; 15 per cent of its agricultural production

SOURCE 2.1 British economist J. M. Keynes, *The Economic Consequences of the Peace, 1919*

I believe that the campaign for securing out of Germany the general costs of the War was one of the most serious acts of political unwisdom for which our statesmen have been responsible.

SOURCE 2.2 Harold Nicholson, British observer at Versailles

Now that we see [the terms] as a whole, we realise that they are much too stiff. The real crime is the reparations and indemnity [compensation] chapter, which is immoral and senseless. There is not a single person among the younger people here who is not unhappy and disappointed at the terms. The only people who approve are the old fire-eaters.

Disarmament

Section V 'In order to render possible the initiation of a general limitation of the armaments of all nations, Germany undertakes strictly to observe the military, naval and air clauses ...' This meant:

- Abolition of conscription and reduction of army to 100,000. No tanks or military aircraft allowed
- Navy limited to 6 battleships, 6 cruisers, 12 destroyers, 12 torpedo boats. No submarines allowed

War guilt

The principle of war guilt and the resulting reparations was laid down in Article 231:

'The Allied Governments affirm and Germany accepts the responsibility of Germany and her allies for causing all the loss and damage to which the Allied Governments and their nationals have been subjected as a consequence of the war imposed upon them by the aggression of Germany and her allies.'

The estimated cost of the war

Costs	France	British Empire	Germany
Dead (m)	1.3	1	2
Wounded (m)	4	2	6.3
Physical damage	300,000 buildings destroyed 21,000 km² farmland destroyed	Small	Small

	Allies	Germany
Financial costs	£29,000m	£8,500m

The process

1918	Oct	The German government seeks an armistice on the basis of Wilson's Fourteen Points. Britain and France broadly accept but stipulate that there should be compensation for damage to the civilian population
1919	Jan	Peace Conference begins. Germany not invited
	7 May	Terms formally presented. Germany allowed fifteen days (later extended to 21) for observations
	29 May	German counter-proposals lead to only minor changes
	16 June	Germany presented with the final terms; acceptance required within seven days. The German government discusses the possibility of renewed fighting; Hindenburg says success is impossible, but favours heroic defeat
	20 June	Chancellor Scheidemann resigns rather than sign terms; President Ebert persuaded not to resign
	22 June	Constituent Assembly accepts terms by 237 to 138
	28 June	Foreign Minister Müller signs the treaty. Nineteen minutes before the deadline the German fleet is scuttled at Scapa Flow

Reparations

Germany was made liable to pay for physical damage caused in the war (most of which would go to France and Belgium), but also for war pensions (so Britain would gain major reparations). The actual amount of compensation was left to a commission to decide. In the meantime, 20,000 million marks of reparations (mainly paid in kind, e.g. industrial goods) were paid. In April 1921 the Allies fixed the total amount at 132,000 million gold marks over 30 years. See pages 82–3

■ Learning trouble spot

The Rhineland and the Ruhr

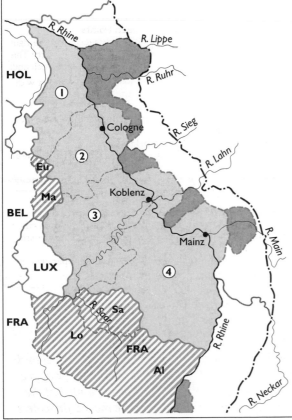

The Rhineland

The economically and militarily strategic area of the Rhineland played a crucial part in German history from 1919 to 1936. Under the Treaty of Versailles the areas either side of the river Rhine were DEMILITARISED, that is Germany could not keep troops there and had to disband fortifications. This was stated to be permanent. In addition, to ensure German compliance with Versailles, especially the paying of reparations, the four Allied powers occupied the west bank and a few areas on the other side. This was expected to last for fifteen years. There was the possibility of phased withdrawal or extended occupation depending upon Germany's behaviour. From 1924 some troops were withdrawn.

In the Locarno Pact of 1925 (see pages 81 and 85), Germany voluntarily accepted her western borders, including permanent demilitarisation; and France agreed not to invade unilaterally as she had done in 1923 (see below). The Allies withdrew their last troops in 1930.

The Ruhr

France and Belgium extended their occupation of Germany by marching into the adjacent Ruhr region briefly in 1921 and for over a year in 1923 in reaction to Germany's technical infringement of reparations payments. The French invasion provoked a major crisis in Germany.

Key

~·~ Left bank of Rhine and 50 km of right bank up to this limit permanently demilitarised

Occupied in 1918 by:
1 Belgium
2 Britain
3 France
4 USA

Occupied by French and Belgian troops, January 1923–5

Territory lost by Germany at Versailles:
Sa Saar (until 1935 plebiscite)
Lo Lorraine
Al Alsace
Eu Eupen
Ma Malmédy

HOL Holland LUX Luxembourg
BEL Belgium FRA France

The political effects of the peace treaty on the Weimar Republic

ACTIVITY

1 Look at Sources 2.3–5. Which aspects of the treaty did the cartoonists resent?
2 **a)** According to Source 2.6, how did the treaty affect German attitudes to the Weimar Republic?
   b) How valuable a witness is Preuss (Source 2.6) for the attitudes of the German people?
3 Read Sources 2.7 and 2.8. According to these historians how did the treaty affect
   a) the German economy
   b) German attitudes to the Republic?
4 To what extent do the historians agree with Preuss?

TALKING POINT

What are the benefits and problems of using political cartoons as historical evidence?

SOURCE 2.3 Captioned 'Clemenceau the Vampire', this cartoon appeared in the conservative German newspaper *Kladderadatsch* in July 1919

SOURCE 2.4 Signing the Diktat: a German cartoon

SOURCE 2.5 This picture appeared in a German school textbook published in 1933

SOURCE 2.6 Hugo Preuss, the lawyer chiefly responsible for writing the Weimar constitution in 1919, on the effects of the Versailles settlement, 1923

. . . the German Republic was born out of . . . terrible defeat. This . . . cast from the first a dark shadow on the new political order, as far as national sentiment was concerned; but initially the belief still predominated that the new order was necessary for the rebirth of Germany. That is why the democratic clauses of the Weimar constitution met with relatively little resistance, despite the unrivalled severity of the armistice terms. For everyone still expected a peace settlement in accordance with Wilson's Fourteen Points, which all the belligerent [fighting] countries had bindingly accepted as the basis for the peace . . . The criminal madness of the Versailles Diktat was a shameless blow in the face [to hopes of political and economic recovery]. The Reich constitution was born with this curse upon it. That it did not collapse immediately under the strain is striking proof of the intrinsic [genuine] vitality of its basic principles; but its implementation and evolution were inevitably fatefully restricted and lamed thereby.

SOURCE 2.7   A. Nicholls, *Weimar and the Rise of Hitler*, 1979, p. 44

Much more important than the fairness or unfairness of the treaty was its impact on the new German Republic. How far is it true that the Versailles Treaty wrecked German democracy? That Germany's economy was ruined by reparations and her security undermined? ... Economically and DEMOGRAPHICALLY *speaking there was no foundation in these assertions ...*

Much more serious was the political demoralisation which the treaty caused within the Reich itself ... The real damage the treaty did to Germany was to disillusion more moderate men who might otherwise have supported their new republic ... The peace settlement continued to poison the political atmosphere in Germany for many years.

SOURCE 2.8   J. Hiden, *The Weimar Republic*, 1974, p. 14

It is no longer acceptable to blame the ultimate failure of the Republic on the Treaty of Versailles, and even its economic effects are disputed, given the economic 'recovery' of Germany in the mid twenties ... The pernicious [evil] effects of the Treaty of Versailles lie ... in the way it created added dimensions to existing internal conflicts and contradictions which had, to some extent, survived the revolution.

The cartoons opposite show German hatred for the Allied peacemakers, but that hatred was transferred to the German politicians who had signed the treaty. The government's acceptance of the terms, though realistic, made it seem weak and reinforced the stab-in-the-back myth. Therefore, the Treaty of Versailles reinforced the hostility of many Germans to the new Weimar system. Hatred of Versailles allowed the radical Right to gain support and helped inspire two right-wing challenges in 1920 and 1923. The disarmament issue was the precipitant for the Kapp Putsch (see page 42), and reparations helped cause the hyperinflation of 1923. A. J. Ryder (*Twentieth Century Germany*, 1973, pp. 204–5) concluded: 'In extracting the republicans' signature to the treaty, the Allies had practically forced them to sign the death warrant of German democracy. Nor did public resentment lessen with time: subsequent events, notably the occupation of the Ruhr, exacerbated [worsened] it. Ten years after the signing of the Versailles treaty a German pastor (who was no nationalist) declared, "This war educated our German people to peace; this peace has educated it to war." '

However, recent analysis has stressed an alternative perspective, arguing that Germany was not that harshly treated. In this view Germany was in a potentially strong position after Versailles for three reasons:

- The break-up of the Tsarist, Austro-Hungarian and Turkish empires created opportunities for Germany, since it was now surrounded by small, weak states, especially in the east.
- France failed to achieve its aims of a permanently weakened Germany and a secure border.
- Reparations were not so burdensome that they destroyed the German economy (see pages 82–3).

Furthermore, the hope that as time progressed the Allies might modify at least the reparations terms proved justified. By the mid-1920s the issue of Versailles by itself was probably not a major obstacle to the consolidation of the Weimar Republic. However, when a major problem hit Germany, such as hyperinflation in 1923 and the Depression in 1929, Versailles could easily be blamed by DEMAGOGIC politicians who could rapidly revive German hatred of reparations and the loss of territory. Thus it remained a potentially deep flaw throughout the Weimar period.

TALKING POINT

The harsh treaty the Allies imposed on Germany has been blamed on the fact that these countries had popularly elected democratic governments. Can you explain this comment?

ACTIVITY

1   'The practical impact of Versailles was not very burdensome; but what mattered was how the Germans felt about it.' How accurate is this interpretation?
2   'Too harsh to be acceptable to most Germans but not harsh enough to keep Germany suppressed.' How valid is this criticism of the Treaty of Versailles?

FOCUS ROUTE

Complete the first two columns of your copy of the table on page 33.

B Did Weimar democracy face a serious challenge from the Left?

As you have seen (page 21), the new Weimar government had used the army to crush the Spartacist rising of January 1919. However, opposition was not completely suppressed and for the next four years the government faced a series of threats from the extreme Left. Workers were angered by economic problems and disillusioned by the lack of real gains from their revolution. In the spring of 1919 the industrial areas of Germany were wracked by radical unrest. A wave of strikes occurred in the Ruhr mines, central Germany and Berlin. The strikers demanded shorter hours, the socialisation of industry and a government based on councils. However, the wave of protests was uncoordinated, with radical 'leaders' desperately following rather than leading the protests. The KPD had neither strong leadership with a clear strategy nor a tightly organised party structure, as the Communists did in Russia. Furthermore, it lacked support, both in terms of numbers and depth of commitment. Eventually, a mixture of government promises and the use of the army and Freikorps quelled the unrest, with considerable loss of life in some places.

Only in Bavaria did the revolutionaries temporarily gain control. After the overthrow of the Bavarian monarchy and the creation of a republic on 7 November 1918, there had been considerable political confusion. In March 1919 a soviet republic was proclaimed, which created RED GUARDS and workers' councils. In May 1919, this was bloodily suppressed by the Freikorps, with over 700 killed, and a right-wing government was established.

By the summer of 1919, the best chance of establishing communism in Germany had gone, even though Marxists considered Germany the country most ripe for revolution. For the next three years unrest continued but it never seriously threatened the government's control. There were numerous demonstrations and strikes, some of which developed into attempted insurrections, especially in the key industrial areas in the Ruhr and central Germany. Workers felt that their gains from the revolution of 1918, especially the symbolic eight-hour day, were under threat and that the revolution needed to be deepened. Some looked to Russia and argued the need for a German 'OCTOBER' – a second-stage revolution that would establish a true communist state. In the aftermath of the Kapp Putsch (see pages 42–3), attempts were made to exploit the fragility of the Republic to establish a more revolutionary regime but they came to nothing.

The KPD's approach has been described as a combination of foolhardiness and hesitancy. It failed to exploit the post-Kapp MILITANCY. Then in 1921 it rushed into a poorly supported rising. It reacted to this by being overcautious during the mass protests of mid-1923, then acted too late in October 1923. Inadequate leadership, poor organisation, internal divisions, lack of support and government repression (accompanied by minor concessions) meant that the revolts of 1920–3, just like those of 1919, failed.

■ Learning trouble spot

Coup (d'état) or putsch

These terms, the first French and the second German, literally mean a blow. They are used to refer to a secretly plotted and sudden attempt to overthrow a government, usually by force. A coup is normally organised by a small group of people, such as generals or a political party, who try to take control, initially by seizing the key centres of power.

In contrast to a revolution, a coup does not need mass support to succeed. Normally, a coup or putsch comes from the political Right, attracting support from the elite, and a revolution from the Left, attracting support from the lower classes.

ACTIVITY

With which of these statements do you agree? Explain your reasons.

a) Left-wing challenges had a strong chance of overthrowing the Weimar government.
b) Left-wing challenges did not seriously challenge the Weimar government but did help to reduce the confidence of many Germans in the government.

Left-wing revolutionaries from the Ruhr 'Red Army' fighting the Freikorps in 1920

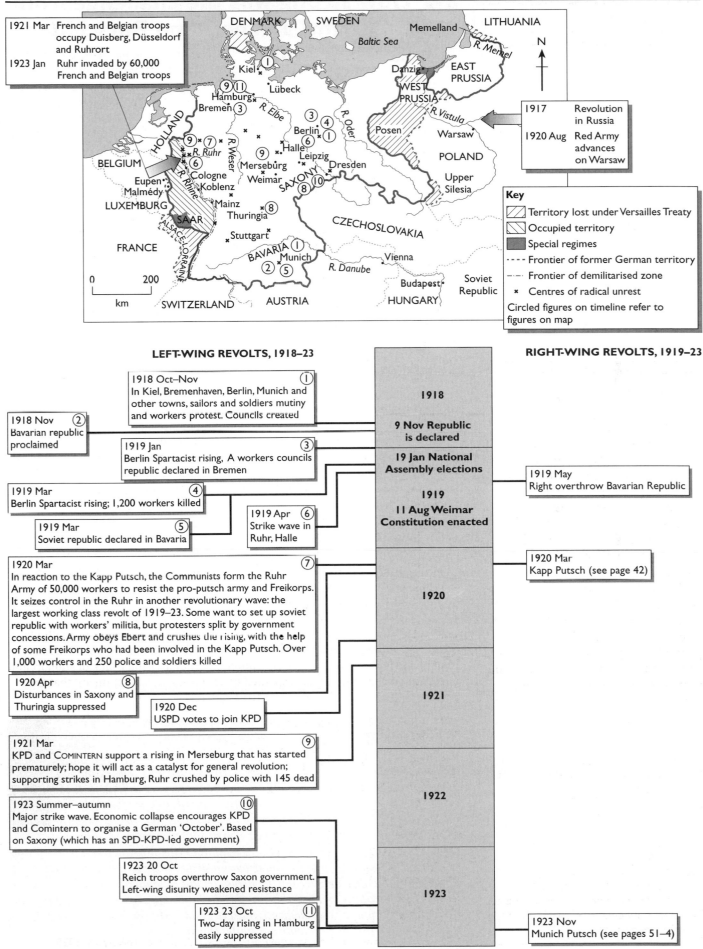

1921 Mar French and Belgian troops occupy Duisberg, Düsseldorf and Ruhrort

1923 Jan Ruhr invaded by 60,000 French and Belgian troops

1917 Revolution in Russia

1920 Aug Red Army advances on Warsaw

Key

▨	Territory lost under Versailles Treaty
▧	Occupied territory
▦	Special regimes
- - - -	Frontier of former German territory
-·-·-	Frontier of demilitarised zone
✕	Centres of radical unrest

Circled figures on timeline refer to figures on map

LEFT-WING REVOLTS, 1918–23

1918 Oct–Nov ①
In Kiel, Bremenhaven, Berlin, Munich and other towns, sailors and soldiers mutiny and workers protest. Councils created

1918 Nov ②
Bavarian republic proclaimed

1919 Jan ③
Berlin Spartacist rising, A workers councils republic declared in Bremen

1919 Mar ④
Berlin Spartacist rising; 1,200 workers killed

1919 Mar ⑤
Soviet republic declared in Bavaria

1919 Apr ⑥
Strike wave in Ruhr, Halle

1920 Mar ⑦
In reaction to the Kapp Putsch, the Communists form the Ruhr Army of 50,000 workers to resist the pro-putsch army and Freikorps. It seizes control in the Ruhr in another revolutionary wave: the largest working class revolt of 1919–23. Some want to set up soviet republic with workers' militia, but protesters split by government concessions. Army obeys Ebert and crushes the rising, with the help of some Freikorps who had been involved in the Kapp Putsch. Over 1,000 workers and 250 police and soldiers killed

1920 Apr ⑧
Disturbances in Saxony and Thuringia suppressed

1920 Dec
USPD votes to join KPD

1921 Mar ⑨
KPD and COMINTERN support a rising in Merseburg that has started prematurely; hope it will act as a catalyst for general revolution; supporting strikes in Hamburg, Ruhr crushed by police with 145 dead

1923 Summer–autumn ⑩
Major strike wave. Economic collapse encourages KPD and Comintern to organise a German 'October'. Based on Saxony (which has an SPD-KPD-led government)

1923 20 Oct
Reich troops overthrow Saxon government. Left-wing disunity weakened resistance

1923 23 Oct ⑪
Two-day rising in Hamburg easily suppressed

(timeline centre)

1918

9 Nov Republic is declared

19 Jan National Assembly elections

1919

11 Aug Weimar Constitution enacted

1920

1921

1922

1923

RIGHT-WING REVOLTS, 1919–23

1919 May
Right overthrow Bavarian Republic

1920 Mar
Kapp Putsch (see page 42)

1923 Nov
Munich Putsch (see pages 51–4)

FOCUS ROUTE

1 Complete the third column in your copy of the table on page 33.
2 Make notes on the assassinations of this period. What do they, and the reaction to them, reveal about attitudes to the Weimar Republic?

C How strong was the challenge from the Right? 1: The Kapp Putsch and assassinations

In addition to the left-wing threat to Weimar democracy, there was strong right-wing opposition. This came partly from powerful conservative forces such as the army, industrialists and landowners and other members of the elite. There were also the Freikorps and paramilitary groups which thrived in post-war Germany and the numerous VÖLKISCH groups that had their roots in the pre-war period. These groups felt great bitterness towards the Weimar regime, and their activities weakened the new parliamentary democracy.

The Kapp Putsch

The first major crisis from the Right was the Kapp Putsch in March 1920. After some order had been restored by the end of 1919, the Socialist-led government had less need for the Freikorps. It was also trying to reduce the size of the army to conform to the disarmament requirements of Versailles. So in February 1920 the Defence Minister ordered two Freikorps brigades (about 12,000 men) to disband. One of their leaders, General Walther von Lüttwitz, refused. Along with other disgruntled army officers and Wolfgang Kapp, leader of the Fatherland Party, he planned to overthrow the government. He contacted other generals, including Seeckt and Ludendorff, but they were non-committal.

On 12 March, 12,000 Freikorps marched twelve miles to Berlin where, crucially, the army refused to support the government. General Hans von Seeckt told Ebert: 'Troops do not fire on troops; when REICHSWEHR fires on Reichswehr all comradeship within the officer corps has vanished.' The government had no alternative but to flee and the Freikorps entered Berlin. A new government headed by Kapp was proclaimed. However, it failed to gain widespread support, even from most conservatives. In a few places, the army supported the putsch; in most areas, it was neutral.

The Left organised a general strike in Berlin and elsewhere in protest at the putsch. Berlin was paralysed. Even civil servants and bankers refused to recognise Kapp's government. It was occupying government buildings but was not able to govern. After four days the Kapp government fled and Ebert's government returned to Berlin. In the aftermath, there were several clashes between workers and the army, especially in industrial areas such as the Ruhr, Halle and Dresden, as some workers tried to extend the successful strike to impose more radical changes on the restored government.

The government took no action against Seeckt and other army leaders for their lack of support. It realised it might still need them against the Communists. Kapp died before he could be prosecuted, but those actually involved in the putsch were treated leniently as Source 2.9 shows.

Wolfgang Kapp, 1868–1922

- A right-wing journalist and civil servant, Kapp helped found the right-wing Fatherland Party during the First World War.
- In 1919 he was elected to the Reichstag as a monarchist.
- Rather surprisingly, Kapp became Chancellor of the new government briefly established by the Kapp Putsch, though the Freikorps leader Captain Hermann Ehrhardt and General Lüttwitz had been its main organisers.
- After its failure, he fled to Sweden where he died in 1922.

SOURCE 2.9 Prosecution of the 705 people involved in the Kapp Putsch

Granted amnesty	412
Proceedings discontinued	285
Proceedings reviewed	7
Punished	I

SOURCE 2.10 A poster proclamation issued by the government in response to the Kapp Putsch. It was issued in the name of the SPD members of the government, including Ebert, and was probably sanctioned by him

Workers, Party comrades! The military putsch has started. The Baltic MERCENARIES, fearing the command to dissolve, are trying to remove the republic and to form a military dictatorship. Lüttwitz and Kapp [are] at their head ... The achievements of a whole year are to be smashed, your dearly bought freedom to be destroyed. Everything is at stake! The strongest countermeasures are required. No factory must work while the military dictatorship of Ludendorff and Co rules! Therefore down tools! Come out on strike! Deprive the military clique of oxygen! Fight with all means for the Republic! Put all quarrels aside. There is only one way against the dictatorship of Wilhelm II: paralysis of all economic life. No hand must move! No proletarian must help the military dictators. General strike all along the line! Proletarians unite! Down with the counter-revolution!

Walther Rathenau, 1867–1922

Assassinations

Between 1919 and 1923 Weimar politicians lived in fear of assassination. The brutalising effect of war, the revolutionary origins of the Republic, the political struggles of the period and the challenge to traditional values encouraged some right-wing Germans to resort to murder to weaken the democratic regime. The lenient attitude to such actions of conservative judges, who had been kept in their posts in the new Republic, reinforced this trend. The Republic lost hundreds of devoted servants through assassination, including one of its greatest statesmen, Walther Rathenau.

Walther Rathenau

Rathenau was head of the massive AEG electrical firm. He developed imaginative views about industrial organisation and the co-operation of workers and employers. During the Second Reich he had been a strong monarchist, favouring German expansionism, and had played a major role in running the war economy. He participated in arranging the armistice and attempts to improve the Treaty of Versailles. Like his more famous successor Stresemann, his political ideas became more progressive. He was a founder of the Democratic Party. In 1921 he became Minister of Reconstruction and Foreign Minister in February 1922.

Rathenau's involvement at Versailles and his Jewish background made him a target for nationalist extremists. Some Rightists chanted, 'Shoot down Walther Rathenau, that God-damned son of a Jewish sow.' After several failed attempts he was assassinated in June 1922 by a right-wing terror group, Organisation Consul. His death was seen as a major blow to the stability of the Weimar Republic but it led to a general revulsion against these tactics. Over 700,000 people demonstrated in Berlin against his assassination and the murderous Organisation Consul was forced to disband. After 1923 political assassinations declined.

Although there was a strong reaction against these murders, all the revolts and assassinations served to foster disillusionment with the new regime. Most Germans had the opportunity to express their opinions in elections in 1920 after the Spartacist rising and the Kapp Putsch. Source 2.16 compares their reactions one year into the regime with their initial feelings for the Republic.

SOURCE 2.12 Political assassinations

	Left	Right
Murders committed	22	354 (326 unpunished)
Number convicted and sentenced to death	10	0
Number convicted and sentenced to severe punishment	17	1

SOURCE 2.13 Finance Minister Matthias Erzberger, who had sponsored the Reichstag Peace Resolution in 1917 and had signed the Armistice, was wounded in January 1922 and killed in August. After his murder the Chancellor, Wirth, told the Reichstag

A state of political bestiality [beast-like behaviour] prevails. I need only to mention poor Frau Erzberger who is constantly receiving letters announcing the intention to defile her husband's grave. Is it surprising, then, that I also received letters yesterday, headed 'on the day of Rathenau's execution', and declaring: 'You men of FULFILMENT mania have not listened to the voices of those who have tried to dissuade you from a bad policy. Let hard fate, therefore, take its course, so that the fatherland may prosper.'

SOURCE 2.14 Kurt Tucholsky, left-wing satirist

When the Republic was created, these judges held over from the monarchy found it impossible to transfer their allegiance to the new organisation of the state . . . They created a private law and subverted [undermined] the public law of the Republic by refusing to administer justice in an equal manner to all people.

SOURCE 2.15 Cartoon of judges passing sentence on right-wing rebels. Many were reluctant to convict them. In 1926 a judge surveyed the political allegiance of his colleagues and reported the following results: 5 per cent republican, 15 per cent reactionary, 80 per cent waverers

SOURCE 2.16 Election results 1919–20 (% of votes cast)

Main pro-Weimar parties	January 1919 (%)	June 1920 (%)
SPD	38	21
DDP	19	8
Z	20	18

Anti-republican parties	January 1919 (%)	June 1920 (%)
USPD/KPD	8	19
DVP	4	14
DNVP	10	15

ACTIVITY

1 From the point of view of Weimar's survival what were
   a) the most encouraging aspects
   b) the most ominous aspects
   of the Kapp Putsch and the assassinations?
2 What did the political opponents of Weimar hope to achieve by these assassinations?
3 What evidence do Sources 2.12–15 provide of the problems for democracy in Weimar Germany caused by
   a) the limited nature of the 1918 Revolution
   b) the Treaty of Versailles?
4 How successful were the right-wing attacks on the Republic in the period 1919–22?

FOCUS ROUTE

1 Why did the Weimar Republic suffer a major inflationary crisis in 1923?
2 How did inflation affect the German people?
3 How seriously did it harm the prospects for Weimar democracy?

D Did the hyperinflation crisis of 1923 undermine Weimar democracy?

The impact of inflation

'Two women were going to the bank with a washing basket filled with notes. They passed a shop and saw a crowd standing round the window, so put down the basket for a moment to see if there was anything going that could be bought. Then they turned round and found that all the notes were there, untouched, but the basket had gone.'

It is difficult to believe that such a theft actually happened but it did – in Berlin in 1923. It happened because the German people had lost all confidence in their currency. Monetary systems are based on confidence. In Britain today, you can be confident that a £5 note will be accepted in a shop in return for a purchase. Both you and the shopkeeper are confident about the value of a banknote. If that confidence is lost, the shopkeeper might only hand over what you want if you offer him more paper money, so in effect the price goes up. Once confidence in a currency is lost, its value plummets and inflation soars.

This is what happened in Germany in 1923 when the Weimar Republic was hit by one of the worst inflationary crises in history. By November 1923 the German mark was worthless, as confidence in the economy collapsed. Inflation was so extreme that at one stage an egg cost 80 million marks and a glass of beer 150 million marks. People resorted to barter, for example, using coal or sausages as currency. Workers rushed to spend wages before they lost even more value with prices rising between 20 and 100 per cent in a day. There were major food shortages, since farmers were reluctant to sell food for worthless money.

SOURCE 2.17 The awful statistics of hyperinflation

	Marks to the $	**Wholesale prices**
1914 Jul	4.2	1 (1913)
1919 Jan	8.9	2
1920 Jan	14.0	4
Jul	39.5	
1921 Jan	64.9	14
Jul	76.7	
1922 Jan	191.8	37
Jul	493.2	100
1923 Jan	17,792	2,785
Jul	353,412	74,787
4 Aug	620,455	
Sep	98,860,000	23,949,000
25 Oct	260,208,000	7,095,800,000
4 Nov	200,000,000,000	750,000,000,000

SOURCE 2.18 Money as waste paper

SOURCE 2.19 K. Heiden, *Der Führer: Hitler's Rise to Power*, 1944. Heiden was a German democrat who lived through Weimar and Nazi Germany; he carefully collected evidence to use in his anti-Nazi writings

On Friday afternoons in 1923, very long lines of workers waited outside the pay windows of the big German factories, department stores, banks and offices, watching the clocks until at last they reached the pay window and received a bag full of paper bank notes.

According to the figures on the notes, they were worth anything from 700,000 marks up to 380 billion or even 18 trillion marks; the figures rose month by month, then week to week, then day to day.

People began running as soon as they could. They dashed to food stores where there were further slow queues. Had you got there first, a half kilo of sugar might have been bought for 2 million marks. If you were at the back, by the time you got to the counter, 2 millions would buy only a quarter kilo.

The government printing presses could not keep up. People carried their money around in sacks or prams. Life was madness, nightmare, desperation, chaos.

SOURCE 2.20   Notice in a Berlin shop window: 'No sales to foreigners'

SOURCE 2.21   Letter from a bank to a German about his savings built up during a life of hard work under the Second Reich. The envelope bore a 5 million mark postage stamp

The bank deeply regrets that it can no longer administer your deposit of 68,000 marks since the costs are out of all proportion to the capital. Since we have no bank-notes of small enough denominations at our disposal, we have rounded out the sum to one million marks. Enclosed: one 1,000,000 mark bill.

Who benefited and who lost out

You are probably used to being told by governments that inflation is bad. However, many Germans actually benefited from the collapse in the value of the mark. Many people in debt, such as mortgage holders, paid off their loans with the devalued currency. Many entrepreneurs with access to cheap credit, especially via the Reichsbank, used loans to extend their holdings, and then easily repaid the loans when their income had increased in money terms. People who rented property with long-term rents gained as the real value of their payments fell. Owners of foreign exchange and foreigners in Germany who converted their money into millions of marks also greatly benefited. Exporters gained from the mark's falling exchange rate.

However, hyperinflation was catastrophic for the majority. The greatest losers were those with savings, especially many pensioners who lived off fixed-interest investments. The value of their hard-earned savings disintegrated. Those who had patriotically purchased WAR BONDS (with fixed rates of interest) found their investments and the interest paid lost almost all their value. Those relying on welfare benefits and landlords receiving fixed rents found the value of their incomes fall. By 1923, the cost to a landlord of one window replacement might be greater than all the rents received in the last ten years.

Workers initially secured compensatory wage rises, but these lagged behind rising prices. It has been estimated that unskilled workers lost 30 per cent of their spending power between 1913 and September 1923. Civil servants, who initially made gains in 1920–2, found their real income declining again.

These were the main groups of winners and losers from hyperinflation, but the historian Peukert (in his book *The Weimar Republic*, 1991, p. 66) has warned against simple class-based generalisations such as 'the destruction of the middle class': 'Two individuals from the same broad social class might be affected very differently, depending on the precise period in question, the part of the country in which they lived and their exact role within the fabric of the economy. Indeed, it was precisely through the confusion experienced by individuals and their fears for their social status that the real psychological impact of the inflation made itself felt. A profiteering ethic became common among people who had previously prided themselves on their rectitude [good behaviour]. Others turned to crime out of sheer hardship. The shifts in the relative standing of the different social groups ... made individuals uncertain about their social status.'

SOURCE 2.22   Impoverished middle-class Germans selling their household possessions to raise money in 1922

SOURCE 2.23   Cartoon from the German magazine *Simplicissimus*, 1923. Drowning in a sea of paper money, the mother screams, 'Bread! Bread!'

Under the Second Reich Hugo Stinnes owned businesses in the coal, iron and electrical industries. Despite his conservative views, he compromised during the revolution, granted workers more rights and became a DVP member of the Reichstag. As inflation increased, Stinnes used his ties with the Reichsbank to gain cheap credit to buy up struggling competitors. He converted foreign currency gained from selling his products abroad into millions of marks to expand and re-equip his plant. He paid off loans in near valueless marks. By 1924 'the King of the Ruhr' owned 1,535 companies, an estimated 20 per cent of Germany's industries, covering coal mines, steelworks, paper mills, chemical concerns, newspapers, hotels, land and shipping lines. His wealth, in the midst of despair, aroused great resentment. His economic power was matched by his political ambitions. The American Assistant Secretary of State Castle described him as 'the strongest man in Germany . . . and one of the most dangerous men in the world'. He hoped to support a dictator capable of 'speaking the language of the people' who would defeat Bolshevism and restore Germany to greatness. Stinnes died in 1924 but his vision was supported and taken on by other industrialists. After his death, his industrial empire crashed.

SOURCE 2.25   Hugo Stinnes, 1870–1924

ACTIVITY

1   Explain how Stinnes benefited from inflation.
2   Did this success make him more supportive of the Weimar Republic?
3   What criticism did the Left make of him?

SOURCE 2.24   A 1922 left-wing cartoon satirising the industrialist Hugo Stinnes

Stinnes repariert — — seine Finanzen.

Only the ten-hour day can solve this mess.
Of course we'll pay the worker less.

Pay reparations – quickly, without pain
And then – fill our pockets once again.

The unemployed out on the streets
Have nothing now at all to eat.

For the fatherland (and our profits) to bloom
All! All must meet their doom!

SOURCE 2.26   A cartoon from the Nazi weekly newspaper *Der Angriff* (The Attack), 19 March 1928, shows Stinnes as a victim of the Jews. The caption reads: 'The mighty Stinnes – eaten up by Jacob Goldsmith.'

Den mächtigen Stinnes —   — fraß Jakob Goldschmidt

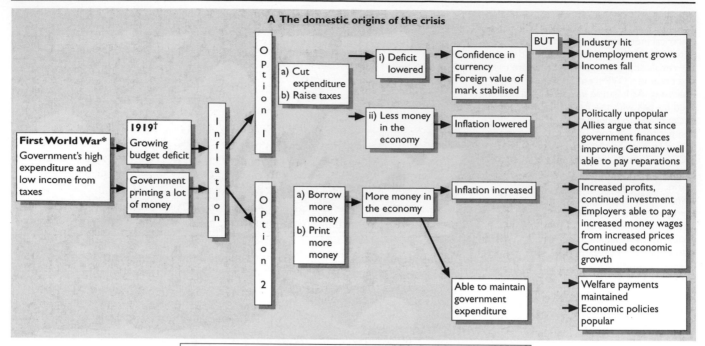

A The domestic origins of the crisis

The government chose option 2. Initially, inflation had economic and political benefits. However, by 1923 it had reached such levels that the whole economy was disrupted. Why did this happen?

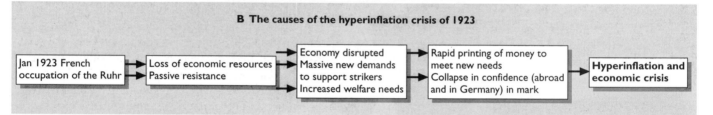

B The causes of the hyperinflation crisis of 1923

* Government did not fund the war mainly from increased taxation, but by borrowing and printing money

† New, insecure democratic government lost major raw material and population resources. It also faced extra financial demands, e.g. war pensions, extended welfare, reparations

Inflation and Reparations
Contrary to what many historians say, the government did not encourage inflation in order to be able to pay off reparations in devalued marks. Reparations had to be paid in goods, gold or foreign currency. However, rising inflation did lead to a lack of confidence in the German economy which could be used to argue that Germany was unable to pay reparations.

The causes of inflation

Many people, both at the time and later, blamed the Allies for causing the hyperinflation crisis of 1923. Chart 2F, however, tries to show how the French occupation of the Ruhr was only one factor, exacerbating an inflationary problem that had its origins in the German government's actions in the First World War. Then, from 1919, Weimar governments faced a growing budget deficit. There were two broad policy options, the tough policies of Option 1 in Chart 2F or the more attractive, but inflationary, policies of Option 2. The insecure Weimar governments opted for the second approach. This contributed to the hyperinflation crisis of 1923.

ACTIVITY

Match up the methods with the disadvantages of each method of funding the war.

Method	Disadvantage
a) Raise taxes	**d)** Causes inflation
b) Borrow money	**e)** Politically unpopular
c) Print money	**f)** Leaves government with a large debt

■ **Learning trouble spot**

The German government's funding of the war, and its consequent financial problems

Wars cost governments a lot of money. To cover the cost, three main approaches can be taken, but each has its problems. They are:

a) raise taxes   **b)** borrow money   **c)** print money.

The German government relied mainly on b) and c). It did not worry too much about getting into debt as it assumed it could repay debts with the money and resources it would receive from its defeated enemies. So when Germany was itself defeated, this plan collapsed; Germany had a large debt, worsened by having to pay reparations rather than receive them. The government also faced a large post-war pensions bill. Faced with these problems, the new democratic regime followed its predecessor by printing more money rather than greatly increasing taxes.

Thus, though in 1923 most Germans blamed the economic crisis on the French and British demands for reparations, in many ways German governments were responsible. In some respects the government actually favoured inflation, since it reduced the real burden of its internal debt – interest and debt repayments on money borrowed from its citizens. (Reparations were payable in gold or goods so their real value would not be affected by inflation.) Modest inflation can be beneficial to stimulate an economy, and some historians, for example Holtfrerich (in *Weimar: Why Did German Democracy Fail?*, ed. I. Kershaw, 1990), argue that the German government's economic policy in 1919–21 was economically rational as well as politically wise.

The government continued to print money. By 1923, 300 paper mills and 2,000 printing firms, including newspaper firms, were working 24-hour shifts to produce money. The government needed money to pay compensation to war victims and to those who had lost land under the Treaty of Versailles. It also needed to pay wages to civil servants, welfare benefits and subsidies and provide cheap credit to help industry readjust and maintain full employment. Another factor was the hope that continuing economic problems would reinforce the argument that Germany could not pay reparations and so influence Allied governments to lower the level of their demands.

Foreign governments must also share some blame for the crisis. The French and Belgian occupation of the Ruhr in January 1923 came as the final blow to the faltering mark. Sixty thousand troops took control of all industries and railways in order to seize resources in lieu of payments that were overdue. However, it was not so much the invasion itself as the government's response to it that let loose hyperinflation. The government called for passive resistance, that no one should co-operate with the invaders. Civil servants, miners and others went on strike, financed by the government. In places resistance was far from passive and over 140 Germans were killed in clashes with French troops. Revenues to the government fell as Germany's industrial heartland was disrupted but expenditure on welfare increased rapidly, again funded by increased printing of money.

The end to hyperinflation

The inflationary crisis, a long time in the making, was actually solved remarkably quickly. In November 1923 the new Chancellor, Stresemann, took decisive action to restore confidence in the currency. He appointed the expert financier Hjalmar Schacht to the Reichsbank. The old currency was replaced with a new one, the Rentenmark. One Rentenmark replaced 1,000 billion paper marks. The supply of new currency was strictly limited to 3,200 million Rentenmarks. The new currency was quickly accepted. In November, the weekly *Berliner Illustrierter Zeitung* cost 1 billion marks. In December, it cost 20 pfennigs! The government showed its determination to prevent a recurrence of inflation by cutting expenditure, partly by dismissing many civil servants.

ACTIVITY

1 To what extent was hyperinflation caused by:
   a) the policies of the Second Reich during the war
   b) the policies of Weimar governments
   c) the French/Belgian occupation of the Ruhr
   d) reparations?
2 Look at Chart 2F. What reasons are there why the government did not try to fight inflation?

The effects of the inflationary crisis

The inflationary crisis had major economic, social, political and psychological effects, some of which left deep scars that help to explain the eventual collapse of the Republic. Most Germans suffered badly. Basic values were challenged. With millions desperate, it was easy for DEMAGOGUES to offer simple explanations and solutions. Thus the crisis was variously blamed on Jewish finance, the Versailles Treaty, Weimar democracy and Socialists. The inflationary crisis also helped provoke increased unrest in 1923. However, despite the fact that millions of Germans lost their savings, radical right-wing groups did not win mass support.

The German state actually gained financially since it lost its debt (the new currency meant a government debt of 150,000 million marks was reduced to 15 pfennigs). However, the Weimar Republic was weakened politically, since the great financial losses that people with savings suffered turned many of them against the democratic regime. Health too suffered, especially among the elderly, as a result of inflation-induced poverty, and this also was blamed on the Weimar government. The hyperinflation crisis thus inflicted wounds that in the long term contributed to Weimar's death.

SOURCE 2.27 Mary Fulbrook, *Fontana History of Germany*, 1991, p. 34

The savings, hopes, plans and assumptions and aspirations of huge numbers of people were swept away in a chaotic whirlwind ... Even when the worst material impact was over, the psychological shock of the experience was to have longer lasting effects, confirming a deep-seated dislike of democracy, which was thereafter equated with economic distress, and a heightened fear of the possibility of economic instability.

SOURCE 2.28 General John Hartment Morgan, Disarmament Commission, December 1923

Inflation has destroyed the equipoise [balance] of society. It has ruined the middle classes and impoverished the workers ... It has been a tremendous solvent [weakening agent] of society ... Inflation has undermined the political basis of the Republic and concentrated all real power in the hands of a few, namely the great industrialists ... In no country in the world is capital so strong or politically so DESPOTIC. The economic form of society fails to correspond to the political theory; a republic in name, it is capitalist despotism in fact.

SOURCE 2.29 Gustav Stresemann, Foreign Minister, 1927

The intellectual and productive middle class, which was traditionally the backbone of the country, has been paid for the utter sacrifice of itself to the state during the war by being deprived of all its property and by being PROLETARIANISED.

ACTIVITY

Choose four phrases from Sources 2.27–9 that sum up the crucial effects of the great inflation.

■ **Learning trouble spot**

Why did Germany not suffer mass unemployment, 1919–23?

The period 1919–23 was primarily an inflationary crisis with no major unemployment problems until the virtual collapse of the economy in 1923. The end of the First World War led to a drop in demand for war-related products, and mass demobilisation returned millions to the labour market. Furthermore, Germany lost some of its major economic resources. However, Weimar governments managed to control unemployment. This was partly due to the need to restock after the war, but primarily because the initially mild inflation served to stimulate the economy. In addition, reparations may actually have helped since they were paid in goods, the supply of which required labour.

The second major economic crisis of the Weimar Republic, that of 1929–33, took a very different form. Then the major problem was mass employment. There was no inflationary problem; in fact, prices fell.

E How strong was the challenge from the Right? 2: Hitler's Munich Putsch, 1923

FOCUS ROUTE

Complete the fourth column of your copy of the table on page 33.

Gustav Stresemann became Chancellor of Germany in August 1923 as the leader of a coalition ranging from the SPD to the moderate conservative DVP. By November his government was having some success in tackling the economic crisis. The new currency was restoring stability to the economy and passive resistance to the French occupation of the Ruhr (which had only worsened the economic situation) had been called off. However, Stresemann still faced major political problems.

The Bavarian state government opposed his decision to call off passive resistance and regarded the national government as too weak to withstand threats from the Left. Bavaria had been one of the most turbulent areas in Germany since 1918. It had experienced both a brief soviet republic and a right-wing regime opposed to Weimar democracy. Traditionally, Bavaria was hostile to Prussia, had its own cultural traditions and acted independently, having kept its own monarch during the Second Reich.

In September 1923 right-wing politicians in Bavaria, backed by the Bavarian Reichswehr commander, Otto von Lossow, considered marching on Berlin to replace the central government. Only the Weimar government's action in driving Communists from the Saxon and Thuringian governments finally dissuaded the Bavarian government from challenging Berlin. However, this was not the end of the threat from the Right. In November 1923 the little-known Nazi Party tried to seize power in Munich, an attempt which is the main focus of this subsection.

■ 2G The crisis facing the Weimar regime in autumn 1923

Economic crisis
The French occupation of the Ruhr, and the German government's policy of passive resistance was causing hyperinflation.

The threat from the Left
Communists had joined Socialists in the state governments of Saxony and Thuringia. There was talk of a 'German October'.

The threat from the Right
i) The army
Many Conservatives still looked to the army to replace the democratic system.
ii) Bavaria
The right-wing government of Bavaria was defying the federal government in Berlin. The army in Bavaria had sworn loyalty to Gustav von Kahr, not the Reich government. The Bavarian leaders were worried by Communists in neighbouring states. There was talk of the Bavarian government trying to overthrow the federal government.
iii) The Nazis
Hitler's Nazis and other right-wing Bavarian groups were also considering trying to seize power.

General Erich von Ludendorff, popular hero from the First World War, had virtually run the government 1916–18; a determined opponent of democracy. He had been involved in the Kapp Putsch

General Hans von Seeckt. Most powerful general. Suspicious of democracy, but also concerned about the danger of civil war. Ambiguous attitude: known as 'the Sphinx'. He wanted the army kept above politics; he felt it should obey legitimate government provided it protected the army's interests

Otto von Lossow, commander of the Reichswehr in Bavaria. Very conservative, he favoured a strong national state

Gustav von Kahr, the Bavarian leader (State Commissioner). A reactionary monarchist, he considered re-establishing a German emperor, or an independent Bavarian kingdom. Muddle-headed

Adolf Hitler. Leader of small Nazi Movement (55,000 members), one of many right-wing Bavarian groups. He had a paramilitary force, the SA

Stresemann's actions
Action: He bravely called off passive resistance, since it had failed to force a French withdrawal.
Result: This infuriated the Right who saw Stresemann's action as giving in to the French. There was more talk of a right-wing putsch.
Action: He sent the army into Saxony and Thuringia and overthrew the left-wing governments; but he did nothing about the right-wing government in Bavaria which was defying his authority.
Result: This upset the SPD who left the coalition government in protest. It pleased the Bavarian government, which now lost enthusiasm for a putsch.

The rise of the Nazis

In 1923, Adolf Hitler emerged from obscurity. (If you wish to read about his background, you can turn to page 55.) Before we study his first and unsuccessful attempt to come to power it will be useful to see what his Nazi Party stood for.

ACTIVITY

1 Identify clauses in Source 2.30 that are
   - a) nationalist
   - b) racist/anti-semitic
   - c) socialist/anti-capitalist
   - d) opposed to parliamentary democracy.
2 Which of the following groups might be more likely to be:
   - a) attracted by the programme
   - b) alienated?
   - i) People in debt
   - ii) Small business people
   - iii) Big industrialists
   - iv) War profiteers
   - v) Ex-soldiers
   - vi) Industrial workers
   - vii) Generals
   - viii) Lower middle class
3 Use your answers to questions 1 and 2 to suggest whether the Nazis might be a threat to Stresemann.

SOURCE 2.30   The Programme of the German Workers' Party, Munich, 24 February 1920

1 We demand the union of all Germans . . . to form a Great Germany.

2 We demand equality of right for the German People in its dealings with other nations, and abolition of the Peace Treaties of Versailles and St Germain.

3 We demand land and territory [colonies] for the nourishment of our people and for settling our surplus population.

4 Only members of the nation may be citizens of the State. None but those of German blood, whatever their creed, may be members of the nation. No Jew, therefore, may be a member of the nation . . .

6 The right of voting . . . is to be enjoyed by the citizens of the State alone. We demand, therefore, that all official appointments shall be granted to citizens of the State alone. We oppose the corrupt Parliamentary custom of the State of filling posts merely with a view to Party considerations . . .

9 All citizens of the State shall possess equal rights and duties.

10 It must be the first duty of every citizen of the State to perform mental or physical work. The activities of the individual must not clash with the interests of the whole, but must proceed within the framework of the community and must be for the general good.

We demand therefore:

11 Abolition of incomes unearned by work. Abolition of the thraldom [slavery] of interest.

12 We demand therefore the ruthless confiscation of all war profits.

13 We demand the nationalisation of all businesses.

14 We demand that there shall be profit-sharing in the great industries.

15 We demand a general development of provision for old age.

16 We demand the creation and maintenance of a healthy middle class, immediate communalisation of wholesale warehouses, and their lease at low rates to small traders.

17 We demand a land reform suitable to our national requirements . . . the abolition of interest on mortgages, and prohibition of all speculation in land . . .

18 We demand an all-out battle against those who damage the common interest by their actions; criminals against the nation, profiteers, racketeers, etc. should be punished by death, without regard to religion or race.

19 We demand the replacement of the system of ROMAN LAW, which serves the materialistic world order, by a system of Germanic COMMON LAW.

20 In order to make it possible for all capable and diligent Germans to receive a good education . . . the state must carry the burden of a thorough overhaul of the national education system. The curricula of all institutions of education must adapt to the practical requirements of life. We must aim to instil national ideas from the earliest age in lessons [in citizenship]. We demand that the brightest children of poor parents should be supported by the state irrespective of their class or job.

21 The state must ensure the general good health of its citizens, by providing for mothers and children, by banning child labour, by encouraging the development of physical fitness, by making it a legal obligation to participate in sport and gymnastics.

22 We demand the abolition of the professional army and its replacement by a people's army.

23 . . . Newspapers which are deemed to be against the common good should be banned. We demand a legal battle against any art and literature which exerts a harmful influence on public life.

24 We demand the freedom of religion in the Reich so long as it does not endanger the position of the state or adversely affect the moral standards of the German race. As such the Party represents a positively Christian position without binding itself to one particular faith. The Party opposes the materialistic Jewish spirit within and beyond us and is convinced that a lasting recovery of our people can only be achieved on the basis of:
Common Good before Personal Gain.

25 In order to achieve all the foregoing requirements we demand the creation of a strong central power of the Reich, unconditional authority of the politically central Parliament over the entire Reich and its organisation in general.

The leaders of the Party swear to proceed regardless of consequences, if necessary at the sacrifice of their lives, towards the fulfilment of the foregoing Points.

■ **2H   How did Hitler first try to gain power? The Munich Putsch**

53

8 November 1923
Otto von Lossow and Gustav von Kahr address a meeting of 2,000 right-wing supporters in a Munich beer-hall.

Hitler and his stormtroopers burst into the meeting. They declare a national revolution. Gun in hand, Hitler forces Kahr and Lossow into a side room. The two men are forced to state their support for a march on Berlin to impose a new government, with General Ludendorff as the new Commander-in-Chief.

Meanwhile, thousands of stormtroopers seize other members of the Bavarian government; they terrorise their opponents but they fail to gain control of the army barracks.

After Lossow and Kahr promise loyalty to the putsch, Ludendorff allows them to leave the beer-hall.

9 November
Berlin: President Ebert declares a national state of emergency because of the treason in Munich. General Seeckt orders Lossow to crush the revolt.

Lossow and Kahr now issue a proclamation denouncing the putsch.

Ludendorff persuades Hitler not to give up and to march into Munich to seize power, as a first step to marching on Berlin. Ludendorff is convinced that soldiers will support their former commander, and certainly not fire on him.

At noon 2,000 armed Nazis, gaining some public support, march to a military base in Munich.

They are met by armed police and Bavarian soldiers. A shot is fired, probably by a Nazi, and police return fire.

Fourteen Nazis are killed, including the person next to Hitler. Most Nazis fall to the ground and take cover. Hitler dislocates a shoulder in his fall, then flees. Ludendorff continues to march up to the police. He is arrested.

Aftermath
11 November: Hitler is arrested. Seeckt bans the Nazis.

February 1924: Hitler, Ludendorff and other leaders are tried for treason which carries the death penalty. Hitler turns the trial into an opportunity to attack the Weimar regime and expound his views. Hitler achieves national fame. The trial, just before the elections, helps the Nazi vote. The Nazis become the third largest group in Bavaria. The judges are sympathetic. Ludendorff is acquitted. Hitler is sentenced to the minimum possible sentence of five years in prison. The judges accepted Ludendorff's explanation that he had only been present 'by accident' (an excuse he had also successfully used in 1920 over his involvement in the Kapp Putsch).

Hitler kept in good conditions in Landsberg prison. While there he dictates *Mein Kampf*.

The Nazis nearly disintegrate without their leader. On 24 December 1924 Hitler is released after nine months.

Why did Hitler's putsch fail?

SOURCE 2.31   A. Bullock, *Hitler and Stalin: Parallel Lives*, 1992, p. 100

Hitler proved singularly ineffective. Nothing had been properly planned, and when Hitler was forced to recognize that von Lossow and von Kahr had resumed their freedom of action and were taking measures to suppress the rising he suffered a nervous collapse in which he passed through a whole succession of moods – anger, despair, apathy, renewed hope, hesitation. He remained shut up in the Beer Hall, isolated from the crowds from which he had always drawn strength, and unable to make up his mind whether or not to risk a demonstration. It was Ludendorff who decided for him, and at noon next day led out Hitler and the other Nazi leaders at the head of a column of several thousand men, which ... marched into the centre of the city. Eyewitness accounts strongly suggest that Hitler had already lost all faith in what they were doing. When a police cordon opened fire, 14 in the procession and 3 policemen were killed, and many more wounded. While Ludendorff marched on and pushed through the cordon, Hitler, after being pulled to the ground and dislocating his shoulder, scrambled to his feet and fled ... The chances of bringing off a coup in 1923 comparable with Mussolini's March on Rome the year before had never been more than marginal.

ACTIVITY

What, according to Bullock, were the main reasons for the failure of the putsch?

Was the Munich Putsch a complete failure?

SOURCE 2.32   Hitler comments in 1933 on the failed coup

It was the greatest good fortune for us National Socialists that the Putsch collapsed because:

1   *Co-operation with General Ludendorff would have been absolutely impossible.*
2   *The sudden takeover of power in the whole of Germany would have led to the greatest of difficulties in 1923 because the essential preparations had not even been begun by the National Socialist Party.*
3   *The events of 9th November 1923 with their blood sacrifice have proved the most effective propaganda for National Socialism.*

SOURCE 2.33   Hitler talking to Kurt Lüdecke in 1924, from *I Knew Hitler*, 1938. Lüdecke, a former Nazi supporter, broke with Hitler in 1934 and became a bitter critic

When I resume active work it will be necessary to pursue a new policy. Instead of working to achieve power by an armed coup we shall have to hold our noses against the Catholic and Marxist deputies. If out-voting them takes longer than outshooting them, at least the results will be guaranteed by their own Constitution! ... Sooner or later we shall have a majority – and after that, Germany. I am convinced that this is our best line of action, now that conditions in the country have changed so radically.

SOURCE 2.34   William Shirer was an American journalist living in Germany in the 1930s. His book *The Rise and Fall of the Third Reich* was published in the US in 1960

Hitler was shrewd enough to see that his trial would provide a new platform from which he could ... for the first time make his name known far beyond the confines of Bavaria and indeed Germany itself ... By the time it ended ... Hitler had transformed defeat into triumph ... impressed the German people by his eloquence and the fervour of his nationalism, and emblazoned his name on the front pages of the world.

ACTIVITY

Look at Sources 2.32–4.

1   Why did Hitler consider the Nazis not ready for power?
2   In what ways did the failure help the Nazis?
3   Does Source 2.33 show that after the Munich Putsch the Nazis became a democratic party, and accepted the Weimar constitution?
4   Was the Munich Putsch a complete failure?

ACTIVITY

Write a police report on Hitler and the Munich Putsch. Use pages 51–4 and the page opposite giving you information about Hitler. Refer to the following areas:

a)   Background: general political, economic situation in Bavaria; Hitler and Nazi Party
b)   Aims of the putsch
c)   Why the putsch failed
d)   Assessment: degree of threat in 1923 and whether the Nazis are likely to be a threat in the future.

BACKGROUND

Who was Hitler?
In 1939, after Germany had taken over Austria, the village of Döllersheim was wiped from the map. Its inhabitants were forcibly removed and the village destroyed by artillery and tanks. Döllersheim was the birthplace of Alois Schicklgruber, father of Adolf Hitler. In this manoeuvre, Hitler was trying to obliterate traces of his ancestry, as he feared that his grandmother may have been made pregnant by a Jew. For Hitler, obsessed with hatred of Jews, the terrible suspicion that he was one-quarter Jewish had to be suppressed.

Character
- Shy, awkward, moody; unable to form loving ties (due to repressive father, pampered by mother?)
- Profoundly lonely, isolated
- Contemptuous of mankind, suspicious
- Admired strength and success
- Absorbed in fantasies, became convinced he was destined to play a great role

General skills, abilities
- Commitment
- Tremendous energy
- Remarkable willpower
- Single-minded fanatic

PROPAGANDA skills
- Great orator
- Had hypnotic effect on audience
- Supreme master of psychology of mass politics
- Gift for exploiting anxiety/discontent
- Put into words what crowd longing to hear

Hitler's basic ideas
- Anti-semitism. The purity of German blood was being defiled by Jews. They should be excluded from Germany.
- Social Darwinism/survival of the fittest. Germans should form a *Herrenvölk* or Master Race to dominate others.
- Pan-Germanism. All Germans should join together.
- LEBENSRAUM. Germany must expand to take over more territory (living space) to feed her population.
- Anti-Marxism. Hostile to the ideas of Karl Marx, the German philosopher, economist and revolutionary. Marx was a non-religious Jew.
- Anti-democracy/*Führerprinzip*. Democracy provided weak government; it should be replaced by a one-party state based on the principle of an all-powerful leader.

Other ideas Hitler frequently expressed
- Anti-capitalism. He disliked what he called finance capitalism, i.e. the power that came from being very rich; this again was associated with Jews. He also initially criticised big business, i.e. large firms which often harmed small producers.
- Socialism. Although he hated Marxism, he spoke in favour of socialism, in the sense of stressing the needs of the national community.

1837 Alois, Hitler's father, born to unmarried cook Maria Anna Schicklgruber. (The Jewish Frankenberger family whom she has worked for pays her an allowance for fourteen years.)

1842 Maria Schicklgruber marries miller Johann Georg Hiedler. His brother, Johann Nepomuk, fosters Alois

1876 Alois' birth certificate is altered to show Johann Georg Hiedler (misspelt Hitler) as his father

1885 Alois, a customs official, marries Klara Pölzl, his third wife

1889 Adolf Hitler born in Braunau-am-Inn, Austria

1895 Adolf attends local choir school. Wishes to become a priest

1903 Alois dies; freed from tight control, Adolf becomes wayward; unhappy at school in Lintz, his record is poor, except in gym and art. Uses a school report as toilet paper

1905 Leaves school with no qualifications

1907 Goes to Vienna; fails to gain a place at Academy of Fine Arts; very upset over death of his mother

1907–13 Drifts for six years; slums it in Vienna; lives in Jewish quarter, develops anti-semitic, anti-Marxist, anti-democratic feelings; supports PAN-GERMANISM and racism

1913 Moves to Munich, perhaps to avoid being conscripted into the Austro-Hungarian army

1914 Feb Recalled to Austria, but is found medically unfit for army
Aug Ecstatic when war breaks out, he joins Bavarian regiment; has found real purpose in life – exemplary soldier; but only rises to corporal; is considered to lack leadership qualities

1916 Oct Wounded – awarded Iron Cross, Second and First Class

1918 Oct Gassed and then hospitalised where he hears of Germany's defeat. Hysterical at news. Feels betrayed

1919 Employed as 'education officer' (that is, a spy) by Bavarian army's political section
Sept Goes to a German Workers' Party (DAP) meeting and joins; becomes a committee member

1920 Feb With DAP leader Drexler, draws up Twenty-five Point Programme; party name changed to NSDAP. His powerful speeches help build up membership

1921 Jul Becomes chairman and Führer after he threatens to resign
Aug Sets up the SA

1922 Jan Is let off leniently after being convicted of breaking up a meeting

Hitler's family tree

Maria Anna Schicklgruber (1796–1847) = Johann Georg Hiedler (1792–1857)

Johann V Nepomuk Hiedler (1807–88) = Eva Maria Decker (1792–1873)

Johanna Hiedler (1830–1906) = Johann Pölzl (1828–1902)

Franziska Matzelberger (2) = Alois Schicklgruber (illegitimate; legitimised in 1876 as Alois Hitler; 1837–1903) = (3) Klara Pölzl (1860–1907)

Angela Hitler = Leo Raubal
Alois Hitler
Leo Raubal
Friedl Raubal
Angela Raubal

Gustav Hitler (1885–6)
Ida Hitler (1886–7)
Otto Hitler (1887–lived only a few days)
Adolf Hitler (1889–1945)
Edmund Hitler (1894–1900)
Paula Hitler (b. 1896 d. 1960)

F Review: Why did the Weimar Republic survive the crises of 1919–23?

The new republic had faced major political, international and economic problems but it had survived. This was partly because the extremist forces of both Left and Right failed to attract much support and were both divided and disorganised. Although many in the army and elite were not committed to democracy, they were not yet prepared to overthrow it as they feared this could lead to greater chaos. President Ebert used Article 48, as intended, to take firm action against threats to the regime, and Stresemann tackled hyperinflation successfully. By the end of 1923, it looked as if the worst was over and that, having survived such turbulence, Weimar democracy had a chance of taking root.

FOCUS ROUTE

Look back at the table on page 33. Identify why

a) the left-wing
b) the right-wing

revolts failed.
Did they fail for the same reasons? Explain your answer.

KEY POINTS FROM CHAPTER 2: Why did the Weimar Republic survive the crises of 1919–23?

1 The imposed Treaty of Versailles was hated by virtually all Germans. The new democratic government was blamed for accepting it.
2 Germany lost land, all its colonies and was partially disarmed.
3 The war-guilt clause and reparations were especially hated. Reparations remained a running sore.
4 The Kapp Putsch of 1920 was resisted by a general strike as the army stayed neutral.
5 The Bavarian authorities suppressed Hitler's ill-organised Munich Putsch in 1923.
6 Between 1919 and 1923 the Communists made several uncoordinated attempts to overthrow the Weimar government; they were suppressed by the army and the Freikorps.
7 Inflation, beginning in 1914, reached astronomic levels in 1923 when the value of the mark collapsed.
8 Millions of Germans lost savings; others exploited the crisis to build up assets.
9 The inflationary crisis left permanent scars.
10 By the end of 1923 the worst of the economic and political turmoil was over.

Part 1.1 Review

Chapters 1 and 2 have covered the early, turbulent years of the Weimar Republic in some detail. The following exercises look at the period 1918–23 in overview.

REVIEW ACTIVITY I

Explain which of the following issues posed the greatest threat to the consolidation of democracy in Germany:

a) The limited nature of the German revolution
b) The nature of the Weimar constitution
c) The Treaty of Versailles
d) Right-wing extremism
e) Left-wing extremism
f) The economic crisis
g) The attitudes of the German elite
h) The attitudes of ordinary people.

This task allows you to think about your own views on the first four years of the Weimar Republic. The table on the right gives contrasting viewpoints on various aspects of the Weimar Republic, 1919–23.

Identify the statement in each pair with which you most agree. (Are there any where you feel both alternatives have considerable merit?) Discuss your views, then write a brief summary of your assessment of each issue.

Event/issue	Comment
1 Setting up of the Weimar Republic	**a)** The fact that many of the old elite were prepared to support the new regime was promising. **b)** The initial support from the elite for the new regime was purely tactical and might be ominous for the prospects for secure democracy.
2 Nature of the German Revolution	**a)** The events of 1918–19 can be seen as a series of complex revolutions: initially one from above, then a limited, unrevolutionary revolution from below, followed by the defeat of the real revolutionaries. **b)** The creation of a democratic republic must be considered as a real revolution.
3 Ebert's role	**a)** Ebert must be considered a traitor to the cause of the working class for his deal with the army and the crushing of the Spartacist rising. **b)** Ebert correctly judged the mood of the majority of the German people and was justified in using the army to maintain the new government.
4 The Armistice	**a)** An armistice was sought by the generals and cannot be blamed on the new civilian politicians. **b)** The new republican government was unwise to accept the Armistice as the peace terms were bound to be harsh and unpopular.
5 Versailles Treaty	**a)** Considering the context, the terms of the Versailles Treaty were understandable, though the Allied diplomats could have shown greater wisdom. **b)** The Treaty of Versailles was an act of criminal irresponsibility by short-sighted, vengeful politicians.
6 The Weimar constitution	**a)** The constitution was far too democratic for the situation facing Germany in 1919. **b)** The Weimar constitution was a well-considered mix of democracy and protective measures against anarchy; the regime's greatest weaknesses lay elsewhere.
7 Kapp Putsch	**a)** Although a failure, the Kapp Putsch suggests how it might be only a matter of time before the Weimar Republic was overthrown. **b)** The defeat of the Kapp Putsch illustrates the strength of democratic forces in Germany.
8 Communist threat	**a)** The Communists posed a major threat in 1919–23 to the infant democratic regime. **b)** The Communists aroused the fears of moderate Socialists and conservatives but were far too weak to gain power.
9 Causes of the inflationary crisis	**a)** The Allies bear sole responsibility for the German inflationary crisis. **b)** German governments were partly to blame for the inflationary crisis of 1923.
10 Significance of the inflationary crisis	**a)** The fact that the Weimar regime overcame the crisis of hyperinflation means it cannot be considered a factor in the Republic's later collapse. **b)** The 1923 inflationary crisis might have caused the regime's collapse and its aftermath was to contribute to the Republic's eventual disintegration.
11 Hitler's Munich Putsch	**a)** Hitler's putsch was a minor event. Its importance lies in the lessons Hitler learned from it. **b)** The Munich Putsch was important in causing the eventual collapse of the Weimar Republic.
12 Overall judgement	**a)** The fact that the Weimar Republic survived so many crises in its first four years suggests it had considerable strengths. **b)** Although the Weimar Republic survived its turbulent first four years, it was permanently scarred by the experience, and the prospects for democracy were poor.

REVIEW ACTIVITY 3

Essay: What problems faced the new republic in Germany from 1918 to 1923? Why did it survive?

In an exam, you are likely to be asked for a two-stage essay on this topic.

The first part is easier. You have to describe the problems (the left-wing revolts, the right-wing revolts, the economic crisis, etc.). As well as displaying your knowledge of the problems, you would gain extra marks for making judgements about the comparative seriousness of the problems.

The second part is more complex. You could go through each problem in turn, analysing how it was overcome. Alternatively, you could make general points about why the Weimar regime survived, such as the weakness and divisions of its opponents as well as its own actions, and substantiate (back up) your opinions with relevant examples from the various problems. The second approach is probably best if you are going for the highest grade. What matters is that you approach the essay in a structured way.

PART 1.2
The Weimar Republic 1924–9: Years of recovery and achievement?

By 1924 the Weimar Republic had survived a series of attempted coups and revolts from both the Right and the Left. These had been serious threats, not so much because of the strength of the various opposition groups, but because of the sense of national humiliation following the Treaty of Versailles and then the economic crisis of 1923. However, the Republic survived and entered a more stable period that lasted until 1929. On the surface these were years of recovery and achievement – or do they only seem successful in contrast to the turmoil of 1918 to 1923? An alternative view is that, behind the superficial promise of these years, major weaknesses still existed in the Weimar Republic, weaknesses that would later contribute significantly to the downfall of democracy. Chapters 3–5 therefore examine whether the middle years of the Weimar Republic were really years of recovery and achievement by looking at the topics shown in Chart A below.

TALKING POINT

Why might it be difficult to reach an objective conclusion about the extent of stability and recovery between 1924 and 1929?

■ A   Alternative views of the period 1924–9

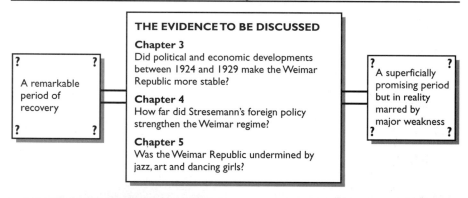

A remarkable period of recovery

THE EVIDENCE TO BE DISCUSSED

Chapter 3
Did political and economic developments between 1924 and 1929 make the Weimar Republic more stable?

Chapter 4
How far did Stresemann's foreign policy strengthen the Weimar regime?

Chapter 5
Was the Weimar Republic undermined by jazz, art and dancing girls?

A superficially promising period but in reality marred by major weakness

ACTIVITY

Chart B summarises the main events of this period. Which events might be used as evidence to support either of the interpretations in Chart A?

■ B   Timeline of key events 1923–9

1923	**Aug**	Stresemann becomes Chancellor
	Oct	Radical left-wing governments in Saxony and Thuringia are overthrown
	Nov	Hitler's Munich Putsch fails
		Rentenmark is introduced and ends the inflationary crisis
		Stresemann's government falls; but he remains Foreign Minister
1924	**Apr**	Dawes Plan reorganises reparations in Germany's favour
	May	Election: extremist parties improve their positions
	Dec	Election: moderate parties make gains at expense of extremists
1925	**Feb**	President Ebert dies
	Apr	Field Marshal Hindenburg is elected President
	Oct	Locarno Conference. Germany voluntarily accepts its western borders

Cartoon from the German magazine *Simplicisimus* in 1924

Signing the Locarno Treaty in 1925

1926	**Apr**	Treaty of Berlin with the USSR builds on relationship established by Rapallo Pact 1922
	Sept	Germany joins the League of Nations
1927		Agricultural prices begin to fall
	July	Unemployment insurance law benefits working classes
1928	**May**	Moderate parties make gains in elections
	Oct–Dec	Ruhr lockout of workers by employers
1929	**June**	Young Plan eases reparations burden but is hated by many Germans
	3 Oct	Stresemann dies
	29 Oct	Wall Street Crash
	Dec	Anti-Young Plan referendum wins 5.8 million votes (14 per cent of voters)

German army practising with model tanks on manoeuvres

Farmers blockade entrance to a farm to prevent the eviction of a farmer for debt

FOCUS ROUTE

As you read Chapters 3, 4 and 5 complete the relevant sections in your own copy of the table below.
This will help you in the debate in the Review on page 98.

	A remarkable period of recovery	A superficially promising period but in reality marred by major weaknesses
Politics		
Economics		
Social policy		
Foreign policy		
Culture		

■ **Learning trouble spot**

Assessing sources

Content and provenance

When assessing sources, you clearly need to consider a source's **content**. This involves considering both what it says, and what it does not say that might have been said. You might also need to consider what can be implied or inferred from the source; that is, deduced from it, without it being explicit. You might need to assess how far the source is factual and how far opinion. Often how the ideas are conveyed (for example, the language and techniques used) will also need considering.

You are frequently asked to comment on the **origins**, PROVENANCE or **attribution** of a source. These three words all cover the same issue, that is, who created the source. To assess a source effectively, you need to consider what sort of source it is, who produced it, when, for whom and why.

Language, style and tone

The way a written source is composed often causes students problems. If asked to comment on **language**, you need to identify and quote particular, often emotive, words to illustrate your discussion. But you are sometimes also asked about **style** and **tone**. Style refers to various techniques that might be used, such as exaggeration, repetition, exclamation. Tone is the overall atmosphere created by a source. Thus it will cover both what is expressed, and how, to create an overall impression.

It is important when asked about specific aspects such as tone that you do directly address that issue, using the word tone in your answer. Of course, merely using the word is not sufficient; as with any historical analysis, the tone must be assessed with supporting evidence.

Reliability and value of a source

You are often asked to assess the **reliability** and **value** of a source. These two issues are related but not identical. **Reliable** means that it can be relied upon, that it is accurate. **Value** means how useful, which may be partly based on reliability, but covers broader issues. When assessing either of these qualities, you need to consider the purpose for which the historian is using the source, as it may be reliable for some purposes, but not others. Again, its value will partly depend upon the use to which it is being put.

Remember that an unreliable source may also be valuable: for example, a propaganda poster about Jews may be very misleading about Jewish behaviour, but it could be a valuable piece of evidence about Nazi propaganda.

You may often, at the end of a number of source-based questions, be asked an overall question about the value of the sources as evidence about an event. A common error students make is simply to discuss this in relation to the content of the sources, neglecting issues of reliability stemming from who wrote the sources and how ideas are presented, even though they may already have answered quite effectively specific questions on these issues. Do ensure you consider all such aspects when discussing the value of a collection of sources.

See also pages 72, 177 and 367 for further advice on other aspects of source-based questions.

3

Did political and economic developments between 1924 and 1929 make the Weimar Republic more stable?

CHAPTER OVERVIEW

In 1923 the Weimar Republic had faced severe crises but it had survived and was to last for another ten years. Indeed, the Republic in fact lasted longer than Hitler's Third Reich. Some historians therefore argue that Weimar Germany could have developed into a secure parliamentary democracy if it had not been for the Great Depression after 1929. This chapter examines the mid-1920s, the 'golden years' of the Weimar Republic, to see whether a firm political and economic foundation had really been established for the long-term survival of parliamentary democracy or whether the events justify the opposing view that the Weimar Republic was a 'republic without republicans' and was doomed to failure.

This chapter also includes a range of information on political developments during Weimar Germany as a whole (pages 62–4), as well as a Guide to Economic Terms (page 73).

A 'A republic without republicans.' How far did the German people support the Republic? (pp. 61–70)

B How secure was the economic recovery? (pp. 71–6)

C Did the Weimar welfare state strengthen or weaken the regime? (pp. 76–7)

D Review: Did political and economic developments between 1924 and 1929 make the Weimar Republic more stable? (p. 77)

'A republic without republicans.' How far did the German people support the Republic?

Governments, parties and elections – the pattern of events

Pages 62–70 give you a range of information about the political developments during the Weimar Republic. You can use the Activities on these pages to work out whether the Weimar Republic had become politically more stable by 1929 or whether major weaknesses remained.

SOURCE 3.1   Weimar governments 1919–33

Elections	Date of appointment of new government	Chancellor (party)	SPD*	DDP	Z	DVP	BVP	DNVP	NSDAP	% of deputies in Reichstag in parties supporting the government
Jan 1919	Feb 1919	Scheidemann (SPD)	●	●	●					78
	June 1919	Bauer (SPD)	●		●					60
	Mar 1920	Müller (SPD)	●	●	●					78
June 1920	June 1920	Fehrenbach (Z)		●	●	●				37
	May 1921	Wirth (Z)	●	●	●					45
	Nov 1922	Cuno†		●	●	●	●			41
	Aug 1923	Stresemann (DVP)	●	●	●	●				59
	Nov 1923	Marx (Z)		●	●	●				37
May 1924	June 1924	Marx (Z)		●	●	●				29
Dec 1924	Jan 1925	Luther†		●	●	●	●	●		56
	Jan 1926	Luther†		●	●	●	●			35
	May 1926	Marx (Z)		●	●	●	●			35
	Jan 1927	Marx (Z)			●	●	●	●		49
May 1928	June 1928	Müller (SPD)	●	●	●	●	●			61
Sept 1930	Mar 1930	Brüning (Z)	Presidential government including DDP, Z, BVP, DVP							35–28
July 1932 Nov 1932	June 1932	Papen (Z)	Presidential government, including DNVP							6–10
	Dec 1932	Schleicher†	Presidential government, including DNVP							9
Mar 1933	Jan 1933	Hitler (NSDAP)						●	●	43 53 after March

* On many issues the government was dependent on the support of the SPD, even when it was officially in opposition.
† Not a member of a party.

ACTIVITY

Study Source 3.2. Did the vote for parties supporting the Republic increase, fall or stay the same between 1924 and 1929?

SOURCE 3.2 Support for democracy

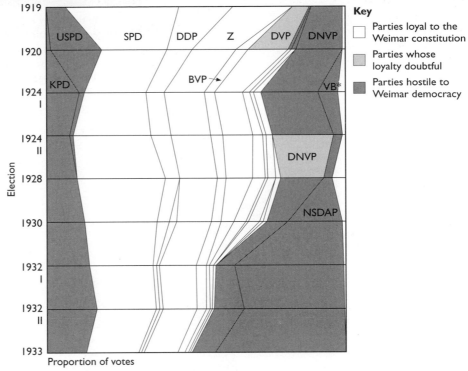

Key

☐ Parties loyal to the Weimar constitution

▨ Parties whose loyalty doubtful

▪ Parties hostile to Weimar democracy

*Völkischer Block (Racial–Nationalist Alliance)

SOURCE 3.3 Reichstag elections, 1919–33

Parties	% of vote won by each party								
	Jan 1919	Jun 1920	May 1924	Dec 1924	May 1928	Sept 1930	July 1932	Nov 1932	Mar 1933
KPD	–	2.1	12.6	9.0	10.6	13.1	14.5	16.9	12.3
USPD	7.6	17.9	0.8	0.3	0.1	0.0	–	–	–
SPD	37.9	21.7	20.5	26.0	29.8	24.5	21.6	20.4	18.3
DDP*	18.6	8.3	5.7	6.3	4.9	3.8	1.0	1.0	0.9
Z	15.9	13.6	13.4	13.6	12.1	11.8	12.5	11.9	11.2
BVP	3.8	4.2	3.2	3.8	3.1	3.0	3.7	3.4	2.7
DVP	4.4	13.9	9.2	10.1	8.7	4.7	1.2	1.9	1.1
DNVP	10.3	15.1	19.5	20.5	14.2	7.0	6.2	8.9	8.0
NSDAP	–	–	6.5	3.0	2.6	18.3	37.4	33.1	43.9
Others†	1.6	3.3	8.6	7.0	13.9	13.8	2.0	2.6	1.6
Turnout (%)	83	79	77	79	76	82	84	81	89
Number of deputies	421	459	472	493	491	577	608	584	647
Total vote (millions)	30.4	28.2	29.3	30.3	30.8	35.0	36.9	35.5	39.6

* From 1930 known as the German States Party.
† Others consisted of a number of special interest parties formed to protect a narrow segment of the population, such as the Völkischer Block (Racial–Nationalist Alliance). Such parties were encouraged by the system of proportional representation.

64

DID POLITICAL AND ECONOMIC DEVELOPMENTS BETWEEN 1924 AND 1929 MAKE THE WEIMAR REPUBLIC MORE STABLE?

TALKING POINT

How valuable are such posters to historians seeking to explain election results?

ACTIVITY

1 Study the party election posters in Sources 3.4–11 and the list of slogans. The names of the parties have been replaced by a dash. Chart 3A on page 66 may help you answer these questions:
   a) Which poster belongs to which party?
   b) Which slogan belongs to each poster?
2 Identify the public moods and concerns to which each party was seeking to appeal.

SOURCE 3.4

SOURCE 3.5

SOURCE 3.6

SOURCE 3.7

Poster slogans

1 'Against a new inflation; for German unity and the Republic. Away with our enemies. The – brings recovery. Vote –.'

2 'Free from Versailles! Away with the Jewish-Socialist Front. For Freedom and Fatherland. Your solution: –.'

3 'This is how it was in 1918. This is how it is in 1928. So vote –.'

4 'Away with the system.'

5 'These are the enemies of democracy! Away with them! So vote list 1!'

6 'Every vote counts against civil war and inflation!'

7 'We are building! Our building bricks: Work. Freedom. Bread. The others' building plans ... unemployment, spending cuts, corruption, terror, lying ... Therefore vote –.'

8 'Who will save our children for us Christian mothers? Vote for the –.'

65

DID POLITICAL AND ECONOMIC DEVELOPMENTS BETWEEN 1924 AND 1929 MAKE THE WEIMAR REPUBLIC MORE STABLE?

SOURCE 3.8

SOURCE 3.9

SOURCE 3.10

SOURCE 3.11

■ 3A   Political parties in Weimar Germany

Parties generally committed to Weimar democracy	Parties with a more fluctuating attitude to Weimar democracy	Parties hostile to Weimar democracy
SPD (Sozialdemokratische Partei Deutschlands). Founded in 1875, this party was the main creator of the Weimar Republic, and for much of the period gained the greatest electoral support, largely from the working class. Yet for long periods it did not participate in the coalition governments, although it did help maintain the government in office. There was tension between advocates of keeping the SPD a Marxist, class-based party of the proletariat, aiming for genuine socialism, and those modernisers who wanted a more broadly based, reformist party. The SPD continually worried about losing votes to the KPD but was also wary of frightening potential democratic allies amongst middle-class moderates. The SPD was strong not just in the federal Reichstag, but in many states. From 1918 to 1932 it led coalition governments (with the Z) in the key state of Prussia, using its position in power there to appoint officials supportive of democracy.	**DVP (Deutsche Volkspartei).** A moderate conservative party, under Stresemann's leadership it became committed to the Weimar system and moderate social reform, whilst retaining a more right-wing stance. Its main support came from the Protestant middle class and industrialists who favoured free trade. Despite Stresemann's diplomatic achievements, his party never became a major force in Weimar politics. After his death, the DVP moved to the right, and helped bring down Müller's SPD government in 1930.	**KPD (Kommunistische Partei Deutschlands).** This was a revolutionary Marxist party committed to a soviet-style system. Formed from the Spartacists and radicals from the USPD, the KPD attempted a series of revolts between 1919 and 1923. It failed to overthrow the Republic, so then it concentrated on building up mass support. From 1924 the KPD became a disciplined bureaucratic party under Ernst Thaelmann. It gained between 9 and 17 per cent of the vote, overwhelmingly from the working class. The KPD had 360,000 members by 1932. The KPD became increasingly dominated by the USSR, which through the Third COMMUNIST INTERNATIONAL (or Comintern) sought to influence the tactics of communist parties throughout Europe. Stalin encouraged it to be hostile to the SPD, so left-wing forces in Germany were divided.
Z (Zentrum) – Centre Party. This party, created in 1870, existed primarily to protect the interests of the Catholic Church. It regularly attracted the support of about two-fifths of voting Catholics. It had a broad appeal across the classes, and so it had left and right wings. From 1928, under Kass and Brüning, it moved to the right. Catholics who supported the Z considered protecting Catholicism the most important issue and tended to vote for the Centre Party regardless of changing economic circumstances. Bavaria had its own Catholic Party, the Bavarian People's Party (BVP).	**DNVP (Deutschnationale Volkspartei).** This was the main conservative party. Initially hostile to the Republic, the DNVP became more pragmatic, and joined the government in 1925 and in 1927–8. It remained split between reactionaries and moderates. The majority came to realise the benefits of co-operation in government to protect the interests of the industrialists and large landowners that the party represented. Initially it also attracted support from smaller farmers and artisans. After major election losses in 1928 when it was part of the government, it moved to the right under its new leader Alfred Hugenberg, an industrialist and media tycoon.	**NSDAP (Nationalsozialistische Deutsche Arbeiterpartei).** In 1924 the Nazis were part of a racialist grouping, but from 1928 onwards they campaigned on their own. Like the KPD, the NSDAP tried to use legal electoral methods to gain power, having failed to overthrow the regime by force. The NSDAP received reasonable support in some regional elections, especially in farming areas in 1928, but overall there was little mass support before 1930.
DDP (Deutsche Demokratische Partei). This liberal, middle-class party might have been the main base for a secure parliamentary system, if liberalism had had deeper roots in Germany. Its members played a major role in drawing up the constitution, but it failed to attract the majority of the more conservative-minded middle classes. Preuss and Rathenau were leading members.		

FOCUS ROUTE

1   Study Chart 3A. Copy and complete this table. (You will be able to add more information by the end of Chapter 4.)

2   Copy out the names of the following parties, arranging them in order from left wing to right wing:
   - NSDAP
   - DDP
   - DVP
   - KPD
   - DNVP
   - Z
   - SPD
   - BVP

Party	German name	Prominent figures	Political position	Main supporters
Nazis				
Nationalists				
People's Party				
Centre Party				
Democratic Party				
Social Democrats				
Communists				

FOCUS ROUTE

As you read pages 67–9, note down in the 'politics' section of your own copy of the table on page 60 evidence that supports the two opposing views (which you were introduced to on page 58). Include election results, the voting system, developments in the Reichstag, governments, the presidency and the attitudes of ordinary Germans and the elite. Remember, things that *don't* happen can be important too.

Did the German voters, parties and politicians strengthen the Weimar Republic?

After 1923 politics became more peaceful. There were no attempted coups, from right or left, between 1924 and 1929 and no major political figures were assassinated. However, political violence did not completely disappear. Although extremist parties did not gain mass support, they still made an impact on the streets. There were frequent fights between the Nazis, with their SA, and the KPD, with its paramilitary Red Fighting League. Over 50 people were killed and many more were injured.

Elections also gave some encouraging signs to supporters of the Republic. As the economic situation stabilised in 1924, so Germans switched back to voting for the main democratic parties. These made gains in the 1928 election, as you can see in Source 3.12. However, behind this broadly positive pattern, the liberal DDP, which could have formed the basis for representing middle-class interests within the parliamentary system, lost ground. Peukert (in *The Weimar Republic*, p. 210) argues that 'The electoral decline of the liberals was the decisive event of Weimar politics because it undermined the pro-republican centre from within.' Furthermore, the Centre Party moved to the right in the late 1920s, and some of its leaders, like Brüning, began to favour establishing a more authoritarian system.

SOURCE 3.12 Votes (in %) in Reichstag elections in 1924, 1928 and 1933

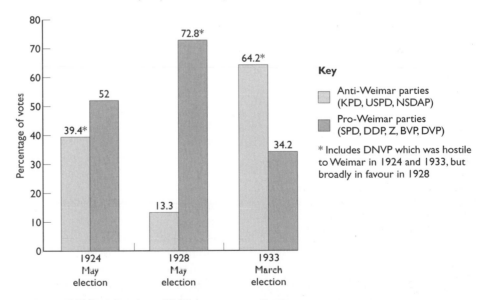

The likelihood of an increased sense of stability was reduced by the fact that there were six Weimar governments between 1924 and 1929, each one a short-lived coalition. Most did not have a secure majority in the Reichstag. These coalitions were the product of the proportional representation electoral system. Ideally, the politicians from different parties should have co-operated in government but many found this difficult. They often stuck to their political principles rather than accept the compromises necessary for effective government. As a result, no Chancellor was able to hold a government together for more than two years. Even when politicians tried to work together, the need for constant bargaining to stay in power discredited parliamentary government in the eyes of many Germans who came to see politics as a matter of manoeuvring by politicians rather than a process that they themselves controlled. The so-called 'political stability' of 1924–8 only appeared stable in comparison to the turmoil of 1918–23.

Another cause of public dissatisfaction with politicians was the voting system. Voters, in 35 vast electoral regions, voted for a party list rather than individual politicians. It was therefore the party machine that decided who actually became a Reichstag deputy, on the basis of the number of votes the party list had won. The voters therefore had not chosen their own deputy and thus there was not a close tie between voters in an area and the deputy.

The political parties can also be blamed for public disenchantment. The moderate parties were inconsistent in their attitudes to governments. The only way for governments to gain approval for policies in the Reichstag, given the presence of the radical opposition groups on the Left and Right, was by building a majority around the middle ground. However, on any issue the moderate Left (SPD) and moderate Right (DVP) might join forces with the radicals to defeat government policy. Furthermore, within the Reichstag, parties were also often divided amongst themselves. On one occasion in November 1928, SPD government ministers voted with their party against their own government which was proposing the funding of a new battleship. Such manoeuvres, critics argued, showed that parliamentary government was a charade.

The prospects for stable government were further reduced during this period by the growth of narrow sectional interest parties which gained a total of 78 deputies at their peak in 1930. (They then dramatically lost support to the Nazis who, as a form of 'super-interest group', took over their role.) Such sectional groups were encouraged by the proportional representation system because only 60,000 votes were needed to get representation in the Reichstag. Their advocacy of narrow interests, such as compensation for the losers from hyperinflation (the Reich Party for People's Rights and Revaluation), reduced the chances of the broader compromises required for effective democratic government.

In addition, a series of apparently minor issues showed the deep divisions within Germany. One example was the fierce controversy over the new national flag of black, red and gold, originally adopted by the 1848 revolutionaries but opposed by conservatives who used the old imperial flag of black, white and red. The Weimar regime might have won broader support if it had developed symbols that appealed to popular emotions, but it had no heroes and very few commemorative days. It only created a less than inspiring 'Constitution Day' in 1928. No myths of heroic leadership were fostered; and the negative one of the 'stab in the back' retained its hold. Weimar lacked a CHARISMATIC leader to deepen people's support. It was served by able politicians, like Rathenau and Stresemann, but no leader built up a dynamic of support for the regime. As a result, as the historian Bookbinder has argued in *Weimar Germany* (p. 150), 'Pride was in short supply during the Weimar years', echoing the views of Edgar Jung (secretary to Papen, leader of the Centre Party), who said in 1927: 'If there were to be an opinion survey, not of those who support today's Republic, but of those who love it, the result would be devastating.' A growing number of Germans began to look for charismatic, inspiring leadership and were attracted to what has been called the 'totalitarian temptation'.

Further evidence about the stability of the Weimar regime comes from the first election to the presidency in 1925. The presidency was crucial in the Weimar Republic's development, given its power to appoint and dismiss chancellors and to issue decrees under Article 48. The committed democrat Ebert had been chosen as President by the Assembly in 1919 and his period of office was renewed in 1922 for three years. Ebert was expected to win the election due to be held in 1925 but, when he died, the question of who should become President became a major issue.

The electoral system said that if no candidate gained over 50 per cent in the first round, a second round, in which new candidates could stand, had to be held. The candidate then winning most votes would become President. After an indecisive first round where most parties put forward their own candidate, the

69

DID POLITICAL AND ECONOMIC DEVELOPMENTS BETWEEN 1924 AND 1929 MAKE THE WEIMAR REPUBLIC MORE STABLE?

parties regrouped. The influential SPD Prussian leader Braun withdrew in favour of the drab Wilhelm Marx, leader of the Centre Party, in the hope of consolidating support for a reforming republic. The Right, in an attempt to broaden its support, rallied behind a new candidate, Paul von Hindenburg. (He had asked the ex-Kaiser's son for permission to become President!) The Communists refused to withdraw to help a united Left against the Right. The voting figures suggest this may have been vital in determining the result.

The election of the ultra-conservative Hindenburg can be seen as both a positive and an ominous sign for Weimar democracy. Hindenburg did nothing unconstitutional and abided by his oath to uphold the constitution. The presence of the conservative former field marshal, as opposed to a socialist ex-saddler, as head of the Republic, may have attracted some conservatives to the Republic. On the other hand, it was ominous to have someone who was uncommitted to democracy with such great powers. Hindenburg increasingly became the focus of powerful groups who wanted a more authoritarian system.

SOURCE 3.13 Presidential election, March–April 1925

First round 29 March			Second round 26 April		
Votes (millions)	Candidate (party)	Votes (%)	Votes (millions)	Candidate (party)	Votes (%)
10.8	Jarres (DVP)	39	14.7	Hindenburg (DNVP)	48
7.8	Braun (SDP)	28	13.8	Marx (Z)	45
4.0	Marx (Z)	14	1.9	Thaelmann (KPD)	6
1.9	Thaelmann (KPD)	7			
1.6	Hellpach (DDP)	6			
1.0	Held (BVP)	4			
0.2	Ludendorff (Volk)	1			

Note: 2.5m extra people voted in the second round; total vote was 69% of electorate.

The elite and the parliamentary system

We have seen how many in the elite had initially supported the Republic only through fear of a worse alternative. For its consolidation a more positive commitment would be important, but this did not develop even during the calmer days of the mid-1920s.

Many industrialists resented what they saw as the growing burdens of the welfare state and, as in the 1928 Ruhr lockout, tried to reassert greater control of wages. The landed aristocracy resented its loss of influence. The army was dominated by generals who at best wanted to keep the army as 'a state within a state', supposedly above politics, or who desired a more authoritarian system. Many of the employees of the state, such as judges and civil servants, retained a distaste for democracy. Few among opinion formers, such as church leaders, teachers and newspaper editors, tried to win support for democracy. Thus the people in key German institutions failed the Weimar Republic during the 'golden years'. The historian Bookbinder (*Weimar Germany*, p. 159) has summarised the situation as follows: 'With the schools not being geared to create critically thinking citizens and with newspapers not doing what they might to clarify issues, citizenship development did not progress very quickly. This was especially unfortunate during the peaceful period of the Republic. It was under these conditions, when people were not continually beset by crisis and when the shrill voices of the extremists created less resonance, that real progress towards the creation of Republicans could have been made ... With little inspiration from political leaders and little encouragement for democracy from the pulpit or the teacher's desk, the political education of many Germans made little progress.'

70

DID POLITICAL AND ECONOMIC DEVELOPMENTS BETWEEN 1924 AND 1929 MAKE THE WEIMAR REPUBLIC MORE STABLE?

ACTIVITY

Below are some statements that might have been made by members of the elite and other influential groups in 1928. Match each one up with the person most likely to have made that statement. (This exercise illustrates some of the attitudes amongst these groups; these were probably the predominant attitudes, but remember that there would be a considerable variety of opinion within each group.)

a) General   **b)** Teacher   **c)** Industrialist   **d)** Junker   **e)** Judge   **f)** Protestant pastor   **g)** Newspaper editor

h) Economic growth is not sufficient to finance welfare reforms as well as maintain the profitability of our businesses. We must follow the example of employers in the Ruhr lockout and regain our proper control over the workers.

k) Even though we don't like this new democratic system, at least we've kept our jobs. We will have to enforce laws we dislike, but we should take every opportunity to let good German nationalists not be harshly penalised for trying to save their country.

i) Our traditionally dominant political and social position has been undermined by the establishment of democracy. What's worse, our economic position has been weakened by the fall in world prices. I know our party, the DNVP, has recently joined the government, but I trust this is to try to secure government subsidies, not to bolster the regime!

l) We have lost the special position we had under the Second Reich, but at least the regime allows free religious activities. I and many of my colleagues, though, are concerned about the decline in moral standards and behaviour. Some people seem to want to break with tradition just for the sake of it; and there's still the danger of atheistic communism.

m) I, and most of my rivals, can't develop any enthusiasm for this new democracy. When you compare Germany now with what it was like under the Kaiser, it's hard to fathom. For the moment there seems no alternative, but I don't see it as my job to try to explain to our readers how the system works or to rally support for the present drab state of affairs.

j) Our priority is to maintain our beloved Reichswehr, and not let it be contaminated by democracy. We must, of course, defend the government against communist subversives, and it would be unwise to assist some of these harebrained conservative plotters. For the moment, we should concentrate on developing Germany's military position, and exploit our links with Russia. There's something to be said for strengthening the position of the President compared to the Reichstag, but let's bide our time for the moment.

n) At least this new regime has not yet interfered too much, but I am concerned that the spirit of democracy if taken too far could undermine discipline and respect for authority amongst youth. We must uphold traditional German values. We must foster pride in our country, though not in our current weak government.

B How secure was the economic recovery?

FOCUS ROUTE

As you read pages 71–6, note down in the 'economics' section of your own copy of the table on page 60 evidence that supports the two opposing views (which you were introduced to on page 58). Use Chart 3D to check that you have covered all the relevant points.

Traditionally, the period 1924–8 has been seen as one of considerable economic advance that might have secured the future of the Weimar regime if it had not been for the catastrophic impact of the Wall Street Crash and consequent world depression. You have already read (pages 49–50) how Stresemann's policies, helped by foreign assistance, restored the stability of the currency and public confidence. The Allies wanted the German economy to recover so that reparations could be paid. The USA, in particular, which had lent millions to Britain and France, wanted economic recovery so that it could retrieve its war loans. Under the Dawes Plan of 1924 (see page 82 for fuller details), Germany received massive American loans to help recovery; and reparations were rearranged, extending their repayment period. The prospects for economic growth made Weimar Germany a magnet for foreign investment until 1929. This traditional, positive interpretation has, however, been challenged by some historians who argue that continuing, fundamental problems in the German economy were of more significance for the future of the Weimar Republic.

■ 3B The Weimar economy in the 1920s

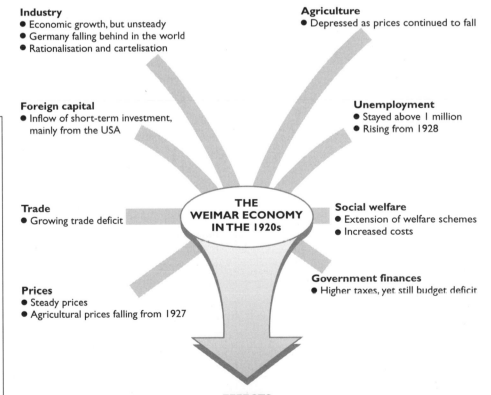

Industry
- Economic growth, but unsteady
- Germany falling behind in the world
- Rationalisation and cartelisation

Agriculture
- Depressed as prices continued to fall

Foreign capital
- Inflow of short-term investment, mainly from the USA

Unemployment
- Stayed above 1 million
- Rising from 1928

Trade
- Growing trade deficit

THE WEIMAR ECONOMY IN THE 1920s

Social welfare
- Extension of welfare schemes
- Increased costs

Prices
- Steady prices
- Agricultural prices falling from 1927

Government finances
- Higher taxes, yet still budget deficit

EFFECTS
- Peasant farmers and Junkers increasingly hostile to the regime; the former looked to the Nazis; the latter to a more authoritarian system of government
- Employers increasingly resented high welfare costs at a time of limited growth
- Workers made only modest gains
- The economy was dependent on the US economy

■ Learning trouble spot

Marks, Rentenmarks and Reichsmarks!

Until 1923 Germany's currency was called the mark. In November 1923, to stabilise the German currency, Stresemann and Schacht introduced a temporary currency called the Rentenmark. It was issued in limited numbers. Normally currencies are backed by gold, but the Rentenmark was based on a mortgage of Germany's entire industrial and agricultural resources. In theory, a Rentenmark could be exchanged for a piece of land or industry. In practice, people had confidence in it, so no one wanted to do this. In 1924 the Rentenmark was converted into a new currency, the Reichsmark (RM), backed by gold.

72

DID POLITICAL AND ECONOMIC DEVELOPMENTS BETWEEN 1924 AND 1929 MAKE THE WEIMAR REPUBLIC MORE STABLE?

Germany's economic performance

The effects of inflation were long lasting. Pressure groups, including a whole political party, were set up demanding the revaluation of old loans and compensation for those who had lost money. The government unwisely accepted the principle of compensation but pleaded inability to pay fully, offering various schemes. It established a lottery to decide in which order people were paid compensation. This gave creditors hope without ruining government finances. Debts were generally reassessed at 15 per cent of their original value, a compromise which upset both creditors, who got only part of their money back, and debtors, who still had to find money to pay off their debts. The long-running saga of revaluation weakened the Weimar Republic, since it kept bitterness over hyperinflation alive.

Although after 1923 the economy improved, its rate of growth was erratic. In 1926 there was a downturn and unemployment grew, but the economy then recovered. Overall, the rate of industrial growth was low. Spending was no longer financed by simply printing money. Expenditure and the circulation of money were tightly controlled. These were orthodox policies but as a result there were insufficient resources to finance the ambitious welfare state built into the Weimar constitution (see page 76).

■ **Learning trouble spot**

Economic not economical

These two adjectives can be confused.

Economic means to do with the economy, for example, economic policy. This is the word you will usually use.

Economical means making economies, that is, savings, or using as little as possible.

■ **Learning trouble spot**

Handling statistics

As a historian, you are likely to encounter many statistics, either in the form of figures or transferred into column or linear graphs.

You must be as critical of statistics as of any other source. You have to ask who produced them, and why. Statistics may be deliberately inaccurate: Hitler issued exaggerated figures for his military forces to try to intimidate opponents. They may be unavoidably inaccurate, due to lack of precise information or poor classification. The published statistics may be misinterpreted by the historian. They may be technically accurate but distorted due to careful selection by the historian to argue a case. The debate over the state of the German economy in 1939, and its connection with the outbreak of war, is a notorious case here (see page 222).

When you use statistics, bear these points in mind. There are also some other problems students may encounter.

- You must give specific dates to statistics you use as evidence; to say that the economy grew by 10 per cent means something only if you give the dates for the period.
- Be careful about base lines. Some statistics are given in absolute terms, for example production figures in Reichsmarks (RM). Often historians want to compare how the economy is doing in one year compared to another. Here they often use not absolute figures but relative ones. Thus they choose a particular year as a base line, call this figure 100, and then convert figures for other years into proportions of that base line; for example, 85 shows it has gone down 15 per cent, 135 shows it has increased 35 per cent. Such figures are easier to understand quickly, but much depends on the base line chosen.

A further problem with base lines is that if you choose a year when an industry is only just starting, for example Buna (a synthetic rubber) production in 1936, you can demonstrate very impressive growth rates; whereas if you choose a baseline when the industry was well established, the growth rate would be far smaller.

Inflation

- Inflation is when prices go up. A certain amount of inflation can be beneficial for an economy, as it normally means levels of profit increase, and this may encourage increased investment. Money wages may also go up, boosting demand. However, increased prices for goods purchased may outweigh the advantages for workers, though this is less likely for industrialists and investors who have more surplus money.
- If inflation is too great, then people may not be able to increase their income in line with rising prices. This was classically the case with investors (whose interest rate on savings might be fixed), and with groups with little economic muscle, for example tradesmen, artisans, non-unionised workers, etc.
- Inflation is normally caused by a loss of confidence in the economy. This can happen for several reasons:
  a) a continuing balance of trade deficit (see below)
  b) a growing budget deficit (see below), and an inability of the government to pay its debts (which might also encourage the government to print money, see c below)
  c) an increased amount of banknotes in circulation due to the government printing too much paper money. (This can lead to the classic inflationary problem of too much money chasing too few goods.)

Deflation

- Deflation is the opposite of inflation: that is, prices fall. This happens during a slump or depression when there is a fall in production and a rise in unemployment. In such situations there are normally too many goods for the demand, so prices fall to try to attract buyers. In such circumstances government income from taxes falls and expenditure on welfare rises, causing budgetary problems.
- Deflationary policies, as pursued by Weimar governments during the Great Depression, aimed to tackle this budgetary problem by cutting welfare benefits and increasing taxes to balance the budget in the hope that the economy would naturally recover.

Deficit financing

- This is when the government spends more money than it receives in order to expand the economy. The resultant expansion should then improve the government's tax revenues which would help restore the government's finances.

Reflation

- Reflation is the policy to counteract deflation. Reflationary policies are designed to stimulate economic growth, especially by government spending money to boost demand, leading to increased jobs, higher wages and rising prices, and so restoring confidence in the economy. Such interventionist policies were most notably advocated by the economist J. M. Keynes in the 1930s, though for a long time most governments rejected such an approach.

Budget deficit

- A budget deficit is when the government's income (from taxes, tariffs, etc.) is lower than its expenditure (for example, on welfare, defence, interest payments). If the government's annual budget stays in deficit (with the gap between income and expenditure met by increased borrowing) then the **national debt** (that is the accumulated annual budget deficits) will increase. Most governments can function with a large national debt, but it means that they will have to spend a lot of money on interest payments to their creditors. If the economy is expanding, this may not be a problem (as after 1933 in Germany), but if the economy is contracting (as between 1929 and 1933 in Germany) it can be a major concern.

Balance of trade deficit

- This is when the value of a country's exports (in goods and services) is lower than the value of the country's imports. This may mean that imports have to be obtained by using up **currency reserves**, rather than being covered by money obtained from exports. It is rather similar to the budget deficit: there the government is losing money; here the country is losing money.

Currency reserves

- The money held by a government is its currency reserves. They could be in the form of gold (normally the safest form of money), or foreign currencies (preferably one in which there is confidence, such as the pound or dollar). These reserves have been built up by trade surpluses. If they are large, then it encourages confidence in the country's economy; if they are low or non-existent, then the economy looks weak.

Gross National Product (GNP)

- GNP is the monetary value of all that is produced (normally in one year) in a country, that is the value of all goods and services. If GNP is increasing, this is the best indication of a growing, and thus healthy, economy. Historians also use GNP to analyse the comparative importance of different economic activities, for example how much of GNP comes from military production, how much from agriculture, etc.

National Income

- National Income is similar to GNP but is a measure of the overall income of all people in a country (largely dependent upon GNP). Income here covers, for example, wages for workers, investment income for savers, profits for industrialists/shareholders. Again, if it is increasing this means people on average are better off (though this needs to be related to the inflation rate). Analysing what proportion of National Income is going to particular social groups, for example workers, gives historians a good indication of which groups are benefiting most from a regime. The proportion of National Income spent by the government on various areas (for example, welfare or rearmament) can also be a useful statistic.

Money wages and real wages

- Money wages is the amount of money someone is paid; it is an absolute term. Real wages is a relative term, used to show how wages relate to prices; in other words, it is an indication of how much a worker can buy with his/her wages.
- Changes in real wages are useful indications to the historian as to how well workers are doing under a regime.

Direct and indirect taxes

- Direct taxes are taxes paid by workers/investors in money to the government, for example, income tax.
- Indirect taxes are paid indirectly to the government, for example taxes on goods. This means people pay a higher price for what they buy; then the shopkeeper gives some of the price to the government. VAT is the most famous current example. Indirect taxes are normally **regressive**, that is they hit poorer people comparatively more; and direct taxes are more **progressive**, hitting richer people more. (But it does depend upon what goods are taxed, for example food or luxury cars; and whether direct taxes are a fixed proportion of income.) The balance between the two can thus tell a historian about the nature of a regime.

Tariffs, quotas and protection

- Tariffs (or import duties) are taxes placed on imported goods. They can have two purposes: **i)** to raise government revenue; **ii)** to discriminate against imports by making them more expensive, thus reducing demand for them. This serves as a form of **protection**: that is, measures taken to protect home industries from foreign competition. This can also be done by **quotas** – formal limits on the amount of particular goods that can be imported.

Industry did make some advances, but the picture in agriculture was far worse. There was a world surplus of grain and prices fell dramatically, affecting both large estates and smaller farms. Indebtedness and bankruptcies grew and there were outbreaks of peasant violence against evictions. In 1928, in what has been called 'the farmers' revenge', many farmers voted for the Nazi Party. Other groups who did not benefit from the so-called prosperity were state employees, savers and tradesmen, the urban MITTELSTAND, who now saw organised workers making gains, diminishing the crucial gap between the middle class and the proletariat. They too were soon to express their resentment politically.

Overall, Germany's economic performance during this period was mixed. Prosperity and confidence returned for many but others harboured resentments at their loss of savings and felt insecure. Most crucially, economic recovery was fuelled by foreign, short-term loans and, when these were withdrawn, the economy was to plunge into crisis. As Kolb argues, in *Weimar Republic* (p. 165), 'It is generally accepted that the economic situation in Germany was highly

■ 3D   Comparative statistics for the Weimar economy

SOURCE 3.14   Working days lost in strikes. (Working days lost = the number of people involved multiplied by the number of days they were on strike)

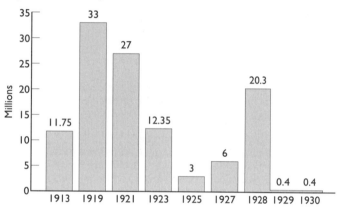

SOURCE 3.15   Wages 1924–32 (1925 = 100)

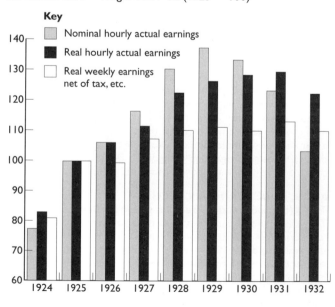

SOURCE 3.16   The burden of reparations and annual budget deficits as a percentage of GNP (Gross National Product)

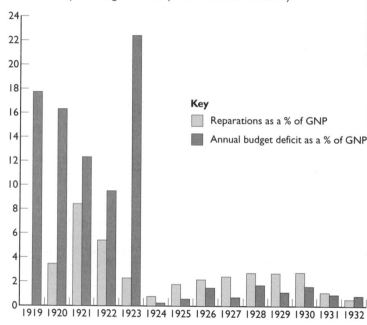

SOURCE 3.17   Industrial production

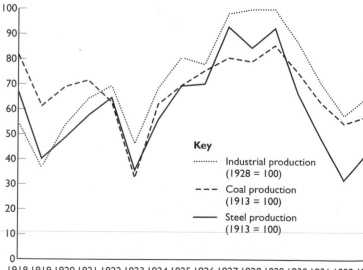

precarious even before the world depression.' Even Stresemann admitted in 1928: 'Germany is dancing on a volcano. If the short-term credits are called in, a large section of our economy would collapse.'

Who was responsible for the problems in the Weimar economy?

A conservative view

The German economic historian Borchhardt is critical of Weimar Germany's economic performance in the 1920s. He argues that the state was living beyond its means, with both subsidies and the redistribution of wealth harmful to economic growth. He argues wages increased unrelated to productivity, due to the strength of trade unions and state arbitration. Profits and thus investment income were therefore squeezed which led to low internal investment, with growth lower than might be expected. He stresses the persistence of high unemployment (over 1 million). Recession began at different times, in different

ACTIVITY

1 Do the statistics (especially Source 3.15) support the view that the Weimar Republic favoured the working class at the expense of the elite?
2 Study Chart 3D and identify optimistic and pessimistic trends.

SOURCE 3.18 Unemployment 1921–33

SOURCE 3.19 Balance of trade 1913–29

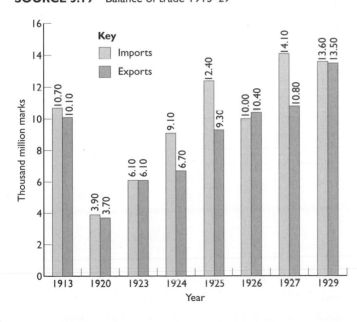

SOURCE 3.20 Flow of money into and out of Germany 1924–31

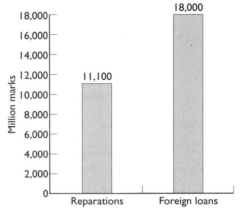

SOURCE 3.21 Economic growth 1913–29

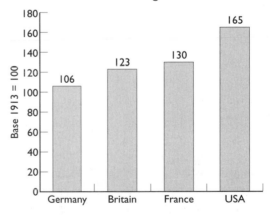

SOURCE 3.22 Agricultural prices 1927–30

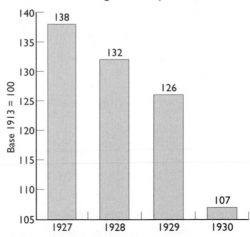

76

DID POLITICAL AND ECONOMIC DEVELOPMENTS BETWEEN 1924 AND 1929 MAKE THE WEIMAR REPUBLIC MORE STABLE?

sectors, but set in well before the October 1929 crash. He points to an 'abnormal, in fact a sick economy, which could not possibly have gone on in the same way even if the world depression had not occurred'.

An alternative view

Other historians, such as the left-wing Holtfrerich, reject what they see as Borchhardt's stress on working-class greed and argue that the main reasons for Germany's limited economic performance lay with a lack of entrepreneurial attitude and inadequate investment from the industrial elite. Low productivity was primarily caused by government subsidies, and by industrialists' formation of cartels which reduced entrepreneurial spirit. Thus failures were the responsibility more of cautious and cosseted industrialists than of hard-pressed workers who were striving to maintain their position.

A synthesis

Recent research, partly fuelled by new work in local archives available after the collapse of the east German state, the German Democratic Republic, in 1989, suggest that both workers and employers contributed to economic weakness. Both groups sought to defend their position and were unwilling to co-operate with each other. Wages did rise, but this was due more to local shortages of skilled labour than to greedy workers and overpowerful trade unions. Low investment was caused by savers' lack of confidence in lending their money and by the government's priority of trying to balance the budget.

TALKING POINTS

You will often come across disagreements between historians during your course. How do you decide what you think? Do you simply assume the correct answer lies part-way between the two views?

If historians' views over the reasons for Weimar Germany's poor performance reflect their political outlook, does this discredit their analysis?

C Did the Weimar welfare state strengthen or weaken the regime?

Another area of debate for historians is the impact of the developing welfare state on support for the Weimar Republic. The principles of a welfare state had been written into the constitution (see page 27) and so expectations had been high amongst the poorer classes. Early success came in November 1918, when workers won agreement from employers to an eight-hour working day and a system of industrial tribunals. Considerable advances were made in social services. State governments, often using foreign loans, improved hospitals, schools, housing, roads and electricity supplies. In addition, approximately 40 per cent of federal government expenditure went on war-related pensions to invalids, widows and orphans, in all over 2.5 million people. A further major advance in welfare provision was made in 1927, when the social insurance scheme was extended to protect over 17 million workers in the event of unemployment. Although such measures probably strengthened support amongst many ordinary Germans, the regime also suffered from exaggerated expectations. The competing demands on welfare could not be met, even before the slump ruined the economy. This was especially the case with unemployment insurance which, introduced just before the slump, had its financial basis ruined by mass unemployment.

FOCUS ROUTE

As you read pages 76–7 complete the social policy section on your copy of the chart on page 60.

SOURCE 3.23 Development of welfare during the Weimar Republic

Unemployment insurance	Introduced in 1927, financed by a levy, half paid by employers, half by employees. It was viable unless the total of unemployed went above 800,000		
Social expenditure	**1913**		**Late 1920s**
	15% of GNP		26% of GNP
Public spending on housing (compared to 1913 level)	**1913**	**1925**	**1929**
	100	2,525	3,300
Tax burden (as % of income)	**1919***		**1925**
	9%		17%
Health	**1913**		**1928**
Deaths per 10,000	TB	143	87
	Pneumonia	119	93

* There was progressive taxation for the first time and a general increase in taxes.

77

DID POLITICAL AND ECONOMIC DEVELOPMENTS BETWEEN 1924 AND 1929 MAKE THE WEIMAR REPUBLIC MORE STABLE?

Welfare reforms also affected the elite's attitude to the Republic. The resulting high taxation and comparative redistribution of resources away from the elite reinforced its suspicions of the new democratic system. Some employers sought to pull back their earlier concessions. Before the slump, the eight-hour limit to the working day was changed to a ten-hour limit to help employers. There were also attempts to cut wages. The arbitration system set up under the Weimar Republic protected workers but it aroused the resentment of employers who complained at 'political wages', that is wages set by arbitrators appointed by a government wanting to win working-class votes. In 1928, Ruhr industrialists rejected an arbitration award and locked out 250,000 workers in a clear attempt to break the power of the unions and defeat compulsory arbitration. The government did eventually arrange a compromise, but the original award had been undermined. This typified the growing tension between employers and workers that was to become acute with the impact of the Depression. The historian Abelshauser, in *German History since 1800* (ed. Fulbrook, p. 250) concluded that 'the Weimar Republic was an over-strained welfare state', as the economic growth of the recovery period was insufficient to meet growing aspirations, and, arguably, served to retard industrial advance, and to increase the elite's alienation from the new democratic regime.

ACTIVITY

In what ways and for what reasons do historians disagree on the causes of the weaknesses in the German economy of the 1920s?

D Review: Did political and economic developments between 1924 and 1929 make the Weimar Republic more stable?

You have studied how there were both promising and worrying aspects of the political and economic history of the period. This pattern will be repeated as you study the diplomatic and cultural developments of this time.

ACTIVITY

'Economic developments were more encouraging for the Weimar regime than political ones.' Do you agree with this statement?

KEY POINTS FROM CHAPTER 3: Did political and economic developments between 1924 and 1929 make the Weimar Republic more stable?

1 The success of democratic parties in the Reichstag elections in December 1924 and May 1928 was an optimistic sign, though middle-class liberal parties remained small.

2 Political calm was restored to Germany and there were no attempts to overthrow the system, but there was continued governmental instability.

3 The election of Hindenburg as President in 1925 put great power in the hands of someone not committed to the parliamentary system.

4 Influential groups failed to foster commitment to democratic values.

5 Inflation was cured in 1924, never to return.

6 Reparations were reorganised on a more reasonable level in the Dawes Plan and later the Young Plan, but they still caused great nationalist resentment.

7 The economy was heavily dependent on short-term American loans.

8 By 1929 production was back to 1913 levels, but growth lagged behind that of other countries.

9 Unemployment remained around 1 million, and farmers became increasingly harmed by low food prices.

10 The welfare state was extended and the working class made gains, but this alienated powerful groups in the elite and aroused expectations that could not be met.

4

How far did Stresemann's foreign policy strengthen the Weimar regime?

CHAPTER OVERVIEW

'The Stresemann Era' is the name sometimes given to the history of the Weimar Republic between 1923 and 1929. It reflects the importance of Germany's Foreign Minister, Gustav Stresemann, and his diplomacy which was an important factor in the public's attitude to the Weimar regime. A successful foreign policy was needed. This would reduce the public hatred of the Republic's acceptance of the Versailles Treaty. It would also help Germany's economy, since sorting out reparations would be essential if the new Rentenmark was to maintain its value.

In this chapter we examine Stresemann's aims and strategy, how successful he was and whether his policy strengthened the Weimar Republic. In addition, you will decide whether he was a 'good European', an idealistic politician, committed to European co-operation or whether he was a 'good German', a determined nationalist, committed to establishing Germany's domination in Europe.

A What foreign policy did Stresemann pursue? (pp. 80–3)

B Was Stresemann a 'good European' or a 'good German'? (p. 84)

C How successful was Stresemann's foreign policy? (pp. 85–6)

D Review: How far did Stresemann's foreign policy strengthen the Weimar regime? (pp. 87–8)

■ 4A Gustav Stresemann, 1878–1929

Born the son of a Berlin publican, Stresemann studied economics at university, before going into business. Attracted to both liberalism and German nationalism, he became the youngest member of the Reichstag when elected in 1907 as a National Liberal. He became party leader in 1917. During the war, he took a very assertive line and was nicknamed 'Ludendorff's young man'. He supported unrestricted submarine warfare, opposed the 1917 peace resolution, and supported the Treaty of Brest-Litovsk.

In 1919 the National Liberal Party split into the German National People's Party, which Stresemann rejected as too conservative, and the German Democratic Party, which rejected Stresemann as he was too nationalist. Stresemann therefore formed the moderate conservative German People's Party (DVP), which favoured constitutional monarchy. Over the next few years Stresemann moved the DVP into a more constructive attitude to the new republic, seeing it as the best available alternative to left- or right-wing dictatorship.

Stresemann's abilities as speaker and administrator and the assassination of other leaders such as Erzberger and Rathenau meant that he emerged as the most effective Weimar politician. In August 1923 he was appointed Chancellor to deal with the economic crisis. He tackled the challenge with firm and realistic policies and although he lost the Reichstag's confidence as Chancellor in November 1923 he remained as Foreign Minister from 1923 until his death in October 1929.

In 1926 Gustav Stresemann was awarded the Nobel Peace Prize for his diplomatic work.

TALKING POINTS

1 Which aspects of Stresemann's early experience might prove valuable as Foreign Minister?

2 Can you draw conclusions from his early career about his likely policies as Foreign Minister?

Various foreign policy options were open to Stresemann in 1923. In this exercise you are going to consider what foreign policy problems he faced and how he might tackle them in Germany's best interests.

1 Choose one option in each row of the table that you think Stresemann should adopt. Remember to consider the effects of your policy both on other countries' attitudes to Germany and on the German people's support for the Weimar Republic.

Issues facing the Weimar government	Options		
1 French occupation of the Ruhr	**a)** Call off passive resistance unconditionally	**b)** Promise to call off passive resistance if France withdraws	**c)** Maintain passive resistance to force France to withdraw
2 Reparations	**d)** Follow fulfilment policy to show they cannot be fully paid. Try to get foreign loans to help economic growth	**e)** Claim you are trying to pay them but in practice obstruct them	**f)** Publicly declare they are unjustified and refuse to pay
3 Relations with France	**g)** Try to improve relations by accepting western borders	**h)** Offer to guarantee western borders if France makes concessions	**i)** Accuse France of being a hate-driven enemy of Germany and vow to change your western borders
4 Relations with Poland	**j)** Make a treaty with Poland accepting each other's borders with guarantees for minorities	**k)** Refuse to accept existing borders but promise not to change them UNILATERALLY. Continue to raise question of Germans living in Poland	**l)** Threaten war unless Poland gives back German territory
5 Disarmament	**m)** Keep to Versailles restrictions	**n)** Publicly keep to restrictions and urge other countries to disarm but secretly rearm	**o)** Publicly renounce disarmament and build up military might
6 Relations with the USSR	**p)** Keep contacts with this outcast regime to a minimum	**q)** Develop economic and military contacts with the USSR as a useful counter to the West	**r)** Form a firm alliance committing both parties to mutual military support to revise the post-war settlement
7 League of Nations	**s)** Join this new body, and fully participate in its operations, in letter and in spirit	**t)** Join this new body and raise the issue of German self-determination	**u)** Denounce the League as an instrument for the victors to hold on to their ill-gotten gains
8 Allied occupation of the Rhineland	**v)** Try to get an earlier phased withdrawal by arguing occupation no longer needed	**w)** Insist that no agreements can be made until Germany has full sovereignty over all its territory	**x)** Insist Allied occupation is an infringement of German sovereignty and threaten renewed civil disobedience
9 Relations with the USA	**y)** Try to get the USA involved in Germany and win it over to revising Versailles	**z)** Accept that an isolationist USA is not a major player in Europe, but try to get American funds	**aa)** Ignore the USA as irrelevant to Germany's needs
10 Public opinion	**bb)** Criticise excessive German nationalism	**cc)** Publicly criticise nationalism but use it as an argument for the West to make concessions	**dd)** Stir up nationalism by XENOPHOBIC rhetoric

2 After making your choices, decide which of the following strategies best fits your overall approach:
   a) total conciliation and APPEASEMENT of the Allies, accepting Germany is in no position to have an active foreign policy
   b) a mixed approach, appearing conciliatory, but working to revise the Treaty of Versailles, and playing off various countries against each other
   c) a hard-line assertive policy, threatening to use armed force to achieve your objectives.
3 Explain your objectives and the thinking behind your strategy.
4 What problems do you think Stresemann might have faced in winning public support for conciliatory policies?
5 Turn to pages 80–1 and 88. In what ways does Stresemann's actual policy seem to have been similar to or different from your proposals?

80

HOW FAR DID STRESEMANN'S FOREIGN POLICY STRENGTHEN THE WEIMAR REGIME?

FOCUS ROUTE

On your copy of your chart from page 60, make notes on Stresemann's achievements in foreign policy. Note:

- his aims (linking domestic and foreign policy)
- strategies he used
- his successes and failures
- key developments in reparations
- responses in Germany to his actions
- different interpretations of his motives/achievements.

ACTIVITY

1 Explain why Stresemann wanted to have agreements with both the West and the USSR.
2 Locarno reaffirmed the western borders established at Versailles. What, then, was the significance of the Pact?
3 Why was the USA so prepared to help Germany financially?

TALKING POINT

What evidence is there here that Stresemann was either a good European or a German nationalist? Why might his actions make it difficult to decide on his real objective?

A What foreign policy did Stresemann pursue?

Aims and strategy

Stresemann's broad aim was to restore Germany's power and prosperity but he accepted that Germany was in no position to challenge the Allies militarily and revise the Treaty of Versailles by force. He rejected the argument of those such as General Seeckt who saw the future for Germany primarily in terms of building up the country's military might. Instead he pursued a pragmatic policy of co-operation with the West, and a mixture of conciliation and mild pressure on the other powers. Pressure came from using Germany's economic potential (as a purchaser of other countries' food, as a supplier of coal to France, as a market for Britain and as an opportunity for investment for the USA) as a lever that he hoped would produce revision of the treaty and restore Germany's great power status. Stresemann realised that other countries could not afford to let the German economy collapse completely and so made great use of the close interdependence of economic and foreign policy.

Stresemann's realistic strategy is known as *Erfüllungspolitik* (fulfilment), which meant complying with or fulfilling the terms of Versailles to improve relations with Britain and France and thus encourage them to revise the treaty. This policy entailed:

- negotiation because Germany lacked military power
- gaining the confidence of the Western powers and ending Germany's diplomatic isolation
- using Germany's economic rather than military potential as a means to get Versailles revised
- close co-operation with the USA to gain economic aid
- satisfying the French demand for security
- building links with the USSR and so putting slight pressure on the West to improve relations through fear of further German moves towards the USSR.

As a result of this strategy, Stresemann hoped that:

- the reparations problem would be solved
- the 1923 Ruhr and Rhineland occupations would end
- military control of Germany would end
- Germany's eastern borders would be revised.

■ 4B The attitudes of the major powers towards Germany

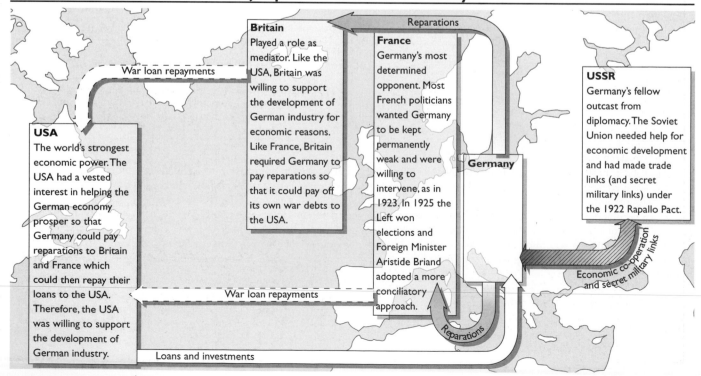

Britain
Played a role as mediator. Like the USA, Britain was willing to support the development of German industry for economic reasons. Like France, Britain required Germany to pay reparations so that it could pay off its own war debts to the USA.

France
Germany's most determined opponent. Most French politicians wanted Germany to be kept permanently weak and were willing to intervene, as in 1923. In 1925 the Left won elections and Foreign Minister Aristide Briand adopted a more conciliatory approach.

USSR
Germany's fellow outcast from diplomacy. The Soviet Union needed help for economic development and had made trade links (and secret military links) under the 1922 Rapallo Pact.

USA
The world's strongest economic power. The USA had a vested interest in helping the German economy prosper so that Germany could pay reparations to Britain and France which could then repay their loans to the USA. Therefore, the USA was willing to support the development of German industry.

Germany

Reparations

War loan repayments

War loan repayments

Loans and investments

Economic co-operation and secret military links

Reparations

Reparations	• Stresemann negotiated the reorganisation of reparations through the Dawes Plan in 1924 and the Young Plan in 1929 (see page 82 for details).
Locarno Pact, 1925	• Stresemann signed at Locarno, Switzerland, in October 1925 a series of treaties (known collectively as the Locarno Pact) with Britain, France, Belgium and Italy. • Stresemann accepted Germany's western (not eastern) borders; all countries renounced the use of invasion and force, except in self-defence. • The Pact reassured France about its borders and Germany about further French invasion (such as had happened in 1923). • Germany also signed arbitration treaties with Poland and Czechoslovakia, renouncing the use of force, but this did not involve Germany accepting its eastern borders.
League of Nations, 1926	• In September 1926 Germany joined the League of Nations, the international organisation set up by the Treaty of Versailles. Germany was given great power status on the League Council with veto power. • Germany was allowed not to participate in collective action against aggression if it was unrealistic, given the military limitations that had been imposed on the country by the Treaty of Versailles. • Germany used its position to raise matters of German interest.
Treaty of Berlin, 1926	• In April 1926 Stresemann signed this treaty with the USSR. The treaty had both public and secret clauses. • Like the 1922 Rapallo Pact, the treaty helped to develop good relations between Germany and the USSR, with further economic and military exchanges. • Stresemann used the treaty to put mild pressure on the West to improve its relations with Germany through fear of Germany moving closer to the USSR.
Allied occupation	• By calling off passive resistance, Stresemann persuaded the French to withdraw from the Ruhr during 1924–5. • Following the Locarno Pact, the Allies had left Zone 1 around Cologne by December 1925. • As part of the Young Plan negotiations of 1929, the Allies agreed to end their occupation early. This success of Stresemann's policy actually happened after his death in October 1929: a month later, Zone 2 was evacuated and the final zone was evacuated in June 1930.
Disarmament	• Stresemann pressed for the issue of general disarmament (as mentioned in the Versailles Treaty) to be addressed. In 1926 a preliminary disarmament meeting was held at Geneva but no progress took place. • In 1928 Germany, along with over 70 other countries, signed the Kellogg–Briand Pact renouncing the use of force, but it had no practical effect. • In 1926 Stresemann gained a minor success when the Inter-Allied Military Control Commission (monitoring Germany's compliance with the military terms of Versailles) was withdrawn. • Germany secretly rearmed beyond the restrictions imposed at the Treaty of Versailles.

82

HOW FAR DID STRESEMANN'S FOREIGN POLICY STRENGTHEN THE WEIMAR REGIME?

The reparations issue 1919–32

Any discussion of reparations and American loans is usually conducted in a swirl of figures and dates with students often being none the wiser on three crucial issues:

- How much did the Allies demand?
- How much did Germany actually pay?
- What form did reparations take?

How much did the Allies demand?

You may come across a bewildering variety of figures on the amount of reparations. This may be because they are in different currencies, but the calculations themselves were also very complex and differed over time.

Versailles 1919
- At Versailles the principle of compensation was established but no actual sum was fixed.

1921
- The sum to be paid was initially fixed at 226,000 million gold marks, payable over 42 years.
- In April 1921, the total was reduced to 132,000 million marks, or £6,600 million. This was arranged as 50,000 million marks (plus 6 per cent interest) to be paid over 50 years, followed by a second-phase payment of 82,000 million marks, or 82 milliard. (One milliard equals 1,000 million.)
- The annual payments were estimated to be about 7 per cent of Germany's national income.

1924 and 1929
- Reparations were reorganised by the Dawes and Young plans (see Chart 4D).

1931–2
- In 1931 payments were suspended for one year as part of a general MORATORIUM on debts. The next year, at the Lausanne Conference, agreement was reached on a final payment of 3,000 million marks, to be paid in a one-off payment in 1935. This was never paid.

FOCUS ROUTE

Use the reparations data for the foreign policy section of your copy of the table on page 60.

■ 4D The Dawes Plan (1924) and the Young Plan (1929)

ASPECT	DAWES PLAN, 1924	YOUNG PLAN, 1929
Overall amount of reparations	The sum of 132,000 million marks fixed in 1921 was confirmed	The total sum to be paid was reduced to 37,000 million marks
Schedule	Over five years annual payments would rise from 1,000 million marks to 2,500 million, then at varying levels according to economic performance	Annual payments, lower than under the Dawes Plan, to be made over 58 years
Conditions	Allies maintained control of the railways, the Reichsbank and customs duties. Sanctions for non-payment must be agreed by all Allies, not France alone, as in 1923	Allied supervision discontinued
Other points	Seen as a temporary arrangement. Germany given 800 million mark loan to help stabilise the currency	Intended as final settlement. Germany participated in these reparations negotiations for the first time
Impact	Helped economic recovery; led to reparations being paid as scheduled	Allied troops were withdrawn in June 1930. Major internal opposition; referendum campaign

How much did Germany actually pay?

Overall, it has been estimated that Germany paid one-eighth of the original sum. Following the Dawes Plan Germany actually received more in loans than it paid in reparations. This appears generous, but remember that whereas reparations were permanent losses to Germany, American loans to Germany had to be repaid. Between 1924 and 1930, Germany received 135 long-term loans totalling $1,430 million ($1,293 million from the USA), plus short-term loans totalling $1,560 million. All payments were suspended in 1932.

83

HOW FAR DID STRESEMANN'S FOREIGN POLICY STRENGTHEN THE WEIMAR REGIME?

■ 4E   Germany's reparations payments, 1925–32

Date	Plan	Requirement (bn marks)	Actual payment (bn marks)	Payment as % of National Income
1925	Dawes	1.00	1.06	1.8
1926	Dawes	1.22	1.19	2.0
1927	Dawes	1.50	1.58	2.3
1928	Dawes	2.50	2.00	2.8
1929	Dawes	1.94	2.34	3.2
1930	Young	1.70	1.71	2.6
1931	Young	1.69	0.99	1.8
1932	Young	1.73	0.16	0.4

■ 4F   The balance of reparation payments and loans 1918–31

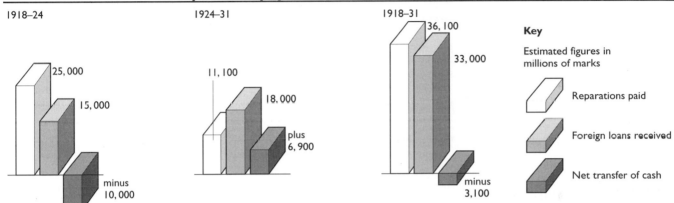

What form did reparations take?

Reparations took the form of payments in kind, for example coal and manufactured products, and money in the form of gold, but not paper money. The German government bought the materials from German manufacturers and gave them to nine foreign governments, primarily France (about 50 per cent of the total), Britain (20 per cent), Italy (10 per cent) and Belgium (8 per cent). As payments were not in paper money, inflation did not reduce the real burden.

The Allied governments received the products and money and kept some for their own use (including paying compensation to those harmed during the war, for example via war pensions), but also paid back some of their loans to the USA.

American loans came direct from the government and from private investors. They were lent to both the German federal government and state governments to finance various spending programmes, such as municipal housing. Loans also went to private firms to help their expansion. American firms invested directly, with 79 firms, such as General Electric (GE) and General Motors, establishing factories. In return for this outlay, Americans received interest payments on their loans, or dividends from their investments.

ACTIVITY

1   What were the chief differences between the Dawes and Young plans? Which one treated Germany more leniently?
2   Explain why Stresemann was more concerned about short-term levels of reparation payments than about the final total amount.
3   Study the financial flows in and out of Germany (Chart 4F). How much of a real burden were reparations?

TALKING POINT

Would you agree that reparations were more harmful psychologically than economically?

B Was Stresemann a 'good European' or a 'good German'?

Stresemann's approach has been interpreted differently by historians. Some argue that he had moved away from his assertive nationalist past to become a 'good European'. Thus, although he remained a true German patriot, he accepted that Germany's interests were best protected by becoming part of the European order and co-operating with foreign countries. Others argue that he did not abandon his earlier extreme nationalist position and was essentially a 'good German', putting Germany's interests above all else and determined to exploit the international situation to re-establish German HEGEMONY in Europe. In this light, some historians even argue that there were similarities between Stresemann's and Hitler's foreign policy.

Such different interpretations partly arise from the complex nature of Stresemann's policy of trying to appear moderate to foreign statesmen, whilst trying to maintain domestic support by using nationalist rhetoric (stirring language). Interpretations have also changed with the publication of new research into government archives and Stresemann's complete diaries rather than edited versions of them. These sources have revealed the importance of relations with the USSR, and the extent to which he was prepared to manipulate circumstances to advance Germany's cause.

SOURCE 4.1　Excerpt from a letter from Stresemann to the Crown Prince Wilhelm Hohenzollern, the former Kaiser's son, 7 September 1925

In my opinion there are three great tasks that confront German policy in the immediate future:

1　*The solution of the reparations problem in a way that is tolerable for Germany.*

2　*The protection of those ten to twelve million Germans who now live under foreign control in foreign lands.*

3　*The readjustment of our eastern frontiers; the recovery of Danzig, the Polish Corridor, and a correction of the frontier in Upper Silesia . . .*

The question of the option between east and west is not affected by our entry into the League of Nations. Such options only become viable when we have military force behind us. Unfortunately that we do not have . . .

The most important task for German politics is to free German soil from foreign domination. We have to free the stranglehold on our throat. Therefore, German policy must be one of machination [scheming] and the avoidance of any fundamental decision . . . I ask your Royal Highness to allow me to restrict myself to this short résumé, and further request that you fully appreciate the frank tone of this letter since I am naturally obliged to practise the utmost restraint in my public utterances. Should your Royal Highness give me the pleasure of an hour of your time to discuss these questions . . . then I will gladly make myself available.

SOURCE 4.2　Stresemann's address to the League of Nations, 10 September 1926

It is . . . the task of the present generation to look to the present and to the future . . . The co-operation of the peoples in the League of Nations must and will lead to just solutions for the moral questions which arise in the conscience of the peoples. The most durable foundation of peace is a policy inspired by mutual understanding and mutual respect between nation and nation.

Even before her entry into the League, Germany endeavoured to promote this friendly co-operation. The action which she took and which led to the Pact of Locarno is a proof of this . . . The German Government is resolved to persevere unswervingly in this line of policy and is glad to see that these ideas, which at first met with lively opposition in Germany, are now becoming more and more deeply rooted in the conscience of the German people. Thus the German Government may well speak for the great majority of the German race when it declares that it will wholeheartedly devote itself to the duties devolving upon the League of Nations . . .

In many respects the League is the heir and executor of the treaties of 1919. Out of these Treaties there have arisen in the past, I may say frankly, many differences between the League and Germany. I hope that our co-operation within the League will make it easier in future to discuss these questions. In this respect mutual confidence will, from a political point of view, be found a greater creative force than anything else . . . Germany desires to co-operate on the basis of mutual confidence with all nations represented in the League . . .

ACTIVITY

1　How can
　　a) Locarno and
　　b) Germany's joining the League of Nations
　　be seen as evidence of Stresemann as a 'good European' and as a 'good German'?

2　**a)** Read Source 4.1. What are Stresemann's aims and how does he propose to achieve them?
　　b) To what extent does Source 4.2 confirm this view?
　　c) Compare the tone of Sources 4.1 and 4.2. How might these differences be explained?
　　d) What light do these two sources shed on the 'good European' versus 'good German' debate about Stresemann?
　　e) With reference to the origin and content of these sources, discuss which you consider provides the more reliable evidence about German foreign policy.

C How successful was Stresemann's foreign policy?

International success?

In many ways Stresemann was very successful. The Dawes Plan made a vital contribution to German economic recovery. The Young Plan then reduced both current payments and the total burden, and the rescheduling of payments over a longer time span reduced the likelihood of payment being fully implemented. Perhaps Stresemann's greatest achievement was the Locarno Pact. On the face of it, this looked like capitulation, giving France a greater sense of security for its Versailles borders. However, Stresemann realised that France must feel secure if it was to allow Germany to recover fully. Germany lost nothing by signing Locarno, as it had no sound national claim to Alsace–Lorraine. On the other hand, Stresemann also won advances on the evacuation of the Rhineland. Furthermore, by voluntarily accepting its western borders, Germany was able to concentrate on revision in the east.

Entry into the League of Nations was required in order for the Locarno Pact to come into operation. Because of Stresemann's insistence on only entering as a permanent member of the Council, Germany's status as a great power was formally acknowledged. Furthermore, Stresemann subtly used Germany's position to weaken the provision for collective security, and he raised the issue of German minorities living in other states. In practice, Germany made no real sacrifice, but gained prestige and the goodwill vital for securing revision. The Treaty of Berlin did arouse some suspicion in the West (as had Rapallo), but it was not sufficient to stop DÉTENTE and as a form of mild pressure probably assisted in gaining concessions from the West. Thus Stresemann transformed Germany from being a distrusted outcast to being actively involved in European diplomacy. His contribution to the new atmosphere of co-operation (the 'Spirit of Locarno') earned him the Nobel Peace Prize in 1926.

However, the concrete gains from his diplomacy were not great. He did gain French withdrawal from the Ruhr by 1925 and, in 1929, an agreement on the final withdrawal of Allied troops from the west bank of the Rhine. This came five years before the original schedule of 1935, but full withdrawal only happened after his death. There was no formal agreement changing the demilitarisation terms of Versailles, although Germany secretly broke them.

Some historians argue that Stresemann's basic approach was fundamentally flawed, as Germany lacked the power to insist on revision but could not gain international support for the territorial changes required. Peukert has argued that Stresemann should have accepted Germany's eastern borders and concentrated on building up economic and political influence in the new states in eastern and south-eastern Europe. Furthermore, Peukert argues that by 1929 it was clear that Stresemann's policy of combining REVISIONISM with RAPPROCHEMENT had failed. The only way forward for him was to abandon either his method or his aim.

Other historians point to the concessions gained and argue that this process would have intensified. Whether the Stresemann approach, if continued, would have led to major Versailles revision cannot be known, as his death was followed by the adoption of a more assertive foreign policy, and the Wall Street Crash in October 1929 changed the whole atmosphere.

Domestic success?

Although historians are divided over how successful Stresemann's policy was in making gains, most accept that he failed to strengthen significantly the Weimar regime. He hoped that the successful diplomacy that had strengthened the economy and had led to revision of the Versailles Treaty would win greater domestic support for the regime. There is considerable evidence, however, that his policy failed to rally Germans to the regime, because the concessions he gained were not sufficiently dramatic, as you can see in Chart 4G on page 86.

■ **4G**   **Stresemann's strategy and its weaknesses**

The aim: German greatness

STRATEGY	a) Conciliatory diplomacy	b) Rearranging reparations	c) Economic recovery	d) Stronger Germany	e) Changes to Versailles	f) Increased support for Weimar regime

PROBLEMS	a) His conciliatory approach was seen as a sell-out by nationalists	b) Nationalists opposed any payment of reparations	c) The economy was too dependent on American loans	d) Germany was not strong enough to exert real pressure	e) Very few real concessions were achieved	f) Support for the regime remained fragile

OVERALL WEAKNESSES   The success of Stresemann's strategy would depend upon: i) the co-operation of the Allies
ii) winning over extreme German nationalists

Anti-Locarno demonstration

Many Germans, especially on the Right, saw Stresemann's policy of fulfilment of the terms of the Versailles Treaty as capitulation. They believed that Locarno only benefited the French and also that Germany should have nothing to do with the League of Nations which they regarded as simply the enforcer of Versailles. To them, Stresemann's concessions achieved little because Germany remained occupied and disarmed. Even the Young Plan was opposed because it confirmed that Germany still had to pay reparations. Nationalist groups mounted a major campaign to force the government to reject the Young Plan, using the constitution (which, ironically, most of them despised) to arrange a referendum on its acceptance. Although only 5.8 million (14 per cent) voted to reject the Young Plan, the campaign helped make Hitler a nationally known politician. His fierce condemnation of the Plan contributed to the surge in the Nazi vote in the 1930 elections, when both high unemployment and the economic slump were blamed on reparations and the Young Plan.

Although, as the vote for the anti-Young Plan referendum showed, outright critics were a small, if vocal, minority, Stresemann's policy did not win the support of the silent majority of Germans. They did not feel that the Weimar regime had successfully restored Germany's pride or escaped from its association with the hated Versailles Treaty. Stresemann's achievements were too subtle to be greeted enthusiastically by the majority.

SOURCE 4.3
A placard urging voters to reject the Young Plan. The caption is: 'You must slave into the third generation!'

SOURCE 4.4   A poster advertising a meeting to protest about the Young Plan. The text reads: 'People's meeting against the Young Plan ... We do not want to pay 80 gold marks every second for 60 years!'

Bis in die dritte Generation

Geht zum Volksbegehren!
Wehrt Euch!

müßt ihr fronen!

Volksversammlung
gegen den
Youngplan
am 26. September 1929, abends 8 Uhr
Aula der Herderschule, Charlottenburg, Bismarck Bayern-Allee 2

60 Jahre jede Sekunde 80 Goldmark wollen wir nicht zahlen!

D Review: How far did Stresemann's foreign policy strengthen the Weimar regime?

SOURCE 4.5 A 1929 cartoon from the SPD newspaper *Vorwärts*. The Nazis and nationalists following Hugenberg are carrying a stink bomb, bucket of manure and placards saying 'Traitor' and 'Stresemann, rot in hell'. The nurse is saying 'You're too late, gentlemen! He's already dead.' The caption of the cartoon is 'Their quarry has escaped them.' What can you learn from this cartoon about German attitudes to Stresemann's policies?

Entgangenes Ziel.

„Sie kommen zu spät, meine Herren! — Er ist tot."

SOURCE 4.6 Stresemann to an English journalist a few months before his death

I gave and gave some more till finally my countrymen turned against me. If I had received a single concession after Locarno, I would have been able to win over my people. I still could, but you Englishmen gave nothing, and the only concessions you did make always came too late ... The future now lies in the hands of the young generation – the youth of Germany whom we could have won over to peace and the new Europe. If both have been lost – that is my tragedy and a great error on your part.

ACTIVITY

1 What do the tone and content of Source 4.6 suggest about Stresemann's own assessment of his foreign policy?

2 Does this source prove that Stresemann himself considered his foreign policy had failed?

3 What light do Sources 4.5–7 shed on whether contemporaries saw Stresemann as a 'good German' or a 'good European'?

4 In Source 4.8 Marks makes a very positive assessment of Stresemann's foreign policy. How far do you agree with her assessment?

5 Write an obituary of Stresemann, either for a DVP-leaning newspaper or for *The Times*, or write a right-wing nationalist critique of Stresemann.

SOURCE 4.7 An obituary of Stresemann published in the German newspaper *Vorwärts* on 6 October 1929

Stresemann's achievement was in line with the ideas of the international socialist movement. He saw that you can only serve your people by understanding other peoples. To serve collapsed Germany he set out on the path of understanding. He refused to try to get back land which had gone forever. He offered our former enemies friendship. Being a practical man he saw that any other path would have left Germany without any hope of recovery. He covered the long distance from being a nationalist politician of conquest to being a champion of world peace. He fought with great personal courage for the ideals in which he believed ... It is no wonder that right-wingers watched with horror as he went from his original camp to the opposite one. They could not accept him because doing so involved accepting that the Republic created by the workers had brought Germany from devastation to recovery.

SOURCE 4.8 S. Marks, *Illusion of Peace*, 1976, pp. 64 and 65

It is often said that a diplomat must lie for his country and Stresemann was a superlative liar, dispensing total untruths to the ENTENTE, the German people, and his diary with even-handed aplomb [coolness, composure]. He had substantial political difficulties, as the German left distrusted his conservative past and the German right thought he was conceding too much to the Entente; Stresemann made the most of these to gain foreign concessions. Entente leaders, anxious to keep in office this 'good European' (who was in fact a great German nationalist), generally gave way. Stresemann invariably had a list of concessions to Germany necessary to achieve the pacification of Europe. As he achieved one concession from the top of the list, two or three more were always added at the bottom. Stresemann gained most of his list, and no man in the Weimar Republic did more to destroy the Versailles Treaty ...

[He] worked himself to death at the age of fifty-one. In his last days he had recognised the rising tide of strident [noisy], BELLIGERENT German nationalism and had known that the days of his indirect and patient policy were numbered ... In his six years as architect of German foreign policy, he had liberated the Ruhr and the Rhineland, ended military inspection, twice reduced reparations, and transformed Germany from the pariah [outcast] to the pre-eminent member of the European family of nations. He had further demonstrated the futility of imposing upon a great power a treaty it will not accept.

88

HOW FAR DID STRESEMANN'S FOREIGN POLICY STRENGTHEN THE WEIMAR REGIME?

SOURCE 4.9 This DVP poster for the 1930 election shows Stresemann the bridge-builder

ACTIVITY

How might a historian interpret the DVP's use of the poster in Source 4.9 in the 1930 election and the election result (see page 63) as evidence of the success of Stresemann's work?

KEY POINTS FROM CHAPTER 4: How far did Stresemann's foreign policy strengthen the Weimar regime?

1 Stresemann as Foreign Minister from 1923 to 1929 was determined to improve Germany's international position.

2 He believed the key to success would be a strong economy.

3 He pursued a policy of fulfilment in order to show that the burden of reparations was unworkable.

4 He helped negotiate the Dawes and Young plans which aided the German economy.

5 Germany accepted its western borders at Locarno, and joined the League of Nations.

6 Stresemann also maintained good relations with the USSR and extended the Rapallo Pact with the Berlin Treaty in 1926.

7 He gained agreement for the Allies to withdraw from the Rhineland by 1930.

8 Stresemann's conciliatory policy upset German nationalists without winning major concessions from the Allies.

9 Stresemann has been seen as both a 'good European', working for European harmony, and as a 'good German', working to secure Germany's dominance.

10 Stresemann died before he had been able to win sufficient changes to the Treaty of Versailles to strengthen the Weimar Republic.

5

Was the Weimar Republic undermined by jazz, art and dancing girls?

CHAPTER OVERVIEW

SOURCE 5.1   *The Waltz* by George Grosz; it was painted in 1921

Have you ever had an argument with your parents about any aspect of your lifestyle? If so, you might be able to understand the cultural clashes that occurred in Germany in the 1920s. The Weimar period saw an explosion of new cultural ideas, both in traditional forms of high culture (such as painting, literature and music) and in the newly developing mass culture. This atmosphere of innovation and democratisation was partly a general European trend, helped by technological developments, but it was particularly strong in Germany. Many welcomed a new culture that they thought would reflect and foster their infant democracy and so traditional values in culture came under attack. There was a general spirit of experimentation, whether in theatre or science or sexual behaviour. Many felt that the arts should both reflect and help shape a new world. In the age of democracy art should be accessible to the masses.

But for all those who welcomed the new cultural climate there were many more who hankered after the past, resented change and saw cultural experimentation as leading to Germany's cultural and national degeneration. The old order and traditions had already suffered the shock of military defeat and sudden political change, closely followed by economic crisis that had undermined traditional values such as hard work and thrift. To many traditional Germans, scenes like those in Source 5.1 were the last straw: they thought their country was doomed unless something drastic was done. For these people, the Weimar cultural explosion reinforced their hostility to the regime.

In this chapter we try to give you some insight into the cultural vitality of the Weimar period, and to examine the effect this had on the prospects for the new democratic regime.

A   What kinds of cultural experimentation took place? (pp. 90–3)

B   How did Germans react to cultural experimentation? (p. 94)

C   Review: How significant was cultural ferment in weakening the Weimar Republic? (pp. 94–5)

TALKING POINTS

1   How do you think someone from the German middle classes, who had perhaps lost his or her savings in the economic crisis of 1923, would react to this painting?

2   'Culture reflects the society that produces it.' Do you agree?

FOCUS ROUTE

1   Study the material on pages 90–5 and use it to complete your own copy of the table below, noting evidence for each of the following aspects of Weimar culture:

    A   A spirit of experimentation and challenge to traditional culture

    B   An attempt to democratise 'art' by making it more accessible to the masses, and to make it reflect the spirit of the age

    C   The development of new technology.

Aspect	Painting	Literature	Music/opera	Theatre	Architecture	Film	Cabaret	Radio
A								
B								
C								

2   Use the information in this chapter to complete the culture section of your copy of the chart on page 60.

A What kinds of cultural experimentation took place?

ACTIVITY

Research the careers of these famous people, who contributed to Weimar culture. Do their careers suggest that new cultural ideas won or lost support for the democratic regime?

- Bertolt Brecht
- George Grosz
- Walter Gropius
- Emil Nolde

Traditional art forms
Painting

The visual arts saw an explosion of innovation in form and subject matter, with EXPRESSIONISM developing alongside a new emphasis on social comment. New media such as collage and photomontage developed. Artists such as George Grosz and Otto Dix were part of the *Neue Sachlichkeit* (new objectivity) movement, which believed art should comment on society and be understood by ordinary people.

SOURCE 5.2 *Pillars of Society* by George Grosz

SOURCE 5.3 *Big City* by Otto Dix

91

WAS THE WEIMAR REPUBLIC UNDERMINED BY JAZZ, ART AND DANCING GIRLS?

SOURCE 5.4 John Heartfield and George Grosz, *The Art Scab*, 1920. John Heartfield was a German artist who had changed his name in 1916 in protest against the extreme nationalism of the time

What is the worker supposed to do with art? Have painters given their works the appropriate content for the working people's struggle for liberation, the content that would teach them to free themselves from the yoke of a thousand years of oppression?

No, despite this disgrace they have painted the world in a calming light. The beauty of nature, the forest with the twitter of birds and evening twilight! Do they show that the forest is in the oily hands of the profiteer, who declares it far and wide to be his private property, over which he alone disposes, who chops it down when his wallet requires it, but fences it in, so that freezing people cannot fetch wood?

SOURCE 5.5 A still from the film of Erich Maria Remarque's novel *All Quiet on the Western Front*

Literature

There was a reaction against writing linked to the personal experience of the author in favour of literature with a social and political purpose. The essential worth of writing was its usefulness. Such UTILITARIANISM itself provoked a reaction from both rightist writers and apolitical avant-garde writers, such as Gottfried Benn. Overall, however, there was an explosion of publishing, with bestseller lists, paperbacks and book clubs encouraging greater reading. Several major novelists wrote during the Weimar Republic, such as Arnold Zweig, Hermann Hesse and Thomas Mann. Erich Maria Remarque's anti-war novel *All Quiet on the Western Front* challenged the 'stab in the back' view of how Germany lost the war. Published in 1929, it sold half a million copies in three months and the American-made film was a popular success.

Music and opera

The experimental mood was also evident in music, with Schoenberg's use of atonality. Other musicians advocated *Gebrauchsmusik*, music with a practical purpose. They welcomed opportunities to reach a new mass audience with sound films, the radio and the gramophone. *Zeitopera* (opera of the time) developed, reflecting modern issues from a radical left perspective, notably at the famous Kroll Opera, Berlin.

Theatre

A new school of *Zeittheater* (theatre of the time) developed, employing realistic techniques, such as actors sitting on the toilet, to convey a generally critical message of bourgeois society, and seeking to involve the audience directly. Street theatre developed to take political drama to a mass audience. Drama became the most explicitly political art form, with many left-wing playwrights, most famously the Marxist Bertolt Brecht who believed that 'a theatre that makes no contact with the public is nonsense'.

SOURCE 5.6 Kroll Opera House

SOURCE 5.7 A scene from *Die Dreigroschenoper* (The Threepenny Opera) by Kurt Weill and Bertolt Brecht. Based on John Gay's *The Beggar's Opera*, an eighteenth-century satire of London society set in the world of pickpockets, prostitutes and highwaymen, *Die Dreigroschenoper* has a similar low-life setting which Brecht uses to satirise Weimar society. Kurt Weill's music, with its jazz rhythms and cabaret style, made the work an instant success

Architecture and design

SOURCE 5.8 This apartment block in Stuttgart was designed by Bauhaus architects

SOURCE 5.9 The Einstein Tower, designed by Bauhaus architect Erich Mendelsohn, was built in 1921 in a Potsdam suburb

SOURCE 5.10 A Bauhaus tubular chair

Architecture was one of the most innovative areas, with some architects seeing architecture as the spatial expression of a new age. Familiar materials were used in innovative ways: whole buildings were constructed out of concrete, for example. There was great stress on functionalism. The most famous school was the Bauhaus under Walter Gropius. Using the slogan 'Art and Technology – a new unity', members used new materials in bold new designs, seeking to unite art and craft in a utilitarian approach. Their work covered both architecture, especially public buildings, and design, especially furniture.

SOURCE 5.11 W. Gropius, *Programme of the Bauhaus, 1919*

The Bauhaus strives to bring together all creative effort into one whole, to reunify all the disciplines of practical art – sculpture, painting, handicrafts, and the crafts – as inseparable components of a new architecture. The ultimate, if distant, aim of the Bauhaus is the unified work of art – the great structure – in which there is no distinction between monumental and decorative art.

How did mass culture develop?

Germany's existing forms of popular culture, such as religious and folk festivals, largely reflected a rural world. Now urbanisation, the growth of consumer goods and new means of communication fostered a modern mass culture. The radio, gramophone and cinema allowed music, drama and new forms of artistic expression to reach ordinary people. Increased public funding of the arts, with subsidies for exhibitions, also helped to involve more people.

Spectator sport and consumerist attitudes were also part of this mass culture, much of which derived from the USA rather than from traditional German roots. Many looked to 'swinging twenties' America, with its mass production of consumer goods and advertising, its new musical forms, especially jazz, and its dazzling film industry, as the way to the future. There was a craze for all things American, from the Charleston to chewing gum, described by one commentator as 'the cheapest way to Americanise oneself'.

Other traditions, such as the subordinate position of women, were challenged. Some women broke traditional norms by smoking, having short hair styles and wearing modern, American-style dress, and they campaigned for sexual liberation. This accompanied a continued expansion of employment opportunities for women in the growing professional and service sectors. The 'modern woman' was becoming far more visible. However, although the Weimar constitution had given women the vote, the regime retained the criminal code against abortion and contraception.

Film

SOURCE 5.12 A scene from *Metropolis*, Fritz Lang's vision of the future, of a mechanised society in which the oppressed workers live a robotic life underground ruled by an upper class of Thinkers who make the plans but don't know how to realise them without the enslaved workers

During the 1920s the cinema developed as a form of mass entertainment. It was welcomed by many as a symbol of the new plebeian, democratic age, using modern technology to involve the masses in culture. By the end of the 1920s there were 500 cinemas in Germany. There was considerable variety in the films made for the German cinema, with a general shift from early expressionism to a greater stress on social reality. There was also a growth in American imports. Marlene Dietrich, flaunting her sexuality, became a worldwide star. The most famous German filmmaker was Fritz Lang, who produced *Metropolis*, a powerful critique of modern society. By the late 1920s, right-wing filmmakers were exploiting this new medium to produce stirring, patriotic films, such as *Fridericus Rex* (Frederick the Great), which Germans flocked to see.

Radio

Radio developed quickly as a form of mass communication. Radio broadcasts began in 1923, and were controlled by the state; by 1930 there were 4 million sets. Many people were enthusiastic over the opportunities this new medium gave to democratise culture, and new music and plays were specifically created for radio.

Cabaret and dance

Berlin, with its 40 theatres and 120 newspapers and magazines, challenged Paris as the cultural centre of Europe. Berlin became notorious for its nightclubs, where naked dancing, subversive songs and open homosexuality lured many, but horrified more. The Charleston became popular, reflecting the mechanisation and democratisation of life.

SOURCE 5.13 Dancing girls

SOURCE 5.14 Stefan Zweig, in his autobiography *The World of Yesterday*, remembers Berlin in the 1920s

Bars, amusement parks, pubs shot up like mushrooms. Made-up boys with artificial waistlines promenaded along the Kurfürstendamm [one of Berlin's main streets]. In the darkened bars one could see high public officials and high financiers courting drunken sailors without shame. At the Berlin transvestite balls, hundreds of men in women's clothes and women in men's clothes danced under the benevolent eyes of the police. Amid the general collapse of values a kind of insanity took hold of those middle-class circles which had hitherto been unshakeable in their order.

B How did Germans react to cultural experimentation?

Many Germans welcomed the atmosphere of optimism and experimentation. For many others, however, social and cultural change reinforced fears that their world was collapsing. These fears of cultural decay were politicised by the Right and blamed on the lazy, un-German Weimar Republic. The Centre and nationalist parties campaigned against 'tides of filth'. Bodies such as the Nazi-supported *Kampfbund für Deutsche Kultur* were created to campaign against nudism, homosexuality, birth control, Americanisation and female emancipation, and in favour of traditional activities such as churchgoing and family prayers. The Nazis organised disruption of performances of 'unpatriotic' films such as *All Quiet on the Western Front* and decadent theatrical productions at the Kroll Opera House. The prominence of Jews amidst the cultural experimentation was seen by the Right as proof of the harm the COSMOPOLITAN Weimar Republic was doing to Germany.

Although it is always hard to judge popular opinion, particularly in such a diverse field as culture, it seems probable that more Germans reacted against many of the new cultural activities than were attracted by them. There are several indications of a growing reaction against Weimar cultural experimentation. As early as 1926 the Reichstag passed a law to 'protect youth from pulp fiction and pornography', and state governments drew up lists of publications not to be sold to under 18-year-olds, for example true crime, erotic magazines and sex education books. There are reports of audiences booing experimental plays and concerts. Public-spending cuts from 1929 onwards affected the arts: local government withdrew subsidies from avant-garde (experimental) productions, and theatres had to concentrate on more popular productions, relying on income from tickets not subsidies. The increased participation of conservative politicians in state governments after 1929 resulted in several measures against new cultural forms. Wilhelm Frick, who as Thuringian Interior Minister became the first Nazi in a state government in 1930, ordered modern art removed from museums and tried to restrict jazz performances.

C Review: How significant was cultural ferment in weakening the Weimar Republic?

In many ways Weimar culture was very significant, as it contained artistic forms that were greatly to influence later cultural development, most famously the Bauhaus, which has been a major inspiration for modern architecture and design. However, here we are concerned with the short-term effects of cultural experimentation on the prospects for the Weimar Republic's survival. As Peter Pulzer has written in *Germany 1870–1945* (1997, p. 116): 'To most Germans ... the energy, the experimentation, the chaotic creativity which made Weimar culture the envy and Mecca of so many foreigners represented *Kulturbolshewismus* (cultural communism), the overturning of forms and values in a world in which too much had been overturned already. The predominant cry was in favour of ... "a conservative revolution".'

Many conservatives blamed the government for allowing traditional German culture to be undermined. This was further evidence of the unpatriotic nature of the new regime. But it was not only the Right that attacked the Weimar regime. Some left-wing artists criticised it as grey and uninspiring; some were attracted to more dynamic communism. In culture, as in politics, Weimar was assailed from both extremes. In return, the state used its control of the radio to limit radical programmes. George Grosz was fined for defaming the military, corrupting public morals and blasphemy.

FOCUS ROUTE

Complete the culture section of your copy of the table on page 60.

It is also worth noting that the experimentation was largely confined to towns. In 1932, 46 per cent of households in large cities could receive radio, compared with just 10 per cent in small villages. More Germans continued to go to or take part in traditional forms of entertainment, such as church festivals, choral societies and beer halls, than attended new plays or watched cabaret. However, Weimar culture did reinforce many people's hostility to the regime. Weimar Germany was not ruined by female wrestlers or disfigured paintings, but such activities seemed for many Germans to symbolise all that was wrong with their country and so made them more likely to vote against the Weimar regime or simply not vote at all.

SOURCE 5.15   Women wrestlers

TALKING POINT

Do you feel that your study of Weimar culture has enhanced your understanding of the conflicts in Weimar Germany and the prospects of the regime's survival?

KEY POINTS FROM CHAPTER 5: Was the Weimar Republic undermined by jazz, art and dancing girls?

1   Weimar Germany was marked by an explosion of cultural experimentation in various forms.
2   This reflected the new optimism, democratisation, challenge to tradition, excitement and modernism of the period.
3   Berlin, with its lively culture and night life, became the cultural centre of Europe.
4   There was also the development of a mass culture, with the growth of films, radio and consumerism.
5   Many Germans were horrified by what they saw as the collapse of traditional moral and cultural standards. This reinforced their hostility to the regime.

Part 1.2 Review: How secure was the Weimar Recovery 1924–9?

ACTIVITY

1 Look at the points jumbled up in the table below.
   Sort them out into three lists:
   i)   promising developments
   ii) worrying aspects
   iii) mixed (i.e. it could be argued to be either i) or ii) or both).

Developments 1924–9	
a) Dawes Plan	m) Attitude of army
b) Allied occupation of Ruhr/Rhineland	n) League of Nations
c) Young Plan	o) Coalition governments
d) Employers' attitude and Ruhr lockout	p) Wage levels
e) Attitude of administrative elite	q) 'The new woman'
f) Public expenditure	r) Inflation
g) Agriculture	s) Putschs
h) The SPD	t) Election of President Hindenburg
i) Unemployment and the Unemployment Insurance Scheme, 1927	u) Cultural experimentation
j) Locarno Pact	v) Treaty of Berlin
k) Extremist parties	w) Attitude of DNVP
l) Industrial investment and production	x) Support for DDP

2 Essay: 'By the beginning of 1929, the prospects for the survival of the Weimar Republic looked good.' Discuss.

Essay-writing exercise: developing a structured, well-supported argument

One major technique when writing an essay is to organise your ideas into neat paragraphs, each covering a major idea. It is often very effective to make the basic point in the first sentence of the paragraph, then develop this idea in the rest of the paragraph.

1 First, try to write down between five and seven basic points that could be used to answer question 2 above, some agreeing with the statement, some disagreeing. Later, compare your points with those in the exercise below.
2 Opposite are a series of sentences that could form part of the essay. Part one covers the first part of the essay and includes a possible brief introduction. Here the optimistic viewpoint is argued. Part two covers the last part of the essay, where points challenging the quotation are made, and includes a possible brief conclusion.
3 Take one set of sentences. Try to pick out the three key idea sentences that could be used as the opening sentence of a paragraph. Then find the two sentences that develop this key idea. Identify the possible introduction/conclusion.
4 Compare your results with those of other students.
5 Try to place the key sentences in an order. There is no one fixed way of ordering the points. Discuss various possibilities.
6 Study the facts in the 'Possible Supporting Evidence' section, and find evidence to support each paragraph.

NB The completed essay would require these ideas to be further developed with more supporting detail.

The paragraphs do not cover all the possible points that could be made.

When written as an essay, some sentences would be slightly rephrased in places to read more fluently.

Instead of writing the essay in this way (arguing in favour of the question, then against), you could discuss each area (political, economic, diplomatic) in turn, making optimistic and pessimistic points in each one.

Structuring paragraphs for essay: 'By the beginning of 1929, the prospects for the survival of the Weimar Republic looked good.'

Part One: The Optimistic Case

a) By 1929 the Weimar system of government seemed to have become well established.

b) Inflation had been cured, there had been five years of virtually continuous growth in production, and unemployment remained low.

c) Reparations had been reorganised once, and the improved terms of the Young Plan were near finalisation.

d) Many historians would agree with the above quotation and take an optimistic view of the Weimar Republic's prospects, arguing that it was strong by 1929 and could have survived if the Depression had not occurred. Others disagree, and stress some key weaknesses in the Weimar Republic that were still present in 1929.

e) More money was entering Germany through foreign loans than was leaving through reparations, and this investment boosted industrial expansion and social expenditure.

f) The 1928 elections had seen a growth in support for parties committed to democracy, with extremists of Left and Right doing badly. There had been no coups since 1923, and by 1929 Germans had had ten years of democratic, republican government.

g) By 1929 there were many encouraging signs in the economy.

h) Stresemann's conciliatory foreign policy can be seen as laying the basis for the long-term consolidation of the Weimar Republic.

i) The election of Hindenburg as President in 1925 reassured many conservatives that the Republic might protect their interests.

j) Germany could use its membership of the League of Nations to raise the issue of German minorities in its lost lands, and links with the USSR strengthened Germany's bargaining position.

Part Two: The Pessimistic Case

aa) Although extremists posed no direct threat, the Republic still faced opposition from both left- and right-wing parties who were biding their time.

bb) There were some crucial underlying weaknesses in the economy.

cc) The Weimar regime was still blamed for accepting the Treaty of Versailles, and there had been no major revision of the hated treaty.

dd) Close examination suggests that fundamental political problems still remained.

ee) Although there had been some successes, Stresemann's diplomatic achievements looked paltry to many Germans.

ff) We will never know whether the Weimar Republic could have developed into a stable parliamentary system if it had not been for the impact of the Depression. Some argue that the success of parliamentary government in Germany since 1945 illustrates how democracy could flourish in Germany, but the evidence identified above does seem to suggest that there were major weaknesses within the Republic even before the double blow of the death of Stresemann and the Great Depression of 1929.

gg) Any payment of reparations, no matter how repackaged, would be resented by most Germans.

hh) No party had been able to achieve a majority in the Reichstag, so the Weimar Republic was still plagued by weak, short-lived coalition governments.

ii) Industrial production grew at a far slower rate than in other European countries, and unemployment remained a running sore. Employers considered their prospects for expansion were hindered by the too powerful trade unions.

jj) From 1927 farmers were increasingly hit by falling food prices, and were getting into debt.

Possible supporting evidence

i) There were six changes of government during 1924–8.

ii) The Young Plan reduced the overall figure for reparations from 132,000 million marks to 37,000 million.

iii) Overall industrial production by 1927 had recovered to 1913 levels.

iv) The pro-Weimar parties' share of the vote went up from 52 per cent in May 1924 to 73 per cent in May 1928.

v) Germany's share of world production fell from 14.3 per cent in 1913 to 11.6 per cent in 1926–9.

vi) President Hindenburg stuck to his oath to uphold the Weimar constitution.

vii) Allied troops still occupied much of the west bank of the Rhine; Germany had not regained any of the land lost in 1919.

viii) In the 1928 elections the KPD gained over 10 per cent of the vote; the Nazis made significant gains in northern rural areas.

ix) Between 1924 and 1931 Germany received 18,000 million marks in foreign loans and paid out 11,100 million marks in reparations.

x) Under the Treaty of Berlin Germany provided the USSR with economic expertise in return for Soviet help with rearmament.

xi) Under the Young Plan Germany would be paying reparations until 1988.

xii) From 1928 over one-third of farms were running at a loss.

98

THE WEIMAR REPUBLIC 1924–9: YEARS OF ACHIEVEMENT AND RECOVERY?

Historians' assessments

We can now finally assess whether the Weimar Republic experienced a secure recovery during this period. Read the historians' assessments in Sources 1–4 and complete the Activity below.

SOURCE 1 R. Bessel in M. Fulbrook (ed.), *German History Since 1800*, 1997, pp. 252–3

Even during the years of 'relative stabilisation' all was not well with the Weimar Republic. The profound social, economic, political and psychological destabilisation which had set in with the First World War had not really been overcome; underlying economic problems remained, and the relative political stability of Weimar's 'golden years' rested on shaky foundations . . .

While the two liberal parties saw their popular support dwindle and the (moderate) conservatives lost roughly a third of their supporters, many voters turned to special-interest parties – betraying a lack of faith in a democratic politics which focused on the common good.

SOURCE 3 M. Fulbrook, *The Fontana History of Germany, 1918–1990: The Divided Nation*, 1991, pp. 7–8

To moderate observers, it might appear that under Stresemann's guidance, a considerable amount had been achieved . . . Yet many observers in Weimar Germany were far from moderate. Each of the measures negotiated under Stresemann was highly contentious. Moreover, under the façade of apparent stabilisation there were many cracks, both political and economic.

SOURCE 4 P. Pulzer, *Germany 1870–1945*, 1997, p. 3

The era of Stresemann was the high noon of the Weimar Republic. Tempers dropped, political extremism subsided. In large part this was due to the return of prosperity. Between 1924 . . . and 1928 money wages doubled and the value of the currency was maintained. The standard of living was higher in 1928 than in 1913. Unemployment was generally below one million. In 1927 the expansion of the German state culminated in the introduction of a comprehensive unemployment insurance scheme. German industry regained its technical and organisational lead. The Dawes loan . . . encouraged modernisation.

SOURCE 2 K. Fischer, *Nazi Germany. A New History*, 1995, pp. 179–87

The middle years of the Weimar Republic, sometimes referred to as the Roaring or Golden Twenties, saw a temporary return of domestic prosperity and a concurrent relaxation in international relations . . . Many western loans were made to Germany, creating an impressive boom that persuaded many that the crisis of 1923 had been resolved. Germany used the borrowed capital in two profitable ways: financing a program of public works and investing in the modernization of industry. In 1923 German industrial output had fallen to 47 percent of 1913 levels, but by 1929 it surpassed 1913 levels by 4 percent.

The return of prosperity brought with it a corresponding improvement in international relations, partly because the Western powers recognized that their economic well-being in an increasingly interconnected economic order rested on cooperation rather than on conflict and partly because a group of more moderate statesmen now took the helm in foreign policy in the major Western nations . . .

This relaxed atmosphere in international relations, combined with the return to prosperity, also lowered the political temperature in Germany . . . In 1925 . . . the Weimar Republic gained new respectability with the election as president of the venerable [old and distinguished] Paul von Hindenburg, who would painstakingly observe his oath to the republic despite his monarchist convictions.

The political life of the republic . . . still had not stabilized or matured. Between 1924 and 1929 governments were glued together by tenuous coalitions of center to moderate right-wing parties . . . The republic had come into being as . . . an accidental republic, with a democratic constitution that few Germans understood or appreciated. Tarnished by its opponents with the stigma of Versailles and saddled with staggering socio-economic problems, the republic found few passionate supporters . . .

Political parties reflected the traditional social, religious, and regional cleavages that had divided the German people from each other in the past. Even parties located close to each other on the political spectrum found greater strengths in their differences than their similarities . . . Out of some ten major parties, none displayed a passionate commitment to the republic . . .

The political foundation of the republic was also under attack by Germany's elite institutions and groups . . . The overwhelming majority of judges were unsympathetic to the republic . . . The universities were bastions [strongholds] of institutionalized conservatism and elitism . . .

The military, of course, was the most powerful bulwark [defence] against democratization . . . The Reichswehr had managed to preserve its traditional structure and conservative ethos [spirit], though officially it pretended to stay above politics . . .

The leaders of heavy industry also wanted to dismantle the Weimar system because it supported the costly welfare state . . . German big business gradually mounted a counterattack against labor by trying to reduce wages and benefits . . .

In addition to these political and institutional cleavages, the Weimar Republic also faced intense cultural divisions stemming from the . . . process of modernization . . . [with] rapid urbanization and mass education . . . and new forms of expression suitable to a mass audience . . .

The republic, certainly in the eyes of cultural conservatives, became causally associated with every threatening wind of change in fashion, mores [customs] or intellectual attitudes . . . In the field of culture, as in so many other fields, Germany became radically polarized between the traditionalists . . . and the cultural pluralists.

ACTIVITY

Hold a debate: Which is the more accurate view of the Weimar Republic from 1924 to 1929:
- 'A remarkable period of recovery'
- 'A superficially promising period, but in reality marred by major weaknesses'?
Use the information on your completed chart from page 60 to support your arguments.

PART 1.3
Germany 1929–33: Why did the Weimar Republic fail and Hitler gain power in 1933?

Adolf Hitler, in 1930. After hearing Hitler speak, a 16-year-old boy commented: 'Nobody will vote for him; such ranting can't convince anybody.'

Have you ever made a major misjudgement of someone's ability and prospects? Well, don't worry! You are in good company. Many people misjudged Hitler. Although the Nazis' share of the vote increased from 3 per cent in 1928 to 37 per cent in July 1932, President Hindenburg advised Schleicher in August 1932: 'Put him in charge of the Post Office. That's the best job he'll ever get.' Five months later, in January 1933, Hindenburg appointed Hitler Chancellor.

Chapters 6–8 explain this phenomenal rise to power. Our attention will focus on three broad developments:

- the effects of the Great Depression on the stability of the Weimar Republic
- the reasons why the Nazis grew to be the largest political party
- the decline of parliamentary government in 1930–2.

These all help to explain why Hindenburg appointed Hitler Chancellor in January 1933.

These chapters will also complete our investigation into the reasons why the Weimar Republic failed. We began by asking whether the long-term problems you can see in Chart A on page 100 doomed the Weimar Republic to failure and we finish by investigating the short-term causes of the Republic's collapse, culminating in Hindenburg's decision in January 1933 to appoint Hitler as Chancellor. In Chapter 9 you will need to decide whether all the causal factors shown in Chart A were a necessary part of the Weimar Republic's fall and Hitler's success. If you took one away, would events have turned out in the same way?

100

GERMANY 1929-33: WHY DID THE WEIMAR REPUBLIC FAIL AND HITLER GAIN POWER IN 1933?

■ A   Germany 1918–33. Factors contributing to the decline of parliamentary government and the appointment of Hitler

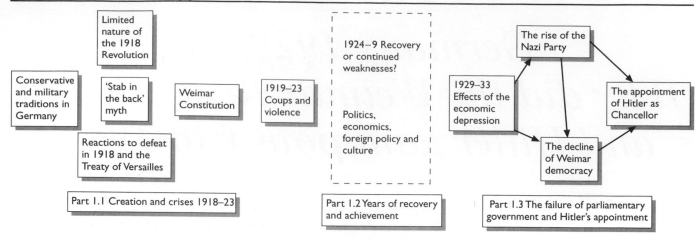

■ B   The pattern of events 1929–33

1929	
3 Oct	Stresemann dies
29 Oct	Wall Street Crash

1930	
27 Mar	SPD coalition government led by Müller resigns
29 Mar	Brüning is appointed Chancellor
30 Mar	Reichstag approves Young Plan
30 June	Rhineland is finally evacuated by Allied troops
16 July	Brüning is defeated in the Reichstag when it votes to overturn his austerity budget which had been issued by presidential decree
	Hindenburg dissolves the Reichstag
14 Sept	New elections; Nazis and Communists make major gains

1931	
Mar	France blocks Brüning's proposed Customs Union with Austria
6 July	Hoover moratorium (suspension) on all debts, including reparations
13 July	Failure of Danat bank marks the beginning of a financial crisis
11 Oct	Nazis and DNVP co-operate in the HARZBURG FRONT

1932	
27 Jan	Hitler meets industrialists and reassures them about Nazi policies
Feb	Unemployment peaks at 6,128,000
	Geneva Disarmament Conference
10 Apr	Hindenburg defeats Hitler in presidential elections
13 Apr	Brüning bans the SA in an attempt to reduce street violence
24 Apr	State elections in Prussia result in the Socialist-led coalition government losing its majority, but it continues as a caretaker government
12 May	Defence Minister Groener forced to resign
30 May	Brüning resigns
	Papen is appointed Chancellor of a new government of 'national concentration'
4 June	Reichstag is dissolved
16 June	Papen lifts ban on the SA
9 July	Lausanne Conference ends reparations
20 July	Socialist-led Prussian state government is removed by Chancellor Papen
22 July	Germany withdraws from the Geneva Disarmament Conference
31 July	Nazis become largest party in Reichstag elections with 37 per cent of vote; extremist parties win a majority in the Reichstag
13 Aug	Hindenburg rejects Hitler's demand to be made Chancellor
30 Aug	Goering elected leader of Reichstag
12 Sept	Papen loses a Reichstag confidence vote by 512 to 42. Reichstag is dissolved
6 Nov	Reichstag elections: Nazi vote falls to 33 per cent
17 Nov	Papen resigns as Chancellor
2 Dec	General Schleicher becomes Chancellor
11 Dec	Allies accept the principle of equal disarmament

1933	
4 Jan	Hitler and Papen make a deal to try to form a government
15 Jan	Nazis make gains in Lippe state elections
28 Jan	Hindenburg refuses to back Chancellor Schleicher, who then resigns
30 Jan	Hindenburg appoints Hitler as Chancellor

ACTIVITY

1. List the Chancellors that held power during this period.
2. Find evidence of each of the following:
   a) the harmful effects of the Great Depression
   b) the rise of the Nazi Party
   c) the decline of parliamentary government.

6

Was Weimar democracy undermined by the world economic depression?

CHAPTER OVERVIEW

'When America sneezes, Europe catches a cold.' This saying was especially true in Germany after the American Stock Exchange crash of October 1929. In fact, it would be fairer to say that after 1929 Germany caught pneumonia. The massive impact of the Great Depression (also known as the World Slump) on Germany is the essential context for the collapse of the Weimar Republic and the rise of Hitler. Such is its importance that the historian William Carr wrote that: 'It is inconceivable that Hitler could ever have come to power had not the Weimar Republic been subjected to the unprecedented strain of a world economic crisis.' To assess the accuracy of this view we will investigate:

A How was Germany affected by the slump? (pp. 102–4)

B How did German governments react to the slump? (pp. 104–5)

C How did German voters react to the slump? (pp. 106–7)

D Review: Was Weimar democracy undermined by the world economic depression? (p. 108)

ACTIVITY

1 **a)** What would you expect to happen in a country if it experienced an economic depression or slump? Read the lists of possibilities in the table and choose either A or B from each pair.
   b) Discuss your choices with the rest of the class.

Economic developments	
A	**B**
Inflation	Fall in prices
Rise in wages	Fall in wages
Rise in world trade	Fall in world trade
Rise in government income	Fall in government income
Rise in government debt	Fall in government debt

Political effects	
A	**B**
Increased co-operation amongst political parties	Greater divisions within coalition governments
Increased votes for moderate parties	Increased votes for extreme parties
Increase of extreme nationalism	Decline in nationalism
Increase in despair	Growing optimism

A How was Germany affected by the slump?

FOCUS ROUTE

1 Explain briefly what happened to each economic indicator in Source 6.1.
2 What does Source 6.2 reveal about the government's response to the slump?
3 Look at Source 6.3. How was Germany affected compared to other countries?
4 List the effects of the slump on the German economy.

SOURCE 6.1 Key indicators of the state of the German economy, 1928–33

Aspect	1927	1928	1929	1930	1931	1932	1933
Industrial production (1913 = 100)	110	113	114	99	82	66	74
Exports (bn RM)		12.3	13.5	12.0	9.6	5.7	4.9
Imports (bn RM)		14.0	13.5	10.4	6.7	4.7	4.2
Unemployment (m)		1.4	1.8	3.1	4.5	5.6	4.8
Wages (nominal) 1913 = 100	145	164	169	155	137	113	115
Agricultural prices 1913 = 100	138	132	126	107	89	77	84
Industrial prices 1913 = 100		159	157	154	142	118	111
Government income bn RM*		9.0*				6.6*	6.8*

* Income crosses year, i.e. 1928 figure covers 1928–9, etc.

SOURCE 6.2 Government expenditure: per capita state expenditure (at all levels, i.e. federal, states, local) at 1900 prices (M) (i.e. so fluctuations in prices are taken into account)

Items	1913	1925	1929	1932
Economy, e.g. transport	17	16	22	18
Welfare services	20	65	102	106
Public housing	0.4	10	13	4
Education	17	20	28	24
Interest payments on National Debt	6	1	4	7

SOURCE 6.3 International comparisons

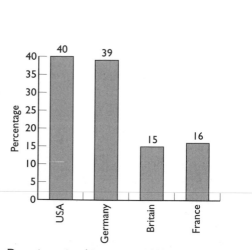

Drop in national income in 1932 compared to 1929 (%)

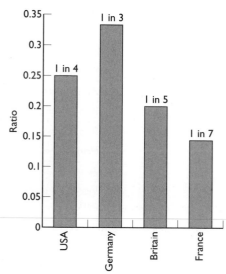

Ratio of unemployed in 1933

The effects of the slump were widespread. Many farmers had already been hit by high interest rates and falling agricultural prices. Their position worsened and by 1932 18,000 farmers had gone bankrupt. Industry equally suffered from the depression with 50,000 businesses going bankrupt between 1930 and 1932. The crisis had worsened in 1931 when five major banks closed down.

Just as significant was the fact that by 1932 over 6 million people were unemployed. For most, it was a disaster. Not only did they lose the income that they relied on, but they also felt unwanted and rejected, which had a deep psychological effect on many. In addition, millions of other people were affected by the job losses. Members of workers' families were hard hit, and traders suffered because of reduced demand for their goods. Even those who managed to keep their jobs had their wages reduced or lived in fear of losing their jobs.

■ 6A   How the slump became a vicious circle

The depression in Germany after 1929 is often blamed on external events, chiefly the Wall Street Crash. However, as this chart shows, the internal situation in Germany played a major part in the crisis.

Germany   USA   World

Offstage: the Government

No government was prepared to intervene in a major way to reflate the economy.
Müller's coalition government 1928–30 could not agree on cuts.
Brüning's government 1930–2 tried to use the slump for its own political and foreign policy purposes.

The component parts of the economic crisis

a) Agriculture: many farmers, hit by high interest rates, were going bankrupt by 1927; they were then hit by falling prices.
b) Industry suffered a trade recession from 1929 on.
b) Finance was hit by a banking collapse in the summer of 1931 when five banks went bankrupt.

■ **Learning trouble spot**

The Great Depression and the fear of inflation

1 Many students understand that Germany suffered major economic problems in 1929–33 but remember the inflationary crisis of 1923 and assume that this also happened in 1929. In fact, prices actually fell. The economic crisis of 1929–33 was a depression or slump: that is, industries suffered from a loss of demand and laid off workers. The chief problem was unemployment not inflation. In fact, the lack of demand tended to lower prices.

2 Other students understand the above, but then argue that inflation was thus unimportant in the collapse of the Weimar Republic. This view is misleading. Although the 1923 inflationary crisis was over by 1924 and there was no inflationary problem between 1929 and 1933, the inflation of 1923 still played a role in the slump because the government (along with most Germans) was determined to avoid another inflationary crisis. This was a major influence on its policies during the slump. In addition, the bitter memories of hyperinflation still influenced voting behaviour.

3 Some students think that all the problems of the Great Depression developed instantly in 1929. In reality, the depression in Germany was not a sudden event resulting from the Wall Street Crash. There had been major economic problems before October 1929, as you saw in Chapter 3, and these and other problems kept accelerating for two years after October 1929. Even in 1931 most politicians expected the economy to recover naturally, as it had from the 1926 downturn. However, in the summer of 1931 a major banking crisis deepened the slump and particularly hit the middle class. Depression was thus an escalating problem from late 1929 to 1932.

4 Some students believe that all foreign funds were taken from Germany right after the Wall Street Crash in October 1929. Foreign investors could not normally withdraw their money immediately but had to wait until the agreement ended. (Many of these agreements were short term, for example for two years, which allowed quicker withdrawal.) The biggest withdrawal of investment actually occurred late in 1930, partly as a reaction to the success of extremist parties in the September elections.

B How did German governments react to the slump?

FOCUS ROUTE

1 Why was it difficult for Weimar governments to follow a policy of intervention in the economy?
2 What measures were taken to reduce the impact of the slump?
3 How effective were these measures?

ACTIVITY

As a government, you need to decide how to tackle the problems of the economy. Will you try to break out of the vicious circle by reflating the economy?

1 Which of the following two strategies would you adopt? Look closely at the individual policies and identify the benefits and dangers of each.
2 Explain your choice, referring to:
   a) individual policies
   b) past events in Germany
   c) possible political consequences of your actions.

Strategy 1	Strategy 2
A general policy of non-intervention, waiting for a natural recovery, as in 1926. Give priority to maintaining government finances to keep confidence in the currency	Intervention to assist economic recovery. Use deficit financing (see page 73) to stimulate demand, help recovery and reduce people's misery
a) Cut welfare benefits b) Cut state employees' wages c) Raise welfare insurance contributions d) Raise taxes e) Argue that Germany cannot pay reparations	f) Stimulate the economy by starting a programme of PUBLIC WORKS g) Maintain the rates of unemployment relief and wages h) Extend welfare to those not covered i) Borrow money j) Print money

You might have expected the German government to take a range of actions to help the economy recover. However, like the governments of most other countries hit by the slump, for a long time it did very little. This was partly due to the widespread international belief that governments were fairly powerless to help. There were also particular factors operating in Germany:

- Germany had recovered from the minor slump of 1926 without the government taking action.
- It was hard for a coalition government to agree on action, particularly if this called for sacrifices. In March 1930 the Müller SPD-led government collapsed when it failed to agree on what cuts in unemployment relief to make.
- Most crucially, the government was terrified by the thought of a recurrence of the hyperinflation crisis of 1923. It believed that spending its way out of the crisis (for example, by maintaining welfare levels and increasing expenditure on public works) without raising taxes could provoke another inflationary crisis.
- Legal restrictions on the Reichsbank (as part of the Dawes and Young plans) meant it could not greatly increase the amount of money printed nor devalue the mark.
- The government found it difficult to borrow money. Many potential German investors had lost their savings in 1923 and were unable or reluctant to lend money. Foreigners shared this lack of confidence in German finances. Foreign governments who might have made loans insisted on terms that were unacceptable to the government.
- Evidence now suggests that Brüning (Chancellor, 1930–2) deliberately allowed the economic crisis to continue as part of his campaign to get reparations ended and to dismantle the welfare state.

The main approach of governments after 1929 was to reduce expenditure to cope with the fall in tax revenue as economic activity declined. For example, between 1928 and 1933 the budget for war victims' pensions was cut by one-third, embittering thousands of people who felt betrayed by the system. They voted accordingly. The economic crises made governments appear weak and divided. Blame fell not only on individual politicians and parties but on the whole democratic system of the Weimar Republic.

Eventually, but too late, the government became more interventionist. Once reparations were suspended in 1931 (see page 82), Chancellor Brüning set up some public works schemes and his successor Papen began to allocate unused land to dispossessed peasants and workers. But these measures were a classic example of 'too little, too late'. The economy did start to improve late in 1932, but this was too imperceptible to influence the voters. It was to be Hitler who built on this recovery and took all the credit.

Protectionism

During the Depression, many governments faced demands for measures to protect their national economy. One method was to restrict imports from other countries, especially if they were cheaper than home-produced goods. This was called protectionism, a policy of protecting your own industries and farms from foreign competition (see page 73). It was a break from free trade policies, where countries trade with each other without artificial restrictions.

The normal form of protectionism was to impose taxes on imported goods to make them more expensive; or to impose restrictions on the number of imported goods. There were, however, problems with such an approach. Other countries might retaliate and adopt similar moves against your exports. This could harm parts of your economy that were dependent upon exporting goods. Also, moves which put up the cost of goods, especially food, would be unpopular with consumers. Different groups also made conflicting demands on governments. Whereas farmers wanted high food prices, workers wanted low food prices. Industries that exported goods favoured free trade, whereas industries and farms supplying the home market tended to want protectionist policies.

ACTIVITY

1 Study the voting figures in Source 3.3 on page 63. Select evidence to support the view that the slump weakened support for Weimar democracy.

2 'Increased unemployment led to increased support for extremism in Germany.' Do Sources 6.4–8 prove this?

C How did German voters react to the slump?

By the winter of 1932 about one-third of the German workforce was unemployed. This scale of unemployment overwhelmed the new unemployment insurance scheme. An increasing number of workers had to be given temporary relief, and were then forced back onto local authority handouts. Many were forced out of their homes, and lived in shanty towns. Mass unemployment had a great impact on the views of all Germans and how they consequently voted. Between 1930 and 1932 there were five major national elections, as well as numerous state elections. The effect of the slump can clearly be seen in German voting behaviour.

SOURCE 6.4 Unemployment 1928–32

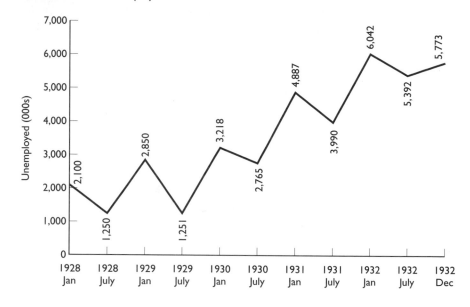

SOURCE 6.5 'Our last hope: Hitler.' A Nazi election poster from 1932

SOURCE 6.6 Nazi vote in Reichstag elections 1928–32

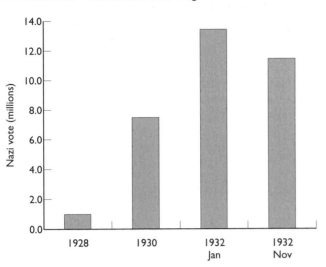

SOURCE 6.7 KPD vote in Reichstag elections 1928–32

SOURCE 6.8 'Open the factories': a communist poster from 1932

D Review: Was Weimar democracy undermined by the world economic depression?

The slump had a major effect on the Weimar Republic. It induced a general feeling of gloom and reinforced many Germans' hostility to what they saw as a feeble and failing democratic system. As we shall see, it contributed in March 1930 to the fall of the last Weimar government (Müller's SPD coalition) that had a majority in the Reichstag. In September 1930, it led to a large increase in the number of anti-democratic deputies (especially the Nazis) in the Reichstag, a trend that continued in 1932. This meant that it became virtually impossible for any government to gain the support of the Reichstag, and parliamentary government declined.

Some historians argue that the Weimar Republic was fundamentally flawed, containing major weaknesses even before the impact of the slump. Others argue that it was the slump that killed a system just beginning to establish itself. Most would agree, however, that the economic effects of the slump reduced the chances of Weimar democracy surviving to virtually nil, even if it was still not certain that a Nazi government would take power.

ACTIVITY

Complete a spider diagram to show what you think were the main consequences for Germany of the economic slump.

KEY POINTS FROM CHAPTER 6: Was Weimar democracy undermined by the world economic depression?

1 Germany's economy was already suffering difficulties before 1929 and was heavily dependent on American loans, many of which could be withdrawn.

2 From October 1929, Germany was badly hit by the effects of the Wall Street Crash.

3 Between 1929 and 1932 production nearly halved and unemployment rose to 6 million.

4 Governments were terrified of sparking off inflation if they spent extra money, and so took little action to counter the Depression.

5 The slump led to growing support for extreme parties in the 1930 and 1932 elections.

7

Why did the Nazis become the largest party in Weimar Germany?

CHAPTER OVERVIEW

'In spite of their very well-prepared and thoroughly organised propaganda . . . their successes remain . . . very modest . . . This is a party that isn't going anywhere. Today it is a numerically . . . insignificant, radical, revolutionary splinter group that is incapable of exerting any noticeable influence on the great mass of the population or on the course of political developments.' That is how a confidential Interior Ministry report described the Nazi Party, the NSDAP, in 1927. Yet within five years it was the most popular German party ever, with 37 per cent of the vote. How did this transformation come about?

First we investigate the Nazis' own contribution to their success, including Hitler's skills as leader, the quality of their organisation and propaganda and the effects of their use of violence. Then we look at who voted Nazi and why they did so. Was class a major determinant of voting behaviour? How influential were the actions and arguments of the Nazis, or did they gain support mainly because of the growing economic crisis? Therefore this chapter consists of:

A What role did Hitler play in the rise of the Nazis? (pp. 112–13)

B How well organised were the Nazis? (pp. 114–15)

C How important were the SA and the role played by violence? (pp. 116–17)

D Who supported the Nazis? (pp. 118–23)

E Why did people support the Nazis? (pp. 124–7)

F Review: Why did the Nazis become the largest party in Weimar Germany? (pp. 128–30)

ACTIVITY

Using Chart 7A on pages 110–11:

1 Identify two events that appear important in Hitler gaining control of the Nazi Party.
2 **a)** Identify six occasions when the Nazis strengthened their position.
  b) For which of these were they responsible? Which were outside their control?

FOCUS ROUTE

Why did the Nazis become the largest party in Weimar Germany? Make a large display chart covering all the key points to answer this question. You could use the following headings.

- Role of Hitler
- Nazi message
- Nazi organisation
- Nazi strategy (including propaganda, violence)
- Role of the SA
- Nazi supporters (who, why)
- Overall context (especially the Depression and the failings of Weimar parliamentary government)

WHY DID THE NAZIS BECOME THE LARGEST PARTY IN WEIMAR GERMANY?

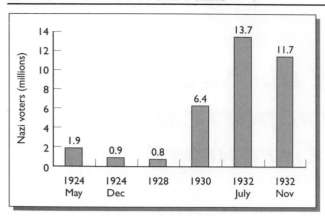

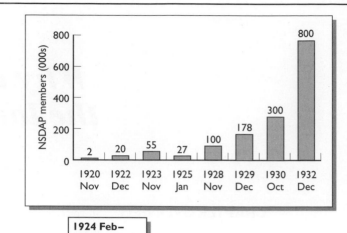

1924 Feb–March Hitler's trial becomes a great propaganda success. Hitler is imprisoned. He writes *Mein Kampf*, vol 1. Many Nazis make small election gains in aftermath of inflationary crisis. Party nearly falls to pieces in Hitler's absence. **Dec** Hitler is released early from prison

1925 Hitler refounds party

1925–8 Party organisation improved, so it was in a strong position to exploit discontent when the slump hit Germany

1926 Feb At Bamberg meeting Hitler finally gains control and establishes a Führer party: the 'Heil Hitler' salute is adopted

1919 German Workers Party (DAP) founded by Anton Drexler **Sept** Hitler joins as 55th member

1920 Feb DAP is renamed NSDAP; Hitler drafts the 25 Point Programme

1921 Hitler becomes party leader. SA set up. Newspaper *Völkischer Beobachter* set up

| 1919 | 1920 | 1921 | 1922 | 1923 | 1924 | 1925 | 1926 |

1923 Nov Munich Putsch fails, but lessons learnt. Party reorganised to prepare for power legally, under all-powerful Führer

1924 Dec Nazis lose votes as economic growth continues

Bamberg meeting 1926 Hitler faced criticism from northern, more socialist wing of party, centred on Strasser brothers. Pressure to change 25 Point Programme in a more socialist direction, and to make the leader bound by it.

The early development of the Nazi Party
Helped by upper-class contacts, e.g. Ludendorff, publisher Lehmann, piano-manufacturer Bechstein; Röhm's links with army obtains weapons for SA

ECONOMIC

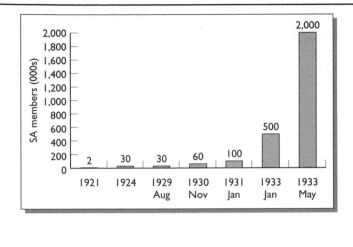

Key

Text	Nazi Party advances
Text	Nazi Party setbacks
Text	Independent events

27 Jan 1932 Hitler enthusiastically received by German industrialists at Düsseldorf Industry Club; promises to guarantee the existing social order and property rights, and to weaken trade unions

1931 Feb SA is purged of Berlin SA leader Stennes and other dissidents Goebbels is put in charge of more centralised Reich Propaganda Leadership **Oct** Harzburg Front. Nazis join with DNVP, STAHLHELM and some of the elite

1930 Otto Strasser is forced out of the party **Sept elections Nazis make major gains** Hitler is able to soothe discontent and appoints radical Röhm as leader. Hitler builds up his disciplined SS as a rival

1929 local election gains; Nazis gain their first ever majority in city of Coburg. Hitler helps lead the Anti-Young Plan referendum campaign

1928 elections; slight overall losses, but significant gains in some rural areas

1932 March Hitler gains 37% of the vote in presidential elections **July elections. Nazis gain 37% of the vote**

1933 Jan Hitler is appointed Chancellor Nazis make gains in Lippe local state elections

1927	1928	1929	1930	1931	1932	1933

1930 Oct Berlin SA mutiny at reactionary tendencies in the NSDAP

1932 Aug Hitler meets Hindenburg and demands to be made Chancellor; Hindenburg refuses. **Nov Nazis lose 2 million votes in elections Dec** Nazis face a serious internal crisis. They have growing financial problems; there is radical pressure to seize power. Gregor Strasser resigns

1929 Anti-Young campaign Nationalist outcry against 1929 Young Plan

Farmers hit by falling prices

RECOVERY   WALL STREET CRASH

TALKING POINT

Hitler's membership card had the number 555 on it, since membership started at 501. Why do you think the founders of the DAP did this?

A What role did Hitler play in the rise of the Nazis?

FOCUS ROUTE

Make notes on:

a) Hitler's leadership qualities

b) Hitler's skills as a communicator.

SOURCE 7.1 Adolf Hitler, *Mein Kampf* (My Struggle), 1925

Politics is the art of using men's weaknesses for one's ends.

Since the masses have only poor acquaintance with abstract ideas, their reactions lie more in the domain of feelings ... And the driving force which has brought about the most tremendous revolutions on this earth has never been a body of scientific teaching which has gained power over the masses, but always a devotion which has inspired them, and often a kind of hysteria which has urged them into action. Whoever wishes to win over the masses must know the key that will open the door to their hearts.

The receptive powers of the masses are very restricted, and their understanding is feeble. On the other hand, they quickly forget. Such being the case, all effective propaganda must be confined to a few bare necessities and then must be expressed in a few stereotyped formulas.

The art of leadership consists of consolidating the attention of the people against a single adversary [opponent] and taking care that nothing will split that attention ... The leader of genius must have the ability to make different opponents appear as if they belonged to the one category.

SOURCE 7.2 Otto Strasser, *Hitler and I*, 1940. Otto Strasser and his brother Gregor were early supporters of the Nazi Party and held leading positions in its organisation. Otto became disillusioned and left the party in 1930

Adolf Hitler enters a hall. He sniffs the air. For a minute he gropes, feels his way, senses the atmosphere. Suddenly he bursts forth. His words go like an arrow to their target, he touches each private wound on the raw, liberating the mass unconscious, expressing its innermost aspirations, telling it what it most wants to hear ... If he tries to bolster up his argument with theories or quotations from books he has only imperfectly understood, he scarcely rises above a very poor mediocrity. But let him throw away his crutches and step out boldly, speaking as the spirit moves him, and he is promptly transformed into one of the greatest speakers of the century.

SOURCE 7.3 E. A. Buller, *Darkness over Germany*, 1943. Buller was an anti-Nazi German teacher who left Germany

At one of the early congresses I was sitting around surrounded by thousands of SA men and as Hitler spoke I was most interested at the shouts and more often the muttered exclamations of the men around me, who were mainly workmen or lower-middle-class types. 'He speaks for me, he speaks for me.' 'Ach Gott [Oh, God], he knows how I feel.' Many of them seemed lost to the world around them and were probably unaware of what they were saying. One man in particular struck me as he lent forward with his head in his hands, and with a sort of convulsive sob said, 'Gott sei Dank [God be thanked], he understands.'

ACTIVITY

1 List the main points Hitler is making in Source 7.1 about how to win support.

2 Which of Sources 7.2 and 7.3 do you think is more reliable as evidence of Hitler's skills?

3 What can you learn from Sources 7.2–4 about Hitler's skills in winning support?

113

WHY DID THE NAZIS BECOME THE LARGEST PARTY IN WEIMAR GERMANY?

SOURCE 7.4 Audience listening to Hitler speaking at a rally in Munich in 1922

In 1924 Hitler was in gaol, sentenced to five years for treason. His future looked bleak and it was possible that he might even be deported to Austria. However, within one year he had been released and was able to turn his failure at Munich to his advantage. He had gained national publicity from his bold defence at his trial. He had also used the time in prison to reflect on politics and to write *Mein Kampf.*

Furthermore, the chaos into which the Nazi Party fell during his absence showed his indispensability to the movement. He virtually refounded the party in February 1925 and based it round the *Führerprinzip* (see page 55). This gave Hitler supreme power over both policy and strategy. He reorganised the party's strategy, structure and symbols. Only the Twenty-five Point Programme remained fixed, although its interpretation would become flexible. The Nazis would now use Weimar democracy to gain mass support rather than attempting another putsch.

The *Führerprinzip* made the party an obedient tool of Hitler's will. He introduced the brown shirt for his SA storm troopers, adopted the outstretched right arm as a salute and personally designed the Nazi flag with the swastika and striking yet traditional red, black and white colours. At the party congress at Bamberg in 1926 he defeated more socialist-inclined rivals and became the undisputed Führer of the party.

Hitler himself was central to the success of the Nazis. He provided charismatic leadership with his MESSIANIC mission to build a new Germany. He seemed to possess almost demonic willpower, which was both infectious and inspiring to others who accepted that what he said could come true. He was a powerful speaker; his timing, expression and the content of his speeches impressed his listeners. His hypnotic gaze from protuberant [staring] blue eyes helped fix his audience. He was able to identify with their emotions and expectations and gave people faith – an attractive commodity, particularly amidst the despair of economic crisis when other political parties appeared to lack a sense of direction.

Along with Josef Goebbels, Hitler realised the importance of propaganda and used it to target many Germans' specific grievances. He was very flexible in what he actually said to the German people. He was able to tailor his message to his audience, and was able to appeal both to the socially downtrodden and to the agrarian and industrial elites. He was the central rallying figure that gave the various groups within the party cohesion and attracted wider support. Hitler also had a good sense of opportunity and timing. However, he was clearly not infallible, as was exemplified by his near-disastrous meeting with Hindenburg in August 1932 (see page 111). Furthermore, in 1930 the Nazis did as well in areas where they had not organised mass rallies as in those where they had. It must also be said that many people who encountered Hitler were not impressed.

TALKING POINT

Some have argued that modern advertising tactics are partly inspired by Hitler's views and approaches. Do you think there is a case for this?

B How well organised were the Nazis?

The Nazis' success partly stemmed from their organisational structure throughout Germany. The party was organised in a series of areas, or GAUE, headed by a local leader, the GAULEITER, appointed by Hitler and subordinate to his orders. Outside these orders, the *Gauleiter* enjoyed considerable latitude to develop the party according to local circumstances. The Nazis also built up a series of associated organisations for young people, women, students, lawyers, factory workers, etc. Especially important was the Nazi Welfare Organisation which ran soup kitchens and organised food donations to people in distress, putting into practice their idea of a *VOLKSGEMEINSCHAFT* or national community. Under its organisation chief, Gregor Strasser, the party built up an efficient structure that allowed it to exploit the economic deterioration after 1929.

Although the Nazis had a centralised party propaganda machine under Goebbels, they also paid great attention to local propaganda. Most Nazi members and voters were won over by personal contacts or by attending a meeting addressed by a local speaker, not through direct contact with Hitler, despite his energetic campaigning. The Nazis targeted key individuals in a local community, such as a butcher or teacher, and hoped he would influence others. Their growing membership allowed them to organise concerted door-to-door campaigning and leafleting. They also used direct mailing and the publication of pamphlets. For example, they distributed 600,000 copies of their Immediate Economic Programme during the July 1932 election campaign. Posters conveyed simple messages: simple in both what was offered and how they portrayed their opponents.

The Nazis put great effort into training speakers. Over 6,000 had passed through their training school by 1933. Speakers were licensed by the party to ensure quality and were provided with booklets on policies and propaganda techniques. The Nazis used the latest technology – loudspeakers, slide shows, films and even planes – as in, for example, the 1932 presidential election campaign, 'Führer over Germany'. Initially, they relied on traditional forms, such as mass rallies, marches in uniform and drill. Music, lighting and the display of disciplined enthusiasm fostered the message as much as the words. Once in power, they made great use of radio and films.

Success was also due to the campaigning effectiveness of the Nazi Movement (*Bewegung*). (The Nazis called themselves a movement to distinguish themselves from other parties.) Firstly, they developed a powerful message. The Nazis promised to restore hope and create a new national community for all Germans (*Volksgemeinschaft*). Economic problems would be solved and the people provided with work and bread. The interests of all Germans would be looked after, but especial attention was given to the needs of the true German peasant and small trader who would be saved from 'the clutch of Jewish moneylenders'. The feeble Weimar democratic system would be replaced with strong leadership, which would smash communism, end Jewish influence, destroy the Versailles settlement and end reparations. Germany's new military might would allow it to secure vital living space (*Lebensraum*) and Germany would be a great nation once more.

Nationalism was crucial to the Nazi appeal, providing a form of ideological cement to hold together potentially diverse and conflicting interest groups. Anti-semitism was prominent in the early stages in the 1920s, but was not a major reason for their mass support in the 1930s.

The Nazis' ability to convey their message gained a great boost from their 1929 anti-Young Plan alliance with Alfred Hugenberg's Nationalist Party. This alliance gave Hitler access to Hugenberg's vast media empire. Their ideas now reached beyond the party's own paper, *Völkischer Beobachter*, to a range of mass-circulation papers. Funds were also attracted so that the party could compete in the numerous Reichstag, presidential and state elections that marked the final years of the Weimar Republic. Initially, the Nazi Party had some funding from the army and wealthy patrons, but most of its money came from ordinary members, through donations and charges for attending meetings.

115

WHY DID THE NAZIS BECOME THE LARGEST PARTY IN WEIMAR GERMANY?

The party did receive some funding from industrialists, most notably Thyssen, but it was not a major factor in its success.

The rapid expansion of the Nazi Movement created an aura of success, which further boosted membership and resources. After their startling electoral success of 1930, the Nazis immediately intensified their propaganda in readiness for the next elections. In the following year, membership rose from 390,000 to 800,000. On the other hand, turnover was rapid, as some apparently became disillusioned, especially late in 1932, with their apparent failure to gain power.

TALKING POINT

What do you think is the difference between a movement and a party?

SOURCE 7.5 Report of the Prussian state police, in June 1930, on the NSDAP's speakers' school

The training of speakers is accomplished by correspondence course in the form of monthly instruction packages ... A participant at the Speakers' School is only finally recognised as an official party speaker after participating in the correspondence course for 12 months and speaking publicly thirty times within 8 months.

This year it is planned to hold a further, oral course in Herrshing. The precondition for attendance is a minimum of 6 months satisfactory participation on the correspondence course ... Speakers in possession of a 'certificate of aptitude' are permitted to hold local training evenings at which they can train speakers according to the methods of the speakers' school.

SOURCE 7.7 A Nazi meeting, July 1931, described in the Nazi monthly journal, *Wille und Weg* (The Will and the Way)

The first meeting in a village must be prepared in such a way that it is well attended. The prerequisite [essential thing] is that the speaker is fairly well informed about specifically rural questions. Then, it is most advisable to go to a neighbouring village some time after but to advertise the meeting in the first village there as well, then many people will certainly come across. After this, one holds a big German Evening in a central hall for a number of villages with co-operation of the SA and the SA band ... The German Evening, provided it is skilfully and grandiosely [with a great show] geared to producing a big public impact, primarily has the task of making the audience enthusiastic for our cause, and secondly to raise the money necessary for the further build-up of propaganda. The preparation of the village meetings should best be carried out in the following way: most effectively through written personal invitations to every farmer or inhabitant; in the bigger villages by a circular, which is carried from farm to farm by party members.

SOURCE 7.6 Report for the 1930 accounts of the town group in Preussisch Holland, East Prussia

Preussisch Holland 8.3.1931

Receipts	Marks	Expenditure	Marks
Subscriptions from members	616.10	**Subscriptions paid to central party**	248.05
		SA insurance	170.40
Donations Voluntary and collections	1,620.68	**Administrative expenses**	468.97
Meetings Sale of admission tickets to meetings; donations at meetings to fighting fund	1,957.70	**Propaganda** Advertisements, leaflets, speakers' fees, travel, rent, etc.	2,249.64
		Extras SA/Hitler Youth damages at meeting	896.61
General	475.95	**General**	298.50
Total	**4,670.43**		**4,332.17**

SOURCE 7.8 Extracts from the course held by the National Propaganda Directorate II, 17–31 August 1931

Saturday 22 August
09.30–11.30 Dr Konopath, Chief of the Cultural Policy Section of the National Directorate: Blood and Race in the German Nation
15.00–18.30 Town Councillor Fiehler, Specialist in Community Politics Issues within the National Directorate: National Socialist Community Politics
22.00–23.00 Plenary [attended by all members] Session. Speaker: Dr Konopath
Sunday 23 August
07.30–10.00 Reinhardt: The National Socialists in the Reichstag: the others and us
10.30–12.00 Alfred Rosenberg: National Socialist Foreign Policy
14.00–15.30 Alfred Rosenberg: The Militant League for German Culture
16.00–18.00 Walther Darré, Chief of the Agricultural Policy Section of the National Directorate: National Socialist Agricultural Policy.
Tuesday 25 August
Wednesday 26 August
Whichever of these days sees good weather will be kept free to allow the party comrades time to participate in a long-distance tour of the Bavarian Alps.

[Other sessions included 'Tribute, Currency and Economy'; 'National Socialism and Support for War Victims'; 'Work and the Shaping of Social Life'; 'Hitler Youth'; 'National Socialist View of the State'; 'Educational and Religious Policy'; 'Military Policy'; 'The Jewish Question'.]

116

WHY DID THE NAZIS BECOME THE LARGEST PARTY IN WEIMAR GERMANY?

C How important were the SA and the role played by violence?

FOCUS ROUTE

1 Who joined the SA and why?
2 Why did the SA make a positive impression on many Germans?

'We must struggle with ideas, but if necessary also with fists.' Hitler's words neatly summarise the main role of the *Sturm-Abteilung,* or SA. They were formed in 1920 as the *Sportabteilung,* or sports detachment of the Nazi Party, intended primarily to protect Nazi speakers. More aptly renamed the *Sturm-Abteilung* (storm detachment) in 1921, they had developed into a mass organisation of 500,000 by 1933. SA members were provided with a distinctive brown shirt, emblazoned with the swastika after, in 1924, the Party bought a stock of cheap, surplus German army tropical shirts. This was the origin of their other name, the Brownshirts.

From 1921 to 1923 and from 1930 to 1934, they were led by Ernst Röhm, who had participated in the 1923 Munich Putsch and was a friend of Hitler. He was eager for the Nazis to seize power and saw the SA as the army of a new Nazi state. Röhm represented the more radical, socialist aspect of Nazism, although, unlike fellow radicals the Strasser brothers, he was not a sophisticated thinker. He once explained his approach: 'Since I am an immature and wicked man, war and unrest appeal to me more than good bourgeois order.'

The original core of ex-soldiers expanded into a vast army of young men, attracted for a variety of reasons, ranging from hatred of communism, commitment to Hitler and love of excitement and violence to a desire for free soup and a new purpose in life. Over half came from the working class, especially the unemployed. Many were just ruffians and bullies. They were provided with a uniform, meals and sometimes accommodation in SA hostels. The SA ran occasional camps, with the stress on sport and military training. As an SA leader explained, the SA offered recruits 'what they almost always lack at home, a warm hearth, a helping hand, a sense of comradeship'.

The SA's work entailed distributing propaganda leaflets, protecting Nazi meetings and trying to drive the hated Communists from the streets. From 1930 to 1932 city streets saw increasing violence between political paramilitaries. Although these groups were not allowed to carry arms, many members were killed – nearly 100 in July 1932 alone. SA casualties were held up as martyrs for the cause. In 1932 Chancellor Brüning banned the SA. They formally obeyed but paraded without shirts. Brüning's successor as Chancellor, Papen, in an attempt to appease the Nazis, ended the ban.

The SA played a major role in Hitler's success. Their 'propaganda by deed' focused attention on the communist threat and the Nazis' determination to smash it. Despite the violence and disorder they caused, their disciplined marches created the impression that the Nazis would offer firm government to restore Germany to law and order. The fear of an SA seizure of power persuaded some in the elite to favour Hitler playing a role in government, since they thought he was the only one who could control the SA.

SOURCE 7.9 A leader explains the power of the SA

The only form in which the SA appears to the public is that of the military formation. This is one of the most powerful forms of propaganda. The sight of a large number of calm, disciplined men whose total will to fight may be seen or sensed makes the most profound impression on every German, and speaks to his heart in a more convincing and inspiring language than writing and speech and logic can ever do. Where whole hosts march purposefully, stake life and existence for a cause, all must be great and true.

ACTIVITY

Draw a left-wing caricature of an SA man.

FOCUS ROUTE

Draw up two lists of evidence for and evidence against the Nazi Party being a socialist party.

■ **Learning trouble spot**

How socialist was the National Socialist German Workers' Party?

Students often have trouble with the word socialist in the full name of the Nazi Party because it seems to contradict the fact that it is considered a right-wing party. Here we try to clarify this issue.

1 **In what sense were Hitler and the Nazis Socialists?** There is a strong argument that the Nazis, as their name states, were national Socialists, as opposed to Marxist international Socialists. By socialism they meant a system that put the needs of the community before the needs of individuals. However, they saw community (*Volksgemeinschaft*) in national not class terms. In this respect they were similar to Fascists in Italy.

2 **Were the Nazis anti-capitalist?** Unfortunately the answer is yes – and no! The Nazis were certainly not left-wing Marxist Socialists. There were, though, anti-capitalist elements in the Nazi Movement (see, for example, their 1920 programme, page 52), but increasingly this anti-capitalism was modified, focusing only on some types of capitalism. There was hostility to FINANCE CAPITALISM, where wealthy people used their money to exploit others; finance capitalism was often synonymous with (considered the same as) Jewish capitalism. This view was attractive to indebted farmers. Nazism also opposed big business at times. This appealed to the petty bourgeoisie of artisans and small traders, who could not compete with department stores and mass production. The danger was that anti-capitalism might alienate the business elite, but Hitler reassured industrialists that it would not threaten their interests. In power, Hitler's ambitions were achieved through developing industrial might, not by protecting the petty bourgeoisie.

3 **Was Hitler a Socialist?** Unlike Mussolini, Hitler had never been a member of a socialist party. Issues of wealth distribution and class were never important to him. His concern was with a racially pure, ideologically unified and powerful Germany. He used the word socialist in the sense identified above but opposed party members with a traditional view of socialism.

4 **Were there genuinely left-wing Socialists in the Nazi Party?** Yes. They were strongest in the north where the Strasser brothers were based. They looked to attract workers by supporting strikes, and talked of social change, favouring ordinary Germans, not the economic elite. For them socialism meant a new order of society in which the material position of workers would be greatly improved. Some advocated co-operation with Communists, hoping to win them over to a national form of socialism. In 1932, some Nazis in Berlin co-operated in a strike with Communists. Schleicher's attempt in 1932 (page 135) to split the Nazis and gain the co-operation of trade unionists and the Strasserite Nazis was based on understanding this left wing of Nazism, and was not as unrealistic as is sometimes portrayed.

Revolutionary socialist Nazis were strongly represented in the SA, whose leader Röhm favoured radical change. Tension continued between them and the mainstream movement until the Night of the Long Knives which effectively decapitated Nazi social radicalism (see pages 173–9). Left-wing elements were also strong in the NSBO, the National Socialist Factory Cell Organisation. These were bodies set up from 1925 by factory workers as a Nazi rival to socialist unions. They provided services for members and ran strikes. By 1933 they had 250,000 members.

5 **Were the Nazis a workers' party?** Right from its creation, the Nazi Party had 'workers' in its name, but the Nazis initially failed to gain much support from workers. The first sign of it becoming a mass party was in rural areas in 1928, when it shifted its emphasis to target farmers, whilst seeking a broad, pan-class (across class) base. Increasingly, the term 'workers' was interpreted loosely as all Germans working for the good of Germany, by hand or brain. Thus the Nazis could still appeal to industrial workers on a more socialist basis (see Source 7.11), whilst reassuring industrialists that their interests would also be looked after.

Otto Strasser, 1897–1974
■ A former member of the SPD, he became a Nazi in 1925.
■ Born in Bavaria to a middle-class family, Otto was on the left wing of the Nazi Party. He advocated a nationalist and racist form of socialism that appealed to the lower middle classes and workers.
■ Otto became disillusioned when he realised that the party as it was evolving under Hitler was neither socialist nor for the workers. He left in 1930.
■ In 1934 he survived the Night of the Long Knives and went into exile.

Gregor Strasser, 1892–1934
■ The brother of Otto, Gregor joined the NSDAP in 1920.
■ In 1923 he took part in the Munich Putsch and led the party during Hitler's imprisonment.
■ A gifted public speaker and organiser, he built up a mass movement in northern Germany with the help of his brother and the young Josef Goebbels.
■ By the early 1930s he was second only to Hitler in power and popularity and a potential rival.
■ Opposed to Hitler's anti-semitism and his courting of big business, Gregor resigned in 1932.
■ On Hitler's orders, he was murdered during the Night of the Long Knives.

118

WHY DID THE NAZIS BECOME THE LARGEST PARTY IN WEIMAR GERMANY?

FOCUS ROUTE

1 Which groups of people were most likely to:
   a) be members of the Nazi party
   b) vote for the Nazis?
2 How has the debate developed among historians over who voted for the Nazis?

D Who supported the Nazis?

ACTIVITY

1 Who voted Nazi? Before you examine some detailed evidence about Nazi supporters, try this preliminary exercise based on your current impressions. We will then see how far you will need to modify your views.
   a) Study the following list of different sorts of German people.
   b) Divide them into two groups: those most likely to vote Nazi, and those least likely to. Then put each group in a column, with the strongest supporters/opponents at the top and the weakest at the bottom.
   c) Discuss your results with the rest of the class. Compare them with the detailed evidence on pages 118–23.

Low-ranking civil servant	Industrial worker
Retired professor	High-ranking civil servant
Army general	Protestant student
Shopkeeper in northern Germany	Small farmer
Female industrial worker	Catholic unemployed worker
Junker	Unemployed ex-soldier
Catholic priest	Unemployed artist
Protestant small retailer	

2 What attracted people to vote Nazi?
   a) Write down on separate slips of paper four different Nazi slogans illustrating how the Nazis appealed to the German people.
   b) Mix up all the slips from the whole class. Then sort them out into four or five categories, such as economic, political, nationalist, etc., and see how many slogans there are in each category.
   c) As a class, discuss whether the proportion of your slogans in each category does actually reflect the main emphasis of Nazi appeal.

How can we tell?

Nazi support rose dramatically between 1928 and 1932. There has been much debate over exactly who supported this extremist party because historians are hampered by the absence of modern opinion polls. Several types of source are available, beginning with election results. However, the results of secret ballots do not tell us who voted for whom, just how many votes a party list got in any region. One exception is that the constitution allowed states to hold separate ballots for men and women. A few did so, with blue ballot papers for men and pink for women! Thus in a few areas we have figures available by gender.

Historians' analyses of electoral support for the Nazis from particular social or religious groups are normally based on comparing how well the Nazis did in areas that differed by religious or social composition. For example, if the Nazis got 37 per cent of the national vote, but only 25 per cent in a strongly Catholic area, it seems reasonable to argue that Catholics were less likely to vote Nazi. Similarly, if they gained 45 per cent in a predominantly farming area, and several areas show this pattern, then it would seem that farmers were more likely to vote Nazi. But caution is still needed because there could be a whole range of variables affecting the result.

Other evidence is more direct. We have membership records of the Nazi Party and the SA that give some personal details, for example of occupations, although not generally of religion. Even here there are problems, as classifying people's class position is not an exact science, and people do not complete forms in a consistent way. Historians have also used Nazi propaganda, such as leaflets, posters and speeches, as an indication of whom they were trying to attract and why. We also have autobiographies of some Nazi members. One of the most valuable, but still potentially flawed, sources is Abel's survey of 581 autobiographies of Nazi members. In 1934 this American academic offered prizes to Nazi Party members who wrote accounts of why they joined. They provide fascinating insights, but are not necessarily representative and may not be an accurate reflection of their authors' motives. There are also accounts by Germans and foreigners who lived in Germany and commented on the growing Nazi Movement and memoirs of former Nazi supporters. All such sources need to be treated cautiously.

119

WHY DID THE NAZIS BECOME THE LARGEST PARTY IN WEIMAR GERMANY?

ACTIVITY

1 Using Source 7.10, identify two groups that were over-represented in the Nazi Party and two that were under-represented.
2 How did the membership of the Nazi Party change between 1929 and 1933 and then again after 1933? Why might this be?
3 What do Chart 7B and Source 7.11 show about Nazi support from the working class?
4 What do Sources 7.12, 7.13 and 7.15 tell you about the nature of Nazi support?
5 Were there differences between those who were members of the Nazi Party and those who voted for the Nazis?
6 Using Source 7.14 and Chart 7C on page 121:
   a) How does support for the Nazi Party differ by region?
   b) Why do you think it differed in this way?
7 Study Source 7.16. To what extent do these earlier sources confirm Hitler's claim that the Nazis were successful in appealing to 'every German'?

SOURCE 7.10 This table gives detail of Nazi Party members. Columns A–F divide them according to when they joined the party. Column G gives estimated percentages of each social group in Germany in 1933

	Before Nov 1930		Nov 1930–Jan 1933		Total Jan 1935		1933
	A **Number**	**B** **% of total members**	**C** **Number**	**D** **% of total members**	**E** **Number**	**F** **% of total members**	**G** **Estimated % of society**
Workers	33,944	26.3	233,479	32.5	755,967	30.3	46.3
White-collar workers	31,067	24.0	147,855	20.6	484,054	19.4	12.4
Self-employed, including artisans	24,563	18.9	124,579	17.3	475,223	19.0	9.6
Civil servants, including teachers	10,015	7.7	46,967	6.5	307,205	12.4	4.8
Peasants	17,181	13.2	89,800	12.5	255,291	10.2	20.7
Others	12,793	9.9	76,766	10.7	216,130	8.7	6.2
Total members	**129,563**		**719,446**		**2,493,870**		

SOURCE 7.11 Internal KPD document discussing the NSDAP and SA, December, 1931

The betrayal of socialism, of the German working people and thereby of the German nation by the SPD's leaders has led millions of proletarians, rural workers and impoverished members of the middle classes into the ranks of the NSDAP. In particular the ... SS and SA boast a high percentage of proletarians. For sure the NSDAP, supported by finance capital, uses bribery to win over the unemployed masses. Unemployed who join the SA receive clothing and sometimes accommodation and board. But this bribery is not the decisive factor behind the flow even of the proletarian masses into the NSDAP. Decisive is the SPD's betrayal of socialism and the lying, pseudo-socialist demagogy of Hitler's party. We have to recognise that a large proportion of the Nazi proletarians are misled workers who honestly believe that they are fighting against capitalism and for socialism.

■ 7B The occupational structure of Nazi Party membership compared to national patterns

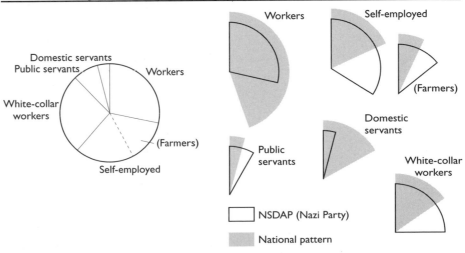

The pie chart on the left shows the occupational structure of the Nazi Party. The segments and shading on the right show the proportion of the German population for each social group overlaid by the proportion of Nazi Party members who were of that group.

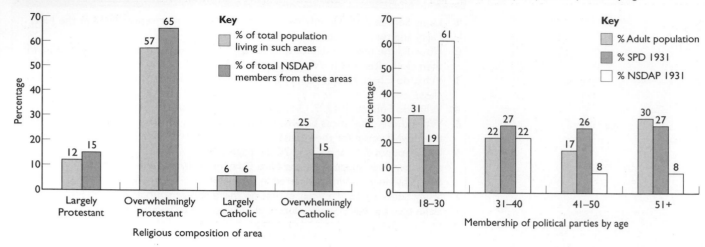

SOURCE 7.12 Membership of the NSDAP, 1925–33, by religion

Key
- % of total population living in such areas
- % of total NSDAP members from these areas

Religious composition of area

SOURCE 7.13 Membership of political parties by age

Key
- % Adult population
- % SPD 1931
- % NSDAP 1931

Membership of political parties by age

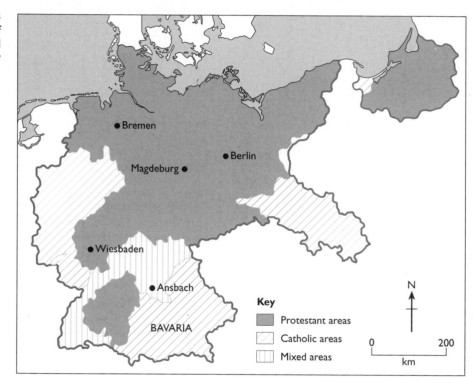

SOURCE 7.14
The distribution of Protestants and Catholics in Germany

Key
- Protestant areas
- Catholic areas
- Mixed areas

SOURCE 7.15 Percentage of German males/females voting Nazi

Area	1930		July 1932		November 1932		January 1933	
	Male	Female	Male	Female	Male	Female	Male	Female
Bremen	12.9	11.1	29.9	30.9	20.8	20.9	30.8	34.4
Bavaria	18.9	14.2	29.2	25.6	27.4	24.7	36.2	34.4
Ansbach	34.6	33.3			47.6	50.0	51.2	55.6
Magdeburg	19.8	18.7	36.3	38.9	31.1	34.0	38.1	43.3
Wiesbaden	29.1	26.0	43.0	43.7	36.1	36.8	44.9	47.3

SOURCE 7.16 Hitler, November 1928

[The NSDAP is] not the movement of any particular class or of a particular status group or profession ... [instead it is] in the highest sense of the word a German national party. It aims to encompass all elements of the nation and to embrace all occupational groups, to address each and every German of good will.

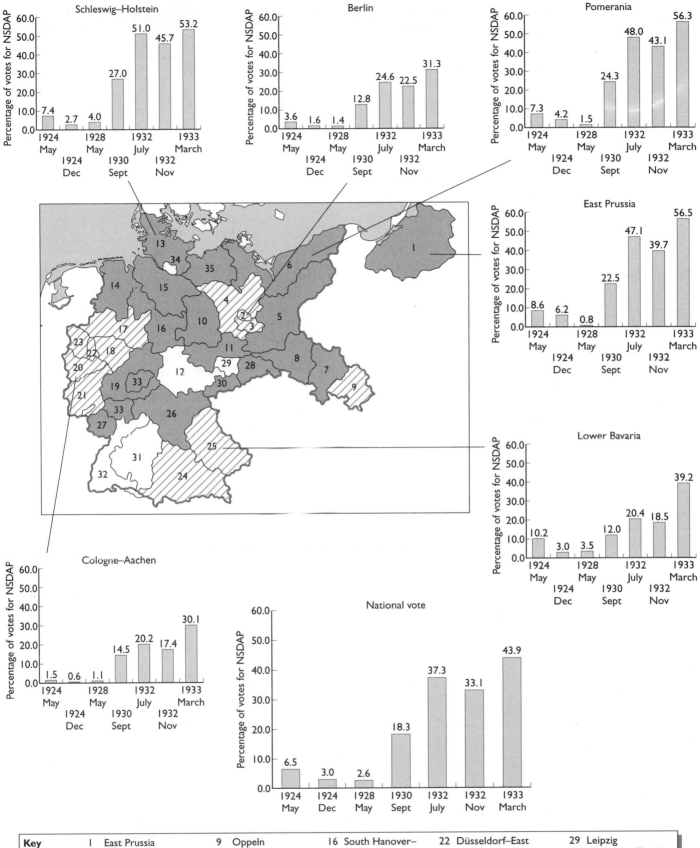

Schleswig–Holstein

Percentage of votes for NSDAP

	7.4	2.7	4.0	27.0	51.0	45.7	53.2
1924 May	1924 Dec	1928 May	1930 Sept	1932 July	1932 Nov	1933 March

Berlin

Percentage of votes for NSDAP

3.6	1.6	1.4	12.8	24.6	22.5	31.3
1924 May	1924 Dec	1928 May	1930 Sept	1932 July	1932 Nov	1933 March

Pomerania

Percentage of votes for NSDAP

7.3	4.2	1.5	24.3	48.0	43.1	56.3
1924 May	1924 Dec	1928 May	1930 Sept	1932 July	1932 Nov	1933 March

East Prussia

Percentage of votes for NSDAP

8.6	6.2	0.8	22.5	47.1	39.7	56.5
1924 May	1924 Dec	1928 May	1930 Sept	1932 July	1932 Nov	1933 March

Lower Bavaria

Percentage of votes for NSDAP

10.2	3.0	3.5	12.0	20.4	18.5	39.2
1924 May	1924 Dec	1928 May	1930 Sept	1932 July	1932 Nov	1933 March

Cologne–Aachen

Percentage of votes for NSDAP

1.5	0.6	1.1	14.5	20.2	17.4	30.1
1924 May	1924 Dec	1928 May	1930 Sept	1932 July	1932 Nov	1933 March

National vote

Percentage of votes for NSDAP

6.5	3.0	2.6	18.3	37.3	33.1	43.9
1924 May	1924 Dec	1928 May	1930 Sept	1932 July	1932 Nov	1933 March

WHY DID THE NAZIS BECOME THE LARGEST PARTY IN WEIMAR GERMANY?

Key

Consistently

■ High

▨ Low

1	East Prussia	9	Oppeln	16	South Hanover–Brunswick	22	Düsseldorf–East	29	Leipzig
2	Berlin	10	Magdeburg	17	Westphalia–North	23	Düsseldorf–West	30	Chemnitz–Zwickau
3	Potsdam II	11	Merseburg	18	Westphalia–South	24	Upper Bavaria–Swabia	31	Württemburg
4	Potsdam I	12	Thuringia	19	Hesse–Nassau	25	Lower Bavaria	32	Baden
5	Frankfurt an der Oder	13	Schleswig–Holstein	20	Cologne–Aachen	26	Franconia	33	Hesse–Darmstadt
6	Pomerania	14	Weser–Ems	21	Koblenz–Trier	27	Palatinate	34	Hamburg
7	Breslau	15	East Hanover			28	Dresden–Bautzen	35	Mecklenburg
8	Liegnitz							

122

WHY DID THE NAZIS BECOME THE LARGEST PARTY IN WEIMAR GERMANY?

SOURCE 7.17 J. Noakes, 'The Rise of the Nazis', *History Today*, January 1983, p. 11

The Nazis did best in the rural areas and small towns of the Protestant parts of Germany, particularly in the north and east. They won much of their support from the most rooted and traditional section of the German population – peasant farmers, self-employed artisans, craftsmen and small retailers ... In urban areas the party did best in those towns and cities which were administrative or commercial centres with large civil servant and white collar populations, rather than in industrial centres; and they tended to win most support in upper-middle-class districts. Nazi support also tended to be strongest among the younger generation. This was particularly true of the membership, which was also overwhelmingly male.

SOURCE 7.18 J. Falter, 'How likely were workers to vote for the NSDAP?', in *The Rise of Nationalism and the Working Classes in Weimar Germany*, ed. C. Fischer, 1996, pp. 34 and 40

According to our estimates, probably one in three workers of voting age backed the NSDAP ... From July 1932 onwards more workers would have voted NSDAP than voted KPD or SPD ... On a regular basis more than a quarter of National Socialist voters were workers ...

In terms of its electoral support the NSDAP was clearly Protestant dominated, but otherwise in social terms it was a distinctly heterogeneous [mixed] party ... There is unmistakable over-representation of voters from the middle classes, a fact certainly disputed by no one as yet. On the other hand, it no longer appears admissible, given so high a proportion of voters from the working class, to speak of a middle class party. The National Socialists' electoral successes were nourished by so many different sources, that the NSDAP might really best be characterised as an integrative [all-embracing] protest movement ... Its composition was so socially balanced ... that ... it possessed the character of a people's party or national party more than any other large Weimar party.

Historical debate: who voted Nazi?

ACTIVITY

The issue of who voted for the Nazis has been the subject of great historical controversy. To some extent this is because behind it lies the extremely sensitive question, 'Who was to blame for Hitler?' This activity will help you to identify the main trends in historians' explanations.

1   Copy the table below. Mark a tick if the historian identifies a group as prone to vote Nazi.

Group	1 Noakes (Source 7.17)	2 Peterson (Source 7.19)	3 Fischer (Source 7.20)	4 Falter (Source 7.18)	5 Geary (Source 7.21)
Working class					
Petty bourgeoisie/ middle class, e.g. shopkeepers, white-collar workers					
Wealthy, i.e. upper middle class					
Protestants					
Wide range, i.e. a people's movement					

2   What degree of historical consensus about Nazi support emerges from this exercise?
3   These are only extracts from the analyses of these historians so care has to be taken when assessing their views. However, the paragraph from Peterson (Source 7.19) is complete. Is there any surprising omission from his discussion of Nazi supporters? How might this be explained?
4   'The traditional stress on the petty-bourgeois base of Nazi support need not be discarded, but instead incorporated into a broader picture.' How far do these extracts substantiate this opinion?

SOURCE 7.19 B. Peterson, 'Regional Elites and the Rise of National Socialism' in *Radical Perspectives on the Rise of Fascism in Germany*, 1989, p. 172

Most [historians] now generally agree that the social class most inclined to join and vote for the National Socialists was the petty bourgeoisie, including artisans, shopkeepers, and peasants. Substantial support, however, has been shown to have come from higher social strata. Recent studies have demonstrated that residents of affluent neighbourhoods, vacationers, cruise ship passengers, civil servants and RENTIERS – all arguably elite – supported the National Socialist German Workers Party. On the other hand, big business and Junkers – the core groups of the ruling class in Weimar Germany – were generally disinclined to join or vote for the Nazis, although some of them gave various other kinds of direct and indirect support.

SOURCE 7.20 Conan Fischer, *The Rise of the Nazis*, 1995, pp. 63 and 99

[The Nazis] intended to MOBILISE all 'ethnic' Germans, tried to do so and enjoyed a degree of success in crossing class, regional, confessional [religious], gender and age barriers which was unprecedented in German political history ...

An impressive body of evidence ... supports the overall picture of National Socialism as a predominantly Protestant, middle-class rassemblement [movement], and this line of interpretation has provided the starting point and the conclusion for most of the general histories of Nazism ... The latest EMPIRICAL work on the National Socialist constituency [voters] has now created problems for this long-standing consensus which have yet to be fully addressed. It appears that some 40 per cent of voters and party members were working class and some 60 per cent of SA members were working class, leading to the typification of Nazism as a popular or people's movement instead of a class movement.

123

WHY DID THE NAZIS BECOME THE LARGEST PARTY IN WEIMAR GERMANY?

SOURCE 7.21   R. Geary, *Hitler and Nazism*, 1993, p. 27

The NSDAP was most successful where it did not have to cope with strong pre-existing IDEOLOGICAL and organisational loyalties. Where these did exist, as in Social Democratic and Communist strongholds, it did far less well. The same applied to Germany's Catholic community, strongly represented over decades by the Centre Party (or the BVP in Bavaria). Loyalty to the party was reinforced by a plethora [great range] of Catholic leisure organisations which penetrated daily life and also by the pulpit, from which the NSDAP was sometimes denounced as godless. On the other hand, Nazi success in Protestant rural and middle class Germany was facilitated by the fact that political loyalties there were either weak or non-existent.

Until the 1980s the predominant view was that the key group was the petty bourgeoisie (*Mittelstand*) who provided the Nazis with mass support. They shared responsibility with the elite (who intrigued to get Hitler appointed) for the catastrophe of the Nazis coming to power. Left-wing historians could thus blame the Right and portray the working class as largely without blame. By the 1990s two developments challenged this view. Firstly, the centrality of the whole concept of class has been questioned. The phenomenon of many workers voting for right-wing governments in Britain and the USA led to more sophisticated analysis of political support and voting behaviour. Other factors, such as religion and the local community, have been identified as additional important influences on voting. The end of the Cold War and the decline of Marxism as a major force in Western universities have also encouraged a more empirical approach.

Secondly, more sources have been examined, with new techniques. The use of computers and refined statistical methodology have allowed more data to be viewed in different ways. There has been a growth in local studies, so the German people have been looked at in small groups and as individuals, not as classes. This has inevitably led to more complex views emerging. The collapse of the East German communist regime has further opened up many records. As a result, recent historians such as Falter, Conan Fischer and Brustein have all produced convincing arguments that German workers were far more attracted to the Nazis than many have argued in the past.

This does not mean, however, that the long-standing stress on the importance of support from the petty bourgeoisie can be rejected. The evidence does powerfully suggest that this class voted disproportionately for the Nazis, but far less than used to be thought. Religion and local community influences seem to have been a greater determinant of voting behaviour than class.

SOURCE 7.22   J. Falter, 1996, p. 10

The range of living and working conditions concealed behind the collective term 'worker' was huge. Thus the East Prussian or Pomeranian farm labourer who was paid largely in kind [goods] and received an hourly cash payment of 10 pfennig or less belonged to this group as much as the factory-employed craftsman or the highly specialised skilled worker who might earn ten times as much in the industrialised conurbations. Similarly, the foreman who had worked in the same Württemberg family for thirty years was as much a 'worker' according to the census as the young labourer in an Upper Silesian ironworks, the homeworker from the Erzgebirge or the daily help in a villa in Berlin-Zehlendorf. One might be in everyday contact with 'his' trade union and the workers' parties, while the other might have scarcely heard of either and align his voting intentions according to the political preferences of the estate manager or the proprietor of the small workshop with whom he went to school and who, possibly, belonged to the same hunting association or sporting club. In view of this it appears all the less likely that the working class as a whole would manifest even a degree of homogeneity in its voting behaviour.

■ 7D   The working class and Nazism

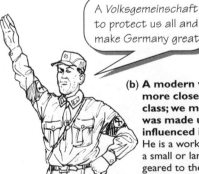

(a) **The traditional view: class is crucial**
He is an industrial worker and this will determine his voting. He will not vote Nazi.

(b) **A modern view: we must look more closely at the working class; we must examine how it was made up and what influenced it**
He is a worker, but does he work in a small or large factory? Is his work geared to the export or the domestic market? He also has a religion, an age, a family. He lives in a particular community (city, small town, village). He has a particular outlook; does he identify with fellow workers or is he ambitious? He belongs (or does not belong) to a trade union and other bodies, e.g. choral group. He may vote SPD or KPD, but he might vote NSDAP!

124

WHY DID THE NAZIS BECOME THE LARGEST PARTY IN WEIMAR GERMANY?

FOCUS ROUTE

1 List the range of reasons why people voted for the Nazis.
2 Which of these reasons do you consider the most important?
3 How have historians' interpretations changed in recent years?

E Why did people support the Nazis?

ACTIVITY

We will begin to investigate the reasons why some people voted for the Nazis by examining Nazi propaganda in the form of leaflets and posters.

1 Draw and complete a table like the one below, using Sources 7.23–32.

Source	Group directed at	Their grievances	What the Nazis offered	Other comments

2 What overall conclusions can you reach from these sources?
3 How valuable are these sources as evidence of why people voted for the Nazis?

SOURCE 7.23 Nazi publication, *Der Betriebs-Stürmer*, 1931

The years 1914-18 involved the destruction of the German Reich's economic pre-eminence and thus the freedom of German labour. November 1918 did not result in the deposition [overthrow] of the FEUDAL lords to the benefit of the workers. Instead the 9th November brought the defeat of Germany as a state. But the German worker paid the price.

His masters today are the irresponsible, faceless, international big capitalists and the Jews of the banking world ... National Socialism demands a transformation from the utterly unscrupulous profit-motivated economy to an economy geared to need.

SOURCE 7.24 A leaflet from July 1932

GERMAN WOMEN! GERMAN MOTHERS!
Our Young People Defiled.

The present Prussian Welfare Minister ... has confirmed ... that in a German Grammar School for Girls 63 per cent of the girls had experienced sexual intercourse and 47 per cent had some form of sexual disease ... The number of sexual offences and cases of incest pile up in the most gruesome manner! ...

This is the result of the many years during which our people, and in particular our youth, have been exposed to a flood of muck and filth, in word and print, in the theatre and in the cinema. These are the result of the systematic Marxist destruction of the family ...

The National Socialists must win the election so that they can put a halt to this Marxist handiwork, so that once again women are honoured and valued, and so that the cinema and the theatre contribute to the inner rebuilding of the nation.

German women and mothers. Do you want your honour to sink still further?

Do you want your daughters to be playthings and the objects of sexual lust?

If NOT, then vote for a National Socialist majority on July 31st.

Then vote for

LIST TWO
HITLER-MOVEMENT   **NAT.SOCIAL GERMAN WORKERS PARTY**

SOURCE 7.25 A Nazi election poster, 1932: 'We want work and bread!'

SOURCE 7.26 A 1924 Nazi poster: 'First bread! Then reparations'

SOURCE 7.27 A 1932 Nazi election poster showing Marxism as the guardian angel of big business. The angel has SPD on his helmet – the Nazis called the moderate Socialists Marxists to discredit them

SOURCE 7.28   A 1929 leaflet

TRADERS !
SMALL PRODUCERS! ARTISANS!

For a long time you have kept out of sight and let corruption, favouritism and the NEPOTISM of others run all over you. You believed that obeying law and order was the first duty of the citizen.

But what has this led to? Ever more exploitation by those in power. The tax-screw being turned ever tighter. You are HELOTS of this system. Your only job is to work and pay taxes which go into the salaries and pensions of ministers.

What have your parties done for you? They promised the world but did nothing. They made coalitions, prattled away before the elections then disappeared into parliament until the next.

They didn't unite against the treacherous leaders of Marxism.

They horse-dealt over ministerial posts and never gave you a thought.

They have ruled with Social-Democrats and forgotten the aim of that party – Death to the Middle Class!

Have you forgotten the inflation? How you were robbed of your savings and commercial capital?

Have you forgotten how taxes have slowly throttled your businesses?

Have you forgotten how the Department Stores and Co-operatives have ruined you?

… Middle classes, why is it so bad? Why are your shops empty? Why are you out of business?

Look at the banks and their massive profits! They are eating you out of existence!

Marxism is guilty of pawning the German economy to international high finance. Therefore citizens, you belong to the ranks of those who make no pact with Marxism, but fight it wherever it is to be found.

GERMAN NATIONAL SOCIALIST WORKERS PARTY

SOURCE 7.29
'We're for Adolf Hitler!'

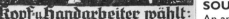

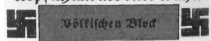

SOURCE 7.30
An anti-Jewish poster. It says: 'The puppet master. All workers vote Nazi.'

SOURCE 7.31
A 1932 Nazi poster: 'Women! Millions of men without work. Millions of children without a future. Save the German family. Vote Adolf Hitler!'

SOURCE 7.32   A 1929 leaflet

GERMAN FARMERS!

Farmers, it's a matter of your house and home!

Factories, forests, railways, taxes and the state's finances have all been robbed by the Jew. Now he's stretching his greedy fingers towards the last German possession – the countryside.

Insatiable [never satisfied] Jewish race-lust and fanaticism are the driving forces behind this devilish attempt to break Germany's backbone through the annihilation [destruction] of the German farming community.

Doesn't it open your eyes when you see the economy of the countryside being crippled by unnaturally high taxes, while you have insufficient income to set off against this because of low prices for livestock and grain?

Huge imports of frozen meat and foreign grain, at lowest prices, undercut you and push down your earnings … You cannot obtain credit to tide you over these hard times. If you want money the usurious [very high] interest rates will wring your neck. Under the protection of the state it won't be long before the greater part of the land-owning farmers will be driven from their farms and homes by Jewish money lenders.

Help us build a new Germany that will be
NATIONALIST AND SOCIALIST

NATIONALIST because it is free and held in respect.

SOCIALIST because any German who works and creates will be guaranteed not just a slave's ration of bread, but an honourable life, decent earnings and the sanctity of his hard-earned property.

Farmers, it is a matter of the most holy possessions of a people, **THE LAND AND THE FIELDS WHICH GOD HAS GIVEN US.**

Farmers, it is a matter of house and home,
Of life and death, of our people and our fatherland!

THEREFORE FARMERS – WAKE UP!

JOIN THE RANKS OF OUR DEFENCE FORCE. FIGHT WITH US IN THE NATIONAL SOCIALIST GERMAN WORKERS PARTY

Historians' assessments of Nazi support
Mood, manipulation or money: why did Germans vote Nazi?

Some historians have laid great stress on the emotional appeal of the Nazis, via a charismatic leader, symbols and rallies, to the many people who felt alienated in Germany at the time. The petty bourgeoisie was particularly attracted by this. It felt threatened by big business and by the powerful working class. These atomised (divided up, isolated) individuals in a new, mass society were looking for security and a sense of direction. The Nazis tapped this sense of unease and offered a bright future. The high turnover of Nazi Party membership has also been taken to indicate how many joined for emotional reasons, which could not be sustained on deeper reflection.

This stress on irrationalism (not based on reason) as the crucial factor in the Nazi appeal can also be used to support more recent interpretations that put stress on the broad base of Nazi support, that is a true *Volkspartei*. The prospect of firm action to take Germany out of the economic and psychological depression made Nazism attractive to millions of worried Germans, regardless of class. The Nazis were particularly successful with those Germans who had weak, unsupportive communities.

Many historians also stress the importance of propaganda organised to appeal to the emotions, especially mass meetings and rallies. Here there was no political discussion. What mattered was being there, surrounded by thousands of others, exhilarated by the carefully choreographed (designed) display. 'How could 20,000 be wrong?' 'Stop thinking, just believe!' As Goebbels said in 1934: 'Propaganda was our sharpest weapon in conquering the state, and remains our sharpest weapon in maintaining and building up the state.'

By stressing the power of Nazi propaganda it was possible to some extent to make excuses for Germans. They were manipulated: it could happen to anyone.

However, the recent work of Noakes and others has introduced a corrective to what they see as an excessive stress on propaganda. They argue that the Nazis had major electoral successes in some areas where there was little propaganda, and vice versa. Therefore, propaganda was more successful in reinforcing existing sympathies and feelings than in creating them.

An alternative view has recently come from other historians – notably Brustein – who have challenged the stress on emotions as an explanation for Nazi success, and have instead argued that Germans voted Nazi for rational economic reasons. Between 1930 and 1933 the Nazis put forward a series of economic policies, offering a third way between Marxist state planning and LAISSEZ-FAIRE capitalism. They said the economy should serve the needs of the state, not individuals. They advocated public investment in industry to boost the economy; financial controls to protect those in debt; economic AUTARKY to put the interests of Germans above those of foreigners and the creation of a continental economic zone dominated by Germany. They would support farmers through controls on prices, imports and debt, and help some resettle on unused land in the east. This package of policies, developed from 1928 to exploit the rising tide of protest in some farming areas, was reinforced by the SA and others taking action to defend farmers' interests, for example by disrupting auctions of bankrupt farms.

Brustein also sees economic factors as the reason for working-class support for the Nazis. Blue-collar workers in depressed industries were particularly attracted to their interventionist economic policies. Aspiring workers, those who had benefited from the social reforms of Weimar and were looking for further advance beyond their working-class origins, might be attracted by a Nazi future.

One commonly held view that is no longer propounded by historians is that virulent (poisonous/bitter) anti-semitism was a major contributor to Hitler's mass support. It was indeed a powerful attraction for many of the original Nazis and for some who joined the party, but not especially for voters. Other parties, such as the DNVP, were also anti-semitic. Hitler was deeply anti-semitic but played down Nazi anti-semitism as the prospects for power increased, instead stressing anti-communism which was much more attractive to the elite upon whom his chances might depend. Even the American Jewish historian

Goldhagen, who caused a storm in 1996 with his book *Hitler's Willing Executioners* (see page 350) where he argued that Germany alone developed a strong desire to eliminate Jews, accepts that anti-semitism was not crucial in the Nazis' electoral success.

127

WHY DID THE NAZIS BECOME THE LARGEST PARTY IN WEIMAR GERMANY?

SOURCE 7.33 In a survey of Nazi Party members, the following reasons were given as the main factor for joining the Nazis

Reasons for joining the Nazi Party	% of those surveyed
Anti-Marxism	65
National community	32
Supernationalism	22
Hitler cult	18
Anti-semitism	14

SOURCE 7.34 A. Bullock, *Hitler and Stalin: Parallel Lives*, 1992, p. 249

[Nazism was] a movement that was deliberately designed to highlight by every manipulative device – symbols, language, ritual, hierarchy, parades, rallies . . . the supremacy of the dynamic, irrational factors in politics: struggle, will, force, the sinking of individual identity in the collective emotions of the group, sacrifice, discipline.

SOURCE 7.35 W. Brustein, *The Logic of Evil. Social Origins of the Nazi Party 1925–33*, 1996, p. 184

The Nazi Party did not gain its phenomenal mass constituency because of its emphasis on xenophobia but rather because the party designed a series of innovative programs that appealed to material interests of a broad constituency overwhelmed by the Depression. Xenophobia alone could not have brought the Nazis to power.

I must conclude that evil may have ordinary and rational origins. This applied to pre-1933 Germans as much as to all other peoples.

TALKING POINT

Why do you think Brustein called his book *The Logic of Evil*?

ACTIVITY

Study Sources 7.34 and 7.35.

1 Explain the differences between Bullock's and Brustein's views.
2 'Complementary rather than competing.' Using the sources and your knowledge, explain how far you agree with this comment on Brustein's and Bullock's opinions on the reasons for the Nazis' support.

F **Review: Why did the Nazis become the largest party in Weimar Germany?**

Chart 7E tries to summarise what you have learnt about the extent to which different social groups supported the Nazis, and what the Nazis offered. Then, to conclude, we look at two contemporary sources that shed light on the nature of support for the Nazis.

■ **7E   Who supported the Nazis and why?**

Make Germany great!

Away with reparations!

Help us build a *Volksgemeinschaft*!

Restore traditional values!

Smash communism!

Away with feeble Weimar democracy!

Smash the chains of Versailles!

Rebuild the economy!

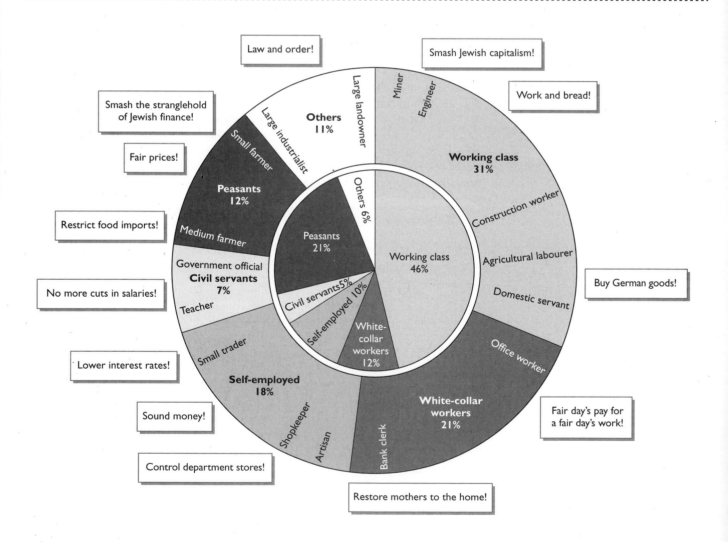

Law and order!

Smash Jewish capitalism!

Work and bread!

Smash the stranglehold of Jewish finance!

Fair prices!

Restrict food imports!

No more cuts in salaries!

Lower interest rates!

Sound money!

Control department stores!

Restore mothers to the home!

Buy German goods!

Fair day's pay for a fair day's work!

Key

Inner circle: German population in 1933 by social group (%)

Outer circle: members of Nazi Party in 1932 by same social groups

General slogans

Slogans targeted at particular social groups

REVIEW ACTIVITY

1 a) Which reasons for the growth of support for the Nazis are shown in Source 7.36?

   b) Which reasons are not reflected?

2 a) What can you learn from Source 7.37 about the reasons for the rise of the Nazis?

   b) What can be deduced from this poem about Brecht's political position?

3 A key reason for the Nazis' electoral success was that they offered both big ideas that could appeal to any German and also particular policies aimed at specific groups. How does Chart 7E support this view?

4 Do you think the actions and skills of Hitler and the Nazi Movement were more important in winning support than factors outside their control such as the economic depression?

SOURCE 7.36 'Why I became a Nazi.' An extract from an autobiography of a Nazi member submitted in 1934 to a prize competition organised by Professor Abel at Columbia University, New York, USA. The writer was a farmer and fought in the First World War against the Russians

Then came November 9 [1918]. Slowly and more strongly there grew up in me a hatred of this band of traitors and their followers. Soon the consequence of this betrayal of the nation became more and more evident.

[We lost West Prussia and Danzig; were hit by inflation; Jews became rich.] My inward aversion [hostility] to these men of a foreign race which had crucified the saviour and which now was betraying our people increased until one day it grew into hatred. The Jew was at fault for all the misery.

Then came November 9, 1923. Great and brilliant, the name of Adolf Hitler, which we heard not for the first time in these agitated days, appeared before us. We were all marching in step; we all had the same desire to wipe out the existing system which had come into power by betrayal of the people and country. We wanted something that was to grow out of the common experience of the war and the front, that would know no estates [social groups] and classes but only the German people. The word, Hitler, became for me a symbol of our future.

These first members are still our best. They grasped National Socialism not with their minds but with their emotions. They had not learned National Socialism from books. Their blood, their natural instinct drove them to the movement. Like myself, they sought the road to the people and, like myself, found it by ridding themselves of class consciousness and seeing only the fellow-countryman in every German.

In July the leader came to Tilsit. I saw him for the first time. About 40,000 people from near and far had gathered to greet him. I wore the brown shirt for the first time. Those hours are never to be forgotten. The Leader spoke. For the first time I heard his voice. His words went straight to the heart. From now on my life and efforts were dedicated to the Leader. I wanted to be a true follower. The Leader spoke of the threatened ruin of the nation and of the resurrection under the Third Reich. What matter personal interest, and social status? How insignificant had all parties become to my eyes. How despicable [vile] was Communism.

Another thing the Leader gave us was faith in the German people. If we won, Germany was saved; if we were defeated, a gate would open up and Moscow's Red hordes would swarm in and plunge Europe into night and misery.

SOURCE 7.37 'Song of the SA Man' by Bertolt Brecht (translated by John Willett)

My hunger made me fall asleep
With a belly ache.
Then I heard voices crying
Hey, Germany awake!

Then I saw crowds of men marching:
To the Third Reich, I heard them say.
I thought as I'd nothing to live for
I might as well march their way.

And as I marched, there marched beside me
The fattest of the crew
And when I shouted 'We want bread and work'
The fat man shouted too.

The chief of staff wore boots
My feet meanwhile were wet
But both of us were marching
Whole heartedly in step.

I thought that the left road led forward
He told me that I was wrong.
I went the way that he ordered
And blindly tagged along.

And those who were weak from hunger
Kept marching, pale and taut
Together with the well-fed
To some Third Reich of a sort.

They told me which enemy to shoot at
So I took their gun and aimed
And, when I had shot, saw my brother
Was the enemy they had named.

Now I know: over there stands my brother
It's hunger that makes us one
While I march with the enemy
My brother's and my own.

So now my brother is dying
By my own hand he fell
Yet I know that if he's defeated
I shall be lost as well.

130

WHY DID THE NAZIS BECOME THE LARGEST PARTY IN WEIMAR GERMANY?

REVIEW ACTIVITY

This activity brings together your work in Chapter 3 and in this chapter on the rise of the Nazis and voting behaviour in general in the Weimar Republic.

1 Study the data on Weimar elections on page 63. Compose a linear graph showing the election results for all the parties 1919–33. You might like to do this using a computer.
2 Identify and explain the trend in support for the Nazis.
3 Which parties lost support as the Nazis gained it? Does this automatically mean that the Nazis took votes from these parties?
4 What happened to support after 1928 for
  a) the SPD
  b) the KPD
  c) both left-wing parties together?
5 What happened to support for the Z/BVP throughout the Weimar period?
6 Explain what this exercise shows about why the Nazis became the largest party.

KEY POINTS FROM CHAPTER 7: Why did the Nazis become the largest party in Weimar Germany?

1 After the failure of the Munich Putsch of 1923, Hitler reorganised the Nazi Party on the *Führerprinzip*.
2 The Nazis were well organised in the regions, and established associations covering most groups in German society.
3 The Nazis used skilful propaganda techniques, and exploited Hitler's ability as a speaker.
4 In 1928, the Nazis were still on the fringe of politics.
5 In 1930, as a result of the impact of the slump, the Nazis became the second-largest party.
6 Success built up a momentum, and in July 1932 the Nazis won 37 per cent of the vote.
7 However, in August 1932 Hitler failed to be made Chancellor, and in November 1932 the Nazis' share of the vote dropped to 33 per cent.
8 The Nazis gained particular support from the petty bourgeoisie, but were a true people's party, gaining support from all groups. For some their appeal was emotional; others were attracted for reasons of material self-interest.
9 The Nazis made least impact amongst groups that had a strong sense of community, such as Catholics and Socialists.
10 The Nazis offered a solution to Germany's problems, were well organised, and rallied around an inspiring leader.

8

Why did parliamentary government decline in Germany 1930–3 and why was Hitler appointed Chancellor in January 1933?

CHAPTER OVERVIEW

We now come to the last part of our study of the key years 1929–33 that led to Hitler's appointment as Chancellor. We have seen how, mainly owing to the influence of the Depression, the Nazis had become the largest party in the Reichstag. However, 37 per cent of the vote was not sufficient in itself for Hitler to become Chancellor. He either had to obtain a majority in the Reichstag, or, more likely, he had to persuade President Hindenburg to appoint him.

In this chapter, we focus on what was happening in the Reichstag and within governing circles. We look at the problems facing the parliamentary system, and how the elite increasingly looked to establish a more authoritarian regime. This will enable you to decide whether effective parliamentary government was over before Hitler was appointed. Was Hitler indeed more the beneficiary than the cause of the Weimar Regime's failure?

It is important to avoid the assumption that Hitler's appointment as Chancellor was inevitable. In these years there were various ways in which German politics and government could have developed, as you can see in Chart 8A.

A Why did parliamentary government decline after 1930? (pp. 132–5)

B Brüning: potential saviour or destroyer of Weimar democracy? (pp. 136–7)

C Was Hitler's rise to power inevitable? (pp. 138–41)

D Why was Hitler appointed Chancellor in January 1933? (pp. 142–44)

E Review: Why did parliamentary government decline in Germany 1930–3 and why was Hitler appointed Chancellor in January 1933? (pp. 145–50)

ACTIVITY

Before you begin this chapter in detail, think yourself into the political situation in 1930. Consider each of the four outcomes at the bottom of Chart 8A. List the reasons for and against each outcome taking place.

■ 8A The Weimar regime in crisis

Long-term problems

a) Germany's authoritarian tradition

b) Nature of the Weimar regime
● Limited nature of 1918 Revolution
● Proportional representation
● Article 48

c) The Versailles Treaty
● Territorial losses
● Reparations
● Disarmament
● Allied occupation

d) Opposition from left and right
● Revolts 1919–23
● Armed opposition died away 1924–8, but potential still there
● Elites increasingly hostile

Problems in 1929–33

1929 Great Depression (and agrarian crisis)

Growth of KPD Up to 17% 1932

WEIMAR REGIME IN CRISIS 1930–3

Growth of Nazis Up to 37% 1932

Reichstag 1932: no majority support for parliamentary government

Weak democratic centre DVP, DDP lose support

Opposition from the elites Growing support for a more authoritarian system

Possible outcomes

| Communist state | Continuation of parliamentary democracy | More authoritarian system, e.g. a restored monarchy | Nazi dictatorship |

132

WHY DID PARLIAMENTARY GOVERNMENT DECLINE IN GERMANY 1930–3 AND WHY WAS HITLER APPOINTED CHANCELLOR IN JANUARY 1933?

A Why did parliamentary government decline after 1930?

You are now entering a danger zone. Not only was this a hazardous period for the Weimar regime, but it is also one that has seen many a history student become confused. You have already seen how, in the 1924 and 1928 elections, parties loyal to the Weimar system did well. These elections produced a series of coalition governments that managed to get their legislation passed by the Reichstag. Potentially the strongest of these was the 'grand coalition' government led by the Socialist Hermann Müller that took office in 1928. However, even before the Depression, there were worrying signs for the parliamentary system. President Hindenburg and his associates were discussing a more authoritarian system to 'put an end to the impotence [powerlessness] of politics'. This new form of government would not negotiate with parties in the Reichstag, but instead would rely on using Article 48 to issue decrees and would threaten DISSOLUTION of the Reichstag if it opposed the government.

So let us first try to establish a clear, basic view of the period and then look at the detailed chronology of the changes in government.

This period saw the gradual decline of democracy, as Germany moved from parliamentary government to presidential government, and then to dictatorship under Hitler. Article 48 of the constitution, giving the President powers to issue decrees, had been intended to be used only in an emergency, to defend the regime against potential enemies. After 1930 it was increasingly used to sustain governments that were unable to get their legislation through the Reichstag.

The prospect of parliamentary government surviving was further weakened by the Reichstag elections of 1932. In both July and November the majority of voters supported the two extremist parties who were hostile to the parliamentary regime.

FOCUS ROUTE

1 Explain the difference between parliamentary and presidential government.
2 Explain how presidential government came to replace parliamentary government in 1930–2.

■ 8B The decline of parliamentary government

Parliamentary Government 1928–30
Müller led a coalition government with majority support in the Reichstag.

Presidential Government, 1930–3
Hindenburg dismissed Müller. He was succeeded by a series of Chancellors (Brüning, Papen, Schleicher) who had little support in the Reichstag and depended upon President Hindenburg for support and to issue decrees. There was a growing move to change the Weimar system, by reducing the power of parliament and establishing a more authoritarian government.

Dictatorship
In 1933 Hindenburg appointed Hitler, leader of the largest party, as Chancellor. Within a year he set up a dictatorship.

SOURCE 8.1 The role of the Reichstag and the President 1930–2

	1930	1931	1932
Presidential decree laws	5	44	66
Reichstag laws	98	34	5
Reichstag: days sitting	94	42	13

Chart 8C introduces you to five of the most important politicians in 1930–2.

Paul von Hindenburg, 1847–1934

A somewhat reluctant President, Hindenburg played a key role, through his appointment of Chancellors and the use of Article 48. Having refused to appoint Hitler after his election success of July 1932, he reluctantly did so in January 1933. Hindenburg was the last potential obstacle to Hitler as dictator, but died in 1934.

Paul von Hindenburg

Hermann Müller, 1876–1931

As Foreign Minister, Müller signed the Treaty of Versailles for Germany in 1919. He was briefly Chancellor after the Kapp Putsch in 1920 and from that year onwards was leader of his party, the SPD. In May 1928 he became Chancellor for the second time and formed a grand coalition government ranging from the SPD to the DVP. It failed to agree on how to fund the rising unemployment payments brought about by the Depression. When President Hindenburg refused to support him, he resigned in 1930. His was the last genuine parliamentary government. He died within a year of leaving office.

Heinrich Brüning

Heinrich Brüning, 1885–1970

The son of a Catholic merchant, Brüning became a teacher and from 1915 to 1918 served as an infantry officer. In 1924 he was elected to the Reichstag and became the Centre Party's Reichstag leader in 1929. He was appointed Chancellor in 1930. In July 1930, in order to win Reichstag support, he called a new election which led to major gains for extremists. He failed to take action to reduce the impact of the Depression, and his austerity programme earned him the nickname of the 'Hunger Chancellor'. He was forced to resign when he lost the confidence of Hindenburg over plans to divide up bankrupt estates in east Germany. He emigrated in 1934 and settled in the USA. See also pages 136–7.

Franz von Papen, 1879–1969

Born into a Catholic noble family, Papen married the daughter of a Saar industrialist. He became a cavalry officer. In 1921 he was elected as a Centre Party candidate to the Prussian LANDTAG. He was chairman of the conservative newspaper *Germania*. At heart, Papen remained a monarchist. A friend of Hindenburg, he had limited political experience but was asked to be Chancellor in 1932. After his dismissal, he intrigued with Hitler to replace Schleicher. In January 1933 he was appointed Vice-Chancellor. He resigned in July 1934, becoming ambassador to Austria, then Turkey. He was tried at Nuremberg (see page 426) but acquitted. In 1947 a German denazification court sentenced him to eight years in a labour camp, but he was released in 1949.

Franz von Papen

Kurt von Schleicher, 1882–1934

From a noble family, he became an officer in Hindenburg's regiment. General Schleicher considered the army the true embodiment of the nation, far more so than the new Weimar Republic. He became a confidant of Hindenburg and his son. Between 1919 and 1932 he held various posts, linking the army and governments. He also cultivated links with key individuals, wanting to make the army the centre of power. This upset other generals, such as Blomberg, who wanted the army to have a lesser political role. Schleicher was responsible for getting Hindenburg to appoint Brüning, then Papen and then, reluctantly, himself as Chancellor. By 1932, worried about the power of the Nazis and the danger of civil war, he tried to tame them by including them in government. He was murdered by the Nazis in the Night of the Long Knives, 1934 (see page 173).

Kurt von Schleicher

TALKING POINT

By the time of his re-election as President in 1932, Hindenburg was 85. How might that have affected developments in 1932–3?

■ **Learning trouble spot**

The Brüning, Papen and Schleicher governments

In many ways it is more important to grasp the overall nature of the period than to get bogged down in detail. The three chancellorships had a lot in common: all were looking to reorder the Weimar parliamentary system into a more authoritarian form of government. The key differences between the various governments can be summarised as follows:

- Brüning was probably more prepared to accept a greater role for the Reichstag than Papen or Schleicher. He tried to work with the Reichstag but found this increasingly difficult. Brüning included trade union leader Adam Stegerwald in his government and planned agrarian reforms, yet his austere (harsh/severe) policies and inability to inspire the masses meant he was unpopular and his agrarian reforms upset some in the elite. His position was also weakened by his hostility to co-operation with the Nazis.
- Papen was the most hostile to the Reichstag. His 'government of barons' had no real chance of getting Reichstag support on any positive basis.
- General Schleicher was a complex character. He considered Papen's approach was too narrow and that it risked civil war, which as a general he was concerned to avoid. He described himself as a 'socially minded general' and tried to create a broader based government through links with trade unions and the more socialist wing of the Nazis. This failed and, like Brüning, his preparedness to consider agrarian reform upset the elite.

■ **Learning trouble spot**

Papen's coup against the Prussian state government

This event often causes confusion, and many students decide not to bother about it as it seems unimportant. All historians have to decide which events are significant, so why not discard this complex one? However, it was not only important in its own right but it also illustrates much about the Weimar Republic.

Firstly, it reminds us that the new Weimar Republic remained a federal state. Prussia was by far the most important state government. Since 1919 it had been run by an SPD–Z coalition which had acted effectively to reform the state. This has been seen as an example of what could have happened nationally if parties had co-operated. However, in 1932, under the impact of the Depression, the SPD–Z lost its majority in the Prussian Assembly, continuing as a caretaker government. During this period there were political fights in the streets of Berlin. Papen used this decline of law and order to intervene under Article 48 to depose the state government and put it under federal control. A parliamentary system was thus replaced by an authoritarian government. This shows how Article 48, designed to protect democracy, could be used to replace it. Furthermore, Papen's coup was a massive blow to the morale of the Left. The SPD lost its last stronghold without resisting. The deposed Prussian government stuck to the course of legality and just appealed to the courts. It was intimidated by the threat of the Reichswehr and refused to organise mass protest, since high unemployment weakened the prospects for a general strike as had happened in 1920 against the Kapp Putsch.

When Hitler became Chancellor in 1933 he inherited control of the Prussian state and used the precedent of Papen's actions to overthrow other state governments. Once again, the Left did not resist. Papen's coup has thus been seen as a mortal blow to the Weimar regime.

ACTIVITY

1 For each government between 1928 and 1933, list:
   a) how it came to power
   b) its main policies and actions
   c) the reasons for its fall.
2 How did German voters harm the prospects for parliamentary government? (Source 3.2 on page 63 will also help you answer this question.)

ACTIVITY

Study Chart 8D. Match each of the descriptions below to the correct Chancellor.

1 He was lucky to be appointed, since his support was falling. However, he did have a good chance of getting support in the Reichstag. Appointed through intrigue amongst the elite, he was underestimated.
2 The scheme behind his government was too ingenious in attempting to attract support from the Nazi and socialist Left, whilst also being concerned to buttress the elite. He became a victim of intrigue amongst the elite.
3 His was the last genuinely parliamentary government. This illustrates the key role of the Depression and shows Hindenburg's hostility to the SPD.
4 His two-year chancellorship marked a decisive shift away from parliamentary government. Eventually, some major improvements were seen, but he lost the support of the elites. A victim of intrigue, both his appointment and his fall show the key role of Hindenburg.
5 His chancellorship was a blatant attempt at authoritarian government with no hope of Reichstag support. He enacted a major blow against the SPD yet made concessions to the Nazis. A victim of intrigue amongst the elite.

1928–30 MÜLLER'S GOVERNMENT

1 March 1930: the fall of Müller's government
Once Müller's SPD-led coalition had got the Young Plan through the Reichstag, Hindenburg began looking to replace him as Chancellor. The government was divided over measures to deal with the slump, particularly over whether to increase unemployment contributions (from 3 to 3.5 per cent) to fund the increased numbers needing relief. The SPD argued employers as well as workers should bear some of the extra costs; the DVP argued relief benefits should be cut. In March 1930 Müller resigned when President Hindenburg refused to use Article 48 to support his government.

This was to be the last coalition government with a working majority in the Reichstag. It marks the effective end of parliamentary government.

1930–2 BRÜNING'S GOVERNMENT

2 The appointment of Brüning as Chancellor
In March 1930 Hindenburg, on General Schleicher's advice, appointed Heinrich Brüning, a prominent member of the Centre Party, as Chancellor. He formed a government from the centre–right, but one without a majority in the Reichstag.

In July, the Reichstag rejected the government's finance bill. Instead of trying to compromise to win parliamentary support, Brüning had the bill issued by Article 48. The Reichstag demanded its withdrawal. Brüning then persuaded Hindenburg, unwisely as it turned out, to dissolve the Reichstag in the hope of gaining more support in a new Reichstag.

3 September 1930: Reichstag election
In the new election the Nazis caused a shock by making major gains. The increase in deputies from extremist parties (Nazis 107, KPD 77) harmed the effective working of the Reichstag.

Any government would find it hard to get a majority in the Reichstag. Frightened foreigners withdrew 800 million marks in investment funds.

4 Brüning's government struggles on
Despite the election setback, the Brüning government survived. It relied on presidential decrees, rather than the Reichstag. The SPD tolerated Brüning's government for fear of another election and further gains by extremists. As they said, 'Anything but Hitler.'

Brüning tried to use the worsening economic situation to get reparations ended, and to reorder the Weimar welfare state. He took little action to reduce the impact of the slump that was causing a massive rise in unemployment. In 1932 after the suspension of reparations, he belatedly began modest reflation via public works and land reforms. In April 1932 Brüning banned the SA in an attempt to reduce street violence.

5 March–April 1932: the presidential election
In the scheduled presidential election, Hindenburg, now supported by the moderate Left and Centre, defeated Hitler. Hitler gained 37 per cent of the vote. The rise in the Nazi vote led some to believe that the Nazi Party must be included in government.

6 The fall of Brüning's government
General Schleicher, who had supported Brüning's appointment in 1930, now turned against him. He felt that Brüning's opposition to the Nazis was wrong and that some co-operation was needed. Brüning's proposals to break up bankrupt Prussian estates finally persuaded Hindenburg to dismiss him in May 1932. Brüning was not dismissed after losing a confidence vote in the Reichstag, but merely because Hindenburg had turned against him.

MAY–DEC 1932 PAPEN'S GOVERNMENT

7 The formation of Papen's government
In May 1932, Schleicher persuaded Hindenburg to ask Franz von Papen to form a non-party government of 'national concentration'. It consisted of the elite, or 'barons'. The government did not contain any members of the Reichstag; it was seen as a presidential government. Papen hoped to gain support from the Nazis to help sustain his government.

8 July 1932: Papen's coup against Prussia
In June, Papen lifted the ban on the SA. Next month he used emergency powers to depose the Socialist-led coalition government in Prussia. This was a further blow to democracy in Germany. The Reich Chancellor became Prussian Minister-President, with a Reich Commissioner as Prussian Interior Minister. Papen also agreed to Hitler's demand to call for new elections.

9 July 1932: Reichstag election
With deadlock in the Reichstag, Hindenburg agreed to dissolve it and hold an election. The results were a disaster for the Weimar regime. Extremists made further major gains. The Nazis and Communists won over half of the Reichstag seats.

10 Hitler demands to be made Chancellor, August 1932
After his party's success in the Reichstag election, Hitler, with 37 per cent of the vote, demanded that Hindenburg should make him Chancellor, with an Enabling Act allowing him to issue decrees. Hindenburg, who disliked the upstart 'Bohemian corporal', bluntly refused. (Hindenburg had apparently been misinformed that Hitler came from Bohemia, part of Czechoslovakia since 1919, not Austria. But Hitler had only been a German citizen since February 1932.)

11 September 1932: Papen humiliated in the Reichstag
Papen carried on and tried to gain support in the Reichstag. It was a hopeless task. In September the new Reichstag voted no confidence in him by 512 votes to 42. (Only the DNVP and DVP supported him.) Hindenburg dissolved the Reichstag after one day; Papen and Hindenburg originally planned not to call a new election (contrary to the constitution), but Schleicher was afraid this would cause civil war and he persuaded Hindenburg to allow new elections. This, however, was unlikely to solve anything.

12 November 1932: election
In the new election the Nazis lost 2 million votes (their share fell from 37 to 33 per cent). The KPD made further gains. The new Reichstag would be as unworkable as the old.

13 Attempts to end the deadlock
The elite discussed a possible new government. Schacht and industrial leaders asked Hindenburg for a government led by Hitler; Hindenburg said only if Hitler could get a Reichstag majority; Hitler refused to make the necessary compromises; he wanted a strong government. Papen wanted to continue as Chancellor and proposed permanently to replace the Reichstag, and to use the army to suppress opposition. There would be a new authoritarian constitution.

Schleicher was hostile to this drastic option, and advised Hindenburg that it risked civil war. Schleicher was developing links with the trade unions and sections of the NSDAP around Gregor Strasser in a 'diagonal front' stretching from Right to Left to try to gain popular support for major constitutional change.

DEC 1932–JAN 1933 SCHLEICHER'S GOVERNMENT

14 Schleicher's attempt to form a stable government
In December 1932 Schleicher persuaded Hindenburg to dismiss Papen and appoint himself as Chancellor. He tried to get support for his plans by making the Nazi Gregor Strasser Vice-Chancellor and developing Brüning's land resettlement schemes. However, Schleicher not only failed to win support on the Left he also alienated the elite who warned Hindenburg of 'agrarian Bolshevism'.

15 Papen's intrigue against Schleicher
Papen now took the initiative against Schleicher; he wanted revenge. In January 1933 he met Hitler several times. Hitler still insisted on being Chancellor; Papen could be Vice-Chancellor. Hindenburg's son, Oskar, also now favoured a Hitler-Papen government, as did others in the elite.

HITLER BECOMES CHANCELLOR

16 January 1933: the appointment of Hitler
Hindenburg refused to back Schleicher's request to rule by decree and suspend further elections. After discussions, and after he had gained the support of the army with General Werner von Blomberg agreeing to be Defence Minister in a Hitler government, Hindenburg appointed Hitler Chancellor, with Papen as his deputy.

FOCUS ROUTE

Outline Brüning's approach to governing and the problems facing the Weimar regime in 1930–2. What arguments can be made for and against his strategy?

B Brüning: potential saviour or destroyer of Weimar democracy?

Although there were personal and strategic disagreements between Schleicher, Papen and Hindenburg, most historians agree that they all favoured replacing the Weimar system of parliamentary democracy and played a crucial role in its death. There has, however, been considerable debate about Brüning's motives and role. Was he the last defender of Weimar democracy or its enemy?

Supporters of Brüning would argue that he was trying to defend the Weimar parliamentary regime in adverse circumstances. They would say that he was near to succeeding when he was forced to resign. Critics of Brüning say he was planning to establish a more authoritarian, non-parliamentary system. Furthermore, they say there were alternatives to his deflationary policies which could have been tried if he had wanted democracy to survive.

What do you think? For Brüning? Against Brüning?

Let us now examine Brüning's chancellorship in more detail.

Brüning's chancellorship, March 1930–May 1932

In March 1930, Brüning's Cabinet contained most of Müller's ministers, except those from the SPD. In July, when the Reichstag rejected some of his austerity measures, Brüning began using Article 48 of the constitution to govern by presidential decree. He dissolved the Reichstag and held new elections, in the hope that the new assembly would support his policies. However, this turned out to be a major mistake. In the September elections both the Communists and the Nazis increased their representation, making it far harder for Brüning to gain the co-operation of the Reichstag. Instead he had increasingly to rely on presidential decrees.

Brüning's economic policy

Brüning was prepared to worsen the effects of the Depression to achieve his aim of ending reparations. He told a meeting of Centre Party Reichstag deputies in August 1931 that 'only deflation would convince the world that Germany could not afford to pay reparations'. He also tried to use the Depression to reverse earlier Weimar governments' interventionist welfare policies and to create a leaner, more competitive economy. As he told Hitler in October 1930: 'The first country prepared to implement all the unpopular domestic measures necessary will rise to the top.'

Brüning rejected inflationary policies financed by large-scale borrowing. Instead, he opted for deflationary policies, which included government expenditure cuts, especially targeting civil servants' wages, and tax increases. Brüning cut the government deficit drastically (it was 38 per cent lower in 1932 than in 1928). He lowered prices to help exports, but since other countries' prices were also falling and protectionism was widespread he achieved little. Real incomes fell. These harsh measures earned him the nickname 'Hunger Chancellor'. Brüning has been greatly blamed for Hitler's eventual appointment as Chancellor. Firstly, Brüning's decision to call unscheduled elections in 1930 gave the Nazis an opportunity to break into the political mainstream, and his deflationary policies 1930–2 drove millions to vote Nazi.

Late in 1932, after reparations had been suspended, he embarked on a programme of public works and the economy began to improve.

Foreign policy

With the backing of Hindenburg and the army, there was an overall shift under Brüning from Stresemann's conciliatory approach to a more assertive one. Brüning hoped to improve the economy, and then to use Germany's economic might to get the Treaty of Versailles overturned. He had several foreign policy successes.

- In June 1930 the last Allied troops left the Rhineland (as had been agreed in 1929).

- Brüning took a strong line on reparations: partly as a result of the Depression, reparations were suspended in July 1931 under the Hoover moratorium (a temporary legal suspension of debt repayment). Reparations were finally cancelled a month after Brüning lost office.
- Brüning pressed for equal treatment for Germany over disarmament, as laid down by the Treaty of Versailles. The Disarmament Conference finally met at Geneva in February 1932. In December 1932, seven months after Brüning had resigned, parity (equality) was declared, though no action by the other powers was forthcoming.

Brüning's fall

On 30 May 1932 Brüning was forced to resign. His proposal for land reform had upset the agrarian elite. Hindenburg, himself an eastern landowner, considered it Bolshevist and withdrew his support.

Brüning lost office not through a vote of no confidence by the Reichstag, but because he had lost President Hindenburg's support. Brüning felt he had been brought down 'a hundred metres before reaching the goal'.

Historians' assessments

There are various interpretations of Brüning's chancellorship, all of which can be supported by reference to his policies. The terms of the debate were significantly changed with the posthumous (after his death) publication in the 1970s of his memoirs. Here he claimed he had been trying to restore the monarchy. Some historians, however, argue that this was a retrospective (after the event) attempt to give greater coherence to his chancellorship than it deserves. The picture of him as a desperate improviser, who might yet have helped some form of parliamentary system to survive, still retains support.

SOURCE 8.2 E. Feuchtwanger, *From Weimar to Hitler*, 1995, p. 277

Brüning was the last chancellor to govern with any kind of constitutional legitimacy. His personal integrity, intelligence and devotion to duty have never been doubted by men of goodwill. He was also secretive and sometimes paranoid. The debate about his place in history is focused on two main issues. The first question is whether his method of government by decree can be regarded as a last attempt to preserve a non-dictatorial political system or should be seen as a stepping stone to dictatorship. The second question is whether there were any realistic alternatives to Brüning's policies.

SOURCE 8.3 K. Bracher, quoted in Kolb, *Weimar Republic*, 1988, p. 182

[Brüning] was not . . . the last chancellor before the break-up of the Weimar Republic, but the first chancellor in the process of destroying German democracy.

TALKING POINT

What are the dangers of adopting a strategy of relying on matters to get worse in order to achieve one's aims?

SOURCE 8.4 H. Mommsen, *Weimar to Auschwitz*, 1991, pp. 125, 140

He deliberately intended his policies to deepen the economic crisis as he hoped this would enable Germany to get over the worst of the crisis before other comparable states . . .

Breaking the spirit of the constitution, and replacing it with formal legalisms [strict conformity to the letter of the law] was his doing. This contributed to the final destruction of the Weimar Republic just as surely as the systematic escalation of the economic crisis, which he deliberately engineered, produced the atmosphere of utter hopelessness . . . which Hitler could exploit more effectively than any other.

SOURCE 8.5 R. Henig, *The Weimar Republic 1919–1933*, 1998, p. 67

Many commentators, at the time and since, have argued that there were alternatives to Brüning's deflationary policies, that measures could have been introduced to stimulate credit formation and to create comprehensive job-creation schemes. But such alternatives would have undermined Brüning's main objectives, to use the crisis to end Germany's reparation payments, to dismantle Weimar's comprehensive and elaborate system of welfare provision and to reduce Germany's manufacturing costs in order to make her industry more competitive than that of her European neighbours.

ACTIVITY

1 'In the circumstances, Brüning's policies were well judged and could have helped the Weimar regime survive.' Do you agree?
2 Read the historians' assessments in Sources 8.2–5. Do they agree with you?

C Was Hitler's rise to power inevitable?

Some commentators would give a clear 'yes' to this question. However, one would then need to consider when Hitler's appointment became inevitable – in 1930, or 1932, or not until the last days of January 1933, or was it inevitable as far back as 1919 when the new Weimar government signed the Treaty of Versailles?

Many historians object to this degree of DETERMINISM. If one argues that Hitler's rise was inevitable right from the beginning, it undermines the reasons for studying the events of 1920 to 1933. One would just be tinkering with a development that had already been determined. Partly for this reason, most historians are very cautious about the word 'inevitable'. Some react against it to such an extent that they maintain that nothing is inevitable until it happens. It is probably wiser to use phrases such as 'more likely' or 'highly probable' rather than 'inevitable'.

Here we are going to look at two issues that shed light on the possible inevitability of Hitler's appointment as Chancellor.

- Was Hitler lucky to be appointed Chancellor just as the Nazis were on the verge of disintegration?
- Were there viable alternatives, either authoritarian, liberal or communist?

One intriguing aspect of the debate on the inevitability of Hitler's coming to power is the evidence that the Nazi Movement was in severe difficulties by late 1932: it seems possible that if Hitler had not been appointed Chancellor in January 1933 the Movement might well have declined. Hitler's options in those circumstances might also have been limited. For example, he might have tried to repeat his putsch of 1923. Given his greater mass support, his prospects for success looked brighter, and there were radical elements in the Nazi Party, and especially the SA, who urged a seizure of power after he had been refused the chancellorship in August 1932. Hitler himself, however, seems to have abandoned the idea of a putsch. His strategy was based on winning electoral support to gain the chancellorship, ideally through controlling a majority of the Reichstag, but, if that proved impossible, by being in such a position that there was no alternative to Hindenburg's appointing him. With Nazi electoral support falling, if Hindenburg had not appointed him Hitler's prospects looked bleak.

■ 8E The Nazis' position in late 1932 and early 1933

1 Election results

a) Reichstag
- In November 1932 the Nazis lost 2 million votes and 34 seats, partly because some voters were disillusioned as they had failed to gain power. Their protest vote seemed to be getting nowhere.
- The inexorable (unstoppable) advance of the Nazi Movement had thus been reversed.
- Some middle-class voters were alienated by Nazi moves to attract more working-class support, e.g. by supporting the Berlin transport strike in November 1932, and by the party's radical propaganda.
- The Nazis were still the largest party in the Reichstag where anti-parliamentary parties had a majority.

b) State elections
- The Nazis did badly in local elections in November and December 1932, e.g. they lost 40 per cent of their vote in the Thuringian municipal elections.
- In January 1933 the Nazis poured resources into the elections in the small state of Lippe; they increased their vote and claimed a comeback.

2 Finances
- By the end of 1932, Nazi finances were very low due to the cost of competing in so many elections.

3 Organisation
- The SA had 400,000 members in 1932 – making it four times larger than the Reichswehr.
- Party membership stood at 850,000, but there was a high turnover.

4 Internal disagreements
- There was considerable discord in the party and SA; some in the party criticised the SA's unruly behaviour and its lack of commitment to electioneering in November.
- The internal disagreements in the Nazi Party were evident enough for General Schleicher to believe that he could split the Nazi Movement.
- Hitler's 'all or nothing' tactics worried some: e.g. Gregor Strasser, who resigned in December 1932.
- There were internal Nazi Party reports of low morale.

5 Other points
- The SPD newspaper *Vorwärts* predicted in December 1932: 'The decline [of the NSDAP] will hardly be less rapid than its rise has been.'
- The Nazis had to be successful to keep the party together and to maintain their sense of momentum.
- In April 1932 Goebbels said, 'We must come to power in the foreseeable future. Otherwise, we will win ourselves to death in elections.'
- Apart from the KPD, the Nazis were the only party not associated with a discredited government.

FOCUS ROUTE

1 Study Sources 8.6–9 and Chart 8E. What evidence is there that
   a) the Nazis would have been in difficulty if Hitler had not been appointed Chancellor in January 1933
   b) the Nazi Party was still a powerful movement that could influence the course of German history?
2 Explain why the awareness of Nazi weaknesses and divisions in late 1932 might actually have encouraged the elite to risk recommending Hitler's appointment.

SOURCE 8.6   Secret report by the Reich Propaganda Leadership (a Nazi organisation), November 1932

We are of the opinion that little can be salvaged by way of propaganda ... New paths must be taken. Nothing more is to be done with words, placards and leaflets. Now we must act ... It must not come to another election. The results could not be imagined.

SOURCE 8.7   Extracts from Josef Goebbels' diary for 1932

13 Aug: *Nothing is more difficult than to tell victory-flushed troops that victory has been snatched out of their hands.*

14 Aug: *Great hopelessness reigns among the party comrades.*

15 Oct: *Party workers become very nervous as a result of these everlasting elections. They are overworked.*

8 December: *Severe depression prevails ... Financial worries render all systematic work impossible ... The danger now exists of the whole Party going to pieces ... Dr Ley telephones that the situation in the Party is becoming more critical from hour to hour ... [Gregor Strasser's] letter to the Führer [resigning his offices] is dialectic pettifoggery [argumentative quibbling] ... Treason! Treason! Treason! ... For hours on end the Führer walks anxiously up and down the hotel room ... Once he stops and merely says: 'If the Party should ever break up, I'll make an end of things in three minutes with a revolver.'*

15 December: *It is hard to hold the SA and the Party officials to a clear course ... If we succeed in holding the movement together we shall also succeed in saving the situation.*

29 December: *It is possible that in a few days the Führer will have a conference with Papen. There a new chance opens.*

SOURCE 8.8   H. Heiber, *The Weimar Republic*, 1993, p. 205

[By late 1932 the Nazis were in barren opposition] wavering between claims to legitimacy and revolutionary slogans, between socialistic promises and conservative contacts.

SOURCE 8.9   T. Childers, *The Formation of the Nazi Constituency*, 1986, p. 254

After an ascent of unparalleled swiftness, the NSDAP had reached the limits of its electoral potential and now [in December 1932] faced almost certain decline. The policy of legality, of mass mobilisation for electoral campaigning had reached a dead end.

The political situation in 1932

During 1932 the Brüning, Papen and Schleicher governments embarked on public works programmes. Unemployment reached its peak in December 1932, then started to fall. To some, it seemed that the worst of the crisis was over and that the Weimar Republic had weathered the storm. For example:

- Allied troops had withdrawn from Germany in 1930.
- Reparations had been virtually ended in July 1932.
- In December 1932 Germany was granted the right to equality of armaments at the Geneva Disarmament Conference.

However, these developments did not stop the communist vote increasing in the November 1932 Reichstag election.

Was there an alternative to Hitler?

FOCUS ROUTE

1 Copy and complete the following table to assess the political possibilities in Germany from 1932, using the material below and any other knowledge you have.
2 a) Which of the options do you consider provided the most realistic alternative to the appointment of Hitler as Chancellor?
   b) How strong was your choice of alternative?
3 When, if at all, did Hitler's appointment as Chancellor become inevitable?

Possible form of government	Factors favouring this option	Factors against this option
Nazi dictatorship		
More authoritarian system, e.g. restored monarchy		
Parliamentary democracy		
Communist dictatorship		

Was there an authoritarian alternative?

In many ways the most likely outcome to the political crisis of 1930–2 was some form of more authoritarian government, involving a permanent reduction in the powers of the Reichstag and the formation of a government less dependent upon popular elections. This, of course, was what had been happening in an improvised way with the Brüning, Papen and Schleicher governments reliant on Article 48. The elite were actively exploring revision of the constitution, and perhaps even a return to something similar to the Second Reich with a powerful monarchy.

The problems with this approach were that to carry it out constitutionally needed a two-thirds majority in the Reichstag, and this reactionary programme had limited mass appeal. To revoke (overthrow) the constitution unilaterally (on their own initiative) might have provoked civil war, and the politically powerful army was very concerned about such an eventuality. Papen was prepared to risk civil war, but Hindenburg initially favoured Schleicher's ingenious scheme to try to get a broader basis of support. When this failed, Hindenburg's options were clearly limited.

However, many ordinary Germans were as disillusioned with Weimar democracy as were the elite, so a restoration of the successful Second Reich might be attractive to many. In the end, Hindenburg took the advice of Papen and others by trying to use Hitler, with his popular appeal, to enhance their own power. This turned out to be a fatal, though understandable, miscalculation. Many historians consider this decision was a very narrow one and that other authoritarian options might well have succeeded.

Could Weimar parliamentary democracy have survived?

This seems a more unlikely option, given the problems the Weimar system was already facing, even before the Great Depression. The mass misery this caused was largely blamed on the weak Weimar governments and their acceptance of the Treaty of Versailles and reparations. With the majority of Germans in 1932 voting for parties hostile to the parliamentary system, with the decline of liberal parties and with key elements within the two largest democratic parties (SPD and Z) hostile to each other, the prospects looked bleak. Many historians also stress that Weimar had a fundamental problem in its lack of legitimacy in the eyes of millions of Germans. Many of the elite had never been committed to parliamentary democracy and by 1930 they had moved decisively against it.

However, the economic and international situations were improving by the end of 1932. If these trends had continued, it is possible that the moderate parties might have regained their electoral support at the expense of the extremists (as they had done in 1928) and formed a government backed by a majority in the Reichstag.

Could Germany have gone communist?

Fear of communism was a vital factor in the history of the Weimar Republic. The first socialist government had won the provisional support of the elite in order to co-operate against the Bolshevik threat. The Communists probably had their best chance of gaining power in the chaos of 1919 and 1923, but failed to exploit the situation. From 1930 communism seemed on the advance again but its efforts were concentrated on elections rather than on organising a revolution. However, its renewed electoral support and massive presence in the streets (especially its paramilitary wing) encouraged members of the elite in their hostility to the weak Weimar state and their preparedness to co-operate with the anti-communist Nazis.

The Communists were never able to gain more than 20 per cent of the vote, as their appeal was mainly to the working class, who made up about 50 per cent of the population but who were split politically. Membership of the KPD was very fluid. The limited appeal of the Communists was in stark contrast to the cross-class appeal of the Nazis. Further, Hitler, as the leader of a nationalist, anti-communist movement, could reasonably look for potential co-operation from the elite and the authorities, whereas the KPD was an explicitly revolutionary movement which could not gain their co-operation. Thus the KPD would have to obtain power either through gaining a majority electorally or joining a coalition (neither of which was likely), or by seizing power in a revolution.

The Communists could only have gained power legally in co-operation with the Socialists, but the two Marxist parties remained bitter enemies. Ebert's SPD-led government had suppressed the communist risings of 1919–23 and in the eyes of the Communists had betrayed the working class and sold out to the elite. The SPD remained the main supporter of the Weimar democracy it had founded, whereas the Communists rejected the parliamentary system. The KPD's close identification with the Soviet Union also alienated some potential supporters. In the late 1920s the KPD followed the line laid down in Moscow by the Communist International, which viewed Socialists as rivals and delayers of the world revolution. This reinforced the split between the KPD and SPD, as illustrated in the KPD's slogan: 'All party forces must be thrown into battle against social democracy.' The KPD further crucially underestimated the power of fascism, considering it would be the prelude to a communist victory. 'After Hitler, us,' they chanted.

SOURCE 8.10   Membership of the KPD

Date	Numbers		
	Joined	**Left**	**Total members**
1923	250,000		
1929	50,000	39,000	130,000
1930	145,000	95,000	180,000
1931	210,000	130,000	260,000

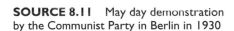

SOURCE 8.11   May day demonstration by the Communist Party in Berlin in 1930

SOURCE 8.12   'Religion is the opium of people': a 1923 communist election poster on the side of a lorry. Beneath it says 'There is no higher being, no God, no Kaiser, no tribune to save us'

D Why was Hitler appointed Chancellor in January 1933?

FOCUS ROUTE

Explain the reasons why key members of the elite eventually favoured the appointment of Hitler as Chancellor.

On 30 January 1933 President Hindenburg summoned Adolf Hitler to Berlin and appointed him Chancellor. In many ways this was a surprising development. Hindenburg disliked Hitler. In August 1932 he had refused to appoint him Chancellor after the Nazis' great electoral success. Since then Nazi support had declined and the movement had been torn by divisions. Many in the elite were also wary of the radicalism and the generally vulgar nature of the Nazi Movement.

Despite this, in January 1933, members of the elite persuaded Hindenburg to appoint Hitler Chancellor. By 1932, key industrialists and landowners were very concerned about the lack of effective government. They had never been committed to parliamentary democracy and now believed their fears were confirmed. Some saw the possibility of using the Nazis' popular support to channel the political system in a more authoritarian direction. The Junkers were also upset by Brüning's and later Schleicher's reform proposals to buy up bankrupt estates to resettle poor farmers. This was seen by landowners as 'agrarian Bolshevism', and contributed to the intrigue that persuaded Hindenburg to dismiss both Brüning and Schleicher.

Members of the elite used a number of tactics in what has been called their 'taming strategy' for the Nazi Party.

1 The first tactic was to make Hitler Vice-Chancellor under Papen; this was put forward in August 1932, but Hitler rejected it, demanding to be Chancellor. Hitler's rejection was risky, since he did not get the chancellorship, and it was seen as a great defeat by many Nazis.
2 The second tactic was used in December 1932. Schleicher, hoping to split the Nazis, proposed the idea of himself as Chancellor, with the Nazi Gregor Strasser as Vice-Chancellor. This failed, and Strasser left the Nazi Party.
3 The final tactic (arranged by a Cologne banker, Kurt von Schröder, members of the Reich Agrarian League, industrialists and Oskar von Hindenburg) was to put Hitler in office as Chancellor, but surrounded by Papen as Vice-Chancellor and other conservatives. The Nazis' current difficulties would make them easier to control. Hindenburg agreed, against his own judgement. Papen commented to a friend, 'We've hired him', but he was fatally wrong.

■ 8F Factors bringing the elite and the Nazis together – and factors that kept them apart

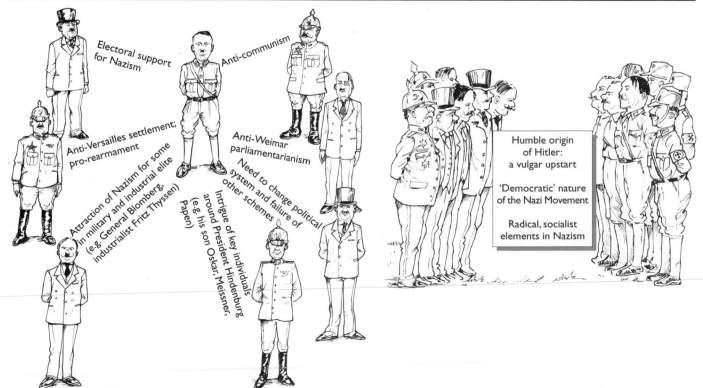

Electoral support for Nazism

Anti-communism

Anti-Versailles settlement; pro-rearmament

Anti-Weimar parliamentarianism

Attraction of Nazism for some in military and industrial elite (e.g. General Blomberg, industrialist Fritz Thyssen)

Need to change political system and failure of other schemes

Intrigue of key individuals around President Hindenburg (e.g. his son Oskar, Meissner, Papen)

Humble origin of Hitler: a vulgar upstart

'Democratic' nature of the Nazi Movement

Radical, socialist elements in Nazism

Hindenburg – a personal motive?

Some historians argue that Hindenburg's decision to appoint Hitler as Chancellor was partly a selfish move.

In the late 1920s, German agriculture suffered from low prices for farm products. Large landowners in the east used their influence on governments to get financial help. This resulted in the *Osthilfe* (Help for the East) programme. Funds were allocated to large landowners to help them stay afloat. Hindenburg had been given back his family's formerly bankrupt estate at Neudeck in East Prussia in 1927 as an eightieth birthday present. This was intended, successfully, to tie him close to Junker interests. However, in 1932 a Reichstag committee investigating the misuse of *Osthilfe* funds for gambling, supporting mistresses, etc. implicated the Neudeck estate in the scandal. This may have influenced Hindenburg's decision to appoint Hitler in the hope that the investigation would be ended.

SOURCE 8.13   Industrialists' letter to Hindenburg, November 1932

Your Excellency! Like you, we are imbued [filled] with an impassioned love of the German people and the Fatherland ... together with Your Excellency, we agree that it is necessary to create a government independent of the parliamentary parties ...

The outcome of the Reichstag elections of 6 November has demonstrated that the present cabinet, whose honest intentions no one among the German people would doubt, has failed to find sufficient support among the German people for its actual policies.

... It is quite apparent that another dissolution of parliament, leading to yet another general election with its inevitable frenzied party-political struggles, would be inimicable [harmful] to political as well as economic peace and stability. But it is also apparent that any constitutional change that does not have widespread popular support would have even greater negative economic, political and moral effects.

We therefore consider it to be our duty, Your Excellency, to humbly beg you to consider reconstituting the cabinet in a manner which would guarantee it with the greatest possible popular support.

We declare ourselves to be free from any specific party-political interests. But we recognise in the nationalist movement, which is sweeping through our people, the auspicious beginning of an era of rebirth for the German economy which can only be achieved by the surmounting of class conflict. We know that the rebirth will demand great sacrifices. We believe that these sacrifices will only be made willingly when the greater part of this nationalist movement plays a leading role in the government.

The transfer of responsibility for leading a Presidential cabinet to the leader of the largest nationalist group would remove the waste and slag that inevitably clings to any mass movement. As a result millions of people who at present still stand on the sidelines would be swept into active participation.

Fully trusting in Your Excellency's wisdom and Your Excellency's feeling for the unity of his people,

We greet Your Excellency with the greatest respect,
Bosch Schacht Thyssen Krupp [and 20 other industrialists]

SOURCE 8.14   An account by Otto Meissner, State Secretary in Hindenburg's office, made to the Nuremberg Tribunal after the Second World War

Despite Papen's persuasions, Hindenburg was extremely hesitant, until the end of January, to make Hitler Chancellor. He wanted to have Papen again as Chancellor. Papen finally won him over to Hitler with the argument that the representatives of the other right-wing parties which would belong to the government would restrict Hitler's freedom of action. In addition Papen expressed his misgivings that, if the present opportunity were missed, a revolt of the national socialists and civil war were likely.

ACTIVITY

1   Why do the industrialists in Source 8.13 favour a government led by Hitler?
2   According to Meissner (Source 8.14), why was Hindenburg persuaded to appoint Hitler as Chancellor?
3   With reference to the origins and content of Sources 8.13 and 8.14, how valuable are they in explaining Hitler's appointment?

SOURCE 8.15
A 1932 DNVP poster. It says: 'More power to the presidency! Away with the supremacy of Parliament (Article 54). Vote Nationalist'. (For Article 54, see page 26)

SOURCE 8.16 A September 1932 cartoon by John Heartfield

SOURCE 8.17 A 1932 cartoon: the big wheel of politics. The cartoon is captioned 'A breakdown: a pleasing phenomenon'

ACTIVITY

Explain what each of Sources 8.15–17 shows about the Weimar Republic at this time.

TALKING POINTS

1 It has been said that proportional representation was crucial in helping Hitler gain power. It has also been said that proportional representation would have stopped him gaining power, if it had not been for President Hindenburg. Can you explain both views?

2 Does Hitler's rejection of parliamentary democracy disqualify him from being considered a democratically elected leader?

■ **Learning trouble spot**

Did Hitler come to power legally and democratically?

It is sometimes said that Hitler was elected into office. This is not really the case. The way of being elected into office in a parliamentary system is to win a majority of members of parliament. Hitler never did this in free elections. As the Weimar Republic had a proportional representation electoral system, unlike Britain's first-past-the-post method, Hitler could only have become Chancellor directly through elections by winning 50 per cent of the vote. He peaked at 37 per cent.

Hitler came to power because Hindenburg, legally, appointed him Chancellor. If Hindenburg had not made this decision, Hitler could not legally have become Germany's leader. However, he did win 37 per cent of the vote (far more than any other party except the SPD in 1919); he led the largest party in the Reichstag, and thus had a 'moral' (if not constitutional) claim to be Chancellor. Having 'won' both Reichstag elections in 1932 he was appointed constitutionally by the democratically elected President.

However, some historians argue that Hitler's use of violence means that he cannot be seen as coming to power legally. The violence committed by the Nazis in the streets that intimidated communist opponents contributed both to the Nazis' electoral success and to the preparedness of the elite to use the Nazis and then tame them. This violence helped create an atmosphere where many favoured strong government to restore law and order, and also won the support of many of those who were worried by the threat of communism.

Some also consider the fact that Hitler's programme was fundamentally undemocratic relevant to this issue.

E Review: Why did parliamentary government decline in Germany 1930–3 and why was Hitler appointed Chancellor in January 1933?

In this chapter you have studied the decline of parliamentary government and how within that context Hitler became Chancellor. Students can be confused about the relationship between the failure of the Weimar Republic and the appointment of Hitler. Was his appointment an abrupt end to Weimar democracy? Most historians now argue that seeing 30 January 1933 as marking the end of Weimar democracy is too simple. Indeed, it is argued that Weimar democracy was already in deep, perhaps terminal, trouble from 1930 onwards and that some form of authoritarian government was virtually inevitable. This could have taken many forms; the appointment of Hitler as Chancellor was just one of the options. In this view, the failure of the Weimar Republic happened for far deeper reasons than those behind Hitler's appointment, which might have been avoided.

Students also sometimes assume that they need to explain why many Germans wanted to create a totalitarian Nazi dictatorship. However, you need not look for deep reasons why Germany succumbed to totalitarianism. This was not the intention of the elite, but the result of its miscalculation of how it could use Hitler for its own purposes. In addition, the millions of Germans who voted for Hitler did not do so because they wanted to kill millions of Jews or start a world war. These were the eventual results of their actions, but not the reasons for them.

Our final two sources are powerful testimony to why many ordinary Germans were prepared to support the Nazis and have Hitler as their leader.

SOURCE 8.18 The distinguished banker Johannes Zahn, writing in 1997, explains his feelings in the early 1930s

You have to consider Germany's general position [in] 1930–33. An unemployed man either joined the Communists or became an SA man, and so business believed it was better if these people became storm troopers as there was discipline and order ... you really have to say this today, at the beginning you couldn't tell whether National Socialism was something good with a few bad side-effects, or something evil with a few good side-effects; you couldn't tell.

Finally, we end this chapter by reading Kershaw's summary of the reasons for Hitler's appointment.

SOURCE 8.19 I. Kershaw, *Hitler*, 1991, p. 55

Access to Hindenburg was the key to power. Accordingly, the presidential palace became the focal point of intrigues of power brokers, who, freed from institutional constraints, conspired with guile and initiative in private wheeler-dealings to further their own power ambitions. And behind the maverick power-brokers stood the lobbying of important elite groups, anxious to attain a political solution of the crisis favourable to their interests.

Few ... had Hitler as their first choice. But by January 1933, with other options apparently exhausted, most, with the big landowners to the fore, were prepared to entertain a Hitler government. Had they opposed it, a Hitler chancellorship would have been inconceivable. Hitler needed the elite to attain power. But by January 1933, they in turn needed Hitler as he alone could deliver the mass support required to impose a tenable authoritarian solution to Germany's crisis of capitalism and crisis of the state.

TALKING POINT

Which of the statements in question I of the Activity are facts and which opinions? Is what constitutes a fact sometimes a matter of opinion?

ACTIVITY

1 Take each of the following statements and explain why you agree or disagree with it.
   a) After 1930 all Chancellors realised parliamentary government was not working and were looking for a more authoritarian solution.
   b) By 1932 Hindenburg, Papen, Schleicher and probably even Brüning all shared the same broad aims, but disagreed on the best way to achieve them.
   c) Once the Nazis became the largest party Hitler had to be appointed Chancellor.
   d) Schleicher and Papen each thought he could use the Nazis for his own purposes.
   e) Members of the elite preferred to change the political system by gaining support in the Reichstag or through using Article 48, as they were afraid of civil war if they just tore up the constitution.
   f) After 1930, and even more by 1932, the composition of the Reichstag made reliance on Article 48 virtually inevitable.
   g) Weimar democracy was safe in the hands of German voters; it was the elite who killed it.
   h) Communism posed no real threat in 1932 and so is unimportant in explaining events.
   i) By late 1932, tensions within the Nazi Party were in danger of causing a decline as rapid as its rise had been; it was saved by Hitler's appointment.
   j) The decline in support for the Nazis in November 1932 actually helped Hitler's appointment as Chancellor.
   k) Hitler's insistence on only joining a government as leader was a risky strategy that eventually paid off.
   l) Hindenburg can be held primarily responsible for giving Hitler power, since in 1933 he still had a wide range of options.
   m) The elites had good grounds for considering they could control Hitler as Chancellor.
   n) Hitler benefited from the collapse of parliamentary government rather than being the cause of it.

2 There is a popular radio programme called *Just a Minute* where contestants have to talk for 60 seconds on any topic, without deviation, hesitation or repetition. This is surprisingly difficult. So we have been kind and you can talk for just 30 seconds on one of the following issues:
   a) The impact of the Depression
   b) The reasons why the Nazis became the largest party
   c) The nature of German governments, 1930–2
   d) The attitude of many of the elite to the Weimar Republic – and to the Nazis
   e) The reasons why Hindenburg appointed Hitler Chancellor.

3 Essay: 'Why did Hindenburg appoint Hitler as Chancellor in 1933?' Include:
   • how Hitler became undisputed leader of the Nazi Party
   • the effects of the Great Depression on Germany after 1929
   • why the Nazis became the largest parliamentary party in 1932
   • the failure of Weimar governments 1929–32
   • why the elite looked for a more authoritarian alternative to parliamentary democracy
   • Hindenburg's reluctant appointment of Hitler.
   Chart 8G will help you.

4 Imagine it is January 1933. Hold a debate in front of a key adviser to President Hindenburg over whether he should appoint Hitler as Chancellor or not.
   Select four to five people for each side of the debate. Possible characters could be:
   • general
   • industrialist
   • professor
   • major landowner
   • small farmer
   • worker
   • ex-soldier
   • diplomat
   • economist.

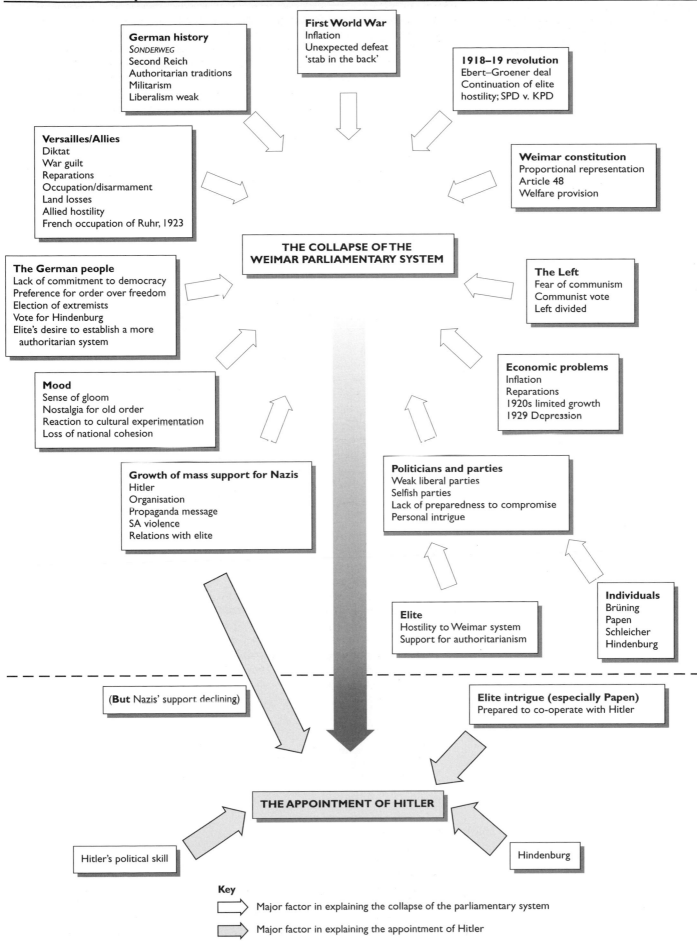

German history
SONDERWEG
Second Reich
Authoritarian traditions
Militarism
Liberalism weak

First World War
Inflation
Unexpected defeat
'stab in the back'

1918–19 revolution
Ebert–Groener deal
Continuation of elite
hostility; SPD v. KPD

Versailles/Allies
Diktat
War guilt
Reparations
Occupation/disarmament
Land losses
Allied hostility
French occupation of Ruhr, 1923

Weimar constitution
Proportional representation
Article 48
Welfare provision

THE COLLAPSE OF THE WEIMAR PARLIAMENTARY SYSTEM

The German people
Lack of commitment to democracy
Preference for order over freedom
Election of extremists
Vote for Hindenburg
Elite's desire to establish a more
  authoritarian system

The Left
Fear of communism
Communist vote
Left divided

Mood
Sense of gloom
Nostalgia for old order
Reaction to cultural experimentation
Loss of national cohesion

Economic problems
Inflation
Reparations
1920s limited growth
1929 Depression

Growth of mass support for Nazis
Hitler
Organisation
Propaganda message
SA violence
Relations with elite

Politicians and parties
Weak liberal parties
Selfish parties
Lack of preparedness to compromise
Personal intrigue

Individuals
Brüning
Papen
Schleicher
Hindenburg

Elite
Hostility to Weimar system
Support for authoritarianism

(But Nazis' support declining)

Elite intrigue (especially Papen)
Prepared to co-operate with Hitler

THE APPOINTMENT OF HITLER

Hitler's political skill

Hindenburg

Key

Major factor in explaining the collapse of the parliamentary system

Major factor in explaining the appointment of Hitler

WHY DID PARLIAMENTARY GOVERNMENT DECLINE IN GERMANY 1930–3 AND WHY WAS HITLER APPOINTED CHANCELLOR IN JANUARY 1933?

ACTIVITY

Who killed Weimar democracy? A mock trial

You have now investigated in detail the collapse of parliamentary government in Weimar Germany. You will probably have concluded that, although the appointment of Hitler as Chancellor put the last nail in the coffin of Weimar democracy, parliamentary government was doomed well before that – fatally wounded by the votes of the German people and the manoeuvrings of Weimar politicians. You have probably formed your own view as to who bears most blame for its demise. You now have the chance to review all you have studied as you put the main culprits on trial. Chart 8H shows the main culprits and summarises their contributions to the power struggles of 1930–3. The following four defendants are on trial for their role in destroying Weimar democracy:

- Brüning
- Papen
- Schleicher
- Hindenburg.

There are two charges to consider at the trial:

a) that this person deliberately undermined Weimar democracy
b) that this person was most to blame for bringing Adolf Hitler to power.

These charges are closely related but at the trial they are each to be considered and answered separately.

Before the trial

1 Allocate the following roles:
   - *Judge:* one person to preside over the court and run the trial.
   - *Four defendants:* Brüning, Papen, Schleicher, Hindenburg. (If you have enough people, each defendant could also have a defence lawyer.)
   - *Four prosecutors:* one to present the case against each defendant.
   - *The jury:* the rest of the group. You will be deciding how guilty each person is on a scale of 0–5.
2 The defendants and prosecutors will need to prepare their case in advance using the information in Chart 8H and in the rest of this chapter. They should refer particularly to pages 133 and 135, which outlines the attitudes and careers of the four accused.

At the trial

3 The first prosecutor makes his or her case on both charges.
4 The defendant and/or his lawyer replies, making a brief speech in his defence to explain his aims and actions.
5 The defendant is then cross-examined by the prosecutor.
6 The jury then gives the defendant a score out of 5 for each of the two charges (0 being not at all guilty, 5 being very guilty).
7 Steps 3–6 are repeated for the other defendants.
8 The jury then discusses the issues and reaches an overall conclusion as to who is the most guilty on each count. They can revise their own original score for a defendant if they wish.

After the trial

9 As a group, discuss the results of the trial and the issues that have emerged from it.
10 Copy and complete the chart below to give you a written record of what you have learned from the trial.

Person	Aims	Actions	Responsibility for undermining democracy	Responsibility for bringing Hitler to power
Brüning				
Papen				
Schleicher				
Hindenburg				

■ **8H**   **Who killed Weimar democracy? The main players and their moves**

149

GENERAL PAUL VON HINDENBURG
President 1925–34
- Key power of appointing and dismissing chancellors
- Able to issue decrees
- Influenced by Schleicher, key civil servants, Junkers, bankers and his son Oskar
- Acted within the letter of the constitution
- Favoured a more authoritarian system
- Concerned about investigations into his estate
- Failed to support the Müller government in 1930
- Supported presidential governments 1930–3
- Hostile to Hitler, seeing him as an upstart
- Refused to make Hitler Chancellor in August 1932
- Appointed Hitler Chancellor in January 1933

HEINRICH BRÜNING
Chancellor March 1930–May 1932

- Tried to gain support from the Reichstag
- Came to favour more authoritarian system, possibly a monarchy
- Called elections July 1930 in which extremist parties such as the Nazis made major gains
- Tolerated by Reichstag for two years but had no working majority
- Increasingly used presidential decrees rather than Reichstag laws to govern
- Failed to take action to reduce impact of slump (nicknamed the 'Hunger Chancellor')
- Hoped to use the Depression to change the regime and end reparations
- Made some reforms, but upset Junkers and Hindenburg with agrarian reform plans
- Forced to resign by Hindenburg

WHO KILLED WEIMAR DEMOCRACY?

FRANZ VON PAPEN
Chancellor May–November 1932
- Formed a non-party 'cabinet of barons' from the elite
- Had no Reichstag members in his government
- Had very little support in the Reichstag
- Relied on presidential decrees to govern
- Overthrew democratic government in Prussia
- After July 1932 elections favoured dissolving the Reichstag and not holding new elections; idea rejected by Schleicher who secured his dismissal
- In January 1933 did a deal with Hitler to become his deputy if Hitler was appointed Chancellor
- Helped persuade Hindenburg to replace Schleicher with Hitler
- Became Vice-Chancellor

ADOLF HITLER
Chancellor January 1933 onwards
- Avowed enemy of democracy
- Tried to overthrow the Weimar Republic in 1923
- Led massive campaigns against the Weimar regime
- Nazis tried to disrupt the Reichstag
- Nazis violently attacked their opponents
- Leader of the largest party in 1932
- Papen intrigued to get him appointed
- Schleicher resisted his appointment
- Hindenburg appointed him as Chancellor
- Hindenburg backed him with emergency decrees
- Once in power, finally destroyed Weimar democracy
- When Hindenburg died in 1934 he declared himself President – and dictator of Germany

GENERAL KURT VON SCHLEICHER
Chancellor December 1932–January 1933
- Concerned to protect the interests of the Reichswehr
- Great influence on Hindenburg
- At the centre of intrigues
- Responsible for the dismissal of Brüning and Papen
- Preferred to exercise power behind the scenes, but in December 1932 reluctantly became Chancellor
- Tried to gain support from the Gregor Strasser wing of the Nazi Party and trade unions
- Dismissed when Papen intrigued against him

WHY DID PARLIAMENTARY GOVERNMENT DECLINE IN GERMANY 1930–3 AND WHY WAS HITLER APPOINTED CHANCELLOR IN JANUARY 1933?

KEY POINTS FROM CHAPTER 8: Why did parliamentary government decline in Germany 1930–3 and why was Hitler appointed Chancellor in January 1933?

1 In 1930, Müller's SPD-led coalition fell; it was the last government to be based on support in the Reichstag. This can be seen as the real end to Weimar parliamentary democracy.

2 After 1930 the popular vote for extremist parties made it hard for any government to get majority support in the Reichstag.

3 Brüning has been accused of exacerbating the situation to achieve his own conservative ends.

4 From 1930 onwards, Chancellors Brüning, Papen and Schleicher had to rely on presidential decrees under Article 48.

5 Members of the elites looked for alternatives to Weimar democracy. They increasingly realised they might have to use the mass support behind Hitler to establish a more authoritarian system.

6 After his election success of July 1932, Hitler failed in his demand for the chancellorship.

7 Hitler needed the support of the elites to get appointed, just as the elites needed his popular support to achieve their aims.

8 Both Papen and Schleicher failed to persuade the Nazis to join a government in a subordinate role.

9 Eventually, elements in the elites persuaded Hindenburg to appoint Hitler Chancellor, hoping to use, then discard, him.

10 Thus under the dual challenge of the masses who voted for radical parties and the elites who disliked democracy, the Weimar Republic declined and Hitler took over.

9

Review: Interpretations of Weimar Germany 1918–33

CHAPTER OVERVIEW

'One doesn't read history, one reads historians.' This saying reminds us that history has two meanings: the past, and the historian's account of the past. In order for us to study the past we have to rely on historians who investigate evidence, make selections and assessments and write their accounts. Thus in the second meaning of history, all history is interpretation. Given that every historian has his/her own outlook, it follows that different views and controversy are inherent in history. This is especially the case with the Weimar Republic.

A Historical controversy (pp. 151–2)

B The controversy over the Weimar Republic and the rise of Hitler (pp. 153–7)

C Historians' assessments (pp. 158–60)

FOCUS ROUTE

Using the material on these pages and your own knowledge, explain why the Weimar Republic has been the source of so much historical controversy.

A Historical controversy

Chart 9A identifies many of the reasons why historical controversies arise. Of course, not all points are relevant in all cases.

■ 9A Reasons for historical controversy

1 THE HISTORIAN

The following points about a historian may influence his/her interpretation.

A Viewpoint
- The individual historian's political, moral, religious beliefs; gender; nationality; personality; experience
- Historians' different theories as to the nature of history
- Historians' different assessments of the value of different types of source

B Purpose
The purpose and nature of the account a historian makes will also lead to different views, e.g. a textbook or research article or TV, etc; is it to entertain, convert, enlighten or make a profit?

C Approach
Some historians may be more careful in handling sources than others.

D Context
- The context in which the historian lives, e.g. period, place, ideological climate

2 THE SOURCES

A The amount of sources
Too many/too few
- Too few sources leave gaps which the historian can fill with different interpretations; too many sources require the historian to make a selection.

Availability
- New sources can emerge which may allow later historians to have a better picture of a past event than earlier ones; sources which once existed may be destroyed.
- New techniques, e.g. computers, aerial photography, can enable historians to make better use of existing sources.

B The nature of sources
Ambiguous
Sources are open to different interpretations and selections, and may contain no clear message.
Contradictory
Sources may contradict each other.

3 THE NATURE OF THE TOPIC BEING STUDIED
Some topics attract more debate.

■ **Learning trouble spot**

What determines the particular historical viewpoint of a historian?

Students nowadays are quite adept at detecting differences in historians' views and at understanding the nature of historical research that can lead to a great variety of interpretations. They often have more trouble when asked to explain why a particular historian holds a particular view. There is a tendency to retreat into generalisations: for example, 'He is a German, therefore he will argue . . .' or 'She is writing in the 1960s, so her view will be . . .'

Sometimes such an assessment, based on a general point about the historian, may be reasonable – for example, for a Marxist – but even here one must add a note of caution. Not all Marxist historians hold the same views, and you need to be very cautious when attributing a historian's views simplistically to, for example, her/his nationality. German history reveals this well. Some of the greatest exponents of the continuity view of German history, identifying authoritarian and aggressive trends within German history, have been German historians: for example, Fritz Fischer and Hans-Ulrich Wehler. So it is best to be cautious: to analyse the information you have about a historian in an open-minded way and to suggest tentative judgements.

Some historians stress the German nature of the Third Reich, and explain it largely as a product of Germany's history. Others see Nazism as one manifestation of a broad authoritarian trend in Europe in the 1920s and 1930s, which saw a series of dictatorships established. Yet other historians stress the 'bad luck' of Hitler gaining power: that it was fortuitous (a matter of luck) rather than the product of deeper forces. Chart 9B shows these varying viewpoints in diagrammatic form.

■ 9B Why the Third Reich: German history or general trend?

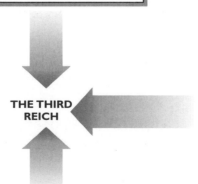

GERMAN HISTORY

Prussian militarism
Germany created by force
Aggressive Second Reich
Lack of a democratic tradition
'German mind' favouring strong leadership
Advanced economy but backward political structure
Desire for strong leadership and national greatness

THE THIRD REICH

GENERAL EUROPEAN INTERWAR PROBLEMS

Dislocation of First World War
Fear of communism
Nationalist resentments
Weaknesses of parliamentary government
Desire for strong leadership
Impact of Depression
Crisis of modernisation

CONTINGENCY/CHANCE

Particular minor events in 1930–3 caused Hitler's appointment, e.g. Papen's intrigue; *Osthilfe* scandal

B The controversy over the Weimar Republic and the rise of Hitler

Since the 1980s, an explosion of new historical techniques, along with access to new sources, particularly after the collapse of communist East Germany in 1990, has added to the diversity of historical interpretation. In the 1990s the influence of Marxism, once powerful not just in communist regimes but also (in more varied forms) in Western European universities, has declined. This has led to greater criticism of class-based perspectives. Closer examination of local areas and access to new sources have led to more diversified interpretations. Much research has been done into the actions and attitudes of Germans at the local level, with historians stressing how heavily people were influenced by their experience in their local community, rather than as members of a general group.

Some historical topics, such as the Weimar Republic, are particularly controversial. As we saw in the introduction to this book, the horrors of the Third Reich cast a shadow over the study of German history in general and the Weimar Republic in particular. Although some historians try to look at Weimar Germany in its own right, the reasons for its failure are vital in trying to understand how Hitler came to power. It is a sensitive issue and has raised great controversy, as the following comments by one of the most interesting but provocative historians of Germany illustrate.

ACTIVITY

Select points from Source 9.1 to support the view that Taylor was:

a) a flawed historian
b) an unfairly criticised historian.

SOURCE 9.1 A. J. P. Taylor in the 1961 Preface to *The Course of German History*, first published in 1945

This book was written in the last days of the Second World War. It had a curious origin. The chapter on the Weimar Republic was written as a separate piece to be included in one of the many compilations which were being put together in order to explain to the conquerors what sort of country they were conquering. My piece proved unacceptable; it was, I learnt, too depressing. The Germans were enthusiastic for a demagogic dictator and engaged on a war for the domination of Europe. But I ought to have shown that this was a bit of bad luck, and that all Germans other than a few wicked men were bubbling over with enthusiasm for democracy or for Christianity or for some other noble cause which would turn them into acceptable allies once we had liberated them from their tyrants. This seemed to me unlikely. I therefore went further back into German history to see whether it confirmed the argument of my rejected chapter; and this book was the result. It was an attempt to plot the course of German history; and it shows that it was no more a mistake for the German people to end up with Hitler than it is an accident when a river flows into the sea, though the process is, I daresay, unpleasant for the fresh water. Nothing, it seems to me, has happened since to disturb the conclusions at which I then arrived.

When the book appeared, some reviewers expostulated [complained] that it 'indicted' [condemned] a nation and that no country's history could survive such hostile scrutiny. I made no indictment; the facts made it for themselves ... Far from treating Germans as barbarians or eternal aggressors, I was anxious to discover why a nation so highly civilised have failed to develop political balance. On almost every test of civilisation, philosophy, music, science, local government, the Germans come out at the top of the list; only the art of political behaviour has been beyond them.

This essentially critical view of Germans, though largely rejected now by most academic historians, still survives in more populist versions and appeals to some deep sentiments in British society. Study of the Weimar Republic also raises a range of other issues, as identified by Richard Bessel who has written: 'The debates about Weimar Germany are not just arcane [obscure] disagreements amongst historians. They involve fundamental questions about the viability of democracy, the relationship of economics to politics, the degree to which a society and economy can bear the costs of social welfare programmes, the relationship between state and society, the stability of modern industrial society.' (*Weimar Germany: The Crisis of Industrial Society, 1918–1933*, 1987, p. 5.)

REVIEW: INTERPRETATIONS OF WEIMAR GERMANY 1918–33

View 1: Hitler as a product of Germany's history

Hitler and Nazism were a natural product of Germany's authoritarian history and the Germans' worship of power. The Germans failed to develop a democratic tradition, preferring instead a strong state led by a powerful individual. Hitler was the natural, even inevitable, culmination of this trend.

View 2 is a particular variant of View 1.

View 2: Germany deviates from the proper course of European development

Germany developed a *Sonderweg*, a peculiar path of development, compared to the rest of western Europe. Although Germany became economically advanced, the aristocratic ruling elite kept power and failed to democratise. The middle class, which elsewhere fostered representative government, merely supported the successful AUTOCRATIC state. The limited 1918 revolution failed to break free from these authoritarian tendencies, and so Weimar failed. Some form of authoritarianism was thus likely to occur.

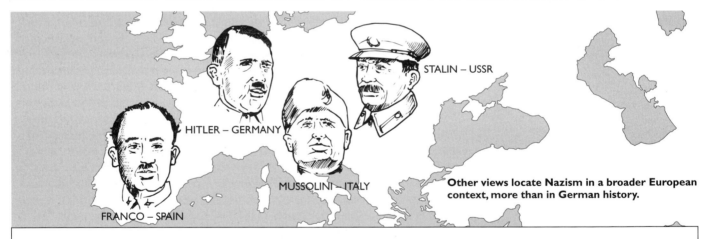

STALIN – USSR

HITLER – GERMANY

MUSSOLINI – ITALY

FRANCO – SPAIN

Other views locate Nazism in a broader European context, more than in German history.

View 3: In Germany, as elsewhere in Europe, war and the Depression create dictatorship

Conditions after the First World War fostered dictatorship in many countries. Hitler's success must be seen in the light of Fascism's rise in Italy and the drift to dictatorship in much of Europe.

View 4: Nazism as a product of capitalism in crisis

Many Marxist historians see Nazism as part of a general crisis of capitalism that hit Europe after 1929. The Weimar Republic was overthrown by frightened Big Business, who used Hitler to protect their threatened interests and to delay the final crisis of capitalism.

View 5: Nazism as an emotional response to a crisis

Disorientated Germans, hit by an economic and political crisis, sought firm leadership and were emotionally attracted to a strong, charismatic leader, offering the 'totalitarian temptation'.

Other views see Nazism's success as due to particular rather than general factors.

View 6: Nazism as the product of the fanatical determination of one man, Adolf Hitler

Hitler was a brilliant demagogue who fooled many Germans into supporting him, and then outmanoeuvred the elite to establish a personal dictatorship. The key to explaining Nazism is thus not German history and society but the evil genius of one man.

View 7: Hitler was just bad luck

Hitler came to power due to chance events that might well not have happened. If only Brüning had not called elections in 1930, or if Papen had not intrigued against Schleicher, or Hindenburg had not been persuaded to appoint Hitler, then German history would have been very different.

TALKING POINT

What lessons, if any, can be learnt from studying the failure of Weimar and the rise of Hitler? Are any of these relevant to the modern world?

ACTIVITY

Match up each of the following criticisms with one of the seven views expressed in Chart 9C.

a) Such a major event as Hitler's coming to power cannot be seen as a mere accident. This view looks suspiciously like an attempt to avoid the question of the Germans' responsibility for Hitler rather than being a proper historical perspective.

b) German history must be studied in its own right, and not compared to some supposed 'normal' form of development.

c) Nazism was a unique phenomenon, developing in a particular national context, and cannot be seen primarily in general terms.

d) There was considerable variety in German history, with a rich cultural mix, rather than trends all developing in one particular direction.

e) Mass support was more important than that of the elites in putting Hitler into power. Hitler reflected a deep feeling in Germany and was not just a capitalist stooge.

f) Nazism gained support from rational calculation, not as a form of psychological fix.

g) Nazism cannot be dismissed as just the product of one man; it reflected deeper trends in history at that time.

TALKING POINT

When you encounter Germans are your thoughts and reactions ever influenced by Hitler?

TALKING POINTS

1 One attempt to understand the past is known as hypothetical (conjectural) history. Do you think it is useful for historians to speculate on what might have happened if one particular event had not happened?

2 A. Doblin wrote in 1924: 'An age is always a farrago [mixture] of different ages. Whole parts of it are unleavened and undercooked; it contains the husks of old forces, and the seeds of new ones.' What do you think he meant? What relevance has this comment to the debate on the nature of the Weimar Republic?

3 The historian Heiber, in his conclusion to his book *The Weimar Republic* (p. 218), has wistfully commented: 'The Weimar state, even decades after its demise, still has many more friends than it ever had during its lifetime.' Why do you think he said this?

SOURCE ACTIVITY

(Marks are given in brackets.)

I Read Source 9.2.
a) What traits in the 'German mind' does Shirer identify? What political results did this have? (3)
b) Referring to specific phrases, discuss the tone of the source. (4)

2 a) How does Wehler (Source 9.3) explain Germany's comparative political and social backwardness under the Weimar Republic? (3)
b) To what extent does Wehler agree with Shirer about the nature of German history? (4)

3 To what extent does Blackbourn (Source 9.4) agree with Wehler's view of continuity and the concept of a *Sonderweg*? (4)

4 a) What different perspective on the explanation for Nazism does Ritter (Source 9.5) have? (3)
b) Explain whether you think Ritter would agree more with Wehler or Blackbourn. (4)

5 Where does Kershaw (Source 9.6) put the emphasis in his explanation of the Nazis' success? (3)

6 Of which of the other historians would Anderson (Source 9.7) probably be most critical? Why? (4)

7 a) Briefly explain:
i) which two historians imply that both the failure of Weimar democracy and the rise to power of Hitler were inevitable
ii) which two historians make the clearest distinction between the failure of Weimar democracy and Hitler's rise to power. (4)
b) What possible reasons could you suggest for this difference in perspective? (4)

8 Using these sources and your own knowledge, explain why historians disagree on the likelihood of Hitler coming to power in Germany. You might like to refer to the following issues, as well as others:
- possible continuities in German history
- the relationship between German history and that of other countries
- deterministic views of history and the role of chance
- racial stereotyping in history
- the particular perspective and approach of individual historians. (10)

(Total: 50 marks)

Some of these different views on German history are illustrated in the extracts below. (When you tackle the Source Activity, you may find it useful to refer to the Learning trouble spot on historical interpretation on page 367.)

SOURCE 9.2 William Shirer, *The Rise and Fall of the Third Reich*, 1960, p. 29

The mind and the passion of Hitler – all the aberrations [mental disorders] that possessed his feverish brain – had roots that lay deep in German experience and thought. Nazism and the Third Reich, in fact, were but a logical continuation of German history...

Acceptance of autocracy, of blind obedience to the petty tyrants who ruled as princes, became ingrained in the German mind. The idea of democracy, or rule by parliament... did not sprout in Germany. This political backwardness of Germany... set Germany apart from and behind the other countries of the West. There was no natural growth of a nation. This has to be borne in mind if one is to comprehend the disastrous road this people subsequently took and the warped state of mind which settled over it. In the end the German nation was forged by naked force and held together by naked aggression...

There thus arose quite artificially a state born of no popular force nor even of an idea except that of conquest, and held together by the absolute power of the ruler, by a narrow-minded bureaucracy which did his bidding and by a ruthlessly disciplined army... The state, which was run with the efficiency and soullessness of a factory, became all: the people were little more than cogs in the machinery...

In contrast to the development of other countries, the idea of democracy, of the people SOVEREIGN, of the supremacy of parliament, never got a foothold in Germany, even after the twentieth century began... The middle classes, grown prosperous by the belated but staggering development of the industrial revolution and dazzled by Bismarck's policy of force and war, had traded for material gain any aspiration for political freedom they may have had. They accepted the Hohenzollern autocracy. They gladly knuckled under to the Junker bureaucracy and they fervently embraced Prussian militarism. Germany's star had risen and they – almost all the people – were eager to do what their masters asked to keep it high.

SOURCE 9.3 Hans-Ulrich Wehler, *The German Empire 1871–1918*, 1985, pp. 245–6. Wehler is the most famous German historian to argue the case for a special German *Sonderweg*

The ruling elites [of the Second Reich] showed themselves to be neither willing nor able to initiate the transition towards modern social and political conditions when this had become necessary. This... culminated in the breakdown of the German Empire in revolution and the end of the old regime [in 1918]... The fact that this break with the past did not go deep enough and that the consequences of the successful preservation of outworn traditions remained everywhere visible after 1918, accounts for the acute nature of the problem of continuity in twentieth-century German history...

In the years before 1945, and indeed in some respects beyond this, the fatal successes of Imperial Germany's ruling elites, assisted by older historical traditions and new experiences, continued to exert an influence. In the widespread susceptibility towards authoritarian policies, the hostility towards democracy in education and political life, in the continuing influence of the pre-industrial ruling elites, there begins a long inventory [list] of serious historical problems... A knowledge of the history of the German Empire between 1871 and 1918 remains absolutely indispensable for an understanding of German history over the past decades.

SOURCE 9.4 English historian D. Blackbourn, *The Peculiarities of German History: Bourgeois Society and Politics in Nineteenth Century Germany*, 1984, pp. 290–2

I have not sought to deny the elements of continuity that link the history of Imperial Germany with the Weimar Republic and the Third Reich. It would hardly be necessary to make such a disclaimer, perhaps, had apologist [sympathetic] historians not insisted on portraying the Third Reich as an 'accident'. The real question about continuity is not 'whether' but 'in which ways'?...

We should not write [the history of Germany] as if it were quite unlike the history of anywhere else. The distinctiveness of German history is probably best recognised if we do not see it [before 1945] as a permanent falling away from the 'normal'. In many respects . . . the German experience constituted a heightened version of what occurred elsewhere. This is true of Germany's dynamic capitalism, and of the social and political consequences it generated . . . It is true of a widespread sentiment like cultural despair . . . And it is true, I believe, although not all want to accept this, of the way in which these and other phenomena . . . combined to produce Germany's exceptionally radical form of fascism . . . Germany was much more the intensified version of the norm than the exception . . . There is much to be said for shifting our emphasis away from the Sonderweg *and viewing the course of German history as distinctive but not* sui generis *[the only one of its kind].*

SOURCE 9.5   German historian G. Ritter, 1955, pp. 22–3

The Weimar Republic failed because it did not succeed in winning general confidence, in becoming genuinely popular through successes which could be appreciated from a distance. So the rejection of democratic slogans became one of the essential conditions for the rise of Hitler's party. But to attribute this rejection simply to 'the Germans' lack of sense of liberty' explains nothing; it only disguises with a grand phrase the true historical problem: the reasons why the chances of liberals have much diminished in this century, particularly in Germany after the First World War . . .

. . . in order to examine the historic foundations of National Socialism, one must first of all see what [it] was in twentieth-century Europe that gave the totalitarian state, composed of one single party, such a good opportunity of taking the place of the constitutional liberal parliamentary state. For the totalitarian state, composed of one single party, is a European, and not solely a German phenomenon.

SOURCE 9.6   British historian I. Kershaw, *Hitler*, p. 38

There was nothing inevitable about Hitler's triumph in January 1933. Five years earlier, the Nazi Party had been a fringe irritant in German politics, but no more . . . External events, the Young Plan to adjust German reparations payments, the Wall Street Crash, and Brüning's entirely unnecessary decision to have an election in summer 1930 – put the Nazis on the political map. Though democracy had by that time an unpromising future, a Nazi dictatorship seemed far less likely than some other form of authoritarian dictatorship or even a reversion to a Bismarckian style of government, possibly under a restored monarchy. In bringing Hitler to power, chance events and conservative miscalculation played a larger role than any actions of the Nazi leader himself.

SOURCE 9.7   American historian E. Anderson, 'The Struggle for Democracy in Germany', in J. Snell and A. Mitchell (ed.), *The Nazi Revolution: Germany's Guilt or Germany's Fate?*, 1959, p. 194

It would be wrong to conclude that Nazism grew inevitably from the German past. This theory would imply fatalism [that an event must happen] which is entirely out of place in any serious study of history. A careful analysis of the events of 1932–1933 shows that at that time a substantial majority of the German people favored an extraordinary increase in governmental authority necessary to solve their problems but opposed National Socialism, that this majority was increasing, and that the recession [lessening] of the economic crisis would have entailed further losses of Nazi popular support. A relatively small group of Junkers, industrialists, and militarists actually achieved Hitler's appointment as chancellor and utilized the senility of President von Hindenburg to accomplish its purpose. The group expected to control the Nazis and to exploit the Nazi power for its own purposes; but the National Socialists proved too clever and too ruthless for it.

TALKING POINT

What are the advantages and disadvantages of using brief extracts, such as these, from historians' work?

C Historians' assessments

We conclude with a selection of short extracts from the work of a number of historians, showing the different emphases they place on the various factors in Weimar's collapse and Hitler's rise.

THE FAILURE OF THE WEIMAR REPUBLIC

SOURCE 9.8 Jackel

The principal predicament of the Weimar Republic was not defeat nor the difficulties which its government faced in the post-war years, but the social and political structure of German society . . . [with] their origins in the nineteenth century.

SOURCE 9.9 Geary

No one in their right mind would claim that the terms of the Treaty of Versailles did not play a major role in the collapse of the Weimar Republic.

SOURCE 9.10 Craig

The Republic's basic vulnerability was rooted in the circumstances of its creation, and it is no exaggeration to say that it failed in the end partly because German officers were allowed to put their epaulets [i.e. uniforms] back on again so quickly and because the public buildings were not burned down, along with the bureaucrats who inhabited them.

SOURCE 9.11 Kolb

The first German republic was encumbered [hampered] by a basic weakness due to the circumstances of its foundation. In the form it took in 1919, parliamentary democracy was truly accepted and zealously defended by only a minority of the population.

SOURCE 9.12 Raff

Without the sympathy and assistance of the various [foreign] powers, the republic had proved unable in the end to withstand the stresses and strains of the lost war. The Allies' lack of sympathy burdened the fledgling republic from its earliest days with handicaps which even a firmly entrenched government, heir to a long democratic tradition, could scarcely have borne. How much less . . . in Germany, habituated to an omnipresent [always there] and authoritarian government.

SOURCE 9.13 Geary

The Weimar Republic had failed to build on the fundamental compromises achieved in 1918 and to use them to create a deep rooted legitimacy of its own: it had lost the struggle for the hearts and minds of the people.

SOURCE 9.14 Peukert

Perhaps the miracle of Weimar is that the Republic survived as long as it did . . . The Republic had already been heading for the crossroads before the immediate crisis of 1929–30 occurred. Everything had been pointing towards a possible crash.

SOURCE 9.15 Geary

The economic crisis acted as a trigger, occasioning the abandonment of a political system that had already lost its legitimacy.

SOURCE 9.16 Kershaw

The future [for Weimar] looked promising. And without the onset of the world economic crisis from 1929 it might have remained so.

SOURCE 9.17 Salmon

If Weimar had some chances of survival before [the Depression], it had very little chance afterwards.

SOURCE 9.18 Ardagh

Gloom was such that already by the mid 1920s many Germans were losing faith in the very principle of parliamentary democracy; this was above all the cancer that killed Weimar . . . A growing number of politicians . . . came to feel that democracy was unworkable . . . Probably by 1930 a period of authoritarian rule had become inevitable.

SOURCE 9.19 Hiden

No single problem 'caused' the downfall of the Weimar Republic . . . the interaction of . . . problems, many of which pre-dated the Republic, progressively weakened the new German state.

HITLER'S RISE TO POWER

SOURCE 9.20   Holtfrerich

The Nazi rise to power was essentially linked to the Great Depression which was a world-wide phenomenon and had little to do with the domestic conflict.

SOURCE 9.21   Salmon

Nazism came to power as a result of a miscalculation by conservative politicians and the military after a large number, but by no means a majority, of the electorate had put it in a position to contend for power.

SOURCE 9.22   Kershaw

The handover of power to Hitler on 30th January 1933 was the worst possible outcome to the irrecoverable crisis of Weimar democracy. It did not have to happen. It was at no stage a foregone conclusion.

SOURCE 9.23   Kolb

It can no doubt be said that the Nazi seizure of power was not objectively inevitable even after the summer of 1932. But, given the attitudes, aims and relative strength of the parties and individuals concerned, and the degree to which the constitution had been undermined, the trend towards a Hitler solution was unquestionably very strong from then on.

SOURCE 9.24   Taylor

There was nothing mysterious in Hitler's victory; the mystery is rather that it had been so long delayed.

SOURCE 9.25   Laffan

There was nothing predestined [inevitable] about Hitler's triumph in 1933. Like the democrats in 1918, the National Socialists came to power more because of their enemies' weakness and failures than because of their own strength.

SOURCE 9.26   Nicholls

[Hitler's] appointment was quite unnecessary . . . The Nazis could not have threatened the state if they had been denied power. Their movement was waning [declining], a further period of frustration might have finished them off.

SOURCE 9.27   Feuchtwanger

The personality of the Führer became a significant historical factor. [He had a] combination of demagogic gifts and political instinct . . . Luck was also with him, mainly because all other players in the field turned out to be so inadequate and mistaken in their judgements.

SOURCE 9.28   Harman

The generals and industrialists estimated late in 1932 that ruling with a Nazi movement that would destroy the working class organisations was preferable to ruling with a Social Democratic movement that would try to buy off the workers.

SOURCE 9.29   Klaus Fischer

The rise of Nazism [was due] to special conditions within a sixty-year span – anti-Semitism, nationalism, imperialism, defeat in war, the Versailles Treaty, the vindictive attitude of the Western powers, catastrophic economic circumstances, Germany's unstable political institutions and parties, the myopia [short-sightedness] of Hindenburg and his conservative clique, and the charismatic genius of Adolf Hitler.

ACTIVITY

1   From Sources 9.8–29, pick out what you consider to be
   a)   the five most important reasons why the Weimar Republic failed
   b)   the five most important reasons why Hitler was appointed Chancellor in January 1933.
   Write a paragraph explaining the importance of each.
2   Find examples of quotations which disagree on
   a)   the importance of the Great Depression
   b)   the likelihood of Hitler coming to power.
3   Find examples of historians who stress the importance of
   a)   broader trends in German history
   b)   external factors
   c)   chance.

ACTIVITY

1　Was Weimar doomed? Divide into two groups. One should draw up a list of reasons why the Weimar Republic was unlikely to succeed, the other should identify reasons why it might well have done so. Debate the issue.

2　If Weimar was doomed, from when was it doomed? List dates when it has been said that Weimar was doomed. Explain your preferred option to the class.

3　'Instead of seeing the Weimar Republic as a prelude to the Third Reich, it should be seen as a considerable success.' Do you think such a statement can be justified?

4　Plan or write one of the following essays:
　a)　Why did Hitler fail to gain power in the 1920s yet succeed in the 1930s?
　b)　Why did the Weimar Republic fall to the Nazis and not the Communists?
　c)　Why did parliamentary government survive in the period 1918–23 but fall in the period 1930–3?
　d)　'The collapse of the Weimar Republic was inevitable. Hitler's rise to power was not.' Discuss.

KEY POINTS FROM SECTION 1: Germany 1918–33: Why did Weimar democracy fail?

Part 1.1 Weimar Germany 1918–23: Creation and crises. Chapters 1 and 2

1　The Weimar Republic was set up in the aftermath of Germany's defeat in the First World War. It was burdened with blame for the much resented Treaty of Versailles. Although it had a new, democratic constitution creating parliamentary government, key structures in Germany were not changed as the 1918–19 German Revolution was very limited.

2　Between 1919 and 1923 the Republic faced a series of revolts from the extreme Left and Right, and a major inflationary crisis, but it survived.

Part 1.2 The Weimar Republic 1924–9: Years of recovery and achievement? Chapters 3, 4 and 5

3　From 1924 the economy recovered, and moderate parties gained more support in elections.

4　Stresemann's conciliatory foreign policy brought Germany back from diplomatic isolation, but it aroused opposition from nationalists.

5　Weimar Germany became famous for its cultural experimentation, but this alienated many traditionalists.

Part 1.3 Germany 1929–33: Why did the Weimar Republic fail and Hitler gain power in 1933? Chapters 6, 7 and 8

6　The Wall Street Crash led to a major depression, with 6 million unemployed. The Depression made it harder for parliamentary government to work, and created a mood of despair.

7　Extremist parties did well in the 1930 elections; in 1932 they obtained a majority of Reichstag deputies, with the Nazis gaining 37 per cent.

8　After 1930 parliamentary government declined, as a series of presidential governments tried to solve Germany's mounting economic and political problems. In January 1933, influenced by sections in the elite, President Hindenburg reluctantly appointed Hitler Chancellor.

Review: Interpretations of Weimar Germany 1918–33. Chapter 9

9　Historians disagree as to whether the Weimar Republic could have survived, why it failed and why Hitler came to power.

10　When explaining Hitler's appointment it is important to realise that the people behind it did not intend to create a murderous, totalitarian Nazi state.

General Ludendorff's prophecy

In January 1933, Ludendorff commented to Hindenburg just after the President had appointed Hitler to be Chancellor: 'You have delivered up our holy German Fatherland to one of the greatest demagogues of all time. I solemnly prophesy that this accursed man will cast our Reich into the abyss and bring our nation to inconceivable ruin. Future generations will damn you in your grave for what you have done.'

　Let us now turn to consider how accurate Ludendorff's prophecy was.

GERMANY 1933–45: What impact did Nazism have on the German people?

SOURCE I A Nazi rally in 1935. What does this picture suggest about the Third Reich?

Section 2 looks at the impact of Nazism on Germany in its twelve years in power. We have divided the section into two parts. Chapters 10–13 look at how Hitler secured his regime; they concentrate on political and economic developments. Chapters 14–18 examine the success of the Nazis in creating their much vaunted *Volksgemeinschaft*, a new, unified Germany or 'community of the people'. These chapters concentrate on social policy and the extent to which the Nazis changed the way Germans thought.

162

A Political map of the Third Reich

GERMANY 1933–45: WHAT IMPACT DID NAZISM HAVE ON THE GERMAN PEOPLE?

DENMARK

SWEDEN

GREAT BRITAIN

Kiel

Lübeck
Hamburg

Ravensbrück

Sachsenhausen

The 1942 Conference on the 'Final Solution'
was held at Wannsee, a suburb of Berlin

Danzig

EAST PRUSSIA

HOLLAND

Bergen-
Belsen

Wannsee

Berlin

Headquarters of Chancellery government

R. Vistula

Hanover

R. Elbe

R. Oder

Posen

Münster

Goering Salzgitter
Stadt

GERMANY

Chelmno

Warsaw

BELGIUM

Düsseldorf   Essen
Cologne

R. Ruhr

Weimar

POLAND

Bonn

RHINELAND

Buchenwald

Breslau

Kreisau

Nazi Party held its annual rallies here

Cracow

Würzburg

Bayreuth

Prague

Auschwitz

Saarbrücken

R. Rhine

Flossenbürg

Nuremberg

BAVARIA

First concentration camp opened 1933

Fortress where Hitler was imprisoned after
the failure of the Munich Putsch in 1923
and where he wrote *Mein Kampf*

Hermann
Dachau

CZECHOSLOVAKIA

Landsberg   Munich

R. Lech

Linz   Mauthausen

Braunau

Vienna

HUNGARY

SWITZERLAND

R. Inn

Bad
Wiessee

Berchtesgaden
Obersalzberg

Hitler's birthplace

R. Danube

FRANCE

N

AUSTRIA

Nazi Party headquarters

Mountain in Bavarian Alps where Adolf Hitler,
Hermann Goering, Martin Bormann and other
Nazi leaders had villas 500 metres above the
town of Berchtesgaden. Hitler's private retreat,
the 'Eagle's Nest', was at the top of the mountain.

1923 Munich Putsch

ITALY

June 1934: SS killed SA leaders
in Night of Long Knives

0   100 km

YUGOSLAVIA

Berchtesgaden, a German town in the Bavarian Alps,
is in a deep valley surrounded on three sides by
Austrian territory; Hitler's villa, the Berghof, was on
the Obersalzberg mountain high above it.

Key

Germany 1933

Greater Germany 1942

Autobahns built by early 1939

Chief concentration camps

Extermination (death) camps

Wolfsschanze (Wolf's Lair): Hitler's field headquarters during the Second World War were at Rastenburg in a heavily wooded, remote and gloomy part of East Prussia. Strongly fortified and surrounded by barbed wire, the bunkers and barracks that made up the Wolf's Lair were described by Alfred Jodl, one of Hitler's generals, as a blend of monastery and concentration camp.

LITHUANIA

stenburg

U S S R

reblinka

Colonel Stauffenberg attempted to kill Hitler at the Wolf's Lair in the July 1944 Bomb Plot

Lublin ▲

Sobibor ▲

Belzec ▲

ROMANIA

BULGARIA

B Key events of the Third Reich

CONSOLIDATION

1933 Jan	President Hindenburg appoints Hitler as Chancellor
Feb	Reichstag fire: Communists blamed. A presidential decree, entitled Protection of the People and State, suspends civil liberties and prepares the way for a state of emergency
Mar	Nazis win 44 per cent of the vote in new elections. Enabling Act gives Hitler dictatorial powers for four years
May	Destruction of trade unions and arrest of leaders
Jul	One-party state is established as other parties are banned
1934 Jan	Power of local government reduced
Jun	Night of the Long Knives: Hitler weakens the SA, his potentially revolutionary supporters, in a PURGE
Aug	Death of President Hindenburg enables Hitler to combine the posts of President and Chancellor

RADICALISATION

1935 Mar	Hitler announces that Germany is rearming; return of military conscription
Sept	The Nuremberg Racial Laws deprive Jews of citizenship
1936 Mar	Hitler sends troops into the demilitarised Rhineland and reclaims it for Germany
Sept	Four-Year Plan is introduced to prepare the economy for war
1938 Feb	Army is reorganised to increase Hitler's control over it
Mar	*Anschluss*: Germany annexes Austria
Sept	At the Munich Conference Hitler's threats gain him the Sudetenland from Czechoslovakia
Nov	*Kristallnacht* (the Night of Broken Glass or Crystal Night): a wave of attacks on Jews throughout Germany
1939 Mar	Hitler seizes Czechoslovakia

WAR

1939 Sept	BLITZKRIEG against Poland starts the Second World War
1940 Apr	Germany invades Denmark and Norway
May	Germany invades Holland, Belgium and Luxembourg
Jun	France is conquered by the Nazis
1941 Jun	Germany invades the Soviet Union
1942 Jan	At the Wannsee Conference, Reinhard Heydrich and other leading Nazis meet to discuss the implementation of the 'Final Solution' of the Jewish question. A full war economy is established
1943 Jan	German defeat at Stalingrad becomes the turning point of the Second World War
1944 Jul	The Bomb Plot by army officers to murder Hitler fails
1945 May	Germany defeated; Hitler commits suicide

ACTIVITY

1 To gain an initial idea of some of the chief features of the Third Reich, study Charts A and B and Sources 2–16. What can you learn from this evidence about
   a) the role of Hitler and how Germans viewed him
   b) the collaboration of the elite with Nazism
   c) Nazi propaganda
   d) the Nazi belief in a strong, united, national community or *Volksgemeinschaft*
   e) anti-semitism and the abuse of people's rights
   f) an aggressive foreign policy?
2 Does the evidence suggest that Hitler succeeded in creating a *Volksgemeinschaft*?

164

GERMANY 1933–45: WHAT IMPACT DID NAZISM HAVE ON THE GERMAN PEOPLE?

SOURCE 2 Nazi slogans

> Germany is Hitler! Hitler is Germany!

> You are nothing; your nation is everything.

SOURCE 3 Ernst Huber, Nazi lawyer and theorist, 1935

> *The Führer is the bearer of the people's will ... he embodies the political unity and entirety of the people in opposition to individual interest.*

SOURCE 4 1938 poster: 'One people, one empire, one leader!'

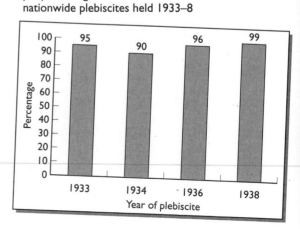

SOURCE 5 Judges in court making the Nazi salute

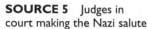

SOURCE 6 The percentage of people voting in favour in four nationwide plebiscites held 1933–8

165

GERMANY 1933–45: WHAT IMPACT DID NAZISM HAVE ON THE GERMAN PEOPLE?

SOURCE 7 The SS

SOURCE 8 NSDAP People's Community poster: 'Fellow members of your community will give you advice and help, so go to your local community group'

SOURCE 9 A 1936 law

All German young people ... will be educated in the Hitler Youth physically, intellectually, and morally in the spirit of National Socialism to serve the nation and the community.

SOURCE 10 Nuremberg Laws, 1935

A Jew cannot be a citizen of the Reich. Any marriages between Jews and citizens of German and kindred blood are herewith forbidden.

SOURCE 11 Poster: 'The whole of Germany listens to the Führer on the people's radio'

166

GERMANY 1933–45: WHAT IMPACT DID NAZISM HAVE ON THE GERMAN PEOPLE?

SOURCE 12 Catholic bishops' statement, 1933

The Führer can be certain that we bishops are prepared to give all moral support to his historic struggle against Bolshevism. We will not criticise things which are purely political.

SOURCE 13 'Now you too can travel!': a poster for the Kraft durch Freude (Strength through Joy) Nazi programme for subsidised workers' holidays

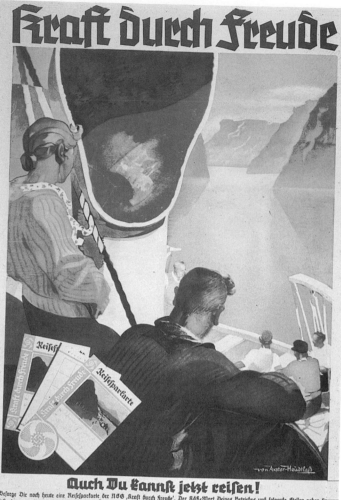

SOURCE 14 Ceremonial burning of books, 1933

SOURCE 15
Wedding rings taken from people killed at Buchenwald concentration camp

SOURCE 16 Leaflet written by Professor Kurt Huber before his execution in 1943

In the name of German youth we demand of Adolf Hitler that he return to us the personal freedom which is the most valuable possession of each German, and of which he has cheated us in the lowest possible manner.

PART 2.1

How did Hitler secure his regime?

10

Why was Hitler able to consolidate his position in power?

CHAPTER OVERVIEW

SOURCE 10.1
A contemporary cartoon from the London evening newspaper *The Standard*. What insight does this cartoon give into who held power in Germany in 1933?

"LET THE GERMAN PEOPLE DECIDE!"

(Copyright in all countries.)

On 30 January 1933 torchlight parades celebrated the appointment of Adolf Hitler as Chancellor of Germany. The millions who had voted for the Nazis were looking to him to restore hope to the German people and re-establish Germany's position after the shame of Versailles. The elite groups around Hindenburg who had actually secured Hitler's appointment hoped to use him to secure their position and then discard him. Vice-Chancellor Papen said to a conservative friend in February 1933: 'I have Hindenburg's confidence. Within two months we will have pushed Hitler so far into a corner that he'll squeak.'

This was one of the most famous, and disastrous, misjudgements in history; for Hitler was to turn into a Frankenstein's monster who inflicted mass destruction on most of Europe and finally on Germany itself. All this, however, lay in the future. In 1933 many saw Hitler as Germany's last hope, while others, from both the Left and Right, did not expect Hitler to last for more than a few months. This chapter examines how Hitler outmanoeuvred Papen and the conservatives and established his Nazi dictatorship so that, by late 1934, it was impossible to remove him legally.

A How did Hitler set up a dictatorship? (pp. 168–72)

B How significant was the Night of the Long Knives? (pp. 173–9)

C Review: Why was Hitler able to consolidate his position in power? (pp. 180–2)

FOCUS ROUTE

1 Choose five or six of the most important events from January 1933 to August 1934 that helped Hitler to establish his dictatorship.
2 Explain why each of these events was important.

A How did Hitler set up a dictatorship?

Hitler lost no time in using his power as Chancellor to gain access to the radio in order to rally support for his government.

SOURCE 10.2 Millions of Germans listened to Hitler's 'Appeal to the German people', broadcast on the radio on 31 January

Over fourteen years have passed since the unhappy day when, dazzled by promises made by those at home and abroad, the German people forgot its most precious possessions, our past, the Empire, its honour and freedom, and thus lost everything. Since those days of betrayal the Almighty has withdrawn His blessing from our people. Discord and hatred came among us. With the deepest sorrow millions of the best German men and women from all walks of life saw the unity of the nation founder and disappear in a confusion of politically egotistical [selfish] opinions, economic interests and ideological conflicts . . . The breakdown of the unity of mind and will of our nation at home was followed by the collapse of its political position abroad . . . With an unparalleled effort of will and of brute force the Communist method of madness is trying as a last resort to poison and undermine an inwardly shaken and uprooted nation . . . Fourteen years of Marxism have undermined Germany. One year of Bolshevism would destroy Germany . . .

. . . It is an appalling inheritance which we are taking over. The task before us is the most difficult which has faced German statesmen in living memory. But we all have unbounded confidence, for we believe in our nation and in its eternal values. Farmers, workers, and the middle class must unite to contribute the bricks wherewith to build the new Reich.

The National Government will therefore regard it as its first and supreme task to restore to the German people unity of mind and will. It will preserve and defend the foundation on which the strength of our nation rests. It will take under its firm protection Christianity, as the basis of our collective morality, and the family as the nucleus of our people and state. It will rise above position and class to bring our people again to an awareness of its racial and political unity and the duties arising from this . . . It will make national discipline govern our life . . . Within four years the German farmer must be free from impoverishment. Within four years unemployment must be overcome permanently . . .

In foreign policy the National Government will see its highest mission in the preservation of natural rights and thus in regaining the freedom of our people. By its resolution to end the chaotic conditions in Germany it will help to introduce into the community of nations a state of equal worth and thus, of course, with equal rights. In doing this it is inspired by the greatness of the duty to support this free nation in maintaining and strengthening, as an equal, that peace which the world needs as never before . . . Now, German people, give us four years and then judge us and give your verdict!

Following the order of the Generalmarschall [Hindenburg] let us make a start. May Almighty God look graciously on our work, direct our purpose, bless our understanding and enrich us with the trust of our People. For we have no desire to fight for ourselves; only for Germany!

ACTIVITY

1 Source 10.2 contains a powerful description of what Hitler was opposed to and what he aimed to do.
   a) Explain how he portrayed the Weimar Republic.
   b) Explain what he claimed the new Germany would be like.
2 With reference to the language and tone of the speech, explain how Hitler tried to win support for his government.

How do you think Hitler would try to consolidate his position after his appointment as Chancellor in January 1933? Remember that Hitler's survival in power would be determined by his position in 1933 and by the actions both he and his opponents would take.

1 Make a list of
   a) the problems he faced
   b) his advantages.
   Refer to the Nazi Movement, its supporters and opponents, the overall context, etc.

2 a) Decide which one of each of the alternatives a)–n) in the table below you would expect him to take in the first eighteen months, and be prepared to explain your decision.
   b) Then choose a statement from o) to describe his overall approach.

3 Decide on several more measures Hitler could take: for example, what might his initial foreign policy be?

4 How do you think his potential opponents would act?

		Radical option	Cautious option
a)	Reichstag	Abolish the Reichstag	Call new elections
b)	Chancellor's position	Declare himself as Chancellor and Führer to be omnipotent (all-powerful)	Use Article 48, and get Reichstag to grant emergency powers
c)	Political parties	Ban other parties; create one-party state	Promise to restore democratic rights
d)	Left-wing opposition	Arrest left-wing leaders and imprison them in new camps	Promise opponents that only traitors will be persecuted
e)	Catholic Church	Take over control of the Catholic Church	Arrange a deal with the Catholic Church
f)	Local government	Ensure Nazi control of local government	Respect local democracy
g)	President Hindenburg	Remove Hindenburg	Appease Hindenburg
h)	Civil service	Replace all top officials with Nazis	Use most of the existing officials
i)	Army and the SA	Replace army with expanded SA	Weaken SA and reassure army
j)	Cabinet	Abolish the Cabinet	Keep most of the original Cabinet
k)	Economic policy	Develop a major programme of public works to create jobs	Reduce government expenditure to balance the budget
l)	Jews	Round up Jews and put them in concentration camps	Allow limited anti-semitism
m)	Trade unions	Ban free trade unions	Respect trade union rights
n)	The press	Create propaganda ministry to control information and repress criticism	Respect press freedom

o)	Overall	Embark on a full-blooded Nazi revolution	Combine both cautious and radical measures in a 'legal revolution'	Abandon revolution to appease the elite

WHY WAS HITLER ABLE TO CONSOLIDATE HIS POSITION IN POWER?

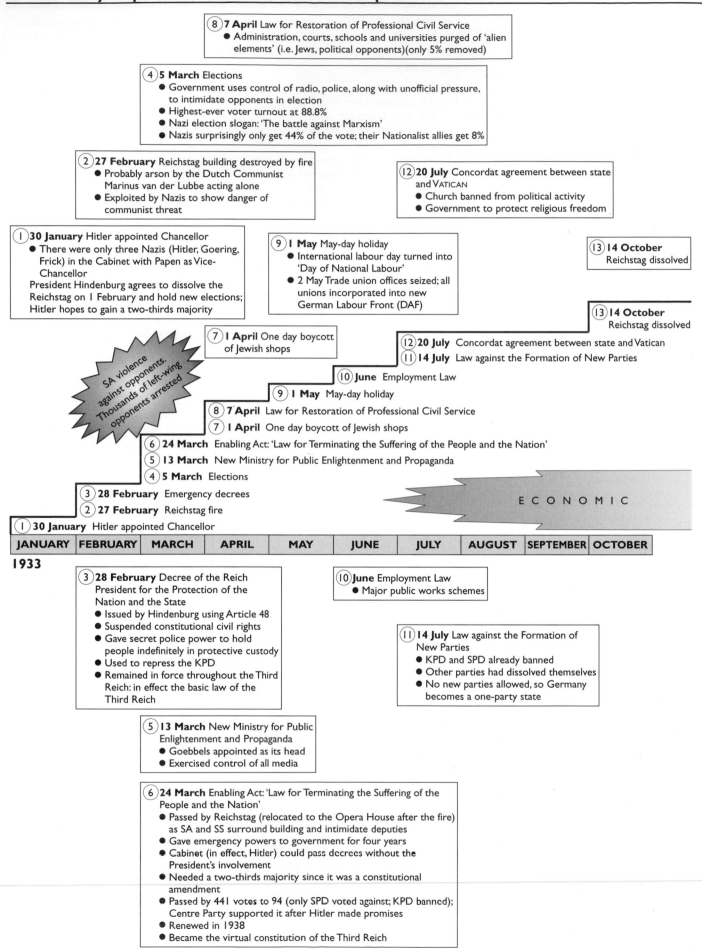

(8) 7 April Law for Restoration of Professional Civil Service
- Administration, courts, schools and universities purged of 'alien elements' (i.e. Jews, political opponents)(only 5% removed)

(4) 5 March Elections
- Government uses control of radio, police, along with unofficial pressure, to intimidate opponents in election
- Highest-ever voter turnout at 88.8%
- Nazi election slogan: 'The battle against Marxism'
- Nazis surprisingly only get 44% of the vote; their Nationalist allies get 8%

(2) 27 February Reichstag building destroyed by fire
- Probably arson by the Dutch Communist Marinus van der Lubbe acting alone
- Exploited by Nazis to show danger of communist threat

(12) 20 July Concordat agreement between state and VATICAN
- Church banned from political activity
- Government to protect religious freedom

(1) 30 January Hitler appointed Chancellor
- There were only three Nazis (Hitler, Goering, Frick) in the Cabinet with Papen as Vice-Chancellor
President Hindenburg agrees to dissolve the Reichstag on 1 February and hold new elections; Hitler hopes to gain a two-thirds majority

(9) 1 May May-day holiday
- International labour day turned into 'Day of National Labour'
- 2 May Trade union offices seized; all unions incorporated into new German Labour Front (DAF)

(13) 14 October Reichstag dissolved

(13) 14 October Reichstag dissolved

SA violence against opponents. Thousands of left-wing opponents arrested

(7) 1 April One day boycott of Jewish shops

(12) 20 July Concordat agreement between state and Vatican

(11) 14 July Law against the Formation of New Parties

(10) June Employment Law

(9) 1 May May-day holiday

(8) 7 April Law for Restoration of Professional Civil Service

(7) 1 April One day boycott of Jewish shops

(6) 24 March Enabling Act: 'Law for Terminating the Suffering of the People and the Nation'

(5) 13 March New Ministry for Public Enlightenment and Propaganda

(4) 5 March Elections

(3) 28 February Emergency decrees

(2) 27 February Reichstag fire

(1) 30 January Hitler appointed Chancellor

E C O N O M I C

JANUARY	FEBRUARY	MARCH	APRIL	MAY	JUNE	JULY	AUGUST	SEPTEMBER	OCTOBER

1933

(3) 28 February Decree of the Reich President for the Protection of the Nation and the State
- Issued by Hindenburg using Article 48
- Suspended constitutional civil rights
- Gave secret police power to hold people indefinitely in protective custody
- Used to repress the KPD
- Remained in force throughout the Third Reich: in effect the basic law of the Third Reich

(10) June Employment Law
- Major public works schemes

(11) 14 July Law against the Formation of New Parties
- KPD and SPD already banned
- Other parties had dissolved themselves
- No new parties allowed, so Germany becomes a one-party state

(5) 13 March New Ministry for Public Enlightenment and Propaganda
- Goebbels appointed as its head
- Exercised control of all media

(6) 24 March Enabling Act: 'Law for Terminating the Suffering of the People and the Nation'
- Passed by Reichstag (relocated to the Opera House after the fire) as SA and SS surround building and intimidate deputies
- Gave emergency powers to government for four years
- Cabinet (in effect, Hitler) could pass decrees without the President's involvement
- Needed a two-thirds majority since it was a constitutional amendment
- Passed by 441 votes to 94 (only SPD voted against; KPD banned); Centre Party supported it after Hitler made promises
- Renewed in 1938
- Became the virtual constitution of the Third Reich

⑮ **January** Law for the Reconstruction of the State
- From March 1933 many state (local) governments overthrown by SA violence allowing the Reich government to appoint commissioners. New laws formalise the situation
- Elected state assemblies dissolved
- Reich Governors (often Nazi *Gauleiter*) created to run states

⑰ **2 August**
Hindenburg dies. Hitler becomes Head of State

⑭ **12 November** Nazi candidates for Reichstag win 92% of votes

⑯ **30 June** Night of the Long Knives

⑮ **30 January** Law for the Reconstruction of the State

⑭ **12 November** Nazi list of candidates for Reichstag win 92% of votes

Other measures
- very few changes to original Cabinet of January 1933
- more assertive foreign policy
- October Germany withdrew from Disarmament Conference, and from League of Nations

⑯ **30 June** Night of the Long Knives
- SS shoot many SA leaders and other people seen as threat

RECOVERY

NOVEMBER	DECEMBER	JANUARY	FEBRUARY	MARCH	APRIL	MAY	JUNE	JULY	AUGUST

1934

⑰ **August** Hitler becomes undisputed head of government
- 1 August Law Concerning the Head of State of the German Reich merges the offices of the President and the Chancellor in the new position of 'Führer and Reich Chancellor'. Confirmed by a plebiscite
- 2 August Hindenburg dies
- Army takes oath of personal loyalty to Hitler: 'I swear by God this sacred oath: I will render unconditional obedience to Adolf Hitler, the Führer of the German nation and people, Supreme Commander of the armed forces, and will be ready as a true soldier to risk my life at any time for this oath.'

ACTIVITY

1 Study Chart 10A. Compare your predictions (in the Activity on page 169) with what actually happened.
2 **a)** Which groups did Hitler appear to conciliate and which did he suppress?
   b) Why did he treat them differently?
3 With which of the following statements on the period 1933–4 would you agree:
   a) 'Once in power, nothing prevented Hitler from imposing his ideas on Germany.'
   b) 'Hitler took a mixture of radical and more cautious measures.'
   c) 'Where he took more drastic measures, it tended to be policies which the elite welcomed, and which weakened the Left.'
   d) 'Within the first year Hitler established complete control of all key institutions.'
   e) 'Hitler was prepared to compromise on areas not crucial to him.'

The key events 1933–4

Within eighteen months of being appointed Chancellor, Hitler had turned himself into a dictator. He had the power to issue decrees and there was no legal way to replace him. His conservative, liberal and socialist opponents were divided, demoralised and weakened by repression. Potential opponents were intimidated by both violence 'from below' (by the SA, who murdered an estimated 500 people in 1933) and terror 'from above', as the Nazis could now use the power of the state machine. By the end of 1933 over 100,000 potential opponents had been arrested. In addition, the elite politicians who had sought to use Hitler had been outmanoeuvred. The only potential threat came from the army, but it had committed itself to the new government.

Chart 10A on pages 170–1 covers the key steps chronologically, as it is important that you develop a clear understanding of the pattern of events between January 1933 and August 1934, by which time the fundamentals of the dictatorship were in place. The process by which Hitler gained control of Germany was called GLEICHSCHALTUNG (co-ordination). He ensured the government had control of all key aspects of society, so that there would be little opposition. The regime developed organisations that Germans had to join: for example DAF (German Labour Front), the Hitler Youth, the German Lawyers' Front. This ensured the regime's control and that the members would work to fulfil the government's objectives.

SOURCE 10.3 Decree of the Reich President on the Protection of the People and the State, 28 February 1933 (see pages 26–7 for the Weimar Constitution)

On the basis of Article 48, paragraph 2 of the Constitution of the Reich, the following is decreed as a protection against communist acts of violence endangering the state:

1 *Sections 114, 115, 117, 118, 123, 124 and 153 of the Constitution of the German Reich are suspended until further notice. Thus restrictions on personal liberty, on the right of free expression of opinion, including freedom of the press, on the right of assembly and association . . . are permissible beyond the legal limits otherwise prescribed [laid down].*
2 *If in any German state the measures necessary for the restoration of public security and order are not taken, the Reich Government may temporarily take over the powers of the supreme authority in such a state in order to restore security . . .*

This decree applies from the day of publication, Berlin 28th February 1933.

SOURCE 10.4 Enabling Act, March 1933

Article 1 In addition to the procedure for the passage of legislation outlined in the Constitution, the Reich cabinet is also authorised to enact Laws . . .
Article 2 The national laws enacted by the Reich cabinet may deviate from the Constitution provided they do not affect the position of the Reichstag and Reichsrat. The powers of the President remain unaffected.
Article 3 The national laws enacted by the Reich cabinet shall be prepared by the Chancellor and published in the official gazette. They come into effect, unless otherwise stated, upon the day following their publication . . .

ACTIVITY

Read Sources 10.3 and 10.4.
a) On what grounds are the government's new powers justified?
b) To what extent did the emergency decrees and Enabling Act undermine the Weimar constitution, in spirit and in fact?

B # How significant was the Night of the Long Knives?

FOCUS ROUTE

1 Explain how the Night of the Long Knives helped consolidate Hitler's position by
   a) removing a left-wing threat to him
   b) winning the support of the army
   c) reducing the conservative opposition to him.
2 Why was Hitler able to get away with such blatant lawlessness?
3 Why was this event so significant?

Why did Hitler turn on the SA in the Night of the Long Knives?

A convoy of lorries moved quietly through the night. Moonlight glistened on numerous silvery revolvers, contrasting with the sinister black uniforms. The SS was moving into position for the first of its many deadly tasks. The night was 29 June 1934, the Night of the Long Knives.

This was the most dramatic and most significant single event during the establishment of Hitler's supremacy. The main victims, unsuspecting in a lakeside hotel at Bad Wiessee, were the leaders of the SA, Hitler's own storm troopers. Now Hitler was in power he had less need of these potentially rebellious shock troops with their radical ideas. The dazed SA leaders were brutally pulled from their beds, taken to Nazi headquarters and gunned down. At the same time, in Berlin and other cities, the SS moved on others whom Hitler disliked or feared. The scheming Schleicher, the potential rival Gregor Strasser and Hitler's old enemy of 1923 Gustav von Kahr as well as the 'arch traitor' SA leader Röhm died in the bloodbath. Figures for the numbers of victims vary, with some estimates as high as 1,000. Most historians now say about 90, including over 50 SA leaders.

Hitler proudly defended his actions to the Reichstag and took full responsibility. He said he was defending Germany against a plot by Röhm and the degenerate homosexuals around him. Ten years earlier in Fascist Italy the murder of one man, Giacomo Matteotti, had nearly caused the early collapse of Mussolini's regime, yet this bloodbath strengthened Hitler's regime. Why was this?

The main victims were the SA, feared by the conservative elite and resented by the Reichswehr. Röhm had talked of merging his 3 million-strong SA, the 'brown flood', with the 'grey rock' of the army into a vast people's militia. But Hitler had other ideas. Now he was in power, he needed the SA far less than the support of the elite. Mussolini, at his first meeting with Hitler in June 1934, had advised him to eliminate his left wing.

SOURCE 10.5 Photomontage by John Heartfield; published in Prague on 19 July 1934

30. JUNI 1934

HEIL HITLER!

Fotomontage: John Heartfield

Nazi infighting also played a major role. Since the early 1920s there had been tension between Röhm's view of the SA, as the key body for seizing and retaining power, and Hitler's view of it as having a subordinate role to the party. In addition, Heinrich Himmler was ambitious for his SS to break away from the formal control of the SA. Goering also resented Röhm and led Hitler to believe that the SA leader was planning a coup to embark on a 'second revolution'. Although Röhm said some things to suggest this (see Chart 10C), it was far more likely that he hoped to persuade Hitler to take more radical measures. Instead, Hitler, more concerned to reassure the elite, especially the army, decided to destroy this pressure for a 'second revolution'.

There was a second, and less well noticed, purpose to the coup. Some conservatives, centred around Vice-Chancellor Papen and his 'Reich Complaints Ministry', were increasingly worried at the growing lawlessness of the regime and the power of the SA. They realised that Hitler was not playing his anticipated PUPPET role. Hitler would be in trouble if these groups gained the support of Hindenburg or the army. So, to deter a conservative backlash, the conservative critic Edgar Jung was murdered; Papen, placed under house arrest, was fortunate to survive. By acting against the SA, Hitler had reassured his conservative supporters but he had also intimidated his conservative critics.

■ 10B Pressures on Hitler in the lead-up to the Night of the Long Knives

> **Hitler's aims**
> - to increase his own power
> - to control the left-wing of the Nazi Party
> - to win over the army

Threat from the Nazi Left	Threat from the Right
• 3-million strong SA: many of them expecting a 'second revolution' • Concerned about Hitler selling out to the Right	• Elite, especially the army, worried about Nazi radicals, especially the SA • Growing criticism of Nazi excesses

Ernst Röhm, 1887–1934

Röhm was a professional soldier who rose to the rank of captain in the First World War but found it hard to adjust to the post-war world. After the war he joined the Freikorps for excitement and was used by the General Staff of the German army to gather political intelligence on opposition groups. Röhm recruited Hitler to infiltrate the German Workers Party but was impressed by his oratory, became his friend and joined the Nazi Party. Röhm helped form the SA and after the failure of the Munich Putsch he was jailed but released on probation.

Röhm was a natural rebel who held revolutionary views, though of an instinctive not ideological kind. He once commented that he had more in common with Communists than with the bourgeoisie. In his autobiography he wrote: 'Since I am an immature and wicked man, war and unrest appeal to me more than good bourgeois order.' He drank heavily and was homosexual.

In 1925 he went to Bolivia as a military instructor. In 1930 Hitler called him back to Germany to train and gain tighter control of the unruly SA. He built up a tough, committed leadership, and vastly expanded the membership. In 1933 he was appointed to the Cabinet, but tension grew over his view that the SA should be a major force for radical revolution. His riotous behaviour further worried the conservatives whom Hitler needed to appease. Hitler let his political sense override his longstanding friendship and decided to eliminate Röhm. Arrested on 30 June 1934, Röhm refused to commit suicide and was shot in prison two days later. Just before he died he commented, 'All revolutions devour their own children.'

■ **Learning trouble spot**

In what sense did Röhm and the SA represent the radical Left, and the SS the radical Right?

Röhm and the SA are sometimes described as left-wing, socialist Nazis or as radical Nazis, a description also used of the SS who are described as the radical Right. This can appear confusing but it is a valid view in some respects.

Röhm was a radical or extremist who disliked bourgeois society and wanted to reorder Germany, especially by replacing the army with the SA. However, neither he nor other SA leaders had a clear socialist view of the future, but arguably just wanted power for themselves. As the historian Fest has commented in *The Face of the Third Reich* (1979, p. 222), 'The slogan "Second Revolution", so often misinterpreted as indicating a predominantly socialist programme ... was merely an expression of the aim of many individuals to enrich themselves or to regain a place in society.' There were, however, some more genuinely socialist elements in the Nazi Party that do justify the term 'Left' (see page 117).

The SS were also Nazi radicals, but it is even more inappropriate to use the term Left or Right for them. Unlike Röhm, Gregor Strasser and other 'left-wing' Nazis, the SS did not talk in class terms, nor did they attract members disproportionately from the working class. They prided themselves on forming a disciplined elite. If one describes Nazism as a right-wing movement, then as radical Nazis they can be described as the radical Right. However, the term Right is perhaps best used to describe the conservative groups who had hoped to use Nazism for their own purposes, not the radical SS. Both the SA and the SS can be seen as revolutionaries, but the former were impatient and overreached themselves. The SS, under Heinrich Himmler's careful leadership, sought a racial revolution and achieved the dominance in the Third Reich ('the SS state') that Röhm had wanted for the SA.

■ **10C   Political tension in the lead-up to the Night of the Long Knives**

> Anyone who thinks the tasks of the SA have been accomplished will have to get used to the fact that we intend to stay. The SA is the Nazi Revolution.

> The SA and SS [will] not permit the German revolution to lose its momentum or be betrayed by the non-fighters halfway to the goal. It is in fact high time the national revolution stopped and became the National Socialist one.

SOURCE 10.6 Ernst Röhm speaking in 1933

> Adolf is rotten. He's betraying all of us. He only goes around with reactionaries. His old comrades aren't good enough for him. So he brings in these East Prussian generals. They're the ones he pals around with now ... Are we a revolution or aren't we? ... Something new has to be brought in, understand? A new discipline. A new principle of organisation. The generals are old fogies. They'll never have a new idea ... But Adolf is and always will be a civilian, an 'artist', a dreamer. Just leave me be, he thinks. Right now all he wants to do is sit up in the mountains and play God. And guys like us have to cool our heels, when we're burning for action ... The chance to do something really new and great, something that will turn the world upside down – it's a chance in a lifetime.
> But Hitler keeps putting me off. He wants to let things drift. Keeps counting on a miracle. That's Adolf for you. He wants to inherit a ready-made army all set to go. He wants to have it knocked together by 'experts'. When I hear that word I blow my top. He'll make it National Socialist later on, he says. But first he's turning it over to the Prussian generals. Where the hell is revolutionary spirit to come from afterwards?

SOURCE 10.7 Röhm privately in a drinking session with friends

> He wants to use it at will, as pressure on the German Army and on big business here and abroad. But if he thinks he can squeeze me for his own ends forever, and some fine day throw me on the ash heap, he's wrong. The SA can also be an instrument for checking Hitler himself.

SOURCE 10.8 Ernst Röhm in conversation with the Nazi Kurt Lüdecke, June 1933, describing Hitler's attitude to the SA

SOURCE ACTIVITY

(Marks are given in brackets.)
Sources 10.6–11 give an indication of the views of three of the key tendencies in Germany in 1933: Röhm and the SA radicals, Chancellor Hitler and the conservative elite.

1   Explain Röhm's distinction in Source 10.6 between a 'national revolution' and a 'National Socialist' revolution.   (2)
2   What do Sources 10.6–8 show about Röhm's view of the SA?   (3)
3   'Just as the elite were trying to use Hitler for their own ends, so Hitler did the same with the SA.'
    What evidence is there in Sources 10.8 and 10.9 to support this view?   (4)
4   With reference to the provenance and content of Source 10.10, explain what this shows about Hitler's view
    of the new state.   (3)
5   **a)**   What criticisms of developments in Germany does Papen make in Source 10.11?   (2)
    b)   To what extent might Hitler share these concerns?   (3)
6   How fully do these sources explain why Hitler turned against the SA in the Night of the Long Knives?   (8)

(Total: 25 marks)

My dear Chief of Staff,
The fight of the National Socialist movement and the National Socialist Revolution were rendered possible for me by the consistent suppression of the Red Terror by the SA. If the army has to guarantee the protection of the nation against the world beyond our frontiers, the task of the SA is to secure the victory of the National Socialist Revolution and the existence of the National Socialist State and the community of our people in the domestic sphere ... It is primarily due to your services ... this political instrument could develop that force which enabled me to face the final struggle for power and to succeed in laying low the Marxist opponent. At the close of the year of the National Socialist Revolution, I feel compelled to thank you, my dear Ernst Röhm.

SOURCE 10.9 Letter,
1 January 1934: Hitler to Röhm, SA Chief of Staff

Revolution is not a permanent state of affairs and it must not develop into such a state. The full rush of revolution must be guided into the secure bed of evolution. The ideas of the [Nazi] programme do not oblige us to act like fools and upset everything.

SOURCE 10.10 Hitler to
Reich Governors July 1933

There appears to be endless talk of a second wave which will complete the revolution ... There is much talk about socialisation. Have we experienced an anti-Marxist revolution in order to carry out the programme of Marxism ...? No nation that would survive before history can afford a permanent uprising from below.

At some stage the movement must come to an end; at some point there must emerge a firm social structure held together by a legal system secure against pressure and by a State power that is unchallenged. A ceaseless dynamic creates nothing ... Confidence and willingness to co-operate will not be furthered by incitement ... nor by threats against the defenceless classes of the community, but only by discussion based upon mutual confidence. The people ... will follow the Führer with unshakeable loyalty, provided they are allowed to have a share in the making and carrying out of decisions, provided every word of criticism is not immediately interpreted as malicious, and provided that despairing patriots are not branded as traitors.

SOURCE 10.11 Vice-Chancellor Papen in a speech, 17 June 1934, to the university of Marburg
This was to be the last speech openly critical of the regime. It was written by Edgar Jung, Papen's associate. Jung was warned of the dangers of a critical speech; he considered he was too well known to be in danger. A few days after the speech he was murdered in the Night of the Long Knives

■ **Learning trouble spot**

Tackling sources: the much ignored 'to what extent?' question – assessing degree

Students often lose marks by failing to understand the importance of certain key phrases in questions. This is frequently the case with questions such as 5b) and 6 (opposite). Another key phrase is 'how much light' does a source shed on an issue.

All these questions ask you to make a judgement as to degree. You should not just identify what the sources say or have in common, and where they contradict or say different (but not necessarily conflicting) things. You must also make a judgement as to how far they do this. To answer these questions effectively you need to express your opinion. The following phrases can be useful: 'Whereas both sources agree on the key issue of ..., they disagree considerably over ... Therefore overall they disagree to a large extent' or 'Although A sheds much light on ..., it does not ... nor ... Thus overall it is surprisingly limited in what it reveals about ...'.

In the case of Question 6, you should refer to the views of Röhm, Hitler, Papen and the elite about the nature of the state (as revealed here and using any other knowledge you have). Then refer to other reasons for Hitler's actions that are not revealed here to make your judgement of 'how fully'.

To help your overall assessment in Question 6, you need to assess the reliability of the sources as well as the content.

SOURCE 10.12 Law passed by the Reichstag, 3 July 1934, legalising the action

The measures taken on 30th June, and 1st, 2nd July to strike down the treasonous attacks are justifiable acts of self-defence by the state.

SOURCE 10.13 Extracts from Hitler's address (lasting several hours) to the Reichstag, 13 July 1934, broadcast on the radio

Everyone will know in future that if he lifts his hand against the state certain death is his fate, and every National Socialist will know that no rank and no position allows him to escape punishment . . .

If anyone reproaches me and asks why I did not resort to the regular courts of justice for conviction of the offenders, then all I can say to him is this: in this hour I was responsible for the fate of the German people, and thereby became the Supreme Judge of the German people . . .

SOURCE 10.16 Defence Minister Werner von Blomberg, 5 July 1934

The Führer with soldierly decision and exemplary courage has himself attacked and crushed the traitors and murderers. The Army, as the bearers of arms of the entire people, far removed from the conflicts of domestic politics, will show its gratitude through devotion and loyalty.

SOURCE 10.18 President Hindenburg on the Night of the Long Knives

Through your decisive intervention and your courageous personal commitment you have nipped all the treasonable intrigues in the bud. You have saved the German nation from serious danger and for this I express to you my deeply felt gratitude and my sincere appreciation.

SOURCE 10.20 A Saxon small businessman

The main thing is that he has freed us from the Marxists [and has] got rid of the harmful influence [of the] dreadful SA . . . even if he is a mass murderer.

Why was Hitler able to get away with murder in the Night of the Long Knives?

It is not easy for us to understand how Hitler managed to get away with state-organised murder. Some of the reasons can be deduced from Sources 10.12–20.

ACTIVITY

1 What reasons can you infer from each source as to why Hitler got away with the Night of the Long Knives?
2 What other reasons can you think of? (In particular, consider whether the Nazis had got away with violence during the Weimar Republic. Who were the main victims then? Who were they now? What did they have in common?)
3 How reliable do you think each of Sources 10.15 and 10.17 is as evidence of public opinion?
4 Construct a spider diagram to record your conclusions about why Hitler was not opposed over the Night of the Long Knives.

SOURCE 10.14 Intelligence reports from socialist party agents within Germany to SOPADE (Social Democratic Party in exile) on public reactions

Wide sections of the population have gained the impression from Hitler's [13 July] speech that through his brutal energy Hitler has prevented a much greater bloodbath.

[He has] paved the way for a moral renewal [and] elevated [his] standing as the cleanser of the Movement all the more as the muck was raked out into full view.

SOURCE 10.15 Gestapo and other government reports on public reactions

The suppression of the Röhm revolt has been like a purifying thunderstorm. The nightmare which has burdened the people has been followed by a liberating sigh of relief . . . Wide sections of the population, however, have been deeply shocked by the shooting of persons unconnected with the Röhm revolt. It is realised these were excesses, which took place without the knowledge and against the will of the Führer.

SOURCE 10.17 A German citizen interviewed in a 1980s TV programme

After June 30th everyone was frightened. Everyone felt that he in turn might share the fate of the SA men. The name of Himmler sent shivers down the spine . . . The ordinary German no longer felt free.

SOURCE 10.19 The caption at the top of this cartoon, a photomontage by John Heartfield, reads: 'The whole nation stands behind me.' Underneath it says: 'I don't see parties, I just see prisoners' – a parody of Kaiser Wilhelm II's remark, 'I don't see parties, I just see Germans'

How significant was the Night of the Long Knives?

The Night of the Long Knives marked a major shift in the development of Hitler's dictatorship. In different ways, he had triumphed over both the Left and the Right. He had tamed his radicals in the SA and won the support of the elite, most crucially the army. The generals were conciliated by the weakening of the army's rival, the SA, and a promise that they would retain a monopoly of armed force. They hoped that with the SA weakened the army's influence would increase. Some generals proposed the army take an oath to tie Hitler and the army together. So, when Hindenburg died, all soldiers took a new oath of personal loyalty to their Führer, replacing the traditional oath of loyalty to the constitution (see page 171). But the generals' plan backfired. As Kershaw has recently argued (in *Hitler*, p. 525), 'Far from creating a dependence of Hitler on the army, the oath marked the symbolic moment where the army chained itself to the Führer.' It was the SS, not the army, which made the real gains. In July 1934 it became independent of the SA, under Hitler's personal and direct command.

The greatest winner of all was undoubtedly Hitler. He had gained the acceptance of the legalised murder of opponents. This served to intimidate future opponents and to embolden him. The traditional organs of the state had acquiesced in (accepted) his actions. Most of the German people accepted the view that as their Führer he would act only for the good of the nation. The Night of the Long Knives showed that the new state was not to be a traditional authoritarian one, but a new dictatorship, where the rule of law was to be replaced by the dictates of one man – a man who, contrary to appearances in 1933, had a horrific vision of the future.

■ 10D   The significance of the Night of the Long Knives

ACTIVITY

Choose one of the following:
a) an associate of Röhm who escaped the death list
b) an associate of Papen
c) a Reichswehr general
d) a German Socialist in exile
e) Himmler
f) Hitler
g) an ordinary German (you may decide what type).
Using the sources and your own knowledge, explain this individual's feelings before June 1934 about the SA and his or her reaction to the Night of the Long Knives.

C Review: Why was Hitler able to consolidate his position in power?

You have studied how Hitler established himself in power, choosing to reassure the elite and control his more radical supporters. As Chart 10E shows, in some

10E Routes to power

	Before 1933	**After January 1933**
Radical approach	**SEIZE POWER IN PUTSCH** Tried 1923, but failed. Some, especially in SA, still urged this method until Hitler's appointment as Chancellor in 1933	**CONTINUE REVOLUTION** Nazis and SA gain full power
	Danger: The army would suppress any putsch, as it had done in 1923	**Danger:** The elite would turn against Hitler and remove him from office
More cautious approach	**GAIN POWER LEGALLY** **Win mass support** Win over 50 per cent of votes to gain a majority in Reichstag: Hitler could then demand to be made Chancellor **Win support of the elite** Negotiate with key groups to be appointed Chancellor	**CO-OPERATE WITH ELITE** Rely largely on inherited administrative, economic and military machine to fulfil aims **Control radical elements** Use the SS to control the SA **Appease elite** Establish personal dictatorship
	Danger: Heterogeneous (varied) Nazi Movement could disintegrate if power not achieved and if economic conditions improved	**Danger:** Hitler would be used (as planned by the elite) to smash communism and move the system in a more authoritarian direction; then would be discarded

■ 10F How Hitler consolidated his position

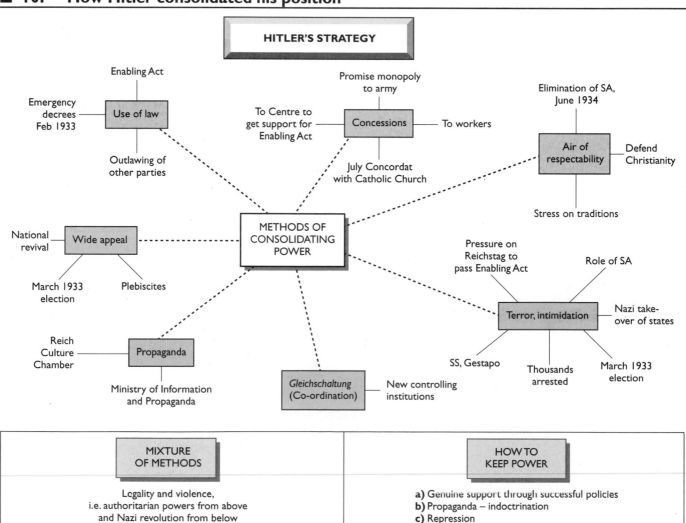

MIXTURE OF METHODS
Legality and violence, i.e. authoritarian powers from above and Nazi revolution from below

HOW TO KEEP POWER
a) Genuine support through successful policies   b) Propaganda – indoctrination   c) Repression

ways this was following the cautious route he had chosen since his failure in 1923. Once he became secure, however, he was more prepared to embark on his own radical vision of the future.

We have looked chronologically at the measures Hitler's government took. Chart 10F identifies the methods Hitler used to gain full power and the reasons why he faced little opposition. With the benefit of hindsight, we can see that the best time to have removed Hitler would have been right at the beginning, in 1933. There were a few attempts by some on the conservative Right to move against Hitler once they realised how violent he was becoming, but they were intimidated by the Long Knives massacre.

ACTIVITY

1 **a)** Study Chart 10F. Elaborate (orally or in writing) on the various methods Hitler used to consolidate his position, giving examples of each method.
   b) Why was there so little opposition to Hitler in his first crucial eighteen months in power?
2 Hitler talked of a 'legal revolution' and a 'national revolution'. Röhm, on the other hand, advocated a 'second revolution'. Explain what each meant by these phrases.
3 Bullock describes the way Hitler consolidated his power as a 'symbiosis [mixture] of legality and terror ... a characteristic interplay of "legal" authorisation from the highest level of government with a mixture of threats, blackmail and terrorism at local level.' What evidence is there to support this view?

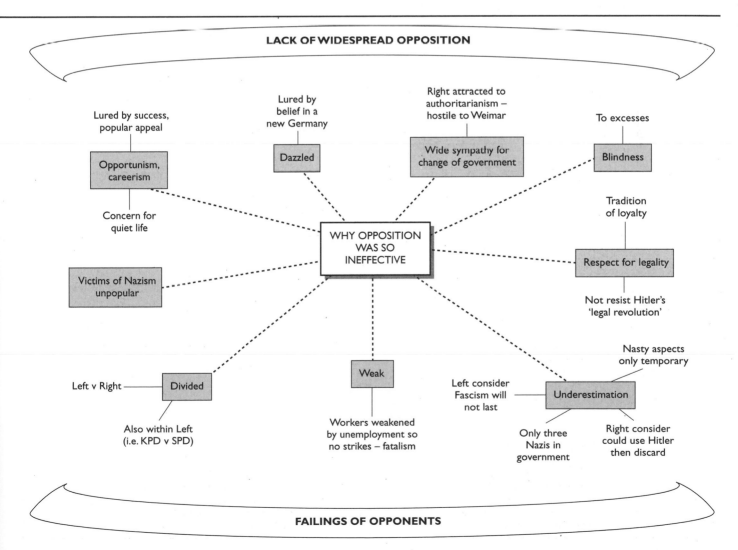

LACK OF WIDESPREAD OPPOSITION

Lured by success, popular appeal

Opportunism, careerism

Concern for quiet life

Victims of Nazism unpopular

Lured by belief in a new Germany

Dazzled

Right attracted to authoritarianism – hostile to Weimar

Wide sympathy for change of government

To excesses

Blindness

Tradition of loyalty

Respect for legality

Not resist Hitler's 'legal revolution'

WHY OPPOSITION WAS SO INEFFECTIVE

Left v Right — Divided

Also within Left (i.e. KPD v SPD)

Weak

Workers weakened by unemployment so no strikes – fatalism

Left consider Fascism will not last

Underestimation

Nasty aspects only temporary

Only three Nazis in government

Right consider could use Hitler then discard

FAILINGS OF OPPONENTS

FOCUS ROUTE

Essay: Why was Hitler able to consolidate his position in Germany between January 1933 and August 1934?

■ **Learning trouble spot**

Time scale

Students often confuse the events of 1933 and 1934, in particular by merging the key Enabling Act of March 1933 with the Night of the Long Knives and Hindenburg's death, June–August 1934, forgetting there was over a year in between. Although Hitler acted far quicker than Mussolini in establishing his dictatorship, it was not until August 1934 that his power was secure. After that it was impossible to remove him legally.

KEY POINTS FROM CHAPTER 10: Why was Hitler able to consolidate his position in power?

1 At first there were only three Nazis in the government, and Hindenburg could have dismissed Hitler at any stage.

2 Hitler exploited the Reichstag Fire to pass a law granting him emergency powers.

3 Hitler used his command of the state machinery to gain 44 per cent of the vote in the March 1933 elections.

4 Despite this failure to win a majority, he persuaded and intimidated the Reichstag into passing a key Enabling Act which changed the constitution by giving the Cabinet the right to issue decrees.

5 In a series of decrees Hitler established a centralised, one-party state.

6 There was little opposition as Hitler skilfully increased his power legally from above, combining this with ARBITRARY violence from below.

7 Hitler mixed fierce repression of his potential opponents with conciliation towards the elite.

8 In the Night of the Long Knives in June 1934 Hitler weakened the radical wing in his SA and reassured the army.

9 When Hindenburg died in August 1934 Hitler combined the office of Chancellor with that of President.

10 After August 1934 there was no legal way to remove Hitler.

Where did power lie in the Third Reich?

CHAPTER OVERVIEW

SOURCE 11.1
A Nazi Party poster:
'Yes! Leader, we will
follow you!'

After 1933 there were three potential centres of power in Germany: Hitler, the Nazi Party and traditional institutions. After the Night of the Long Knives a fourth emerged, the SS. This chapter examines the roles of these different groups to see where power really lay in Nazi Germany.

A   How powerful was Hitler?

FOCUS ROUTE

Explain the nature of Hitler's power in the Third Reich. Refer to:

a) his formal position as Führer and his claimed relationship to the German people
b) the nature and effects of the Hitler myth
c) Hitler's role in decision-making.

Hitler's relationship with the German people

ACTIVITY

Decide which of the statements below best summarises the views of the prominent Nazis in Sources 11.2 and 11.3:

a) Hitler is an absolute dictator who is free to do whatever he wants.
b) Hitler is all powerful because he represents the will of the people.
c) Hitler has to act according to popular wishes.

SOURCE 11.2   Nazi theorist Ernst Huber in 1935

The Führer is the bearer of the people's will; he is independent of all groups, associations and interests, but he is bound by laws which are inherent in the nature of his people ... In his will the will of the people is realised ... He shapes the collective will of the people within himself and he embodies the political unit and entirety of the people in opposition to individual interests.

SOURCE 11.3   Justice Minister Hans Frank in a speech in 1938

The Führer is supreme judge of the nation ... The Führer is not backed by constitutional clauses, but by outstanding achievements which are based on the combination of a calling and of his devotion to the people. The Führer does not put into effect a constitution according to legal guidelines laid before him but by historic achievements which serve the future of his people ... Constitutional law in the Third Reich is the legal formulation of the historical will of the Führer.

All historians agree that Hitler dominated Germany from 1933 to 1945, though they do not agree on how he exercised such power. After the Enabling Act he was formally able to issue decrees. This gradually became the normal way laws were made, bypassing the Reichstag. But, in addition, his wishes, and even his officials' interpretations of his wishes, served as laws. For Hitler's power was based on his unique relationship with the German people. He alone knew what the Germans wanted and he alone could fulfil their needs. His will was absolute because it was the will of the people. Thus Hitler's power did not rest just on his formal position within a system of government. It was much more elemental. It was based on his mission in history and the will of the Führer as a revelation of the German people's destiny. There should thus be no power overriding this force. There were no institutional restraints on him.

This system may seem absurd, but after fourteen years of weak, divided government, and economic and international humiliation, many Germans looked for a MESSIAH. The Nazi Party had been built on this *Führerprinzip* (leadership principle), and now it was applied to all Germany. Helped by successful policies and a powerful propaganda machine, Hitler built up a peculiar form of charismatic leadership, sustained by a powerful Hitler myth. Ian Kershaw's *The 'Hitler Myth'. Image and Reality in the Third Reich* analyses the powerful position Hitler had in the Third Reich due to the image of Hitler that was portrayed. Kershaw's view is summarised in Chart 11A.

TALKING POINTS

1   Can one individual ever represent the wishes of a whole people?
2   Do you believe that any individual, however important, should be above the law?

ACTIVITY

Read Sources 11.4 and 11.5.

1   How did Hitler's obvious popular support strengthen his position at home and abroad?
2   What effect did his popularity have on the overall development of the regime?
3   In Source 11.4, what reasons does Kershaw give for Hitler's popularity?
4   'Even now millions of Germans draw a distinction between the Führer and the party, refusing their support to the latter while believing in Hitler.' What key aspect of the Hitler myth does this comment by Goebbels in 1941 illustrate?
5   Why do you think most Germans did not see through the myth?

What was it?

A carefully cultivated image which much evidence suggests was widely believed. Hitler was portrayed as someone who

- personified the nation and stood aloof from selfish interests
- understood the German people
- was the architect of Germany's economic miracle
- was the representative of popular justice
- defended Germany against its enemies, e.g. Jews, Bolsheviks, corrupt SA, extremists
- was responsible for all the major successes of government.

In foreign affairs, he

- was the rebuilder of Germany's strengths
- was a mighty bulwark against the nation's enemies.

Why did the myth develop and gain credence?

Kershaw identifies the following reasons:

- It was a reaction to the divisions and weaknesses of the old Weimar system.
- It satisfied people's emotional need for strong government.
- It reinforced a German tradition of authoritarian leadership.
- It developed from the long-established Führer principle in the Nazi Party.
- It was sustained by Hitler's successes after 1933.
- It was enhanced by propaganda.

How was it conveyed?

Through the powerful propaganda machinery headed by Goebbels (see pages 245–53).

What were its effects?

The myth contributed to Hitler's great personal popularity. By the late 1930s an estimated 90 per cent of Germans admired him. Only a small minority rejected the Hitler myth. It sustained the regime, and brought most Germans together through its strong emotional appeal. It also helped to cover up the regime's inconsistencies and failures. Thus day-to-day failings could be blamed on minor party leaders, not on their great leader.

However, the myth eventually contributed to the decline of the Third Reich. Such a personalised system, without formal constraints, was inherently unstable. Hitler's popularity gave him more freedom from the elites and led to a radical momentum that weakened the regime. Furthermore, in a sense, Hitler became the victim of his own myth; he came to believe himself infallible (never wrong). He thus moved away from being a calculating, OPPORTUNIST politician. As Kershaw comments: 'The day on which Hitler started to believe in his own myth marked in a sense the beginning of the end of the Third Reich.' Moreover, major military failures after 1941 led to declining belief in the myth.

THE 'HITLER MYTH'

IMAGE AND REALITY IN THE THIRD REICH

IAN KERSHAW

'[a] major contribution to the study of the Third Reich' TLS

Extracts from Kershaw's *The 'Hitler Myth'. Image and Reality in the Third Reich*

SOURCE 11.4 The support it gained (p. 171)

Although the extremes of the personality cult had probably gripped only a minority of the population ... elements of the personality cult had attained far wider resonance and ... affected the vast majority of the population ... Hitler stood for at least some things they admired, and for many had become the symbol and embodiment of the national revival which the Third Reich had in many respects been perceived to accomplish. He had evoked in extreme measure and focused upon himself many irrational, but none the less real and strong, feelings of selfless devotion, sacrifice, and passionate commitment to a national ideal ...

SOURCE 11.5 Its nature and effects (p. 1)

The adulation [praise] of Hitler by millions of Germans who might otherwise have been only marginally committed to Nazism meant that the person of the Führer, as the focal point of basic consensus, formed a crucial integratory [bringing together] force in the Nazi system of rule. Without Hitler's massive personal popularity, the high level of plebiscitary acclamation [support in referenda] which the regime could repeatedly call upon – legitimating its actions at home and abroad, defusing opposition, boosting the autonomy of the leadership from the traditional national–conservative elites who had imagined they would keep Hitler in check, and sustaining the frenetic [fevered] and increasingly dangerous momentum of Nazi rule – is unthinkable. Most important of all, Hitler's huge platform of popularity made his own power position ever more unassailable, providing the foundation for the selective radicalization process in the Third Reich by which his personal ideological obsessions became translated into attainable reality.

ACTIVITY

1 What role did Hitler play in decision-making?

2 What were the results of the absence of formal decision-making?

3 What different reasons are given in Sources 11.7 and 11.9 for Hitler's unwillingness to take decisions?

How were decisions taken in Nazi Germany?

A surprising picture emerges when one examines how decisions were actually taken in Nazi Germany. Hitler acted as a kind of absolute monarch, surrounded by officials competing with each other to implement the leader's wishes. Thus Hitler provided the overall vision, which was then interpreted and turned into detailed policies by those around him. Yet he was remarkably uninvolved in actual decision-making and administrative matters. Most decisions in Nazi Germany were not made by Hitler, even though it was his will that was being implemented. The Führer system meant that there was no need for a formal power or decision-making structure; Hitler's will was law.

Hitler's own work style was haphazard, and reflected his unbureaucratic approach. He often watched films well into the night, went to bed at 2.30 a.m. and got up late. He spent far more time making rambling monologues (speeches) to his entourage (attendants/followers) than in discussing detailed policy. Furthermore, he was often away from the capital Berlin, a city he disliked. He preferred his mountain retreat, the Berghof, where he had lived from 1928 onwards. From 1938 he withdrew even more, and concentrated on foreign policy. After 1941, with few successes to announce, Hitler was seen far less in public.

The historian Peterson has provided a striking description of how the Third Reich operated at the top:

SOURCE 11.6 Edward Peterson, *The Limits of Hitler's Power*, 1969, pp. 432, 446

This view of Hitler – the man who does not decide – would help explain the eternal confusion of the men working for him, a literal anthill of aspiring and fearing people trying to please the 'great one' or escape his wrath or to avoid notice altogether, and never quite sure ... what he wanted them to do after they had said 'Heil Hitler' ... The result was the division of domination into thousands of little empires of ambitious men, domains that were largely unchecked by law [for this] had been replaced by Hitler's will, which was largely a mirage.

If a minister ordered something to happen it could just be on the basis of Hitler's will; it was thus obeyed. If, as often happened, there was disagreement amongst the people at the top, then whoever managed actually to get (or to convince the others that he had!) Hitler's direct approval won. Many of Hitler's decisions amounted to a quick grunt of approval to a summary recommendation from State Secretary Hans Lammers who then conveyed the decision back to those involved. Much of this was done orally rather than on paper.

The Berghof, Hitler's villa on the Obersalzberg, was built with the profits of *Mein Kampf*. After the Nazis came to power, it was developed into an elaborate complex, with twelve underground storeys and one above ground. Designed by Hitler, it reflected his passion for huge rooms, and was built by slave labour. It had five rings of fortifications, and was defended by 20,000 troops.

Hitler preferred to live at the Berghof, rather than the Chancellory in Berlin. Important conferences were held there, including his meeting with Chancellor Schuschnigg of Austria in February 1938 (see pages 387–9) and with Neville Chamberlain, the British Prime Minister, in September 1938 (see page 391).

The Berghof was destroyed in an Allied air raid in April 1945. The ruins were levelled in 1952 and trees planted on the site. Today, a lift cut into the rock face takes visitors to Hitler's mountain-top retreat, the 'Eagle's Nest', which is now a teahouse

The Chancellery in Berlin illustrates much about how the Third Reich operated. In 1938 Hitler's massive new building was completed, symbolising power and order. Yet inside there was chaos. At one stage there were five Chancellery offices (Reich Chancellery under Hans Lammers; Chancellery of the Führer under Philipp Bouhler; Presidential Chancellery under Otto Meissner; Office of Hitler's personal adjutant under Wilhelm Brückner; Office of the Führer's Deputy under Martin Bormann), all claiming to represent Hitler.

Hitler was generally preoccupied with foreign affairs, especially during the war, or with building projects, and left his fellow ministers and PLENIPOTENTIARIES to make decisions. The rivalry of different groups, without formal controls, trying to implement Hitler's will led to a growing lawlessness and brutality. This radicalisation culminated in the HOLOCAUST.

In his book *Hitler 1889–1936. Hubris* (pp. 529–30), Kershaw describes the development of the 'System' between 1934 and 1938 as follows: 'One feature of this process was the fragmentation of government as Hitler's form of personalised rule distorted the machinery of administration and called into being a panoply [array] of overlapping and competing agencies dependent in differing ways upon the "will of the Führer". At the same time, the racial and expansionist goals at the heart of Hitler's own WELTANSCHAUUNG began in these early years gradually to come more sharply into focus, though by no means as a direct consequence of Hitler's own actions.' Chart 11B on page 188 tries to show these 'overlapping and competing agencies' in diagrammatic form.

SOURCE 11.7 From *Twelve Years with Hitler*, the memoirs of Otto Dietrich, Hitler's Press Chief, published in 1955

In the twelve years of his rule in Germany Hitler produced the biggest confusion in government that has ever existed in a civilised state. During his period of government, he removed from the organisation of the state all clarity of leadership and produced a completely opaque network of competences. It was not all laziness or an excessive degree of tolerance which led the otherwise so energetic and forceful Hitler to tolerate this real witch's cauldron of struggles for position and conflicts over competence. It was intentional. With this technique he systematically disorganised the upper echelons [levels] of the Reich leadership in order to develop and further the authority of his own will until it became a despotic tyranny.

SOURCE 11.8 Werner Willikens, State Secretary in the Food Ministry, in a speech in February 1934

Everyone who has the opportunity to observe it knows that the Führer can hardly dictate from above everything he intends to realise sooner or later. On the contrary, up till now everyone with a post in the new Germany has worked best when he has, so to speak, worked towards the Führer ... in fact, it is the duty of everybody to try to work towards the Führer along the lines he would wish. Anyone who makes mistakes will notice it soon enough.

But anyone who really works towards the Führer along his lines and towards his goals will certainly both now and in the future one day have the finest reward in the form of the sudden legal confirmation of his work.

SOURCE 11.9 Fritz Wiedemann, one of Hitler's adjutants in *Der Mann, der Feldherr Werden Wollte* (The man the soldier wanted to be), 1964, p. 69

Hitler normally appeared shortly before lunch, quickly read through Reich Press Chief Dietrich's press cuttings, and then went into lunch. So it became more and more difficult for Lammers and Meissner to get him to make decisions which he alone could make as head of state ... He disliked the study of documents. I have sometimes secured decisions from him, even ones about important matters, without his ever asking to see the relevant files. He took the view that many things sorted themselves out on their own if one did not interfere.

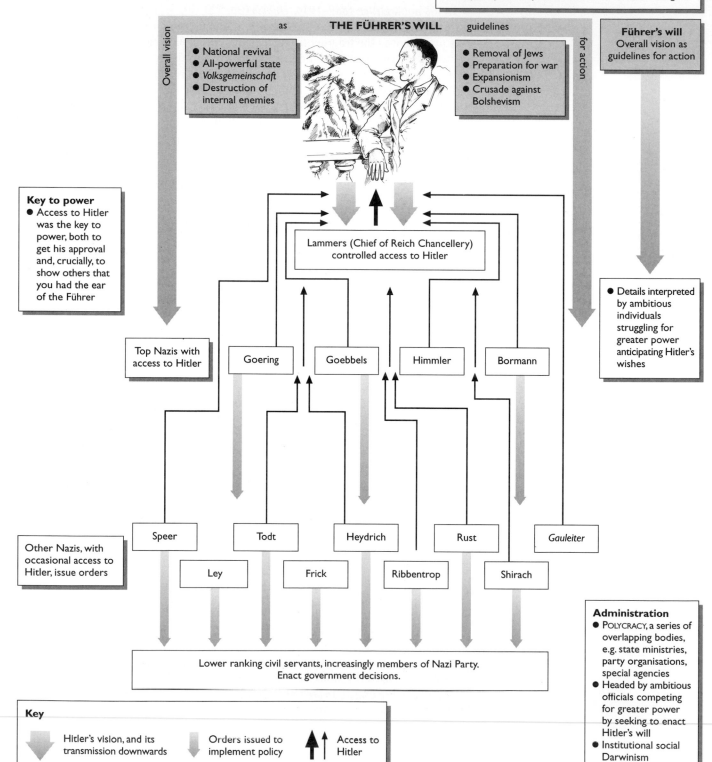

The operation of Hitler's government:
'Working towards the Führer'

Hitler's image
● Great national leader, knows what Germans want
● Above factional disputes
● Responsible for regime's success

Hitler's style of ruling
● Lazy, spent much of the day sleeping, eating, walking, endless monologues
● Rarely intervened in policy debates/decisions
● Signed series of decrees
● Increasingly involved in foreign policy
● Frequently far away from Berlin at his villa, the Berghof

Overall vision

as

THE FÜHRER'S WILL

guidelines

for action

● National revival
● All-powerful state
● *Volksgemeinschaft*
● Destruction of internal enemies

● Removal of Jews
● Preparation for war
● Expansionism
● Crusade against Bolshevism

Führer's will
Overall vision as guidelines for action

Key to power
● Access to Hitler was the key to power, both to get his approval and, crucially, to show others that you had the ear of the Führer

Lammers (Chief of Reich Chancellery) controlled access to Hitler

● Details interpreted by ambitious individuals struggling for greater power anticipating Hitler's wishes

Top Nazis with access to Hitler

Goering   Goebbels   Himmler   Bormann

Other Nazis, with occasional access to Hitler, issue orders

Speer   Todt   Heydrich   Rust   *Gauleiter*

Ley   Frick   Ribbentrop   Shirach

Lower ranking civil servants, increasingly members of Nazi Party.
Enact government decisions.

Administration
● POLYCRACY, a series of overlapping bodies, e.g. state ministries, party organisations, special agencies
● Headed by ambitious officials competing for greater power by seeking to enact Hitler's will
● Institutional social Darwinism

Key

Hitler's vision, and its transmission downwards

Orders issued to implement policy

Access to Hitler

Why were Nazi policies actually implemented?

During the Third Reich, most existing officials kept their posts. They implemented Nazi policies for the sort of reasons given in Chart 11C.

■ 11C Why were Nazi policies actually implemented?

Bureaucrat

I want to keep my job. I want promotion.

Small businessman

My firm will do better if Jewish rivals are forced out.

General

We need to restore Germany's might and smash Bolshevism.

Doctor

This mentally ill patient is a drain on my resources.

Judge

These criminal types have had it too easy for too long.

Industrialist

A war of conquest will boost orders for my firm.

Housewife

My neighbour's far too bossy; he must be an enemy of the state.

Scientist

This search for different industrial substitutes is an interesting chemical challenge.

ACTIVITY

Explain why some Germans were prepared to implement Nazi policies.

Was Hitler an all-powerful dictator?

Chart 11D illustrates a major historical debate that has raged over the Third Reich. Nazi Germany used to be seen, alongside Stalin's USSR, as the classic case of a totalitarian regime. In this view Hitler was an omnipotent dictator; he made a decision, which was smoothly implemented by his disciplined subordinates. Since the 1960s, much detailed study of the actual operation of the Nazi system of government has challenged this view. The Nazi regime has now been compared to a feudal structure, with Hitler as a 'weak dictator'. Thus he frequently did not intervene in many areas. He permitted, and even encouraged, considerable argument amongst his subordinates, and might intervene merely to endorse the decision of whoever emerged as winner.

■ 11D Three views of a dictator

Traditional interpretation – Hitler as strong leader
● Makes all major decisions

Revisionist interpretation – Hitler as weak dictator
● Little involved in most government directives
● Allows others to decide
● Unwilling to take decisions

Rich: 'The point cannot be stressed too strongly: Hitler was master in the Third Reich.'
Bracher: 'The omnipotent power of the Führer, abrogating [breaking] all state and legal norms and sanctioning [authorising] all deeds, was the basic law of the Third Reich.'

Mommsen: '[Hitler was] unwilling to take decisions, frequently uncertain, exclusively concerned with upholding his prestige and personal authority, influenced in the strongest fashion by his current entourage [followers], in some respects a weak dictator.'

Current consensus – a more complex picture, as propounded (put forward) by Kershaw

● Hitler is the key activator
● Policy reflects Hitler's overall vision
● No effective opposition to his will
● He is the mobiliser, legitimator of policies, but does not specifically initiate many policies

Kershaw has argued that elements of both views are correct; that Hitler was often uninvolved in decisions, but that this illustrates his great power. To maintain his image as the infallible leader, he could not be involved in factional struggles, but just let the strongest official win. All his subordinates worked along the lines the Führer would wish; nothing would have been done without these central ideas. So Hitler was crucial, but he did not need to send out a stream of directives. Whenever he did intervene, his view was unchallenged. For most of the time, his subordinates competed with each other to 'work towards the Führer'.

ACTIVITY

Study the four examples of decision-making on the opposite page and assess what they show about the role of Hitler in the Third Reich. What evidence, if any, do they provide of the following roles for Hitler:

a) the direct initiator of action
b) controlling policies
c) the overall inspirer of policy
d) responding to others' proposals and actions
e) opting out of a clear decision.

Clearing up after *Kristallnacht*

SOURCE 11.10 Hitler's note to Bouhler and Brandt authorising them to carry out 'mercy killings'. The note reads: 'Reichsleiter [Reich leader] Bouhler and Dr med. Brandt are charged with the responsibility to extend the powers of specific doctors in such a way that, after the most careful assessment of their condition, those suffering from illness deemed to be incurable may be granted a mercy death.' The note was written in October 1939 but backdated to 1 September

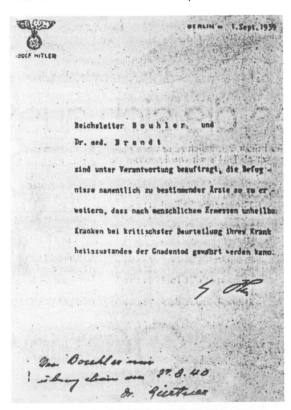

Decision-making in Nazi Germany: four examples

1 The 1935 Nuremberg Laws (see also Chapter 18)

Hitler's anti-semitism was well known, but apart from some actions in 1933 there had not been many moves against the Jews. By 1935 there were strong pressures from within the party – especially from the *Gauleiter*, reflecting pressure from below – to enact the party's 1920 programme and remove Jews from citizenship. In 1935 there was a wave of SA attacks on Jews. Other leading officials saw this as distasteful, and wanted the situation regularised. Schacht, for example, was worried about the effects of such action on exports. So there was pressure for legislation to satisfy two groups, radicals and moderates. Hitler eventually intervened. At the last minute he switched his Nuremberg speech from foreign policy (mainly about Abyssinia) to anti-Jewish legislation, leading to the so-called Nuremberg Laws (see pages 342–3). These were written overnight by civil servants and passed by the Reichstag meeting at Nuremberg. In 1936 there was even worse street violence than in 1935; but Hitler was concerned about the approaching Olympics, and ordered it to be stopped, which it was.

2 *Kristallnacht* (Night of Broken Glass or Crystal Night) 1938

In 1938 there was again growing anti-semitic action on the streets. Goebbels, in particular, fired it up in Berlin. There was also violence in Hesse and Magdeburg. On 8 November the assassination of a Nazi official in Paris by a Jew was used to extend the action. The next day, at the Munich Putsch anniversary meeting, Goebbels suggested to Hitler that in the wake of such anti-semitic demonstrations they should encourage such measures; Hitler gave his approval, and that night there was the wave of anti-Jewish violence known as *Kristallnacht*. See page 342 and Chapter 18 for Hitler's role in the Final Solution.

3 Euthanasia (see also Chapter 18)

It was fairly widely known that Hitler favoured the removal of what he saw as feeble, inferior people in order to foster the German master race. In 1938 a father wrote to Hitler requesting that his ill son be put out of his misery. This letter was just one of hundreds of personal petitions Germans sent to their leader every week, most of which were dealt with by his subordinates. Chancellery Secretary Philipp Bouhler, seeing the adoption of this proposal as an opportunity to increase his own power, got Hitler's verbal permission. Through the Party Chancellery, Hitler's personal physician, Dr Karl Brandt, sent out a letter to doctors inviting nominations for EUTHANASIA. Without any pressure, 60,000 were nominated. However, doctors asked for clear authorisation. Unusually, Hitler wrote a few lines authorising Bouhler to organise it (see Source 11.10). This is the only existing document signed by Hitler authorising killing, although since it was simply a note the process was still technically illegal because it was not authorised in a law. Under the code name 'Aktion T4', 100,000 were killed over the next three years. In 1941, following Bishop Galen's public protest (see page 338), the programme was formally suspended, but it was soon resumed.

4 Horse racing

In 1943 Goebbels, responding to workers' complaints, sought a directive from Hitler to ban horse racing. Hitler issued a series of conflicting directives, responding to different local situations, and after five months of confusion it was decided to leave the matter to local *Gauleiter*.

Why did the Third Reich become more radical?

SOURCE 11.11   I. Kershaw, *Hitler 1889–1936. Hubris*, p. 198

Hitler's personalised form of rule invited radical initiatives from below and offered such initiatives backing, so long as they were in line with his broadly defined goals. This promoted ferocious competition at all levels of the regime, among competing agencies, and among individuals within those agencies. In the Darwinist jungle of the Third Reich, the way to power and advancement was through anticipating the 'Führer's will', and without waiting for directives, taking initiatives to promote what were presumed to be Hitler's aims and wishes . . .

Through 'working towards the Führer', initiatives were taken, pressures created, legislation instigated – all in ways which fell into line with what were taken to be Hitler's aims, and without the dictator necessarily having to dictate. The result was continuing radicalisation of policy in a direction which brought Hitler's own ideological imperatives [requirements] more plainly into view as practicable policy options. The disintegration of the formal machinery of government and the accompanying ideological radicalisation resulted then directly and inexorably [unstoppably] from the specific form of personalised rule under Hitler.

It is also argued that, far from being the basis for what was proclaimed as a Thousand Year Reich, the Nazi regime could not have become stabilised; it was inherently self-destructive. The chaotic structure and competition between groups and between individuals led to a war of all against all. Hitler was surrounded by officials, all seeking to win his favour by advocating the most radical option to fulfil his ideological goals. The lack of any institutional restrictions meant the regime experienced a process that has been called cumulative radicalisation, that is the adoption of increasingly extreme policies. In this view, if it had not been brought down from without, the Third Reich might well have imploded from the effects of this radicalisation.

■ 11E Why did the Third Reich become more radical?

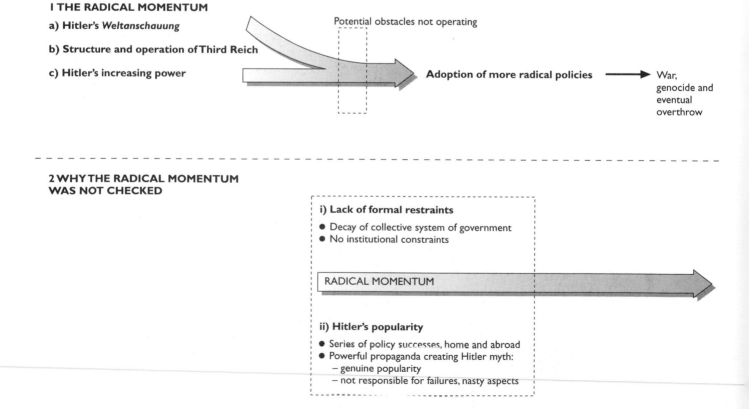

1 THE RADICAL MOMENTUM

a) Hitler's *Weltanschauung*

b) Structure and operation of Third Reich

c) Hitler's increasing power

Potential obstacles not operating

Adoption of more radical policies ⟶ War, genocide and eventual overthrow

2 WHY THE RADICAL MOMENTUM WAS NOT CHECKED

i) Lack of formal restraints

• Decay of collective system of government
• No institutional constraints

RADICAL MOMENTUM

ii) Hitler's popularity

• Series of policy successes, home and abroad
• Powerful propaganda creating Hitler myth:
  – genuine popularity
  – not responsible for failures, nasty aspects

B What happened to the traditional power structures?

After August 1934, when Hitler took over the presidency on the death of Hindenburg, there were no formal restraints on his power. However, he kept most of the existing structures of the Weimar Republic, even if some became unimportant. The Interior Minister Wilhelm Frick drew up schemes for major administrative reform, but Hitler was not interested in developing a new coherent structure; his improvised approach would suffice for policy implementation, and flexibility would enhance his own power. Just as most officials from the Second Reich had stayed in post in the Weimar Republic, so they were content (and many were happier) to work under the Third Reich.

FOCUS ROUTE

1 Complete column 2 of your own version of the table by matching up the eight institutions described in this subsection with the descriptions of their changing role under Hitler's dictatorship in column 1.
2 To what extent did the traditional elites maintain their power in Nazi Germany?

a) Lost its proper role, rarely met after 1933, and contained only Nazis	
b) Central government body which was kept but which fell into disuse	
c) The old democratic system was replaced by centrally appointed officials	
d) A conservative body whose members eventually had to join the Nazi Party	
e) Initially kept intact but bypassed by Nazi bodies, and eventually staffed by Nazis	
f) Traditionally independent from government and protecting the rights of the individual, this institution was co-ordinated to follow the government's will more closely	
g) Hitler worried about this body as a rival and did not reorganise it until he felt totally established in 1938	
h) This government office developed into a massive bureaucratic machine	

The Reichstag

Under the Enabling Act, the Reichstag had granted LEGISLATIVE powers to Hitler, and only seven more laws were passed by the Reichstag. Every four years it renewed the Enabling Act. In November 1933, a Nazi list of candidates was approved in a virtual plebiscite. This was one of a series of such votes, designed, successfully, to show the popularity of the regime. The Reichstag rarely met, and when it did it was mainly used as an applause machine for Nazi leaders' speeches.

Cabinet

Meetings of the Cabinet, 1933–9	
1933	72
1934	19
1935	12
1936	4
1937	7
1938	1
1939	0

Like the Reichstag, the Cabinet was retained but increasingly lost its purpose. Initially, it contained only three Nazis, but this gradually increased, though some non-Nazis remained throughout the regime. This was partly a reflection of the unimportance of the Cabinet. Hitler did not believe in an orderly system of government, and increasingly decisions were made on an *ad hoc* (individual) basis, depending on who had the ear of the Führer. Although the Enabling Act gave the Cabinet legislative powers, in practice laws were just issued through Hitler, having been drawn up by the Reich Chancellery.

Reich Chancellery

This central administrative body greatly expanded its role, since after the Enabling Act most laws/decrees were drawn up by Chancellery officials. It was responsible for co-ordinating the responses of departments to new legislation. New sections, both party and state, were created within this bureaucratic centre. These dealt with the increase in paperwork, such as letters written to Hitler, and issued government decrees. Its head, Lammers, had a major impact on the flow of information to and from Hitler, and thus on policies.

Civil Service

Most civil servants traditionally had been conservative and anti-parliamentary; they had welcomed presidential governments from 1930, and were committed to serving the state. They thus transferred reasonably happily to the Third Reich, and remained throughout the regime. Under 5 per cent were purged in the Law for the Restoration of the Civil Service, 1933. The Civil Service gradually became more Nazi, partly as Nazis were appointed, but mainly as existing bureaucrats joined the party. This became compulsory in 1939, as was the wearing of uniforms. Civil servants generally enacted Nazi laws, but some tried to weaken the impact of arbitrary commands. By the late 1930s they were losing influence as increasing use was made of special agencies, bypassing the ministries and their civil servants.

Local government

Despite Hitler's promise not to abolish elected state governments, they were taken over by centrally appointed officials. State governments became agents of the central government. Real power was exercised by the Reich governor, a post often held by the local *Gauleiter*.

The courts and legal system

Franz Gürtner, the non-Nazi Justice Minister from 1933 to 1941, supported an authoritarian state, but one that still operated on a system of law. He wanted to keep the police and judiciary separate. Most lawyers and judges thought accommodation to the regime was the best way of maintaining their position and controlling excesses. However, as Hiden has pointed out in *Republican and Fascist Germany* (p.190): 'In embarking on self-co-ordination in order to preserve the principles of law, the judiciary effectively worked in favour of the regime.'

Inevitably, Nazi ideas penetrated. Gürtner was unable to prevent ordinary courts losing power to the SS and Gestapo. The established courts still remained, but they adapted to the new system. Initially, some judges defied the government's wishes in their verdicts, so they were increasingly bypassed with the new People's Court and Special Courts created in March 1933.

Lawyers were co-ordinated in the German Lawyers Front. In October 1933, 10,000 lawyers gave the Nazi salute and swore 'by the soul of the German people ... to strive as German jurists to follow the course of our Führer to the end of our days'. Under a new penal code, judges were to act 'according to popular feeling'. From 1936 the eagle and swastika had to be worn on judges' robes. So the existing law was debased, and arbitrary actions were taken by authorities outside the law.

As in other areas, Hitler did not replace the existing legal code with a new Nazi one. New laws reflecting the Nazis' political views were passed, and judges were expected to interpret all laws according to Nazi values. The Interior Minister Wilhelm Frick summarised the Nazi view of the law thus: 'Everything which is useful for the nation is lawful; everything which harms it is unlawful.'

■ **Learning trouble spot**

How were the laws made in the Third Reich?

Students sometimes get confused over how laws were made after 1933. Federal laws were made in three ways, two of which were the same as under the Weimar Republic: that is, laws could be passed by the Reichstag or issued by presidential decree. Both these methods gradually died out (the Reichstag passed seven more laws, the President three more decrees), since after the Enabling Act of March 1933 the Cabinet (in effect Hitler) could just issue decrees. This became the main source of laws in the Third Reich.

Chart 11F opposite shows in diagrammatic form how laws were made in Nazi Germany. It also shows, as a comparison, how laws are made in a democracy.

a) HOW LAWS ARE MADE

Formulating laws in Britain

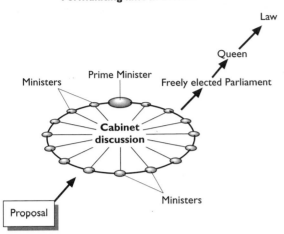

Formulating laws in the Third Reich

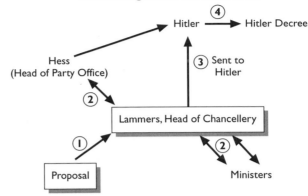

Individual consideration – no collective government

1 Cabinet meets regularly to discuss proposals for laws, which normally originate from government departments.
2 Proposal is discussed by all ministers and a collective decision made. This is a key stage.
3 Law (in white paper) is drawn up by civil servants, then presented to Parliament, which may pass, amend or reject it.

1 Individual ministers (or other agencies) submitted proposal to the Head of Chancellery, Hans Lammers.
2 Lammers circulated a draft to other ministers separately and to Rudolf Hess, Nazi Party Chief and Hitler's deputy, for comments.
3 Lammers then presented a new version to Hitler. He normally agreed.
4 The formal decree was drawn up, signed by Hitler and issued as law. However, many proposals were not made formal decrees or laws, but were just decisions. In this case, Hitler's approval might just be oral.

b) HOW DIFFERENT LEGAL SYSTEMS OPERATE

Liberal democracy		Nazi dictatorship
Very hard to be dismissed since meant to be independent of government influence	**i) Judges**	Existing judges mainly kept, but co-ordinated; made to take loyalty oath to Hitler
		Judges could be replaced
		Old legal system supplemented by new courts with Nazi Party members as judges
Laws to protect individual rights	**ii) Legal principles**	Laws to be interpreted in the interests of the community
		Individual rights suspended by Feb 1933 decree and never restored
Letter of law to be upheld		Letter of law could be overridden for national need; law to be interpreted subjectively
No retrospective laws		Laws could be applied retrospectively (to actions or events that took place before law passed)
Accused innocent until proved guilty		Accused seen as enemies of the *Volksgemeinschaft*
All equal in eyes of law		Law to protect citizens but not outsiders
Long-established courts	**iii) How administered**	New people's courts alongside traditional courts
		New agencies with powers to enforce their policies
Police obey and enforce laws		Gestapo-SS system operating outside the law
Appeals system		No appeals from some courts
Clear guidelines for punishment		Arbitrary punishments

The Foreign Office

One key part of the traditional bureaucracy that initially remained largely intact was the Foreign Office. Brüning's Foreign Minister Konstantin von Neurath remained until 1938. However, foreign policy was increasingly conducted outside the foreign ministry by individual Nazis – for example Goering, Goebbels, Ribbentrop – and by special missions. Furthermore, as part of a general radicalisation of the regime, key personnel changes occurred in 1938, with the Nazi Joachim von Ribbentrop replacing Neurath as Foreign Minister. Younger officials, more sympathetic to the Nazis, were promoted.

Army

A key institution that Hitler had to treat warily was the army. We have seen how initially Hitler reassured the army by weakening the SA, thus gaining the crucial personal oath of loyalty. Even so, Hitler realised the army posed a major potential danger to the regime if it felt threatened. So he left it structurally largely unchanged until 1938, although increased in size. The army generally co-operated, since most generals shared Hitler's anti-Bolshevism, anti-liberalism, strong nationalism and desire to restore Germany's military might. Hitler said the army and the Nazi Party were two columns supporting the state. Military leaders issued internal decrees adjusting to Nazism: for example, revising the army's training guidelines to reflect a Nazi approach. The army also benefited from rearmament: with conscription, the army increased twentyfold between 1933 and 1939.

In 1937 Hitler's aggressive plans in the 'Hossbach Memorandum' (see pages 378–9) received a cool reaction from military leaders. They felt Hitler was planning to expand too quickly. However, by 1938 Hitler felt secure enough to make major changes. In February 1938 he exploited Defence Minister Blomberg's marriage to an ex-prostitute and the alleged homosexuality of Werner von Fritsch, the Commander-in-Chief of the army, to replace them, along with over 100 other generals. Hitler himself took direct command of all the armed forces, as Commander-in-Chief, supreme over a new High Command of the Armed Forces, the Oberkommando der WEHRMACHT (OKW) headed by Wilhelm Keitel. Hitler now for the first time had direct military powers (see page 383).

The consolidation of the regime was now concluded. Nazism now had sufficient power over the army, the last potential instrument of conservative power. However, elements in the army remained hostile to many aspects of Nazism, especially when the war began to go badly (see Chapter 17).

C What role did the Nazi Party play in the Third Reich?

FOCUS ROUTE

Explain the role of the Nazi Party in the Third Reich both at the national and local level.

After 1933 the Nazi Party was the only party in Germany. Most of the government were members of the party, and civil servants, judges and other administrators increasingly joined. However, it would be misleading to say that the Nazi Party ran Germany. Power lay with Hitler and individual Nazi Party members, not with the party itself. There was no ruling party body like the POLITBURO in the Soviet Union. The party itself did not have a policy-making role. Decisions were made by Hitler and the people around him. The power of individual Nazis depended more upon their relationship with Hitler than on the formal office they held.

Relations between the party and the state machine were complex. Alongside traditional institutions were party bodies and other new agencies (see Chart 11N on page 208) creating a confusing administrative system. Most traditional ministries were headed by Nazis, though some top officials, such as Finance Minister Schwerin von Krosigk, were not members of the Nazi Party, yet kept their positions throughout the regime.

Beneath ministerial level, at both national and state level, many, but by no means all, top positions were given to Nazis.

Whilst an opposition party, the Nazi Party had tended to attract only those committed to its vision for Germany. Once it established itself in power, it attracted many CAREERISTS. These people were more concerned with personal advancement than with social change. Goebbels once wryly commented that NSDAP might stand for *Na Suchst Du Auch ein Pöstchen?* (Well, are you looking for a job, too?). Chart 11G shows both the growth in membership of the Nazi Party and the increasing number of full-time party officials.

■ 11G The growth of the Nazi Party

Party membership	
Jan 1933	850,000
1935	2,500,000
1943	6,500,000 (about 10 per cent of the population)
Numbers of full-time party bureaucrats	
1935	25,000
1937	200,000
1940	2,000,000

Note: In March 1933 there was a large influx of people joining the party, the so-called 'March converts'. In May 1935 restrictions were put on joining the party to stop careerists.

The increased power gained by some Nazi Party members encouraged some to abuse it and to lord it over their areas. Many Germans resented the approach of these 'little Hitlers', and there is strong evidence that, though Hitler was highly regarded by most Germans, the Nazi Party was not very popular. They hated busybody Nazi officials and this hostility was reinforced by the aura of corruption that surrounded many party officials.

The party's main roles were to help spread Nazi ideas, to help the implementation of government policies and to check up on the population. Some of the most important party members were the *Gauleiter*, who virtually ran their provinces.

The role of the *Gauleiter*

Gauleiter, or regional party bosses (for example Karl Hanke in Lower Silesia, Karl Kaufmann in Hamburg and Fritz Sauckel in Thuringia), were very influential in determining how Germans experienced Nazi rule. The *Gau* area normally coincided with the Reichstag electoral district and the Nazi *Gauleiter* normally became the Reich governor, exercising effective control in the province. It was his job to ensure that the people in his region kept in line. He headed a mini-bureaucracy running a hierarchical party machine.

SOURCE 11.12 Report of an address by Hitler to a conference of *Gauleiter* in February 1934

The Führer stressed:

The most essential tasks of the party were:

1 *To make the people receptive for the measures intended by the Government.*
2 *To help carry out the measures which have been ordered by the Government in the nation at large.*
3 *To support the Government in every way . . .*

ACTIVITY

1 Study Sources 11.12–14 and list the various roles identified for the Nazi Party.
2 What light does Chart 11I shed on the role and organisation of the Nazi Party?

Gauleiter also communicated directly with Hitler and attended top national party meetings. All claimed to be committed to Hitler but many resisted the implementation of central government instructions. Contrary to what one might expect in a so-called totalitarian regime (but typical of the administrative chaos that was the true nature of the Third Reich), they almost invariably triumphed in their conflicts with central directives.

SOURCE 11.13 Hitler praising the *Gauleiter*, as recorded in *Hitler's Table Talk, 1941–4*, 1953

I have made the Gauleiter *true kings, inasmuch as they receive from central headquarters only very schematic instructions . . . [Their decisions are irrevocable] even if they come into conflict with . . . the Ministry of the Interior. Only in this way is it possible to arouse fresh initiative. Otherwise, one permits a stupid bureaucracy to develop and prosper.*

SOURCE 11.14 The NSDAP 'Organisation Book' describing the role of the *Blockleiter* (block leader) in 1943

It is his duty to find people spreading damaging rumours and to report them to the local leader so that they may be reported to the state authorities.
   The Block Leader must . . . be a preacher and defender of National Socialist ideas.
   The Block Leader must continually remind Party members of their particular duties towards the people and the State.
   Furthermore, the Block Leader must complete a list about the households.
   It is the Block Leader's aim . . . that the sons and daughters of families within his zone become members of the various formations of the Hitler Youth, SA, SS and the German Labour Front, and that they visit National Socialist meetings, rallies, celebrations, etc.

The Nazi Party had a series of sections, reaching right down to local block units, seeking to ensure that all Germans complied with the regime. The key positions were the *Gauleiter*, at the top of the regional structure, and the block leader at the bottom. Both the party's membership and its component organisations expanded greatly, but its power did not develop to pose any challenge to Hitler. The Nazi Party remained essentially a Führer party.

■ 11H Political and party map of Nazi Germany

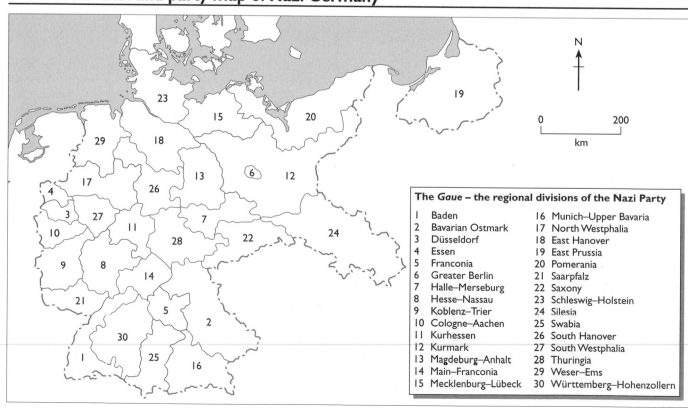

The *Gaue* – the regional divisions of the Nazi Party

1	Baden	16	Munich–Upper Bavaria
2	Bavarian Ostmark	17	North Westphalia
3	Düsseldorf	18	East Hanover
4	Essen	19	East Prussia
5	Franconia	20	Pomerania
6	Greater Berlin	21	Saarpfalz
7	Halle–Merseburg	22	Saxony
8	Hesse–Nassau	23	Schleswig–Holstein
9	Koblenz–Trier	24	Silesia
10	Cologne–Aachen	25	Swabia
11	Kurhessen	26	South Hanover
12	Kurmark	27	South Westphalia
13	Magdeburg–Anhalt	28	Thuringia
14	Main–Franconia	29	Weser–Ems
15	Mecklenburg–Lübeck	30	Württemberg–Hohenzollern

Nazi Party organisation	
Gaue	30
Kreise	760
Ortsgruppen	21,000
Zellen	70,000
Blöcke	400,000

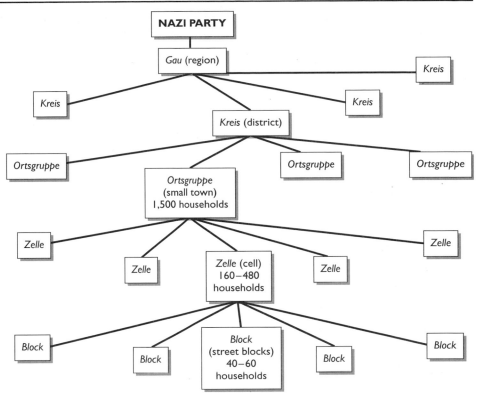

NAZI PARTY

Gau (region)

Kreis

Kreis

Kreis

Kreis (district)

Ortsgruppe

Ortsgruppe

Ortsgruppe

Ortsgruppe
(small town)
1,500 households

Zelle

Zelle

Zelle

Zelle (cell)
160–480
households

Zelle

Block

Block

Block
(street blocks)
40–60
households

Block

Block

TALKING POINT

Why do you think the magazine *Signal*
printed this picture?

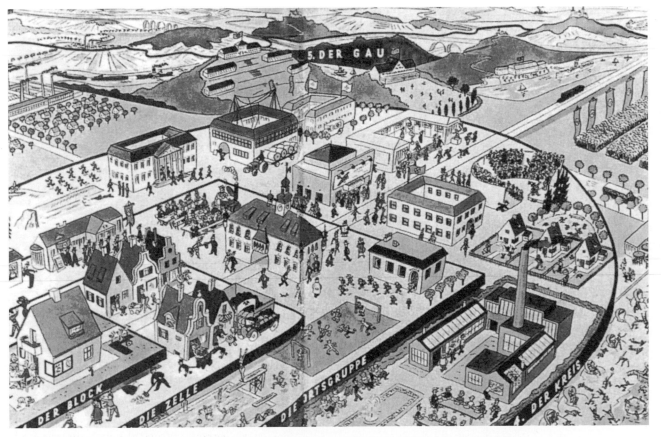

This illustration from the German propaganda magazine *Signal* shows the above diagram in picture form

■ 11J Key leaders of the Nazi Party

Rudolph Hess (1894–1987): the sycophant or flatterer

The son of a merchant, Hess served in the same regiment as Hitler during the First World War. In 1919 he joined the Freikorps and subsequently the Nazi Party. Hess took part in the Munich Putsch and was imprisoned with Hitler at Landsberg, helping him write *Mein Kampf*, particularly the concept of *Lebensraum* (living space). In 1925 he became Hitler's secretary in a reorganised party. Hess then gained many posts, including in 1932 that of Chairman of the Nazi Central Political Commission; he was also elected a Reichstag deputy. Later he became an SS general and in April 1933 Deputy Führer of the Nazi Party. Copies of decrees had to be submitted to his office before being published, and in December 1935 he was given power to select all senior Nazi officials. In 1939 he was made successor to Hitler after Goering. However, Hess had little real influence and was increasingly eclipsed by Bormann.

Hess's main significance was in developing the cult of the Führer. He possessed a religious fervour for his leader, believing his chant at the Nuremberg rallies: 'Hitler is Germany! Germany is Hitler!' Hitler favoured Hess as head of the party organisation because he was a weak, submissive character, totally dependent on Hitler as a father figure. He had few political skills, possessing neither intelligence, the capacity for political intrigue nor oratorical ability, but he compensated for this by his total belief in the infallible Führer, 'pure reason in human form'.

From 1939 Hess's power declined, as Hitler became more absorbed in the war. Feeling increasingly cut off, he made the dramatic decision to fly to Scotland in June 1941, hoping to arrange peace, seeing no conflict between Germany's need for *Lebensraum* and the British Empire. In 1946 he claimed 'I can't remember' to most questions at the Nuremberg trials, but maintained that Hitler was Germany's 'greatest son'. Sentenced to life imprisonment, he was the only prisoner in Spandau prison for the last 21 years of his life. In 1987 he strangled himself with heater cable.

Martin Bormann (1900–45): the power broker

In many ways the most mysterious and sinister figure in the Third Reich, Bormann used the party machine and the trust of Hitler to become eventually the second most powerful person in Germany. The son of a civil servant, Bormann dropped out of school. He fought in the First World War, joined the Freikorps and in 1925 joined the Nazis; he was made *Gauleiter* of Thuringia in 1928. He was a member of the supreme command of the SA and became Chief-of-Staff to Hess in 1933.

Bormann was a brutish, ruthless and ambitious man, a tireless administrator able to thrive in the labyrinthine (maze-like) Nazi machine. He built up his power base in the Nazi Party and became Hitler's secretary in 1943. By controlling Hitler's appointments and access to the Führer, he had tremendous power. From May 1941 he headed the new Party Chancellery, which organised party matters, whilst Hitler dealt with the war. He cut the Führer off from more cautious opinions, allowing Hitler to indulge his fanaticism, which Bormann shared. He pushed forward the Holocaust and the struggle against Christianity.

In 1945 Bormann vanished. He was rumoured to have committed suicide, to have been killed fleeing in a tank, and to have escaped to South America. In 1946 he was sentenced to death *in absentia*. In 1973 bones found in Berlin were officially stated to be his. This was confirmed by DNA tests in 1998.

Hans Heinrich Lammers (1879–1962): the powerful bureaucrat

Lammers, who joined the Nazi Party in 1932, was a civil servant in the Interior Ministry from 1921 to 1933. Chief of the Reich Chancellery from 1933 to 1945 and an honorary SS general from 1940, he was an efficient, unimaginative bureaucrat, whom Hitler trusted as his chief legal adviser and expert on state matters. Lammers acted as the main link between Hitler and the Reich ministers and thus had considerable influence. He summarised ministers' ideas for Hitler, received a grunt of approval from the Führer, then issued instructions. From 1943 Hans Lammers formed, with General Wilhelm Keitel and Martin Bormann, a Committee of Three, filtering problems into Hitler. He was tried in 1946, sentenced to twenty years' imprisonment but was released in 1952.

ACTIVITY

What do the careers of Hess, Bormann and Lammers show about how one gained and exercised power in the Nazi state?

D How powerful were the SS and Gestapo?

What was the connection between the Gestapo and the SS?

This is a very complex issue that can cause confusion. They originated as distinct bodies. The Gestapo was a state body, the Prussian secret police. The SS was a party body, created in 1925 as Hitler's personal bodyguard. It shared with the Gestapo a police role of rooting out enemies of the state but had a wider role for developing the new Nazi racial community. Kershaw describes it as 'the ideological power house of the Third Reich and executive organ of the "Führer will" '.

In 1936 Himmler was made Chief of German Police, adding control of the Gestapo to that of the SS and thus reinforcing the overlap. Kershaw comments on this link that 'The most powerful agency of repression thus merged with the most dynamic ideological force in the Nazi Movement.' Thus both the Gestapo and the SS can be seen as powerful police forces, with the SS having additional roles. It is convenient simply to refer to the SS–Gestapo complex.

Traditional interpretations of the Third Reich see it as a totalitarian state, supported by terror. This view has now been challenged. Undoubtedly, the state possessed a massive repressive machine and it did ruthlessly suppress opponents, but you also need to consider the following points:

- There is evidence that most Germans supported the regime.
- Many Germans did not encounter repression and believed that which did occur was generally justified.
- Thousands of Germans assisted the Gestapo and other repressive agents in their work.
- Repression was somewhat random; some people were actually moved out of Auschwitz; some were acquitted in the courts.
- Some people did protest and escaped punishment.

It is still controversial to make some of these points. However, with more histories influenced by the *Alltagsgeschichte* approach (the study of everyday life) and the expansion of detailed local studies, there is a growing body of evidence to support these views. Hitler's regime can thus be seen as partly based on popular support and co-operation as well as on intrusive and arbitrary terror.

How was the police organised in Nazi Germany?

Until 1933 each state in Germany had its own police force. By 1936 they had been centralised under Himmler as Chief of Police.

The Nazis developed a typically confusing variety of repressive agencies that overlapped and developed over time. Chart 11K clarifies the system. You may encounter references to any of these agencies, but the ones you need to understand are highlighted on this chart. The key points to grasp are:

i) After the Night of the Long Knives, the **SA** was disarmed and restructured, and many members were purged. Its revolutionary power broken, it became a subservient body. However, it remained as an intimidatory force against potential opposition. It retained a visible presence on the streets, periodically beating up alleged opponents and NONCONFORMISTS.

ii) The **SS** developed into the main terror instrument of the regime. From an elite bodyguard it became a mass organisation, with a wide variety of roles.

iii) The **Gestapo**, originally the Prussian secret police, eventually covered all German states. In 1933 SS Leader Himmler was appointed as the head of the Gestapo, so it came under SS control. From 1936 it became the most important security agent of the state, able to decide for itself what the law was.

iv) The **SD** or Security Police was the internal security/intelligence service of the SS, headed by Heydrich; in some ways it was the elite of the elite. Its reports on public opinion in Nazi Germany have become a useful source for historians.

v) The **RHSA** (Reich Main Security Department) was created in 1939 to try to draw together state and party security apparatus into one umbrella organisation.

■ **11K The police state: the Gestapo–SS complex**

- Gestapo*: Geheime Staatspolizei
- Kripo: Kriminalpolizei
- Orpo: Ordnungspolizei ('order' police), including Schutzpolizei and the gendarmerie
- RHSA: Reichssicherheitshauptamt (Reich Main Security Department)
- SA: Sturm-Abteilung
- SD*: Sicherheitsdienst (Security Service)
- Sipo: Sicherheitspolizei (Security Police)
- SS*: Schutzstaffel (defence echelon)

* Most significant agencies

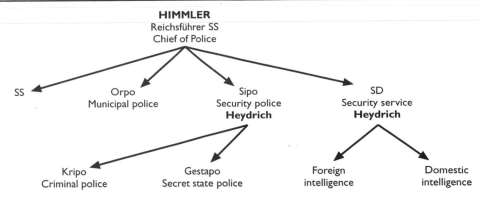

HIMMLER
Reichsführer SS
Chief of Police

SS

Orpo
Municipal police

Sipo
Security police
Heydrich

SD
Security service
Heydrich

Kripo
Criminal police

Gestapo
Secret state police

Foreign intelligence

Domestic intelligence

FOCUS ROUTE

1 What roles were played under the Nazi regime by the SS and Gestapo?
2 Explain how Himmler and the SS became so powerful in the Third Reich.
3 What do recent historians' analyses of the Gestapo suggest about the nature of the Nazi state?
4 What evidence is there that the Nazi police forces were not alien institutions imposed upon the German people?

A 1941 Waffen-SS poster. The wording says 'Admission after 17th birthday'

How did the SS become so powerful?

SS – the two most sinister initials in the world. The blackshirted Schutzstaffel were originally Hitler's personal bodyguard. In 1929 there were only 280 members, but by the late 1930s it had become a vast organisation, a virtual state within a state, involved in most aspects of the Third Reich. In fact, the Third Reich has been called the 'SS State'. It was, alongside the Gestapo, the most powerful and feared of the organs of repression in Nazi Germany.

On Hitler's accession to power, the SS was authorised to act as auxiliary police. It used the Emergency Power Decree of February 1933 (which remained permanently in force) to take suspects into 'protective custody' and, after the weakening of the SA, the SS emerged as the chief police arm of the Nazi Party. Between 1933 and 1939 about 225,000 Germans were convicted and imprisoned for political crimes. By 1939 another 162,000 were in 'protective custody' without trial. It directed its energies against all enemies of Nazism, whether political or racial, later taking over responsibility for concentration and extermination camps. It also established a vast economic empire.

By 1939 there were 240,000 members organised into divisions. The main branch was the Waffen-SS, primarily a military organisation. The Death's Head Formations (SS-Totenkopfverbände) administered the concentration camps and formed Panzer units. At the Nuremberg trials, the SS was declared to be a criminal organisation.

SOURCE 11.15 The American historian Sax has powerfully summarised how the role of the SS grew in *Inside Hitler's Germany*, 1992, p. 329

The SS was not merely a police, surveillance, and paramilitary organisation. Its main objective, from which it derived its 'legitimate' use of force, was to create the racially pure Volksgemeinschaft ... The SS evolved from a police organisation, operating within an administrative whole to become an independent organisation ... [It] became the active part of the political community, making all decisions of any political importance ...

Yet the SS did not simply safeguard the new political order; in Himmler's words, it was also charged with 'creating' the new order. Police power became creative power within the Third Reich, its protective role enlarged so as to allow it to make policy beyond the limits of legitimate state activity and to fuse elements of the new racial community together ... The police could do anything in the name of Volksgemeinschaft.

■ 11L The rise of Himmler and the growth of the SS

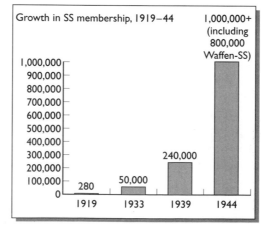

Growth in SS membership, 1919–44

1,000,000+ (including 800,000 Waffen-SS)

	280	50,000	240,000	1,000,000+
	1919	1933	1939	1944

July SS independent of SA
June Night of the Long Knives: SS weakens rival SA
April **Himmler Inspector of Gestapo**

Himmler Head of Bavarian police then other police forces

Himmler head of SS

SS created; part of SA

1925	1926	1927	1928	1929	1930	1931	1932	1933	1934	1935

Heinrich Himmler (1900–45): the exterminator

One of the most notorious Nazis, Himmler looked more like a bank clerk than a ruthless dictator. His evolution from conscientious, popular schoolboy into heartless exterminator remains something of a mystery. Noakes describes him as 'a bizarre combination of naive crank, pedantic [fussily precise] schoolmaster, and coldly efficient bureaucrat, a master at accumulating power in the administrative jungle of the Third Reich'.

The son of a teacher, Himmler joined the officer cadets in 1918 but did not see any war action. Bitter at Germany's defeat, he joined a nationalist paramilitary group and participated in the Munich Putsch. He failed as a poultry farmer, and by 1925 was becoming more active in the NSDAP. Himmler's real chance came when he became head of the SS in 1929. In 1933 he took over the Bavarian police and within three years had unified all the police and security forces under his control as Chief of German Police and Reich Leader SS. This enormous power was further extended when in 1939 he was made Reich Commissioner for Strengthening German Nationhood, with major powers over conquered territory in the east. There he was able to try to enact his aim of purifying the German nation by first removing alien elements, and then turning the SS by selective breeding into a racial elite.

Himmler ran the concentration camps. He also expanded the Waffen-SS to rival the Wehrmacht. In 1943 he became Minister of the Interior, and in July 1944 his power peaked when he was appointed Commander of the Reserve Army. In April 1945, hoping to preserve some form of Nazi state, on his own initiative he tried to negotiate an armistice with the West, and was dismissed by Hitler for treachery. Captured by the Allies, he committed suicide on 23 May 1945.

Himmler presided over the vast repressive machinery of the Third Reich, and had overall control of the Holocaust. His character reflected the contradictions of Nazism. A coldly efficient administrator, he suffered psychosomatic (caused by mental stress) illnesses, and nearly fainted when once observing mass executions. He firmly believed in the occult, in homeopathic medicine and in a romanticised view of history, with the need for pure Germans to 'return to the soil'. Yet he organised inhuman scientific experiments and 'modernised' murder. He inculcated strict discipline and a perverted idealism into the SS which made them see committing mass murder as a form of sacrifice for the cause of a pure German master race.

THE SS STATE: ROLE OF SS BY 1940s

Defend Hitler
Root out enemies
Arbitrary arrests; special courts; camps
SD intelligence reports on public feelings

Elite military force
Waffen-SS grew to rival the Wehrmacht
Suppressed Warsaw Uprising 1943

To create master race
Ran much of conquered lands
Organised labour/extermination camps
Organised *EINSATZGRUPPEN*
Enacted Holocaust
Ran elite schools
Set up 12 *Lebensborn* clinics to breed pure race

All areas, especially
slave labour, armaments,
construction, V-weapon production
Over 150 firms

Security / Racial/Ideological / Military / Economic / SS Empire

July Increased power after Bomb Plot. Supreme Commander of People's Army

Himmler Interior Minister

Himmler Reich Commissioner for Strengthening of German Nationhood
November Waffen-SS created

Himmler head of German Police and Reichsführer SS
He finally wins two-year struggle with Goering and Frick for full control of security forces

April Himmler secretly opens negotiations with Allies
May Himmler flees but captured; takes cyanide

1936	1937	1938	1939	1940	1941	1942	1943	1944	1945

SOURCE 11.17 Origins of denunciations of people for committing race crimes against the German Race in Würzburg, 1933–45

Source	%
Reports from the general population	57
Statements extracted by interrogation	15
Information from NSDAP and other control organisations	14
Observation by Gestapo agents	0.5
Others (unspecified)	13.5

SOURCE 11.19 The Gestapo

Interviewed in the 1990s for the BBC programme The Nazis, *an old man from Würzburg commented: 'They [the Gestapo] were everywhere.'*

Records show that there were 28 Gestapo officials covering the million people living in Würzburg and surrounding Lower Franconia.

The Gestapo badge

Was the Gestapo the all-powerful agent of a terror state?

SOURCE 11.16 The installation of a new police chief in Essen in 1937

SOURCE 11.18 Jacques Delarue, *Nazism and German Society*, ed. D. Crew, 1994, p. 169

Never before, in no other land and at no other time, had an organisation attained such a comprehensive penetration [of society], possessed such power, and reached such a degree of 'completeness' in its ability to arouse terror and horror, as well as in its actual effectiveness.

Source 11.18 is the classic description of the power of that dread organisation, the Gestapo. But were the German people really held down in this way? The Gestapo itself fostered its image as an all-powerful body that brought dread to the enemies of the regime. Such a belief in itself helped the Gestapo to intimidate the population. This view was also propounded (put forward) after the war by many Germans, who could thus excuse their passivity and broad acceptance of the regime by their fear of the all-powerful Gestapo.

However, some historians now argue that this image of the Gestapo is a myth, and that the reality of repression in Nazi Germany was far more complex and, in a way, more disturbing. The might of the Gestapo was in fact much weaker and its power rested on popular consent more than on terror. This change of view has come about from studying the actual operation of the Gestapo on the ground in certain areas, rather than examining the impressive-looking directives of the Gestapo HQ and the reports of the Social Democratic Party in exile (SOPADE) which stress a potentially rebellious working class held down by Gestapo spies and terror.

Several major weaknesses have been seen in the Gestapo as a repressive body. Firstly, it lacked the personnel effectively to enact central directives. Major areas such as Frankfurt, Hanover and Bremen had under 50 officers each. Düsseldorf, covering the west Ruhr industrial area with a population of 4 million, had 281 agents in 1937. At its peak the Gestapo had only 30,000 officers for the whole country. Equally importantly, most Gestapo officers were recruited from existing police forces, with few SS members. In 1939 only 3,000 of 20,000 were in the SS. Furthermore, most of these were office workers not field agents. Gestapo officials were increasingly bogged down in paperwork in a highly bureaucratic system. Its activities were far more directed at ordinary Germans than high status ones, even though Hitler realised many of the latter were not committed to the regime.

However, this apparent weakness of the Gestapo must not be overplayed. The image of power, however unjustified, served to intimidate potential opposition. Even more importantly, its own meagre resources were greatly enhanced by

SOURCE 11.20 Record of a denunciation by Maria Kraus of her neighbour Ilse Totzke in July 1940

Ilse Totzke is a resident next door to us in a garden cottage. I noticed the above-named because she is of Jewish appearance ... I should like to mention that Miss Totzke never responds to the German greeting [Heil Hitler]. I gathered from what she was saying that her attitude was anti-German. On the contrary she always favoured France and the Jews. Among other things, she told me the German Army was not as well equipped as the French ... Now and then a woman of about 36 years old comes and she is of Jewish appearance ... To my mind, Miss Totzke is behaving suspiciously. I thought she might be engaged in some kind of activity which is harmful to the German Reich.

SOURCE 11.21 Maria Kraus to Laurence Rees, the documentary film-maker, who in the 1990s showed her the above denunciation with her signature

I do not know. My signature is correct. But where it comes from I do not know ... I was talking to a friend of mine and she said 'Good God! To think that they rake it all up again fifty years later' ... I mean I did not kill anyone. I did not murder anyone.

co-operation from the public. Local studies have revealed that over half, and in some cases over 80 per cent, of investigations stemmed from voluntary denunciations. This could suggest strong commitment to Nazism by the German people but Professor Gellately (in *Gestapo and German Society*, 1990) has shown convincingly that most denunciations were inspired by personal rather than political factors. Denunciation to the Gestapo could be a way of getting rid of an unwanted husband or an unpleasant neighbour or gaining the resources of a Jew. Hate, greed and spite were more the motive than Nazi faith.

The flood of denunciations contributed to a radicalisation of the Gestapo's actions. Increasingly, the Gestapo could not investigate cases properly, so it resorted to arbitrary arrest, preventative custody and torture. Gestapo operations became more random, dependent upon the decisions and priorities of individual officers. Ironically, this created greater opportunities for opposition and non-conformist behaviour.

Thus the Gestapo was essentially a reactive institution, dependent upon the willing co-operation of the Germans. In fact, the authorities became increasingly concerned about denunciations for personal motives. Overwhelmed by a sea of accusations, they tried to reduce their flow. In an ironic twist, Himmler threatened makers of malicious denunciations with being sent to concentration camps! As Mallman and Paul have written (in 'Omniscient, Omnipotent, Omnipresent?' in *Nazism and German Society 1933–45*, ed. D. Crew, 1994): 'The Nazi regime was quite definitely not in the position to engage in comprehensive surveillance or perfect repression. Although the Nazi regime's aspirations were totalitarian, the reality was not.'

Although the Gestapo was not as all-powerful as is often proclaimed, and evidence suggests considerable support for the regime, the brutality of the Third Reich must not be underestimated. Basic individual freedoms were removed in 1933. Thousands of Germans were rounded up into concentration camps, and those the Nazis viewed as outsiders to their new society were imprisoned, sterilised and eventually murdered. Courts were increasingly expected to come to judgements in line with the wishes of 'true Germans' and the Führer. There was no authority that could protect individuals from the secret police.

TALKING POINT

Can informing on your neighbours ever be justified?

■ 11M Forms of repression

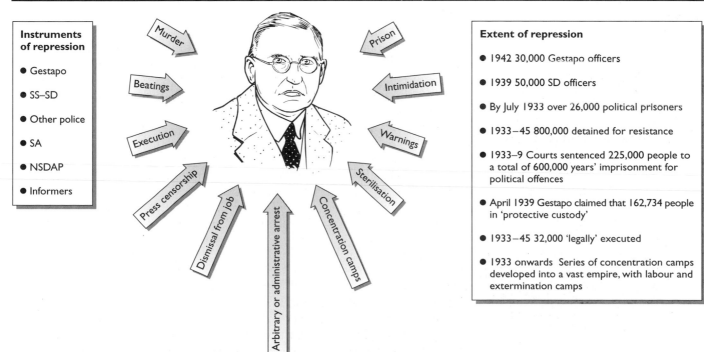

Instruments of repression
● Gestapo
● SS–SD
● Other police
● SA
● NSDAP
● Informers

Murder · Beatings · Execution · Press censorship · Dismissal from job · Arbitrary or administrative arrest · Concentration camps · Sterilisation · Warnings · Intimidation · Prison

Extent of repression

● 1942 30,000 Gestapo officers

● 1939 50,000 SD officers

● By July 1933 over 26,000 political prisoners

● 1933–45 800,000 detained for resistance

● 1933–9 Courts sentenced 225,000 people to a total of 600,000 years' imprisonment for political offences

● April 1939 Gestapo claimed that 162,734 people in 'protective custody'

● 1933–45 32,000 'legally' executed

● 1933 onwards Series of concentration camps developed into a vast empire, with labour and extermination camps

E Review: Where did power lie in the Third Reich?

By August 1934 Hitler had consolidated his position and had begun to construct a totalitarian regime. Many people have an image of such regimes as extremely efficient. When this is combined with the stereotypical images of supposed German efficiency it is easy to see how the popular view of the extremely efficient Third Reich has developed. This indeed was the image the Third Reich portrayed of itself. However, we need to examine critically such views and look beyond the Nazi propaganda to see how the system actually operated.

In the last 30 years historical analysis of the nature of the Nazi state has been radically transformed. The traditional image of a smoothly efficient totalitarian regime, dominated by Hitler, has been considerably modified. A mass of detailed studies of Nazi rule, at local level and in central government agencies, has produced a more complex view. The Nazi machinery of government was a maze of overlapping bodies, and has been described as polycratic, feudal and even chaotic. All these terms have their merits:

- **Polycratic** means there were many different bodies. Overlapping the existing ministries were Nazi bodies. If a problem emerged, Hitler often set up a new body: for example, the Office of the Four-Year Plan to fulfil the autarkic aims of the regime.
- **Feudal** has been used to describe the dominance of Nazi leaders at the head of their agencies, a role similar to that of medieval barons in charge of their followers. Just as the barons owed ultimate loyalty to the king, so the Nazi leaders did to the Führer. Hitler saw loyalty in personal not institutional terms, so he did not mind Goering or Himmler building up great power, as he was convinced of their superior loyalty to him. Of course, this did not stop the 'barons' quarrelling, something which, it has been said, pleased Hitler, since it neutralised any potential threats to him.
- **Chaotic** is used because the overlapping of bodies meant it was unclear where responsibility lay. The confusion was resolved only when Hitler intervened, which he rarely did. The chaos stemmed from the charismatic nature of Hitler's leadership: that is to say, everyone relying on the leader, with no clear power structure. Access to Hitler seemed to be the secret of success, and all the top Nazis had to make regular trips to his residences to keep in with Hitler.

SOURCE 11.22 I. Kershaw, *The Nazi Dictatorship*, 1993 (3rd ed.), p. 74

... the dissolution of the government into a multiplicity of competing and non-coordinated ministries, party offices, and hybrid [combined] agencies all claiming to interpret the Führer's will. Hand in hand with this development went the growing autonomy of the Führer authority itself, detaching itself and isolating itself from any framework of corporate government and correspondingly subject to increasing delusions of grandeur and diminishing sense of reality.

The overall structure of government was reduced to a shambles of constantly shifting power bases or warring factions.

Conflicting interpretations: intentionalist v structuralist

Now that the polycratic view of the Third Reich has won the argument against the totalitarian view, debate has moved to the reasons for this chaotic structure. This has become part of the major debate about the Third Reich between INTENTIONALISTS and STRUCTURALISTS.

This is a reflection of a broader debate about the nature of history. Some historians put more stress on powerful individuals as exercising a major influence on historical development. In this view what major leaders, like Hitler, Stalin and Mussolini, wanted is very important in explaining events, as they were in a position to enact their aims. Other historians tend to put more stress on broader historical developments, especially the economic structure of society, political factors, etc. They do not deny the influence of people, either leaders or

ACTIVITY

The historian Sax has usefully described the power structure as a 'systemless system'. Explain what he meant.

SOURCE 11.23 The historian Stanley Payne has summarised the views in *History of Fascism 1914–45*, 1995, p. 206

The intentionalists hold that Hitler had clear goals from the start and was firmly in charge of all major decisions ... structuralist interpretations assert that the course of events and the major decisions were influenced much more by the structure of institutions, the pressure of cumulative events or economic factors, and the changing international situation.

TALKING POINT

Most historians would argue that history is determined by a combination of the actions of people and broader historical developments; the degree of influence can vary. Karl Marx, who is often assumed, misleadingly, to be a crude economic determinist, once wrote: 'Men make their own history but they make it in conditions determined by their past.' Do you agree with this point?

the masses, but see their actions as determined more by the conditions in which they operated than by their own wishes. These two approaches have played a major part in debates about the nature of the Third Reich.

ACTIVITY

Identify which statement in each pair reflects an intentionalist and which a structuralist position and enter them in your own copy of the table below.

Aspect	Intentionalist position	Structuralist position
a) Hitler's vision		
b) Hitler's power		
c) Reasons for chaotic nature of Third Reich		
d) The Holocaust		
e) Second World War		
f) Nature of Nazism		

A Hitler's vision
i) Hitler had a distinct *Weltanschauung* (world view). He had clear aims, especially anti-semitism, anti-Bolshevism and *Lebensraum*. The key to the Third Reich is Hitler's aims.
ii) Hitler's ideas were not very coherent. He was an opportunist who wanted power.

B Hitler's power
i) Hitler's position within the Third Reich was quite weak; he was wary of potential opposition, and was not able to dominate events.
ii) Hitler had great power, and was gradually able to implement his aims.

C Reasons for the chaotic nature of the Third Reich
i) The administrative confusion arose from the nature of Hitler's charismatic leadership and was not deliberate policy.
ii) The chaotic administrative system was a product of the deliberate intention of Hitler to foster rivalries and competing authorities in order to enhance his own power as the decision-maker.

D The Holocaust
i) Hitler aimed to exterminate the Jews and was eventually able to do so.
ii) The Holocaust developed from a process of radicalisation in the regime and the influence of other events, especially the war.

E The Second World War
i) Hitler aimed at world war, and this desire was the prime determinant of German foreign policy.
ii) Although Hitler had broad overall aims in foreign policy, he had no blueprint for world war.

F Nature of Nazism
i) Nazism should be seen more in the light of the general interwar phenomenon of Fascism.
ii) Nazism can be seen as Hitlerism, dependent upon Hitler's vision, power and decisions.

The Activity identifies broad trends in interpretations but it is a simplification. Few historians would agree with all of the statements in either of the columns in the table. Intentionalism and structuralism should be seen as broad perspectives that may influence historians, rather than distinct SCHOOLS to which historians belong. Some historians call themselves Marxist (though there is considerable variety of opinion within this group), but most historians do not label themselves. Whether their approaches tend towards the EMPIRICAL or the THEORETICAL, they would claim to be studying history to establish as near to the truth as possible, not searching for confirmation of the correctness of a school of interpretation. As a student, you need to be aware of different perspectives but be wary of making simplified statements about historians' views being the result of the school to which they supposedly belong.

How was such an allegedly chaotic system so successful?

As you were reading the description of the chaos of the Third Reich, you might have been asking yourself: 'Well, if it was so chaotic, how on earth did it survive for twelve years? Surely, the fact that there was no real threat to the regime from within Germany, that it conquered most of Europe between 1939 and 1941, and that it was only brought down by the combined might of the USSR, the USA and the British Empire shows how strong and efficient it was.'

This is a good case, but also consider that initially the effects of the inefficiencies of the system were not apparent because:

- The internal rivalries generated a degree of effectiveness.
- The extensive police machine and the popularity of Hitler's policies made opposition difficult.
- Hitler inherited a well-established administrative and industrial structure which he did not disrupt, and which continued to function well. Many of Germany's achievements were despite the regime, not because of it.
- Germany's opponents, especially France, Poland and the USSR, were initially weak.
- The USA did not enter the war to begin with.

■ 11N Structures within the Nazi state

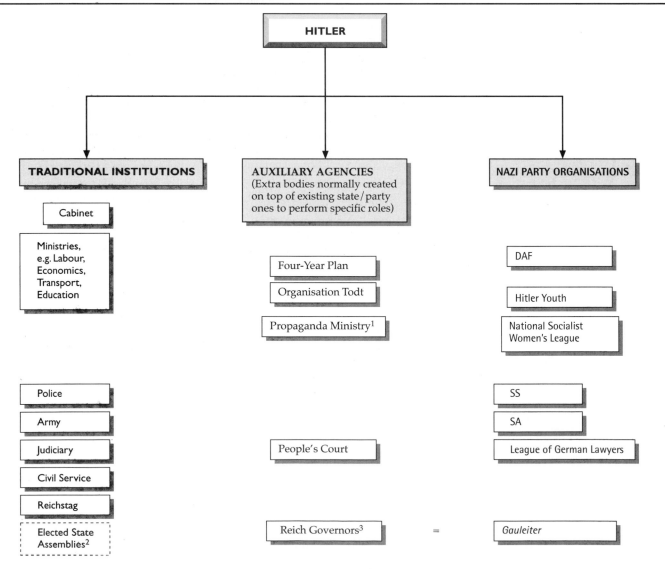

Notes
[1] New ministry created 1933
[2] Elected assemblies abolished
[3] Most Reich Governors were the local *Gauleiter*

ACTIVITY

Historians have been reluctant to represent the chaotic Nazi government system diagrammatically, but we have tried to do this in Chart 11N on the opposite page. It attempts to illustrate the polycratic nature of the regime.

1 Explain in your own words the key points that emerge from Chart 11N.
2 In 1997, in the BBC TV series *The Nazis. A Warning from History*, for which Kershaw acted as a consultant, there was one programme on the nature of the Nazi state and the role of the Gestapo that was called 'Chaos and Consent – the Nazi Rule of Germany'. How appropriate do you consider this title?
3 Essay: 'The Hitler State'. How valid is this view of the Third Reich?

You could tackle this question by splitting it up into the following areas:

i) the direct role of Hitler as Führer within the state: consider his dominance within the party and state, and the extent to which he laid down guidelines and was involved in deciding policies (major/minor)
ii) how far the power of others was dependent upon Hitler
iii) the nature and impact of the 'Hitler myth'
iv) the extent to which Germany as a country was dominated by Hitler.

KEY POINTS FROM CHAPTER 11: Where did power lie in the Third Reich?

1 Hitler did not embark on a major overhaul of Germany's administrative structure.
2 Old institutions such as the Reichstag and Cabinet remained, but were virtually powerless. Traditional institutions co-operated with the new regime and adapted to the Nazi system.
3 Power was concentrated in Hitler as Führer, supposedly representing the will of the German people.
4 Beneath Hitler there was a confusing array of state and party institutions, cutting across each other's jurisdictions but all seeking to work along the lines laid down by the Führer.
5 Such a system of jealous rivalries served to enhance Hitler's power.
6 A powerful Hitler myth developed, which portrayed Hitler as a wonderful leader, responsible for all policy successes. This helped make him genuinely popular, and allowed the regime to become more radical.
7 The Nazi Party was far less admired. It became a vehicle for careerism. It was mainly used to activate the population; it was not a party of rule.
8 A complex police system developed, but its efficiency was partly dependent upon the co-operation of millions of Germans.
9 There was an array of fierce repressive machinery to persecute non-conformists.
10 Nazi Germany was certainly dominated by Hitler, but was not a smoothly run, efficient structure.

How successful was Nazi economic policy?

CHAPTER OVERVIEW

SOURCE 12.1 A German worker explained in 1985 why he joined the Nazis in the 1930s

I was unemployed for many years. I'd have made a pact with the devil to get work. Hitler came along and got me work, so I followed him.

When Hitler was appointed Chancellor there were nearly 6 million people unemployed; by 1935 there were only 2 million, and by 1939 there was a shortage of labour. This remarkable transformation helps explain not only why Hitler was able to consolidate his position in power, but also why he became so popular. Reducing unemployment was an important Nazi success; but Hitler had broader aims. His top priority was to expand the military might of Germany and prepare the country for war.

This chapter studies the main developments in the German economy from 1933 to 1945, considers the importance of ideology in Hitler's economic policies and assesses their success in the subsections listed below.

Pages 212–15 provide an overview of the key developments before we explore them in detail.

SOURCE 12.2
Previously unemployed
workers meet to build
the first autobahn,
September 1933

FOCUS ROUTE

Consolidate your understanding of the overall development of Nazi economic policy by completing your own copy of the following table.

Nazi economic aims	Important individuals	Key measures	Successes and failures
Recovery 1933–6			
Rearmament 1936–9			
War 1939–45			

A Economic developments – an overview

FOCUS ROUTE

What methods did Hitler use to achieve his economic aims? How successful was he? Identify:

a) his aims
b) his methods
c) successes in achieving his aims
d) any counter points.

ACTIVITY

a) List five features you would expect to see in any successful economy.
b) From your knowledge of Hitler, suggest aspects of Germany's economy he might be particularly interested in.
c) Discuss your ideas with the class.

TALKING POINT

Would everyone agree on what constituted strengths and weaknesses in an economy?

Hitler's economic aims

Hitler's initial main aim was to tackle the Depression and restore Germany to full employment. This would improve conditions for millions of Germans and create a broader feeling of optimism, both of which would consolidate his regime politically. Economic recovery would also enable more resources to be utilised to rebuild Germany's military might, as a prelude to territorial expansion. Hitler viewed war as inevitable, and stressed how the German economy must become as self-sufficient as possible.

Hitler's other major priority was creating a *Wehrwirtschaft*, or defence economy, an economy geared to the needs of future war. This idea was widely supported in nationalist circles and by the army. It was to some extent inspired by the realisation that Germany had lost the First World War partly through suffering an economic blockade and because of poor economic and social organisation. The economy was to expand vital war materials, develop substitutes for imports, and train the workforce for skills transferable to war production, to make Germany ready for war.

Other Nazis stressed the importance of fostering the economic interests of the German *Mittelstand* and restricting what they considered to be the harmful influence of finance capital. Some also favoured some form of CORPORATIVIST organisation, as in Fascist Italy, with the economy organised by the state to protect the interests of all groups and ensure maximum production.

At this point, you can gain an overall perspective on the German economy from 1933 to 1945 by studying Chart 12A.

■ 12A Key features of the Nazi economy 1933–45

> **1 RECOVERY** Schacht the dominant figure

> **2 REARMAMENT** Goering the dominant figure

> **3 WAR** Speer the dominant figure 1942–5

Issues to consider
a) Treatment of *Mittelstand*. A few token measures, but really sidelined compared to big business which did well, e.g. iron, coal and especially chemicals
b) Guns v butter debate over the priority of rearmament or the consumer – both expanded, but from 1936 onwards guns a priority
c) Growing role of state; increased state controls, but most firms were not owned by the state
d) Autarky: economic self-sufficiency to prepare for war

AIMS
Economic growth to
i) build up Germany's military might
ii) win support

So:

POLICIES
Reflate the economy via government spending, e.g.
• Public works
• Subsidies to private firms
• Rearmament orders

Led to

PROBLEMS
i) Balance of payments deficit as
   • economic recovery led to rising demand for consumer goods
   • rearmament led to increased demand for raw materials
     (also world protectionism, and the high value of the mark made it hard to increase exports)
ii) danger of inflation, as there was
   • increased demand
   • increased money supply

So tackled by

POLICIES
i) 1934 New Plan: controls on currency, and BILATERAL trade agreements
ii) Government control of wages, prices

Led to

PROBLEMS
Disagreements over priorities: Schacht favoured boosting exports, slower rearmament; Goering, Hitler favoured rapid rearmament

So tackled by

POLICIES
1936 Four-Year Plan
• Prepare for war
• Autarky, by expanding domestic production, developing substitutes, expanding abroad, i.e. Austria, Czechoslovakia
• Extended government controls
• Expanded rearmament

Led to

PROBLEMS
By 1939 danger of economy overheating, as there were labour and raw material shortages, and some prices were rising

So tackled by

POLICIES
i) Initially successful Blitzkrieg 1939–41, with foreign countries plundered for their resources
ii) After the failure to knock out the USSR, the regime tried to organise a Total War Economy 1942–5, with a big increase in production

R E C O V E R Y

R E A R M A M E N T

W A R

■ 12B The German economy 1933–9

SOURCE 12.3 Index of industrial production (1928 = 100)

	Total	Production goods	Consumer goods
1933	66	56	80
1934	83	81	91
1936	107	114	100
1938	125	144	116

SOURCE 12.4 Value of imports and exports (billion marks)

	Imports	Exports
1928	14.0	12.3
1932	4.7	5.7
1933	4.2	4.9
1934	4.5	4.2
1936	4.2	4.8
1938	5.4	5.3

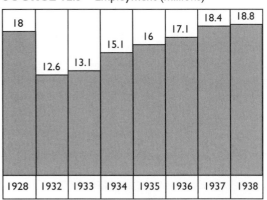

SOURCE 12.5 Employment (millions)

1928	1932	1933	1934	1935	1936	1937	1938
18	12.6	13.1	15.1	16	17.1	18.4	18.8

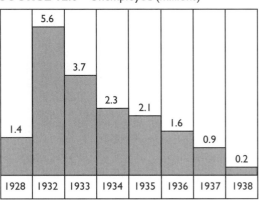

SOURCE 12.6 Unemployed (millions)

1928	1932	1933	1934	1935	1936	1937	1938
1.4	5.6	3.7	2.3	2.1	1.6	0.9	0.2

SOURCE 12.7 National income (billion marks)

1928	72.4
1932	42.6
1933	44
1934	50.4
1936	63.6
1938	79.8

SOURCE 12.8 Wages as percentage of national income

1928	62
1932	64
1933	63
1934	62
1936	59
1938	57

SOURCE 12.9 Real wages (1936 = 100)

1928	102.2
1933	92.5
1934	96.7
1936	100
1938	107.5

ACTIVITY

Study Sources 12.3–18.
a) Note down evidence that suggests the German economy was successful 1933–9.
b) Note down evidence suggesting weaknesses in the economy.
c) Discuss your results. Does this evidence suggest that overall the Nazi economy 1933–9 was successful?

SOURCE 12.10 Money wages index (1936 = 100)

1928	124.5
1933	87.7
1934	94.1
1936	100
1938	108.5

SOURCE 12.11 Prices index (1913 = 100)

1928	140
1933	93.3
1936	104.1
1938	105.8

SOURCE 12.12 Government finances

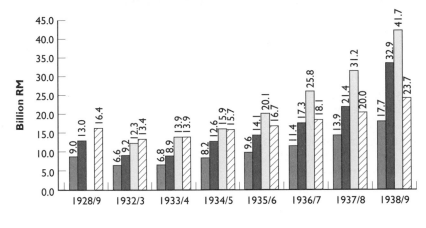

Note: Figures for 1928/9 total national debt not available

SOURCE 12.13 Estimated economic investment 1933–8

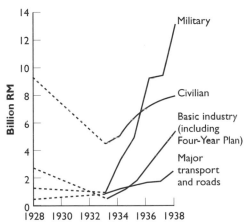

SOURCE 12.14 Public expenditure in Germany by category, 1928–38 (billion RM)

	1928	1932	1933	1934	1935	1936	1937	1938
Total expenditure (central and local)	23.2	17.1	18.4	21.6	21.9	23.6	26.9	37.1
Construction	2.7	0.9	1.7	3.5	4.9	5.4	6.1	7.9
Rearmament	0.7	0.7	1.8	3.0	5.4	10.2	10.9	17.2
Transportation	2.6	0.8	1.3	1.8	2.1	2.4	2.7	3.8
Work creation		0.2	1.5	2.5	0.8	—	—	—

Note: There is some overlap between the categories. Work creation included some expenditure on roads; construction also included some rearmament expenditure.

SOURCE 12.15 Average working week before overtime

	Hours
1933	43
1939	47

SOURCE 12.16 Increase (%) in income 1933–8

Social group	%
Big business	116
Farmers	41
Industrial workers	25

SOURCE 12.17 Self-sufficiency in important foodstuffs 1938–9

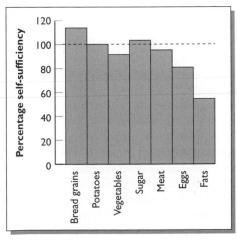

SOURCE 12.18 Food consumption in working-class families 1927–37 (% change)

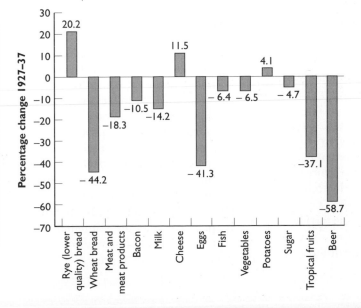

FOCUS ROUTE

1 The main measures Hitler actually took have been classified as follows:
   a) Government funding for new jobs
   b) Encouragement for industrialists to expand production
   c) Reduction of the unemployment figures without actually increasing the numbers employed.

   As you read this subsection note down the main measures introduced by Hitler, under the categories listed above. Then add any additional measures taken.

2 Describe the two main measures taken by Schacht to reduce balance of payments problems.

Mefo bills

A Mefo bill was a credit note, issued by the Reichsbank and guaranteed by the government. They were used by the government to help fund increased expenditure on rearmament by delaying real payment. Schacht set up a new company, the **Metallurgische Forschung**, which gave out credit notes (Mefo bills) to companies providing supplies and services for the government. They were to be converted into Reichsmarks and payable, with interest, after five years from increased government tax revenue. By 1937 the government had paid out 12 billion RM in Mefo bills. They funded about half of Germany's rearmament programme during 1933–8. This ingenious method also disguised military expenditure.

B How did the Nazis stimulate economic recovery 1933–6?

On the face of it, Hitler inherited a difficult situation. The Depression had destroyed the previous regime; Germany was short of certain essential raw materials and did not have the foreign currency to pay for many imports. Exports were hit by the slump in world trade. Confidence had been lost, and investment was low. Almost 6 million Germans were unemployed. However, on the other hand, the mess Germany was in gave Hitler an opportunity to make an impact. Furthermore, it is now clear that the worst of the Depression was over before he was appointed Chancellor. In the longer term, Germany, because of its human and material resources, was potentially the dominant economy in Europe.

The new government took action on a broad front to create jobs. It increased public expenditure and investment, and it tried to stimulate consumer demand. Hitler extended the public works schemes initiated in 1932, especially the building of homes and motorways. Such works, paid for by the state, provided orders for many private companies who took on more workers. Tax concessions and special grants, for example to newlyweds, also stimulated demand. The destruction of independent unions and the new atmosphere of dynamism that the government created helped to restore that vital economic ingredient, confidence. There were subsidies for hiring more workers in the private sector, even domestic servants, and a growth in jobs in the government bureaucracy. Some groups were pressurised out of employment, for example some married women and Jews in public service. Some groups were no longer eligible to register for unemployment relief, for example agricultural workers. The Youth Service (RAD) also took the young off the unemployment register (400,000 in 1934), and from 1935 conscription removed all 18- to 25-year-old males, who were required to do military service for two years. (The armed forces grew from 100,000 in 1933 to 1,400,000 in 1939.)

Hitler appointed Hjalmar Schacht first as President of the Reichsbank in March 1933, then in August 1934 as Economics Minister. These appointments reassured the economic elite with whom Schacht had close links. Schacht's particular skill was in developing ingenious ways of meeting Germany's economic needs. As President of the Reichsbank he used DEFICIT FINANCING (see page 73) to boost the economy. In particular, he pioneered the use of Mefo bills (see left) to finance increased public expenditure without causing inflation. The latter was also prevented by government controls on wages and prices. Hitler benefited from the ending of reparations payments arranged by Brüning. Schacht also suspended debt repayments. The effect of these measures on the unemployment figures was striking and was welcomed by most Germans, as indicated in Source 12.1.

Germany's balance of trade problem

By 1934 the revival of the economy was causing concern because of a balance of trade deficit. Germany was importing more than it was exporting, and its gold and foreign currency reserves were running low. Schacht devised the New Plan of 1934 to tackle the problem. This gave the government strong powers to regulate imports through controlling the allocation of foreign exchange. In effect, imports had to be approved by the government. Schacht also made a series of bilateral trade agreements, especially with Balkan states, which supplied much of Germany's strategic raw material imports. These included some barter (trade by exchange of goods) arrangements that eliminated the need to use scarce foreign currency and also served to increase Germany's economic influence over this key area. Although the New Plan helped overcome the immediate balance of trade problem in 1934, there was still the problem of increased demand sucking in imports, especially as the pace of rearmament grew.

Hjalmar Schacht (1877–1970): Hitler's banker

Schacht had become a Director of the National Bank by 1916. In 1919 he helped found the German Democratic Party but gradually moved to the right. Appointed President of the Reichsbank in 1923, he played a major role in curbing inflation by establishing the Rentenmark. In March 1930 he resigned in protest at the Young Plan.

After reading *Mein Kampf*, Schacht came to see Hitler as Germany's saviour. Although he did not join the Nazi Party, he generated funds for the Nazis from industrialists.

Reappointed President of the Reichsbank in March 1933, Schacht became Economics Minister in August 1934. By using state regulation, he played a major role in the economic recovery and in funding rearmament.

Schacht resigned as Economics Minister in 1937 and Reichsbank President in 1939; he was Minister without PORTFOLIO from 1937 to 1943. He publicly supported the government but privately made contact with the anti-Nazi resistance. After the July 1944 Bomb Plot he was sent to a concentration camp. He was tried and acquitted at the Nuremberg trials in 1945–6.

■ **Learning trouble spot**

Why did Hitler succeed, where the Weimar Republic had failed, in tackling the Depression?

In some respects, Hitler was lucky. Both the German and the world slump had bottomed out by late 1932, and the economy was improving. But it was not just a matter of timing: Hitler was prepared to reject the ORTHODOXIES of ECONOMIC LIBERALISM that had constrained Weimar politicians, and adopt greater state intervention and deficit financing. Much was also due to Hitler's determination, which weak Weimar governments had lacked. For Hitler, reducing unemployment was his top priority, whereas for Brüning unemployment was more a tool to use for his wider aims.

However, it was not just due to greater determination, but also to the context in which the governments were operating. It was more difficult to take decisive action under the Weimar constitution, whereas once Hitler had secured the constitutional change of the Enabling Law, and Hindenburg had died, there were no formal constraints on what Hitler could do. Furthermore, his new government brought a new sense of purpose. The repression of free trade unions meant that business confidence was restored, and the imposition of controls meant that there was far less fear of inflation. To some extent, Hitler just made measures such as public works projects, which Weimar governments had belatedly adopted, more vigorous.

Other factors might seem significant but probably were not. The recovery was not just due to Schacht (who had also helped the Weimar Republic recover from inflation but had resigned in 1930). The ending of reparation payments, which Weimar governments had blamed for the slump, probably had little economic effect, although it might have helped psychologically.

Thus the contrast has to be explained by identifying the reasons why Weimar governments took little action whereas Hitler did; how Hitler benefited from the economic situation; and the greater power and determination of Hitler's government.

SOURCE 12.19 Hitler explains his economic success in a speech to the Reichstag on 21 May 1935

What we have achieved in two and a half years in the way of a planned provision of labour, a planned regulation of the market, a planned control of prices and wages, was considered a few years ago to be absolutely impossible. We only succeeded because behind these apparently dead economic measures we had the living energies of the whole nation. We had, however, first to create a number of technical and psychological conditions before we could carry out this purpose. In order to guarantee the functioning of the national economy it was necessary first of all to put a stop to the everlasting fluctuations of wages and prices. It was further necessary to remove the conditions giving rise to interference which did not spring from higher national economic necessities i.e. to destroy the class organisations of both camps which lived on the politics of wages and prices. The destruction of the Trade Unions, both of employers and employees, which were based on the class struggle demanded a similar removal of the political parties which were maintained by these groups of interest, which interest in return supported them. Here arose the necessity for a new conservative and vital constitution and a new organisation of the Reich and state.

ACTIVITY

1 List all the points that Hitler claims contributed to Germany's economic recovery.
2 What counter points might an opponent of the regime make?

TALKING POINT

Hitler once allegedly commented that the way he had cured inflation was through concentration camps. What do you think he meant?

FOCUS ROUTE

1   Why was the Four-Year Plan created in 1936?
2   What were the successes and failures of the autarky programme?
3   Explain the role of Goering in the economy.
4   How significant was the drive for rearmament during 1936–9?

C   How significant was the drive for rearmament 1936–9?

Why did Hitler establish the Four-Year Plan in 1936?

The year 1936 marked a major turning point in the Nazi economy. Hitler's initial policies had clearly been successful. Confidence was restored and unemployment had been reduced to 1.6 million, so millions of Germans were benefiting. The question now was how to progress. Schacht, who had initially accepted the need for a large increase in public expenditure to reflate the economy and finance rearmament, was becoming increasingly concerned at the distortion of the economy due to rearmament. Severe strains due to a budget deficit and increasing balance of payments problems were occurring. Schacht wanted to encourage exports and slow the increase in arms expenditure. Hitler became impatient with Schacht's caution and on 4 September 1936 put Goering in charge of a new economic organisation, the Office of the Four-Year Plan.

The plan aimed to make Germany ready for war within four years. Priority had to be given to rearmament, and Germany had to be made as self-sufficient as possible in food and industrial production, a policy known as autarky. Emphasis was placed on the development of raw materials and machinery production, providing the base for the later concentration on arms production, ready for war in the mid 1940s. Goering, the Commander-in-Chief of the LUFTWAFFE, now became the major economic figure in Germany. As head of the Four-Year Plan he presided over a vast new organisation, typically cutting across existing economic ministries. The Office of the Four-Year Plan intervened throughout the economy, issuing a series of regulations controlling foreign exchange, labour, raw materials, prices, etc., thus creating a managed economy. The government set overall targets that private industry had to meet.

SOURCE 12.20   An extract from the Four-Year Plan Memorandum, August 1936

I thus set the following tasks:
I The German armed forces must be operational within four years.
II The German economy must be fit for war within four years.
[Underlined by Hitler] ... <u>The extent of the military development of our resources cannot be too large, nor its pace too swift.</u>

How successful was the policy of autarky?

Autarky means economic self-sufficiency, that is a country providing all its economic needs within itself, and thus not being dependent upon imports. Hitler considered this crucial for a country geared for war to avoid the damage inflicted by an economic blockade.

Total autarky is very hard to achieve and it was not envisaged that Germany would be totally self-sufficient. It would, however, lose its dependence on other countries for key commodities. This was initially to be achieved by:

- increasing Germany's own production of key commodities, such as iron and food
- developing ersatz (substitute) products, for example developing Buna (artificial rubber) from acetylene to replace rubber imports, and using coal to produce oil.

However, it took 6 tons of coal to produce 1 ton of oil. By 1939 Germany still depended on foreign imports for one-third of its raw materials, especially iron ore, oil and rubber. Gradually, another method of 'self-sufficiency' was given more stress: conquering other countries to use their resources (for example, Austrian iron and eventually Russian grain).

ACTIVITY

Explain, with reference to content and provenance, what can be inferred about the success of autarky from Sources 12.21–4.

SOURCE 12.21 Figures from the Four-Year Plan launched in 1936

Commodity	Actual output (in thousands of tons)			
	1936	1938	1942	Four-Year Plan target
Oil	1,790	2,340	6,260	13,830
Aluminium	98	166	260	273
Buna rubber	1	5	96	120
Nitrogen	770	914	930	1,040
Explosives	18	45	300	323
Steel	19,216	22,656	20,480	24,000
Iron ore	2,255	3,360	4,137	5,549
Brown coal	161,382	194,985	245,918	240,500
Hard coal	158,400	186,186	166,059	213,000

SOURCE 12.22 Percentage of major foodstuffs produced within Germany

	1927–8	1933–4	1938–9
Grain	79	99	115
Potatoes	96	100	100
Vegetables	84	90	91
Meat	91	98	97
Fats	44	53	57
All food	68	80	83

SOURCE 12.23 A joke circulating in Germany in the late 1930s

A would-be suicide buys a length of rope with which to hang himself but the rope snaps. He jumps into the river, but is kept floating on the surface by the wood in his clothes. Thereupon, he decides to live, only to starve to death after four weeks on normal consumer rations.

SOURCE 12.24 In his book *Account Rendered* (written in 1949), Schacht comments on Goering's approach in 1936

Goering set out with all the folly and incompetence of the amateur to carry out the programme of economic self-sufficiency, or autarky envisaged in the Four-Year Plan. Hitler had given him as chief of the Four-Year Plan operations an order to extend his own influence over economic policy, which he did not find difficult, since he was now of course in a position to place really large contracts ... On December 17th 1936 Goering informed a meeting of big industrialists that it was no longer a question of producing economically but simply producing.

■ **Learning trouble spot**

The Four-Year Plan and the timing of war

Students often put too much stress on 1940 as the final year of the Four-Year Plan preparing Germany for war. In fact, Hitler considered a major war for German control of Europe would be more likely in 1942–3, not 1940. The Four-Year Plan was not based on a plan for a specific war in 1940, but was part of a series of plans aiming at readiness for a major war by the mid 1940s. The first plan had been drawn up in 1933 to tackle unemployment.

What was the impact of Germany's drive for rearmament?

As early as 1933 Hitler put extra resources into industries related to rearmament and this contributed to both economic recovery and balance-of-payments problems. From 1936, with the Four-Year Plan, rearmament became the main focus of the German economy.

Hitler's stress on military requirements was another sign of the gradual radicalisation occurring in the regime. International comparisons (see Source 12.25) illustrate Germany's great stress on rearmament. However, Hitler was unable to subordinate all other areas to the rearmament drive as the tension between 'guns and butter' illustrates (see Learning trouble spot below). Furthermore, as we shall see, the regime faced considerable problems in military supplies when war broke out in 1939.

SOURCE 12.25 Gross National Product and military expenditure in Germany, the USA and Britain, 1929–45

	Germany			USA			Great Britain		
Year	GNP (RMb)	Military expenditure (RMb)	% GNP	GNP ($b)	Military expenditure ($b)	% GNP	National Income* (£b)	Military expenditure (£b)	% NI
1929	89	0.8	1	104	0.7	1	4.2	0.1	2
1932	58	0.8	1	59	0.6	1	–	0.1	–
1934	67	4.1	6	65	0.7	1	3.9	0.1	3
1936	83	10.8	13	83	0.9	1	4.4	0.2	5
1938	105	17.2	17	85	1.0	1	4.8	0.4	8
1940	141	53.0	38	101	2.2	2	6.0	3.2	53
1942	165	91.0	55	159	49.6	31	7.5	4.8	64
1943	184	112.0	61	193	80.4	42	8.0	5.0	63

*Britain's GNP was about £1b above national income, so % of GNP estimates would be lower than national income, e.g. 1938 7%, 1942 57%
Note: 1940–3 figures for Germany include Austria and Sudetenland

Historians talk much about the fats problem in the Nazi economy. This is a reference to the comparative shortage of fats, both for consumption, for example butter, margarine, lard for use in cooking and eating, and for industrial purposes, such as grease for weapons. So fats could be classified as both 'butter' and 'guns'!

■ **Learning trouble spot**

Did the Nazis favour guns or butter?

The phrase 'guns or butter' relates to the tension between putting economic resources into rearmament and supplying consumer goods, especially food fats, to German consumers. No one actually argued for total concentration on one to the abandonment of the other, but there was a debate about priorities. The issue also arouses controversy amongst historians. Originally, it was assumed that Hitler could afford to give priority to guns and neglect butter, since he was the all-powerful ruler of a repressed population. However, as we have seen, many historians now challenge this view of a powerful totalitarian state. Several argue that Hitler was wary of squeezing domestic consumption too far, and that he was concerned to ensure good supplies of butter as well as guns.

The Marxist historian Mason has argued that this need to try to supply both hindered the rearmament programme and made Germany less prepared for war than it would otherwise have been. Different interpretations of economic statistics also lead to divergent opinions on the guns-and-butter issue. Some historians argue that war preparation was a fairly insignificant part of the economy during 1933–9, and that Hitler was only planning for a minor war. Overy has convincingly argued that the key point is to distinguish between the period 1933–6, when public works and a revival of consumer demand were more important in economic recovery, and the period after 1936 when rearmament needs predominated as Hitler geared the whole economy to war.

	Butter (i.e. more stress on consumer goods)	Guns (i.e. more stress on rearmament)
Advocates	Schacht Industrialists, e.g. Krupp* Military*	Goering
Strategy	Develop consumer goods Develop exports Limited rearmament Links with other countries	Major rearmament Autarky, siege economy

*Although industrialists like Krupp were to do very well from Hitler's war-based economy, they initially favoured a more traditional policy. Similarly, most generals advocated caution in foreign policy and over rearmament, and were wary of Hitler's grand aims.

SOURCE 12.26
'Hurrah, the butter is finished!': a cartoon by John Heartfield that appeared in the banned Communist magazine *AIZ* (Workers' Illustrated Paper) in December 1935. It was inspired by a speech by Goering in which he said: 'Would you rather have butter or guns? Shall we bring in lard or iron ore? I tell you, guns make us powerful. Butter only makes us fat'

Hurrah, die Butter ist alle!

Goering in seiner Hamburger Rede: „Erz hat stets ein Reich stark gemacht, Butter und Schmalz haben höchstens ein Volk fett gemacht".

ACTIVITY

1 Explain the point Heartfield is making in Source 12.26.
2 Look at the photograph of Goering below. Do you think his comment would be universally appreciated?

Hermann Goering (1893–1946): economic dictator

Born into a Bavarian gentry family, Goering was decorated for bravery as a fighter pilot in the First World War. In 1922 he joined the Nazi Party, becoming a commander of the SA and was wounded during the 1923 Munich Putsch. Elected to the Reichstag in 1928, he became its presiding officer in 1932. He used his contacts with elite circles to reconcile them to the possibility of a Nazi government. As one of the original three Nazi ministers, he played a crucial role in the Nazi consolidation of power as Minister without Portfolio, Prussian Minister and Interior Minister; he organised the terror that swept Germany in 1933 and the Berlin action in the Night of the Long Knives in 1934.

Goering lived a life of luxury. His first wife, a Swedish aristocrat, died in 1931. In 1935 he married the actress Emmy Sonnemann. Fat, glamorous and charming, he enjoyed his power and wealth, sometimes changing his clothes five times a day. His extravagance and sexual activity were the focus of much humour in the Nazi state.

In 1935 he was made Commander-in-Chief of the new Luftwaffe and in 1936 Commissioner Plenipotentiary for the Four-Year Plan. Although he had no experience or expertise in business, he became the economic dictator of Germany. In November 1937 he became Economics Minister and founded the Reichswerke Hermann Goering (see page 228). In 1939 he was named Hitler's successor, but when his Luftwaffe failed to stop the RAF bombing Germany his influence declined. At the Nuremberg trials in 1945–6 he was found guilty on all charges but killed himself with cyanide the day before his execution. His body was burnt in a Dachau oven.

Was there an economic crisis in Germany in 1939 and did it push Germany into war?

Assessment of the Nazi economy has played a part in debates about the origins of the Second World War. Tim Mason has argued that the German economy was under great strain from the pressures of rearmament. Hitler's expansionist aims meant that the pace of rearmament could not be slowed. According to Mason, the regime felt insufficiently secure to be able to demand the sacrifices necessary from the civilian population, for example in terms of wage reductions, food shortages, and conscription of female workers, to continue rapid rearmament within Germany's existing resources. As it was, there was a danger of major social unrest, led by workers. The only way out was a war of plunder, to gain extra material and human resources.

Mason identified a range of economic problems, and referred to numerous reports on discontent and comments from officials that showed 'a deep and growing anxiety about their own ability to carry out the tasks assigned to them by the rearmament drive'. He also referred to a few concerns expressed by Hitler. For example, Hitler told his generals on 22 August 1939: 'Our economic position, as a result of our restrictions, has become such that we can only hold out a few more years. Goering can confirm that. No other alternative remains open to us, we will have to act . . .' Mason explained the rarity of such comments by stressing the haphazard governing style of the Third Reich, and Hitler's persistent failure to record key discussions on paper. This view has been challenged by Overy (see below).

ACTIVITY

'Although there is evidence that Germany was facing considerable problems as a result of rearmament, they were not sufficient to explain Hitler's decision to go to war in 1939.' Do you agree with this assessment?

■ 12D Mason v Overy

Mason's case rests on the following assessment of Germany's economic problems in 1939	Mason's thesis has come under considerable attack, most notably from Richard Overy
• The excessive pace of rearmament, combined with a massive programme of prestige public building construction, meant the economy was overheating.	• Mason is a Marxist (although an unorthodox one) and this perspective makes him likely to exaggerate the degree of working-class rejection of the government. He has concentrated on 'history from below' with several subjective statements about ordinary people's feelings, whereas the evidence from decision makers does not support the view of concern over a crisis.
• There were growing shortages in 1938–9 of raw materials, food and consumer goods, foreign exchange and skilled labour.	
• These shortages, and the competing demands of different sectors of the armed forces, were slowing the pace of rearmament.	
• There was upward pressure on wages due to labour shortages.	
• Sectors of agriculture were in crisis with structural labour shortages, declining dairy production, and a damaging price freeze.	• The Nazi leadership did not seem aware of a crisis in 1939. Detailed study of economic statistics and the various aspects of rearmament show problems, but hardly a crisis. Production and investment were growing, and the regime was using a variety of controls to direct the economy. State controls, for example of wages and prices, were holding back inflation.
• There was a growing balance-of-payments problem as resources were moved away from export industries, but imports were still growing.	
• There were worries about how to finance the growing public finance deficit.	
• At the 'Hossbach' meeting in November 1937 (see page 379), Hitler referred to mounting inflation, food shortages and lack of foreign exchange.	• There is little evidence of social unrest. According to Overy the decision for war caused, rather than was caused by, a crisis, as the expected local war became a general war, and the regime had to adjust to a long-term war when the economy was not ready.
• Schacht, who was increasingly critical of the priority given to rearmament, had earlier argued that economic problems were leading to war.	
• Economic decisions to tackle these problems were made more difficult due to the government's fear of popular unrest.	
• Elements in the military and economic elite were thinking of replacing Hitler.	• Overy argues that the context of the international situation and Hitler's aims were the crucial factors in the decision for war in September 1939, rather than domestic ones.

FOCUS ROUTE

What light does Germany's wartime economy shed on the success of Hitler's economic policies?

Blitzkrieg 1939–41

While the German economy was being prepared for a major war in the mid 1940s, Hitler was strengthening Germany. Between 1938 and 1939 Germany took over Austria and Czechoslovakia, gaining vital economic resources (see pages 386–92). In September 1939 Hitler invaded Poland. However, he did not expect Britain and France to declare war. By doing so, they turned an anticipated small war into a major one, for which Germany was not fully prepared.

Hitler responded by ordering major economic mobilisation for war, but his hasty change of approach could not remedy major deficiencies of war material during 1939–41. Supply problems became evident by December 1939 and in 1940 Germany was unable to replace planes lost in the Battle of Britain, contributing to Hitler's crucial failure to knock Britain out of the war. Even in 1941 when he invaded the USSR, a third of his troops had inadequate equipment. Indeed, for two years the German economy failed to meet Hitler's military requirements. This was primarily due to the way the economy was 'organised'. Typically, a whole variety of bodies had an economic role, which produced confusion and waste. However, despite this, the Nazis enjoyed great military success in this Blitzkrieg period, partly because they were able to exploit economically the countries they conquered.

The German economy at war 1942–5

It was only when the Nazi armies were stopped at Moscow in December 1941 that the nature of the war began to change. From being a lightning war for plunder, it became a massive economic drain. Goering's vast bureaucratic structure was seen to have failed, and power shifted to a new supremo, Fritz Todt, and after his death in 1942 to Albert Speer. It was not until 1942 that the German economy began to be organised effectively to cope with total war. The approach of Todt and Speer was to relax the constraints and controls previously placed upon industry. A central planning board was established, supported by a series of committees representing every branch of the manufacturers involved. Speer's cadre (body) of 6,000 administrators, drawn from the entrepreneurial and managerial classes, was responsible for a great increase in output, at a time when Germany was enduring a massive Allied bombing campaign targeted at its industry.

Interestingly, this increased war production in Germany during 1942–4 has been used as evidence of the ineffectiveness of Allied bombing. However, Overy has convincingly argued that it can more properly be seen as evidence of the remarkable achievements of Speer, despite serious bombing damage. If it had not been for the Allied bombing, he argues, the German economy might well have outproduced the USSR and UK together, such were the improvements made by Speer. It was not until the military situation deteriorated rapidly in 1945 that the economy proved unable to support the war effort effectively.

TALKING POINT

In the period 1939–41 the economy was not well organised, yet German armies were remarkably successful. From 1942 to 1945 the war economy was far better organised, yet Germany was defeated. How might this be explained?

E How were the major areas of the economy organised during the Third Reich?

Study the information on pages 224–6 and fill in your own copy of the table answering the questions.

	What was the government's role?	How were developments influenced by ideology?	How far was this policy successful?
Agriculture			
Industry			
Transport			
Trade			
Finance			

SOURCE 12.27 Adolf Hitler, October 1933

The future of the nation is solely dependent on the maintenance of the farmer.

Agriculture

The government took some early measures to help peasants, with higher prices and cancellation of some debts. However, it was more concerned with the larger, more efficient estates, whose food production was vital for autarky and the waging of war. It also wanted to avoid excessively high food prices so as to help maintain steady wage rates. Initially, protection and controlled prices helped farmers, but later they served to keep prices below market levels and were increasingly resented. Arable farmers benefited from subsidies, but livestock farmers were hit by shortages and the high cost of fodder, much of it imported.

Farms were increasingly harmed by a flight from the land, and extra labour had to be drafted in. Land values rose, but production failed to meet growing demand. During the war, home production actually fell, but the shortfall was made up from conquered territories.

■ 12E Agriculture under the Nazis

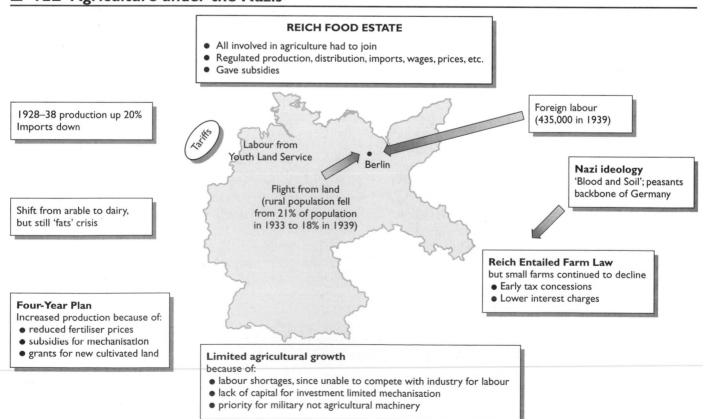

REICH FOOD ESTATE
- All involved in agriculture had to join
- Regulated production, distribution, imports, wages, prices, etc.
- Gave subsidies

1928–38 production up 20%
Imports down

Tariffs

Labour from Youth Land Service

Berlin

Foreign labour (435,000 in 1939)

Nazi ideology 'Blood and Soil'; peasants backbone of Germany

Flight from land (rural population fell from 21% of population in 1933 to 18% in 1939)

Shift from arable to dairy, but still 'fats' crisis

Reich Entailed Farm Law but small farms continued to decline
- Early tax concessions
- Lower interest charges

Four-Year Plan
Increased production because of:
- reduced fertiliser prices
- subsidies for mechanisation
- grants for new cultivated land

Limited agricultural growth because of:
- labour shortages, since unable to compete with industry for labour
- lack of capital for investment limited mechanisation
- priority for military not agricultural machinery

Industry

Industry was brought under state supervision in the interests of national unity. All firms were members of the Reichsgruppe for Industry, part of the Reich Economic Chamber. The state controlled most resources but industry remained largely privately owned. Large firms had to join cartels and they expanded to meet government requirements. However, despite Nazi rhetoric about the *Mittelstand*, over 300,000 small businesses, unable to compete, went bankrupt.

■ 12F Industry under the Nazis

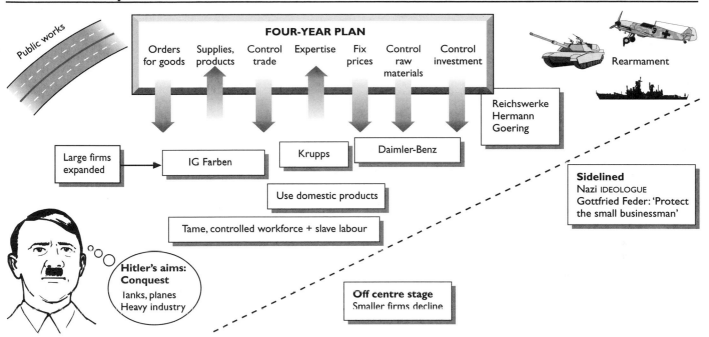

Transport

The greatest Nazi effort went into a massive autobahn creation scheme that symbolised the new Germany. However, typically, there was confusion and overlap in railway administration, particularly during the war.

■ 12G Transport under the Nazis

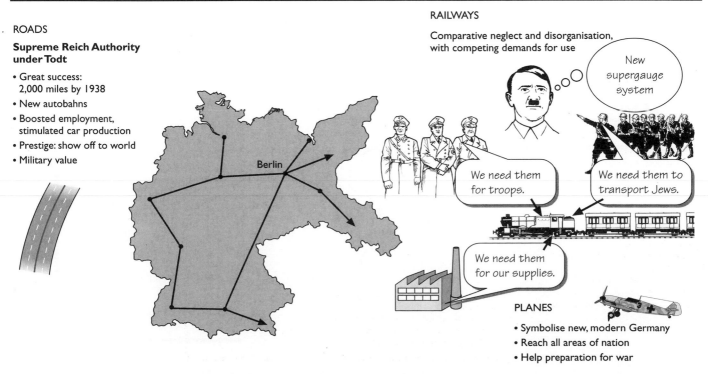

Foreign trade

There was no major growth in foreign trade during the 1930s. Schacht's series of bilateral deals was replaced by more stress on autarky. Less importance was given to external trade; instead, the government looked to domestic production and foreign conquest to obtain the necessary resources.

■ 12H Trade

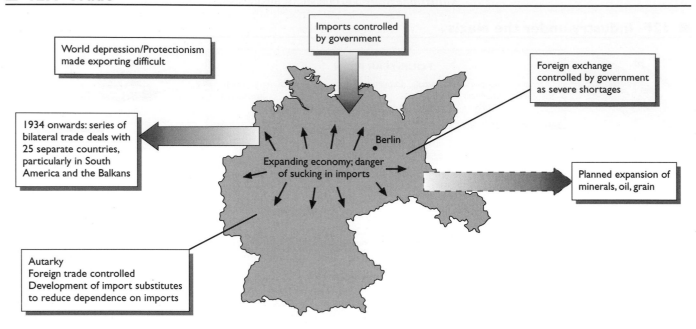

Government finances

The government needed to spend large amounts of money to revive the economy and prepare Germany for war. Finance was raised through increased taxes, and by various forms of credit, such as Mefo bills. General confidence in the expanding economy and strong government allowed the government to attract the loans necessary to maintain a growing budget deficit.

■ 12I Finance

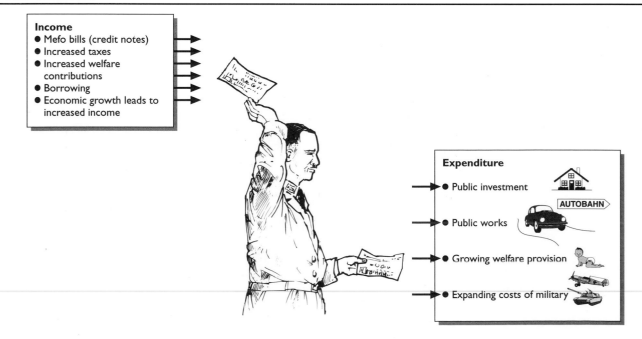

FOCUS ROUTE

There are grounds for expecting three main social groups to make considerable gains from Nazi rule. Hitler owed his appointment to the elite and big business. The Nazis had promised much to the *Mittelstand* and they claimed to be a workers' party.

I   Complete your own copy of the table below for each of the groups discussed in this subsection.

Social group	Benefits of Nazi rule	Drawbacks of Nazi rule
Elite and big business		
Mittelstand		
Workers		

2   Which group to you consider gained most and which the least?
3   Explain the role of DAF.

Nazism and big business

In general, relations between the Nazi government and the economic elite were good. Major landowners benefited from the growing demand for food, although they lost their traditional political influence. Industrialists benefited from the smashing of the independent labour movement and the government's expansion of the economy to help rearmament. Businesses were thus prepared to tolerate a previously unheard of degree of intervention. The private ownership of (non-Jewish) business was not threatened provided firms conformed to requirements; and some firms benefited considerably from the regime.

Relations varied, depending on the firm, the product it produced and whether it was geared to exports. In 1937 the government threatened some industrialists with a charge of sabotage if they opposed self-sufficiency. Relations with coal firms were generally hostile. Others benefited more: for example, Daimler-Benz gained greatly from rearmament; its new aeroplane factories were paid for by the state; and between 1932 and 1941 its production rose over 800 per cent. The chemicals company IG Farben is the classic case of a firm benefiting from the Nazi regime. As Hiden says (*Republican and Fascist Germany*, 1996, p. 129), 'Profits went above all to the industries who were prepared to collaborate actively with the regime.'

Some industrialists were critical of the degree of state control. Fritz Thyssen, the iron baron who had initially welcomed the advent of Hitler, fled to Switzerland in 1939, claiming: 'Soon Germany will not be any different from Bolshevik Russia.' However, Thyssen was very much the exception. Although there were grounds for major industrialists to be critical of the Nazis and for the Nazis to be hostile to industrialists, generally they realised they needed each other. There was no one from business amongst the anti-Hitler plotters of July 1944. Only as Germany was being invaded did major industrialists desert the regime by defying Hitler's demand to sabotage industry. In his book *A Social History of the Third Reich* (1974, p. 238), Grunberger has forcefully described the attitude of German business to the regime as that of a 'conductor of a runaway bus who has no control over the actions of the driver but keeps collecting the passengers' fares right up to the final crash'.

Case study: Reichswerke Hermann Goering (RWHG)

Steel was, for military reasons, a crucial industry for the Nazis and one where it was important that autarkic principles were followed. After the steel industry had shown reluctance to develop plant for processing low-quality domestic ores, the state commissioned the establishment of the national Hermann Goering Steelworks (sited at Salzgitter in Brunswick). The private steel industry was pressurised to invest 130 million marks in the 400-million-mark project, thus in effect financing a rival operation. When industrialists criticised the plans, Goering threatened to charge them with sabotage; they soon backed down.

Once in place, the Hermann Goering Steelworks had priority over established private industry and there was little the latter could do about it. Thus, when the steel industry wanted to expand at the end of 1938, it was told that the national works had pre-empted all available materials and labour. Ironically, the RWHG works director had flagrantly exceeded his brief by smelting high-grade Swedish ores at the plant. By 1939 RWHG was the largest industrial firm in Europe, and was involved in the production of coal, heavy machinery and synthetic fuels as well as steel. Despite the vast expansion of the firm, the German economy failed to meet its steel production target in the Four-Year Plan.

The Hermann Goering Steelworks constituted only one, though undoubtedly the most dramatic, example of the way in which the regime exacted heavy tribute from industrialists to finance schemes harmful – or at least not advantageous – to themselves. Expanding throughout Europe, the company was to become the continent's largest business.

SOURCE 12.28 In *Atlas of Nazi Germany*, 1987, p. 116, M. Freeman sums up the Hermann Goering Steelworks

Like so many other organisations of the Hitler state, it developed a force and momentum of its own, becoming a massive, almost capitalistic, industrial conglomerate through new development, partnership and amalgamation, particularly in occupied territories, and bearing increasingly little relation to the aims of the Four-Year Plan Organisation under which it was born.

Case study: IG Farben

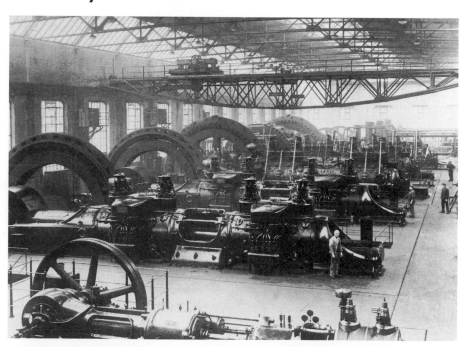

The chemical firm IG Farben, which had been very cautious towards the Nazis in the 1920s, benefited greatly from the regime. In the 1920s it had experimented with the synthetic manufacture of oil and rubber, but Weimar governments had failed to support this costly programme. In 1933, however, it

gained increasing government support. IG Farben lent its expertise to the Office of the Four-Year Plan, and in return received well over 50 per cent of government investment. By 1943 IG Farben owned 334 plants and its officials played a major role directing the Four-Year Plan.

TALKING POINT

Do you think companies should be able to donate money to political parties?

SOURCE 12.29   Political contributions and profits of IG Farben

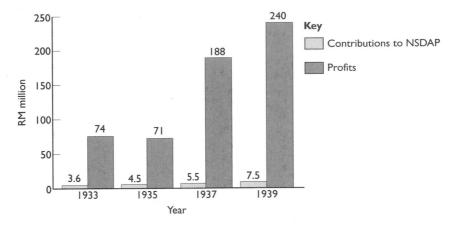

However, even Farben had increasingly to conform to government priorities that it would not have chosen. The company felt compelled to expand into the eastern territories to protect itself; and disruption caused by war was unwelcome. However Farben, which produced gas for extermination camps and had half its labour force in camps, illustrates the extent to which business had become impregnated with Nazi values and had sold its soul for the sake of profits.

ACTIVITY

1   What do the case studies of RWHG and IG Farben show about
   a) the state's relationship with big business
   b) the role of the state in the economy?
2   List the following under the correct heading in your own copy of the table below.
   i) Economic recovery
   ii) Control of wages
   iii) Weak labour force
   iv) Government contracts
   v) State control of imports
   vi) Autarkic policies
   vii) Danger of being taken over if not conforming to government requirements
   viii) Improved profits
   ix) Control of prices
   x) Wartime use of slave labour
   xi) High taxes
   xii) Limits on profits

INDUSTRIALISTS' BALANCE SHEET	
Benefits to industrialists of Nazi rule	**Disadvantages to industrialists of Nazi rule**

TALKING POINT

Does the distribution of the items under the two headings in the Activity necessarily reflect the overall balance of advantages and disadvantages?

Nazism and the *Mittelstand*

Nazi theorists like Gottfried Feder and Otto Wagener advocated policies to protect the interests of the German *Mittelstand*, the small farmer or trader. From 1928 such groups had voted in large numbers for the Nazis. Initially, they appeared to be favoured by the Law to Protect Retail Trade in 1933 which placed special taxes on large stores and banned new department stores. Though many small businesses benefited from the economic recovery, factors such as tight credit, the influence of big business and the slowness of official agencies in paying bills meant that many went bankrupt, and their overall role in the economy declined.

The number of independent artisans (skilled craftsmen) fell from 1,645,000 to 1,500,000 in the period 1936–9 (although the value of their trade nearly doubled). Many went bankrupt due to increased costs and through finding it impossible to compete with larger firms when prices were fixed. The CARTELISATION process encouraged by the government did not help their cause.

SOURCE 12.30 Social Democratic Party in exile (SOPADE) report from central Germany, July 1939, on the reaction of small businessmen

The small businessmen are in a condition of gloom and despondency. These people, to whom the present system to a large extent owes its rise, are the most disappointed of all. The shortages of goods restrict their turnover, but they cannot respond by putting up their prices because the price decrees prevent them from doing so. The artisans complain about raw material shortages . . . and the burden of taxes and other contributions grows. The compulsory maintenance of very detailed accounts, which are frequently checked, has a very demoralising effect. In addition, the indignation of the consumers about goods being unobtainable and contracts not being fulfilled on time often finds expression in a very unpleasant fashion. Thus the mood is often strained.

But if a small artisan has reached the point where his business can no longer provide him with a living, the authorities are quick to close it and pass him on to the employment exchange. The loss of their imaginary independence and the fact that they are compelled to take up a new job to which they are not used, possibly in a strange place, hangs like a threat over the small men and takes away their courage to face life. One can say of many of them that inwardly they have long since turned away from the system and would welcome its fall . . .

Peasants received some protection from creditors, and some gained from the Reich Entailed Farm Law, but they suffered from labour shortages and came to resent government restrictions. Life on farms remained hard, with long hours, low incomes and poor facilities. Despite Nazi rhetoric about the rural population being the backbone of the nation, it fell from 21 to 18 per cent of the total population.

The Reich Entailed Farm Law

The May 1933 Entailed Farm Law was designed to protect traditional small farms (those of 18–30 acres), about 35 per cent of all farms. These family farms could not be sold or mortgaged, and had to be passed on to one person. (They were thus entailed, that is fixed in ownership.) It tied much of the peasantry to the land and discouraged innovations. Such peasants found it hard to get new loans, since they could not use their entailed farms as security. Although the law is a useful illustration of the Nazis' ideological commitment to the small German farmer, in practice it failed to help such farmers prosper.

SOURCE 12.31 Government report from Bavaria on the Reich Entailed Farm Law

Although the Entailed Farm Law was passed for the protection of the peasantry it does not receive wholehearted approval even among farmers. It is naturally welcomed by those peasants whom it saved from foreclosure [losing their farm through debt]. On the other hand, the efficient farmers . . . are unpleasantly surprised when banks etc. no longer grant them credit precisely because they are owners of entailed farms [with fixed ownership].

SOURCE 12.32
A 1935 poster for farmers'
day – Reichsbauerntag

GOSLAR 10. bis 17. November 1935

3.REICHSBAUERNTAG

SOURCE 12.33 Reports for SOPADE in 1937 on farmers' views

The 'production battle' [for autarky] ... has limited even further the right of the farmer to market his products freely. He can see that he is no longer master over his own estate, and that he must more and more follow the commands of the National Food Corporation bureaucracy ...

Greatest dissatisfaction can be found primarily among older farmers ... They remember the great promises with which they were persuaded to vote for Hitler prior to the seizure of power. These promises have been largely unfulfilled ...

[Report from Rhineland–Westphalia] The control over agriculture has been increased tremendously. Officials of the National Food Corporation tell the farmer how much milk his cow has to produce, how many eggs his hen must lay, how many pounds of seed to deliver, how much wool his sheep has to produce, how many acres he should plant of what type of crops ... and how much he should harvest under what weather conditions.

[Report from Bavaria] [One farmer] felt that the regime did bring certain advantages for farmers, especially for those who were heavily in debt and faced imminent forced sale of their property. The Hereditary Farm Law had its advantages as well as disadvantages; the same was true of market regulations ... Many are facing heavier financial pressure than before, while others are better off.

Overall, the *Mittelstand* failed to make the gains it expected from the Nazi regime. In the last resort a nation of peasants and shopkeepers, for all Hitler's 'blood and soil' rhetoric, would not conquer *Lebensraum.*

ACTIVITY

1 What evidence do Sources 12.31 and 12.32 provide of how the regime viewed peasants?
2 Referring to the provenance and content of Sources 12.30, 12.31 and 12.33, assess their value as sources of evidence on the effects of Nazi economic policies on the *Mittelstand.*
3 'For all its rhetoric favouring the petty bourgeoisie, the Nazi regime betrayed its greatest original supporters.' How far would you agree with this statement, in the light of these sources?

The Third Reich and workers

The key to looking at the relationship of workers to the regime is employment. Workers benefited from the increased employment. By 1939 only 35,000 of 25 million male workers were officially unemployed. Indeed, labour shortages meant that there were already 435,000 foreign workers in Germany in 1939. Although wages were officially frozen at 1933 levels, as demand for skilled labour increased, many employers bypassed wage freezes by giving Christmas bonuses and providing insurance schemes. Some employers even provided their workers with free motorcycles as a non-wage perk. Getting round restrictions was an important skill in Nazi Germany, and many industrialists and workers proved remarkably successful at it.

The question of living standards is difficult. It is hard to generalise, given the variety of experience of workers. Workers in some industries such as armaments were far better off, with wages in consumer industries and agriculture lagging a long way behind. When take-home pay did rise, this was often due to overtime rather than higher rates of pay. Although the proportion of national income going to workers declined, at the time this would not have been realised by workers, who had more immediate personal concerns. The rapid improvement in employment and the small but perceptible rise in the living standards of many people meant that many Germans felt they had a better life under the Nazis. (Crucially, comparisons tended to be made with the depressed years immediately preceding Nazi rule rather than the more prosperous mid 1920s.) By 1936 the average wage for a worker was 35 marks a week, ten times more than the dole money which 6 million had been receiving

■ 12J The working class and Nazi organisations

Deutsche Arbeitsfront (DAF): the German Labour Front

DAF was set up on 6 May 1933 after independent trade unions were banned. It took over the unions' assets and workers were now represented in one national body. Membership included employers as well as employees. Headed by Robert Ley, it was the largest organisation in the Third Reich. Membership increased rapidly, since it was hard to avoid joining: from 5 million in 1933 to 22 million in 1939. DAF provided a range of facilities and was intended to restore social peace, win workers over to Nazism and increase production. It was thus a key means for achieving the new *Volksgemeinschaft*.

In November 1933 **Kraft durch Freude (KdF)** or 'Strength through Joy' was created by DAF to improve workers' leisure opportunities, with subsidised activities such as holidays, hikes, sport, theatre and cinema visits. This was described by Ley as 'the quickest means of bringing National Socialism to the workers'. In 1938 over 10 million took KdF holidays, most within Germany. KdF had its own subdivision, **Schönheit der Arbeit (Beauty of Work)** which improved work facilities. Ley argued that it was 'of great political importance that the community spirit associated with physical exercise can make a considerable contribution to the highest principle of National Socialist working life – the unity of the plant in the spirit of the plant community'. He believed this was a major blow against the class system.

In 1938 DAF organised the Volkswagen (people's car) scheme, giving workers an opportunity to subscribe 5 marks a week to a fund eventually allowing them to acquire a car. In practice, the scheme's chief impact was to reduce the danger of inflation by boosting savings and cutting domestic expenditure; no worker actually received a car and in 1939 production was switched to military needs.

From 1936 DAF provided vocational training courses, attended by 2.5 million workers, and the Ordensburgen (Castles of Order) Nazi Party training schools.

Unlike the trade unions it replaced, DAF was not involved in wage bargaining. Ley argued that DAF should have a major influence on social and economic policy, but in practice it was not influential. The possibility of increasing DAF's power was used by the government as a potential threat to business if employers did not conform to government wishes.

DAF is important as a good example of Nazi *Gleichschaltung*, that is Nazi control of all key areas. It illustrates how independent workers' organisations were replaced by Nazi controlled ones. Although primarily a propaganda institution to integrate the working class into the totalitarian state, it did provide benefits for working people. The Nazi state was not purely exploitative of workers, even if its claims about its benefits were greater than the reality. Some historians do argue that DAF was not just a control and propaganda device, but that it did also serve as an agency advocating and providing benefits for workers.

Other bodies affecting workers
Trustees of Labour

Twelve trustees, with officials each in charge of an area, were created by a 1933 law. They were appointed by and directly responsible to the Ministry of Labour. They had the power to set wages, fix holidays, and regulate working conditions. They supervised the operation of Councils of Trust.

Councils of Trust

These councils were created in January 1934 to replace the Weimar system of works councils. Members were nominated by the plant leader, DAF officials, and in a few cases some members were elected by the plant 'retinue' (workers). They discussed plant output, safety, workers' welfare and 'the strengthening of the ties between the members of the plant, and their ties with the plant'. They were subordinate to Trustees of Labour.

Reichsarbeitsdienst (RAD) or Reich Labour Service

RAD developed from a voluntary scheme under the Weimar Republic. A June 1935 law made six months' labour service compulsory for all men aged between 19 and 25. In 1939 it was extended to women. RAD, which was predominantly working class, was 'intended to educate German youth in the spirit of National Socialism, to membership of the national community and to acquire a true conception of work, above all respect for manual labour'. Most members were employed in agriculture or public works. It might mean living in barracks away from home, with low pay.

NSBO (National Socialist Factory Cell Organisation)

Leaders of this Nazi workers' organisation (created in the 1920s) expected to play a major role once Hitler gained power. Instead, many were imprisoned as 'Marxist gangsters'. The organisation declined into insignificance, as DAF 'represented' workers.

Dr Robert Ley (1890–1945): workers' leader

A farmer's son, Ley became a student and fought as a pilot in the First World War. His brain was injured when he was shot down, and he was left with a stutter. He worked as a chemist for IG Farben before being dismissed for drunkenness. He joined the Nazis in 1924 and became *Gauleiter* of Cologne in 1928. He saw Hitler as a Messiah and gained his trust.

As a young Nazi, Ley excelled at rabble-rousing and Jew baiting. In 1930 he was elected to the Reichstag and in 1932 replaced Gregor Strasser as Reich Organisation Leader. He used this position to help organise the Nuremberg party rallies. His main power base, however, was as leader of DAF from 1933. For twelve years this vast organisation was controlled by an incompetent, temperance-preaching alcoholic nicknamed 'Reich Drunkard'. He was unstable, proud of his humble origins and hostile to bourgeois customs. He was pretentious and highly ambitious, but had little talent except for lining his pockets and for a lavish lifestyle.

Ley had grand ambitions to build up DAF as his personal empire, as well as to make it the chief vehicle for creating a new *Volksgemeinschaft*, providing real benefits for German workers. But his personal failings and the hostility of the elite and rival party leaders meant his grand plans failed, and the social radicalism inherent in DAF never developed fully.

In 1945 Ley was captured whilst trying to escape, and hanged himself before he could be tried. The historian Smelser has effectively summarised the significance of Ley: 'He ... embodied the National Socialist Revolution – its apocalyptic [wildly unrestrained] quasi-religious spirit, its social idealism, its racist and IMPERIALIST core, and its flawed and criminal nature ... His restless ambition embodied its dynamism. His venality [willingness to be bribed] its corrupt nature. His failures its administrative inadequacy.' ('Robert Ley: the Brown Collectivist' in *The Nazi Elite. Twenty-two Biographical Sketches* (ed.) R. Smelser and R. Zitelmann, 1993).

in 1932. Average paid holidays rose from three days per year in 1933 to between six and twelve days per year in 1939.

However, Grunberger has argued in his *Social History of the Third Reich* (p. 242) that hourly wages increased by only 1 per cent a year during the period of the Nazi regime. Workers' real incomes were also depressed by the compulsory exaction of membership dues for the German Labour Front, *Winterhilfe* (see page 275) and NSV contributions (see page 297), in addition to insurance and tax deductions. In all, deductions from industrial pay packets in the Third Reich have been estimated at 18 per cent: up from 15 per cent under the Weimar regime.

Generally, workers lost freedom but gained some improved facilities. Thus, they lost any political power, with the suppression of free trade unions and non-Nazi political parties. Even the Nazi factory cell organisation, the NSBO, whose leaders had great hopes of considerable power, was purged of radicals and subordinated to the new DAF. In February 1935 every worker was issued with a workbook, which was needed for employment. In 1938 the government took powers to direct workers wherever they were needed, although these were rarely used. On the other hand, there was some compensation in improved facilities, many of which were provided by DAF. The regime tried to build up the community idea in the workplace. Instead of the works councils created during the Weimar Republic to settle wage disputes, each factory now had Councils of Trust to represent the workers in discussions with the 'plant leaders'. An appeal could be made to the Trustees of Labour who could intervene in disputes but this was unlikely.

SOURCE 12.34 Two contrasting pictures of work breaks before and after 1933, from a Nazi magazine

ACTIVITY

1 According to Source 12.36, what was the purpose of DAF?

2 According to Source 12.37, what benefits did the government claim to have brought to workers?

3 What do Sources 12.34 and 12.38–41 show about the services the Nazis provided for workers?

4 What can be inferred from Source 12.37 about working-class discontent during the Third Reich?

5 What does Source 12.43 suggest about the impact of the Nazi view of the *Volksgemeinschaft*?

6 Select three different types of source and assess their value as evidence of Nazi policy towards ordinary Germans.

SOURCE 12.35 From a speech by Robert Ley on 2 May 1933

Today we are opening the second chapter of the National Socialist revolution. You may say, 'You have absolute power, what more do you want?' True. We have power but we do not yet have the whole nation, we do not have you workers 100 per cent, and it is you whom we want. We will not let you alone until you give us your entire and genuine support. You too shall be freed from the last Marxist manacles, so that you may find your way to your people.

For we know that without the German worker there is no German nation ... Workers, I swear to you we shall not only preserve everything which exists, we shall build up even further the protection of the worker's rights, so that he can enter the new National Socialist State as a completely worthwhile and respected member of the nation.

SOURCE 12.36 Government statement on the role of DAF in November 1933

The German Labour Front is the organisation for all working people without reference to their economic and social position. Within it workers will stand side by side with employers, no longer separated into groups and associations which serve to maintain special economic or social distinctions or interests ...

In accordance with the will of our Führer, Adolf Hitler, the German Labour Front is not the place for deciding the material questions of daily working life ...

The high aim of the Labour Front is to educate all Germans who are at work to support the National Socialist State and to indoctrinate them in the National Socialist mentality.

SOURCE 12.37 Report of a speech by Rudolf Hess at the Reich Chamber of Labour in 1938

The Deputy Führer began by making the point that he was aware that some employees still hold against us that, whereas we are always talking about the increase in production and the growth in the national product, our wages have not been correspondingly increased so that in reality the employees are not sharing the fruits of this increase in production. 'I can only reply to them that the swimming pool in his plant, the canteens, the improvements in working conditions, all the advances in the social field ... all these things are in the final analysis the result of the increase in production from which the individual benefits as part of the community. And the individual could only properly assess the significance for him of the increase in production if its main result, namely, the weapons of our forces, did not exist.

It is therefore of great importance that we should assess the social position of the German worker not on the basis of an increase in wages or no increase in wages, but from a consideration of what position the workers, the employees or the small tradesmen now hold within the national community. And in this case one need only go through Germany with one's eyes open to discover that the ordinary citizen can do things which in other countries are open only to a privileged class but never to the workers.'

SOURCE 12.38 Official figures for participants in Strength through Joy activities in 1938

Cruises	131,623
Hikes	1,937,850
Other holidays	8,259,238
Films	857,402
Exhibitions	1,595,516
Concerts	2,515,598
Operas	6,639,067
Theatre	7,478,633
Variety shows	7,980,973
Popular entertainments	13,660,015
Various sports	22,379,631
Other activities	13,776,791

SOURCE 12.39 DAF estimates of the results of a Beauty of Work campaign for improved working facilities in 1939

Total number of factory inspections	67,000
Improvements to workrooms	26,000
Improvement to factory yards, creation of lawns	17,000
Provision of washing facilities, changing rooms	24,000
Provision of canteens, rest rooms	18,000
Provision of sports facilities	3,000
Total cost	**900m RM**

SOURCE 12.40 SOPADE report on a KdF spa in north Germany

It is of monumental proportions ... It is one of the most effective advertisements for the Third Reich. However, nine-tenths of all German workers will probably see the spa only in pictures.

SOURCE 12.41 Beauty of Work drawing from *Unter dem Sonnenrad* (Under the Swastika), 1938, a Strength through Joy publication

SOURCE 12.42 Cartoon from *Humanité*, a French left-wing paper, in 1934 and captioned: 'What? Bread? Don't you know the National Socialist revolution is over?'

SOURCE 12.43 Bernt Engelmann recalls a conversation on a train in 1936

Two autobahn workers were grumbling about the back breaking work, poor housing and bad food they had to put up with. Then a woman aged about thirty and wearing a Nazi Women's League badge entered the train compartment. The two men continued their conversation. After just a few minutes she gazed sternly at the two workers and remarked, 'Is this whining really necessary? You should be grateful that you have work and thank the Führer for getting rid of unemployment!'

The older of the two said quietly, 'Listen here, young woman, we work outdoors in all kinds of weather, shovelling dirt for 51 pfennigs [1 pfennig would be worth about 2 pence] an hour. Then there are the deductions and the voluntary contribution they take out automatically, and 15 pfennigs a day for a straw mattress in a draughty
wooden barracks, and 35 pfennigs for what they ladle out of a cauldron and call dinner . . . Six months ago we were still getting 66 pfennigs an hour, and now they're pushing us harder and harder.'

. . .The woman . . . soon felt compelled to reply . . . 'You can't expect that the misery brought about by fourteen years of mismanagement will be cured in the twinkling of an eye! But now people have hope. They're off the streets, and Germany is strong and powerful again. We've regained our honour – that's the main thing! In three years Adolf Hitler has accomplished miracles, and from year to year things are getting better. Maybe next year you can take a holiday with your family on Madeira with Strength through Joy. You must have faith in the Führer.'

ACTIVITY

1 Consider the possible effects of Nazi economic policies on various people, by completing your own copy of the following table with policies and effects from the list below. Then discuss your results. (A wide variety of answers could be justified.)

Social group	Positive impact	Harmful impact
Major industrialist		
Small business person		
Peasant farmer		
Industrial worker		

Policies and effects

a) Orders connected with rearmament
b) Public works programmes
c) Controlled food prices
d) Higher wages
e) Government contracts
f) Government regulations
g) Longer working hours
h) No independent trade unions
i) Restrictions on food imports
j) Suspension of agricultural debts
k) Increased cartelisation
l) Reich Entailed Farm Law
m) Law to Protect Retail Trade
n) Growing demand for labour

2 Hold a debate between two small traders, two farmers or two workers; one is fully supportive of what the Nazi government has done for him/her, the other is more critical.

G Was Nazi economic policy ideologically driven?

FOCUS ROUTE

1 What evidence supports the views that Hitler
   a) had a largely instrumental view of economics
   b) put ideology before economic effectiveness?
2 Match up the following points:
   Ideology
   i) Support the *Mittelstand*
   ii) Militarisation, i.e. prepare Germany for war, psychologically, economically and militarily
   iii) Autarky
   iv) Corporativism, to ensure nation/state predominates over private interests
   v) Racism
   Economic policy
   a) Priority given to rearmament
   b) State economic controls, e.g. Reich Food Estate
   c) Reich Entailed Farm Law and Law for Protection of Retail Trade introduced
   d) After 1938 Jewish businesses aryanised and sold off to Germans
   e) Develop own resources and economic substitutes
3 Overy has commented that Hitler wanted an economy that performed rather than one that conformed to ideology. How far do you agree?

SOURCE 12.44 Hitler speaking to building workers, May 1937

A lot is talked about the question of a private enterprise economy or a co-operative economy, a socialised economy or a private property economy. The decisive factor is not the theory but the performance of the economy ... It is in the nation's interests for its economy to be run only by able people and not by civil servants ... I place orders. Who completes them I regard as irrelevant.

SOURCE 12.45 Hitler speaking in 1939, quoted in H. Rauschning, *Hitler Speaks*, 1939, p. 134

The proper limits to private property and private enterprise must be [established by] the state and general public according to their vital needs ... The needs of state, varying according to time and circumstances, are the crucial factor.

Hermann Rauschning
- Joining the Nazis in 1932, he became Hitler's confidant.
- He became President of the Danzig Senate, but became critical of Nazi policy towards Danzig.
- In 1936 he fled to Switzerland and eventually the USA.
- In a series of books, he denounced Nazi brutality. Some historians consider his evidence about Hitler's views to be unreliable, since he exaggerated his contact with Hitler.

When Hitler was appointed Chancellor in 1933 there was no clear Nazi economic programme. During the Weimar Republic, the Nazis had exploited the Depression to gain support and had promised 'bread and work'. Some Nazi leaders, such as the Strasser brothers, and some Nazi programmes, such as the original party platform of 1920, did have some distinct Nazi economic ideas. From 1928 to 1930 the Nazis had targeted the German *Mittelstand*, especially small farmers, crucial in Nazi ideology as the pure 'blood and soil' of the true German *Volk*. The Nazis had promised to protect these potentially weak groups against the threat of a powerful working class and big capitalists.

However, once in power Hitler's priorities were different. As Sources 12.44 and 12.45 show, he held an INSTRUMENTAL view of the economy; it was a means to achieve his ends. In the late 1920s his aim was power, so he had emphasised help for the *Mittelstand* to get their support. However, as the Nazi prospects for gaining power increased, Hitler had reassured the elite that Nazism would not threaten their interests. This trend continued in power. His initial priority was to revive the economy. To achieve this, he realised he needed the support of the business community; this was far more important to him than satisfying the ideological desires of the more radical Nazis. His ultimate aim of conquest similarly demanded the development of heavy industry rather than small-scale farms and workshops. A few minor measures were taken to assist the *Mittelstand*, such as the Reich Entailed Farm Law (see page 230–1) and the Law for the Protection of Retail Trade (see page 230), but these measures were largely ineffective.

Initially, Hitler was even prepared to override his anti-semitism in the interests of economic revival. Thus the Jewish Hertie department stores were given government assistance to prevent redundancies. It was only in 1938, with the economy prospering, that business was ARYANISED and Jews were squeezed out of the economy, being forced to sell their firms to Aryans (see page 342).

Hitler's political aims of military might and autarky had major implications for the economy. However, rearmament was not a distinctly Nazi policy. Most political and economic interests within Germany favoured rearmament as a means to reassert Germany's great power status. For Hitler and many leading Nazis, however, it was a vital part of their vision of an enlarged Germany, eventually dominating the world. Similarly, encouraging home production to reduce dependence on imports attracted wide support, given Germany's experience of economic blockade during the First World War. It was the degree of stress placed on rearmament and autarky that separated the Nazis from other groups.

Although rearmament and autarky were key policy objectives, they were to some extent mutually contradictory. Hitler's rearmament programme required more raw materials than Germany could produce. This problem was overcome by extending German territory through a series of quick wars of plunder; resources thus gained would increase Germany's military might and allow the final achievement of *Lebensraum* (living space) in the east.

The Nazis believed in a strong state where all Germans were committed to national goals, and individual interests were subordinated to this aim. This clearly might imply state control of industry, as did the socialist part of their name. However, one must distinguish between state control and state ownership. There was an increase in regulations issued by the state to control key economic activities, with the creation of bodies such as the Reich Food Estate and Reich Economic Chamber. This partly reflected a corporativist view, that the economy should be regulated in the interests of the whole nation. The German Labour Front (DAF) had the potential to develop into a new form of economic organisation, controlling many aspects of production. Robert Ley's grandiose schemes, however, were not realised (see page 233). Most industry remained in private hands. What mattered for Hitler was that the economy was geared to his aims, not the question of who owned companies. If private industrialists conformed to his requirements, fine. If not then, as with the steel manufacturer Thyssen, the state took them over, through a new company or by nationalising the firm.

Although the role of the state in the economy increased considerably in the Third Reich, justifying the description of it as a 'managed economy', this was more for practical than ideological reasons. Thus, reducing unemployment involved state intervention, as did greater stress on rearmament and autarky. The Four-Year Plan explicitly increased state intervention, and by 1939 a vast array of government controls existed. However, this was still on the basis that private enterprise would be utilised; only where it failed would the state take over. This is well illustrated by the Reichswerke Hermann Goering (see page 228). Overall, it can be argued that the Nazi economy in 1933–6 was dominated by a pragmatic approach, with the needs of recovery predominant. The adoption of the Four-Year Plan in 1936 marked a major turning point, with priority being given to the ideological imperative of rearmament (militarism) and imperialism, accompanied by racism.

H Review: How successful was Nazi economic policy?

In many ways Hitler's economic policy was very successful. He restored full employment to Germany and built up its economic strength which allowed him to dominate Europe by 1941. This success helped make him arguably the most popular ever German leader. However, many historians have debated the extent to which Hitler was responsible for the recovery. It had begun before 1933 and other policies, such as continued development of consumer and export markets rather than rearmament, might have led to a more sustained and faster growth. Hitler's priorities meant the mass of the German people failed to benefit greatly from economic growth.

The most impressive achievement was recovery from the Depression rather than spectacular growth beyond 1920s levels. Autarky was not achieved, and rearmament was wasteful and disorganised until Albert Speer finally rationalised the system. Neither the Weimar Republic nor the Third Reich achieved economic growth rates above the average in inter-war Europe or as great as those before 1914 or after 1950. Nazi economic policy was increasingly geared to the needs of war, and in this Germany ultimately failed.

SOURCE 12.46 R. Overy, *Modern History Review*, 1996, p. 11

Hitler's vision of a powerful militarised economy clearly failed the test of war. Recovery from the Slump had been real enough. But at the point where that recovery might have been used to improve living standards and expand trade ... Hitler chose to divert economic development towards massive militarisation in a short term gamble that he could create a new political and economic order out of the one which had failed in 1929. In 1946 Germany was once again plunged into poverty and economic stagnation – where Hitler found it in 1933.

SOURCE 12.47 R. Overy, *The Nazi Economic Recovery 1932–1938*, 1982, pp. 2–3, 63

It was the exceptional decline of the depression years from 1929 to 1932 which gave the subsequent revival its rosy complexion ... The policies actually pursued in 1933 had much in common with those adopted in other countries, and with the policies of the pre-Hitler governments ...

By any long-term measurement the achievement of the 1930s was not very remarkable. Even by 1937 the economy was only just above the level reached some 25 years before. From 1936 onwards all the indices of growth began to slow down. If the short term recovery had been achieved with remarkable speed, the longer term prospects for growth were more muted. The switch to war preparation did not produce any real crisis in the economy before September 1939, but it did increasingly compromise the achievements already made.

SOURCE 12.48 J. Noakes, G. Pridham, *Nazism 1918–45. A Documentary Reader*, 1984, p. 295

The regime had succeeded in gearing much of Germany's economic activity to rearmament and the country was better prepared for war than it had been in 1914. At the same time it had also managed to sustain tolerable levels of consumption. This was largely because it had been able to mobilise the vast amount of resources in terms of plant, labour and technology which had been idle during the slump. Nevertheless, the goal of achieving a 'defence economy' had not been realised. First, the priority of sustaining politically acceptable levels of consumption had prevented full-scale mobilisation of Germany's resources for war. Secondly, the inadequacies of the German planning apparatus, which in turn reflected the flaws within the political system itself, prevented the adoption of a coherent strategy for rearmament. Moreover, the cracks in an economy which was operating beyond its capacity were beginning to show. Although use of the term 'crisis' to describe the German economy in 1939 may be an overstatement, it was already clear to the regime's leaders that a serious economic crisis was indeed just around the corner. However, the remarkable fact was that the regime had succeeded in imposing a massive rearmament burden on the population without either a wages explosion or serious price inflation and above all without mass opposition. As we have seen, one reason for this was the fact that there had been a distinct improvement in most people's material circumstances since 1933. Two further reasons were the regime's monopoly of the media of information and the system of terror which it imposed on its subjects.

ACTIVITY

1 Overy, Noakes and Pridham assess the Nazi economy in various ways, for example:
   a) by comparison with other countries' performance
   b) by comparison with Germany's economy in other periods
   c) by assessing the impact on various social groups
   d) by looking at the use to which the economy was put
   e) by looking at the political effect of economic policies.
   Draw up a table covering these areas, with one column for positive points and one for negative ones. Use Sources 12.46–8 to complete as much as possible of your table.

2 Explain which historian you consider to be most critical, which least. Why do such varied assessments occur?

A SUMMARY OF GERMANY'S ECONOMIC PROBLEMS, 1919–39

a) **Weimar Germany**
  i) Inflation 1923
  ii) Unemployment 1929–33

b) **Nazi Germany**
  After unemployment was tackled, new problems developed.
  i) Shortage of resources
  ii) Potential inflation*
  iii) Potential budget deficits[†]

Notes
* Inflation never materialised as a major problem, since prices were controlled and workers had no bargaining power.
[†] Budget deficits: the government was able to raise credit to finance budget deficits, since there was general confidence in the country's future.

Under the Third Reich, there was an expanding economy in order to fulfil Hitler's aims of gaining political support and rearmament. This created the problem of a great demand for resources, which could be acquired either internally or externally.

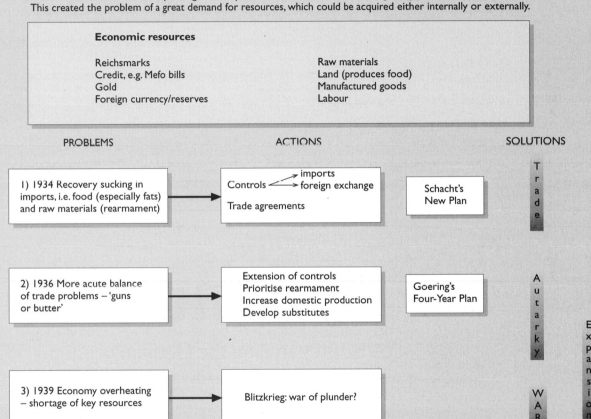

Economic resources

Reichsmarks	Raw materials
Credit, e.g. Mefo bills	Land (produces food)
Gold	Manufactured goods
Foreign currency/reserves	Labour

PROBLEMS — ACTIONS — SOLUTIONS

1) 1934 Recovery sucking in imports, i.e. food (especially fats) and raw materials (rearmament) → Controls → imports / foreign exchange; Trade agreements → Schacht's New Plan

2) 1936 More acute balance of trade problems – 'guns or butter' → Extension of controls; Prioritise rearmament; Increase domestic production; Develop substitutes → Goering's Four-Year Plan

3) 1939 Economy overheating – shortage of key resources → Blitzkrieg: war of plunder?

Trade / Autarky / WAR — Expansion

ACTIVITY

1 Look at Chart 12K. Explain to the rest of the class what the chart shows.
2 Match up question (a–d) and answer (i–iv).
   a) Why did the economy quickly recover?
   b) Why did Hitler's policy not spark off inflation?
   c) Why did industrialists co-operate with Hitler?
   d) Why did Hitler co-operate with industrialists?
   i) Because he needed them to revive the economy.
   ii) Because the government helped private firms and spent government money.
   iii) Because he established government wage and price controls.
   iv) Because they benefited from his policies, especially a tame labour force.
3 Debate: 'Hitler ran an effective economy because he realised that capitalism was the best means of creating wealth, but he knew that the state needed to intervene in the economy to ensure the best distribution of resources in the interests of the nation.' Divide into groups and prepare an argument either in favour or against this proposition.

Exam practice

In your exams you may be asked essay questions on the Nazi economy in two parts:
i) describe and ii) analyse.

Here is such a question on the Nazi economy: Essay: 'What methods did Hitler use to achieve his economic aims? How successful was he?'

You can use your notes for the Focus Route task on page 212 to help with this essay.

KEY POINTS FROM CHAPTER 12: How successful was Nazi economic policy?

1 Hitler had an instrumental view of the economy as a means to prepare Germany for war.
2 The state intervened in the economy to end unemployment.
3 Schacht's New Plan assisted recovery in 1934–6.
4 There was growing tension between the demand for guns or butter.
5 Goering's Four-Year Plan from 1936 stressed autarky and rearmament.
6 The state exercised various controls over the economy but businesses remained largely privately owned.
7 Industrialists benefited more from economic policies than the *Mittelstand* or workers.
8 Although the economy recovered from the Depression, its overall rate of growth was fairly modest.
9 Nazi ideology was subordinated to Hitler's expansionist ambitions.
10 Germany only established a full war economy in 1942.

Germanopoly

A board game on the German economy 1933–45

Although the German economy is a very important topic, you might have found it rather dry. As a reward, you might like to try this board game, which illustrates some of the key events and issues in the economy, as well as the broader nature of the regime. You could use the book as the board, but we suggest you copy and enlarge page 241 to A3 size. See pages 242–3 for instructions on how to play. (Since this game covers many features of the regime, you may wish to play it after you have studied social policies.)

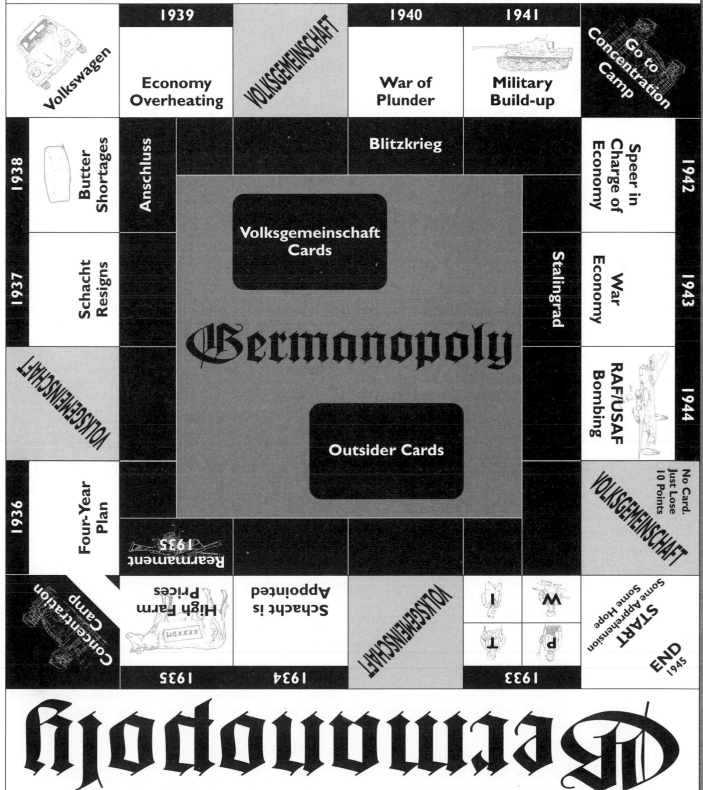

Germanopoly

Volkswagen

| 1939 | | VOLKSGEMEINSCHAFT | 1940 | 1941 | Go to Concentration Camp |

Economy Overheating | **VOLKSGEMEINSCHAFT** | **War of Plunder** | **Military Build-up**

1938 | **Butter Shortages** | **Anschluss** | **Blitzkrieg** | **1942** | **Speer in Charge of Economy**

Volksgemeinschaft Cards

1937 | **Schacht Resigns** | **1943** | **War Economy** | **Stalingrad**

Germanopoly

VOLKSGEMEINSCHAFT | **1944** | **RAF/USAF Bombing**

Outsider Cards

1936 | **Four-Year Plan** | **No Card. Just Lose 10 Points** | **VOLKSGEMEINSCHAFT**

Rearmament 1935 | **START Some Apprehension Some Hope**

Concentration Camp | **High Farm Prices** | **Schacht is Appointed** | **VOLKSGEMEINSCHAFT** | **END 1945**

1935 | **1934** | **1933**

Germanopoly

How to play

1 There are up to four players:

W worker
P peasant
T small trader
I industrialist

2 Each player will need a token or coin that is different from other players' tokens. You will also need dice.

3 You are living in Germany between 1933 and 1945, experiencing the various advantages and disadvantages of so doing.

Each player **starts with 100 points**, and gains or loses points over the twelve years. (Points represent benefits, either material or psychological.)

The winner is the person with the most points in 1945.

When it is your turn, you move round the board a year at a time, landing on every square. (You do not throw the dice to do this as you must not skip a year!) In some years, there is one event that affects all of you; in other years, there are different events for different people.

As you move on to each new year, you gain or lose points depending upon what that year holds for you. In some years, you need to throw a dice to see how you are affected.

In some years there is also reference to important foreign policy events that will affect your life.

4 To start: on every move, you advance one square.

When you land on a *Volksgemeinschaft* space, throw the dice to see whether you are deemed a worthy member of Hitler's new *Volk*. If you throw 3–6, take a *Volksgemeinschaft* card. You are classified as an unwanted outsider if you throw 1 or 2. Take an Outsider card. Some of these cards affect you differently depending upon who you are. If you are not mentioned, then you are not involved.

5 *Volksgemeinschaft* **cards** (even some of these aren't nice!)
There are twelve *Volksgemeinschaft* cards. Make your own cards by copying the following instructions onto separate slips of coloured paper or card.

1 You are chosen for a DAF cruise. W, T, P: gain 20 points; I: gain 5 points.
2 W, T, P: you go to a DAF holiday camp; gain 5 points.
3 W: Beauty of Labour provides a canteen in your factory; gain 5 points.
4 Your wife has her sixth son; gain 10 points.
5 You contribute to *Winterhilfe*; lose 5 points but feel good!
6 You have your monthly *Eintopf* meal; lose 5 points but feel good!
7 W, P, T: your son's turn for RAD comes up; lose 10 points.
8 Your son is pressurised to join the Hitler Youth; lose 5 points.
9 You attend a Nazi rally and get swept away by enthusiasm for Germany's future; gain 5 points.
10 W, P, T: you buy a cheap people's radio receiver; gain 10 points.
11 You stand near Hitler at a rally; gain 20 points.
12 You participate in the 9 November celebrations on the anniversary of the 1923 Munich Putsch; gain 5 points.

6 Outsider cards

There are eight Outsider cards. Make a set using paper or card of a different colour from the *Volksgemeinschaft* cards.

1 You are reported for being friendly to a Jew; lose 10 points.
2 You are discovered to have a Jewish ancestor; lose 10 points.
3 Your son is declared hereditarily mentally ill; lose 20 points.
4 You are accused of being an alcoholic; lose 10 points.
5 I: you are accused of having a Jewish business partner; lose 5 points.
  W, T, P: you are accused of being workshy; lose 10 points.
6 Crucifixes are removed from your church; lose 5 points.
7 You are spotted not giving a Hitler salute and are beaten up by the SA; lose 10 points.
8 Your son is deemed workshy and is sterilised; lose 15 points.

The Board

When you move to a new square with each turn, check the list below to see how the events of the year will affect you.

1933

P: Reich Entailed Farm Law. Throw the dice. Throw 4–6: your debts are reduced, and your fear of having to sell up is ended; gain 15 points. Throw 1–3: you are unable to get a loan to improve your farm; lose 10 points.
T: restrictions under the Law for Protection of Retail Trade are imposed on rival department stores; gain 5 points.
W, I: destruction of trade unions: W: lose 20 points; I: gain 20 points.

Volksgemeinschaft
Throw the dice.

1934

Schacht is appointed Economics Minister.
I: you know he understands business; gain 10 points.
W, T, P: So what? No points.

1935

Farm prices are kept above market levels.
P: gain 10 points.
T, W: lose 10 points.
I: lose 1 point.
Hitler publicly announces rearmament: all gain 5 points.

CORNER SPACE

Pass by a concentration camp. Throw the dice.
Throw 1–2: you hear a friend has been imprisoned and feel ill at ease; lose 10 points.
Throw 3–6: you realise the prisoners are criminals who would otherwise be undermining the government, so you feel secure; gain 5 points.

1936

Four-Year Plan set up. Throw the dice.
I: Throw 5–6: you are a chemicals firm; gain 20 points.
Throw 1–4: you are an exporting firm; lose 10 points.
T: you find it hard to get materials; lose 5 points.
P: your hens fail to produce their egg target; lose 5 points.
W: you find the cost of goods rising; lose 5 points.

Volksgemeinschaft

Throw the dice.

1937

Schacht resigns.

I: lose 10 points.

W, T, P: no points.

1938

There are severe shortages of butter.

T, W: lose 5 points.

I, P: no effect.

Anschluss with Austria.

All: you feel proud of being German; gain 5 points.

I: you see great economic opportunities; gain an extra 5 points.

CORNER SPACE

Volkswagen.

I: you see business possibilities in a new market; gain 10 points.

W, T, P: you join the scheme; lose 5 points.

1939

The economy is in danger of overheating.

W: gain 5 points since there is an increased demand for labour.

T: lose 5 points since you can't obtain raw materials.

I: throw the dice. Throw 1–3: lose 5 points since you too are suffering shortages. Throw 4–6: gain 5 points since the government is controlling supplies and supplying you.

P: you gain from higher food prices; gain 5 points.

Volksgemeinschaft

Throw the dice.

1940

Germany is winning more resources; goods are still available, and taxes remain low; this is a painless war.

All: gain 5 points.

Blitzkrieg is successful: Poland, Holland, France have fallen.

All: gain 5 points.

1941

Military build-up for war against the USSR.

I: great demand for your goods; gain 5 points.

P: you are hit by the high cost of goods; lose 5 points.

W: throw the dice. Throw 1–2: you are called up into the army; lose 10 points. Throw 3–6: you are not conscripted this time; no points.

CORNER SPACE

Concentration camp. Throw the dice.

Throw 1: you are accused of treason; go to camp; lose all your points; game over.

Throw 2: you are informed on, interrogated, but released with a warning; lose 20 points.

Throw 3: you are suspected of treason, but go into hiding; lose 20 points.

Throw 4–6: you are unaffected; no points.

1942

Speer is put in charge of the economy.

I: gain 10 points from better organisation.

W: you have to work longer shifts; lose 10 points.

P: you can't find labour to work on your farm; lose 10 points.

T: you have trouble finding consumer goods; lose 5 points.

1943

War economy. Throw the dice.

I: throw 4–6: you make some goods 'on the side' alongside war material; gain 10 points. Throw 1–3: you suffer from shortages of raw materials; lose 10 points.

T: throw 5–6: you do a 'deal' with corrupt industrialists and gain extra goods to sell; gain 5 points. Throw 1–4: you suffer from shortages of supplies; lose 10 points.

W: throw 5–6: you are a skilled worker exempt from conscription; gain 5 points. Throw 1–4: you are conscripted; lose 10 points.

P: throw 5–6: you are allocated some foreign labourers to work on your farm; gain 10 points. Throw 1–4: you still can't find enough labour; lose 10 points.

News of defeat at Stalingrad.

All: lose 10 points.

1944

RAF bombing. Throw the dice.

W, T: throw 1–2: your house is destroyed in the bombing; lose 30 points. Throw 3–6: your house escapes; no points.

I: throw 1–4: your firm is massively damaged; lose 20 points. Throw 5–6: your firm escapes; no points.

P: you are unaffected; no points.

Volksgemeinschaft

You are all hit by the effects of total war: do not take a card – just lose 10 points.

1945

Throw the dice.

Throw 1–2: you end up in the Soviet occupation zone; lose 30 points.

Throw 3: you end up in the French occupation zone; lose 10 points.

Throw 4–6: you end up in the American or British zones; lose 5 points.

Game review

1 Who 'won'? Was this a likely outcome in Nazi Germany?

2 What points emerged about life in Nazi Germany during 1933–45, and about the different effects of events on different people?

3 What was most effective about the game? What was unrealistic?

4 When you have completed your study of Nazi Germany, you could produce a similar game covering all aspects of life, not just mainly economic issues.

What role did propaganda play in the Third Reich?

CHAPTER OVERVIEW   **SOURCE 13.1**   Nazis assembled in the stadium at Nuremberg to greet Hitler on Party Day, September 1933

Propaganda

Propaganda comes from the word 'propagate', meaning to spread. It means the organised spreading of information to promote the views of a government or movement with the intention of persuading people to think or behave in a certain way.

Mention the Third Reich and one of the first things that people think of is propaganda. For once the stereotype is true. Hitler could not have organised mass meetings such as the one above without a powerful propaganda machine. Propaganda had been vital in winning the Nazis the support that helped them into power. In Hitler and Goebbels, they possessed two great theorists and practitioners of propaganda. Goebbels said in 1934: 'Propaganda was our sharpest weapon in conquering the state, and remains our sharpest weapon in maintaining and building up the state.' The Nazis controlled vast resources with which to

- keep the population contented
- win support for particular policies

and more ambitiously

- indoctrinate the people with their *Weltanschauung* (literally 'view of the world' or philosophy), seeking to turn them into committed members of their *Volksgemeinschaft.*

This chapter will assess the role of Nazi propaganda through the following subsections:

FOCUS ROUTE

Using the information and the primary sources describe
a) the chief aims of Nazi propaganda
b) the means used to achieve those aims.

ACTIVITY

1 Read the views of Goebbels and Hitler on the principles of propaganda (Sources 13.2–5). Draw up a list of bullet points identifying the key points they make about propaganda.

2 How might the following be used to foster support for the values and policies of the regime?

- Sport
- Film
- Painting
- Music
- Architecture

SOURCE 13.2 Goebbels

The finest kind of propaganda does not reveal itself; the best propaganda is that which works invisibly, penetrating into every cell of life in such a way that the public has no idea of the aims of the propagandists.

SOURCE 13.3 Goebbels

It is the task of state propaganda so to simplify complicated ways of thinking that even the smallest man in the street may understand.

SOURCE 13.4 Goebbels

The propagandist must understand how to speak not only to the people in their totality, but also to individual sections of the population: to the worker, the peasant, the middle class. He must understand how to speak to different faiths. The propagandist must always be in a position to speak to people in language that they understand. These capacities are the essential preconditions for success.

SOURCE 13.5 Hitler in *Mein Kampf*

The capacity of the masses for perception is extremely limited and weak. Bearing this in mind, any effective propaganda must be reduced to the minimum of essential concepts, which themselves must be expressed through a few stereotyped formulae ... Only constant repetition can finally bring success in the matter of instilling ideas into the memory of the crowd ... The most important thing ... is to paint your contrasts in black and white.

■ 13A Nazi propaganda: the means

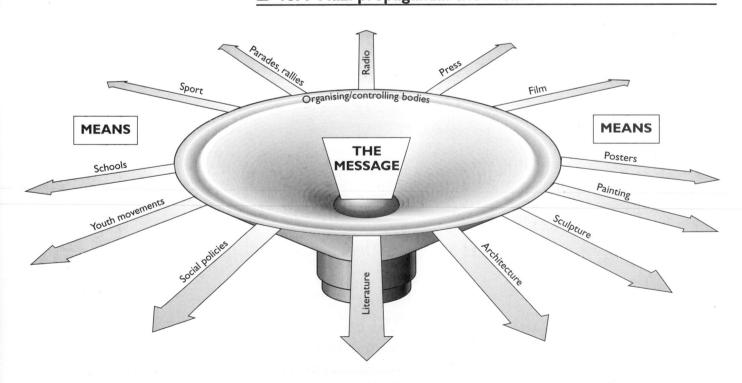

As part of their policy of *Gleichschaltung* (co-ordination), the process by which all German institutions were made to conform to the policies of National Socialism, the Nazi state tried to get control over the media and all cultural activities. Early in 1933 Hitler set up a Propaganda Ministry under Goebbels, who supervised a vast machinery for control of all aspects of the media. The Nazis exercised this through direct ownership of some forms, by controlling those working in the media, by directing the media what to produce, and by prosecuting non-conformist activities. Gaining control of the radio and films was easier than regulating the press where they inherited a diverse system of mainly local papers. The Nazis did not want to deprive the German people of their habitual newspapers, so the state gradually extended its control whilst maintaining many familiar titles.

Most historians argue that totalitarian regimes such as the Third Reich would have been impossible without modern technology. Most crucial was the new medium of radio. Improvements in microphones, loudspeakers and film production also enabled the sounds and images of political leaders to be more readily available to the masses. Hitler in 1932 was the first politician to use aeroplanes ('the Führer over Germany' election campaign) to travel to rallies across Germany. Advances in construction materials and techniques allowed more impressive buildings to be constructed to demonstrate the power of the state.

SOURCE 13.6   The Propaganda Ministry's description of its role, March 1933

The Reich Ministry of Popular Enlightenment and Propaganda is responsible for the entire area of spirituality influencing the nation, through propaganda on behalf of the State, through cultural and economic propaganda and through enlightening the people both at home and abroad; consequently, it is responsible for running all institutions which serve these aims.

■ 13B Goebbels and the propaganda machine

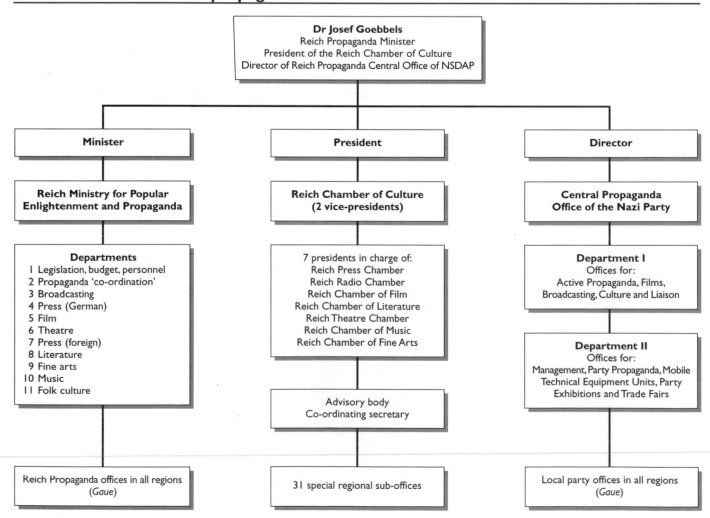

(see Chart 13B).

ACTIVITY

1 Study Chart 13B.
  a) What does this diagram suggest about how the Nazi regime viewed propaganda?
  b) What general impression about the nature of the Third Reich (which you examined in Chapter 11) does this diagram reinforce?
2 Study Sources 13.6 and 13.7.
  a) How important was the Propaganda Ministry according to these sources?
  b) What does this suggest about the aspirations and nature of the new regime?
3 Study Source 13.8. What propaganda vehicles does Hitler mention?
4 What do these sources show about Hitler's and Goebbels' views of:
  a) the relationship between the people and the state
  b) the role of propaganda in that relationship?

SOURCE 13.7   Goebbels at a press conference in March 1933

This Government is, in the truest sense of the word, a People's Government. It arose from the people and will always execute the people's will . . . I see in the newly established Ministry for Popular Enlightenment and Propaganda a link between Government and people, the living contact between the National Government as the expression of the popular will and the people themselves . . . I see the first task of this new ministry as establishing a co-ordination between the Government and the whole people . . . It is not enough for people to be more or less reconciled to our regime, to be persuaded to adopt a neutral attitude towards us. Rather, we want to work on people until they have capitulated to us. The new Ministry has no other aim than to unite the nation behind the ideal of the national revolution.

SOURCE 13.8   Hitler in a speech in March 1933

Simultaneously with this political purification of our public life, the Government of the Reich will undertake a thorough moral purging of the body corporate of the nation. The entire educational system, the theatre, the cinema, the literature, the press and the wireless, all these will be used as means to this end and valued accordingly. They must all serve for the maintenance of the eternal values present in the essential character of our people . . . Art will always remain the expression and the reflection of the longings and realities of an era . . . Blood and race will once more become the source of artistic inspiration.

B How did the Nazis use the media to spread their ideas?

FOCUS ROUTE

1 Explain how the Nazis used the press, radio and film as forms of propaganda.
2 Explain Goebbels' contribution to the creation and development of the Third Reich.

The organisation of propaganda

The regime created a series of new institutions to exercise overall control of propaganda. The most important was the Reichsministerium für Volksaufklärung und Propaganda (RMVP), or Ministry for Popular Enlightenment and Propaganda, created in March 1933, and headed by Goebbels. It developed into a vast organisation (by 1937 employing 14,000 people) and it became a vital prop of Nazi rule.

Alongside this, the government established in September 1933 a Reich Culture Chamber 'to promote German culture for the benefit of the *Volk* and the Reich'. It consisted of seven sub-chambers. Membership was compulsory for people involved in cultural activities. It exercised control of artistic life, as it had to license various activities, such as exhibitions; it could close newspapers and expel members. Typically, alongside these state structures, the party retained its own propaganda organisation, the Central Propaganda Office of the Nazi Party (see Chart 13B).

SOURCE 13.9   Goebbels explained the purpose of the Propaganda Ministry in *Germania*, in November 1933

In future only those who are members of a Chamber are allowed to be productive in our cultural life. Membership is open only to those who fulfil the entrance conditions. In this way all unwanted and damaging elements have been excluded.

Paul Josef Goebbels (1897–1945): master of propaganda

Goebbels was born in the Rhineland to poor Catholic manual worker parents. His leg was crippled by polio and this may have made him feel embittered. He was intelligent and the most educated of the Nazi leaders, in 1921 becoming a doctor of philology (science of language). He tried to make a career as a playwright but failed and became a journalist.

In 1922 he joined the NSDAP. He was attracted to Gregor Strasser's radical wing and in 1925 he demanded that the 'bourgeois Hitler' be expelled from the party. However, in 1926 he sided with Hitler and broke with Strasser. He gradually increased his influence in the party, and became *Gauleiter* of Berlin. In 1927 he founded the paper *Der Angriff*. In 1928 he became party propaganda chief, and in 1930 was elected to the Reichstag. A bitter cynic, Goebbels found his mission in selling Hitler to the German public and organising the Führer cult, with himself as Hitler's faithful servant. He was a powerful public speaker, and this, together with his organisation of propaganda, played a major role in gaining popular support for the Nazis before 1933. In March 1933 he joined the Cabinet as head of the RMVP. He wanted to create 'one single public opinion', and put great stress on the importance of radio and films. An influential adviser to Hitler, he was fiercely anti-semitic and issued the orders for *Kristallnacht*, the night of anti-Jewish attacks in November 1938.

His affair with the Czech (Slav) actress Lida Baarova led to a row with Hitler. Colleagues ridiculed him behind his back and called him the 'little-mouse doctor'. There was bitter rivalry between him, Goering and Ribbentrop. Goebbels' personal life was in stark contrast to his propaganda message. Although he ranted against decadence (decline in moral standards) and stressed the importance of the family, he visited nightclubs and had mistresses. His propaganda for the simple life of the People's Community did not prevent him owning several houses.

After the defeat at Stalingrad in 1943, Goebbels played a major role in organising Germany's domestic war effort. He toured bombed cities, raising morale and organising relief. His February 1943 speech proclaiming 'total war' is one of the most infamous Nazi speeches (see page 418). He was made General Plenipotentiary (with full powers) for the Mobilisation of Total War to organise all manpower for the final effort to stave off the disaster of the Soviet advance. Goebbels helped foil the post-bomb-plot coup in 1944. In May 1945 he persuaded Hitler to make his dramatic suicide. Goebbels poisoned his children, then shot his wife, commenting, 'We shall go down in history as the greatest statesmen of all time, or as the greatest criminals.' He then ended his own life.

TALKING POINT

Do you believe what you read in the press? Would you expect Germans in the 1930s to take a different view from you?

SOURCE 13.10 Speer

Through technical devices like the radio ... 80 million people were deprived of independent thought. It was thereby possible to subject them to the will of one man.

Press

The regime exercised three main methods of control. Firstly, it rigorously controlled all those involved – journalists, editors, publishers – through compulsory membership of co-ordinating bodies. Thus the Reich Press Chamber included the Reich Association of the German Press which kept a register of acceptable editors and journalists. In October 1933 a law made editors responsible for infringements of government directives. Clause 14 obliged editors to exclude from their papers everything 'calculated to weaken the strength of the Reich abroad or at home, the resolution of the community, German defence, culture or the economy, or to injure the religious sensibilities of others, as well as everything offensive to the honour or dignity of a German'. Decrees were issued suspending publications. It was treason to spread false news and rumours.

Secondly, the RMVP controlled the content of the press through the state-controlled Press Agency (Deutsches Nachrichtenbüro) which provided roughly half the content of newspapers. The RMVP held daily press conferences and issued detailed directives on content, including the length and position of articles. Lastly, control was exercised by extending Nazi ownership of the press. The Nazi Party's publishing house, Eher Verlag, gradually took over, directly or indirectly, most of the press. Thus Nazi ownership of the media grew from 3 per cent (of circulation) in 1933 to 69 per cent in 1939 and to 82 per cent in 1944. However, although owned by the Nazis, most of these papers kept their original names.

Radio

Radio had been state regulated since the 1925 creation of the Reich Radio Company (RRG). It was 51 per cent owned by the Ministry of Posts, and 40 per cent by nine regional broadcast companies. These controlled the content. In 1933 they were taken over by Reich governors, and in April 1934 the Nazis established a unified radio system and purged it of hostile elements.

SOURCE 13.11   Goebbels to radio controllers in March 1933

I consider radio to be the most modern and the most crucial instrument that exists for influencing the masses. I also believe . . . that radio will, in the end, replace the press . . . First principle: at all costs avoid being boring. I put that before everything. You must help to bring forth a nationalist art and culture which is truly appropriate to the pace of modern life and to the mood of the times.

SOURCE 13.12   'The Führer Speaks', a painting by Paul Mathias Padua

Radio became one of the most powerful tools for indoctrination. Goebbels described it as the 'spiritual weapon of the totalitarian state'. There was a great extension of the audience, helped by the mass production of the subsidised basic 'people's receiver'. This had just one station and a limited range. In 1935 there were 7 million sets; by 1943 16 million. By 1939 70 per cent of households owned one. There were also communal loudspeakers.

Although mainly used for light entertainment, radio also transmitted Hitler's key speeches. (Hitler speaking alone in a radio studio was found not to be effective; after October 1933 he did not use one; instead he addressed a real audience in outside broadcasts.) In 1933, 50 broadcasts were transmitted, and in 1935 the estimated audience for his speeches reached 56 million (out of a population of just under 70 million). Key speeches were announced by sirens, and work stopped so all could listen to public loudspeakers. Radio wardens organised these important 'national moments', and reported on attendance. Television was in its infancy and was not important, though parts of the 1936 Olympic games were broadcast.

SOURCE 13.13   Newspaper advert, 16 March 1934

Attention! The Führer is speaking on the radio. On Wednesday 21 March, the Führer is speaking on all German stations from 11.00am to 11.50am. The district Party headquarters has ordered that all factory owners, department stores, offices, shops, inns and blocks of flats put up loudspeakers an hour before the broadcast of the Führer's speech so that the whole work force and all national comrades can participate fully in the broadcast.

SOURCE 13.14   Philip Gibbs, a journalist visiting Berlin, in 1934

I remember being in a big Berlin café when Hitler was announced to speak over the microphone. The loudspeaker was turned on. Next to me was a group of German businessmen. They went on talking in low voices. At another table was a woman writing a letter. She went on writing. The only man who stood up was a little fellow with his tie creeping over his collar at the back of his head. No one in the crowded café listened to Adolf Hitler.

SOURCE 13.15
Workers listening to a broadcast by Hitler

ACTIVITY

1   What do Sources 13.11 and 13.13 show about the importance the Nazis placed on the radio as a means of propaganda?
2   Discuss the value of Sources 13.10, 13.12, 13.14 and 13.15 for the historian of propaganda in Nazi Germany.
3   What conclusions can be drawn from Sources 13.10–15 about the effect of the Nazis' use of the radio?

Goebbels and film

■ Goebbels loved films. His favourites, rather surprisingly, were *Gone with the Wind* and *Snow White and the Seven Dwarfs*. He believed in films as entertainment, and that in this way they could be the best form of propaganda. He argued that films could work on the subconscious, reinforcing previously held prejudices in an entertaining way. Films could have several political purposes: getting the public off the streets, and diverting them from their worries and making them feel happy; they also provided opportunities for a subtle political message. Ninety per cent of films produced in the Third Reich had no overt (obvious) propaganda content. Goebbels disagreed with Hitler who wanted more directly political films; Goebbels said let pictures speak for themselves. He rejected blatant political films, and hated the crude *Hitlerjunge Queux* (the story of a Nazi murdered by Communists) and *Hans Westmar*, based on the life of Horst Wessel (see page 283). Goebbels disliked Riefenstahl, and considered her *Triumph of the Will* study of Hitler too serious. He wanted Hitler portrayed via historical parallels, such as Frederick the Great.

■ By 1943 Goebbels realised he could not convince the people that Germany was winning the war, but he could show the country defiantly pulling together. In 1944 in his one final effort, *Kolberg*, a film about heroic national resistance to Napoleon, 100,000 soldiers were diverted from the front to take part. This was considered more important than fighting at the front; it would rally the nation together, and they could achieve victory even in death.

Film

Film was seen more as a means of relaxation than directly for explicit propaganda purposes. The 1930s saw a great growth in productions and audiences. The number of filmgoers quadrupled between 1933 and 1942. The state exercised increasing control both over film companies and the content of films. In 1933 the four major film companies were allowed to remain as private companies, partly as the government did not want to harm export sales. However, the RMVP gradually bought up shares, and increasingly financed films, so indirectly companies became state owned. In 1942 all were nationalised under Ufi (Ufa Film GmbH).

The Reich Film Chamber regulated the content of both German made and imported films. Several American films were banned. Goebbels made himself responsible for approving every film made in Germany. Films were classified – for example, 'politically and artistically valuable', 'culturally valuable', a 'film of the nation', 'valuable for youth' – and given money accordingly.

During the regime over one thousand feature films were produced, with only about one-sixth being overtly propagandist. The most famous producer was Leni Riefenstahl who was commissioned to make detailed recordings of rallies and festivals, to tell people what was happening and to encourage involvement. Her most famous films were *Triumph of the Will* (1935) about the 1934 Nuremberg Rally and *Olympia* (1938) about the 1936 Olympic Games in Berlin. Some films glorified the *Kampfzeit* (struggle for power); others tried to develop racist attitudes. In 1940 three anti-semitic films were released to stress the 'Jewish problem'. The infamous *Der Ewige Jude* (The Eternal Jew) showed Jews as a parasitic race within the nation. It was filmed in Poland, and reworked twelve times, with Hitler insisting it was made more horrific, for example by including rats juxtaposed with Jews. The film included an extract from Hitler's 1939 speech to the Reichstag threatening the destruction of the Jewish race. It turned out to be a disaster at the box office; many fainted. Goebbels arranged an alternative anti-semitic film, *Jud Süss*, in 1940, a story about an eighteenth-century Jew in Württemberg who was hanged, followed by the expulsion of all Jews. This was much more successful as audiences enjoyed it, yet it still tried to justify the removal of Jews. Himmler ordered SS camp guards to see it.

Films were probably more effective in keeping support for the regime than in indoctrinating people with Nazism. The need for entertainment took priority.

SOURCE 13.16
A still from the film *Jud Süss*

ACTIVITY

What can you deduce from Sources 13.16–18 as to the ideas the films were trying to convey?

SOURCE 13.17 Scenes from *Olympia*, Leni Riefenstahl's two-part film of the 1936 Olympic Games. The film was supported by the Olympic Committee and financed by the government. It was dedicated to 'the youth of the world', but was really intended to symbolise the new Germany and its Aryan ideals (linked to classical Greece). The film contributed to the positive way many foreigners viewed Germany in the mid 1930s

TALKING POINT

Do you believe that films can influence people's behaviour?

The more subtle films were more effective, though newsreels were effectively and widely used, being shown before all fictional films. Admission was only allowed at the beginning of the programme. They were used to convey key Nazi ideas, especially that of Hitler as a man apart, who sacrificed himself for the good of the nation.

SOURCE 13.18 Scenes from Leni Riefenstahl's *Triumph des Willens* (Triumph of the Will), 1934: This was filmed at the 1934 Nuremberg rally. Hitler discussed with Riefenstahl many of the details. It was intended to illustrate the *Führerprinzip* (leadership principle), and the fusion of party and nation

SOURCE 13.19 Hitler practising in Heinrich Hoffmann's Munich studio in 1926

SOURCE 13.21 'Hitler': a 1932 poster

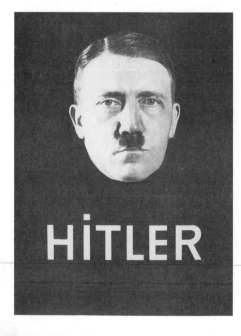

Photographs

Considerable use was also made of photographs. Hitler had an official photographer, Heinrich Hoffmann. Key images were carefully stage managed. Hitler practised expressions and poses before the camera. A series of photographs was widely reproduced, some as postcards, others inside cigarette packets.

SOURCE 13.20 Heinrich Hoffmann took this photo of Hitler posing with children

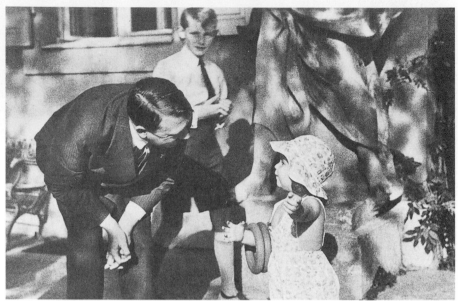

ACTIVITY

1 What supposed qualities in Hitler are portrayed in Source 13.20?
2 Can you see any connection between the images of Hitler in Source 13.19 and Nazi views on the principles of propaganda? (See pages 245–7.)

Posters

The Nazis, like other parties, had made considerable use of political posters during the democratic Weimar Republic. After 1933 they had a monopoly which was used to deepen support.

ACTIVITY

1 Study the Nazi posters in Sources 13.21 and 13.22. Make and complete your own copy of the assessment table below.

Poster	How effective is it in attracting attention? (5 = very, 0 = not at all)	What is the message conveyed?	What techniques are used to convey this message?
Hitler			
A Long live Germany			
B Build youth hostels and homes			
C Young people, serve the Führer			
D All the people say Yes!			
E *The Eternal Jew*			

2 We have asked you to judge the effectiveness of each poster in attracting attention, but not its overall effectiveness. What problems are there in assessing the effectiveness of posters on Germans during the Nazi era?

A 'Long live Germany': a 1930s poster by K. Stanber

B 'Build youth hostels and homes'

C 'Young people, serve the Führer – all ten-year-olds join the Hitler Youth': a 1936 poster

D '*Das ganze Volk sagt ja!*' (All the people people say Yes!) This poster was produced for the plebiscite held after *Anschluss* (union with Austria) in 1938

E A poster for the film *The Eternal Jew*

TALKING POINT

You will probably already be familiar with many of the hundreds of different posters produced by the Nazis. What dangers arise when historians select posters to illustrate their analysis of a period?

FOCUS ROUTE

Explain how the Nazis used the activities described on pages 254–9 as a form of propaganda.

C What other forms of propaganda did the Third Reich use?

Meetings and rallies

One of the most effective ways of gaining support was through mass rallies. Of course, most of the participants were likely to be Nazi supporters, but their commitment would probably be strengthened through attending such rallies. They also attracted bystanders who might be won over. Lastly, films of rallies might make even non-participants feel they wanted to become part of such an impressive movement. Goebbels described how rallies transformed a person 'from a little worm into part of a large dragon'.

The rallies were carefully organised. Speer specialised in choreographing (designing) such displays, using the architecture of light, to create an effect similar to today's pop concerts. The combination of uniforms, disciplined mass movements, stirring music, striking flags and symbols, often at night, created a powerful feeling of wishing to belong. Then came the address by Hitler, the master at manipulating mass emotions.

SOURCE 13.23 A description of the roll-call of political wardens (heads of local party groups) at the 1936 Nuremberg Rally, reported in *Niederelbisches Tageblatt*

As Adolf Hitler is entering the Zeppelin Field, 150 floodlights of the air force blaze up. They are distributed around the entire square, and cut into the night, erecting a canopy of light in the midst of darkness ... The wide field resembles a powerful Gothic cathedral made of light. Bluish-violet shine the floodlights, and between their cones of light hangs the dark cloth of night ... Twenty-five thousand flags, that means 25,000 local, district and factory groups all over the nation who are gathered around this flag. Every one of these flag bearers is ready to give his life in the defence of every one of those pieces of cloth. There is no one among them to whom this flag is not the final command and the highest obligation ... A devotional hour of the Movement is being held here, is protected by a sea of light against the darkness outside.

The men's arms are lifted in salute, which at this moment goes out to the dead of the Movement and of the War. Then the flags [are] raised again.

Dr Ley speaks: 'We believe in a Lord God, who directs us and guides us, and who has sent to us you, my Führer.' These are the final words of the Reich Organisational Leader – they are underlined by the applause that rises from the 150,000 spectators and that lasts for minutes.

SOURCE 13.24 From P. Adam, *The Arts of the Third Reich*, 1992, p. 89

The rallies expressed power, order, solemnity ... Hitler the theatre fanatic, assisted by the mass orator Joseph Goebbels and the architect Albert Speer, who built the settings for these spectacles – created his ultimate stage productions ... The mass became part of the set in a gigantic happening, a communal celebration that eliminated the brain and led to ecstasy ... The timing of pauses and the stage management of climaxes were as important as the music and the banners ...

Few politicians have produced such adoration, even hysteria, as Hitler. He carefully studied his style and the effects he wanted to achieve. People still cannot understand how a man with the face of a psychopath could fascinate so many. Looking at film clips and photographs of him today, we find the image he created ridiculous and incredible. Yet at the time he moved vast crowds of different kinds of people ... His gestures, too, look ridiculous today. They were borrowed from the silent movies. To us, used to the close-up intimacy of television and of microphones, their emotionalism seems ludicrous. The mobilisation of the masses does not happen at mass rallies any more. It takes place in front of the TV screen ...

All the filmed speeches by Hitler, Goebbels and other Party bosses show clearly how these actors drove the people into ecstasy – a mixture of mysticism and eroticism. Screams, shouting, outstretched arms, grimaces – all generated a hysterical response in the audience ...

There was no casual spectator; everyone played a part. Discipline, obedience, self-sacrifice, loyalty, duty – these were the highest virtues. The individual had to enter the mass ...

His message was always of the same triviality. It is hard to understand how he was able to convince anybody with his ideas, and yet his success was overwhelming. Hitler was a man who could deal in simple images. The platitudes [trite remarks] were uttered with a rare energy and charisma [magnetism]. It was not reasoning but passion that made him so convincing.

ACTIVITY

Read Sources 13.23 and 13.24 and study Chart 13C.
1 Explain why the rallies made such an impact on those present.
2 What effect do you think such rallies had on non-participants?

Festivals

Alongside the various party rallies, the calendar in Nazi Germany was peppered with new festivals, celebrating key dates in the Nazi year. On these days rallies were held in numerous cities. On such days streets would be festooned with swastika flags. Failure to support this might be reported to the Gestapo.

■ 13D Annual festivals

30 Jan	'Day of the Seizing of Power'
24 Feb	Anniversary of the Founding of the Party
Mar (1st Sunday)	Day of the Commemoration of Heroes
20 Apr	Hitler's birthday
1 May	National Day of Labour
May (2nd Sunday)	Mother's Day
21 Jun	Summer solstice
July (2nd Sunday)	Day of German Culture
Sept	Reich Party Day rally at Nuremberg
Oct	Thanks for Harvest
9 Nov	Remembrance of Munich Putsch
Dec	Yuletide

SOURCE 13.25 Young German girls dancing around the maypole

SOURCE 13.26 Flags decorating the streets on the Day of German Culture in Munich

Sport

The Nazis also used sport as propaganda. The government co-ordinated the various sporting bodies under a Reichssportsführer. The Hitler Youth and DAF organised sporting activities, especially gymnastics, for the masses. Such activities would help develop the fit bodies that soldiers and child-bearers required. They also encouraged sport as a spectator activity. Mass gym displays were a microcosm (representation in miniature) of a healthy, regimented nation.

The government made great efforts to ensure that the 1936 Olympic Games were a propaganda success. The Olympics had originally been scheduled for Berlin in 1916 and a stadium had been constructed. In 1930 the Olympic Committee rescheduled the games for Berlin in 1936 and construction started on a new stadium in a MODERNIST style. Hitler disliked this 'glass box' and insisted on 'something gigantic'. So the existing steel skeleton was clad in stone. Memorials to dead German soldiers were included, thus linking sport and militarism. Somewhat incongruously (out of place) with the spirit of the Olympics, Hitler was quoted in an Olympic publication as saying: 'He who wishes to live must also fight, and he who will not strive in this world of struggle does not deserve the gift of life.'

SOURCE 13.27 An official German poster advertising the Olympic Games in Berlin, 1936

Hitler saw the Olympics as an opportunity to display the physical superiority of Germans as the master race, their organisational ability and to enhance the country's international status. The new Germany was on show; anti-semitic propaganda was reduced whilst visitors were present. The emphasis was placed on international rather than individual competition. Germany headed the league table, despite the gold medal achievements of the African-American Jesse Owens.

Max Schmeling's success as heavyweight boxing champion (he knocked out the legendary Joe Louis in New York in 1936) was used as a further demonstration of Nazi supremacy. Nazi Germany was unable to match Fascist Italy's footballers' success in winning the World Cup, but gained a boost from the English Football Association's instruction to its players to give the Nazi salute before a 1938 match in Berlin. England, unfortunately for the watching Nazi dignatories, repeated its 1934 success and won 6–3.

SOURCE 13.28 John Heartfield cartoon: 'Goebbels' Puppets', July 1936. The caption reads: 'The object of the exercise – All together, Olympic visitors – quick march!'

SOURCE 13.29
The English soccer team giving the Nazi salute in the Olympic Stadium, Berlin, 1938

ACTIVITY

1 What does Source 13.27 suggest about how the Nazis used sport?
2 Study Source 13.28. How is Heartfield saying that the Nazis are abusing the Olympics?
3 How do you think the Nazi regime exploited Source 13.29? What do you think the reaction to such a photograph might have been in England?

TALKING POINT

Do modern governments seek to use sport for their own purposes?

The autobahns

At first sight, it might appear peculiar to include roads in a section on propaganda, but Hitler's autobahn programme illustrates the propaganda role of many features of the Third Reich. Although autobahns did have an economic and military role, they were a concrete expression of the new united Germany. Imitating Lenin's famous saying about electricity that 'Communism equals Soviet power plus electrification', Nazism has been defined as 'Hitler plus autobahns'.

Motorway construction had begun in the 1920s, but little progress had been made; cars were seen, rightly given the high cost, as an elitist form of transport. At that time the Nazis criticised them as such. Once in power, the Nazi view changed. Hitler in particular was fascinated by cars, and put great stress both on the construction of autobahns and the production of cars.

The actual impact of the autobahn was much exaggerated. Although they did provide much needed employment during the Depression, at the peak of construction in 1936 only 125,000 people were directly employed in construction, with a similar number in supply industries. When the programme was stopped in 1942, 3,870 km had been completed. The much lauded people's car never became available to ordinary people in Germany, where car ownership was far below that of Britain, let alone the USA. (In 1938 1 in 5 Americans owned a car, 1 in 27 Britons and 1 in 44 Germans.) Even the autobahns' military significance has been exaggerated, for although they were used for transporting soldiers and equipment, their surface was too thin for tanks.

**SOURCE
13.30**
Autobahn
poster by
Robert Zinner

The autobahns are of considerable significance architecturally as they illustrate great diversity. Thus modernist functionalism (the idea that function dictates form) co-existed with conservative traditionalism: for example, steel spans on granite plinths and NEO-CLASSICAL bridges alongside Bauhaus-derived service station designs.

The success of the autobahn programme was far more propagandist than real. Photographers, newsreel makers and even painters sold the message of a revived German nation working together for the common good, symbolising the political strength, willpower and achievement of Hitler's Germany. This image was conveyed to an international as well as a domestic audience.

SOURCE 13.31 Speech by Hitler at the start of work on the first autobahn in September 1933

[It is a] milepost for the construction of the community of the German People, a community which, both as a nation and as a state, will deliver to us what we are rightfully entitled to claim and demand in this world ... German workers, on with the job!

ACTIVITY

1 List the various effects of the autobahn programme.
2 What image did the government want the programme to convey?

Social policy as propaganda

Much of Nazi social policy was aimed at transforming people's consciousness far more than their social position. It thus can be seen as an aspect of propaganda policy. A wide variety of schemes was devised to encapsulate the idea of a *Volksgemeinschaft*, working together, protected by the state. Thus DAF, especially through its Beauty of Work and Strength through Joy sections, provided facilities for German workers. The people's car scheme symbolised co-operation to help potentially anyone. The Winter Relief Campaign (*Winterhilfswerk*) and *Eintopf* (one-pot meal) schemes (see page 275) all illustrated the new People's Community in operation.

SOURCE 13.32 A propaganda photo of Goebbels (left) and Hitler (right) with other Nazis having an *Eintopf* meal

FOCUS ROUTE

Explain how the Third Reich used painting, sculpture and architecture for propaganda purposes.

SOURCE 13.33 Dr Kiener in *Art in the Third Reich*, an official art magazine, August 1937

The Führer wants the German artist to leave his solitude and speak to the people. This must start with the choice of the subject. It has to be popular and comprehensible. It has to be heroic in line with the ideals of National Socialism. It has to declare its faith in the ideal of beauty of the NORDIC and racially pure human being.

D How did the Nazis use culture as a form of propaganda?

The Nazis were determined, through the Reich Chamber of Culture, to exercise control of all aspects of culture, to utilise it to reinforce their power and inculcate (instil) their values. After 1933 the arts were compelled to serve as vehicles for the transmission of Nazi ideology, and to help forge the people's collective mind. Other totalitarian regimes also used art in this way, but, partly due to Hitler's own artistic background, it was in Nazi Germany that art was most used.

SOURCE 13.34 Announcement by the Propaganda Ministry of a new theatre law in 1934

The arts are for the National Socialist State a public exercise; they are not only aesthetic but also moral in nature and the public interest demands not only police supervision but also guidance.

Painting

Hitler, the failed artist, took great interest in painting. In 1928 Alfred Rosenberg had set up the Combat League for German Culture, and once in power Hitler began to remove 'degenerate' (corrupt) art and foster 'healthy' Aryan art. Some Nazis, most notably Goebbels and Goering, had a wider artistic taste, but by 1936 Hitler's view was imposed. Modern, reflective, abstract art, which had flourished during the Weimar Republic, was to be replaced by clear visual images that ordinary Germans could understand and be inspired by. Nazi art was to be clear, direct and heroic.

In the new Nazi art people were drawn not as real individuals but just as heroic idealisations: the healthy peasant, the brave warrior, the supreme athlete, the productive woman. Hitler was portrayed as the wise, imperious leader. Landscapes, revealing the source of the *Volk*, and a curiously unmechanised rural life, predominated, followed by nude women, displaying biological purity. Such representation, although superficially realistic compared to the much loathed abstract art, did not in fact reflect the real world so much as Nazi ideology and myth.

Hitler considered true art should be the art of the masses, both in terms of reflecting popular taste and to reach mass audiences. This would make the propaganda role effective. The state was involved both in controlling what was produced and in its dissemination (spread). All working artists had to become members of the Reich Culture Chamber. The state could withdraw licences to teach, to exhibit or even to paint by issuing a *Malverbot* (painting forbidden).

A series of well-attended national and local exhibitions was held. In 1935 there were 120 art exhibitions in factories, and in 1941 over 1,000 art exhibitions overall. Exhibition titles included 'Autobahns of Adolf Hitler through the Eyes of Art', 'To the Glory of Labour', 'German Father: German Land', 'Blood and Soil', 'Race and Nation'. The most famous exhibitions were two contrasting ones in Munich in 1937 (see pages 264–6). The DAF subsection Beauty of Work aimed to build 'bridges between the artist and worker'. It provided paintings in factory canteens. Many paintings were reproduced, full scale or particularly as postcards or stamps, or in journals and newspapers. The magazine *Art in the Third Reich* had a print run of 50,000.

It is hard to judge how widespread real diffusion was, but Lehmann-Haupt has argued (in *Art under a Dictatorship*, 1954, p. 181) that everyone was 'continuously exposed to some form of officially sponsored art activity'. However, from an artistic rather than propagandist viewpoint, German art degenerated under the Third Reich into a mass of stereotyped images, as the best artists left the country, went into 'internal exile' (that is, stayed in Germany but stopped working as artists) or, to maintain their livelihood, joined the Culture Chamber and produced lifeless art to order.

ACTIVITY

Look at the paintings in Source 13.35. All of them were officially approved by the German government. What aspect or aspects of Nazi ideology does each one propound?

SOURCE 13.35

A Portrait of Hitler

B *German Soil*, painting by Werner Peiner

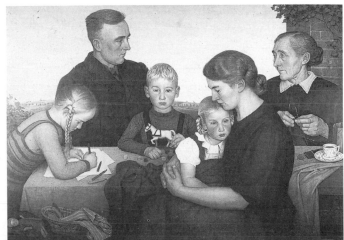

C *Water sport*, by Albert Janesch, 1936

D *Kahlenberg peasant family*, oil painting by Adolf Wissel, 1939

E Mural by Rudolf Hermann Eisenmenger from the office of the Reich Labour Service, Vienna

Sculpture

Sculpture was more immediately accessible to people through the vast statues that adorned many of the new public buildings. In 1934 it was decreed that all new public buildings should be embellished by sculptures conveying the Nazi message. Expressive individualist works now gave way to those portraying stereotyped Nazi virtues, in perfect but lifeless body shapes. The change in style required is well illustrated in two sculptures of 1930 and 1938 by Georg Kolbe (Source 13.37).

A series of massive sculptural muscle men paraded on or in front of Nazi buildings, reflecting the biologically pure, vigorous Aryan race. Hitler's favourite sculptors Arno Breker and Josef Thorak were given vast studios to turn out masses of heroic German figures and dominant animals such as eagles to adorn public buildings. Numerous reproductions made works more accessible.

SOURCE 13.36   Art critic Berthold Hinz, in *Art and Power. Europe under the Dictators 1930–45*, ed. D. Ades, 1995, p. 332

In the career of an artist like Georg Kolbe, who in 1933 was already well established, with a clearly defined personal style, we trace a marked tendency not only to work on a larger scale but to move from the subjective [personal] to the exemplary [illustrative]. Kolbe's earlier work shows mobility and dynamic balance, together with apparently chance irregularities in both anatomy and technique. Later, all this is eliminated: the attitude becomes a pose; stability triumphs; the surface changes from an artistic texture into a smooth, encasing, body-sheathing skin.

ACTIVITY

Explain, with reference to Source 13.37, what Hinz means in Source 13.36 by Kolbe's shift from portraying 'the subjective to the exemplary'.

SOURCE 13.37
Two sculptures by Georg Kolbe: *Night*, 1930 (left) and *The Protectress*, 1938 (right)

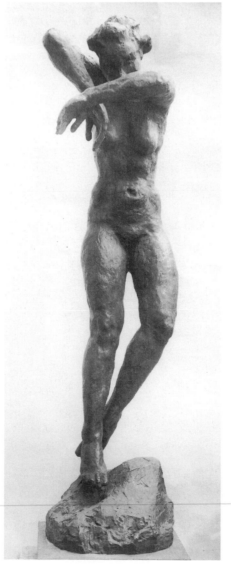

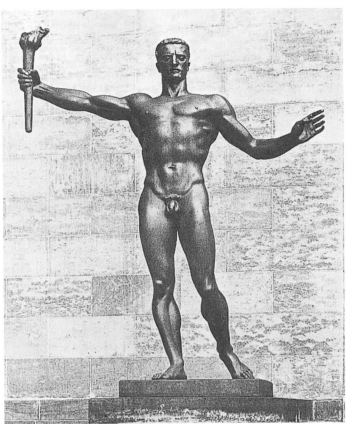

ACTIVITY

Look at the sculptures in Source 13.38. As with painting, sculpture too was meant to foster Nazi values.

a) Match up the following titles to the sculptures:

- *The Party* by Arno Breker
- *Comradeship* by Josef Thorak
- *The Autobahn Worker* by Josef Thorak.

b) Explain what Nazi values they are promoting.

SOURCE 13.39 Catalogue cover for the Exhibition of Great German Art

GROSSE
DEUTSCHE
KUNSTAUSSTELLUNG
1937
IM HAUS DER DEUTSCHEN
KUNST ZU MÜNCHEN

OFFIZIELLER AUSSTELLUNGSKATALOG

SOURCE 13.40 Analysis of the exhibits in the Exhibition of Great German Art

Subject	%
Landscapes	40
Ordinary people	30
Historical figures	11
Animals	10
Still lifes	7
Others	2

SOURCE 13.42 Catalogue cover for the Exhibition of Degenerate Art

ENTARTETE

"KUNST"

Ausstellungsführer

PREIS 30 PFG.

German versus degenerate art

In 1937 two parallel art exhibitions were held in Munich, the city Hitler saw as a 'city of art'. One represented what the regime considered the best of German art, the other what it deemed degenerate art.

Exhibition of Great German Art

The Exhibition of Great German Art was held in a newly built museum, the first of Hitler's prestigious public buildings. The exhibition had two purposes: it was an opportunity for artists to display and sell their work but more importantly for people to see 'true' German art. Over 16,000 works were submitted for inclusion, from which 6,000 were chosen. This art was deemed to represent the healthy instincts of the master race; it was rooted in the people as the true expression of the *Volksgemeinschaft*. More than 600,000 people attended the exhibition.

The exhibition was preceded by a Day of German Art, which became an annual pageant of 2,000 years of German history parading through Munich.

Exhibition of Degenerate Art

A day later, on 19 July, the Exhibition of Degenerate Art was opened by the President of the Art Chamber. The 5,000 exhibits displayed were variously labelled as the work of degenerates, cultural Bolsheviks, fumbling daubers. They reflected the disruption of established values under the Weimar Republic that had brought Germany to its knees. The works displayed distorted forms, unnatural colours and unsettling subjects. They included 1,052 by Emil Nolde, 508 by Max Beckmann, as well as works by Gauguin, Van Gogh, Picasso. Two million attended the exhibition. After later going on a national tour, the works were destroyed, sold abroad or kept by Goering!

SOURCE 13.41 *Gauleiter* and propaganda chiefs viewing the Exhibition of Degenerate Art

SOURCE 13.43 The catalogue for the Exhibition of Degenerate Art classified exhibits in nine groups

1 *general survey of the barbarous methods of representation and the progressive destruction of form and colour*
2 *shameless mockery of religious conceptions*
3 *artistic anarchy*
4 *Marxist propaganda*
5 *whole of reality as a vast brothel*
6–7 *systematic undermining of racial consciousness*
8 *infinite store of Jewish rubbish*
9 *general madness*

ACTIVITY

1 What might one infer about the success of Nazi cultural propaganda from the comparative attendance at the two exhibitions?

2 With reference to the exhibition titles and the classification of exhibits given in Sources 13.40 and 13.43, explain what they show about
   a) the attempt by the regime to use art
   b) the aims of the regime.

3 Look at the paintings and sculptures in Source 13.44. Select those which would have been classified as
   a) true German art
   b) degenerate art
   and explain your choices.

SOURCE 13.44   German art of the 1920s and 1930s

A *Sower*, a painting by Oskar Martin-Amorbach, 1937

B *Man in the dark*, 1934, by Max Beckmann

C *Panama Dancers*, a painting by Ernst Ludwig Kirchner

D *Dancing with fear*, a painting by Paul Klee

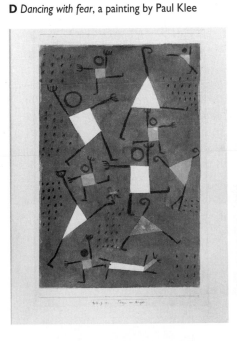

E *Venus and Adonis*, by Arthur Kampf, 1939

F *Readiness* by Arno Breker

SOURCE 13.45 Extracts from Hitler's speech on opening the Exhibition of Great German Art in 1937

It is not Art that creates new ages, but the ordinary life of a People that adopts new forms and accordingly often seeks a new expression ... it is either an outrageous impertinence [offence] or a barely comprehensible stupidity to offer our present age works that might have been made by Stone Age Man some ten or twenty thousand years ago.

Today's New Age is at work on a new type of mankind. Enormous efforts are bearing fruit in countless departments of Life so as to elevate the People, making our men, boys and youths, our girls and women, healthier and thereby stronger and more beautiful. And from this power and this beauty flows a new sense of life, a new joy of Living. Sport, contests and competitions are hardening millions of youthful bodies, displaying them to us more and more in a form and temper that they have neither manifested [shown] nor been thought to possess for perhaps a thousand years. A radiantly beautiful human type is growing up, the most intensive of whose work achievements do honour to that fine old phrase: 'Weeks of sweat, days of joy.'

This human type, which we saw appearing before the whole world last year at the Olympic Games in its proud, radiant physical power and fitness, this human type (O you prehistoric art stutterers!) is the type of the New Age. Meanwhile, what are you manufacturing? Deformed cripples and cretins, women who look merely loathsome, men who resemble beasts rather than humans, children that if encountered in real life would be viewed as a curse of God. And this is what our horrible amateurs nowadays have the effrontery to put forward as the Art of our Age. I would like in the name of the German People simply to forbid such unfortunates, who are clearly having trouble with their vision, from thrusting their erroneous observations on the rest of us as reality, even putting them forward as 'Art'.

I know that when the German People now walks round these galleries it will acknowledge me here too as its spokesman and adviser, because it will observe that for the first time for decades it is not an artistic confidence trick but honest artistic achievement that is being celebrated. And just as it has given approval to our buildings today, so it will be inwardly relieved to express its joyful agreement with the cleansing of our Art. The opening of this Exhibition marks the end of German art craziness and therefore of the destruction of our culture. From now on, let me assure you, all those mutually supportive and thereby still surviving cliques of chatterers, dilettanti [dabblers] and art fakers will be picked out and eliminated. Let those prehistoric cultural cave dwellers and art stutterers creep back into their ancestors' caverns and fill them with their primitive international scrawls.

Today to my great joy I can see that new Masters are arising among our Youth to join the many decent, hitherto terrorised and oppressed, but still at bottom stubbornly German, older artists. A walk through the Exhibition will allow you to find much that once again strikes you as beautiful, and above all decent, and that you will consider good. It may be given to this one house to be able to reveal to the German people many works by great artists in its halls during the centuries to come thereby contributing not only to the fame of this true City of Art but to the honour and standing of the German Nation as a whole. I hereby declare the Munich Great German Art Exhibition of 1937 open!

SOURCE 13.46 Opening speech at the Exhibition of Degenerate Art, by Adolf Ziegler, President of the Reich Chamber of Art

As in all things, the people trust the judgement of one man, our Führer. He knows which way German art must go in order to fulfil its task as a projection of the German character. I open the exhibition of degenerate art.

ACTIVITY

a) How does Hitler describe degenerate art?

b) What role does he see for art? What does he feel should be the relationship between art and the people?

c) How does he describe his New Age?

d) What measures does he suggest against degenerate artists?

e) How does Hitler's campaign against degenerate art fit in with his overall vision for Germany?

Architecture

Of the traditional arts (that is excluding the new medium of film), architecture has been seen as the most important artistic form of propaganda. Hitler described it as 'the word in stone'. Buildings were experienced by large numbers of people, and could be constructed in materials that would last; they could thus represent the Thousand Year Reich the Nazis were building.

Hitler was fascinated by architecture, and spent many hours poring over schemes for new buildings and restructured cities. The pressure for resources for rearmament and consumer goods in the late 1930s did not interfere with Hitler's massive building construction programme. He was planning the rebuilding of Linz as the Russians approached his devastated Berlin in 1945!

Three main styles are evident in the buildings constructed during the Third Reich. By far the most important was that used for the numerous new public buildings. Here Hitler favoured a neo-classical, monumental style: the symmetric simplicity and order of the Greeks but on a vast scale. Such buildings clearly had a propaganda purpose. Hitler once said: 'Our enemies and our followers must realise that these buildings strengthen our authority.' The individual was dwarfed in front of the building, which represented absolute authority. Their actual construction also expressed the collective effort of the people, creating their Thousand Year Reich. For the 1937 Paris International Exhibition of Arts and Technology, Speer designed a massive 65-metre tower, higher than the Soviet one whose plans they had acquired. Built entirely from German materials and weighing more than 100,000 tonnes, this temporary 'pavilion' faced the Soviet pavilion in a clear instance of architectural rivalry.

A permanent 30-square-kilometre complex around Nuremberg was planned and partially built to accommodate vast Nazi rallies, with space for up to half a million participants. Hitler drew up grandiose plans for a complete rebuilding of the centre of Berlin as a new world capital, Germania, as well as plans for over 30 other German cities. His initial interest in workers' housing soon disappeared.

Alongside this monumental style for major public buildings, the regime also fostered a more traditional, vernacular (local) Germanic style for homes and youth hostels. Most Nazis were critical of the experimental modernist style of many of the mass housing schemes built under the Weimar Republic, and instead favoured a more traditional approach, with pitched roofs and shutters. This reflected the backward-looking, pro-countryside aspect of Nazi ideology.

In some areas, however, pragmatism prevailed. There was no destruction of Bauhaus modernist buildings, and some architects still used new techniques, in more purely functional buildings. Thus factories, airports and the autobahns were able to take advantage of new materials and techniques. Alongside public buildings constructed from traditional materials such as marble and granite, the more modernist materials of concrete, steel and glass were employed.

Albert Speer (1905–81): the architect

Albert Speer was born to middle-class parents and like his father became an architect. He joined the Nazi Party in 1931 because 'Hitler promised to free the German nation' from the 'guilt' of the Treaty of Versailles. In 1933 he arranged the Berlin party rally, attracting Hitler's attention. The 1934 Nuremberg Rally was a further triumph when he produced a 'cathedral of light' by borrowing all the Luftwaffe's searchlights. Speer then became Hitler's personal architect and, unusually with Hitler, a personal friendship developed. Speer became Head of the Beauty of Work section of DAF, and as General Architectural Inspector of the Reich (1937) he drew up plans for the rebuilding of German cities.

In February 1942 he replaced Todt as Minister of Armaments and War Production and became arguably the second most important Nazi. He was now virtual dictator of the war economy and dramatically increased armaments production. Towards the end of the war his influence with Hitler waned and in 1945 he opposed Hitler's orders to destroy Germany's industrial base in front of the invading Allies.

He was tried at Nuremberg for the use of slave labour and was the only defendant to plead guilty. Sentenced to twenty years, he was released from Spandau prison in 1966. His book *Inside the Third Reich* (1970), written while in prison, reveals the fragmented nature of the Nazi governing system and, according to recent biographers, is 'economical with the truth' about his role in the Nazi state, particularly on the issue of evicting Jews from Berlin and his knowledge of concentration camps. He always claimed his work was technological and economic not political, and since he was said to charm most of those he met his true role is still being assessed.

SOURCE 13.47   Nazi architecture

A Building new homes for miners, 1937

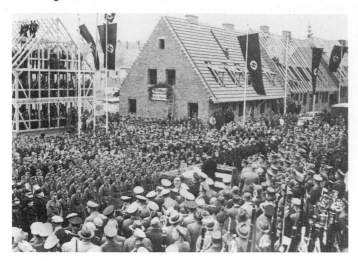

B German pavilion, Paris, 1937

C House of German Art, Munich, designed by P. Troost

D Entrance to the Zeppelin Field, Nuremberg, designed by Albert Speer

E 1923 Munich Putsch memorial, 'Eternal Watch', designed by P. Troost

SOURCE 13.48
Architectural model
for Hitler's Germania:
the planned rebuilding
of Berlin

People's Hall:
300 sq m;
designed to
hold 180,000

It was planned to demolish
25,000 houses to build the
north–south axis; this vast
boulevard was 5 km long
and 120 m wide

Arch: over 120 m high and
170 m wide; it was inscribed
with the names of the dead
of the First World War

Station square: 1 km long and
300 m wide; crowned by the
largest arch in the world

Dome of the People's Hall:
250 m in diameter and 300 m high

ACTIVITY

Look at the photographs of buildings
constructed during the Third Reich
(Source 13.47). How might these be
used as evidence about the Third
Reich? (You could refer to architectural
style, Nazi values and the impression
such buildings were designed to make.)

Hitler's most grandiose architectural project was a plan to rebuild Berlin as the new city of
Germania by 1950. This would give the regime the appearance of power and permanence,
and would last the much proclaimed Thousand Years. Hitler drew up the guidelines, including
the idea of axes, a vast domed hall and a triumphal arch. He put Speer in charge. Parts of
Berlin were demolished, but little was actually built, apart from the new Olympic stadium on
the outskirts. In October 1937 a Law for the Remodelling of German Cities proposed similar
schemes across Germany, to show the regime's economic and technological dominance.

Literature

SOURCE 13.49
Book burning in Berlin,
May 1933: loading
confiscated books onto
a lorry to be taken to
the bonfire

The nature of the new Nazi state was dramatically illustrated in May 1933 with the organised Burning of Books ceremony in Berlin, when 20,000 books, both novels and non-fiction, were burnt, in order to cleanse the new Germany. Similar ceremonies followed in other cities. Several famous novelists, such as Thomas Mann, Stefan Zweig and Erich Maria Remarque, went into exile. Others stayed but were forbidden to publish; some were imprisoned.

Novelists were expected to promote Nazi ideas or at least to be neutral. The regime favoured novels about the comradeship of the trenches, and 'blood and soil' novels, stressing traditional peasant rural values. The best selling book (and arguably the least well written) was Hitler's *Mein Kampf* which sold more than 6 million copies. How widely read it was is another question.

Theatre

As in other areas, the Weimar experimentation in drama was abruptly ended in the Third Reich. Many playwrights and producers emigrated, including Bertolt Brecht and Ernst Toller; others were banned. Officially approved drama concentrated on historical drama, light entertainment and 'blood and soil' stories. Such drama was brought to the people in subsidised theatres run by Strength through Joy, and by touring companies. A new form of drama called *Thingspielen* (literally, assembly) was developed. A combination of pageant and circus, it glorified the pagan past and was performed in specially constructed outdoor amphitheatres.

SOURCE 13.50 'Negroid' jazz was officially condemned, and the saxophone banned, though jazz survived in lightly camouflaged forms. In 1938 the Exhibition of Degenerate Music was held in Düsseldorf. This is the cover of the catalogue

Music

The lively diversity which had characterised German music during the Weimar Republic was quickly ended by the Nazis. The Reich Chamber of Music, headed between 1933 and 1935 by Richard Strauss, controlled production. Experimental music, such as the atonal compositions of Schoenberg, was banned as decadent, and a stream of musicians emigrated. Music, less suitable as a means of explicit propaganda, was still scrutinised to remove Jewish influences. Thus Mendelssohn was removed from the list of permitted composers, and Hitler's favourites, Wagner, Strauss and Bruckner, were given special stress.

Hitler encouraged the annual Bayreuth Festival, which had been started by Richard Wagner and was dedicated to his operas. Folk operas were also fostered. The up-and-coming Carl Orff was commissioned to compose music for the 1936 Olympics, and wrote the popular opera *Carmina Burana*, based on Germanic medieval themes. Stirring music and tales of German heroes were used to stir patriotic emotions, especially in marches and rallies.

TALKING POINT

Can one appreciate the artistic talent of someone who holds unattractive political views?

Reactions to Nazi propaganda

Contemporary views

SOURCE 13.51 Paul Schultze-Naumburg, Nazi IDEOLOGUE, author of *Art and Race*, 1932

A life and death struggle is taking place in art, just as it is in the realm of politics. And the battle for art has to be fought with the same seriousness and determination as the battle for political power.

SOURCE 13.52 From *Swastika Flag*, June 1938

Divine destiny has given the German people everything in the person of one man. Not only does he possess strong and ingenious statesmanship, not only is he ingenious as a soldier, not only is he the first worker and the first economist among his people; but, and this is perhaps his greatest strength, he is an artist. He came from art, he devoted himself to art, especially to the art of architecture, this powerful creator of great buildings, and one who has also become the Reich's builder.

SOURCE 13.53 Hitler's living room in the Führer building, Munich, was designed by Leonard Gall and Gerdy Troost. The painting over the fireplace is *The Four Elements* by Adolf Ziegler

SOURCE 13.54 A 1933 cartoon, 'Memorial to the Sculptors of Germany' by Garvens, from the satirical magazine *Kladderadatsch*

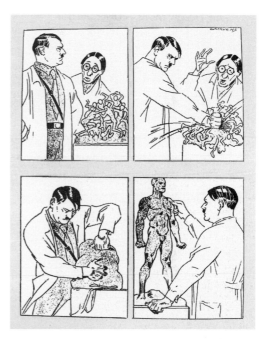

SOURCE 13.55 Stephen Roth cartoon: 'Art has become very spontaneous and sincere under the supervision of National Socialism.' This is a quotation from Goebbels

ACTIVITY

Read Sources 13.56–61.
1 Why did totalitarian regimes become involved in culture?
2 What message did they seek to convey?
3 How did they try and convey it?
4 Explain the contrast between Weimar and Nazi culture.
5 How useful is Source 13.61 in assessing Nazi culture?

Dada (literally, hobby horse in French): an anti-art movement; Marcel Duchamp's work *Bicycle Wheel*, consisting of a wheel mounted on a stool, is a typical work.

Expressionism: a form of art depicting the subjective emotions and personal responses of the artist rather than objective reality. Typical expressionist works show exaggerated, distorted, often violent images.

New Objectivity (*Neue Sachlichkeit*): a style of art reflecting the cynicism in Germany after the First World War of such artists as George Grosz and Otto Dix.

Historians' views on the role of Nazi art

SOURCE 13.56   Frank Whitford in *Art and Power: Images of the 1930s* exhibition catalogue, 1995, p. 4

... culture mattered a great deal to totalitarian governments. They paid it obsessive attention because they believed in its power. They knew that it could, if directed, immeasurably enhance their authority. They also knew that, if uncontrolled, it could undermine and destroy their omnipotence [absolute power]. Culture could only serve their purposes if it were regulated as ruthlessly as every other aspect of life.

SOURCE 13.57   T. Golomstock, *Totalitarian Art*, 1990, p. xii

In a totalitarian system art performs the function of transforming the raw material of dry ideology into the fuel of images and myths intended for general consumption.

SOURCE 13.58   Whitford, p. 5

The central message of totalitarian art and architecture was that individual identity had meaning only in terms of the larger identity of the state, embodied in the charismatic person of the supreme leader. It followed, then, that the most charismatic totalitarian works of art were not buildings, sculpture or paintings at all. They were the meticulously [carefully] planned, brilliantly choreographed [designed] state spectacles – 'mass organisations of atomised [split up] isolated individuals', in Hannah Arendt's phrase – which employed the masses as their medium.

SOURCE 13.59   Adam, p. 21

National Socialist doctrine lived in almost every painting, film, stamp, and public building, in the toys of the children, in people's houses, in tales and costumes, in the layout of villages, in the songs and poems taught in schools, even in household goods. The cultural infiltration of every sphere of life never ceased.

SOURCE 13.60   B. Taylor and W. van der Will, *The Nazification of Art*, 1990

National Socialism was both a regime of brutal destruction and carefully calculated aesthetic presentation. Germany pre-1933 exemplified the culture of modernity within its large cities, particularly Berlin. 'Expressionism', 'Dada', 'New Objectivity', the 'Bauhaus' [see page 92], films such as Metropolis, *the worker culture movement, the struggle for an emancipated femininity, all provided an exciting but to many a disorientating array of cultural creativity. Within the economic and political crisis of the later 1920s and early 1930s a cultural backlash occurred. Hitler's 'revolution' in 1933 put an end to the many faceted pluralism [diversity] of the Weimar Republic. This was now denounced as 'internationalist', 'cosmopolitan' [a mixture of nationalities], 'Jewish', 'negroid' or 'Bolshevist'. The Nazis' dictatorial regime set about replacing it with what it believed to be a truly Aryan, Germanic culture.*

SOURCE 13.61   Helmut Lehmann-Haupt, in *Art Under a Dictatorship*, 1954, p. 287, assessed the degree to which various art forms were dominated by Nazi ideology

Painting 80–90 per cent
Sculpture 70–80 per cent
Architecture 40–60 per cent
Applied arts 20–30 per cent

TALKING POINT

The art historian Peter Adam has said: 'One can only look at the art of the Third Reich through the lens of Auschwitz.' What is his point, and do you agree?

E How successful was Nazi propaganda?

This is a very hard question to answer, for a variety of reasons. Firstly, success is essentially to do with people's attitudes, and what evidence there is of attitudes must be treated with extreme caution. Secondly, people's attitudes would vary depending on numerous factors, such as the period, region, occupation, age, even mood at the time. Thirdly, it is hard to distinguish the extent to which people's favourable or hostile views were a product of Nazi propaganda and how much can be attributed to other influences, such as other Nazi policies, fear of repression, etc. We will thus delay fuller discussion of people's attitudes until we have examined all the Nazis' major policies.

Here we will just note that the effectiveness of Nazi propaganda has, hardly surprisingly, been assessed differently by different historians. Some put great emphasis on Nazi propaganda in explaining the growth of the Nazis under the Weimar Republic. Others say its most important role was in strengthening the regime, for example Herzstein in his book on propaganda entitled *The War that Hitler Won.*

On the other hand, Mason is more sceptical of Nazi propaganda success generally, and especially of its effect upon particular social groups, such as the working class. Welch, in his book on Nazi propaganda (*Third Reich. Politics and Propaganda*, 1993), has argued the need to separate different strands of Nazi propaganda. For example, it had considerable success in strengthening overall support for Hitler and the regime, by reinforcing enthusiasm for a strong leader who was making Germany economically and militarily strong. Its success in gaining support for particular policies, however, was more varied: it probably strengthened latent anti-semitism, without turning Germans into ANNIHILATIONISTS; anti-Church propaganda was probably counter-productive. It probably succeeded in reinforcing militarism, without achieving widespread enthusiasm for the outbreak of war in September 1939. Welch concludes that propaganda was more successful in reinforcing than in countering existing attitudes, and that it was a relative failure in its broader role of indoctrinating Germans with the Nazi *Weltanschauung*, or 'world view'. Geary agrees, arguing (in *Hitler and Nazism*, 1993, p.59) that 'In general Nazi propaganda ... was most successful where it could play upon the traditional prejudices and values of German middle-class society, upon issues such as nationalism, anti-socialism, family values ... But where the regime opposed traditional loyalties, it was far less successful, most obviously in the case of churches, as also amongst the German working class.'

Finally, we must not let ourselves become the victims of Nazi propaganda. The Nazis tried, for example through newsreels of rallies, to convey the impression of a united, disciplined nation, all committed to Nazism. We must examine the reality behind this image, as we now assess the impact of Nazi social policies in the next chapters.

Review: What role did propaganda play in the Third Reich?

ACTIVITY

1 Complete your own copy of the following exercise on a day in the life of a German worker during the Third Reich. It illustrates the various forms of propaganda she/he might encounter. You will need to look back through this chapter to find specific examples for column 2. The first row has been completed for you.

Activity	Specific example of that propaganda form	Possible message from that form	Assessment of impact
Reading a newspaper	*Völkischer Beobachter*	A story about the thriving economy	Confirms belief in Hitler's economic policies
Noticing a poster			
Visiting a library			
Passing a public sculpture			
Visiting a new government building			
Listening to a factory concert			
Listening to the radio			
Visiting the cinema			
Other?			

2 The final column is very hard to complete. Why?

KEY POINTS FROM CHAPTER 13: What role did propaganda play in the Third Reich?

1 Hitler and Goebbels were propaganda experts.

2 From the very beginning, the government created a Ministry of Propaganda headed by Goebbels.

3 Initially the press remained largely in private hands, but it had to contain government news and was censored. Increasingly, it was taken over by the Nazi Party.

4 The government helped the growth of radio and exploited it for propaganda purposes.

5 The Nazis used newsreels as propaganda, but most films were pure entertainment.

6 Festivals, sport and especially stage-managed mass rallies were used to deepen commitment to the regime.

7 Artists had to join a Nazi association in order to continue their work.

8 The Nazis laid down guidelines on approved art; it was to be clear and heroic, illustrating Nazi ideology. 'Degenerate art' was attacked.

9 There was less uniformity in architecture, with modernist and traditional designs. Hitler embarked on a massive building programme. These new official buildings were monumental and classical, designed to impress.

10 Judgements on the effects of propaganda are hard to make, as it did not operate in a vacuum. Although its success has been exaggerated, it probably played a considerable role in increasing the government's popularity.

PART 2.2

How far did Hitler succeed in creating a Volksgemeinschaft?

Hitler did not just want to retain power but to use it to create a *Volksgemeinschaft*, a new German nation. This new society did not entail major changes in the social structure of Germany, but instead required a change in the consciousness of the German people so that they all supported the new German state and acted together. As you will see, this vision also entailed hostility to 'outsiders' who were to be removed from the new community. Chapters 14–18 examine the Nazis' methods of creating a *Volksgemeinschaft* and how effective their methods proved to be, looking particularly at their policies for youth, women and the Christian Churches. Finally, we look at how they treated outsiders, those not part of the national community.

Volksgemeinschaft (literally, people's community) meant a new, unified community based on blood and race, sharing a common world view or philosophy (*Weltanschauung*). Members of this national community, the *Volksgenossen* or 'fellow Germans', would be Aryan, genetically healthy, socially useful and politically committed to the regime. This united national community would make Germany fit for world domination. However, the ideal German was seen as the traditional peasant, working close to the beloved German soil. Therefore this romantic and essentially reactionary vision clashed with the modern industrial economy that Hitler's military ambitions required.

Two Nazi policies, *Eintopf* and *Winterhilfe*, illustrate the working of the *Volksgemeinschaft*. Under *Eintopf*, the state urged national comrades to eat a simple 'one pot' meal on Sunday once a month as 'a sacrifice for the Reich', and to donate the money thus saved to a welfare scheme, such as *Winterhilfe*. This fund was introduced in 1933 to provide extra help to the unemployed during the winter months. Much propaganda was used to encourage donations, and to demonstrate how Germans were uniting to help each other. Collectors went from door to door, sometimes pressurising people to make contributions. Unlike the Volkswagen scheme (see page 232), *Winterhilfe* did actually provide benefits to Germans, with nearly 9 million receiving payments in 1938.

SOURCE 1
Serving stew to Berliners, 1936

14

Did the Nazis succeed in winning the hearts and minds of German youth?

CHAPTER OVERVIEW

SOURCE 14.1 Members of the Hitler Youth (HJ)

You will not be surprised at Hitler's views in Source 14.4 on the ideal characteristics of a Nazi youth, nor that he would have viewed the boys in Source 14.1 with pleasure. Virtually from birth, German children were to be brought up as good National Socialists and loyal followers of Hitler. However, you may be surprised that the young men in Source 14.2 also lived in Nazi Germany. This is an early indication of an important theme in this chapter that, although the Nazis had a great deal of success with youth, they certainly did not have it all their own way. This chapter investigates the extent of the Nazi impact on young people through the following subsections:

A How did the Nazis use youth movements to inculcate their values? (pp. 278–9)

B In what ways was education used as propaganda? (pp. 280–5)

C Alternative youth (pp. 286–7)

D Was Nazi youth policy successful? (pp. 288–9)

E Review: Did the Nazis succeed in winning the hearts and minds of German youth? (pp. 290–1)

SOURCE 14.2 'Swing' youth from a 1941 book on youth criminality

SOURCE 14.3 A Hitler Youth report on a Hamburg music festival in February 1940

The dance music was all English and American. Only swing dancing and jitterbugging took place. At the entrance to the hall stood a notice on which the words 'Swing prohibited' had been altered to 'Swing requested' . . .

The dancers made an appalling sight. None of the couples danced normally; there was only swing of the worst kind. Sometimes two boys danced with one girl; sometimes several couples formed a circle, linking arms and jumping . . . and then, bent double, with the top half of the body hanging loosely down, long hair flopping into the face, they dragged themselves round practically on their knees. When the band played a rumba, the dancers went into a wild ecstasy. They all leaped around and mumbled the chorus in English . . . They all jitterbugged like wild animals. Frequently boys could be observed dancing together, without exception with two cigarettes in the mouth, one in each corner.

SOURCE 14.4 Hitler (quoted in *Hitler Speaks* by Hermann Rauschning, 1939)

In my great educative work I am beginning with the young. We older ones are used up . . . We are rotten to the marrow. But my magnificent youngsters! Are there finer ones in the world? With them I can make a new world.

My teaching is hard. Weakness has to be knocked out of them . . . A violently active, dominating, intrepid, brutal youth – that is what I am after . . . It must be indifferent to pain. There must be no weakness or tenderness in it . . .

I will have no intellectual training. Knowledge is ruin to my young men . . . One thing they must learn, self-command!

FOCUS ROUTE

As you read this chapter, note down points to help you with the following structured essay.

a) What were the aims of Nazi youth and education policy?

b) What methods did they use?

c) How successful were they in achieving their aims?

SEMINAR

You may like to study the topics in Chapters 14 and 15 in a rather different manner.

Divide into groups of three or four. Each group should choose to study either Youth or Women in Nazi Germany.

Read the appropriate chapter, making notes on:

a) Aims of Nazi policy

b) Nazi methods

c) The effectiveness of Nazi policy.

Discuss your findings with your group. Then one group on each topic can report its findings to the rest of the class.

■ 14A Nazi youth policy

SOURCE 14.5 Robert Ley, leader of the Labour Front (DAF)

We start our work when the child is three. As soon as it begins to think, a little flag is put into its hand. Then comes school, the Hitler Youth Movement, the Storm Troop ... We never let a single soul go, and when they have gone through all that, there is the Labour Front, which takes them when they are grown up and never lets hold of them ... whether they like it or not.

The progress of German youth through Nazi organisations

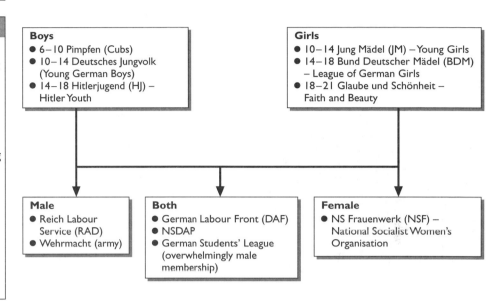

Boys
- 6–10 Pimpfen (Cubs)
- 10–14 Deutsches Jungvolk (Young German Boys)
- 14–18 Hitlerjugend (HJ) – Hitler Youth

Girls
- 10–14 Jung Mädel (JM) – Young Girls
- 14–18 Bund Deutscher Mädel (BDM) – League of German Girls
- 18–21 Glaube und Schönheit – Faith and Beauty

Male
- Reich Labour Service (RAD)
- Wehrmacht (army)

Both
- German Labour Front (DAF)
- NSDAP
- German Students' League (overwhelmingly male membership)

Female
- NS Frauenwerk (NSF) – National Socialist Women's Organisation

Influences on German youth under the Third Reich

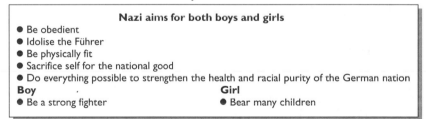

Nazi aims for both boys and girls
- Be obedient
- Idolise the Führer
- Be physically fit
- Sacrifice self for the national good
- Do everything possible to strengthen the health and racial purity of the German nation

Boy
- Be a strong fighter

Girl
- Bear many children

Nazi influences

NSF	NSDAP	Wehrmacht (army)
Faith and Beauty	DAF	RAD
BDM (League of German Girls)	Media	German Students' League
Jung Mädel	Schools	Hitler Youth
		Deutsches Jungvolk
		Pimpfen

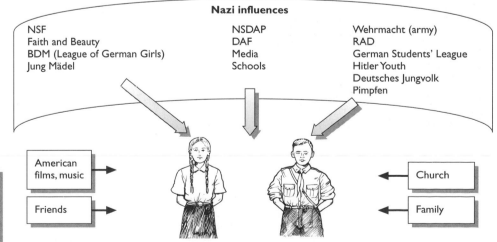

American films, music

Friends

Church

Family

Key

➡ Nazi influences

→ Possibly non-Nazi influences

TALKING POINT

What kinds of sources do you think historians use in investigating the impact of the Nazis on young people?

278

DID THE NAZIS SUCCEED IN WINNING THE HEARTS AND MINDS OF GERMAN YOUTH?

SOURCE 14.6 A young boy in the uniform of the Pimpfen (Cubs)

SOURCE 14.7 A nursery rhyme from the 1930s

What puffs and patters?
What clicks and clatters?
I know, oh what fun!
It's a lovely Gatling-gun.

TALKING POINT

Do you think contemporary youth movements are used for propaganda purposes?

ACTIVITY

What do Sources 14.8–14 show about the following aspects of the youth movements:

a) the aims of the Hitler Youth
b) the methods used
c) the reasons why youngsters joined
d) the reactions of young Germans?

A How did the Nazis use youth movements to inculcate their values?

The Nazis used two major institutions to achieve their aims: the school system and, in particular, youth groups. Furthermore, once youngsters left education and youth movements, they would join other Nazi organisations, such as RAD and DAF (see page 232), to ensure they did not escape control. The Nazis hoped that the influence of such an array of institutions would predominate over the traditional, and possibly hostile, influences of parents and the Church.

Converting any group in society to a way of thinking has long exercised the minds of politicians and advertisers. If you can offer exciting activities, people may become more receptive to your broader aims. Thus the Hitler Youth focused on offering fun and action to the young, but this was backed up by intimidation to persuade members to conform to all the state's demands. The Hitler Youth, created in 1926, expanded rapidly after 1933 with the support of the government. It organised a variety of activities, such as camps, sport and military training.

In 1933 all other youth organisations, except Catholic ones protected by the Concordat (see pages 308–9), were taken over by the Hitler Youth. After 1936 all other youth organisations were banned. Although membership of the Hitler Youth became compulsory, many managed to avoid it, especially after they left school, which many did at fourteen. In addition, some rival groups were set up, which the authorities failed to suppress. As membership became more widespread, the Hitler Youth arguably became less successful, because it included less committed youngsters and because there developed an increasing stress on military preparation at the expense of other, more popular, activities.

SOURCE 14.8 Marianne Gartner joined the Hitler Youth at the age of twelve in 1938. In her memoirs *The Naked Years: Growing up in Nazi Germany* she recalls the change from 'exciting activities' to 'indoctrination' (instruction)

One day, fittingly enough on Hitler's birthday, my age group was called up and I took the oath: 'I promise always to do my duty in the Hitler Youth, in love and loyalty to the Führer.' Service in the Hitler Youth, we were told, was an honourable service to the German people. I was, however, not thinking of the Führer, nor of serving the German people, when I raised my right hand, but of the attractive prospect of participating in games, sports, hiking, singing, camping and other exciting activities away from school and the home. A uniform, a badge, an oath, a salute. There seemed to be nothing to it ... Thus, unquestioningly, I acquired membership, and forthwith attended meetings, joined ball games and competitions, and took part in weekend hikes ...

It was not long, however, before plain-faced leaders taught us marching drill and marching songs. I hated marching ... There were now lectures on National Socialism, stories about modern heroes and about Hitler ... while extracts from Mein Kampf *were used to expound [put forward] the new racial doctrines.*

SOURCE 14.9 A German describes her experience in the BDM, the League of German Girls

I and all the other girls of my age had to attend evening classes twice weekly. We had to be present at every public meeting and at youth rallies and sports. The weekends were crammed full with outings, campaigns and marches, when we carried heavy packs on our backs. It was all fun in a way, and we certainly got plenty of exercise, but it had a bad effect on our school reports. We had no time for homework. The young BDM leaders taught us songs and tried desperately to maintain a certain amount of discipline ... We were marched up and down as though we were soldiers on the barrack square ... We were of course lectured a lot on National Socialist ideology, and most of this went over our heads ... We were told to prepare for motherhood, as the mother of our beloved leader and the National Socialist government was the most important person in the nation. We were Germany's hope and Germany's future.

SOURCE 14.10   Membership of the Hitler Youth

1932	107,956
1934	3,500,000
1936	6,000,000+

SOURCE 14.12   The numbers of participants in nationwide sporting competitions for young people

1935	3.4 million
1939	7 million

SOURCE 14.11   Numbers attending camps

1935–7 973,803 HJ members attended camps
1937   96,699 BDM members attended camps

In 1935, during a rally of 100,000 members of the Hitler Youth and League of German Girls in Nuremberg, 900 fifteen- to eighteen-year-old girls became pregnant.

SOURCE 14.13   A. Klonne, *Youth in the Third Reich*, 1982

What I liked about the Hitler Youth was the comradeship. I was full of enthusiasm ... what boy isn't fired by high ideals such as comradeship, loyalty, honour ... The trips ... off into the countryside ... I was pleased that sport had its place ...

Later when I became a leader the negative aspects became obvious. I found the compulsion and the requirement of absolute obedience unpleasant. It was preferred that people should not have a will of their own ... The Hitler Youth was interfering everywhere in people's private lives ...

In our troop the activities consisted almost entirely of stolid [boring] military drill ... Why didn't we complain to parents and teachers? The explanation I can find is that we were all in the grip of ambition; we wanted to impress our sub-leaders with exemplary [perfect] discipline, with our powers of endurance, with our military bearing.

SOURCE 14.14   Melita Maschmann, former leader in the BDM, *Account Rendered*, 1964

Whenever I probe the reasons which drew me to join the Hitler Youth, I always come up against this one: I wanted to escape from a childish narrow life and I wanted to attach myself to something that was great and fundamental. This longing I shared with countless others of my contemporaries.

Our camp community was a reduced model of that which I imagined our national community to be. It was a completely successful model. Never before or since have I had the experience of such a good community. Among us were peasant girls, students, workers, shop assistants, hairdressers, pupils, clerks, and so forth. The camp was led by an East Prussian farmer's daughter ... She managed us in such a way that, after we had recognised one another's strengths and weaknesses, she led us to accept one another as we were, with everyone endeavouring to be helpful and reliable. The fact that I had experienced this model of a national community intensely created in me an optimism which I held on to stubbornly until 1945. Supported by this experience I believed in the face of all evidence to the contrary that this model could be extended infinitely.

Baldur von Schirach (1907–74): Hitler Youth Leader

Schirach was the son of an aristocratic German father and an American mother. He studied art history and developed anti-semitic and anti-Christian views. In 1925 he joined the Nazi Party. A great admirer of Hitler, he was appointed head of the German Students' League in 1929 and Nazi Youth Leader in 1931. At the age of 26 he became Youth Leader of the German Reich, a post he held until 1940. Photographs of him were much displayed, and he was presented to the Germans as a demigod [outstanding, almost divine person], embodying all that was fine and noble in German youth. Enemies made jokes about his effeminate (feminine-like) behaviour. In 1941 he was made *Gauleiter* of Vienna, where he supervised the deportation of Jews, though at the Nuremberg trials in 1945–6 he denied knowledge of the Holocaust. He was sentenced to twenty years' imprisonment. Released in 1966, he wrote a book which, in an attempt to prevent any rebirth of Nazism, explained the fatal fascination of Hitler.

ACTIVITY

1   Write a report by a sympathetic journalist in 1939 about the role of the Hitler Youth in Nazi Germany.
    or:
2   After reading the rest of this chapter, write a report as a German opponent of Nazism in 1942 for the Social Democratic Party in exile (SOPADE), assessing the extent of the effectiveness of the Hitler Youth.

280

DID THE NAZIS SUCCEED IN WINNING THE HEARTS AND MINDS OF GERMAN YOUTH?

B In what ways was education used as propaganda?

TALKING POINTS

1 What do you consider to be the most important subjects taught in school/college?
2 Do you think a Nazi government would have the same priorities?
3 To gain influence over youth, would it be more important for the Nazis to manipulate the teachers or the curriculum?

FOCUS ROUTE

1 Identify three important changes made by the Nazis to the education system.
2 Explain the purpose of each change.
3 Copy and complete the table below. In column 2, give specific examples of how the Nazis tried in schools to develop the spirit of *Volksgemeinschaft*.

Aims	Methods
Anti-intellectualism	
Anti-semitism	
Indifference to the weak	
Nationalism	
Militarism	
Obedience and discipline	
Hitler worship	

The Nazis' approach stemmed from their anti-intellectual prejudices and the importance they placed on healthy bodies and National Socialist character, as part of a racially pure *Volksgemeinschaft*. Bernhard Rust, the Nazi Education Minister, stated in 'Education and Instruction', the official manual for teachers, 'The chief purpose of the school is to train human beings to realise that the State is more important than the individual, that individuals must be willing and ready to sacrifice themselves for Nation and Führer.'

The Nazi strategy on education had a number of strands. They were initially concerned to exercise greater control over the schools. Regulations were issued, co-ordinating teachers and encouraging local Nazi officials to interfere in schools. Many teachers were already sympathetic to the Nazis and by 1936 over 30 per cent of teachers had voluntarily joined the Nazi Party. To ensure that all teachers followed the party line, they were pressurised into joining the National Socialist Teachers' League (NSLB). By 1937, 97 per cent had done so. Members had to attend one-month training courses, stressing Nazi ideology and physical education. By 1938, two-thirds had attended. Local Nazi officials kept records on individual teachers, and those who were insufficiently committed to National Socialism could be dismissed.

The other major strategy the Nazis used was to change the curriculum. Greater stress was put on physical exercise which, by 1936, took up at least two hours a day. Nazi ideas were incorporated into subjects, particularly biology and history. Religious education was downgraded and eventually replaced. From 1935, all textbooks had to be approved. New textbooks were produced, reflecting Nazi values.

There was also a move away from co-educational schools to ensure the different sexes received their appropriate education. Girls took needlework and music, not Latin; then language and home crafts, to become good homemakers and mothers. Local plebiscites were held, which due to government pressure led to parents voting to end denominational (religious) schools. By 1939 all the denominational schools had been abolished.

As in other areas, the Nazis did not initiate major structural reorganisation. They used the school system they inherited, and supplemented it with new Nazi institutions. Thus some new schools to train the future Nazi elite were created. In 1933 Education Minister Rust announced the formation of National Political Institutes of Education (NAPOLAs) for boys aged 10–18 to develop future leaders. In 1936 the NAPOLAs were taken over by the SS. There were 21 by 1938 and 39 by 1943. They provided a military-style boarding education, with classes called 'platoons' and with the atmosphere of a military camp. There was even more stress on physical education, compulsory manual labour and further political training replaced religious education.

In 1937 Youth Leader Schirach and DAF Leader Ley set up new special leadership schools, the Adolf Hitler Schools. They were intended partly to rival the SS's NAPOLAs and to avoid Rust's interference. Only eleven were created. They were free boarding schools for 12- to 18-year-olds, selected mainly on grounds of physical appearance and leadership potential. In the curriculum physical, political and military training were even more dominant. Many features of normal schools were abandoned. Significantly, Nazi leaders did not send their own children there.

Worthy Nazi youths could finally progress to three new Ordensburgen (Castles of Order), partly modelled on medieval chivalric orders, where their training as future political and military leaders was completed. They were housed in vast castles, which held 1,000 students (called Ordensjunkers) aged 25–30, plus 500 staff. Hitler told Rauschning, 'My Ordensburgen will mould a youth from which the world will shrink in terror.'

There were fewer changes in the nature of higher education. Most significant was a considerable contraction in numbers of students, from 113,000 in 1933 to 57,000 in 1939, reflecting the Nazi downgrading of academic education. Thereafter numbers rose to 82,000 by 1944, mainly due to a large increase in female students (11 per cent of students in 1939 were female; in 1944, 49 per cent) and to a growing realisation of the value of specialist education. In general, the government did not intervene very much in the universities, though some *Gauleiter* interfered more.

As with schools, the government tried to ensure the political compliance of the educators. In April 1933 the Law for the Restoration of the Civil Service led to about 1,200 university teachers (about 10 per cent) being dismissed (33 per cent for racial and 56 per cent for political reasons). There was little reaction to this purge in which the universities lost some of their greatest thinkers. In November 1933 all university teachers were made to sign a 'Declaration in Support of Hitler and the National Socialist State' and join the Nazi Lecturers' Association. New appointees had to attend a six-week ideological and physical training camp.

Students were forced to join the Nazi-controlled German Students' League, but 25 per cent seem to have avoided this. Students had to attend twice weekly sessions for ideological and fitness training. They had to score points in sporting activities (unless given medical exemption). University curricula were modified in some areas, for example, with racial and EUGENIC ideas in medicine, law, politics. However, there was a growing perception that standards were falling. Indeed, by the 1940s some Nazi leaders realised the adverse effects of their education policy and wanted to reverse its anti-intellectual stress, arguing that they needed to train more scientists to compete with other countries in research.

Berlin university students giving the Hitler salute

282

DID THE NAZIS SUCCEED IN WINNING THE HEARTS AND MINDS OF GERMAN YOUTH?

ACTIVITY

Study Sources 14.15–28.

1 What methods did the Nazis use to try to ensure schools were teaching correctly?

2 Schools/colleges today have a statement at the beginning of their prospectuses explaining the main educational aims of the institution. Using the sources, write one for a school in Nazi Germany.

SOURCE 14.15 A National Socialist Teachers' League (NSLB) official explains its role in 1937

Naturally, the German teacher must first be converted to this completely new task of German youth education. The real task of the NSLB is to create the new German educator in the spirit of National Socialism. It is being carried out with the same methods with which the movement has conquered the whole nation: indoctrination and propaganda.

SOURCE 14.16 Dr Schuster, a geography teacher, describes the problems he faced, in an interview in 1938: quoted in E. Amy Buller's *Darkness over Germany*, 1945

There is no longer any intellectual freedom . . . and education is being degraded by political interference . . . Political agents, often ignorant and stupid men . . . interfere with my teaching of geography. Some of them don't seem to realise that any countries exist except Germany . . .

My headmaster, who is new and young and a very keen Nazi – in fact he would not have the post if he were not a Party man – greatly hopes that I will leave. That is obvious, for he will get high praise if he can quickly establish an all-Nazi staff.

SOURCE 14.17 A British teacher in Germany describes the situation in schools in 1933

Nazis were sent to schools, where they walked into the classes and cross-examined the teacher in front of his pupils. If they thought it necessary they arrested him at once.

SOURCE 14.18 From a newspaper report in Oldenburg

The State Ministry has ordered: the Hitler Greeting is also to be used in conversation between teachers and pupils . . . Every day at the beginning of the first lesson the pupils will get up from their places as soon as the teacher enters the class, stand to attention and raise their outstretched arm level with their eyes. The teacher will go to the front of the class and offer the same greeting accompanied by the words 'Heil Hitler!' The pupils will reply 'Heil Hitler!'

SOURCE 14.19 Teenage girls salute the flag at the start of the school day in 1933

SOURCE 14.20 *Der Angriff*, 27 October 1939

All subjects, German Language, History, Geography, Chemistry and Mathematics – must concentrate on military subjects – the glorification of military service and of German heroes and leaders and the strength of a regenerated Germany. Chemistry will inculcate a knowledge of chemical warfare, explosives, Buna [artificial rubber], etc. while mathematics will help the young to understand artillery calculations, ballistics etc.

SOURCE 14.21   Extracts from a Nazi mathematics textbook

Question 95 The construction of a lunatic asylum costs 6 million RM. How many houses at 15,000 RM each could have been built for that amount?

Question 97 To keep a mentally ill person costs approx. 4 RM per day, a cripple 5.5 RM, a criminal 3.50 RM. Many civil servants receive only 4 RM per day, white collar employees barely 3.50 RM, unskilled workers not even 2 RM per head for their families.

(a) Illustrate these figures with a diagram.

According to conservative estimates, there are 300,000 mentally ill, epileptics, etc. in care.

(b) How much do these people cost to keep in total, at a cost of 4 RM per head?

(c) How many marriage loans at 1,000 RM each ... could be granted from this money?

SOURCE 14.22   From official instructions on the teaching of history, issued by the German Central Institute of Education, 1938

The German nation in its essence and greatness, in its fateful struggle for internal and external identity is the subject of the teaching of history. It is based on the natural bond of the child with his nation and, by interpreting history as the fateful struggle for existence between the nations, has the particular task of educating young people to respect the great German past and to have faith in the mission and future of their own nation and to respect the right of existence of other nations ... It must always show greatness ... the powerless and insignificant have no history.

TALKING POINT

Should history teaching be used to develop pride in one's country's past?

SOURCE 14.23   History curriculum recommended by the *National Socialist Educator*

Weeks	Subject	Relations to Jews	Reading material
1–4	Pre-war Germany. The class war. Profits, strikes	The Jew at large!	Hauptmann: *The Weavers*
5–8	From agrarian to industrial state. Colonies	The peasant in the claws of the Jews	Descriptions of the colonies from Hermann Löns
9–12	Conspiracy against Germany	The Jew reigns. War plots	Beumelburg: *Barrage. Life of Hindenburg* Wartime letters
13–16	German struggle. German want. Blockade! Starvation!	The Jew becomes prosperous! Profit from German want	Manke: *Espionage at the Front* War reports
17–20	The stab in the back. Collapse	Jews as leaders of the November insurrection	*Secret Service in Enemy Country* Bruno Brehm: *That was the End*
21–24	Germany's Golgotha. Erzberger's crimes! Versailles	Jews enter Germany from the east. Judah's triumph	Volkmann: *Revolution over Germany* Feder: *The Jews* *Der Stürmer* newspaper
25–28	Adolf Hitler National Socialism	Judah's foe!	*Mein Kampf* Dietrich Eckart
29–32	The Bleeding Frontiers. Enslavement of Germany. The Volunteer Corps. Schlageter [a young German killed by invading French troops in 1923]	The Jew profits by Germany's misfortunes. Loans (Dawes, Young)	Beumelburg: *Germany in Chains* Wehner: *Pilgrimage to Paris* *Schlageter – a German hero*
33–36	National Socialism at grips with crime and the underworld	Jewish instigators of murder. The Jewish press	Horst Wessel [a young Nazi killed in a brawl in 1930 and turned into a hero]
37–40	Germany's youth at the helm! The victory of faith	The last fight against Judah	The Reich Party Congress

SOURCE 14.24 Nazi School Assignments, from a Munich teachers' book, 1935

6   Collect propaganda posters and caricatures [exaggerated portraits] for your race book, and arrange them according to a racial scheme.
9   Observe people whose special racial features have drawn your attention, also with respect to their bearing when moving or speaking. Observe their expressions and gestures.
10 Observe the Jew: his way of walking, his bearing, gestures and movements when talking.
12 What are the occupations engaged in by Jews of your acquaintance?
13 What are the occupations in which Jews are not found? Explain this phenomenon in the basic character of the Jew's soul.
14 In what stories, descriptions and poems do you find the physical character of the Jew pertinently [relevantly] portrayed? (e.g. Grimms' Fairy Tales, The Merchant of Venice by Shakespeare, etc.)

SOURCE 14.25 Dictation exercise from a Munich primary school in 1934

Just as Jesus saved people from sin and from Hell, Hitler saves the German Volk from ruin. Jesus and Hitler were persecuted, but while Jesus was crucified, Hitler was raised to the Chancellorship. While the disciples of Jesus denied their master and deserted him, the sixteen comrades of Hitler died for their leader. The apostles completed the work of their lord. We hope that Hitler will be able to complete his work himself. Jesus built for heaven: Hitler for the German earth.

SOURCE 14.26 This militaristic timetable from a 1939 schoolbook has the words 'The history of the German people is the history of its infantry' inscribed above it

SOURCE 14.27   A 1937 poster welcoming the decline in the use of Essen's libraries. The translation is on the right

Die Gesundung.
Rückgang der Vielleserei

Im Krisenjahr 1932:
Beängstigendes Ansteigen von Entleihungsziffern und Lesesaalbenutzung:
643000 Buchentleihungen
315000 Lesesaalbesucher=
Arbeitslosigkeit trieb die Menschen in die Büchereien

nach 4 Jahren Aufbau 1937:
Gesundes Verhalten von Entleihungsziffern und
Lesesaalbenutzung:
412000 Buchentleihungen
217000 Lesesaalbesucher

Neue Aufgaben nahmen die Leser in Anspruch:
1. Die Rückkehr an die Arbeitsplätze
2. Die politische Betätigung für
Volk und Staat
3. Die Arbeitsdienstpflicht
4. Der Heeresdienst

Die Ausleiheziffer sank demnach um ein Drittel, die
Zahl der Leser nur um ein Siebentel (1932: 21765 Leser
1937: 18907 Leser). Das bedeutet, daß die Bücher
gründlicher gelesen werden und so eine nachhaltigere
Wirkung ausüben=

Healthy Recovery.
Decline in Indiscriminate Reading

1932, year of crisis:
Disturbing increase in numbers of books
borrowed and in use of the reading room:
643,000 titles borrowed
315,000 reading-room users
Unemployment sends people into the libraries

1937, after 4 years of reconstruction:
Healthy response in numbers of books borrowed and
in use of the reading room:
412,000 titles borrowed
217,000 reading-room users

Readers are engaged in new tasks:
1. The return to employment
2. Political activity for the
people and the state
3. Labour Service duty
4. Military service

Thus, numbers of loans have fallen by one-third,
but the number of readers has fallen only by one-seventh
(1932: 21,765 readers; 1937: 18,907 readers). This shows
that books are being read more thoroughly and will
therefore have a more lasting effect

DID THE NAZIS SUCCEED IN WINNING THE HEARTS AND MINDS OF GERMAN YOUTH?

SOURCE 14.28
Ordensburg cadets on parade

C Alternative youth

Edelweiss Pirates

SOURCE 14.29 Edelweiss Pirates. The edelweiss flower was chosen as a symbol of resistance to Hitler. The pirates wore the edelweiss as a metal badge on their collars

SOURCE 14.30 Edelweiss Pirates' song

Hark the hearty fellows sing!
Strum that banjo, pluck that string!
And the lassies all join in
We're going to get rid of Hitler,
And he can't do a thing.

We march by banks of Ruhr and Rhine
And smash the Hitler Youth in twain.
Our song is freedom, love and life,
We're Pirates of the Edelweiss.

Hitler's power may lay us low,
And keep us locked in chains,
But we will smash the chains one day.
We'll be free again.
We've got fists and we can fight
We've got knives and we'll get them out.
We want freedom, don't we boys?
We are the fighting Navajos.

FOCUS ROUTE

1 Choose five features of the activities of the alternative youth groups and explain what aspects of Nazi ideology they challenged.
2 Why do you think their popularity increased in the later part of the war?
3 Why do you think most of the sources on the alternative youth movements come from agents of the Nazi state?

The growing political and ideological bias of the Hitler Youth diminished its attraction for many young people. The Edelweiss Pirates was the name for a loose collection of subgroups. These bands were mainly of boys aged 14–17 but also included a few girls. They could be recognised by their badges, for example the edelweiss or skull and crossbones; and some wore check shirts, dark short trousers, and white socks. They were largely localised groups with their own names, such as the Roving Dudes, Kittelbach Pirates, the Navajos. Membership was mainly rooted in the working class. The earliest recorded groups existed in 1934 and membership has been estimated at 2,000 by 1939. Numbers grew most rapidly during the war years. In 1945, for instance, the Cologne authorities reported twenty groups of around 100 members.

Their aims are not easy to identify. They were partly just rebellious youth trying to escape the intrusive Nazi system, joining in popular pastimes such as weekend camps, hikes and singing songs about sex and food (not Hitler Youth songs!). However, some groups were highly politicised, establishing links with the KPD and beating up Hitler Youth patrols with the slogan 'Eternal War on the Hitler Youth!' In 1942 the Düsseldorf Hitler Youth complained of 'no go' areas. During the Second World War some groups helped escaped prisoners of war and distributed Allied and communist leaflets. Thus their actions ranged from socially nonconformist behaviour to political resistance.

The response of the authorities became harsher over time. They initially issued warnings with some raids and arrests, but in March 1940 130 Navajos in Cologne were arrested. Later, in December 1942, the Gestapo arrested 739 Edelweiss Pirates in Düsseldorf. They had their heads shaven, were detained, or sent for corrective education or to labour camps. Some were tried and executed. In November 1944 the leaders of the Cologne Edelweiss Pirates were hanged.

Swing

These groups of mainly upper-middle-class youths, unlike the Edelweiss Pirates, had the wealth to frequent night-clubs. Many were nominally members of the Hitler Youth. Swing groups mainly developed in large cities, such as Hamburg, Berlin, Frankfurt and Dresden, during the late 1930s. They rejected Hitler Youth ideals, but were generally anti-politics. Their approach was to develop a counter identity, expressed through forbidden music. They met in bars, night-clubs and houses and played American Black and Jewish jazz and swing, not the officially sanctioned German folk music. The Nazis felt undermined by their activities and closed the bars and made some arrests. Although only a tiny minority of German youths were connected with the Swing groups, they do illustrate, as with the Pirates, the failure of the regime to dominate youth; and for many they were a heartening illustration of non-conformity.

SOURCE 14.31   A newspaper report in the *Rheinische Landeszeitung*, February 1936

Dangerous Pirate Games

On 6 October of last year the police authorities . . . staged a mass raid on the so-called Wolfsberg near Huels. It had become known that a great number of 'Kittelbach pirates' had undertaken a social trip to the Wolfsberg . . . In order to put a stop to their games once and for all, the police patrol of 6 October was made ready. The 80 or so young chaps aged from 16 to 25 who were on the journey were dressed in the typical 'uniform' of the Kittelbach pirates (short summer trousers, white shirt, belt with death's head, death's head ring, lump of porcelain on the trouser buckle, tin whistle in the leg of the boot). They had taken along with them strips of canvas for spending a night in the open, alcohol galore and . . . girls . . .

When the police arrived, they found most of the 'pirates' completely drunk, and the girls in an indescribable state. The whole group (apparently overcome by a false romantic idea of what it is to be an outlaw) was picked up by the police. Perhaps 70 of these wayward young chaps were taken to the law court in Krefeld where they were found guilty of offences against Section 4 of the ORDINANCE of 28 February 1933, wearing a banned uniform. Ten additional ones . . . had to appear before the Düsseldorf special court today . . .

In the main trial, which was conducted 'in camera' [in private], all of the accused (who used nicknames like 'Bobby', 'Jumbo', 'Sonny Boy', 'Black Hand' and the like) admitted their guilt . . . 'Black Hand' was sentenced to two months in prison, 'Bobby' to one month. The other pirates each got a 75 Mark fine . . . The chairman of the court explained that . . . if the accused had been older and had displayed activity which amounted to subversion . . . the death penalty, life imprisonment or a long prison sentence would have been expected. The chairman of the special court concluded that this may serve as warning to any other 'members of other special groups'.

TALKING POINT

Is total youth conformity an impossible task for any regime?

SOURCE 14.32   In 1942 the Reich youth leadership was driven to declare

The formation of cliques, i.e. groupings of young people outside the Hitler Youth, was on the increase a few years before the war, and has particularly increased during the war, to such a degree that a serious risk of the political, moral and criminal breakdown of youth must be said to exist.

TALKING POINT

Some German historians have been accused of exaggerating the significance of the Edelweiss Pirates. Why might they have done so?

SOURCE 14.33   The hanging of Edelweiss Pirates in 1944

288

DID THE NAZIS SUCCEED IN WINNING THE HEARTS AND MINDS OF GERMAN YOUTH?

D Was Nazi youth policy successful?

It is very hard to judge the extent to which the Nazis succeeded in indoctrinating German youth. You have already encountered evidence that some children reacted against Nazi propaganda, whilst others absorbed it. Clearly a whole range of variables would affect the degree of impact.

FOCUS ROUTE

I   Read Sources 14.34–39, then copy and complete the chart below.

Responses to Nazi youth policies	Sources you could use	Evidence
Enthusiasm	14.35	
Conformity for career reasons	14.35, 14.37	
Conformity through fear	14.36, 14.38	
Conformity through apathy/ natural obedience	14.34	
Noncomformity/disillusion	14.36	
Criticism/opposition	14.36, 14.37, 14.39	

2   Do the sources suggest that young people's reactions to the Nazis changed over time?
3   Most of these sources come from either the German opposition or the police. How reliable on this topic do you think these two types of source are?
4   Write your own judgement on the success of Nazi youth policy. Then compare it with those of the historians quoted in the chapter review (pages 290–1).

SOURCE 14.34   A German reflects back on his youth in the Third Reich: quoted in D. Peukert, *Life in the Third Reich*, ed. R. Bessel, 1987, p. 27

No one in our class ever read Mein Kampf. *I myself only took quotations from the book. On the whole we didn't know much about Nazi ideology. Even anti-Semitism was brought in rather marginally at school – for example via Richard Wagner's essay 'The Jews in Music' – and outside school the display copies of* Der Stürmer *made the idea questionable, if anything . . .*

Nevertheless, we were politically programmed: to obey orders, to cultivate the soldierly 'virtue' of standing to attention and saying 'Yes, sir', and to stop thinking when the magic word 'Fatherland' was uttered and Germany's honour and greatness were mentioned.

SOURCE 14.35   A 1934 report to the Social Democratic Party in exile (SOPADE)

Youth is still in favour of the system: the novelty, the drill, the uniform, the camp life, the fact that school and the parental home take a back seat compared to the community – all that is marvellous. A great time without any danger. Many believe that they will find job opportunities through the persecution of Jews and Marxists . . .

The new generation has never had much use for education . . . on the contrary, knowledge is publicly condemned . . . The children and young people follow the instructions of the HJ and demand from their parents that they become good Nazis . . . The parents cannot forbid the child to do what all children are doing, cannot refuse him the uniform . . . The secret of National Socialism is the secret of its youth. The chaps are so fanaticised that they believe in nothing but their Hitler.

Source 14.36 From SOPADE reports, 1935

[Bavaria] The reports dealing with youth and its enthusiasm for the regime are not uniformly in agreement. In as much as most of our colleagues detect tremendous support for the regime among the oncoming generation, some maintain that the sentiments among youth are diverse. It goes without saying that Hitler Youth does its utmost to create enthusiasm, but among working-class youths one can hear much criticism.

[Southwestern Germany] To youth in the secondary schools, the continuous force-feeding of National Socialism is having the same effect as the heavy emphasis on religious instruction in earlier decades. National Socialism is no longer a matter of youthful rebellion but has instead become the state-sponsored school curriculum. Consequently National Socialism has lost much of its appeal, especially since the suppression of political opponents and otherwise orientated youth organisations. This is why today the frequent dodging of the Hitler Youth and its events, as well as the transgression [violation] of National Socialist prohibitions, has become a favourite game for youths who eagerly outfox the authorities.

[Rhineland–Westphalia] Some of the teachers tried everything in order to force children into the Hitler Youth ... Teachers enquire whether or not one's father is a party member or is in the SA ... or which newspapers are read at home. Children whose parents are avowed opponents of the Nazis answer yes many times simply because they are afraid.

... In the rural areas as well as industrial cities one can see an increasing demoralisation of youth. In rural areas there has been a sharp decline in participation at Hitler Youth events. Many have resigned their membership, and membership dues are frequently unpaid. While at first uniforms and war games were quite appealing, the regimented routine is now regarded as burdensome by children. The power of authority which was bestowed upon some children has given rise to discontent and resistance. It is not unusual for a youthful group leader whose position of authority has gone to his head to receive a beating from his charges because he wanted to drill the already exhausted group even harder ...

SOURCE 14.37 From a SOPADE report, 1938

Young people are more easily influenced in terms of mood than are adults. This fact made it easier for the regime to win over young people in the first years after the seizure of power. It appears that the same fact is now making it hard for the regime to keep young people in thrall [submissive] ... They were made particularly large promises which for the most part were incapable of fulfilment. The great mass of young people today can see that the well-paying posts in public administration and the Party apparatus have been filled by comrades who had the good fortune of being a few years older ... in the long run young people too are feeling increasingly irritated by the lack of freedom and the mindless drilling that is customary in the National Socialist organisations ...

SOURCE 14.38 The title page of *Kamaradschaft* (Comradeship), an underground youth magazine of 1938

SOURCE 14.39 The Düsseldorf–Grafenberg branch of the National Socialist Party reported to the Gestapo on 17 July 1943

The said youths are throwing their weight around again. I have been informed that assemblages of young people have become more conspicuous than ever, especially since the last terror [bombing] raid on Düsseldorf. These youngsters, aged between 12 and 17 hang around into the late evening, with musical instruments and young females. Since this riffraff is to a large extent outside the Hitler Youth and adopts a hostile attitude towards the organisation, they represent a danger to other young people ... There is a suspicion that it is these youths who have been inscribing the walls of the pedestrian subway on the Altenbergstrasse with the slogans 'Down with Hitler', 'The OKW is lying', 'Medals for Murder!', 'Down with Nazi brutality', etc. However often these inscriptions are removed, within a few days new ones appear on the walls again.

E Review: Did the Nazis succeed in winning the hearts and minds of German youth?

Assessing the effectiveness of propaganda on the young in a totalitarian society is a notoriously difficult task. There is the problem of people at the time being too frightened to put their real views on paper. On the other hand, there is the danger that people recording their oral testimony at a later date exaggerate their degree of opposition to the regime. Furthermore, when we do find opposition from young people, is it really opposition to the regime or simply the normal rebelliousness of youth? Several historians have attempted to assess the overall impact of Nazi policies.

SOURCE 14.40   G. Mosse, *Nazi Culture*, 1981, p. 265

It is difficult to say just how successful the Nazi reshaping of education proved to be in practice. It must have varied greatly from school to school and depended a great deal on individual teachers and principals.

SOURCE 14.41   A. Wilt, *Nazi Germany*, 1994, p.66

It has been estimated that as many as 95 per cent of the German youth backed the Nazis, or at least Hitler, and that opposition for the most part remained vague and diffuse.

SOURCE 14.42   D. Peukert, *Inside Nazi Germany. Conformity and Opposition in Everyday Life*, 1987, pp. 152, 173

The second half of the 1930s reveals a growing crisis in the Hitler Youth, a crisis which during the war years developed into a massive opposition movement on the part of groups and gangs of young people. The SOPADE reports on Germany for 1938 already recorded this radical shift of attitude among the young, from initial attraction to growing rejection.

... The two central projects of National Socialist social policy – the nullification [cancelling] of class reality through the sentiment of Volksgemeinschaft; *and the mobilisation of the people, militarised and schooled in* CHAUVINISM, *to smash the perceived threat to traditional influences posed by modernity [current fashion] and internationalism – seem to have miscarried even before the end of the Third Reich loomed into sight in the shape of military defeat.*

SOURCE 14.43   K. Fischer, *Nazi Germany*, 1995, p. 353

Nazi educational efforts as a whole turned out to be poorly thought out and lacking in substance. At best, the Nazis put a thin ideological veneer [surface] on German education. It is not surprising that twelve years were not enough to break down 'two thousand years of European cultural heritage'. However, Nazi indoctrination was able to miseducate and misuse a whole generation of young people.

SOURCE 14.44   B. Sax, D. Kuntz, *Inside Hitler's Germany*, 1992, p. 308

Through the training of young men and women, the Nazis procured [acquired] a most impressionable group of individuals on whom to impose their ideas in the hope of creating the new men and women of the Volksgemeinschaft ... *What National Socialist training produced, however, were duller and stupider, though healthier, individuals. By the late 1930s, the authorities became increasingly aware of the fact that while students, no longer able to think for themselves, would therefore not resist the regime, they were incapable of either providing political leadership in the future or contributing the intellectual and technical skills necessary for running a modern industrial society. They proved to be the most willing to sacrifice themselves to the principles of National Socialism.*

SOURCE 14.45 M. Housden, in *Resistance and Conformity in the Third Reich*, 1997, p. 81, summarises reasons for the support for Nazism

There were all manner of reasons for youngsters to support the Third Reich. [1] National Socialism provided a vehicle for conflict between generations. [2] It could be dynamic, exciting and purposeful. [3] Youngsters were socialised into National Socialist ways at school and [4] in the Hitler Youth. [5] When all else failed they could be intimidated. What is more, the longer the Nazi system was in place, the more hazy became the memories of younger Germans of the days before Hitler. Eventually youngsters knew no alternative. And yet, despite all this, support for Hitler was less than total.

ACTIVITY

1 **a)** Explain the limited success of Nazi education. Refer, with supporting evidence, to the following:

   - Nazi ideas on the aims of education
   - the complex institutional structure
   - the reactions of teachers, parents and students
   - the length of time the Nazis held power.

   b) Why are there problems in both finding and assessing the evidence for this question?

2 Find evidence to support all the statements we have numbered in Source 14.45.

3 'Natural youth behaviour' or 'political opposition'. Which is the more appropriate description of groups like the Edelweiss Pirates?

4 Now use your Focus Route answers (see page 277) to do your essay.

KEY POINTS FROM CHAPTER 14: Did the Nazis succeed in winning the hearts and minds of German youth?

1 The Nazis sought to indoctrinate the young from the age of four, using youth movements and the school system to impose their values.

2 The Nazis scorned intellectual learning and placed emphasis on physical strength and obedience.

3 Millions joined the Hitler Youth, initially attracted by adventurous activities. Pressure to join increased, and in 1936 membership was made compulsory.

4 There is evidence of increasing disillusion with aspects of the Nazi youth movements as the years passed.

5 During the war, organised groups of young people directly challenged Nazi orthodoxy, despite the danger of getting caught.

6 There was no major reorganisation of schools, except for a decline in denominational schools and the creation of a few elite schools.

7 The government attempted indoctrination via control of the curriculum and teachers.

8 Many parents disliked the Nazi training but felt it safer outwardly to conform.

9 One effect of the Nazi changes was to reduce the academic quality of the students.

10 There is mixed evidence as to the overall effectiveness of Nazi propaganda on German youth.

15

How successfully did the Nazis impose their ideology on German women?

CHAPTER OVERVIEW

Deutschland wächst aus starken Müttern und gesunden Kindern

HILFSWERK MUTTER UND KIND

SOURCE 15.1 A poster produced in 1935 by the Organisation to Aid Mothers and Children: 'Germany grows through strong mothers and healthy children'

'I have donated a child to the Führer.' Thus proclaimed one German mother upon giving birth. She had clearly absorbed the government propaganda that urged women to have more children as a vital way of strengthening the Nazi *Volksgemeinschaft*. We open this chapter with a selection of sources on attitudes towards women in the Third Reich. You may find them very provocative. However, in order to develop a balanced assessment of women's position in the Third Reich, you must also seek to understand the general perceptions of women at the time, and not read back into history your own views on the position of women in society. You should also understand the extent to which some Nazi views were held by other groups and societies at the time. Finally, you will also need to consider objectively the services the Nazis provided for women.

A What role were women to play in the Nazi state? (pp. 292–5)

B How did the Nazis try to implement their ideas? (pp. 296–301)

C Review: How successfully did the Nazis impose their ideology on German women? (pp. 302–3)

FOCUS ROUTE

Using your work on Sources 15.2–15 and Chart 15A, explain:

a) the proposed role for women and the ideal type of woman in the Nazi state
b) what the Nazis disliked about 'emancipated' women.

SEMINAR

You might like to organise your study of this chapter around a seminar (see page 277).

A What role were women to play in the Nazi state?

ACTIVITY

Split up into four groups. Each study one selection of sources:

a) Sources 15.2–6
b) Sources 15.7–9
c) Sources 15.10–13
d) Sources 15.14 and 15.15.

In your groups, discuss and record what each source shows about Nazi attitudes, identifying what the Nazis thought women should and should not do/be like. Then report back to the class, referring to specific sources.

SOURCE 15.2 *Familienbildnis*: the ideal German family – a painting by Wolfgang Willrich in the 1930s

SOURCE 15.3 A 1937 propaganda poster aimed at German girls: 'You too belong to the Führer'

SOURCE 15.4 Nazi slogan on the role of women

Kinder, Küche, Kirche [Children, kitchen, church]

SOURCE 15.6 German rhyme

Take hold of kettle, broom and pan.
Then you'll surely get your man!
Shop and office leave alone,
Your true life's work lies at home.

SOURCE 15.5 Gertrud Scholtz-Klink, Head of the Nazi Women's Organisation

Woman is entrusted in the life of the nation with a great task, the care of man, soul, body, and mind. It is the mission of woman to minister in the home and in her profession to the needs of life from the first to the last moment of man's existence. Her mission in marriage is . . . comrade, helper and womanly complement of man – this is the right of woman in the New Germany.

SOURCE 15.7 A German newspaper in 1937 explaining why women should be ineligible for jury service

They cannot think logically or reason objectively since they are ruled only by emotion.

SOURCE 15.8 A speech by Hitler to the National Socialist Women's Organisation in 1934

If the man's world is said to be the state, his struggle, his readiness to devote his powers to the service of the community, then it may perhaps be said that the woman's is a smaller world. For her world is her husband, her family, her children, and her home . . . the greater world is built on the foundation of this smaller one. This great world cannot survive if the smaller world is not stable . . . The two worlds are not antagonistic. They complement each other, they belong together just as man and woman belong together.

. . . We consider it natural if these two worlds remain distinct. To the one belongs the strength of feeling, the strength of the soul. To the other belongs the strength of vision, of toughness of decision, and of willingness to act. In the one case this strength demands the willingness of the woman to risk her life to preserve this important cell and multiply it, and in the other case it demands from the man the readiness to safeguard life.

TALKING POINT

What aspects of Nazi views on women are still prevalent today?

294

HOW SUCCESSFULLY DID THE NAZIS IMPOSE THEIR IDEOLOGY ON GERMAN WOMEN?

SOURCE 15.9   Extracts from two contemporary Nazi publications

Marriage

Marriage is the lasting, life-long union of two genetically healthy persons of the same race and of different sexes, which has been approved by the national community, and is based on mutual ties of loyalty, love and respect. Its purpose is the maintenance and furtherance of the common good through harmonious co-operation, the procreation of genetically healthy children of the same race, and the education of them to become hard-working national comrades.

The Function of Sex

Sexual activity serves the purpose of procreation for the maintenance of the life of the nation and not the enjoyment of the individual ... If, however, the desire to have a child has been fulfilled and the continuation and enlargement of the nation has been secured by the production of a sufficient number of children, then, from the point of view of the nation, there is no objection to further satisfaction of the sexual urge.

SOURCE 15.10   Goebbels, 1929

The mission of women is to be beautiful and bring children into the world ... The female bird pretties herself for her mate and hatches eggs for him. In exchange, the mate takes care of gathering the food, and stands guard and wards off the enemy.

SOURCE 15.12   From the Nazi newspaper *Völkischer Beobachter*

The most unnatural thing we can encounter in the streets is a German woman, who, disregarding all laws of beauty, has painted her face with Oriental war paint.

SOURCE 15.14   Himmler

With bigamy, each wife would act as a stimulus to the others so that both would try to be their husband's dream woman.

SOURCE 15.15   From an NSF (National Socialist Women's Organisation) publication during the war

It has always been our article of faith that a woman's place is in the home, but since the whole of Germany is our home we must serve wherever we can best do so.

SOURCE 15.11   'Ten Commandments for Choice of Spouse': advice issued to women

1 Remember that you are a German.
2 If you are genetically healthy you should not remain unmarried.
3 Keep your body pure.
4 You should keep your mind and spirit pure.
5 As a German, choose only a spouse of the same or Nordic blood.
6 In choosing a spouse, ask about his ancestors.
7 Health is also a precondition for physical beauty.
8 Marry only for love.
9 Don't look for a playmate but for a companion for marriage.
10 You should want to have as many children as possible.

SOURCE 15.13   Hess, in a newspaper article, 1939

As all National Socialists know, the highest law in war, as in peace, is preservation of the race. An unmarried mother may have a hard path. But she knows that when we are at war, it is better to have a child under the most difficult conditions than not to have one at all ... the family is the basis of the country, but during a war the highest service which a woman may perform for the continuation of the nation is to bear racially healthy children. Be happy, good women, that you have been permitted to perform this high duty for Germany.

Nazi policy towards women was largely reactionary. The Nazis wanted to reverse many of the recent trends that had increased opportunities for women throughout Europe, such as increased female employment in the non-agricultural sector and a declining birth rate that was partly due to wider access to contraception. These trends had been present in Germany under the Weimar Republic, many of whose supporters advocated further EMANCIPATION. Women had been given the vote and experienced greater cultural freedom, and the growing gender imbalance (considerably increased by war casualties, with an estimated 2.8 million surplus women in 1919) had created further opportunities.

A reaction against these trends had set in during the Depression with some moves to discriminate against women in work, and there was an inevitable fall in female employment. Into this context came the Nazis who had a clear vision of women performing what the Nazis considered to be their traditional role as homemakers and childbearers. In the national struggle for survival, women had a vital, if different, role from the warrior men: to breed genetically pure Germans to ensure German supremacy. The Nazis also emphasised the role of the family as the 'germ cell of the nation', and this had clear implications for the position of women in the state.

However, as in other areas of policy, Nazi ideology came into conflict with broader trends and other economic priorities. The early years of the regime saw the forcing of women out of employment and the encouragement of traditional family structures. However, during the war, because of the need for more workers and more soldiers, the government encouraged the utilisation of female labour, and also childbirth outside marriage. These were just some of the several contradictions you will find within Nazi policy towards women.

TALKING POINT

Does this topic create the same or different problems for male and female students of history?

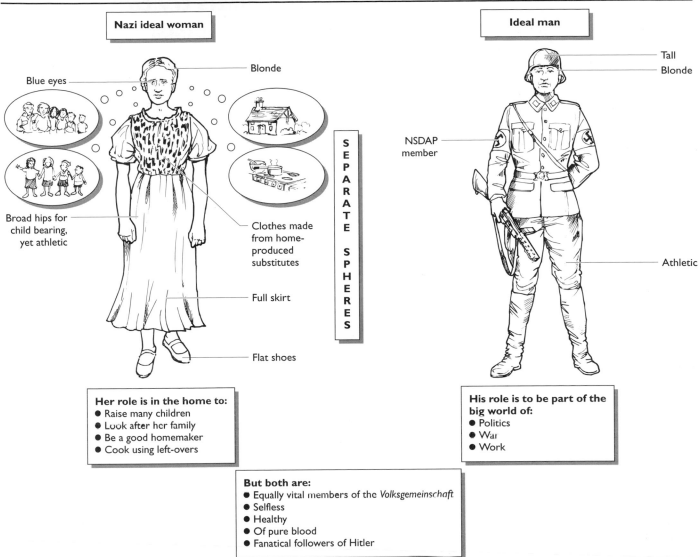

Nazi ideal woman

Blue eyes

Blonde

Broad hips for
child bearing,
yet athletic

Clothes made
from home-
produced
substitutes

Full skirt

Flat shoes

SEPARATE SPHERES

Ideal man

Tall
Blonde

NSDAP
member

Athletic

Her role is in the home to:
● Raise many children
● Look after her family
● Be a good homemaker
● Cook using left-overs

**His role is to be part of the
big world of:**
● Politics
● War
● Work

But both are:
● Equally vital members of the *Volksgemeinschaft*
● Selfless
● Healthy
● Of pure blood
● Fanatical followers of Hitler

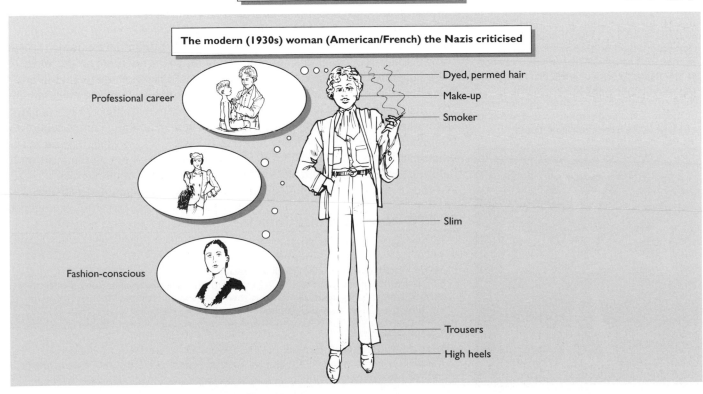

The modern (1930s) woman (American/French) the Nazis criticised

Professional career

Dyed, permed hair

Make-up

Smoker

Slim

Fashion-conscious

Trousers

High heels

296

HOW SUCCESSFULLY DID THE NAZIS IMPOSE THEIR IDEOLOGY ON GERMAN WOMEN?

B How did the Nazis try to implement their ideas?

SOURCE 15.16 In 1943 a Marriage Law was drawn up but not enacted

All single and married women up to the age of 35 who do not already have four children should be obliged to produce four children by racially pure German men. Whether these men are married is of no significance. Every family that already has four children must set the husband free for this action.

SOURCE 15.17 The Honour Cross of German Motherhood, an award given to women for bearing children. It was modelled on the military cross for men. Bronze crosses were given to mothers of four or five children, silver for six or seven, gold for eight or more. Cross bearers were also entitled to a special salute from the Hitler Youth

Soon after the Nazis came to power, women who had experienced new freedoms under the Weimar Republic began to feel the Nazi backlash. In 1933 the Law for the Reduction of Unemployment cleverly linked the fight to reduce unemployment with the introduction of Nazi policies towards women. Marriage loans were granted to women who gave up their jobs. This was soon followed by restrictions on women's employment in the Civil Service. Thus in October 1933 the official guidelines for recruiting civil servants and teachers stated: 'In the event of males and females being equally qualified for employment in public service, the male applicant should be given preference.' In the dire conditions of high unemployment at the time there was not a strong reaction against such a policy.

Marriage too became increasingly influenced by legal changes that both threatened and encouraged German married couples to produce the right racial stock and plenty of it! Divorce became easier, but this was not inspired by concern for women's rights: it was in order to boost the birth rate by ending unproductive marriages that were deemed 'worthless' to the national community. A further example of the Nazi perception of the need for children is shown in Source 15.16.

To help inculcate their values, the Nazis created a series of organisations for girls and women, membership of which eventually numbered millions. However, the Nazi belief in a national community was not mere propaganda. They implemented welfare schemes that supported women and their children. Thus in the *Gau* of Munich–Upper Bavaria, Nazi organisations in one month in 1934 distributed 25,800 litres of milk, 1,500 grocery parcels and 172 sets of baby clothes and linen. Nationally, the number of women attending recuperation homes after childbirth rose from 40,340 in 1934 to 77,723 in 1938. Harvest kindergartens to look after children when their mothers were working in the fields increased from 600 in 1934 to 8,700 in 1941. Prolific mothers were awarded medals in recognition of their contribution to national objectives.

■ 15B Nazi organisations for women

- 10–14 Jung Mädel (Young girls)
- 14–18 BDM (League of German Girls)
- 18–21 Glaube und Schönheit (Faith and Beauty)
- NSF (National Socialist Women's Organisation): an umbrella organisation co-ordinating existing women's organisations to bring them into line with official ideology. It ran the Reich Mothers' Service, which trained housewives and midwives
- DFW (German Women's Enterprise): set up to develop an elite of women committed to Nazi ideology
- RAD and DAF women's sections
- The welfare organisation NSV (National Socialist People's Welfare) relied greatly on paid and volunteer female labour

AREA OF LIFE	Births	Marriage	Welfare	Education	Employment	Public life
A Aims	• Increase pure German births	• Increase suitable marriages	• Develop healthy Germans	• Prepare women for their proper role • Restrict opportunities	• Reduce female employment	• Organise women and incorporate them in the Nazi *Volksgemeinschaft*
B Measures **i) 1933–9**	• Financial incentives, e.g. marriage loans, birth grants • Improved maternity services • Propaganda to raise status and self-esteem of mothers and housewives; awards, e.g. Mother's Cross • Penalties – Higher taxes on childless couples – Tighter penalties on abortion – Restrictions on contraception information – Measures introduced for compulsory sterilisation of 'undesirables'	• 1933 600 RM marriage loan if unemployed • 1937 Loan extended to women in work • 1935 Marriage Law required certificate of 'fitness to marry' before marriage licence issued • Oct 1935 Blood Protection Law: marriage to Jews, Black people, gypsies forbidden • 1938 Marriage Law extended the grounds for divorce	• NS-Volkswohl-schaft (NSV), the National Socialist Welfare Organisation, set up • Vast expansion of health offices, especially in rural areas; improved sanitation, preventative medicine, genetic and racial care	• Limited university enrolment of women to 10%	• 1933 Women in top civil service and medical jobs dismissed • 1936 Banned from being judges, lawyers	• No female Nazi members of Reichstag permitted • Two women's organisations created: NSF, DFW
ii) 1939–45	• *Lebensborn* programme extended. Encouragement of births outside marriage	• 1941 Couples found cohabiting after their marriage had been banned were sent to concentration camps	• Improved childcare facilities, especially for working mothers	• Restrictions dropped as great demand for well-educated workers	• 1939 Compulsory agricultural labour service for unmarried women under 25 • Women exhorted to help war effort, but only in 1942 were women of 17–45 told to register for work (many exceptions)	• Nazi women's organisations support the war effort (e.g. clothes collections for the Russian Front)
C Effects	• 1933–9 Birth rate rose, then slowly declined	• 1932: 516,000 marriages • 1934: 740,000 marriages • Divorces increased after 1938	• Infant mortality dropped: 1933 7.7% 1936 6.6%	• Drop in numbers of women at university until Second World War	• Number of women in employment rose • Further increase during the war	• Increased female participation in Nazi bodies
D Overall assessment	• Increase may have been due more to economic recovery than to Nazi policies/measures • Birth rate rose compared to during the Depression; but did not get back to levels of Weimar Germany • Nazi eugenic policies reduced the population potential	• Increase in marriages may have been due more to economic optimism than to government policies; e.g. average size of family fell • Divorce was extended to help national objectives	• Welfare closely linked to eugenic policies • NSV largely staffed by women; improved opportunities	• Restrictions on opportunities for women were increasingly relaxed as women were needed, since demand for workers and soldiers grew	• Nazi policies had marginal effect on overall female employment • Main impact was on the professions • During the war, women were less mobilised than in the UK or the USA • 1943 Speer's proposal to conscript women fully was opposed by Hitler due to the effect he thought it would have on morale	• In many ways the Nazis gave increased opportunities for (mainly middle-class) women to become involved in public life, although they were excluded from decision-making

298

HOW SUCCESSFULLY DID THE NAZIS IMPOSE THEIR IDEOLOGY ON GERMAN WOMEN?

How effective were Nazi policies?

Gertrud Scholtz-Klink (1902–): the ideal Nazi woman

Scholtz-Klink initially worked for the Berlin Red Cross. Her SA husband died of a heart attack during a demonstration and this inspired her to carry on his work. In 1929 she became the leader of the NSF in Baden and later deputy leader of the Nazi organisation nationwide. In 1934 she was promoted to Reichsfrauenführerin (women's leader) of all Nazi women's organisations (Frauenwerk, Woman's League of the Red Cross, Women's Bureau of DAF, Women's Labour Service). Her leadership was, however, in fact token; although she fronted the organisations, she was subordinate to the top male Nazis.

She was a great supporter of Nazi views on women's role, exhorting women to be enthusiastic breeding machines and beasts of burden for the greater glory of the Reich. She was a good speaker, and was sent abroad to win admiration for the new Germany. Unlike many Nazi leaders, she did actually conform to Nazi ideals: she was blonde, healthy and had four children.

In 1945 she hid from the Allies but was eventually arrested in 1948. She was sentenced to eighteen months' imprisonment for being a 'major offender' as a diehard Nazi, but was acquitted of war crimes. She remained a strong supporter of the Nazi regime whose good she believed outweighed the bad.

SOURCE 15.18   Advertisement in a German newspaper

52-year-old doctor. Fought in World War One. Wishes to settle down. Wants male child through marriage to young, healthy Aryan woman. She should be undemanding, used to heavy work, not a spender, with flat heels, without earrings.

SOURCE 15.19   Advertisement in a German newspaper, 1939

Two vital, lusty, race-conscious Brunnhildes with family trees certified back to 1700 desiring to serve their Fatherland in the form most ennobling to women, would like to meet two similarly inclined Siegfrieds. Marriage not of essential importance. Soldiers on leave also acceptable.

SOURCE 15.20   Letter to Hitler from several women published in a Leipzig newspaper in 1934

Today, man is being educated not for, but against marriage. Men are grouped together in clubs and hostels ... Woman stays back further and further in the shadow of loneliness ... we see our daughters growing up in stupid aimlessness living only in the vague hope of perhaps getting a man and having children ... A son, even the youngest, today laughs in his mother's face. He regards her as his natural servant, and women in general as merely willing tools of his aims.

SOURCE 15.21   Letter of thanks from a woman in a recuperation centre

I would like to thank the Führer heartily with the assurance that I am aware as a German woman and mother of my responsibility to look after my children ... and to educate them into being fit, useful people.

[Note by husband] She has put on 14lb, and the strength she was lacking before her trip has considerably come back again ... March forward, NSV, flourish, prosper and the nation will be healthy.

299

HOW SUCCESSFULLY DID THE NAZIS IMPOSE THEIR IDEOLOGY ON GERMAN WOMEN?

SOURCE 15.22   American journalist, 1937

How many women workers did the Führer send home? According to the statistics of the German Department of Labour, there were, in June 1936, 5,470,000 employed women, or 1,200,000 more than in January 1933 ... The vigorous campaign against the employment of women has not led to their increased domesticity and security, but has been effective in squeezing them out of better paid positions into sweated trades. Needless to say, this type of labour, with its miserable wages and long hours, is extremely dangerous to the health of women and degrades the family.

SOURCE 15.23   A joke told at the time

The father is in the Party; the mother in Frauenschaft [NSF]; the son in the Hitler Youth; the daughter in the BDM. So where does the ideal National Socialist family meet then? At the Reich Party Day in Nuremberg!

SOURCE 15.24   V. Ziemer, *Education for Death*, 1941. An American teacher describes a visit to a Berlin clinic

Hospital beds came and went with methodical precision. The doctors made quick, deft incisions in white abdomen walls.
  'What are they doing?' I asked.
  'These doctors', he said, 'are sterilising women.'
  I asked what type of women ... and was informed they were the mentally sick, women with low resistance, women who had proved through other births that their offspring were not strong ...
  'We are even eradicating colour-blindness,' my SS guide told me. 'We must not have soldiers who are colour-blind. It is transmitted only by women.'

TALKING POINT

In the 1930s France was one of many countries that banned contraception and abortion, and gave rewards for large families. Some states in America and some Scandinavian countries compulsorily sterilised mentally ill people. Does this affect your view of Nazi policies?

SOURCE 15.25   A Social Democrat poster published in December 1930. It says, 'Women, this is what it will be like in the "Third Reich"! Your reply should be: Fight the Nazi for Social Democracy!'

SOURCE 15.26   A female farm worker ploughing during the war

300

HOW SUCCESSFULLY DID THE NAZIS IMPOSE THEIR IDEOLOGY ON GERMAN WOMEN?

SOURCE 15.27 'Introducing Frau Mueller who up to now has brought twelve children into the world.' A German cartoon from the 1930s

SOURCE 15.28 Marriages, divorces, births and deaths

A

Year	Marriages	Live births
1929	589,600	–
1931	–	1,047,775
1932	516,793	993,126
1933	638,573	971,174
1934	740,165	1,198,350
1935	651,435	1,263,976
1936	609,631	1,277,052
1937	620,265	1,277,046
1938	645,062	1,348,534
1939	772,106	1,407,490

Note: 1938–9 figures include extended territory

B Divorce statistics after the 1938 Marriage Law

Reasons for divorce	1938–41
Matrimonial offences, including adultery	197,000
Irretrievable breakdown	31,000
Refusal to procreate	1,771
Premature infertility	383

C Average number of children

1933	3.6
1939	3.3

D Mean marriage rate 1933–9

20 per cent lower than 1923–32

SOURCE 15.29 Women's employment (in millions)

A

Job	1933	1939
Agriculture and forestry	4.6	4.9
Industry and crafts	2.7	3.3
Trade and transport	1.9	2.1
Non-domestic services	0.9	1.1
Domestic service	1.2	1.3

B

	Married women working outside the home
1933	4.2
1939	6.2*

* 35% of married women aged 16–65

SOURCE 15.30 'Join the youth groups': a recruitment poster for Nazi organisations. Membership of DFW and NSF in 1941 was 6 million out of 30 million female adults, i.e. 1 in 5 women

The Nazis' policies towards women suffered from several contradictions, for example over their attitude to marriage and the family. The main burden of their propaganda was to encourage the healthy Aryan family, as a small unit of the *Volksgemeinschaft*. However, several of their policies undermined the family. The demands of the Hitler Youth took youngsters away from the family and encouraged them to challenge any non-Nazi attitudes of their parents. The quest for a genetically pure race led to the encouragement of divorce and sterilisation for those 'unworthy' of marriage: an approach that aroused the anger of the Catholic Church, as did later the policy of 'euthanasia'.

During the Second World War the quest for a larger population of genetically pure Germans led to encouragement of procreation outside marriage, as in the *Lebensborn* (Life Springs) programme. In what were, in effect, state-run brothels, 'Aryan' women had babies by SS men. The programme was set up in 1935 and by 1944 nearly 11,000 children had been born in these special homes.

The Nazis' attempts to drive women back into the home were even less successful. The number of women in all types of jobs increased, mainly due to the economic recovery. By 1936 the economy was suffering from a labour shortage in key areas, and by 1939 this had become acute. Here ideology conflicted with economic need. Increasing numbers of women were attracted back into work, but the government did not encourage this. When war broke out, several Nazis advised Hitler to introduce female conscription, but he rejected this, partly on ideological grounds, but probably mainly because he was concerned at the effect on soldiers' morale of drafting their wives into factories. Not until 1943 were women aged 17–45 compelled to register for state-allocated work. The 'totalitarian' Nazi state was thus far less effective in utilising its resources than the liberal regimes in Britain and the USA.

The extent to which women absorbed Nazi propaganda is hard to judge. Mason has argued that the regime was more popular overall with women than with men, and that most women preferred to stay at home than work in factories. This was one factor increasing Hitler's reluctance to impose conscription. Middle-class women, who suffered greater restrictions on their careers, were probably less enthusiastic.

One must also remember to study the regime in context. Many of the Nazis' ideas were just more extreme or explicit versions of views that were widespread well before the Nazis gained power. Thus the Catholic Church and conservative organisations advocated the separate spheres view of women's role and stressed the importance of procreation.

There is considerable debate amongst the growing number of historians of women's history about the impact of Nazism on women. Initial stress by radical feminist historians on the evil impact of Nazi policies has been challenged by other historians arguing that, even if for questionable reasons, there were advantages for women in Nazi Germany. They argue that the benefits of a policy should not be cancelled out by its unattractive aims. In some areas, such as women's organisations and youth groups, the Nazis widened experiences for women. Social services improved. Opportunities to avoid the drudgeries of paid employment had advantages. Furthermore, several historians now stress the ineffectiveness of many Nazi restrictions. This is not to deny that for many women (though proportionately a small number) as well as men their experience of the regime was horrific.

In many ways this account of Nazi policies towards women illustrates some of the limitations on the totalitarian nature of the regime. The Nazis adopted a fairly cautious approach; thus only a few women were actually forced out of jobs; the regime relied more on financial and moral pressure. When in 1939 the Nazis needed female labour contrary to their previous policies, they proceeded very cautiously, partly because they were afraid of the reaction from women and men.

302

HOW SUCCESSFULLY DID THE NAZIS IMPOSE THEIR IDEOLOGY ON GERMAN WOMEN?

ACTIVITY

Read the historians' assessments in Sources 15.31–4, then answer these questions.

1 What contradictions in Nazi policies towards women do De Grand and Frevert identify?

2 Which historian stresses the success of Nazi policies most?

3 What explanations do Mason and Frevert give for the successes of Nazi policies?

4 Why does Pine see Nazi policy towards the family as evidence of the regime's totalitarian nature?

5 What conclusions can be drawn from these extracts as to the impact of Nazi policies on women?

C Review: How successfully did the Nazis impose their ideology on German women?

We conclude by studying some of the views of historians who have analysed the position of women in Nazi Germany.

SOURCE 15.31 Alexander De Grand, *Fascist Italy and Nazi Germany*, 1995, pp. 57, 63

The fascist position had always been that class distinctions were artificial and superficial but that biologically determined gender roles were immutable [unchangeable] ...

The conservative and stabilising elements of Nazi ideology – to keep women in their place and maintain them as a pillar of the traditional, hierarchical society – could not be reconciled with the political, social and racial ambitions of the regime.

SOURCE 15.32 Tim Mason, 'Women in Germany 1925–1940', in *Nazism, Fascism and the Working Class*, 1995, p. 132

In respect of its attitudes and policies towards women, National Socialism was the most repressive and reactionary of all modern political movements. And yet it seems that the overtly [undisguised] anti-feminist policies of the regime after 1933 were at least partially successful, in that they secured the approval, perhaps gratitude, of many German people, men and women alike; partially successful too in blocking and turning back the social, economic and educational pressures which had been conducive [led] to gradual progress towards emancipation in the preceding decades. At the very least, there is scarcely any evidence that the policies adopted on the family and on women's work were unpopular, despite the fact that they ran directly counter to basic liberal, democratic and socialist principles, principles which seemed to have been widely accepted during the 1920s.

SOURCE 15.33 Lisa Pine, *Nazi Family Policy*, 1997, p. 181

The Nazi regime utilised the family for its own ends. Marriage and childbirth became racial obligations rather than personal decisions, as the National Socialists systematically reduced the functions of the family to the single task of reproduction. They aimed to shatter the most intimate human group, the family, and to place it as a breeding and rearing institution completely in the service of the totalitarian state.

SOURCE 15.34 Ute Frevert, *Women in German History*, 1988, pp. 248, 250

Even if most of the twelve million women in the numerous Nazi organisations of 1939 were not themselves ardent National Socialists, twelve years of being educated and bombarded with propaganda by the Volksgemeinschaft *cannot have left individual consciousness and collective memory unmarked. In addition the impact of welfare measures ... reinforced popular loyalty ...*

National Socialism ... was ... a highly ambiguous period in history which witnessed a unique confluence of 'modernist' and 'traditionalist' tendencies. In a few areas, such as voting rights, access to the upper echelons [levels] of the civil service, and family planning, the fruits of hard fought battles were destroyed; in many areas (most notably with respect to the labour market), the Nazi state represented but a smooth continuation of existing structures and processes, together with all their unfavourable aspects (lower wages and less upward social mobility). By contrast, where youth policy, divorce laws and social organisations were concerned, the Third Reich offered women novel opportunities for participation and recognition in public life, and, indeed, many women benefited in an unprecedented fashion from such socio-political innovation ...

The actual outcome of policy was sometimes different, and often diametrically opposed, to its intended effects ...

The immense ability of the regime to mobilise the population, and the relative rarity of deliberate acts of political resistance, however, suggest that women who satisfied the political, racial and social requirements – and the vast majority did – did not perceive the Third Reich as a women's hell. Much of what it introduced was doubtless appealing, the rest one learned to accept.

TALKING POINT

Is women's history best written by women?

303

HOW SUCCESSFULLY DID THE NAZIS IMPOSE THEIR IDEOLOGY ON GERMAN WOMEN?

ACTIVITY

1 Identify the contradictions between Nazi ideology and some of the developments that the government actually assisted, by linking each belief (a–d) with one or more developments (i–vii).

Ideology
- **a)** Women as producers of babies
- **b)** Women to stay at home
- **c)** Support the family
- **d)** Support traditional, rural society

Conflicting developments
- **i)** Encouragement of birth outside marriage
- **ii)** Development of industrial/military might
- **iii)** Compulsory sterilisation for the hereditarily 'ill'
- **iv)** Fostering youth assertion in Hitler Youth
- **v)** Growth in female employment
- **vi)** New organisations for women
- **vii)** Encouragement of divorce

2 The historian G. Layton has argued (in *Germany: the Third Reich*, 1992, p. 105): 'Nazi policy towards women and the family was contradictory and incoherent, and did little to affect the ongoing sociological trends of an industrialised society.' Do you agree?

3 Hold a debate between two women in 1939, one supporting and one critical of the regime. Give yourself a specific identity, since this could well influence your view of the regime. Consider your class, your age, your religion, your pre-1933 voting behaviour, your home region, etc.

KEY POINTS FROM CHAPTER 15: How successfully did the Nazis impose their ideology on German women?

1 Nazis believed women should concentrate on childbearing and supporting their husbands.

2 This distinct role for women was seen as important and of equal value to the role of men.

3 Many of the Nazis' reactionary ideas were widely held, and many women viewed their policies positively.

4 Nazi policies towards women were in some respects contradictory.

5 The Nazis stressed the role of the family, but increasingly they were prepared to encourage divorce and extra-marital sex to breed more genetically pure Germans.

6 The government provided marriage loans and increased welfare services for mothers.

7 The Nazis initially encouraged and forced women to give up some jobs, but this trend was reversed during the Second World War.

8 Women's opportunities in universities were initially restricted, but this policy too was later reversed.

9 The Nazis set up several women's organisations that involved women outside the family sphere.

10 Women's experience of the Third Reich was complex and varied, and was not simply a reflection of Nazi ideology.

16

Did the Churches collaborate with or resist the Nazi regime?

CHAPTER OVERVIEW

SOURCE 16.1 Hitler in a speech to the Reichstag in March 1933

[Christianity is] the unshakeable foundation of the moral life of our people...

SOURCE 16.3 Archbishop Faulhaber of Munich in 1936

The Reich Chancellor undoubtedly lives in belief in God.

SOURCE 16.2 Hitler in a private conversation in 1933: quoted in *Hitler Speaks* by Hermann Rauschning

For our people it is decisive whether they acknowledge the Jewish Christ-creed with its effeminate [feeble] pity–ethics, or a strong, heroic belief in God in Nature, God in our people, in our destiny, in our blood.

[As in Italy, I will make] peace with the Church. Why not! It won't stop me eradicating Christianity from Germany root and branch. You are either Christian or a German. You can't be both.

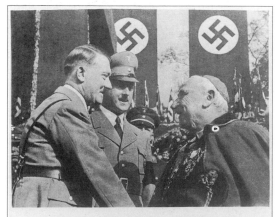

SOURCE 16.4
A poster produced by the government during the 1934 plebiscite campaign, showing Hitler and the Papal Nuncio (diplomat): 'For a long time I didn't understand you. But I have been trying to. And today I do.' Beneath it says: 'And every German Catholic understands Adolf Hitler and will vote Yes! on 12 November'

SOURCE 16.5
'On the founding of the state Church': a 1933 cartoon by John Heartfield. The text beneath says: 'The cross wasn't heavy enough yet'

ACTIVITY

1 What do Sources 16.1–9 suggest about relations between the Churches and the Nazi state?
2 Make a preliminary list of reasons why you might expect the Churches to:
   a) co-operate with the Third Reich
   b) oppose it.
3 Make a similar list of reasons why the Nazi regime might seek to:
   a) co-operate with the Churches
   b) weaken them.

SOURCE 16.8 1934 Nuremberg Rally Hitler Youth song. This song was adopted as a virtual national anthem

No evil priest can prevent us from feeling that we are the children of Hitler.
We follow not Christ, but Horst Wessel.
Away with incense and holy water!
The Church can go hang for all we care,
The swastika brings salvation on earth.
I want to follow it step by step.

SOURCE 16.6 Public statement by Bishop Berning, September 1933

The German bishops have long ago said Yes to the new State, and have not only promised to recognise its authority . . . but are serving the State with burning love and all our strength.

SOURCE 16.7 1934 Declaration by the Confessional Church (a new dissenting Protestant organisation)

We repudiate the false teaching that there are areas of life in which we belong not to Jesus Christ but to another lord . . .
   We repudiate the false teaching that the State can and should expand beyond its special responsibility to become the single and total order of human life.

SOURCE 16.9 Papal ENCYCLICAL, 'With Burning Grief', a message from the Pope circulated in Germany in 1937

He who singles out race . . . [and] the bearers of state power . . . and sets them up as the highest norm above all, including religious values, and reverences them with idolatry, he distorts and falsifies the God-created, God-demanded order of things. Such a person is far from real belief in God and from a conception of life that corresponds to such a belief. Only superficial spirits can fall victim to the false doctrine of a national God, or a national religion.

FOCUS ROUTE

1 What were Hitler's aims for the Churches?
2 Explain the Nazi government's approach to:
   a) the Protestant Churches
   b) the Catholic Church.
3 What were the main reasons why many Christian leaders co-operated with the Nazis?
4 What forms did opposition from the Churches take?
5 What evidence is there to suggest the Nazis failed to replace commitment to Christianity with support for a faith more suited to their *Volksgemeinschaft*?

A Introduction

In most respects, the Christian and Nazi approaches to life seem poles apart. The former advocated love and co-operation, the latter, hate and struggle. However, both organisations shared some common outlooks, most notably in respect for traditional cultural values, such as the importance of family life, and in their hostility to communism. There was also, particularly in Lutheran Protestantism, a tradition of respect for the state and nationalism. Anti-semitism, too, was not totally alien to the Christian tradition.

Hitler had been brought up a Catholic. However, although at times for political reasons he associated Nazism with Christianity, his real beliefs were clearly hostile to that faith. He wanted to replace Christianity, a religion reflecting the values of an inferior race, with a new, assertive Aryan faith. Furthermore, the Churches were a potential obstacle to his reordering of the German people into committed followers of his totalitarian regime.

However, Hitler was a skilled politician as well as a fanatic, and he realised he was not in a position to embark immediately on the implementation of his full vision. For tactical reasons, he talked of the need for a 'positive Christianity'. His initial main concern was to gain some control of, and support from, the Church hierarchies, and then gradually to reduce their influence.

306

DID THE CHURCHES COLLABORATE WITH OR RESIST THE NAZI REGIME?

ACTIVITY

Read the chronological list of events relating to the Churches in the Third Reich in Chart 16A. (To help understand it, you might also want to refer to the **Learning trouble spot** opposite.)

1 First, examine how the Nazi regime treated the Churches, by finding evidence of:
 a) a conciliatory approach by the regime
 b) a hostile approach by the regime.
2 Then examine how the Churches responded to the Nazi state, by finding evidence of:
 a) co-operation with the Nazi regime
 b) opposition to the regime.
 (Different groups of students could look for evidence of one particular feature.)
 Support each answer with evidence from the chronology. Also note down any changes over time in the above areas.
3 Is there any evidence of Hitler modifying his approach in the light of public reactions?
4 Can you draw any initial overall conclusion about relations between the Churches and the Nazi state?

■ 16A Nazism and the Churches: some key events

1933 July	The SA are ordered to attend church ceremonies
	The Catholic Church and the new government sign a Concordat (agreement) respecting each other's role
	The government supports the creation of a Reich Church to co-ordinate all Protestant Churches
Nov	A new Nazi-supported Protestant group, the German Christians, calls for the cleansing of the gospels of un-German elements
1934	A protest Confessional Church breaks away from the state-supported Reich Church
	The Catholic Bishops Conference issues a pastoral letter: 'Religion cannot be based on blood, race or other dogmas of human creation, but only on divine revelation'
Autumn	Two Protestant bishops are arrested, but released after an outcry
1935	700 Prussian Protestant pastors (ministers) are arrested for condemning Nazi neo-paganism (a new form of the 'old religion' based on Nordic mythology)
1936	Galen, Bishop of Münster, thanks the Führer for remilitarising the Rhineland, and asks God to bless his endeavours
	The National Socialist Teachers' League (NSLB) encourages members not to teach religion; religious education downplayed in school reports and lessons reduced
June	Confessional pastors circulate a message criticising Nazi ideology and policies. Hundreds of Confessional pastors are sent to concentration camps; their church funds are confiscated
1937	200 priests are put on trial on currency trafficking offences
	An order banning crucifixes from classrooms is withdrawn after public protest. The Pope criticises racism and the Führer worship of Nazism
1939 Nov	Cardinal Faulhaber orders a special service to celebrate Hitler's survival of an assassination attempt
1941 Dec	The Churches welcome the German attack on the USSR
	Bishop Galen publicly protests against euthanasia. No action is taken against him, but in Lübeck three priests who had circulated his text to soldiers are executed
1943	A SYNOD of the Prussian Confessional Church criticises those involved in the extermination of people on health and racial grounds: 'We cannot permit superiors to relieve us of our responsibility before God'

■ 16B Religious organisations in Nazi Germany

	Christian				Pagan
	Catholic	**Protestant**			
	Catholic Church	**1** Reich Church	Confessional Church	**2** German Christians	**3** Faith Movement
Key individuals	Bishop Galen Pope Pius XII	Bishop Ludwig Müller	Pastor Niemöller Pastor Bonhöffer	Ludwig Müller	Alfred Rosenberg

Note: The numerals 1, 2, 3 show the progressive religious aims of the regime. The Confessional Church was a reaction by some Christians to the first stage of Nazi policies.

■ Learning trouble spot

The Churches in Germany

This topic is complicated because of the large number of different church groupings, and the Nazi regime's gradual approach to replacing traditional Christianity.

A CHURCHES BEFORE 1933

Catholic

- Members: 22 million (32 per cent of population); concentrated in west and south (see map on page 120)
- Powerful institution with range of bodies: e.g. youth organisations (1.5 million members), schools, charities
- The Catholic Z and BVP parties together regularly received about one-fifth of the votes in Weimar elections

Protestants

- Members: over 40 million (58 per cent of population)
- Mainly Lutheran (EVANGELICAL) and CALVINIST
- Organised separately in 28 state-based Churches
- Youth organisations had 0.7 million members

B KEY RELIGIOUS ORGANISATIONS DURING THE THIRD REICH

The Reich Church

The Reich Church was a new umbrella organisation of the Protestant Churches, set up as a means of co-ordinating religion. Within it, the German Christians developed as a powerful movement. Hitler hoped they would dominate the Reich Church. However, the attempt to create a unified, state-controlled Church caused a reaction and the Confessional Church broke away.

German Christians

German Christians wanted to restructure the whole of Protestantism into a new, racially based brand of Christianity. They described themselves as the 'SA of the Church', of a new people's Church. They adopted Nazi-style uniforms and salutes; they had a slogan: 'The swastika on our breasts and the cross in our hearts.' In November 1933 they called for the cleansing of the gospels of un-German elements, especially 'the scapegoat and inferiority theology of Rabbi Paul'.

Confessional Church

In 1934 the Confessional Church broke away from the Reich Church. It was not based on opposition to Nazism as such, but it was concerned to defend the Protestant Church against state interference and the false theology of the German Christians. It had about 5,000 clergy.

German Faith Movement

Whereas the German Christians wanted to nazify Christianity, the Faith Movement went further and wanted to replace Christianity with a new pagan Nazi faith. It encouraged Germans to leave Christianity and adopt pagan rituals: for example the SS held marriages in RUNIC carved rooms. It remained a small sect, but illustrates what the Nazis might have done if they had won the Second World War.

SOURCE 16.11 From the journal of the Faith Movement, 1937

Jesus was a cowardly Jewish lout who had certain adventures during his years of indiscretion. He uprooted his disciples from blood and soil ... At the very end he insulted the majesty of death in an obscene manner.

SOURCE 16.10 Reich Bishop Ludwig Müller, leader of the German Christians, making a speech in September 1934

Key words

Confession: often used to describe a particular type of church

Diocese: church administrative unit centred on a bishopric

Encyclical: formal policy statement issued by the Pope and circulated throughout the Catholic Church

Pastor: Protestant minister

Synod: an assembly of Protestant pastors and laity (ordinary church members)

308

DID THE CHURCHES COLLABORATE WITH OR RESIST THE NAZI REGIME?

ACTIVITY

Find evidence to support the descriptions of the three stages in Chart 16C and use it to complete your own copy of the table below.

Stage	Evidence of the policy
1 Control	
2 Weaken	
3 Replace	

B How did the Nazi regime treat the Churches?

■ 16C Key features of Nazi policy towards the Churches

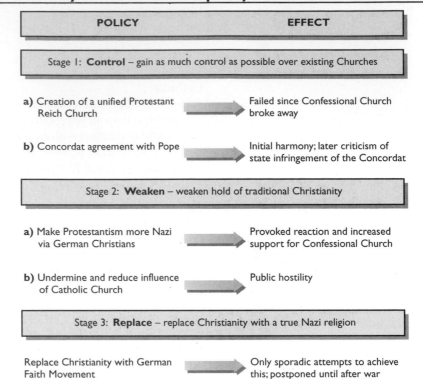

Hitler's overall approach to the Churches of Germany was firstly to seek to control them, then to reduce their influence, and finally to replace them with a faith reflecting Nazi values. It would be easier to gain greater control of the divided Protestant Churches than the international Catholic Church. The Protestant Churches were traditionally nationalist and had supported conservative parties during the Weimar Republic.

The government gave support to a growing movement among Protestants, the German Christians (Deutsche Christen). They wanted to imbue Christianity with the spirit of Nazism. In August 1933 two-thirds of those attending the Prussian synod showed their leanings by wearing Nazi uniforms. They helped establish a new Reich Church, hoping to combine all Protestants within one structure. Hitler hoped the German Christians could be used to co-ordinate the Protestant Churches. Ludwig Müller, Hitler's adviser on Protestant church affairs, was elected to the new post of Reich Bishop in July 1933.

However, this clear attempt to control and nazify Protestantism aroused much opposition. In September 1933 over one hundred pastors created a breakaway movement, which in October 1934 was organised into the Confessional Church (Bekennende Kirche). It was not explicitly anti-Nazi, but wanted to preserve Protestantism from political control and indoctrination.

Some of the German Christians' actions, such as requiring pastors to take an oath of loyalty to Hitler, and the arrest of two Protestant bishops increased the public outcry. Hitler, who could be pragmatic when required, now distanced himself from Reich Bishop Müller. The attempt to create a more nazified, unified Protestant Church had failed. Instead there were now three groups within Protestantism: the official Reich Church, the German Christians trying to control it, and the opposition Confessional Church (see Chart 16B).

Hitler realised it would be even harder to exercise control over the Catholic Church, so instead he looked for an agreement to gain its support. Both sides were initially conciliatory. The Papacy agreed to the dissolution of the Centre Party (Z). In July 1933 the Vatican signed a Concordat with the government. The Vatican recognised the new regime and promised that the Church would

ACTIVITY

What insights do Sources 16.12–14 reveal about Nazi policy towards Christianity?

SOURCE 16.12 Security police measures against 'agitator priests' in 1941

1 *Warning*
2 *Fine*
3 *Forbidden to preach* (Redeverbot)
4 *Forbidden to remain in the parish*
5 *Forbidden all activities as a priest*
6 *Short-term arrest*
7 *Protective custody*

309

DID THE CHURCHES COLLABORATE WITH OR RESIST THE NAZI REGIME?

SOURCE 16.13 An anti-Nazi cartoon on the evolution of Nazi policy for the Protestant (Lutheran) Church

not interfere in politics. In return, the state would not interfere in the Catholic Church which could keep control of its educational, youth and other communal institutions. Catholic leaders generally remained concerned not to provoke the government. However, the Nazis were less conciliatory and did not accept the Concordat limitations on their power for long.

Hitler now tried to reduce the influence of the Churches, partly by attacking what he saw as church interference in politics and partly by discrediting them rather than tackling them head on. Within this broad picture, relations were complicated. This was partly due to the disorganised nature of the Nazi state. Hitler did not impose a clear strategy on all Nazi authorities. Several local *Gauleiter* indulged in radical anti-Church activities that then had to be abandoned due to popular opposition. For example, in Bavaria people continued to use the traditional greeting '*Gruss Gott*' (God greet you) rather than the officially approved 'Heil Hitler', and Bavarian blue-and-white flags rather than swastikas were flown on feast days.

The Nazis particularly targeted the young in their attempts to reduce the influence of the Churches. Young people were encouraged to join the Hitler Youth, not Catholic groups. In 1936 church groups were disbanded and the Hitler Youth made compulsory. Less and less stress was put on religious education in state schools; and Nazi Party officials tried to remove crucifixes from schools. Parents were pressurised to send their children to local state schools, not denominational (mainly Catholic) ones. Whereas 65 per cent of children attended church schools in 1935, only 5 per cent did by 1937, and these schools had virtually disappeared by 1939.

In a more direct attack on the Catholic Church's influence, over 200 priests were accused of sexual and financial misbehaviour in what amounted to SHOW TRIALS, and numerous monasteries were closed down.

In the mid 1930s the Nazi Party launched a 'Church Secession Campaign' to encourage Germans to abandon their Churches. This had some success with government employees. In 1937 over 100,000 Christians left the Church, and in 1939 3.5 million Germans were members of the *Gottgläubig* (God-believing) neo-pagan movement; they had thus rejected what was described as 'Germany's religious Versailles'. However, many of these wanted their names kept secret for fear of ostracism (being rejected by their society), and during the war the tide away from Christianity was reversed.

In the early successful years of the Second World War, there were more aggressive moves against the Churches, particularly against critical priests (see Source 16.12). However, the government pulled back as it became wary of provoking opposition. When the war was won, however, it intended to replace Christianity with a new German Faith Movement.

SOURCE 16.14 Cartoon from the SS magazine *Das Schwarze Korps* (The Black Corps), 1937. The labels on the pigs surrounding the priestly chief 'shepherd' read: 'Rape, sadistic orgies in monasteries', 'Unnatural acts in places of worship' and 'Abuse of children and mental defectives'. The caption running from top to bottom reads: 'Go forth and watch over my – lambs!'

310

DID THE CHURCHES COLLABORATE WITH OR RESIST THE NAZI REGIME?

C How did the Churches react to the Nazi state?

Once again, a complex picture emerges. This is hardly surprising, given the existence of different religious groups, changes over time, and local and individual variations. The overwhelming majority of Germans were Christians and at the same time supported the regime, especially Hitler. Many disliked particular measures the government took against the Churches, and sometimes expressed dissatisfaction that led the government to modify its approach. Christians often blamed anti-Church measures on radicals around Hitler, not on their great leader himself.

■ 16D Religion and Nazism: how seven people responded to the regime

Ludwig Müller

Individuals respond to difficult situations in different ways. The biographies of these seven people illustrate the complex relationship between the state and the Churches in Nazi Germany.

Ludwig Müller, 1883–1946
Müller was the leader of the German Christians. He was a strongly nationalist and anti-semitic Protestant army chaplain. Elected Reich Bishop in July 1933 at the National Synod, he was pushed into the background after the Confessional Church broke away. He committed suicide in 1946.

Alfred Rosenberg, 1893–1946
Rosenberg was an anti-semitic, anti-Christian Nazi ideologue. He promoted the German Faith Movement as a new pagan cult. Within the party he fought hard against Christianity. In 1941 he was made Minister for Occupied Territories. Rosenberg was hanged in 1946.

Alfred Rosenberg

Pope Pius XI, 1857–1939
Pius XI, having allowed the dissolution of the Centre Party and agreed to the Concordat, became disillusioned by the Nazis' failure to keep its part of the agreement. In 1937 he issued the encyclical *Mit Brennender Sorge* (With Burning Grief), which was an outspoken attack on Nazi beliefs and methods. He was preparing an encyclical against anti-semitism when he died.

Pope Pius XII, 1876–1958
As a papal nuncio (diplomat) in Germany, the future Pius XII played a major part in negotiating the Concordat in 1933. In March 1939 he was elected Pope, but did not openly condemn Nazism, only communism. He was silent on anti-semitism, and he refused to excommunicate Catholics participating in GENOCIDE. He was criticised for failing to take a stand against Nazism, but defended his approach on tactical grounds as the best way of maintaining the Church's role.

Pope Pius XI

Pope Pius XII

311

DID THE CHURCHES COLLABORATE WITH OR RESIST THE NAZI REGIME?

ACTIVITY

Read the biographies, then match up each of the following views of the best approach to the Nazi regime to the right individual.

i) The survival of Christianity is more important than criticising the government.

ii) My personal prejudices match the regime's so I can work with it.

iii) My initial co-operation was a mistake, for I now realise that Hitler does not keep his word. I should have realised that Nazism and Christianity are incompatible.

iv) I hate traditional religion. Here is an opportunity to start something new that suits our beliefs.

v) This regime is so evil I will do what I can to overthrow it.

vi) I will use my public position to criticise the regime when it acts against the basic teachings of Christ.

vii) I have reluctantly come to realise that my Christian faith cannot accept this regime and what it has done to the Church. I will support the founding of another, true Christian Church.

The Churches were more concerned with protecting their own institutions and beliefs than in speaking out about the nature of the regime. There were, however, several critical statements from clerics, and in 1937 the Pope issued the encyclical 'With Burning Grief'. It complained about the government's breaking of the Concordat, the harassment of priests and Nazi idolatry (worship) of the state and race. The text was smuggled into Germany and read out from pulpits on Palm Sunday in March 1937. The most famous, and possibly most effective, criticism came from Bishop Galen against euthanasia in 1941 (see below and page 338). This caused great consternation (dismay) within the government and vigorous debate about what action to take. In the end Galen remained unpunished.

Bishop Clemens von Galen, 1878–1946

As Catholic Bishop of Münster, he initially welcomed Hitler's nationalism, but was critical of racism. From 1934 he preached several sermons criticising Nazi policies. In 1941 he criticised euthanasia, but he was seen as too popular to be punished. Known as the 'Lion of Münster', Galen has been described as the only effective protester in the Third Reich. He was arrested after the July 1944 Bomb Plot, but released in 1945.

Bishop Clemens von Galen

Martin Niemöller, 1892–1984

A former U-boat commander and nationalist, Niemöller initially supported Hitler, but was later one of the founders of the Confessional Church. He was arrested in 1937; he remained imprisoned until his release from Dachau by the Allies in 1945.

Dietrich Bonhöffer, 1906–45

Bonhöffer joined the Confessional Church in 1935. In February 1933 he had broadcast a critique of the *Führerprinzip* which he openly regarded as hostile to Christianity. His broadcast was cut off. He taught trainee pastors and encouraged them to resist Nazism; he also tried to get the Confessional Church to condemn the Nuremberg Laws. In 1940 his college was closed and he was banned from preaching and publishing. He worked with the underground and in 1942 met Bishop Bell, a British intermediary, in Sweden. He wanted the Allies to recognise the existence of the opposition, and work with a new government for peace. In April 1943 he was arrested after being named by an ABWEHR agent, and was executed in Flossenbürg concentration camp on 5 April 1945.

Martin Niemöller

Dietrich Bonhöffer

312

DID THE CHURCHES COLLABORATE WITH OR RESIST THE NAZI REGIME?

During the Third Reich an estimated 800 of 17,000 Protestant pastors were arrested, but only 50 received major prison sentences for opposition. Between one-third and one-half of the Catholic clergy are estimated to have been harassed in some way, but only one Catholic bishop was expelled and one imprisoned for a long period.

Many Christians later felt the Churches had failed in their duty during the regime. Although the Churches had institutional structures separate from the government and a set of beliefs to inspire opposition, they were concerned to try to hold on to their members, and not to provoke a crushing retaliation from a government that clearly contained elements hostile to Christianity. Both the Catholic and Protestant Churches were concerned to demonstrate their patriotism and supported the war effort, especially that in the east against the USSR. However, relations between the Catholic Church and the Nazi regime have been described as a state of simmering tension within a war of attrition.

Overall, Church–state relations seem to reflect the fears each side felt towards the other. Despite the regime's totalitarian pretensions (claims), government documents illustrate the fear that undue pressure on the Churches, particularly in Catholic areas, would turn the people against the regime. Ironically, many clerics were afraid that they were losing the battle with Nazism between 1933 and 1939.

Source 16.15 illustrates the complexity of the relationship between the Churches and the Nazi state.

TALKING POINT

In 1998 the Vatican officially apologised for its lack of opposition to the Holocaust. Is it important for governments to apologise for the actions of their predecessors in the past?

SOURCE 16.15   Extract from the Bavarian Catholic bishops' pastoral letter in December 1936

After the deplorable fight carried on by Marxists, Communists, Free Thinkers and FREEMASONS against Christianity and the Church we welcomed with gratitude the National Socialist profession of positive Christianity. We are convinced that many hundreds of thousands are still loyal to this profession of faith and, indeed, we observe with sorrow how others tend to remove themselves from Christian belief and from the programme of the Führer, and by this means put the Third Reich on a new basis, a Weltanschauung *standing in open contradiction to the commandments of Christianity. This formation of National Socialism into a* Weltanschauung *which cuts it away from any foundation in religion is developing more and more into a full-scale attack on the Christian faith and the Catholic Church. All this bodes ill for the future of our people and our Fatherland. Our Führer and Chancellor in a most impressive demonstration acknowledged the importance of the two Christian confessions to state and society, and promised the two confessions his protection. Unfortunately, men with considerable influence and power are operating in direct opposition to those promises and both confessions are being systematically attacked. Certain of those who lead the attack on the Churches wish to promote a united church in which the confession of faith will become meaningless. Most especially they seek to rid Germany of the Catholic Church and declare it to be a body foreign to our country and its people. These folk lack all real understanding of our holy faith and of the Christian religion in any form . . .*

. . . Nothing could be further from our intentions than to adopt a hostile attitude toward, or a renunciation of, the present form taken by our Government. For us, respect for authority, love of Fatherland, and the fulfilment of our duty to the State are matters not only of conscience but of divine ordinance. This command we will always require our faithful to follow. But we will never regard as an infringement of this duty our defence of God's laws and of His Church, or of ourselves against attacks on the Faith and the Church. The Führer can be certain that we Bishops are prepared to give all moral support to his historic struggle against Bolshevism. We will not criticise things which are purely political. What we do ask is that our holy Church be permitted to enjoy her God-given rights and her freedom.

ACTIVITY

Study Source 16.15.

1 Explain the reference to:
   a) *Weltanschauung* (line 7)
   b) 'united church' (line 17).
2 Identify reasons why the bishops support the government.
3 How do they view Hitler and his aims? What do they criticise?
4 What can be deduced from this letter as to the bishops' view of the Concordat of 1933?
5 What support does this source give for
   a) criticism of the Catholic Church for being solely concerned with its own position
   b) recent historians' interpretations of the nature of the Nazi state and the 'Hitler myth'?

ACTIVITY

One group of students read Sources 16.16, 16.17 and 16.19; another group should read Source 16.18. Then compare your answers to the following questions:

1 What appears to be happening to belief and involvement in Christianity?
2 What value does each of these sources have as evidence about the experience of Christianity during the Nazi period?

SOURCE 16.17 Bavarian district police report, June 1939

The uncertainty of the diplomatic situation, the harsh taxation, certain economic difficulties, and in particular the pressure against the Church are at the moment producing increasing apathy among the rural population as far as nationalist issues are concerned. The Catholic Church is reaping the profit from these burdens. The more attempts are made to keep a watch on the Church or such attempts are even suspected, the more the peasantry support their priests. Catholic churchgoing, participation in various events such as processions, the blessing of the fields, pilgrimages, attendance at services during weekdays, and confession remain strong. For the time being the Party's propaganda is helpless in trying to resist this development. The mood is directed less against the State and much more against the Party.

SOURCE 16.19 Gauleiter reports, June 1943

The war, with all its sorrow and anguish, has driven some families back into the arms of priests and the church ...

The districts unanimously report that the church of both confessional orientations is engaging in exceptionally heavy activity. In comparison to the party, the church today still has much manpower at its disposal ...

In their weekly reports, the party regional organisations have repeatedly emphasised that the churches of both confessions – but especially the Catholic Church – are in today's fateful struggle one of the main pillars of negative influence upon public morale.

D How did the German people respond to the uneasy relationship between Church and state?

Finally, let us look at some evidence to help us assess how far the Nazis succeeded in reducing the hold of Christianity.

SOURCE 16.16 Police report in Cologne, March 1934

Politically, it is noteworthy and illuminating that the Catholic population of Cologne ... in recent times have banded together strongly. They are taking part in church celebrations and events in numbers of such a size that have hardly been seen in previous years ... The reason is that people who disapprove of the measures taken against Catholic organisations want to make a show in public that they are loyal to the Catholic Church.

SOURCE 16.18 A 1939 report by the Protestant Church on visits to Bavaria 1937–8

The year 1938 seems to have brought a series of difficulties which have a negative impact on the general attitude of the parish. A dean [commented in spring 1939]: 'The general impression was heavily determined by the catastrophic changes in the school sphere and in that of religious instruction' ... The work of the pastors has become much more difficult than before ...

The problem of the German Christians is already a matter of history as far as the general situation is concerned. A few German Christian clergy have returned to the Confession. Others must at least restrain themselves in their own parishes especially to maintain their position at all ...

The last few years are much more characterised by the fact that after the defensive victory against the German Christians, they find themselves confronted by a new enemy, who is difficult to get to grips with and yet is clearly fighting everywhere against Christianity ...

The danger which threatens our parishes is of being ground down, of becoming dispirited, atrophied [paralysed]. The vast majority of the parishes will not be voluntarily unfaithful to their Christian beliefs, but they continue to believe that 'one cannot do anything' against the new forces, and give up ... The school question has had a particularly deep impact in many parishes: they have felt the danger instinctively but believe they are faced with an 'inevitable' development ...

The trend [is] towards a slight reduction in Church-going and participation in Communion, the prevention of young people, and often the men too, from taking part in parish life because of other events, the putting of obstacles in the way of religious instruction, anti-Christian influence and clandestine [secret] pressure on certain groups to keep a low profile vis-à-vis [with respect to] the Church.

In many areas the events put on by the State youth organisation take less and less account of the Parish Church services and what would have been inconceivable in 1935 has become the norm in some places in 1939. Above all, youth is losing the habit of going to Church regularly. One need not fear that the village youth will be influenced by the German Faith Movement but rather will lose the habit of going to Church through being intentionally kept from Church services which will be followed by an inner estrangement ...

As far as the younger ones are concerned, school is the central problem. While at the time of the visitation in 1936 the confessional school was still in existence, the questionnaire for 1939 reports on the community school, the reduction in religious instruction, the obstruction of such instruction for technical college pupils, the giving up of religious instruction on the part of most teachers. The removal of religious instruction from the core curriculum ...

Church-going is normally satisfactory. Of the 200 reports two-thirds describe churchgoing as good, two-ninths as moderate, and one-ninth as poor and unsatisfactory. However, in contrast to this subjective assessment, it must be said that in comparison with the situation in 1932 a moderate reduction in church-going is the general rule even in village and small town parishes ...

314

DID THE CHURCHES COLLABORATE WITH OR RESIST THE NAZI REGIME?

ACTIVITY

1 a) Why, according to Noakes, were the Churches able to limit the Nazis' control of German life?

   b) What reasons do Geary and Wilt give why the Churches did not resist the Nazis more?

   c) How far do Wright and Housden agree on the nature of Church opposition?

   d) Explain which historian you consider to be most critical and which least critical of the Churches' response to National Socialism.

   e) Why do such differences occur?

2 Summarise in your own words how the Churches responded to Nazism. Would you be prepared to use either of the words *resist* or *collaborate*?

3 'The Nazis were more hostile to the Church than the Church was to them.' Do you agree?

E Review: Did the Churches collaborate with or resist the Nazi regime?

It is now time to return to the question in the chapter title about collaboration and resistance. We need to discuss whether either of these words is an accurate representation of how the Christian Churches responded to the Nazis. You may feel that either of these descriptions would be too simplistic to sum up the response of different Christian institutions and many millions of individuals. Read the following accounts by historians to help you finalise your assessment of the Christian response to Nazism.

SOURCE 16.20 J. Noakes, G. Pridham, *Nazism: A History in Documents*, 1984, p. 582

The churches were the only institutions which both had an alternative 'ideology' to that of the regime and were permitted to retain their own organisational autonomy. This made them a major obstacle to the Nazi attempt to establish total control over German life.

SOURCE 16.21 R. Geary, *Hitler and Nazism*, 1993, p. 55

A similar [to the army] mixture of institutional self-interest, agreement with certain aspects of Nazi policy and yet also principled opposition was to be found in the German churches ... In general the church hierarchy sought to avoid conflict with the regime without endorsing all aspects of its policies.

SOURCE 16.22 A. Wilt, *Nazi Germany*, 1994, p. 81

It is difficult to account for the meagre resistance of most clergy, though the overwhelming acceptance of Nazism by their respective congregations and parishes, their distrust of leftist thinking, their own conservatism, their belief in the separation of political affairs from one's spiritual life, and their tradition of subservience [obedience] to the state, as practised in particular by Lutheranism, all played a part. Whatever the reason, the churches' overall response to National Socialism was timid and half-hearted, and helped erode their influence on German life.

SOURCE 16.23 J. R. C. Wright, 1970s article 'Hitler and the Churches'

Both Christian Churches showed they were not prepared to tolerate Nazi aggression against them passively. In this they compared favourably with other institutions ... However, the purpose of the Church opposition was self-defence, not a wider political opposition; the Churches ... frequently affirmed their loyalty to the state and the Führer.

SOURCE 16.24 M. Housden, *Resistance and Conformity in the Third Reich*, 1996, p. 64

The churches' opposition was 'issue driven' (that is to say involving piecemeal reactions to individual, concrete actions such as the withdrawal of crucifixes from schools, the appointment of a German Christian as Reich bishop, or euthanasia) rather than rooted in a coherent, politically active anti-Nazi morality. The churches and their followers generally were more interested in defending their religious 'space' and surviving attack than in becoming society's moral guardians. They wanted to write themselves into the overall trajectory [course] of the Third Reich rather than alter its direction per se.

TALKING POINT

Is it right to compromise with a government you profoundly disagree with to protect the position of your own institution?

1 Hitler publicly acknowledged the role of Christianity but because of its opposing values privately vowed to eliminate it.
2 Many Christians supported Nazism because of its anti-communism and respect for traditional cultural values.
3 The Nazi approach was initially to try to control the Churches, then weaken them and finally replace them.
4 A Reich Church was created to control Protestantism, but the breakaway Confessional Church rejected government interference.
5 The Catholic Church signed an agreement with Hitler but became increasingly concerned with the government's actions.
6 Some priests were arrested and some Church organisations were threatened, but the Christian faith remained strong, and increased again during the Second World War.
7 The Nazis' efforts to introduce the German Faith Movement failed.
8 The Churches were more concerned to defend their institutions from Nazi attack than to challenge the government on a broader front.
9 There was more criticism of and opposition to the regime from individual Christians than from the Churches as institutions.
10 The Churches could be said to have broadly compromised in order to survive.

17

How much opposition was there to the Nazi regime?

CHAPTER OVERVIEW

SOURCE 17.1 Sophie Scholl, a student at Munich university and one of the leaders of the White Rose group

'What we have written and said is in the minds of all of you, but you lack the courage to say it aloud.' Thus spoke the brave Sophie Scholl during her trial before a People's Court in 1943. She was executed for distributing anti-government pamphlets. Her statement raises a number of issues about the German people's attitude to Nazism and in particular:

- Were most Germans privately critical of the Nazi regime or did public acceptance reflect genuine support?
- Was the limited amount of opposition a reflection of a lack of courage or of the problems potential opponents faced?

In this chapter we examine the difficult and sensitive issue of how much opposition there was in Nazi Germany. The general impression is of little opposition and there is much evidence of Hitler's genuine popularity. Furthermore, the Third Reich was overthrown not by the German people but by the massive military might of the Soviet Union, the United States of America and their allies. Such internal opposition as there was had little effect on the course of events. This has led some historians to follow Sophie Scholl's criticism of the Germans as lacking courage. We must, however, be cautious.

We have already seen that many Germans gained greatly from Hitler's domestic policies, and so had good reason not to oppose the regime. Hitler's undoubted foreign policy successes until 1941 (see Chapters 20 and 21) reinforced this support. (It was not until 1943 that many Germans wavered in their loyalty to the regime.) Furthermore, there was a fierce repressive machinery, reinforced by widespread denunciations (see Chapter 11), that made open criticism of the regime a brave, and perhaps foolhardy, act. Opposition could cost you your job, freedom or life. The dilemma was particularly acute for civil servants. Many welcomed the new regime but others had to decide whether to continue to work for the government while trying to limit its harm, or to dissociate themselves totally from the regime. This could be a hard decision, as the comments in Sources 17.2–5 illustrate. We might like to think that if we had lived in Nazi Germany we would have opposed Nazism, but careful reflection might lead to a different conclusion. We shall try to assess how many Germans, like Sophie Scholl, tried to oppose the regime in the following subsections:

A What opposition was there to the Nazi regime? (pp. 318–25)

B How can the historian judge the degree of opposition and support in Nazi Germany? (pp. 326–9)

C Humour as resistance (pp. 329–30)

D Review: How much opposition was there to the Nazi regime? (pp. 331–3)

Why is the question of the degree of German opposition to Nazism a sensitive one?

ACTIVITY

1 List five groups of people who might have been opposed to the Nazi regime.
2 List the various forms that opposition might take.
3 Consider the tables below of factors favouring opposition to a government and those making opposition difficult. (The factors encouraging opposition cover both reasons why people might be discontented with a regime and possible opportunities for them to organise opposition activities.)
    a) Write down those factors that applied during the Third Reich.
    b) What conclusions do you draw?

Factors encouraging opposition
Rising unemployment
Food shortages
General perception that the country is going downhill
Foreign policy failures
Divided government
Weak leader
Free elections
Range of political parties
Potential opposition groups prepared to co-operate

Factors making effective opposition difficult
Powerful secret police
Arbitrary imprisonment
Government control of the media
One-party state
Tradition of respect for authority
Loyal army
No independent trade unions
Network of government informers

4 Read Sources 17.2–7. What reasons are given why resistance was difficult?

SOURCE 17.2 Foreign Minister State Secretary Bülow who stayed on in his job after 1933

One cannot leave one's country in the lurch because it has a bad government.

SOURCE 17.3 General Werner von Fritsch, Commander-in-Chief of the army, 1934–8

We cannot change politics; we must do our duty silently.

SOURCE 17.4 Ewald von Kleist-Schmenzin, a conservative Prussian landowner

Do you think that when you board an express train, the driver of which is deranged, you can somehow take over the controls?

SOURCE 17.5 Ambassador Prittwitz on resigning in 1933

One must only put oneself at the disposal of a government for which certain basic values of humanity are sacred. Coming to terms with inhuman principles in order to avoid something allegedly worse leads to disaster.

SOURCE 17.6 Dr Schuster, an anti-Nazi teacher, describes his various options

1 Emigrate.
2 Resign, write alternative books for the future.
3 Stay and publicly defy the headmaster, and be sent to prison.
4 [which he adopts] I am trying through the teaching of geography to do everything in my power to give the boys knowledge and I hope later on, judgement, so that when, as they grow older, the Nazi fever dies down and it again becomes possible to offer some opposition they may be prepared ... There are four or five masters who are non-Nazis left in our school now, and we all work on the same plan. If we leave, four Nazis will come in and there will be no honest teaching in the whole school ... If we went to America and left others to it, would that be honest, or are the only honest people those in prison cells? If only there could be some collective action among teachers. But we cannot meet in conference, we cannot have a newspaper.

SOURCE 17.7 Emmi Bonhöffer, sister-in-law of Dietrich Bonhöffer, interviewed in the 1989 TV programme *Führer*

There was no resistance movement and there couldn't be. Nowhere in the world can develop a resistance movement when people feel better from day to day. Resistance: we were stones in a torrent, and the water crashed over us.

FOCUS ROUTE

1 Describe the main forms of opposition to the Nazi regime.
2 Explain why there was comparatively little opposition.

A What opposition was there to the Nazi regime?

In what ways did people oppose the regime?

ACTIVITY

As you read Source 17.8, identify the actions Linnert took and how he tried to escape detection.

SOURCE 17.8 SPD member Ludwig Linnert tried to resist the regime from 1933 until his arrest in 1938

Justice, freedom and culture – and yes socialism – forced us to warn people and arouse their consciences by distributing illegal leaflets, and writing slogans on the streets, in public squares and on walls . . .

Until my imprisonment . . . [a small grocer's] shop acted as a kind of resistance centre . . . Political contacts made themselves known to us by asking for loaf sugar, which we didn't keep and wasn't really available at that time. Or, when they bought other things, they would put their coins down on the counter in a square pattern, with a fifth coin in the middle . . .

We had also begun to make our own leaflets. We had a typewriter with movable typefaces, a copy machine and, most important, stacks of paper, which were purchased cautiously in small amounts from many different shops. We posted the first leaflets, mainly in the letter boxes of flats in working-class districts . . . We wore rubber gloves when we made these leaflets, so as not to leave behind any fingerprints . . .

As late as 1937 we had made leaflets in the flat and then scattered them just before dawn from the back of our motorbike on the streets leading to the factories in Sendling. We knew the dangers of what we were doing. There was no heroism; we didn't want to be martyrs. We wanted to survive to see the better future that we hoped for.

During the 1980s and 1990s, many historians have made great efforts to discover the evidence provided by accounts such as that of Linnert in Source 17.8. They have shifted their focus from the decisions of people in government to the activities of ordinary people that can be classified as popular opposition.

ACTIVITY

1 Read the following list of seven possible reactions to the Nazi regime. Write them out in a line, with the most hostile attitude towards the regime on the left, moving towards the most positive on the right.

Nonconformity
Acceptance
Resistance
Participation
Enthusiasm
Protest
Commitment

2 The three furthest to the left have been classified as opposition activities. Study Chart 17A which illustrates the various forms of opposition activities that have been recorded in the Third Reich. Select two examples of each of the three opposition categories above. (Remember that such classifications are more a matter of degree than of distinct categories.)

Organising a coup

Publicly criticising the regime

Not giving the Hitler greeting

Listening to American jazz

Attempting to assassinate Hitler and other leaders

Spontaneously protesting in public

Distributing anti-Nazi leaflets

Underachieving in the workplace

Spying for foreign governments

Deserting from the armed forces

Emigrating

Hiding Jews

Obstructive collaboration (e.g. remaining as a judge but giving lenient punishments to those 'guilty' of political offences)

Reading banned literature

The variety of opposition in the Third Reich

Listening to the BBC

Printing opposition literature

Going on strike

Applauding potentially subversive speeches in plays

Telling anti-Hitler jokes

Refusing to join the Hitler Youth

Not attending Nazi meetings

Collecting evidence of Nazi atrocities

Refusing to contribute to the *Winterhilfe* collection

Writing anti-Nazi graffiti

Helping victims of Nazism

Privately discussing an alternative government

Pressurising for higher wages

Committing suicide

TALKING POINT

It could be argued that some of these actions might be inspired by purely private or non-political reasons. Which of the above actions might fit into this category?

Opposition, resistance and nonconformity

Until recently, historians studying opposition to the Nazi regime tended to concentrate on public criticism of policies, such as that by Bishop Galen over euthanasia, and attempts to assassinate Hitler, most famously the July 1944 Bomb Plot. Since the 1980s some historians have shifted their focus from these fairly isolated acts of opposition to study the behaviour of ordinary people, and to see opposition in broader terms. They have identified a broad range of opposition activities, from minor to major. Minor opposition might be grumbling at the lack of butter; major could be challenging the whole regime. Minor might take place in private, major in public. Minor could involve people with little power. Major could include powerful leaders.

Assassination attempts

The most drastic acts of resistance that could have led to the collapse of the whole regime were assassination attempts on Hitler. There were numerous individual and group plans to assassinate Hitler, especially from 1939, some of which came very near to success. Some of the best documented are listed in the table below.

ASSASSINATION ATTEMPTS				
Date	**Who**	**Plan**	**What happened?**	**Result**
1935–6	Jewish students	Assassination	Nothing. No opportunity	–
9 Nov 1938	Student: Maurice Bavaud	Shoot Hitler at annual Munich parade	Couldn't get shot in	Executed (1941)
9 Nov 1939	Socialist cabinet-maker Georg Elser	Plant bomb in beer-hall where Hitler was speaking	Hitler left early because of fog. Bomb went off and killed four people	Arrested and executed (1945)
June 1940	Police Chief Friedrich von Schulenburg	Assassination at victory parade	Parade called off	–
Feb 1943	Army Command at Kharkov	Kill Hitler when he visited	Hitler changed his plans	–
March 1943	Major-General Henning von Tresckow and Lieutenant Fabian von Schlabrendorff	Place bomb on Hitler's plane	Fuse worked, but bomb did not ignite as it was too cold	–
March 1943	Colonel Rudolf von Gersdorff	Keep next to Hitler at an exhibition with a bomb	Hitler unexpectedly late	–
Dec 1943	Major Axel von dem Bussche	Blow himself and Hitler up at a uniform exhibition	Building bombed by RAF so the visit was cancelled	–
July 1944	Colonel Claus von Stauffenberg	Three bomb attempts	Briefcase, which exploded on the third attempt, had been moved further away from Hitler. He was shaken but not among the four killed	Over 5,000 people executed

TALKING POINT

Can the assassination of political leaders ever be justified?

Who were the resisters?

The best chance of replacing the Hitler regime was at the beginning. Until his death in August 1934, President Hindenburg could have dismissed Hitler as Chancellor. Alternatively, opposition parties and trade unions might have organised a general strike. However, unemployment was high, opposition elements were divided and many people did not expect Hitler to remain in power for long. The fact that Hitler had been appointed legally reinforced civil servants' instinct to obey the government. The army was appeased (conciliated) by the Night of the Long Knives, and then tied to Hitler by its oath. There was also a widespread hope of a national revival, led by the charismatic Hitler, after the divisions and failings of Weimar governments.

After 1934 there was no legal way to remove Hitler. Opposition activity was banned. Critics who remained in Germany had to resort to clandestine (secret) activity. This made co-ordination virtually impossible. There were various acts of opposition but they remained isolated, partly because of massive support for the government, shown in a series of plebiscites after 1934. Even allowing for intimidation, most historians argue that these reflect considerable popular enthusiasm. In many ways this is not surprising. The early victims of the Third Reich were unpopular: for example Communists, SA leaders, Jews, even political parties and trade unions. Hitler was also careful to control more radical Nazi ideas. Furthermore, his policies were increasingly successful, especially in reducing unemployment and in foreign policy. There was a general wave of optimism, reinforced by effective government propaganda. Critics suffered arbitrary (unjustified) arrest. Thus a mixture of successful policies, propaganda and repression reduced opposition.

During the Third Reich there were some plans to overthrow the government, most notably in the army, but generally opposition took the form of non-co-operation rather than resistance. However, in a totalitarian regime, which aims to mobilise all the people within its structures, non-compliance, even non-commitment, can be deemed opposition. The number of actual resisters was small; their aims and methods varied. The story of 'resistance' is really that of a hundred subgroups and thousands of individuals. This was easier in institutions, such as the Churches and the army, that gave opponents opportunities to meet for apparently legitimate reasons. They had a legal organisation, meeting places and a clear value system; the army also had a code of secrecy at the top.

As historians complete further work on local archives, more evidence of a variety of forms of dissent emerged. Thus the Marxist historian Mason studying the working class identified considerable non-conformism, such as absenteeism, and even wildcat strikes and industrial sabotage. Kershaw's studies of public opinion have highlighted large-scale grumbling, and Peukert's studies of Hamburg and Cologne have identified considerable opposition among young people. The estimated 1.3 million Germans who were sent to concentration camps and the 300,000 who left Germany between 1933 and 1939 have also been used as some indication of widespread opposition to the regime.

Groups providing some opposition to the Nazi regime

The Churches (see pages 306–15)

Amongst Protestants, the Confessional Church fairly successfully resisted nazification, but it was more concerned to defend the Church than to weaken the regime itself.

The Catholic hierarchy initially co-operated, but mass opposition of the laity to government interference modified government attacks on the Catholic Church. Catholic clergy criticised sterilisation, then euthanasia.

Overall, the Churches concentrated on protecting their own positions, and as institutions did not pose a threat to the regime. However, they remained an obstacle to a fully totalitarian state. Some brave individuals resisted and hundreds of pastors and priests were imprisoned and killed.

Youth (see pages 276–91)

Various alternative and opposition youth groups developed, including Swing Youth and the Edelweiss Pirates. There were some organised university groups, for example the White Rose group in Munich from 1941 to 1943: its objective was 'to strive for the renewal of the mortally wounded German spirit'. In contact with groups at other universities, the White Rose was inspired by the sermons of Bishop Galen. Its members secretly distributed leaflets on such topics as 'Is not every decent German today ashamed of his government?' and 'Germany's name will remain disgraced forever unless German youth finally rises up immediately, takes revenge, and atones, smashes its torturers, and builds a new, spiritual Europe.' They printed details about euthanasia programmes and the atrocities on the Eastern Front. They were arrested and their leaders, the brother and sister Hans and Sophie Scholl, were executed.

The army

Aristocratic officers generally remained suspicious of Hitler and Nazism. They initially co-operated, but later relations broke down as concern grew that Hitler was too radical in foreign policy. General Beck's plan to arrest Hitler in 1938 was ruined by Hitler's success at the Munich conference (see page 391). Several officers were subsequently involved in failed assassination attempts, most notably in the July 1944 Bomb Plot.

There was also, surprisingly, considerable opposition activity in the Abwehr, the German military intelligence organisation. From 1935 it was headed by Admiral Canaris who tolerated resistance activities and helped Jews leave during the war. The Abwehr was absorbed into the SS in 1944 during a clampdown on opposition.

Government and the Civil Service

Initially, there were some critics within the government: for example, in June 1934 Papen pleaded in a speech for greater freedom and in August 1935 Schacht deplored anti-semitic violence. Some government officials planned an alternative government and maintained contacts with other opponents.

Judiciary
Some judges tried to maintain proper standards of justice despite an increasingly arbitrary system, with the growing intervention of the SS and the special courts (see page 194).

The workers
German workers had the numerical but not organisational strength to provide major opposition to the regime. Furthermore, many had good reasons to support the new, dynamic government. They had no legal organisations that could be used for opposition, but there were strikes (an estimated 400 between 1933 and 1935) and other forms of pressure were put on the government. Many workers maintained their links with illegal political parties (see below). Overy has also identified some 'no-go' areas for Nazi officials in some working-class districts of industrial cities.

Opposition parties
All political parties (except the ruling Nazi Party) were banned in July 1933, and were hit by a wave of arrests of their leaders; but left-wing parties continued some illegal activities. The SPD in exile (SOPADE) was based in Prague and organised some underground groups, such as the Berlin Red Patrol and the Hanover Socialist Front. They distributed underground leaflets and tried to start a whispering propaganda campaign.

The KPD formed underground cells, even in DAF, but two-thirds of their members were arrested. The Rote Kapelle (Red Orchestra) spy organisation sent information to the USSR. It was smashed in 1942 by the Abwehr.

Traditional elites
Among some of the elites there was considerable discussion of replacing Hitler, especially in the Kreisau Circle on Count Helmuth von Moltke's estate. This was a small group of officers and professionals who had come together in 1933 to oppose Hitler. In August 1943 they drew up the Basic Principles for a New Order, which was a plan for a new Germany, with an open society and equal justice for all.

TALKING POINT
Are there occasions when it is right to break the law?

Some individual opponents of the Nazi regime

The army officer: General Ludwig Beck (1880–1944)

Beck described President Hindenburg's death on 2 August 1934 as the blackest day of his life. Hitler proclaimed himself Supreme Commander of the Armed Forces and made Beck the army's chief-of-staff (1935–8). In May 1938, Hitler told the generals of his unalterable aim to attack Czechoslovakia. Beck was opposed, as the army was not ready for general war. He tried to organise all the chiefs-of-staff to threaten resignation over Hitler's radical approach, but the new Commander-in-Chief General Walther von Brauchitsch failed to give his support. In August 1938 Beck resigned, commenting to a colleague: 'What is that dog doing to our beautiful Germany?' Beck conceived a plan for a march on Berlin, but called it off after Hitler gained the Sudetenland. Many other generals, aware of the plotting, had a wait-and-see attitude to these activities. Beck remained in contact with various opposition circles. In 1944 he was shot for his involvement in the Bomb Plot.

The army officer: Colonel Claus Schenk Graf von Stauffenberg (1907–44)

Colonel Stauffenberg was an aristocratic soldier. An able and ambitious officer, he was in the army High Command by 1940. He had a monarchist distaste for Hitler and was horrified by SS barbarities in the USSR. In September 1942, at the army High Command, one general urged that they must tell Hitler the truth about the military disaster. Stauffenberg replied, 'It is not a question of telling him the truth, but of killing him, and I am prepared to do it.' In 1943 Stauffenberg was wounded in North Africa and lost his right hand, half of his left hand and his left eye. In July 1944 he twice took bombs into Hitler's headquarters, but did not use them as Himmler and Goering were not present. On 29 July he went ahead anyway, but Hitler was only wounded. At least 5,000 people said to be 'involved' were executed.

The army officer: General Hans Oster (1887–1945)

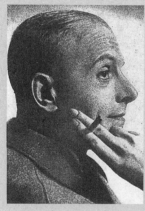

Oster was a member of the General Staff, serving in the Ministry of Defence, and then in the Abwehr. He became alienated by the 1934 killing of General Schleicher in the aftermath of the Night of the Long Knives. In 1938 he advised Britain to stand firm against Hitler and sent the British government details of Germany's military plans. He made contact with trade unionists and Socialists who were actively encouraging resistance and was involved in the 1944 Bomb Plot. He died in Flossenbürg concentration camp four days before Allied troops liberated it.

The pastor: Dietrich Bonhöffer (1906–45)

Bonhöffer criticised Nazism as incompatible with Christianity and defended its victims. He had contacts with Generals Oster and Beck, and other opposition elements. He tried to get help for resistance from abroad, but in 1943 was sent to Buchenwald and then to Flossenbürg where he was executed in April 1945. (See also page 311.)

The civil servant: Carl Friedrich Goerdeler (1884–1945)

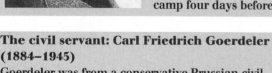

Goerdeler was from a conservative Prussian civil service family. He fought in the First World War, became Mayor of Leipzig from 1923 to 1937, and in 1934 he joined the government, hoping to influence Hitler. Disillusioned when he saw that Hitler was leading Germany to war, he resigned in 1935. He frequently travelled abroad with his anti-Hitler message. He was arrested in the wholesale rounding up of opponents of the regime after the 1944 Bomb Plot, tortured and finally executed in February 1945.

The student: Sophie Scholl (1921–43)

Scholl was the daughter of a former mayor of Forchtenberg and trained as a teacher. At Munich university she joined the White Rose anti-Nazi group, led by her brother Hans and assisted by Professor Huber. In February 1943 she distributed anti-government pamphlets in the university. She was arrested and tortured for over seventeen hours, but refused to give details of others in the group. She was sentenced to death and guillotined. Her brother Hans, Professor Huber and others in the group were also executed.

The actor: Joachim Gottschalk (1904–41)

Gottschalk was a famous actor married to a Jewish woman. He refused to separate from her or perform for Strength through Joy. In 1941 he and his wife killed their 8-year-old son and then committed suicide. At their funeral the priest, despite the presence of Nazi supervisors, rejected criticism of their killing of their child, explaining that they had decided not to leave him alone in such a barbaric world.

The journalist: Carl von Ossietzky (1889–1938)

Ossietzky fought on the Western Front in the First World War and was determined to prevent another war and to defend democracy in Germany. He was secretary of the German Peace Society and editor of liberal newspapers. During the Weimar Republic he criticised Nazism, militarism and communism. In 1931 he was sentenced to eighteen months' imprisonment on a charge of 'treason and betrayal of military secrets' for exposing secret funds, outside parliamentary control, given to the military for use in the USSR. Released in a Christmas amnesty, he was later arrested during the night of the Reichstag fire. Having been sent to a camp, he was offered release if he signed a declaration to say he had revised his opinion. He refused and died in the camp.

The teacher: Adolf Reichwein (1898–1944)

After fighting in the First World War, Reichwein became a professor of history and teacher trainer. He joined the SPD. In 1933 the Nazis removed him from his professorship and he became a village schoolteacher. Concerned over the growth of the terror state, he took an increasingly active part in resistance. He became the main link between the Kreisau Circle and other resistance groups, particularly with those among industrial workers. He used his office at the Folklore Museum in Berlin as a cover for many secret meetings and discussions. He was betrayed by a police spy, arrested and imprisoned and finally condemned by the People's Court on 20 October 1944.

The socialist: Julius Leber (1891–1945)

After a stint as a war journalist, Leber became leader of the Lübeck SPD. He was a Reichstag deputy from 1924 to 1933. He was arrested on 30 January 1933 and sentenced to twenty months' imprisonment, then rearrested and sent to a concentration camp until 1937. He then resumed political activity and became an outstanding leader of the resistance. He joined the Kreisau Circle, but in June 1944 was arrested at a meeting trying to bring together communist opponents and the Stauffenberg conspirators. A Gestapo spy had betrayed him and in January 1945 he was hanged.

ACTIVITY

What do the details of these individuals who resisted show about:

a) who resisted
b) types of resistance
c) the problems they faced
d) the nature of the Nazi state?

B How can the historian judge the degree of opposition and support in Nazi Germany?

Although this is a difficult area to research, there is a range of primary sources available. Here we examine two very important groups of sources, which offer contrasting perspectives. Sources 17.9 and 17.10 are from SOPADE, the Social Democratic Party in exile. Source 17.11 is from the Gestapo.

ACTIVITY

Before you study Sources 17.9–11, consider their likely reliability by answering these questions.

1 How reliable do you expect the SOPADE reports to be about
   a) opposition to the Nazi regime
   b) support for the Nazi regime?
2 How reliable do you expect the Gestapo reports to be about
   a) opposition to the Nazi regime
   b) support for the Nazi regime?

SOURCE 17.9 SOPADE report, June 1934

The regime still controls important instruments of power; the comprehensive propaganda apparatus, hundreds of thousands of supporters whose posts and prosperity depend on the continuation of the regime. At the top of the regime are men who have no scruples in the exercise of power and who in the hour of danger will not shrink from the greatest crimes.

No system of rule collapses by itself. The weakness of the opposition is the strength of the regime. Its opponents are ideologically and organisationally weak. They are ideologically weak because the great mass are only discontented, they are merely grumblers whose discontent springs simply from economic motives. That is particularly true of the Mittelstand *and of the peasantry. The loudest and strongest criticism comes from these groups, but the criticism springs mostly from narrow selfish interest. These groups are least prepared to fight seriously against the regime because they have the least idea of what they should be fighting for ... Fear of Bolshevism, of chaos, which, in the view particularly of the vast majority of the* Mittelstand *and peasantry, would follow Hitler's fall, is still the negative basis of the regime as far as the masses are concerned.*

Its opponents are organisationally weak because it is of the essence of a fascist system that it does not allow its opponents to organise collectively. The forces of 'reaction' [traditional, conservative groups] are extraordinarily fragmented. In informed circles people register no fewer than five monarchist tendencies [supporters of various potential kings]. The labour movement is still split into Socialists and Communists and within the two movements there are numerous factions ...

The attitude of the Church opponents of the regime is not uniform. Their struggle is evidently not least directed towards improving the position of the Churches within the regime ...

SOURCE 17.10 SOPADE report, 1937

The number of those who consciously criticise the political objectives of the regime is very small, quite apart from the fact that they cannot give expression to this criticism. And the fact that discontent (about other matters) makes itself loudly felt on numerous occasions also confirms the 'good conscience' of these people in terms of the National Socialist regime. They do not want to return to the past and if anyone told them that their complaints about this or that aspect threaten the foundations of the Third Reich they would probably be very astonished and horrified ...

It becomes increasingly evident that the majority of the people have two faces;

one which they show to their good and reliable acquaintances; and the other for the authorities, the Party officers, keen Nazis, and for strangers. The private face shows the sharpest criticism of everything that is going on now; the official one beams with optimism and contentment.

SOURCE 17.11 Düsseldorf Gestapo report, 1937

The Communist movement

During the first years after the take-over of power, until about 1936, the Communists tried to expand their party and its various subsidiary organisations. But later they saw clearly that they only endangered those members illegally active inside the country and made it easy for the police to break up the illegal organisations, particularly since the distribution route of a pamphlet could be followed and traced fairly easily . . . Whereas until 1936 the main propaganda emphasis was on distributing lots of pamphlets, at the beginning of 1936 they switched to propaganda by word of mouth, setting up bases in factories, and advocated the so-called popular front [co-operation of anti-Nazi groups].

It became apparent that the Communist propaganda described above was already having some success in various factories. After factory meetings at which speakers of the Labour Front had spoken, some of whom were in fact rather clumsy in their statements, the mood of discontent among the workers was apparent in subsequent discussions. In one fairly large factory the speaker from the Labour Front greeted the workers with the German [Nazi] salute: but in reply the workers only mumbled.

Social Democratic Party

In the period covered by the report the SPD has worked mainly by means of the dissemination [spreading] of news. The information that reaches the leadership of the illegal SPD from their news service in Germany is collected there and distributed as information material in Gothic type. The information material that is smuggled into Germany is produced in postcard size editions in small print. The articles appearing in these information leaflets are biased criticisms of Government measures. They are sent only to reliable old SPD people.

Apart from this, the illegal activity of the SPD is the same as that outlined in the newly published guidelines for the conspiratorial work of the KPD; the setting up of cells in factories, sports clubs and other organisations. Since the former SPD members carry on propaganda only by word of mouth, it is very difficult to get hold of proof of their illegal activities which would be usable in court.

In 1938 we will have to devote particular attention to illegal activity in the factories. Trusted agents have been infiltrated into several big factories in my district who have already provided proof that the KPD and the SPD are carrying out conspiratorial work jointly . . . It is noticeable that no pamphlets whatsoever are distributed; information is only passed on orally.

SOURCE ACTIVITY

(Marks are given in brackets.)

1 Read Source 17.9. What reasons, stated or implied, are given for
   a) why opposition was weak   [3]
   b) the strength of the regime?   [3]
2 Read Source 17.10.
   a) What points could be extracted from this source to argue that opposition was weak?   [2]
   b) What counter points could be made?   [2]
3 Read Source 17.11. What light does this source shed on the nature of opposition to Hitler's regime?   [4]
4 **a)** How far does Source 17.11 confirm the impression given in Source 17.9 of relations between the Socialists and Communists?   [3]
   b) How might this be explained?   [3]
5 How valuable are these sources as evidence of opposition to the Nazi regime?   [5]

(Total: 25 marks)

How can historians make effective use of unreliable sources?

The question of the reliability of the sources on opposition in Hitler's Germany and how far we can make judgements from them is discussed in Source 17.12.

SOURCE 17.12 Kershaw, *The 'Hitler Myth'. Image and Reality in the Third Reich*, pp. 6–8

The sources for the investigation fall into two main categories: firstly, innumerable internal confidential reports on opinion and morale compiled on a regular basis by German government officials, by the police and justice administrations, by Nazi Party agencies, and by the security service (SD); and, secondly, down to the early years of the war, the rich reports filtering out of Germany to the exiled opponents of the Nazi regime, above all those fed to and circulated by the leadership of the exiled SPD (now calling itself the Sopade) in Prague, then Paris, and finally London . . .

Obviously, we cannot quantify Hitler's popularity at any given time during the Third Reich. The reports of the regime's own agents provide us with a large number of varied subjective comments, qualitative judgements on the state of popular opinion. Naturally, people were particularly cautious about making disparaging [critical] comments about the Führer, whatever criticism might be risked about other aspects of Nazi rule. And the citizen's fear of criticising Hitler was compounded [reinforced] by the anxiety of those compiling opinion reports not to offend their superiors. We have to face up to the possibility, therefore, that eulogies [exaggerated statements] of praise in the reports might reflect the opinion – genuine or forced – of the reporter rather than the public.

Even if the reported comments faithfully reflect public attitudes, these attitudes may, of course, be themselves the expression of a more or less coerced [forced] conformity rather than of Hitler's genuine popularity. In the nature of things, it is more difficult to interpret the pro-regime comments of the reports, where scepticism about the underlying elements of fear and coercion is bound to prevail, than it is to evaluate the anti-regime comments and actions of the population, which often speak for themselves. A potential danger, therefore, is an over-estimation of oppositional attitudes and a corresponding playing down of genuine approval and consensus. Given the type of material at our disposal, there is no objective or external criterion for solving this difficulty. However imperfect, the historian's judgement, based on patient source criticism, acquaintance with the complete mass of material available from different reporting agencies, and a readiness to read between the lines has to suffice.

The reports are not, however, beyond echoing direct criticism of Hitler. From the mid-war years on, a body of adverse comment – unmistakable even if veiled in expression – accumulates, strengthening, therefore, the argument that the positive tenor of the reports before this time had on the whole reflected genuine popularity and the absence of widespread and substantial criticism of Hitler. At the same time, there is sufficient witness – for instance, in the proceedings of the political 'Special Courts' as well as in anonymous letters and the reported activities of 'enemies of the State' – to the kinds of negative comments made about Hitler in the Third Reich, even if these seem, until the middle of the war, to have reflected the views of only a small minority of the population.

The Sopade reports naturally contain in-built bias diametrically opposite to that of the internal reports. Sopade reporters gladly seized upon expressions of anti-Nazi sentiment, which they encountered not infrequently in their main milieu of operation among the industrial work-force, and tended at times to err in judgement in the direction of an over-rosy estimation of the extent of underlying opposition to the regime. The editors of the Deutschland-Berichte *(Germany Reports) are well aware of this danger, as indeed were some of the Sopade's 'Border Secretaries' who were sending in the reports. It is all the more striking and suggestive, therefore, that even this oppositional source is on numerous occasions fully prepared to testify to the power and significance of the Hitler cult and to accept that the Führer's massive popularity even extended to working class circles which had recognisably not been won over to Nazism. Though there are some important divergences and a totally different perspective, the* Sopade *material offers for the most part convincing corroboration of the picture of the Hitler image and its impact which can be gained from the internal sources. There is sufficient evidence, then ... to be able to point at least in an imprecise way to the pattern of development of Hitler's image, to the curve of his popularity and the reasons behind it.*

ACTIVITY

1 Why is there a danger of historians underestimating the degree of genuine approval for Hitler?
2 Despite the problems of evidence, how, according to Kershaw, does the historian have to develop his/her account?
3 Why does Kershaw argue that evidence of Hitler's popularity in the SOPADE reports is particularly convincing?

C Humour as resistance

The Third Reich denied Germans free expression in most ways. Humour, though, was a possible outlet to express feelings. Anti-Nazi jokes were a low-key expression of resistance to the regime and have been called a form of therapy. F. Hillenbrand, a German who lived in the Third Reich, argues in his book *Underground Humour in Nazi Germany* that the jokes in Nazi Germany reflected the widespread popular discontent that existed and that 'humour ... reveals most directly the mood of the time' (p. xv).

Telling jokes was a dangerous affair; you needed to take precautions – for example, before whispering, to look suspiciously around in what came to be called 'the German glance'. The penalty for anti-Hitler jokes was death. Jokes were risky and led to many people being sent to camps and executed for undermining morale. Hillenbrand, however, survived. As he explains (p. xviii): 'My point of view is simply that of one who was there and lived in the world which produced these jokes. I laughed at them too, while taking note not to criticise the regime in public, and thus I lived to tell the tale.'

Hillenbrand argues that some jokes were probably produced by the Propaganda Ministry to test underground distribution systems: one, for example, was found to have spread 1,000 miles in one week. Some were also a product of the internecine (bitter) rivalry in the Nazi hierarchy.

On page 330 we give a selection of jokes current in Nazi Germany.

SOURCE 17.13 F. Hillenbrand, *Underground Humour in Nazi Germany*, 1994, pp. xv, xviii

Many people found in the telling of such jokes their only means of protest against the police state in which they lived. These jokes provided welcome emotional release from pressure and restrictions 'from above' and from the daily pinpricks of the hordes of Nazi officials of the lesser order, the 'little Hitlers' in their obscene brown uniforms, who got on the wick of so many Germans. Thus underground humour had some therapeutic value for the millions living in the prison-without-bars which Germany had now become, even in peacetime. This became even more true when war broke out.

Nazi leaders

The ideal German:
As blond as Hitler,
As tall as Goebbels,
As slim as Goering,
and as chaste as Röhm.

Repression

The Munich cabaret artist Weiss-Ferdl:
'Can you imagine, my friend Adolf has given me his picture, and he has even signed it! Now I've got a problem – shall I hang him, or shall I put him against a wall?'

Jews

It is 1933. A Jew appears at a register office with an urgent request to be permitted to change his name. The official seems very reluctant at first but eventually asks the Jew his name.
'My name is Adolf Stinkfoot.'
'Well,' says the official, 'in that case I think I can accede to your request. Which new name have you chosen?'
'Maurice Stinkfoot.'

ACTIVITY

1 Which jokes do you consider the most powerful criticism of the Nazi regime?
2 Explain the role of humour in Nazi Germany.

Nazis abbreviated everything, so some jokes used this practice to create new units of measurement:
'Hit' – the number of promises a man can make in a time-span of fourteen years without keeping any of them.
'Goer' – the maximum amount of tin a man can wear on his chest without falling flat on his face.
'Goeb' – the minimum amount of energy required to switch off 100,000 radio receivers simultaneously, or, alternatively, the maximum extent to which a person can pull his mouth open without actually splitting his face.
'Ley' – the maximum time during which a man can speak without saying a single sensible thing.

The Nazi Party

On a visit to a factory (so the story goes), Ley asked the manager about the political views of the factory workers.
Ley: Tell me, have you still got any Social Democrats with you?
Manager: Oh yes, about half the workforce.
Ley: How dreadful. But surely no Commies?
Manager: Oh yes, about a third of the men.
Ley: Really! What about Democrats etc.?
Manager: They make up the remaining 20 per cent.
Ley: Good gracious! Haven't you got any Nazis at all?
Manager: Oh yes, of course, all of them are Nazis!

Someone opens his mouth too wide and as a result spends several weeks of ideological training in a concentration camp. After his discharge he is asked by a friend what life was like there. 'Excellent!' he replies. 'At 9 a.m. we were served breakfast in our bedrooms. Then some light work for those who wanted to work, and some sport for those who didn't. Lunch was plain but good and afterwards again some light work. For supper we were served some open sandwiches and pudding. In the evening we had lectures or a film, or we played games.'
   The questioner is much impressed. 'Incredible!' he says. 'All those lies we hear about the concentration camps! The other day I met Meier who had just been released from one; he told me rather different stories about his camp!'
   'Well, yes, but then Meier is back in his camp again!'

Some Nazis surround an old Jew and ask him who is responsible for the war. 'The Jews,' he answers. And then he adds, 'and the cyclists.'
'Why the cyclists?' ask the puzzled Nazis.
'Why the Jews?' replies the old man.

An SS officer who has just arrested a Jew says to him, 'I have one glass eye. If you guess correctly which it is, I'll let you go.' To this the prisoner replies, 'It is the left one.' 'Correct!' exclaims the officer. 'How did you manage to guess?' 'Oh,' says the Jew, 'your left eye has such a human, compassionate expression!'

A Jew is arrested during the war, having been denounced for killing a Nazi at 10 p.m. and then eating the brain of his victim. This is his defence: in the first place a Nazi hasn't got any brain. Secondly, a Jew doesn't eat anything that comes from a pig. And thirdly, he could not have killed the Nazi at 10 p.m. because at that time everybody listens to the BBC broadcast.

Hitler Youth

A little boy is crying because he has lost his way. A policeman on his beat tries to console him and asks him what he is doing so far from home. The boy answers between sobs, 'I've just been to a Hitler Youth leadership conference.'

Foreign policy

Q What is the difference between Chamberlain and Hitler?
A Chamberlain takes his weekends in the country, but Hitler takes whole countries in a weekend.

Q Why are the new frontier posts in the Third Reich now equipped with wheels?
A In order to facilitate Hitler's new territorial demands in continental Europe.

D Review: How much opposition was there to the Nazi regime?

Historians continue to debate how Germans responded to Nazi rule. Far more evidence has become available, especially since the collapse of the secretive east German state, the German Democratic Republic. Historians have embarked on a considerable examination of local archives that has led to a fuller picture of what life was like on the ground. Use of oral history techniques has reinforced this 'everyday life/*Alltagsgeschichte*' approach. It has led to greater awareness of the complexity and confusion of the Nazi state in Germany, and the variety of responses possible in varied situations.

This is well illustrated by Reinhard Mann's survey of Gestapo proceedings based on an examination of 825 cases from 70,000 Gestapo files in Düsseldorf. It gives an indication of the nature of everyday opposition within the Third Reich.

SOURCE 17.14 Dissident behaviour as recorded in a random sample of cases in the files of the Düsseldorf Gestapo 1933–45; from R. Mann, *Protest und Kontrolle*, p. 180. Most cases date from 1933–5, with a steady decline after 1937

DISSIDENT BEHAVIOUR	NUMBER	%
Continuation of forbidden organisations:		
Continuation of illegal political parties and associations*	204	
Continuation of forbidden religious associations and sects	15	
Continuation of dissolved associations and activity for the forbidden youth groups	26	
Total	245	30
Nonconforming behaviour in everyday life:		
Nonconforming verbal utterances	203	
Nonconforming work or leisure activities	38	
Total	241	29
Other forms of nonconformity:		
Acquiring or spreading of forbidden printed matter	37	
Listening to foreign radio	20	
Political passivity	7	
Assorted others	75	
Total	139	17
Conventional criminality	96	12
Breaking administrative control measures (e.g. residency requirements)	104	13
Overall total	825	100

* Of the 204 cases, 61 concerned the KPD and 44 the SPD.

ACTIVITY

To what extent does Source 17.14 support the evidence you have already studied about the nature of opposition in Nazi Germany?

ACTIVITY

1 Kershaw has added a new chapter on opposition to the 1993 edition of his 1985 book *The Nazi Dictatorship. Problems and Perspectives of Interpretation*. He has called it 'Resistance without the People'.
   a) What is he implying about the nature of opposition to the Nazi regime?
   b) Why do you think he has only recently added such a chapter to his book?
2 Kershaw has argued that the more totalitarian a regime is, the more opposition there will be. Can you explain this apparent paradox?
3 'The lack of opposition in the Third Reich shows that most Germans supported the Nazi government.' Do you agree?

TALKING POINT

What are the advantages and disadvantages of 'history from below'?

Historians' assessments

SOURCE 17.15 M. Housden, 'Germans and their opposition to the Third Reich' in *History Review*, No. 19, September 1994, pp. 38–40

The most significant efforts at resistance came from the establishment sections of German society, that is to say the minor nobility, civil servants and, most notably, members of the officer corps . . .

In the Third Reich, a person needed courage just to say 'hello' in the street to someone wearing a yellow star. For that reason we must be careful not to undervalue the achievements of anyone who did anything, no matter how small, to subvert the Nazi order. Equally we must stand in awe of the self-sacrificial heroism of a person such as von Stauffenberg. But just as we value bravery, we need to maintain a sense of proportion.

Both workers and Christians refused to conform to Nazi demands in noteworthy ways. It appears, however, that worker unrest never became really unmanageable for the regime. The mixed strategies of propaganda incentives, food on the table when it was most required and Gestapo surveillance for the most part ensured the compliance of the working class in public. What opposition there was seems to have been most significant in private life, with groups of like-minded workers meeting secretly in order to keep alive their hopes for a better future. As far as religious nonconformity was concerned, individual priests and parsons doubtless did do much to keep Christian morality alive. At the national level there were also some victories against Nazi social control and policy. Nevertheless, we are left with the sense that countrywide religious-based opposition never achieved its full potential. So while Christianity and socialism both encouraged people to live as more than 'heroic robots', they never threatened the functioning of the Nazi system as a whole . . .

While very many Germans remained at odds with the Third Reich, only a few exceptional souls, driven by a mixture of bravery and despair, dared express themselves openly. But then, how many of us, today, under similar circumstances, would do different?

SOURCE 17.16 J. Hiden, *Republican and Fascist Germany*, 1996, p. 189

The persecution of hundreds of thousands of Germans by the Hitler regime serves to illustrate that the dissent and nonconformity must have been widespread. Resistance, defined as an organised and sustained attempt to destroy the government, was not.

SOURCE 17.17 A. Leber, *Conscience in Revolt*, 1994, p. xiv

The decision to resist an authority that in the eyes of the public was legally constituted, accepted, and upheld by national institutions and was supported by the broad public was the act of an extremist. Such resistance was perilous both in principle and in reality. No common sense recommended it . . .

It is believed that between 1933 and 1945, 3 million were confined for political crimes; 800,000 were sentenced for active resistance; and 32,600 were executed – of these, 12,000 had been convicted of high treason.

SOURCE 17.18 D. Peukert, *Inside Nazi Germany*, p. 264

We must distinguish the many and varied expressions of nonconformist behaviour: the steadfast non-response of traditional environments to National Socialist pressure, and more far-reaching forms of resistance and non-cooperation. Active resistance was only a minority affair. Certainly, as young people's wartime acts of non-compliance illustrate, conflict with the Nazi authorities did not necessarily remain static, and those involved might move from mere assertion of a dissident style to more deliberate acts of protest. In individual cases we can trace an entire 'career', graduating from nonconformist behaviour, via refusal, to protest and resistance. But the cumulative effect of the use of terror against political opponents proclaimed as enemies, of the fragmentising social processes and of the cross-cutting devices of integration, was to paralyse even the anti-fascist resistance. Although soon robbed of its mechanisms of political expression by Gestapo terror, the resistance mobilised tens of thousands of people into performing acts of courage and sacrifice, but remained decentralised, disorientated and historically ineffectual. The true historical significance of the resistance was its preservation of non-fascist traditions.

... Everyday life under Hitler was thus not mere conformity on the one hand ... and mere 'everyday deprivation', loss of rights and freedoms, on the other: as if there was only a black-and-white division between rulers and ruled, rather than the multiple everyday ambiguities of 'ordinary people' making their choices among the varying greys of active consent, accommodation and nonconformity.

ACTIVITY

Essay:

a) Describe the main forms of opposition to the Nazi regime, 1933–45.
b) Why did Hitler not face more opposition within Germany?
Study the above extracts from the historians' accounts (Sources 17.15–18). Using these and Source 17.14, write your essay. You could organise it around the following points:

1 Discussion of the problems of the evidence
2 Opposition to what? Hitler, the government, the Nazi Party, particular policies?
3 Problems of opposition
   a) nature of the regime
   b) nature of opposition forces
   c) overall
4 Forms of opposition
   a) activities
   b) by whom
5 Effects of opposition

TALKING POINT

Does the fact that German resistance failed to remove Hitler mean that it is historically unimportant?

KEY POINTS FROM CHAPTER 17: How much opposition was there to the Nazi regime?

1 The best moment to have replaced Hitler was in 1933; after 1934 he could not legally be removed.
2 Successful policies, first economic then foreign, made it hard to gain support for opposition activities.
3 The power of the police state, backed up by informers, was a further major obstacle.
4 There was a range of oppositional responses, from emigration to attempted assassination.
5 Most opposition groups were isolated and were unable to co-operate.
6 The war made opposition harder, but Germany's defeats from 1943 inspired more attempts to remove Hitler.
7 Institutions such as the army and the Churches provided the best opportunities for opposition.
8 The most serious moments were probably Beck's plans to remove Hitler in 1938 and the 1944 Bomb Plot.
9 Historians disagree on the extent of opposition and the problems opponents faced.
10 Aside from assassination attempts, the Nazi regime was secure and was only brought down by a vast coalition of enemy powers.

18

Why did the Nazis commit mass murder?

CHAPTER OVERVIEW So far, in your study of Nazi Germany, you have encountered a perhaps surprising number of positive aspects of the regime. As far as many Germans were concerned, Hitler had revived the economy, restored their national pride and improved their lives. They believed they belonged to a *Volksgemeinschaft* that provided for their needs and to which they owed obedience. But, as you have also seen, such benefits were accompanied by the denial of individual rights, an arbitrary repressive political machinery and a haphazard system of government dependent upon the will of an all-powerful leader.

Here we study how the Nazi regime treated 'outsiders': those unwilling or unable to conform to the *Volksgemeinschaft*, the Nazi vision of the ideal community. Beginning in 1933 with the victimisation of the mentally ill, Nazi policies culminated in the murder of an estimated 1 million Germans and 8 million foreigners: of these people, 7 million were Jews. This mass murder is called the Holocaust.

This chapter investigates the following questions:

A How did the Nazis treat 'outsiders'? (pp. 336–9)

B What measures were taken against the Jews? (pp. 340–3)

C How could the Holocaust happen? (pp. 344–53)

D Review: Why did the Nazis commit mass murder? (pp. 354–6)

ACTIVITY

Although most of the Nazis' victims died during the Second World War, they were not soldiers killed in the fighting but defenceless people systematically murdered in extermination camps and other places. It is very hard to understand how thousands of people could commit such crimes and millions of others acquiesce in them. Consider the following groups of questions:

A
Do you think that
a) seriously deformed foetuses should be aborted (if their parents wish)?
b) people who are incurably ill should have the right to die?
c) parents should be able to have life-support machines switched off for incurably injured children?
d) we should prioritise scarce National Health Service resources for providing cheaper kidney transplants rather than for keeping the incurably ill alive?
e) people suffering from serious hereditary illnesses should be sterilised?

?? ?? ??

B
Do you think that
f) killing enemy soldiers in war can be justified?
g) killing enemy civilians in war can be justified?
h) killing people who threaten the existence of your nation is justified?

??

Would you have

This Activity raises many issues. As individuals we have to make a series of choices:

- Are all people equal?
- What actions towards others are we prepared to tolerate?
- What actions are we prepared to take?

Presumably, none of us would admit to being prepared to gas hundreds of naked adults and children, but most of us enjoy overeating at Christmas even though millions of people are dying of malnutrition. We also spend pounds on injecting our pets with medicine, yet fail to give millions of children in the developing world cholera injections that cost 50 pence each.

This Activity also raises the issue of whether one can approach some understanding of the Holocaust by seeing it as resulting from attitudes prevalent not just in the Third Reich but in our own society. The Activity was supposed to raise the idea of the 'thin end of the wedge' – can elevating some people over others lead to such horrors as the Holocaust? Thus **A** and **B** raise the question of whether all human life should be protected or whether there are circumstances where taking life can be justified. The Nazis argued that national needs took precedence over individual rights. These questions also raise the issue of eugenics, of trying to breed a superior race. Most people argue that killing opponents in war is justified; the Nazis considered themselves to be involved in a vital racial war.

Questions in **C** about views on animals and in **E** about races relate to Nazi racial views. They believed there was a hierarchy of groups, with Aryans at the top and Jews and Black people as 'subhumans', sometimes likened to animals, to be destroyed if they posed a threat. Questions in **D** relate to the Nazi belief in social Darwinism: that the laws of 'survival of the fittest' in nature also apply to nations. Nazi propagation of such views deepened the hostility of many Germans to outsiders. Such attitudes, it has been argued, led to the acceptance of increasingly harsh measures, culminating in murder to ensure the survival and supremacy of Germany.

Some of these are difficult moral issues and many people argue they are of no relevance to historians. However, the historian's task is to try to understand the past, and we would argue to use this to understand the present. There is nothing harder to comprehend in human history than the Holocaust. Was it uniquely evil or was it caused by a broad range of factors that could happen again? Some historians argue that the Holocaust was unique, explaining it as the result of Hitler's determination to kill the Jews. Others see the Holocaust in more complex terms: that it developed gradually as the Nazi regime became radicalised and moral restraints on actions were slowly removed. According to this second view, it is possible that similar horrors could happen elsewhere. Cambodia in the 1980s and Rwanda and Yugoslavia in the 1990s have been cited as examples.

C
Do you think that
i) animal pests should be killed?
j) animals should be killed to provide resources for humans?
k) animals should be hunted for pleasure?

D
Do you think that
l) competition is a natural instinct that encourages achievement?
m) nations should compete rather than co-operate with each other?
n) more civilised nations should have power over weaker ones?

E
Do you think that
o) some racial groups are better at sport than other groups?
p) some races are more intelligent than others?
q) some races are superior to others?

allowed the Holocaust to happen?

A How did the Nazis treat 'outsiders'?

FOCUS ROUTE

1 Explain why the Nazis regarded each of the following groups as outsiders:
   a) the mentally ill
   b) ASOCIALS
   c) homosexuals
   d) members of religious sects
   e) gypsies.
2 How was each of these groups treated by the Nazi regime?
3 Explain what the Nazi sterilisation and euthanasia programmes show about the regime and the way it operated.

The Nazis stressed the idea of *Volksgemeinschaft*, a people's community of healthy, vigorous Aryans working for the good of the nation. This concept was reinforced by its opposite: outsiders who did not belong (*gemeinschaftsunfähig*) and who had to be excluded from the people's community. These outsiders were classified on three main grounds:

- Ideological: those threatening the political unity of the nation, such as Communists
- Biological: those whose genes posed a threat to a healthy, pure German race, such as Jews and people with hereditary illnesses
- Social: those whose behaviour conflicted with the norms of the national community, such as the workshy. (Some Nazis would include some of these in the second category, arguing that such behaviour was genetically determined.)

From sterilisation to euthanasia
The mentally ill

SOURCE 18.1 A still from *Erbkrank* (Hereditary Illness), a 1935 film made by the Office for Racial Politics with the purpose of building up dislike and fear of the mentally ill. Such films were seen by 40 million people in 1939

SOURCE 18.2 Law for the Prevention of Hereditarily Diseased Offspring, July 1933

1 (ii) Anyone is hereditarily ill within the meaning of this law who suffers from one of the following illnesses:
(a) Congenital [hereditary] feeblemindedness.
(b) Schizophrenia.
(c) Manic depression.
(d) Hereditary epilepsy.
(e) Huntington's chorea.
(f) Hereditary blindness.
(g) Hereditary deafness.
(h) Serious physical deformities.
(iii) In addition, anyone who suffers from chronic alcoholism can be sterilised.
12 If the [Hereditary Health] Court has decided finally in favour of sterilisation, the sterilisation must be carried out even against the wishes of the person to be sterilised ... In so far as other measures prove insufficient the use of force is permissible.

For the Nazis, race, not class, was the key to history. A healthy, pure race would gain mastery in the struggle for survival in the world. Unhealthy genes weakened the race. The mentally ill were 'burdens on the community', 'life without life, worthless life' and 'unworthy of life'. Therefore, one of the first acts of the Nazi regime was a law allowing compulsory sterilisation of the hereditarily ill, to prevent bearers of such genes from passing them on to children. In the next twelve years about 350,000 people were sterilised, with about 100 dying as a result of the 'Hitler cut'. By 1939 the policy of reducing the numbers of the mentally ill by sterilisation developed into one of murder, described as 'mercy killing' or euthanasia.

This policy had been considered early on by Nazi leaders but was not at first adopted. However, in 1939 Hitler used a father's letter requesting that his deformed son be 'put to sleep' to initiate the policy of killing the incurably ill (see page 191). (This was typical of the random way policy decisions could be made in the Third Reich.) A special unit, T4, was established to kill disabled children. The government registered disabled children, and their records were examined by three doctors who marked the files '+' to die, '−' to survive. Children were killed by starvation, by lethal injection or by gas in mobile vans ('killer boxes') or 'shower' gas chambers. The policy was gradually extended to adults. By 1944, 200,000 people deemed mentally and physically disabled had been murdered. Relatives were informed by letter of the victims' sudden death from diseases such as measles or from 'general weakness', and were sent urns of ashes. Administrative errors, with urns of boys containing hair grips and diagnoses of appendicitis on those without an appendix, increased suspicion of what was occurring. The euthanasia programme contributed in several ways to the Holocaust. The T4 staff, and the techniques learnt, were later used in the Holocaust. Many would also argue that the moral degeneration that allowed such actions to occur eventually led to people permitting genocide.

Although the killings were kept secret, the government tried to prepare the German people for such policies by promoting the pro-euthanasia argument, especially through propaganda films. Some of these were aimed at the staff in the 'euthanasia institutions', others at the general public. The deaths of the disabled were justified mainly on the grounds of ending their misery, but this idea was reinforced by stressing the financial cost of keeping them alive (see Source 14.21, page 283) and the adverse effect such people had on the nation.

SOURCE 18.3 A scene from the film *I Accuse*, which was produced partly to counter Bishop Galen's 1941 protest against euthanasia (Source 18.5). The film centred around the decline of a musician suffering from multiple sclerosis who pleaded for her husband to kill her. When he did so, he was prosecuted. At his trial, he made an impassioned defence of his actions and accused the law of being outdated. The film was a great box-office success, being seen by 18 million people. The SS monitored audiences' reactions, finding that some seemed convinced but that others, especially Catholics, were ill at ease

SOURCE 18.4 From the commentary for the 1937 film *Victims of the Past*, ordered by Hitler to be shown in all 5,300 German cinemas before the main film

All life on this earth is a struggle for existence. Everything that is weak [in] life will inevitably be destroyed by nature. In the last few decades, mankind has sinned terribly against the laws of natural selection. We haven't just maintained life unworthy of life, we have allowed it to multiply ... Whole clans are to be found in asylums. The costs of caring for the hereditarily ill siblings of this one family have so far been 154,000 RM. How many healthy people could have been housed for this sum?

Sterilisation is a simple surgical operation. In the last 70 years our people have increased by 50 per cent while in the same period the number of hereditarily ill has risen by 450 per cent. If this were to continue, there would be one hereditarily ill [person] to four healthy people. An endless column of horror would march into the nation.

SOURCE 18.5 In August 1941 Bishop Galen, in the most famous public criticism of the Nazi regime, preached a sermon, which was printed and widely circulated, protesting at the euthanasia policy

If you establish and apply the principle that you can kill unproductive fellow human beings then woe betide us all when we become old and frail!... Even if it only initially affects the poor defenceless mentally ill ... as a matter of principle murder is permitted for all unproductive people, in other words for the incurably sick, the people who have become invalids through labour and war, for us all when we become old, frail and therefore unproductive.

... Then none of our lives will be safe any more. Some commission can put us on the list of the 'unproductive' who in their opinion have become worthless life ... Woe to mankind, woe to our German nation if God's holy commandment 'Thou shalt not kill'... is not only broken, but if this transgression is actually tolerated and permitted to go unpunished.

Asocials

'Asocial' was a very broad term that could be applied to anyone who did not fit into the *Volksgemeinschaft*. In 1938 asocials were defined as vagabonds, gypsies, beggars, prostitutes, alcoholics, eccentrics, the workshy and juvenile delinquents. The most obvious manifestation of asocial behaviour was unwillingness to work, as this 'gives offence to the community'. In 1933 there was a round-up of half a million vagrants. They were divided into the orderly, who were given work, and the disorderly, who were imprisoned in camps where they were forced to wear black triangles. As unemployment disappeared, pressure on those not working increased. Thousands were sent to concentration camps, where many died. Increasingly, the unemployed were seen as a matter for the police not welfare agencies. The Nazis increasingly stressed the biological origins of asocial behaviour. Thus the asocial became, in the Nazi view, unworthy people who needed to be removed, via sterilisation and murder, in the interests of the community.

Homosexuals

Another group deemed to be asocial were homosexuals. Not only did their behaviour deeply offend traditionally minded Nazis, it was also believed to be against the laws of nature and to threaten Germany's position in the world by reducing the country's birth rate. In 1936 the Reich Central Office for the Combating of Homosexuality and Abortion was created and Himmler tried to establish a register of homosexuals. He was particularly concerned at the discovery of about ten cases a year of homosexuality even in 'the good blood' in the SS. In 1937 he ordered that homosexual SS officers should be sent to concentration camps 'where they will be shot while attempting to escape'. Eventually, between 10,000 and 15,000 homosexuals were arrested and sent to camps where they were forced to wear pink triangles. Some were castrated and became the object of medical experiments designed to correct their 'unnatural' feelings. Lesbians were not subject to formal persecution in the Third Reich since they were not seen as a threat to the nation.

SOURCE 18.6 SS officer Greifelt in January 1939

In view of the tight situation on the labour market, national labour discipline dictated that all persons who would not conform to the working life of the nation, and who were vegetating as work-shy and asocial, making the streets of our cities and countryside unsafe, had to be compulsorily registered and set to work ... More than 10,000 of these asocial forces are currently undertaking a labour training cure in the concentration camps, which are admirably suited for this purpose.

SOURCE 18.7 From a speech by Heinrich Himmler to the SS in February 1937

... There are those homosexuals who take the view: what I do is my business. However, all things which take place in the sexual sphere are not the private affair of the individual, but signify the life and death of the nation, signify world power or 'SWISSIFICATION'. The people which has many children has the candidature for world power and world domination. A people of good race which has too few children has a one-way ticket to the grave, for insignificance in fifty or a hundred years, for burial in two hundred and fifty years ...

In olden times homosexuals were thrown in swamps ... That wasn't a punishment, but simply the extinguishing of abnormal life. It has to be got rid of; just as we pull out weeds, throw them on a heap, and burn them. It was not a feeling of revenge, simply that those affected had to go.

TALKING POINT

Why do you think the Nazis could not accept that there are things that are entirely up to the individual?

SOURCE 18.8 An illustration from a book, *Nation in Danger*. The top row shows the families of criminals; the middle row families with children who need special education; the bottom row the German family with 2.2 children and the academic couple with 1.9 children

Die Drohung des Untermenschen.

Es treffen auf:

Männliche Verbrecher: 4,9 Kinder

Eine kriminelle Ehe: 4,4 Kinder

Eltern von Hilfsschulkindern: 3,5 Kinder

Die deutsche Familie: 2.2 Kinder

Akademikerehe: 1,9 Kinder

SOURCE 18.9 A picture from an SS calendar entitled: 'A nation stands or falls according to the greater or lesser worth of its blood-bound racial substance.' The Nazi regime believed it was vital to increase the number of children born to Aryan parents. In a speech in 1937 Himmler said: 'If you further take into account the facts I have not yet mentioned, namely that with a static number of women, we have two million men too few on account of those who fell in the war, then you can well imagine how this imbalance of two million homosexuals and two million war dead, or in other words a lack of about four million men capable of having sex, has upset the sexual balance sheet of Germany, and will result in a catastrophe'

Ein Volk steht und fällt mit dem Wert oder Unwert seiner blutgebundenen rassischen Substanz.

Juni   Brachet

11	12	13	14	15	16	17
Sonntag	Montag	Dienstag	Mittwoch	Donnerstag	Freitag	Sonnabend

Religious sects

Although the Nazis were fairly cautious in their dealings with the main Christian Churches (see Chapter 16), they acted fiercely against minority sects, especially Jehovah's Witnesses. These had refused to join the army and to swear allegiance. Whole families were arrested. About one-third of Germany's Jehovah's Witnesses died in concentration camps. Other groups, such as Christian Scientists and Seventh Day Adventists, suffered a similar fate.

Gypsies

The Nazis did not initiate hostility to gypsies. With their distinctive appearance and lifestyle, gypsies had long been objects of suspicion in many countries. As a numerically small group of 30,000, gypsies were not seen as a major threat, provided they did not contaminate the German blood pool; but in the late 1930s they became victims of the general radicalisation. In 1938 Himmler issued a 'Decree for the Struggle against the Gypsy Plague'. In 1939 they were sent to camps, before being expelled to Poland. In December 1942 Himmler ordered them to be transferred to Auschwitz, where there was a special gypsy camp. Eleven thousand of the 20,000 gypsies in Auschwitz were gassed. As German control extended throughout Europe, more gypsies became victims of Nazism, and it has been estimated that half a million gypsies were killed.

SOURCE 18.10 Letter to a Frankfurt newspaper from some citizens about the 'Gypsy nuisance'

... Right opposite properties ... Gypsies have settled themselves ... who represent a heavy burden on the community. The hygienic conditions in this area defy description ... We are worried about the spread of contagious diseases. Also, with regard to sexual conduct, these people, and even the children, have no sense of decency ... Almost daily there are fights and the neighbourhood has become so insecure that one has to worry about walking the streets alone after darkness. Because of the Gypsies our properties have greatly depreciated [fallen in value].

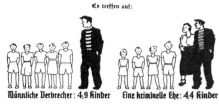

TALKING POINT

Are the attitudes in Sources 18.6, 18.7 and 18.10 still prevalent today?

TALKING POINT

Do you consider prejudice against people with different behaviour and lifestyles inevitable?

FOCUS ROUTE

Explain how anti-semitic measures developed between 1933 and 1939, identifying those periods when discrimination escalated.

SOURCE 18.11 Nobel Peace Prize winner and Holocaust survivor Elie Wiesel

The language to describe the Holocaust does not exist. The more I study, the less I understand.

SOURCE 18.12 The diary entry of Alfred Rosenberg, the Nazi ideologue, for 2 April 1941, after a two-hour meeting with Hitler about the executions of Jews in the east

What I do not write down today, I will none the less never forget.

SOURCE 18.13 Aerial photo of Auschwitz–Birkenau camp taken from an Allied plane in December 1944. Oswiecim is the Polish name which the Germans changed to Auschwitz

B What measures were taken against the Jews?

Anti-semitism was not confined to 1930s Germany. Hostility to the Jews, linked to a belief in their responsibility for the killing of Christ, has a long tradition in Christian history. This hostility was reinforced by resentment at the wealth and position of some Jews and the periodic need for scapegoats to blame for problems. In the late nineteenth century an influx of Jews fleeing persecution in Tsarist Russia, combined with the growth of racist views associated with social Darwinism, led to increased anti-semitic feeling in Germany and other European countries. The problems afflicting Germany after 1918 were attributed by some to a worldwide Jewish conspiracy. The Nazis were one of several parties encouraging anti-semitism, although it seems clear that this was not a major reason for their electoral support.

Once the Nazis came to power, Jews were subjected to increased discrimination (see Chart 18A), though anti-semitic policy developed in a typically haphazard manner. In 1933 some Jews were deprived of their jobs and in 1935 all lost their citizenship. The POGROMS of *Kristallnacht* (the Night of Broken Glass) in November 1938 symbolised the radicalisation of the regime. The Nazis, by then politically and economically secure, were free to pursue their aim of driving Jews out of German life. Jews' economic position, then their individual freedom and ultimately their lives came under threat.

Until 1939 the Nazis favoured emigration as a way to remove the Jewish presence from Germany, but the outbreak of war made overseas emigration difficult. Indeed, the war had a crucial effect on anti-semitic policy, increasing

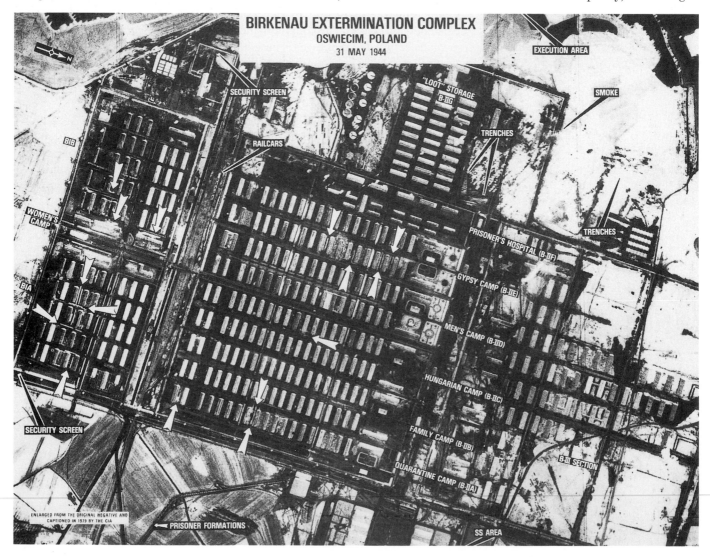

BIRKENAU EXTERMINATION COMPLEX
OSWIECIM, POLAND
31 MAY 1944

Reinhard Heydrich (1904–42): the exterminator

The son of a musician who may have been Jewish, Heydrich later issued many writs for slander over accusations about his ancestry. He served in the navy, but was dismissed over a sexual allegation. Tall, blond and athletic, he thus, unlike many Nazi leaders, typified the ideal Aryan. In 1932 he joined the SS and rose rapidly in its ranks, becoming a close associate of Himmler and playing a major role in the Night of the Long Knives. In 1936 he became Chief of the Security Police and the SD (the Security Service of the SS), organising a vast police network. He became an SS general in 1941 and organised the EINSATZGRUPPEN that carried out killings in the USSR in 1941.

Heydrich established the first Jewish ghetto and became the first administrator of the concentration camp system. At the Wannsee Conference in January 1942 he was chosen to administer the Final Solution. In May 1942 he was killed by a grenade thrown by a special Czech hit squad trained in Britain with the support of the British government. The Nazis responded by executing over 1,000 Czechs and massacring the entire village of Lidice which had sheltered the assassins. This fierce repression permanently alienated the Czechs from Nazi rule.

Heydrich, known as the Blond Beast, was one of the least attractive Nazis, being cold, suspicious and sadistic, with a morbid self-hatred. Along with Himmler, he shared the greatest direct responsibility for organising the Holocaust. His savage treatment of Jews may have been partly caused by his fear that he himself had Jewish blood.

the number of Jews within German-controlled territory and provoking a brutalisation of life that reduced objections to mass murder. By winter 1941, an estimated 700,000 Jews had been killed, mainly in unsystematic mass shootings. The SS then decided gassing was more efficient. In January 1942, at the Wannsee Conference, Nazi policy was co-ordinated and the 'Final Solution' adopted, with the euthanasia programme as a model. Between 1942 and 1945 over 5 million Jews were systematically murdered in extermination camps.

SOURCE 18.14 Painting of Auschwitz by a former inmate, W. Sibek. It shows women being selected for the gas chamber

The aftermath

After the defeat of the Third Reich, many Jews met hostility on their return to their homes. Forty-three survivors of the camps were killed in a pogrom at Kielce in Poland in 1946. Some survivors stayed in camps for displaced persons for up to five years.

Two-thirds of Jewish survivors went to Palestine. In 1948 the Jewish state of Israel was created. It faced hostility from surrounding Arab countries in what has been called 'a clash between total justice and total justice'.

In September 1945 the first of a series of war crimes trials began. Several camp guards were hanged. From November 1945 to October 1946, 22 leading Nazis were tried at Nuremberg (see pages 426–7). By 1949 the Allies had convicted 5,025 people. Most were imprisoned, some were hanged. Trials of those involved have continued in various countries into the 1990s.

■ **Learning trouble spot**

When did the Holocaust happen?

Students often get confused about when the Holocaust actually occurred. Very frequently, they date it too early and believe Jews were being killed in concentration camps before 1939. Most German Jews were still living in their homes in 1939, although increasingly subjected to discrimination and restrictions. They were not deported *en masse* to camps before 1941. The mass killing of Jews began with the invasion of Poland in 1939 and escalated with the invasion of the USSR in 1941 when the true horrors of the Holocaust developed, with random round-ups of innocent civilians.

There has been fierce debate over when the Nazis decided on the Final Solution: the murder of all European Jews. This is complicated by the fact that the euphemism 'final solution' was used in 1940 to refer to the expulsion of Jews to the east and the plan to resettle them in Madagascar. Evidence now suggests that the decision to move from unsystematic mass killings to a systematic programme of elimination of all Jews occurred in either July 1941 or October 1941, and was fully planned at Wannsee in January 1942.

TALKING POINTS

1 Do you think the anti-Nazis were right to assassinate Heydrich, given the reaction it provoked from the Nazis?

2 Do you think it can ever be justified for the government of one country to arrange the assassination of a foreign leader?

■ 18A Descent into Hell: a detailed chronology of anti-semitic measures

1933 Mar   Post-election SA anti-Jewish violence
1 Apr   To try to prevent unruly anti-semitic attacks by radicals, an official boycott of Jewish shops and businesses is declared. It meets with a limited response, and is called off after one day
Apr   Law for the Restoration of the Civil Service bans Jews from employment in the Civil Service (Hindenburg gains some exceptions)
Jul   Law for Compulsory Sterilisation (of the mentally ill)
Sept   Entailed Farm Law: bans Jews from owning farms

1934   Relatively calm year
   SD propose emigration of Jews

1935   Resumption of unofficial attacks on Jews again leads the government to take formal action
Sept   At Nuremberg Rally, Hitler announces:

- **Law for the Protection of German Blood and German Honour** (forbids mixed marriages, sex between Aryans and Jews)
- **Reich Citizenship Law** (deprives Jews of German citizenship)
- **Law for the Protection of the Genetic Health of the German People** (medical examination before marriage; 'certificates of fitness to marry'; a series of centres to be set up by the League for the Propagation of Racial Knowledge where people can have their cranial measurements taken to reassure themselves they are fully Aryan)

1936   Quiet year to help the economy and foreign relations
Aug   Anti-Jewish signs in Berlin removed during Olympic Games
   Himmler put in charge of Jewish emigration

1937   Little action until general radicalisation of the regime in the autumn
Sept   Nuremberg rallies: Hitler makes fierce speech attacking Jews
Nov   Schacht, critical of anti-Jewish economic measures, resigns

1938 Mar   *Anschluss* (union with Austria) gives Germany 150,000 more Jews. Adolf Eichmann forces 45,000 of the Austrian Jews to emigrate
April   Decree on the Registering of Jewish Property (all property valued at over 5,000 RM)
Jun–Oct   Series of anti-Jewish decrees:

- Jewish doctors, dentists, lawyers forbidden to have Aryan patients or clients
- Jews excluded from some commercial activities
- Jews must add Sarah or Israel to their names. Identity cards to be stamped with a J

9–10 Nov   *Kristallnacht* (Night of Broken Glass): a series of anti-Jewish attacks, unofficially encouraged by officials and police. Thousands of Jewish businesses attacked, synagogues burnt, 91 Jews murdered, 20,000 sent to camps. Jews forced to pay 1 billion RM for the damage

Nov   Decree excludes Jews from German economic life:

- Awarding of public business contracts to Jews banned
- Jews banned from trades, shops, businesses
- Jews excluded from schools, universities, cinemas, sports facilities

1939 Jan   Reich Central Office for Jewish Emigration set up to promote emigration
   Hitler refers to annihilation of Jewish race in Reichstag speech
   Hitler tells Czech Foreign Minister that he is going to destroy the Jews
   Major emigration wave
Sept   War against Poland. *Einsatzgruppen* murder thousands of civilians
   German Jews placed under curfew; radios confiscated
Oct   Himmler made Reich Commissioner for Strengthening Germanism
   Polish Jews resettled, moved into ghettos
   Euthanasia programme begins

> The *Einsatzgruppen* were special task forces of the Security Police that operated behind German lines in occupied territory. Their main task was to shoot 'hostile elements', especially Communists and Jews. Between 1939 and 1943 they shot over 2 million innocent civilians, including an estimated one and a half millions Jews.

SOURCE 18.15   Shop boycott. The placard accuses the Jewish owners of damaging German crafts and paying their workers hunger wages

SOURCE 18.16   At the August 1935 rally, in the Berlin Palace of Sport, 16,000 people bought tickets to hear Julius Streicher speak. The anti-semitic slogan reads: 'Women and girls, the Jews are your ruin'

SOURCE 18.17   An advertisement for a 'Jew-free resort': this sign indicated that there were no longer any Jews at the Frisian bathing resort of Nordseebad Norderney

SOURCE 18.18 The entrance to the Warsaw ghetto. The notice reads: 'Jewish area: entrance forbidden'

1940 July	Plan drawn up to transport 4 million western Jews to Madagascar
1940–Aug 1941	70,000 mentally ill people gassed
1941 June	War against the USSR. Political killings ordered. Half a million Jews shot
July (or possibly Oct)	**Decision taken to embark on 'Final Solution'**
Sept	German Jews ordered to wear Star of David
Oct	Emigration banned. Mass deportation of German Jews to the east begins
Dec	Soviet resistance blocks plans to move Jews to beyond the Urals
	Mass gassing of Jews at Chelmno camp begins
1942 Jan	**Wannsee Conference plans Final Solution**
	Beginning of systematic round-up of all Jews under German control
Dec	German gypsies moved to Auschwitz

SOURCE 18.19 Women and girls from Dvinsk about to be shot by a German special force

SOURCE 18.20 Page 1 of a report by an SS official in occupied Lithuania listing the Jews who have been killed by *Einsatzgruppen*

SOURCE 18.21 The crematorium used to burn the bodies after victims had been killed in the gas chambers

THE TOLL OF DEATH
Estimated deaths in camps
6 million Jews
3 million Poles
3 million Soviet prisoners of war
Up to 1 million gypsies
Thousands of homosexuals

1943	**Expansion of extermination camp system**
1944 Nov	Himmler orders end of gassing of inmates and the destruction of Auschwitz. Remaining inmates evacuated west, away from the advancing Soviet troops
1945 Jan	Red Army reaches Auschwitz
Apr	American and British troops reach concentration camps

C How could the Holocaust happen?

The photographs and statistics on pages 340–3 convey some of the horror. Here we concentrate on sources that help us to understand the attitudes of those involved, whether top Nazis, minor civil servants or mere bystanders.

FOCUS ROUTE

1 Read Sources 18.22–34. List the main reasons given in the sources why people were prepared to participate in and tolerate killing Jews.
2 Which three sources do you regard as the most valuable and which three the least valuable as evidence of why the Holocaust happened? Refer to both the origins and the content of the sources.

■ **18B Who was responsible for the Holocaust?**

SOURCE 18.22 Hitler to his staff, autumn 1941

That race of criminals [Jews] has on its conscience the 2 million dead of World War 1, and now already hundreds of thousands more.

SOURCE 18.25 Auschwitz Commandant Rudolf Hoess: Extract from *Commandant of Auschwitz: The Autobiography of Rudolf Hoess*, 1959

In the summer of 1941, I cannot remember the exact date . . . Himmler received me and said in effect: 'The Führer has ordered that the Jewish question be solved for once and for all . . . The Jews are the sworn enemies of the German people and must be eradicated. Every Jew that we can lay our hands on is to be destroyed now during the war, without exception. If we cannot obliterate the biological basis of JEWRY, the Jews will one day destroy the German people.

SOURCE 18.26 Rudolf Hoess's 1946 Nuremberg testimony

It was something already taken for granted that the Jews were to blame for everything . . . It was not just newspapers like the Stürmer *but it was everything we ever heard. Even our military and ideological training took for granted that we had to protect Germany from the Jews . . . We were all so trained to obey orders without even thinking that the thought of disobeying an order would simply never have occurred to anybody and somebody else would have done just as well if I hadn't . . . I really never gave much thought to whether it was wrong. It just seemed a necessity.*

SOURCE 18.29 An extract from a civil servant's memorandum suggesting improvements to special vehicles at Chelmno death camp, June 1942

The van's load is usually nine per square yard. In Saurer vehicles . . . maximum use of space is impossible, not because of any possible overload, but because loading to full capacity would affect the vehicle's stability. So reduction of the load space seems necessary. It must absolutely be reduced by a yard, instead of trying to solve the problem, as hitherto, by reducing the number of pieces loaded. Besides, this extends the operating time, as the empty void must also be filled with carbon monoxide. On the other hand, if the load space is reduced, and the vehicle is packed solid, the operating time can be considerably shortened. The manufacturers told us during a discussion that reducing the size of the van's rear would throw it badly off balance. The front axle, they claim, would be overloaded. In fact, the balance is automatically restored, because the merchandise aboard displays during the operation a natural tendency to rush to the rear doors, and is mainly found lying there at the end of the operation. So the front axle is not overloaded.

. . . Lights could be eliminated, since they apparently are never used. However, it has been observed that, when the doors are shut, the load always presses hard against them as soon as

SOURCE 18.32 Policeman (testifying in 1961)

I believed the propaganda that all Jews were criminals and subhumans and that they were the cause of Germany's decline after the First World War. The thought that one should disobey or evade the order to participate in the extermination of the Jews did not therefore enter my mind at all.

SOURCE 18.33 Soldiers' letters, 1941–2

A *Only when you can see what the Jew has brought about here in Russia, can you really understand why the Führer began the struggle against Jewry. What sort of suffering would not have fallen upon our fatherland if this beast of mankind had retained the upper hand?*

B *There can be no greater and holier task than the ceaseless destruction of Jewry.*

C *We are fighting this war today for the very existence of our Volk . . . Because this war in our view is a Jewish war, the Jews are primarily bearing the brunt of it.*

SOURCE 18.23 International Military Tribunal, Nuremberg, document D-73: notes of a discussion between Hitler and Miklos Horthy, the Hungarian leader, April 1943, recorded by Hitler's interpreter; cited in M. Gilbert, *The Holocaust*, 1986, p. 556

Where the Jews were left to themselves, as for instance in Poland, the most terrible misery and decay prevailed. They are just pure parasites. In Poland this state of affairs had been fundamentally cleared up. If the Jews there did not want to work, they were shot. If they could not work, they had to succumb. They had to be treated like tuberculosis bacilli, with which a healthy body may become infected. This was not cruel, if one remembered that even innocent creatures of nature, such as hares and deer, have to be killed, so that no harm is caused by them. Why should the beasts who wanted to bring us Bolshevism be spared more?

SOURCE 18.24 Himmler to SS officers, Posen, October 1943

We must be honest, decent, loyal and comradely to members of our own blood, but to nobody else . . .

Among ourselves it should be mentioned quite frankly – but we will never speak of it publicly . . . I mean cleaning out the Jews, the extermination of the Jewish race . . . Most of you must know what it means when a hundred corpses are lying side by side, or five hundred or five thousand. To have stuck it out and at the same time (apart from exceptions caused by human weakness) to have remained decent fellows, that is what has made us hard. This is a page of glory in our history which has never been written and will never be written.

SOURCE 18.27 Field Marshal Walther von Reichenau addressing his soldiers, October 1941

In the eastern sphere the soldier is not simply a fighter according to the rules of war, but the supporter of a ruthless racial ideology and the avenger of all the bestialities which have been inflicted on the German nation . . .

Soldiers must show full understanding for the necessity for the severe but just atonement being required of the Jewish subhumans.

SOURCE 18.28 Church leaders

A *[A Protestant theologian and member of the Confessional Church]*
We do not like the Jews as a rule: it is therefore not easy for us to apply to them as well the general love of humankind.

B *[Pastor Otto Dibelius]*
In all the corrosive manifestations of modern civilisation, Jews play a leading role.

rkness sets in. This is because the load naturally rushes *vards the light when darkness sets in, which makes* *sing the doors difficult. Also, because of the alarming* *ture of darkness, screaming always occurs when the* *ors are closed. It would therefore be useful to light the* *mps before and during the first moments of the operation.* *For easy cleaning of the vehicle, there must be a sealed* *ain in the middle of the floor. The drainage hole's cover* *would be equipped with a slanting trap, so that fluids* *n drain off during the operation. During cleaning, the* *ain can sometimes be used to evacuate large pieces of* *t.*

SOURCE 18.30 A civil servant

A rapid dying out of the Jews is for us a matter of total indifference, if not to say desirable.

SOURCE 18.31 Head of Reich Railways Department 33, responsible for 'special' trains. Interview for the film *Shoah* by Claude Lanzmann, 1985

I was strictly a bureaucrat . . . It was said that people were being sent to concentration camps and that those in poor health probably wouldn't survive . . . the extermination. Everyone condemns it . . . But as for knowing about it, we didn't.

SOURCE 18.34 Comments by German civilians from SD reports

A *It is hoped now the last Jews will soon leave the German fatherland.*

B *We have to thank Hitler for freeing us from this pest.*

C *Why should I care about the Jews?*

TALKING POINTS

1 How do you react to Source 18.29?
2 Can the excuse of obeying orders be used as justification for such actions?
3 Is the argument, as in Source 18.26, that 'if I don't do something unpleasant somebody else will, so I might as well do it' a valid one?

■ **Learning trouble spot**

Some key terms

Aryan: technically, this term refers to Indo-European languages, but it has been extended to describe an Aryan race including numerous national groups. In Nazi Germany, Aryan meant non-Jewish. For the Nazis the Nordic or Germanic subgroup was the superior form of the Aryan race.

Eugenics: the belief in improving a race by selective breeding, a widespread idea by the 1920s. Developing from nineteenth-century ideas of social Darwinism (applying Darwin's ideas of survival of the fittest to human races/nations), it was boosted by fears of a declining birth rate, by improved medical advances allowing weaker people to live longer and by scientific theories explaining antisocial behaviour in hereditary terms. Eugenicist ideas were not confined to Nazi Germany. The USA pioneered sterilisation of the mentally ill, and a voluntary scheme was considered during the Weimar Republic. Recently, victims of similar policies in Scandinavian countries and France from the 1930s to the 1960s have been trying to gain compensation as more evidence has come to light of the extent of such practices.

Euthanasia: mercy killing, putting painlessly to death, especially in cases of incurable suffering, with the person involved desiring death. The act is certainly inspired by concern for the person killed, and so it is technically inappropriate to use this term to describe the killing of the mentally ill in Nazi Germany, where the motivation was to help the nation, not the individual concerned, despite a gloss of professed concern to end suffering.

Genocide: the killing of a whole race.

Holocaust: the word comes from the Greek for whole and burnt, and originally was used to describe a sacrifice in which the whole of the victim was burnt. It is now used as a general term to describe the mass slaughter of human life, and in particular (as the Holocaust) to describe the Nazis' murder of 7 million Jews. Some people prefer to use the term 'Shoah' (the Hebrew word for destruction).

Explanations of the Holocaust

We now examine four of the main factors which have been identified as explanations for the Holocaust.

FOCUS ROUTE

Complete the following table, identifying evidence of the contribution each factor made to the Holocaust.

Factor involved	Evidence of an important contribution	Counter points
Hitler		
The nature of the Nazi state		
Anti-semitic attitudes of ordinary Germans		
War		

What was Hitler's involvement in the Holocaust?
Hitler's comments on Jews

SOURCE 18.35 Letter from Hitler to his military superior Adolf Gemlich in 1919

Rational anti-semitism ... must pursue a systematic, legal campaign against the Jews ... But the final objective must be the complete removal [Entfernung] of the Jews.

SOURCE 18.36 Remarks made by Hitler in 1922

As soon as I have the power, I shall have gallows after gallows erected, for example in Munich on the Marienplatz ... Then the Jews will be hanged one after another, and they will stay hanging until they stink. They will stay hanging as long as hygienically possible. As soon as they are untied, then the next groups will follow and that will continue until the last Jew in Munich is exterminated. Exactly the same procedure will be followed in other cities until Germany is cleansed of the last Jew!

SOURCE 18.37 From a speech Hitler made to the Reichstag in January 1939

If the international Jewish financiers outside Europe should succeed in plunging the nations once more into war, then the result will not be the BOLSHEVISING of the earth, and thus the victory of Jewry, but the annihilation of the Jewish race in Europe.

SOURCE 18.38 Extract from Himmler's recently discovered appointment diary

18th December 1941. Meeting with Hitler on the Jewish Question. [Himmler wrote in margin:] to be exterminated as partisans.

SOURCE 18.39 Hitler's New Year message, 1942

The Jew will not exterminate the peoples of Europe; he will be the victim of his own machinations [plots] instead.

ACTIVITY

Do Sources 18.35–9 prove that

a) Hitler wanted to kill all Jews?
b) Hitler was responsible for the Holocaust?

All students know that Hitler was anti-semitic and how central this was to his whole outlook on life. However, whether he really intended to kill the Jews is less clear-cut. This is partly because his long monologue (self-obsessed rant), *Mein Kampf*, is a very indigestible read, from which it is hard to extract clear, brief quotations. There is also the problem of language and translation. Hitler frequently referred to the 'removal' and 'eradication' of Jews and their influence, which could mean resettling them elsewhere, weakening their position or mass killing. When the mass killing of Jews started in 1941 it was deliberately masked behind the language of euphemism (that is, the use of a neutral expression to describe something offensive), such as 'resettlement', 'special handling' and 'final solution'.

A further issue is Hitler's direct role in ordering the Holocaust. No document signed by Hitler ordering that Jews be killed has been found. Although superficially perplexing, this is really not so surprising. Firstly, Hitler did not act in a neat, bureaucratic way. Many of his instructions were purely oral. Secondly, the Nazis tried to keep the Holocaust secret, and from 1944 deliberately destroyed much evidence of it. However, numerous high-ranking Nazis said that Hitler knew about the murders, and several claimed that he authorised them. Furthermore, the whole state was geared to enact the Führer's will, so it is inconceivable that Hitler did not approve of the Holocaust and it is highly probable that he ordered it.

How might the nature of the Nazi state have contributed to the Holocaust?

Some historians see the Holocaust as developing in response to circumstances and as a result of the way the Nazi regime operated. The lack of formal restraints and the institutional social Darwinism with rivals vying to work towards the Führer led to a process of cumulative radicalisation, such that the sporadic murder of 'undesirables' could develop into a system of extermination factories. In such a state, given the lack of formal restraints, euthanasia could easily lead to mass murder. Certainly, the experience gained from the euthanasia programme, in terms of personnel and techniques, was later used in the Holocaust. It is also argued that the totalitarian nature of the state, with the incessant anti-semitic propaganda, the stress on blind obedience and the exercise of arbitrary repression, contributed to the Holocaust. However, there is no evidence of harsh punitive action against those Germans who did refuse to participate.

Source 18.40 is from the official record of a meeting of top Nazis following *Kristallnacht* (10 November 1938). These vicious anti-semitic riots had been partly organised by the authorities. Heydrich had instructed local police to discuss them with the Security Police and to arrest as many Jews as their prisons could contain. This escalation of anti-semitic violence led to further measures, as revealed in Source 18.40 below.

SOURCE 18.40 Stenographic (taken down in shorthand) report of the meeting on the Jewish question, chaired by Goering, on 12 November 1938

Goering: *Gentlemen! Today's meeting is of a decisive nature. I have received a letter written on the Führer's orders, requesting that the Jewish question be now, once and for all, co-ordinated and solved one way or another. And yesterday once again did the Führer request by phone for me to take co-ordinated action in the matter.*

Since the problem is mainly an economic one, it is from the economic angle that it shall have to be tackled. Naturally a number of legal measures shall have to be taken which fall into the sphere of the Minister for Justice and into that of the Minister of the Interior; and certain propaganda measures shall be taken care of by the Minister for Propaganda. The Minister for Finance and the Minister for Economic Affairs shall take care of problems falling in their respective areas.

The meeting, in which we first talked about this question and came to the decision to aryanise the German economy, to take the Jew out of it and put him into our debit ledger, was one in which, to our shame, we only made pretty plans, which were executed very slowly. We then had a demonstration, right here in Berlin, we told the people that something decisive would be done, but again nothing happened. We have had this affair in Paris now [the assassination of a German diplomat by a Jew], more demonstrations followed and this time something decisive must be done!

Because, gentlemen, I have had enough of these demonstrations! They don't harm the Jew but me, who is the last authority for co-ordinating the German economy . . .

If today, a Jewish shop is destroyed, if goods are thrown into the street, the insurance company will pay for the damages, which the Jew does not even have; and furthermore the consumer goods belonging to the people are destroyed. If in the future, demonstrations which are necessary occur, then, I pray that they be directed, so as not to hurt us . . .

I should not want to leave any doubt, gentlemen, as to the aim of today's meeting. We have not come together merely to talk again, but to make decisions, and I implore the competent agencies to take all measures for the elimination of the Jew from the German economy and to submit them to me . . .

The trustee of the State will estimate the value of the property and decide what amount the Jew shall receive. Naturally, this amount is to be set as low as possible. The representative of the State shall then turn the establishment over to the Aryan proprietor, that is, the property shall be sold according to its real value.

Goebbels: *In almost all German cities synagogues are burned . . . I am of the opinion that this is our chance to dissolve the synagogues. All those not completely intact shall be razed by the Jews. The Jews shall pay for it . . . We shall build parking lots in their place or new buildings . . .*

I deem it necessary to issue a decree forbidding the Jews to enter German theatres, movie houses, and circuses . . .

Furthermore, I advocate that Jews be eliminated from all positions in public life in which they may prove to be provocative. It is still possible today that a Jew shares a compartment in a sleeping car with a German. Therefore, we need a decree by the Reich Ministry for Communications stating that separate compartments for Jews shall be available – in cases where compartments are filled up, Jews cannot claim a seat. They shall be given a separate compartment only after all Germans have secured seats. They shall not mix with Germans, and if there is no more room, they shall have to stand in the corridor.

Goering: *In that case, I think it would make more sense to give them separate compartments.*

Goebbels: *Not if the train is overcrowded.*

Goering: *Just a moment. There'll be only one Jewish coach. If that is filled up, the other Jews will have to stay at home.*

Goebbels: *Suppose, though, there won't be many Jews going on the express train to Munich; suppose there would be two Jews in the train and the other compartments would be overcrowded. These two Jews would then have a compartment all to themselves. Therefore, Jews may claim a seat only after all Germans have claimed a seat.*

Goering: *I'd give the Jews one coach or one compartment. And should a case like you mention arise and the train be overcrowded, believe me, we won't need a law. We'll kick him out and he'll have to sit alone in the toilet all the way!*

Goebbels: *I don't agree. I don't believe in this. There ought to be a law. Furthermore, there ought to be a decree barring Jews from German beaches and resorts. [Goebbels then refers to excluding Jews from German forests; then parks.] Furthermore, Jewish children are still allowed in German schools. That's impossible. It is out of the question that any boy should sit beside a Jewish boy in a German high school and receive lessons in German history.*

Goering: *Of course I too am of the opinion that these economic measures ought to be strengthened by a number of police-action propaganda-measures and cultural displays so that everything shall be fixed now and the Jewry will be slapped this week right and left.*

Heydrich: *In spite of the elimination of the Jew from the economic life, the main problem, namely to kick the Jew out of Germany, remains. May I make a few proposals to that effect? Following a suggestion by the Commissioner of the Reich, we have set up a centre for the Emigration of Jews in Vienna, and that way we have eliminated 50,000 Jews from Austria while from the Reich only 19,000 Jews were eliminated during the same period.*

ACTIVITY

1 What does Source 18.40 illustrate about the way the Third Reich operated? Refer to Hitler's role and the way decisions were taken.
2 Some historians argue that the Holocaust developed in a haphazard manner and not primarily as the result of a clear master plan by Hitler. How much evidence does this source provide to substantiate this view?

How far were the German people responsible for the Holocaust?

Most historians have tried to distinguish between Nazi fanatics who ordered and carried out the Holocaust and the mass of Germans who were uninvolved and arguably unaware of what was happening. This view has been challenged, most recently by Daniel Goldhagen, a professor of history at Harvard. His Jewish father, also a history professor, was taken by the Nazis for execution but managed to survive. Goldhagen has made a name for himself with his book *Hitler's Willing Executioners: Ordinary Germans and the Holocaust* (1996) which has aroused fierce controversy. He has not primarily based his study on new sources, but has studied again those used by an earlier research historian Christopher Browning and come up with very different views.

Goldhagen claims ordinary Germans were Hitler's willing executioners. The sources he has studied of the police who followed in the wake of the armies in eastern Europe reveal how thousands of ordinary Germans (most were not Nazi Party members) willingly participated and even revelled in brutality and mass murder. At least 100,000 ordinary Germans were involved in the Holocaust, and all Germans were potentially involved. Such involvement was not conceivable in any other country. Germans were morally responsible for the Holocaust. Goldhagen's view has been well summarised by Richard Evans in Source 18.41.

An alternative view is that most Germans were unaware of the full horrors of the Holocaust which the regime tried to keep secret. Although rumours existed, most Germans turned a deaf ear to them. Only a small number were actively involved, and many of these were Ukrainians and other non-Germans.

Other views accept that knowledge of anti-Jewish atrocities was widespread; it was a secret that could not be kept. However, for a variety of different and complex reasons most Germans did not act to prevent the horrors. Widespread anti-semitism played a part here, strengthened by Nazi propaganda, but this was not the same as most Germans being 'eliminationists'.

The criticisms made of Goldhagen illustrate much about the nature of the historical process. He has been criticised for:

- selective use of evidence: ignoring aspects that do not fit in with his thesis
- sweeping generalisations
- giving a simple answer to a complex question
- his narrow focus; his exaggeration of anti-semitism in Germany and the underplaying of it in other countries
- his subjective approach, as the son of a Jew who survived the camps
- appealing to the emotions by detailing the horrors, to the neglect of critical assessment
- his motivation: he is a careerist out to make a name/money for himself (which has certainly happened for his book became a bestseller)
- the effects of his views, encouraging hatred of Germans (thus fostering racism)
- undermining, by displaying the Holocaust as unique, the attempt to learn lessons from the Holocaust, and to understand similar horrors, and how to prevent them.

Thus he has been criticised for his methods, his motivation, and the possible effects of his work.

SOURCE 18.41   R. Evans, *Rereading German History*, 1997, p. 150

Goldhagen's argument . . . is that Germans killed millions of Jews during the Second World War not because they were forced to, nor because German traditions of obedience enabled a handful of fanatics at the top to do whatever they liked, nor because they were succumbing to peer-group pressure from their comrades-in-arms, nor because they were ambitious careerists, nor because they were acting automatically, like cogs in a machine. Least of all did they carry out extermination of the Jews because they faced death themselves if they refused to obey the order to do so. Goldhagen argues that Germans killed Jews in their millions because they enjoyed doing it, and they enjoyed doing it because their minds and emotions were eaten up by a murderous, all-consuming hatred of Jews that had been pervasive [widespread] in German political culture for decades, even centuries past. Ultimately, says Goldhagen, it is this history of genocidal anti-semitism that explains the German mass murder of Europe's Jews.

TALKING POINT

What are the advantages and disadvantages of using one historian's summary of another's views?

TALKING POINTS

1 How is it that historians looking at the same primary sources can develop contrasting historical explanations?

2 Should the possible effects of historical analysis be used to argue against its validity?

3 In the 1990s there was mass slaughter in Rwanda, Bosnia and Kosovo, and more revelations emerged about the 'Killing Fields' in Pol Pot's Cambodia in the 1970s. Can such contemporary events help us to understand how the Holocaust could happen?

■ 18C Why did the German people allow the Holocaust to happen?

351

WHY DID THE NAZIS COMMIT MASS MURDER?

A variety of claims have been put forward, ranging from evidence of mass ignorance to mass willing participation. Points made include:

- **They were unable to prevent it**

  Nazi Germany was a terror state.

- **They accepted it**

  Many Germans were
  - conformist
  - apathetic
  - influenced by propaganda
  - psychologically prepared
  - influenced by social Darwinist views
  - anti-semitic
  - unconcerned about minority groups
  - brutalised by war, believing 'life is cheap'
  - convinced of the need to prevent Jewish atrocities against themselves
  and saw
  - the Jewish problem in biological not human terms
  - life as a cruel struggle.

  The Holocaust was
  - the culmination of the gradual dehumanising impact of the regime
  - a logical development from euthanasia of the mentally ill
  - something that Germans were gradually sucked into.

- **They were unaware of it**

  The Nazis tried to keep it secret.
  The extermination camps were far away in the east.
  The Nazis used the language of euphemism, e.g. 'special handling', 'final solution'.

  Germans perhaps
  - did not have sufficient evidence of what was going on
  - rejected wild, unbelievable rumours
  - had information, but did not understand or internalise it
  - closed their ears; they were skilled at knowing how not to know
  - deliberately did not find out in order to reduce their responsibility
  - tried to live a normal life by dissociating themselves from it
  - retreated from reality.

ACTIVITY

Debate: 'Were ordinary Germans violently anti-semitic and Hitler's willing executioners?'
The following points have been made in the 'Goldhagen debate'. Arrange them in two lists: those which he might use and those points which could be used by his critics.

a) Eliminationist anti-semitism had deep roots in Germany.
b) At least 100,000 ordinary Germans were involved in the Holocaust.
c) There was considerable opposition to Nazism.
d) Anti-semitism was not an important reason why millions of Germans voted for Hitler in Weimar elections.
e) There is much evidence that many of those involved in killing Jews enjoyed it.
f) No one was executed for refusing to participate in the killings.
g) There were liberal attitudes to Jews in Weimar Germany.
h) Many of those involved in committing atrocities were deeply disturbed by the experience.
i) Germans were under pressure, and had been subjected to propaganda.
j) Other countries, not just Germany, committed anti-semitic atrocities.
k) Jews were involved in operating the Holocaust.
l) Other groups were also systematically killed, e.g. gypsies.

Using these points and others, debate the Goldhagen view.

TALKING POINTS

One German, interviewed in the 1990s about her lack of opposition to the Nazi treatment of Jews, commented: 'I was sorry about that. But really, just like today when you walk away from people in need, you can't help everywhere: it was the same then. You couldn't do anything, could you?'

1 Do you find this a powerful explanation?
2 Can we talk about 'the Germans' attitude' to the Holocaust?

Most historians now accept that knowledge of the mass murder of Jews, even if vague, was increasingly widespread, although far more so in the case of the shootings than of the extermination camps. Too many people were involved – not just the prison guards but front-line soldiers, bureaucrats, railway staff, industrialists – for the atrocities to remain a secret. This is certainly suggested by the following sources.

SOURCE 18.42   Headline from a Hanover newspaper in 1942

The Jews to be exterminated.

SOURCE 18.43   Bishop Theophilus Wurm to the Ministry for Ecclesiastical Affairs

The steps taken in the occupied territories have become known in our homeland. [They] are widely discussed and burden most heavily the conscience and strength of countless men and women among the German people who suffer from it more than from their family sacrifices.

SOURCE 18.44   A foreigner leaving Berlin in 1943, as reported by the British Embassy in Lisbon to the Foreign Office

Feelings were certainly strong against Jews in general, but what the regime had done to them was considered by nearly everyone to be excessive.

SOURCE 18.45   Survey of opinions of a random sample of Germans carried out by American occupation authorities, October 1945

Statement	Percentage agreeing
Hitler was right in his treatment of the Jews.	0
Hitler went too far in his treatment of the Jews, but something had to be done to keep them in bounds.	19
The actions against the Jews were in no way justified.	77

TALKING POINT

What are the limitations of the 1945 American survey of German attitudes on Nazism (Source 18.45)?

Three recent historians have argued quite persuasively on this issue.

SOURCE 18.46   M. Housden, *Resistance and Conformity in the Third Reich*, 1996, p. 160

In the context of a society in which racism formed a background feature of everyday life, very many ordinary Germans indeed played small parts in making a fundamentally flawed system function. Accepting that concrete individual actions always reflect a mixture of motives, during peacetime conformity took the form of both passive acceptance of, and active support for, racial policies and actions which stopped short of the wholesale violence of 'Crystal Night'. With the nation at war, escalating racial policy grew into something people learned to live with; it was for most people a source of indifference. If their job dictated some sort of collaboration in the implementation of racial policy, by and large they conformed to the demand. Naturally there were exceptions to the rule . . . But the impression lingers, as Willy Brandt [Chancellor of the German Federal Republic 1969–74] has said, that far too few people made conscious choices to oppose this particular form of evil. It became normal to conform to highly abnormal expectations.

SOURCE 18.47   D. Bankier, 'German Public Awareness of the Final Solution' in *The Final Solution*, ed. D. Cesarani, 1996, p. 225

The view . . . that very little was known about the extermination at the time, or that only unsubstantiated rumours about the Jews' fate circulated in Germany, is untenable . . . On the basis of the available evidence it is equally untenable that the German people failed to comprehend the significance of the Nazis' genocidal policy . . . The awareness of the extermination shaped the public's reactions to the regime's political stimuli and . . . affected its interpretations of wartime reality.

SOURCE 18.48 I. Kershaw, 'German Popular Opinion during the Final Solution' in *Comprehending the Holocaust*, ed. A. Cohen, 1988, p. 154

The fairly widespread knowledge of the mass shootings of Jews was . . . compatible with a spectrum of responses ranging from overt approval to blank condemnation, and above all with an apathetic shrug of the shoulders, the feeling of impotence, or the turning of the face from unpalatable [unacceptable] truths.

Much suggests, in fact, that this type of reaction – that is non-reaction – was the most commonplace of all. If one term above all sums up the behavioural response of the German people to the persecution of the Jews, it is: passivity [indifference]. The passivity was consonant [consistent] with a number of differing internalised attitudes toward Jews. Most obviously, it corresponded to latent [hidden] anti-semitism, and, arguably, to a mentality of 'moral indifference'. It also mirrored apathy . . . and a willingness to accept uncritically the state's right to take radical action against its 'enemies'. Above all . . . passivity . . . was a reflection of a prevailing lack of interest in the Jewish Question . . . At the time that Jews were being murdered in their millions, the vast majority of Germans had plenty of other things on their mind.

How did war contribute to the Holocaust?

Some historians put great stress on the impact of the Second World War. They argue that but for the outbreak of war the Holocaust would not have happened. Goebbels once described the struggle Germany was in as 'not the Second World War but the great racial war'. The mass killing of Jews began in Poland in the wake of the Nazi advance in 1939 and escalated in 1941 during the invasion of the USSR. There is now overwhelming evidence that it was not just the enthusiastic Nazis of the SS who committed mass murder in the Polish and Russian campaigns, but also ordinary units of the Wehrmacht.

The Second World War contributed to the Holocaust in the following ways:

- It disrupted the Nazi government's plans for mass Jewish emigration.
- It meant Germany gained control of millions more Jews at a time when the Nazi government wanted to remove Jews from its own territory.
- It brutalised people, and accustomed them to killing.
- Since Germans were dying in the war, many felt that killing their enemies was justified.
- It intensified paranoia about the enemy within; it encouraged extremism.
- It removed any concern about international opinion.

German soldiers embarking for the eastern front on 1 September 1939. The graffiti on the train says: 'We're off to Poland – to thrash the Jews'

D Review: Why did the Nazis commit mass murder?

In this chapter you have encountered the full horrors of the Nazi regime. Although millions of Germans supported and benefited from many of Hitler's other policies, his actions against outsiders, especially the Jews, have totally discredited Nazism. We have tried to show how such policies were not just an unfortunate excess but were inherent in the nature of Nazism. Even if the full horrors of the Holocaust were probably not an inevitable result of the Nazis' rise to power in 1933, they stemmed from the Nazis' core view of a blood-based *Volksgemeinschaft* that had to be protected from alien forces within.

Chart 18D below tries to summarise the roots of anti-semitism and the reasons why in Nazi Germany it took such a horrific form.

■ 18D Why anti-semitism? Why the Holocaust?

WHY ANTI-SEMITISM?

a) General reasons

- religious: Jesus killed by Jews
- economic: hostility to wealthy Jews (bankers, industrialists, etc.) or to poor immigrants
- social: popular need to blame someone for problems, to find a scapegoat
- political: government diverts discontent by attacking Jews
- psychological: general hostility to things that are different/alien

b) In twentieth-century Germany

- influence of social Darwinism
- influx of *Ostjuden* from Russia

c) Hitler

- his contact with Jews in Vienna
- his doubts about his own ancestry
- pathological (diseased) aspects of his personality

BUT these are not the major reasons for the Nazis' appeal.

d) In the Third Reich 1933–45

- absolute enemy to unite against
- distraction from problems
- some Nazi leaders pathologically anti-semitic
- anti-semitic propaganda

SO anti-semitism was widespread, but why in 1939–45 did it develop into mass murder?

WHY THE HOLOCAUST?

- Hitler's genocidal intentions
- state lawlessness
- chaotic nature of the Third Reich allowed radicalisation to go unchecked
- persecution of the Jews developed its own momentum
- euthanasia prepared the way for the killing of 'inferiors'
- apathy or deliberate blindness of Germans
- effects of anti-semitic propaganda
- eliminationist anti-semitism deeply engrained in Germans
- brutalisation of war
- sadism of many Nazis
- 'banality of evil' (Hannah Arendt): that is, the capacity of normal people to do evil things

All of the following have been held partly responsible for the Holocaust. Can you explain why?

WHO'S TO BLAME?

- Hitler
- the Nazi leaders
- the camp commanders
- the camp guards
- the SS
- the Wehrmacht
- the German people
- the Allies
- the Jews

TALKING POINTS

1 Which is the more important issue: whether Hitler directly ordered the Holocaust or how much Germans knew about what was going on?
2 Think of other atrocities or massacres. Do you agree with the view that the Holocaust was qualitatively different from all of these?
3 Is the fact that the Nazis used euthanasia a powerful argument against legalising it?

This chapter has raised many historical and moral issues. You might like to conclude by discussing some of the following sources.

SOURCE 18.49 Martin Niemöller

First they came for the Jews
and I did not speak out –
because I was not a Jew.

Then they came for the Communists
and I did not speak out –
because I was not a Communist.

Then they came for the trade unionists
and I did not speak out –
because I was not a trade unionist.

Then they came for me
and there was no one left
to speak out for me.

SOURCE 18.50 The Italian writer Primo Levi, who was himself an inmate of Auschwitz, wrote in *If this is a Man*, 1958

Perhaps one cannot, what is more one must not, understand what happened, because to understand is almost to justify ... No normal human being will ever be able to identify with Hitler, Himmler, Goebbels, Eichmann and endless others ... We cannot understand [Nazi hatred] but we can and must understand from where it springs and we must be on our guard ... Everybody must know or remember that when Hitler and Mussolini spoke in public, they were believed, applauded, admired, and adored like gods ... We must remember that the faithful followers ... were not born torturers, were not (with a few exceptions) monsters: they were ordinary men.

SOURCE 18.51 The writer Arthur Koestler commented in 1944

A dog run over by a car upsets our emotional balance and digestion: 3,000,000 Jews killed in Poland causes but a moderate uneasiness. Statistics don't bleed: it is the detail which counts. We are unable to embrace the total process with our awareness. We can only focus on little lumps of reality.

SOURCE 18.52 Ian Kershaw in 'Studying the Holocaust', ed. R. Landau, 1998, p. 4

The road to Auschwitz was built by hatred but paved with apathy.

SOURCE 18.53 C. Browning, *The Path to Genocide*, 1992, p. 144

The path was a gradual, almost imperceptible, descent past the point of no return.

SOURCE 18.54 The actor Ben Kingsley, after his role in the film about the Holocaust, *Schindler's List*

As we pass into the twenty-first century, the world will inherit an undigestible piece of history, the Shoah, which cannot be understood, may not be forgiven, and must not be forgotten.

TALKING POINT

What point is Martin Niemöller making in the poem? Does it have a message for us nowadays?

TALKING POINTS

1 Do you tend to react in the way described by Koestler?
2 Do you agree with Levi that the attempt to understand may lead to justification?
3 The historian Peter Hayes has said: 'The problem in history is to explain not why bad men do evil, but why good men do.' Explain the thinking behind this point.
4 What insight into the Holocaust do Sources 18.50 and 18.52–4 provide? Do these issues have any relevance for events today?

KEY POINTS FROM CHAPTER 18: Why did the Nazis commit mass murder?

1 The Nazis wanted to create a *Volksgemeinschaft* of healthy Aryans committed to the state.
2 This vision was accompanied by hostility to 'alien elements' that threatened the supremacy of the German people. These aliens were defined in racial–genetic, ideological and social/behavioural terms.
3 This led to the persecution of gypsies, homosexuals, religious sects, the mentally ill, the workshy as well as the Jews.
4 Measures against outsiders included job discrimination, imprisonment, compulsory sterilisation and eventually mass murder.
5 From 1939 the Nazis began to murder mentally ill children in their so-called 'euthanasia' programme.
6 The Nazis used propaganda to win people over to the removal of outsiders, but they tried to keep the Holocaust secret.
7 Measures against Jews escalated in a series of spurts. In 1935 Jews were deprived of citizenship; in 1938 they lost their businesses and from 1941 most were moved to ghettos or camps.
8 Mass murder of Jews began with the invasion of Poland in 1939.
9 From January 1942 the Nazis embarked on their 'Final Solution' of mass gassings.
10 There is considerable historical debate as to how the Holocaust developed, and about the role of Hitler and ordinary Germans in it.

19

Review: What impact did Nazism have on the German people?

This review chapter pulls together the issues that have been discussed in Section 2. Firstly, we will assess the degree of overall control the regime had, to see the extent to which the Third Reich achieved its aim of being a totalitarian state. We then examine the impact of the regime on society, and the extent to which it modernised Germany. We conclude by examining the overall impact of the regime on the minds of Germans, to try to reach conclusions on our overarching debate of how successful the Nazis were in creating a *Volksgemeinschaft*.

A To what extent was Nazi Germany a totalitarian state? (p. 358)

B Was there a social revolution in Nazi Germany? (pp. 359–61)

C How far did Hitler succeed in creating a *Volksgemeinschaft*? (pp. 362–7)

D Conclusions (pp. 368–9)

■ **Learning trouble spot**

Germany 1933–9 or 1933–45?
Section 2 has concentrated on domestic policy in the years 1933–9 since this period is often separated out by historians (and examination boards) as the key one for study. It also enables us to examine the impact of Nazism before the distortions of the Second World War. However, we must balance this by considering whether a major war was inherent in Nazism, and was not just a chance occurrence. Thus some historians argue it is false to make judgements on Nazism during 1933–9 without taking into account the war period. They argue strongly against the view held by many survivors of the Third Reich that overall it was a 'good' period until Hitler went 'wrong' by embarking on war.

   Although this review largely focuses on Nazism's impact by 1939, it must also be realised that the Third Reich was at war for as long as it was at peace. Key points extending to 1945 will be touched upon here and then looked at more fully in Chapter 21.

A To what extent was Nazi Germany a totalitarian state?

SOURCE 19.1 Goebbels

The aim of the National Socialist Revolution must be a totalitarian state, which will permeate all aspects of public life.

SOURCE 19.2 Robert Ley

The only people who still have a private life in Germany are those who are asleep.

A totalitarian state has been defined as a country where the government seeks to control nearly all aspects of life to ensure that the people become committed members of the state. The Nazis, like the Fascists in Italy and Communists in the Soviet Union, aimed to establish a totalitarian state and created a series of organisations to control the people. The essential features of such a regime include:

- a one-party state, led by one powerful leader, the centre of a personality cult
- an official ideology imposed by the state, with no alternative viewpoints permitted
- a government monopoly of the media and culture, used for propaganda
- secret police and a vast repressive machinery
- government control of all key institutions, such as the army, youth movements and the workers' organisations
- the law and the courts dominated by the government, not acting independently
- government control of the economy.

In the following Focus Route we have divided these criteria into more specific areas to help you assess the degree of totalitarianism in Germany. Be aware of developments during the years 1933–9 and again during 1939–45, to see if the degree of totalitarianism developed over time.

FOCUS ROUTE

1 Look back at the key areas of domestic policy covered in Section 2, then complete your own copy of the table below.

Area (chapter)	Evidence of totalitarianism	Limits of state control	Overall assessment (0 = none, 5 = strong)
Political structure (10, 11)			
Repression (11, 17)			
Ideology/propaganda/culture (11, 13)			
Economy (12)			
Social policy (12, 14, 15)			
Religion (16)			
Racial policy (18)			
Other aspects, e.g. opposition (17)			

2 Which areas are
  a) most totalitarian
  b) least totalitarian?
  How do you explain this?
3 Have you detected any changes over time?
4 If you have studied other totalitarian regimes, how do they compare with Nazi Germany?

B Was there a social revolution in Nazi Germany?

Whether the Nazis effected a social revolution in Germany, and the related issue of whether they modernised Germany, has provoked considerable historical debate. Some historians argue that there was great change, others argue that the basics of German society remained largely unchanged. As with other historical controversies, the different ideological positions of historians contribute to contrasting analyses, as do the variety of sources and ways of interpreting them. There are also other problems, such as:

- Definitions: what do we mean by 'social revolution', 'modernisation'?
- Assessment: how does one measure, for example, social mobility and changes in value systems?
- The nature of Nazism: the complex nature of Nazism has caused further problems. The social composition of the Nazi Movement was diverse, and elements of its ideology were contradictory. To get and keep power it had to appeal both to the petty bourgeoisie and also to the elite, while to achieve its foreign policy goals it had to develop modern aspects that clashed with parts of its ideology.
- The importance of ideology: there is also disagreement on the importance one should place on Nazi ideology; was it just propaganda, or did it determine policies?

We must also consider the impact of other trends:

- Longer-term trends: some of the apparent modernisation that occurred during the Third Reich might be due to longer-term developments that were happening anyway, such as the growth of the TERTIARY sector in the economy, improved contraception, the growth of consumerism and improved communications.
- War: for half its time in power Nazism was at war, and it is possible that developments after 1939 were more the product of the pressures of the war than inherent to Nazism. The final effects of Nazism, such as bringing down the Junker order in eastern Germany, were due to its defeat rather than a matter of policy.

ACTIVITY

1 On the right are statements that could be used to describe a modern society or a more traditional one. Sort them out into two lists.

2 Discuss your results, especially points over which you disagree. Is it surprising that there are disagreements?

3 Now use the criteria for a modern society to assess the extent to which the Third Reich modernised Germany.

Economy
a) government greatly concerned with economic issues
b) based on factories and industrial production
c) limited communications
d) based on agricultural and craft production
e) advanced technologies
f) government little involved in the economy
g) simple technologies
h) fast, mass communications

Political
a) power derived from inheritance/God
b) involvement of the masses
c) powerful, intrusive government
d) local power figures important
e) more powerful central government
f) power derived from the people/below
g) dominance by traditional elites
h) formal, impersonal, bureaucratic power structures
i) power derived from personal positions
j) limited reach of government

Values/culture
a) idea of progress and development
b) national loyalties
c) increasingly SECULAR
d) limited media
e) mass media
f) view of society as largely static
g) local loyalties
h) suspicion of variety in behaviour or views
i) religious
j) acceptance of diversity

Society
a) greater gender equality
b) rigid social hierarchies
c) powerful social norms
d) based on status and rank
e) based on class divisions
f) welfare based on church and other local groups
g) mostly rural population
h) greater individualism
i) social mobility
j) welfare state
k) increasingly urban population
l) women in subordinate positions

ACTIVITY

1 Historians have described the developments in the Third Reich shown in the four spider diagrams. Write the points out into two columns: those that could be used to argue that the Third Reich had a modernising impact and those that indicate it maintained or even sought to return to traditional values.

2 Try to substantiate your points with reference to particular developments. Discuss your results with the rest of the class.

3 In which of the four areas do you consider the Third Reich modernised most? In which least?

4 Do you consider there is sufficient evidence to argue that there was a social revolution in the Third Reich? Make an initial assessment, then read the following summary of some historians' views on the issue.

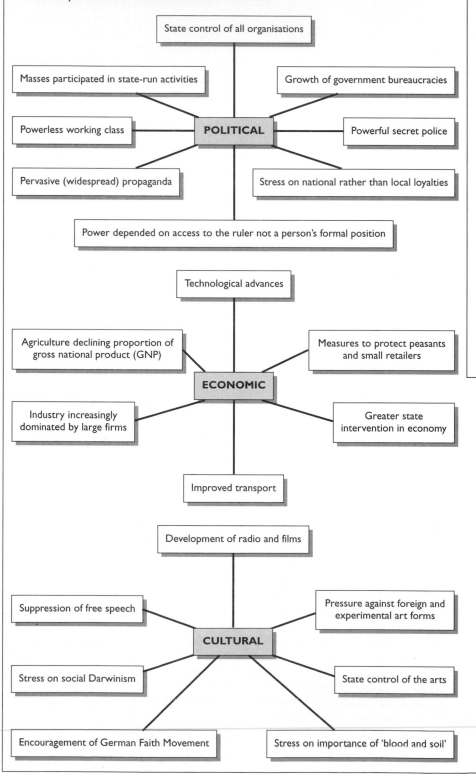

Historians' assessments

There are three broad positions on the issue of Nazism as a social revolution.

i) Some historians, for example the American Schoenbaum in his book *Hitler's Social Revolution* (1960), argue that there were profound changes in the structures of society and in social values, produced directly or indirectly by Nazism, that justify the term 'social revolution' and that paved the way for modern Germany. Although Nazism's ideology was in many ways reactionary, harking back to a rural past of healthy German farmers close to the soil, the actual experience of Nazi rule led to modernisation. For the Nazis' aim of controlling all Germans and creating a major power to compete in the modern world and conquer *Lebensraum* required modern economic and military might. Nazism completed the revolution of the old order that Weimar had failed to do. It created a classless society with unprecedented social mobility and egalitarianism (greater equality).

ii) Other historians reject this view. Although they accept that there were superficial changes to social forms and institutional appearances in the Third Reich, they argue that the fundamental substance of society remained unchanged. Marxists further argue that capitalism was strengthened and the class structure was enhanced, not broken down, by Nazism.

iii) A third position, reinforced by the growth of local studies in the 1980s, is that though there were considerable changes, they did not amount to a 'social revolution' as their effects were contradictory – some 'modernising', others reactionary. Nazism had a greater impact on the attitudes of Germans than on their social position. Some historians do talk of a Nazi revolution, but of a racial rather than a broader social one.

SOURCE 19.3 Kershaw, in *Nazi Dictatorship*, 1993, p. 147, has summarised the position thus

It seems clear, then, that Nazism did not produce a 'social revolution' in Germany during the period of the Third Reich ... It was ... incapable of bringing about a complete and permanent social revolution, short of attaining total and final victory in ... war ... Nazism's intentions were directed towards a transformation of value and belief systems – a psychological 'revolution' rather than one of substance.

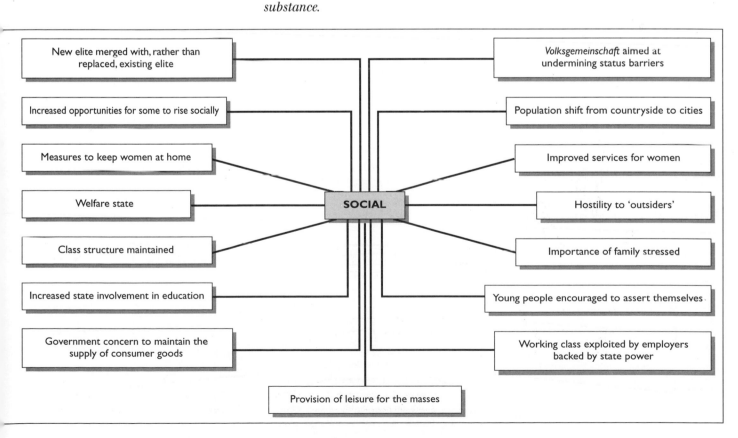

C How far did Hitler succeed in creating a *Volksgemeinschaft*?

FOCUS ROUTE

'Hitler succeeded in creating a genuine *Volksgemeinschaft*.'
Draw up a list of points to argue for and against this statement. Study Sources 19.4–23 and then debate the issue. Consider the time period covered; it could be either 1933–9 or 1933–45.
You might like to consider the following areas:
a) Was the Nazi view of a *Volksgemeinschaft* realisable?
b) What means did Hitler utilise to achieve his aims? Were they sufficient?
c) Does one need to examine the impact of Hitler's policies on particular groups of Germans rather than on Germans as a whole? What might this in itself suggest about his success?
d) Did Hitler gain considerable support without achieving his full vision?

You have seen how most historians have argued that the Third Reich had a limited impact on the structure of society. This is not surprising, since Hitler's priorities lay elsewhere: that is, in the creation of a new united German nation, or *Volksgemeinschaft*. Before assessing Hitler's success in this area, read Sax's excellent summary of the Nazis' aims.

SOURCE 19.4 B. Sax and D. Kuntz, *Inside Hitler's Germany*, 1992, p.178

The type of traditional society that the National Socialists hoped to form was the Volksgemeinschaft. *According to National Socialist ideology, such a community would result from the creative activities of the German* Volk. *Unlike mere society* (Gesellschaft), *which had come to dominate modern industrial life with its impersonal structures and isolated individuals, the* Volk *community was integrated, personal and organic – a national union in which each individual knew his place within the larger whole and in which every aspect of life furthered the good of the community. The notion of* Volk *had a mystical tone. It was at once 'the people', 'the nation', and 'the race'. In National Socialist theory a nation was defined in purely racial terms ...*

... The mission of National Socialism was to re-establish the Volk *community by bringing to full consciousness the awareness of race, blood, and soil among all Germans. At the heart of National Socialist ideology was the idea of creating the 'new man' and the 'new woman', of forming individuals with the strength of character, the awareness of race and soil, and the dedication to follow the Führer necessary to create the* Volk *community. National Socialism aimed to penetrate the very core of individual existence by constructing an organic society in which all people and organisations were 'co-ordinated' under Party control, for the Party was the guardian of the* Volksgemeinschaft. *Class distinctions had to be broken down within the new community, and the very separation between occupational concerns and political existence and even private and public life had to be overcome.*

TALKING POINT

Historians know the horrors committed by the Nazi regime after 1939; how might this distort their assessment of popular reactions to the regime in the 1930s?

SOURCE 19.5 The local structure of the Nazi Party

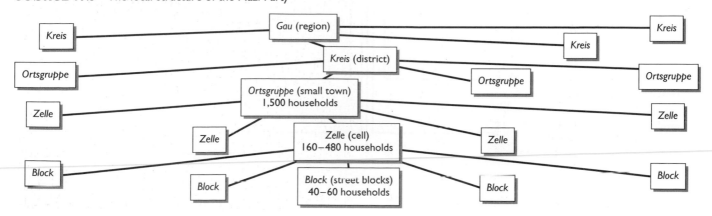

SOURCE 19.6 *Collection for Winterhilfe (Winter Aid)*

SOURCE 19.7 *Winterhilfe (Winter Aid) expenditure graph*

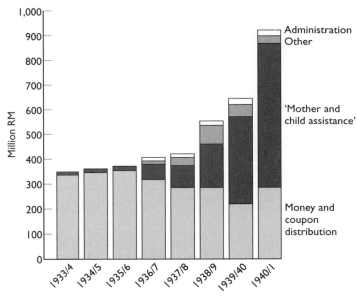

SOURCE 19.9 Mass rally, Nuremberg, 1935

SOURCE 19.8 Membership of the Nazi Party and other Nazi organisations

Membership	1933	1939	1944
NSDAP	850,000	5,300,000	8,000,000
DAF	5,300,000	22,000,000	25,000,000
HY	2,300,000	7,700,000	

SOURCE 19.10 Support for the government in four plebiscites held between 1934 and 1938

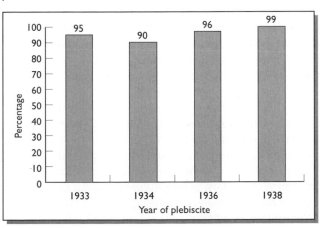

SOURCE 19.11   Festival with banners, Nuremberg, 1937

SOURCE 19.12   A Hitler Youth camp at Nuremberg

SOURCE 19.13   Berliners listening to Hitler making a speech on the radio, 1936

SOURCE 19.14   Shipyard workers in Hamburg in 1936 giving the Heil Hitler salute

SOURCE 19.15   'You have to save 5 marks a week, if you want to drive your own car!' A 1939 poster advertising the KdF scheme

SOURCE 19.16   A December 1936 report to SOPADE

Bavarian Motorworks (BMW), Munich: Since wages are still relatively high in comparison to other metal industries, the mood among workers is accordingly less bitter. One can, however, report that the National Socialists have nothing else that they can announce. Even though the workers do not express it publicly, one senses that the workers will never be conquered by National Socialism. All must, of course, yield to the present pressure, but whenever possible they show that they really have very little interest in all of Hitler's gibberish. This attitude was quite obvious during the last speech by the Führer, at which a communal radio listening had been ordered ... During the speech the workers conversed among themselves so that the factory SA had to intervene in order to restore quiet ... During the last third of the broadcast there occurred a lengthy round of applause over the loudspeaker, whereupon the workers immediately ran for the doors, demanding to be let out as the speech had apparently ended. The gate attendants were taken by surprise as a general race for the exits ensued. Yes, even windows were opened and people squeezed through them as though they were fugitives ... Even the Nazi supporters in the factory, of which there are still a few in every group, say that the broadcasts of the speeches in the factory do more harm than good for National Socialism.

SOURCE 19.17
A 1936 cartoon from the American magazine *The Nation*: 'In these three years I have restored honour and freedom to the German people!'

"In these three years I have restored honor and freedom to the German people!"

SOURCE 19.18   Jew-free resort

SOURCE 19.19   Estimated number of people compulsorily sterilised during the Nazi regime

1933–45	350,000

SOURCE 19.21   Concentration camp inmates

1933	26,000
1939	25,000
1944	700,000

SOURCE 19.20   The growth of the SS 1919–44

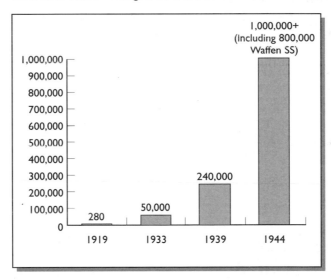

SOURCE 19.23   Estimated number of Germans killed by the Nazi regime

Jews	200,000 of 500,000
Communists	30,000 of 300,000
Gypsies	25,000 of 30,000
Jehovah's Witnesses	10,000 of 30,000
Mentally ill and physically disabled	200,000
Homosexuals	over 5,000

SOURCE 19.22   Nazis 'selecting' Jews arriving at Auschwitz, June 1944

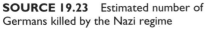

■ 19A Factors advancing and hindering the creation of a *Volksgemeinschaft*

Advancing

- Hitler's great achievements, both domestically and in foreign policy
- The role of propaganda
- The Hitler myth
- Memories of the Weimar Republic
- Longstanding, widespread belief in some Nazi attitudes
- Pervasive Nazi-controlled organisations
- Fear of the Gestapo and repression to enforce conformity

Hindering

- Difficulty of changing attitudes
- Attempt to change minds as a way to change society fundamentally flawed
- Persistence of traditional loyalties
- Contradictions in Nazi ideology
- Hitler's prioritisation of military conquest over recreating a traditional society
- Nazis were only in power for twelve years
- Failure to change the class system
- Hybrid nature of the state

Assessing the success of Hitler's *Volksgemeinshaft*

Clearly, as historians we must be critical of some of the sources we have just studied and be aware of the problems of making judgements, especially over such issues as the opinions of a whole people. There is, however, a strong argument that by the mid 1930s Hitler was personally popular and most Germans seemed to view the regime positively. It had many attractive features that appealed to people's sense of community. Co-operation for the national good was seen in the *Winterhilfe* and *Eintopf* schemes, where Germans were asked to make sacrifices to help less fortunate fellow members of the people's community. The work of oral historians in the 1980s and 1990s indicates that many Germans who lived through the 1930s had positive memories of the period as one of economic success, expanded opportunities and services, and social order.

On the other hand, the reality of achievement did not match the propaganda image, and the formally 'voluntary' nature of such schemes as *Winterhilfe* disguised considerable social pressure to conform. Gestapo reports of grumbling at Nazi officials, government fears of the reaction to falling living standards if rearmament became too prioritised, the regime's hesitant policy towards the Churches and the secrecy over many of the more extreme Nazi actions all suggest a regime that had not won most Germans over to the full Nazi vision. When the tide of war turned from 1943 onwards, there is growing evidence of disillusionment, though perhaps not surprisingly there was no major, large-scale internal threat to the regime during the war.

Recent research has discovered that there was a great variety of reactions to the Nazis, depending, for example, on class, region, gender, age, and religious and personal factors. From this two important ideas become clear: first, that the very need to refer to such categories in itself suggests that the *Volksgemeinschaft* ideal was not truly successful; secondly, that it is notoriously difficult to bring about fundamental changes of opinion in any society.

Historians' assessments

Now let us examine some historians' assessments of the success of the Nazis' *Volksgemeinschaft* policy.

SOURCE 19.24 M. Roseman, 'National Socialism and Modernisation' in *Fascist Italy and Nazi Germany*, ed. R. Bessel, 1996, pp. 216, 223

Recent work suggests that the Nazis were astonishingly successful at integrating very heterogeneous [varied] social groups into the Volksgemeinschaft.

... The regime achieved (and, indeed, attempted) relatively few changes to the structure of society, other than its remarkable efficiency in eliminating those unwanted minority groups it defined as racially undesirable. The structures of class society survived unscathed; inequalities in wealth, life chances and power remained largely undiminished. At the same time, however, it profoundly disrupted established perceptions, patterns of behaviour and allegiances ... It changed consciousness and culture without corresponding changes to the underlying social structure.

SOURCE 19.25 B. Sax and D. Kuntz, *Inside Hitler's Germany*, 1992, p. 183

During the 1930s the Nazi dictatorship only partially realised National Socialist ideology ... These failures resulted both from inner contradictions within the ideology itself and from the tremendous gap between National Socialist ideals and the realities of German society ... Nazi policy often ignored the great difficulties confronting modern industrial societies, and it therefore failed to create a Volksgemeinschaft.

SOURCE 19.26 M. Hughes, *Nationalism and Society. Germany 1800–1945*, 1988, p. 214

The greatest success of the National Socialist regime was in its propaganda. Large numbers of Germans became convinced as a result of Goebbels' efforts that they did live in a genuine Volksgemeinschaft. *This was increased by symbolic devices such as the cheap Volkswagen car and Volksempfanger radio receiver, putting what had previously been luxury goods within the reach of ordinary Germans, and party-encouraged mass participation in the* Winterhilfe *social welfare scheme. The reality was very different. The promise of a 'national revolution', the creation of a classless Germany with equality of opportunity for all and new criteria of worth to the nation, was not fulfilled ...*

The impression of a kind of compulsory national unity was achieved by institutions such as the Labour Service, eventually obligatory for all young Germans, and the process known as 'standardisation' (Gleichschaltung). Under this a large number of National Socialist organisations were given monopoly powers within their own field and commissioned to carry out a political educational role. As membership of such bodies was usually compulsory for people engaged in a given profession, as was involvement in organised activities, a spurious [false] air of unity could be created ...

SOURCE ACTIVITY

Read Sources 19.24–7. (Marks are given in brackets.)

1 According to Roseman, which aspects of society did the Nazis change most, and which least? **[3]**

2 How does Sax explain the Nazis' failure to create a *Volksgemeinschaft*? **[3]**

3 How far does Hughes agree with Roseman on the German people's acceptance of the idea of a *Volksgemeinschaft*? **[4]**

4 a) According to Kershaw, in what areas did the Nazis have some success? **[2]**

   b) What evidence of their failure does he provide? **[2]**

5 Does Kershaw's overall assessment agree more with that of Roseman or Hughes? **[4]**

6 Referring to the sources and using your wider knowledge, explain why historians' assessments of the success of the Nazis' attempt to develop a *Volksgemeinschaft* differ. **[7]**

(Total: 25 marks)

The only aspect of Völkisch *nationalism which was realised was the elimination of the Jews, to which, as time passed, the regime applied more and more of its energies.*

SOURCE 19.27 I. Kershaw, *The Nazi Dictatorship*, 3rd edition, 1993, pp. 145–6

Recent research ... which paints an extremely complex picture of social behaviour and attitudes in the Third Reich, suggests strongly that it is easy to exaggerate the nature of changes in values and attitudes under Nazism, and that here too there can be no suggestion of Nazism having effected a social revolution ...

There was some penetration of Nazi values and attitudes [but] the regime's social propaganda made little serious dent in traditional class loyalties, particularly among older industrial workers ... The hold of the Church and clergy over the population, especially in country areas, was often strengthened rather than weakened by the 'Church struggle' ... Nazi policy failed categorically to break down religious allegiance. Even in their attempt to inculcate the German people with racial, eugenic, and social Darwinist values – the core of their ideology – the Nazis, it appears, had only limited success. Enhancement of existing prejudice against Jews and other racial minorities and 'social outsiders' unquestionably occurred ... but ... exposure to Nazi race values had come nowhere near completely eradicating conventional moral standards.

Much suggests that the Nazis made their greatest impact on young Germans ... but even here the regime had only partial success ... Signs of conflict, tension, and opposition within certain sections of German youth were already apparent by the later 1930s and increased in the war years, suggesting that the Nazis had been only temporarily successful in winning over, mobilising, and integrating young Germans.

■ **Learning trouble spot**

Questions on historical interpretation

You can easily lose marks unnecessarily on such exercises, so try to follow the advice below.

1 Read each source very carefully, and highlight key parts, such as:

- issues directly relevant to the questions set
- powerful statements
- words suggesting a strong viewpoint, etc.

2 Look carefully at the origins of the source.

3 If you are asked to compare two or more historians' views, it may be useful to draw up a rough grid like the one below. Jot down points in the appropriate box, then turn this evidence into a discursive response.

Issue	Historian A	Historian B	Historian C
1			
2			

This will help you make direct comparisons rather than just summarising each view separately, as many students do. Using phrases such as 'Whereas X says ..., Y says ...' can be effective.

4 Always explain the thinking behind your answers.

5 You are frequently asked to explain why historians disagree on an issue; when doing so, make sure you refer to the specific sources given to illustrate disagreement, as well as using your wider knowledge of the area of debate, your understanding of the general reasons why historians disagree (see pages 151–2), and the nature of the historical process. Try to integrate these points together.

D Conclusions

We have tried to shed light on how Germans experienced the Third Reich. We need to be honest over the degree of support for Hitler, without falling into the semi-racist argument that this is evidence of unpleasant national characteristics in all Germans. One must also be able to acknowledge the benefits the regime brought, without being accused of being an apologist for (defender of) Nazism. The sensitivity of this issue was sharply revealed when Bundestag President Dr Philipp Jenninger had to resign in November 1988 after he spoke of the need to try to understand the support Hitler gained. Some useful insights here come from two recent TV series (see Sources 19.28 and 19.29).

As well as looking generally at the extent of change during the Third Reich, it is useful to examine the regime's impact on particular groups, and what each gained and lost, although there were, of course, considerable differences within each group. The horrors of the Nazi regime, especially after 1939, were so great that it is easy to underestimate the extent to which many Germans benefited from the regime, at least until the tide of war turned. The casualties of the system were a minority, and many Germans viewed what they saw as excesses as a perhaps unfortunate but unavoidable byproduct of a largely successful regime.

SOURCE 19.28 Lawrence Rees, the producer of the BBC TV series *The Nazis. A Warning from History*, shown in 1997, wrote in the book of the series (p. 85)

Neither a study of the documents nor the opinions of academics enabled me to understand how it was possible, before World War II, to actually like living in Nazi Germany. But after listening to witness after witness, not hardline committed Nazis, tell us how positive their experiences had been, a glimmer of understanding emerged. If you have lived through times of chaos and humiliation, you welcome order and security. If the price of that is 'a little evil', then you put up with it. Except there is no such thing as a 'little' evil.

SOURCE 19.29 George Clare interviewed in *Führer*, a 1989 TV programme

With all the successes Hitler had, Germany was actually a wonderful place to be alive, unless you were Jewish, you had strong political convictions either as a socialist or a communist, or you believed in individuality and the freedom of the individual; but that never is the majority of any people.

ACTIVITY

1 From the material in the relevant chapters, complete your own copy of the following table to assess the gainers and losers in the Third Reich.

Group (chapter)	Positive impact	Negative impact
Big business (12)		
Army (11, 20, 21)		
Large landowners (12)		
Peasants (12)		
Urban *Mittelstand* (12)		
Working class (12)		
Youth (14)		
Women (15)		
Jews, outsiders (18)		

2 Conclude your study of Nazi domestic policy by organising a debate around the following proposition, linking the regime's achievements to its political structure: 'Given the power of the regime, the domestic achievements of the Third Reich 1933–9 were remarkably limited.'

3 Concluding essay: 'Can a consistent theme be seen in Nazi political, social and economic policies?' Use the following table to help clarify your ideas. On your own copy, fill in details from relevant areas or themes.

Theme	Economy (Chapter 12)	Social (Chapters 12, 14, 15, 18)	Political (Chapters 10, 11)	Churches (Chapter 16)	Other (Chapter 13)
Nationalism					
Führerprinzip					
Militarisation					
Co-ordination					
Reactionary					
Volksgemein-schaft					
Radicalisation					
Other					

Marxists argue that society changes and then people's attitudes change. Others argue that changing minds comes first, then changes can occur in society. Which view do you tend to favour?

The historian Alan Bullock has commented: 'State, economy, society. With the first Hitler never advanced beyond improvisation. The second he treated as instrumental. It was the third, society, in which he was personally involved. Standing Marx on his head, Hitler set out to change the German people's consciousness as the preliminary to changing their material conditions.'

1 Explain what Bullock means.
2 How far do you agree with his view?

KEY POINTS FROM SECTION 2: What impact did Nazism have on the German people?

Part 2.1 How did Hitler secure his regime? Chapters 10–13

1 Hitler moved quickly to strengthen his position and by August 1934 he could not be legally removed.
2 Hitler dominated the Nazi state, though he did not often directly intervene in decisions.
3 The political structure of the Third Reich was confused, with new Nazi bodies cutting across existing ministries.
4 Most major aspects of life were co-ordinated in Nazi-run bodies, such as DAF.
5 The Nazis set up a fierce repressive machine, though many Germans co-operated with the Gestapo.
6 The initial priority of ending mass unemployment was achieved by 1936. From then onwards, the economy was increasingly geared to rearmament.
7 Big business gained more than the *Mittelstand*, despite Nazi rhetoric.
8 The regime established an array of economic controls, but industry remained in private hands as long as it co-operated with the regime's policies.
9 The Nazis developed a vast propaganda system, seeking to control all expression of opinion.

Part 2.2 How far did Hitler succeed in creating a *Volksgemeinschaft*? Chapters 14–19

10 The Nazis used control of the school curriculum, teachers and youth movements to indoctrinate children.
11 Women were seen primarily as childbearers and services were provided for them. Nazi policies for women were not fully consistent, and their impact was limited.
12 Nazi attempts to replace the influence of Christianity failed. The Churches criticised aspects of Nazi policy directed against them, but, apart from a few individuals, generally co-operated.
13 There was a wide range of fairly minor opposition activities, but resistance rarely developed into a serious threat to the regime.
14 The Nazis attempted to create a *Volksgemeinschaft*, and to exclude unwanted groups. Jews and other minority groups were increasingly harshly treated, culminating in mass murder from 1941.
15 The view of the Third Reich as a totalitarian regime that modernised Germany has been undermined, though there is still debate as to how far most Germans absorbed the Nazi view of the *Volksgemeinschaft*.

Hitler's foreign policy: Why did Hitler's initial foreign policy successes turn to catastrophic defeat?

In 1933 the main features of the humiliating Versailles settlement were still largely intact. Yet six years later Germany had unilaterally destroyed the treaty and felt strong enough to invade Poland, an action that led to the Second World War. Within two years Germany had become master of Europe, but by 1945 had suffered catastrophic defeat. Why and how did Hitler lead Germany to such initial triumphs followed by national disaster? Section 3 considers these questions:

- **Why was Hitler's foreign policy so successful 1933–9?**
- **Why did Germany's initial success in war turn to defeat?**

But first, pages 371–5 give you an overview of the main events and issues.

ACTIVITY

(You could work in groups of three, with each of you taking one of the three areas.)
Study Sources 1–12 and the timeline, and find evidence within the following areas:

Aims
a) Hitler's main foreign policy aims

Methods
b) Hitler's ability to appear reasonable and be pragmatic in his approach
c) Germany's use of bilateral diplomatic agreements
d) Germany's use of force

Effects
e) The successes of Hitler's foreign policy, especially in overturning the Treaty of Versailles
f) The domestic effects of foreign policy
g) The eventual failure of his foreign policy.

371

WHY DID HITLER'S INITIAL FOREIGN POLICY SUCCESSES TURN TO CATASTROPHIC DEFEAT?

SOURCE 1 Hitler drives into the Sudetenland in October 1938 to a rapturous welcome from Sudeten Germans

SOURCE 2 Sayings of Hitler

A Point 1 of Nazi Programme, 1920

> We demand the union of all Germans in a Greater Germany on the basis of the right of national self-determination.

B *Mein Kampf*, 1925

> Germany will either be a world power or there will be no Germany.

C *Mein Kampf*, 1925

> We stop the endless German movement to the south and west, and turn our gaze towards the land in the east.

D To Associated Press Agency, 1933

> Nobody wishes peace more than I.

E 1935

> An understanding must be reached between the great Germanic peoples [Germany and Britain] through the permanent elimination of naval rivalry. One will control the sea, the other will be the strongest power on land. A defensive and offensive alliance between the two will inaugurate a new era.

> Everything I undertake is directed against the Russians; if the West is too stupid and blind to grasp this, then I shall be compelled to come to an agreement with the Russians, beat the West, and then after their defeat turn against the Soviet Union with all my forces. I need the Ukraine so they can't starve us like in the last war.

F To League of Nations Commissioner in Danzig, August 1939

> When starting and waging war it is not right that matters, but victory ... Close your hearts to pity. Act brutally. Eighty million people must obtain what is their right. Their existence must be made secure. The strongest man is right.

G 1939

> War is the most natural, the most ordinary thing. War is a constant; war is everywhere. There is no beginning, there is no conclusion of peace. War is life. All struggle is war. War is the primal condition.

H 1939

> No human being has declared or recorded what he wanted more often than I. Again and again I wrote these words – the Abolition of the Treaty of Versailles.

I January 1941

SOURCE 3   This cartoon was published in *The Nation* in 1933

SOURCE 4   From an NSDAP illustrated postcard produced shortly after Hitler introduced compulsory military service in 1935

The one-sided disarmament of Germany seriously endangers her security as long as her neighbours do not also disarm. The German people unanimously demand the same rights and the same security as other nations and claim an absolute equality of status with regard to this vital question.

SOURCE 5   Nazi marching song

If all the world lies in ruins,
What the devil do we care?
We still go marching on,
For today Germany belongs to us
And tomorrow the whole world.

SOURCE 6
German tanks
on parade

■ German foreign policy 1933–45: a chronology

CAUTION 1933–5

1933

14 Oct	**Germany leaves League of Nations and Disarmament Conference** 👤

1934

26 Jan	**Non-Aggression Pact with Poland** 👥👥
14–15 Jun	**Hitler visits fellow Fascist leader Mussolini in Venice**
25 Jul	Austrian Chancellor Engelbert Dollfuss assassinated in attempted coup by Austrian Nazis

1935

13 Jan	In League of Nations' plebiscite (held under terms of Treaty of Versailles), the Saar votes to return to Germany
9 Mar	**Hitler announces expansion of the German air force** 👤
16 Mar	**Hitler announces conscription** 👤
11–14 Apr	Stresa Conference of Britain, France, Italy to unite opposition to German infringement of Versailles
18 Jun	**Anglo-German Naval Agreement on an enlarged German navy** 👥👥
2 Oct	Italy invades Abyssinia; League of Nations votes for (ineffective) sanctions; Mussolini begins to move away from Britain and France towards Germany

ASSERTION AND EXPANSION 1936 to 23 Aug 1939

1936

6 Jan	Mussolini ends Italian guarantee of Austrian independence
7 Mar	**German troops reoccupy the demilitarised Rhineland** 👣
27 July	**Germany starts to send military help to right-wing rebel nationalists in Spanish Civil War** 👣
19 Oct	**Goering in charge of economic Four-Year Plan**
1 Nov	**Rome-Berlin Axis with Fascist Italy announced** 👥👥
25 Nov	**Germany forms Anti-Comintern Pact with Japan** 👥👥

1937

27 Apr	**Luftwaffe destroys Guernica in Spain** 👣
July	Japan–China War
25–9 Sep	Mussolini visits Germany and is impressed
5 Nov	**Hossbach memorandum records Hitler's plans for major expansion**
6 Nov	Italy joins Anti-Comintern Pact

1938

4 Feb	**Ribbentrop becomes Foreign Minister. Generals Blomberg, Fritsch replaced**
12 Feb	**Hitler bullies Austrian Chancellor Schuschnigg to include Nazis in his government** 👥
6 Mar	Austrian plebiscite on *Anschluss* announced
11 Mar	**Germans invade Austria** 👣
13 Mar	***Anschluss* (German union with Austria)** 👣
24 Apr	**German Sudetens in Czechoslovakia demand autonomy**
18 Aug	General Beck resigns
Aug	Great danger of war over Czechoslovakia

29–30 Sep	Munich conference of Germany, Italy, France, Britain grants Germany the Sudetenland 🗣
1–10 Oct	**Germans take Sudetenland** 👥
1 Oct	Czechs cede Teschen to Poland
6–8 Oct	Slovakia, Ruthenia granted autonomy within Czechoslovakia
21 Oct	**Hitler orders plans to invade the remaining part of Czechoslovakia**
1939	
14 Mar	Slovakia declares independence
15 Mar	**Germany occupies Czechoslovakia** 👥
23 Mar	**Germany occupies Memel** 👥
31 Mar	Britain, France guarantee Poland
22 May	**Germany and Italy form the Pact of Steel, a military alliance** 👥
23 Aug	**Nazi Soviet Non-Aggression Pact** 👥

Key

Bold type in chronology represents Hitler's orders and actions

Hitler's methods 1933–9

🧍	Acting unilaterally
🧍🧍	Making bilateral agreements
🗣	Diplomacy with threats
👥	Using troops without fighting
🏃	Troops fighting

WAR 1 Sep 1939 onwards

1939	
1 Sep	**Germany invades Poland** 🏃
3 Sep	France, Britain declare war on Germany
17 Sep	USSR invades Poland. Poland defeated and partitioned between Germany and the USSR
1940	
Apr	**Germany occupies Denmark. Germany conquers Norway in two weeks**
May	**Germany invades Holland (falls in five days), Belgium (eighteen days), France (four weeks)**
June	France capitulates. **Germany occupies the north and west of France**
Aug–Sep	**Germany plans to invade Britain but is defeated in Battle of Britain. Hitler prepares plans to invade the USSR**
1941	
Apr	**Germany invades Yugoslavia and Greece**
June–Dec	**Germany invades the USSR but is stopped at Moscow and Leningrad**
7 Dec	Japanese attack on Pearl Harbor. USA declares war on Japan and Germany
1942	
May	**Major German offensive at Stalingrad, USSR**
June	**Germany and Italy attack Egypt**
1943	
Jan	**Germans surrender at Stalingrad; Hitler's first major defeat**
May	**Germans, Italians, surrender in North Africa. Germans lose tank battle of Kursk in the USSR;** general Soviet advance 1943–5
July	Anglo-American invasion of Italy; Mussolini overthrown, **Germans take over north Italy**
1944	
June	Allies invade west France; general Allied advance 1944–5
1945	
	Germany is invaded from east and west
30 Apr	**Hitler commits suicide**
7 May	Germany surrenders

SOURCE 7
Hitler returning to Germany after the conquest of France, 1940

SOURCE 8 The percentage of Germans voting yes in plebiscites on Hitler's foreign policy

Date	Plebiscite	%
November 1933	Leaving the League/ Disarmament Conference	95
March 1936	After reoccupying Rhineland	98.8
April 1938	*Anschluss* with Austria	99

SOURCE 9 Map of German foreign policy 1933–45. The dates show the years of conquest and Nazi rule

0   500
km

N

NORWAY
1940–5

SWEDEN

FINLAND

ESTONIA
1941–4

LATVIA
1941–4

USSR

DENMARK
1940–5

LITHUANIA
1941–4

GREAT
BRITAIN

HOLLAND
1940–5

GERMANY

POLAND

Occupied by
Germany 1941–43/4

CHANNEL
ISLANDS
1940–5

Sudetenland
1938–45

1939–44   1941–4

BELGIUM
1940–4

CZECHOSLOVAKIA
1939–45

FRANCE
1940–4

AUSTRIA
1938–45

HUNGARY

SWITZERLAND

ITALY

ROMANIA

YUGOSLAVIA

SPAIN

BULGARIA

ALBANIA

GREECE

TURKEY

Key

––·––· German–Soviet border 1939 after Germany
and the USSR divided Poland between them

– – – – Limit of German occupation of the USSR

░░ Sudetenland

SOURCE 10
A satirical comment on the Nazi–Soviet Pact

SOURCE 11
'The conversion of the Fritzes': a 1942 Soviet cartoon

SOURCE 12
Soviet soldiers raise the 'hammer and sickle' flag on the Reichstag in Berlin in May 1945

20

Why was Hitler's foreign policy so successful 1933–9?

CHAPTER OVERVIEW

Hitler was remarkably successful in foreign policy in the 1930s. In this chapter you are going to examine the reasons for his success under the following headings:

A What were Hitler's aims and plans in foreign policy? (pp. 376–9)

B How did the situation in Europe in the 1930s help Hitler? (pp. 380–1)

C Key events and personnel in Hitler's foreign policy 1933–9 (pp. 382–3)

D Why was Hitler able to smash the Versailles settlement? (pp. 384–95)

E How did the major powers react to Hitler's foreign policy 1933–9? (pp. 396–9)

F Was Hitler a master planner or an opportunist? (pp. 400–1)

G Review: Why was Hitler's foreign policy so successful 1933–9? (pp. 402–5)

FOCUS ROUTE

1 What were Hitler's aims?
2 What methods did Hitler use to achieve his aims?
3 How did other powers react to his measures?
4 How successful was Hitler in achieving his aims?
5 Why was he successful?

A What were Hitler's aims and plans in foreign policy?

Sources 20.2–5 are a narrow but important selection of sources that record Hitler's views on foreign policy matters. Some historians consider *Mein Kampf* and Hitler's *Zweite Buch* (see opposite) to be the mere musings of a fringe politician, but most argue that they express broad aims that Hitler still held when he became Führer. His 1936 Memorandum on the Four-Year Plan and his speech to the generals at the 'Hossbach' Conference in 1937 also shed light on his policy.

SOURCE 20.1
A display poster for *Mein Kampf*. This book was written by Hitler when he was in prison in 1924; it was published in 1925–6 and widely available from 1933. References to foreign policy are scattered throughout *Mein Kampf*, and Hitler stresses Russia as Germany's main enemy and *Lebensraum* as the main purpose

SOURCE 20.2 Extract from *Mein Kampf*

The acquisition of new soil for the settlement of the excess population possesses an infinite number of advantages, particularly if we turn from the present to the future. For one thing, the possibility of preserving a healthy peasant class as a foundation for a whole nation can never be valued highly enough. Many of our present-day sufferings are only the consequence of the unhealthy relationship between rural and city population. A solid stock of small and middle peasants has at all times been the best defence against social ills such as we possess today . . .

If land was desired in Europe, it could be obtained by and large only at the expense of Russia, and this meant that the new Reich must again set itself on the march along the road of the TEUTONIC Knights of old [a medieval religious order of knighthood], to obtain by the German sword sod [earth] for the German plough and daily bread for the nation. For such a policy there was but one ally in Europe: England . . . With England alone was it possible, our rear protected, to begin the new Germanic march . . . But we National Socialists must go further. The right to possess soil can become a duty if without extension of its soil a great nation seems doomed to destruction. And most especially when not some little nigger nation or other is involved, but the Germanic mother of life, which has given the present day world its cultural picture. Germany will either be a world power or there will be no Germany . . . And so we National Socialists consciously draw a line beneath the foreign policy tendency of our pre-war period. We take up where we broke off six hundred years ago. We stop the endless German movement to the south and west and turn our gaze towards the land in the east. At long last we break off the colonial and commercial policy of the pre war period and shift to the soil policy of the future.

If we speak of soil in Europe today, we can primarily have in mind only Russia and her VASSAL border states. Here fate itself seems desirous of giving us a sign . . . This colossal empire in the east is ripe for dissolution, and the end of Russia as a state.

Hitler's Second Book

Hitler dictated a second book as a sequel to *Mein Kampf* in May–July 1928. It was then kept at the headquarters of the Nazi Party with orders that it was not to be published until after Hitler's death. The Americans discovered it in 1945, and it was authenticated and published in 1958 in German as *Hitlers Zweite Buch* (Hitler's Second Book) and translated and published in English as *Hitler's Secret Book*. It contains a far more considered view of foreign policy than the sporadic references in *Mein Kampf*. In it, Hitler stressed the need for *Lebensraum* in the east and his explanation of why he thought Britain would not oppose Germany in Europe, since Germany was no threat to the British Empire. He also talked more of the final struggle between German-dominated Europe and the United States of America.

SOURCE 20.3 An extract from *Hitler's Secret Book*

For this earth is not allotted to anyone . . . It is awarded by providence to people who in their hearts have the courage to conquer it, the strength to preserve it, and the industry to put it to the plough . . . Every healthy, vigorous people sees nothing sinful in territorial acquisition, but something quite in keeping with nature. The primary right of this world is the right to life, so far as one possesses the strength for this. Hence on the basis of this right a vigorous nation will always find ways of adapting its territory to its population size . . .

For this, however, a nation needs weapons. The acquisition of soil is always linked with the employment of force.

Four-Year Plan, 1936
This memorandum, rare because it was written by Hitler himself, was produced during the economic troubles of 1936 in order to justify continued massive rearmament, so as to be ready for war in four years.

SOURCE 20.4 The Four-Year Plan, 1936

Since the outbreak of the French Revolution the world has been moving with ever increasing speed towards a new conflict, the most extreme solution of which is Bolshevism; and the essence and goal of Bolshevism is the elimination of those strata of mankind which have hitherto provided the leadership and their replacement by worldwide Jewry.

No nation will be able to avoid or abstain from this historical conflict. Since Marxism, through its victory in Russia, has established one of the great empires as a forward base for its future operations, this question has become a menacing one ... The military resources of this aggressive will are ... increasing from year to year ... Germany will as always have to be regarded as the focus of the Western world against the attacks of Bolshevism ... we cannot ... escape the destiny ... Apart from Germany and Italy, only Japan can be considered as a Power standing firm in the face of the world peril ...

This crisis cannot and will not fail to occur, and ... Germany has the duty of securing her existence by every means in the face of this catastrophe ... For a victory of Bolshevism over Germany would lead not to a Versailles Treaty but to the final destruction, indeed to the annihilation, of the German people ... In the face of the necessity of warding off this danger, all the other considerations must recede into the background as completely irrelevant.

SOURCE 20.5 Extract from the Hossbach Memorandum

The aim of German policy was to make secure and to preserve the racial community and to enlarge it. It was therefore a question of space ... before turning to the question of solving the need for space, it had to be considered whether a solution holding promise for the future was to be reached by means of autarky or by means of an increased participation in the world economy ...

The question for Germany ran: where could she achieve the greatest gain at the lowest cost? German policy had to reckon with two hate-inspired antagonists, Britain and France, to whom a German colossus in the centre of Europe was a thorn in the flesh, and both countries were opposed to any further strengthening of Germany's position either in Europe or overseas ... Germany's problem could only be solved by means of force, and this was never without attendant risk ... there remain still to be answered the questions 'when' and 'how'? In this matter there were three cases to be dealt with ...

Case I: period 1943–45. After this date only a change for the worse, from our point of view could be expected ... Our relative strength would decrease in relation to the rearmament which would by then have been carried out by the rest of the world ... Nobody knew today what the situation would be in the years 1943–45. One thing only was certain, that we could wait no longer ... If the Führer was still living, it was his unalterable resolve to solve Germany's problem of space at the latest by 1943–45. The necessity for action before 1943–45 would arise in cases II and III.

Case II: if internal strife in France should develop into such a domestic crisis as to absorb the French army completely and render it incapable of use for war against Germany, then the time for action against the Czechs had come.

Case III: if France is so embroiled by a war with another state that she cannot 'proceed' against Germany.

For the improvement of our political and military position our first objective, in the event of being embroiled in war, must be to overthrow Czechoslovakia and Austria simultaneously in order to remove the threat from our flank in any possible operation against the West ...

The Hossbach Memorandum

This controversial document was a record of a three-hour meeting in the Reich Chancellery on 5 November 1937 attended by Hitler and military leaders Hermann Goering (air), Werner von Fritsch (army), Erich Raeder (navy), Werner von Blomberg (defence) and Foreign Minister Konstantin von Neurath. Tension with Hjalmar Schacht, who was critical of excessive rearmament, was at its peak, and Hitler tried to convince his listeners of the need for a more aggressive approach in foreign policy. Hitler's speech was recorded by Colonel Friedrich Hossbach five days later, from notes made at the time (he took the official minutes of the meeting). Blomberg filed the document without showing it to Hitler. The original disappeared, but various copies were used at the Nuremberg trials as evidence of planned Nazi aggression.

In his speech Hitler argued that Germany needed to solve her space problems by 1943–5. He did not though refer specifically to war with the USSR. The speech was poorly received by his cautious audience and within three months most had been replaced. Most historians consider the memorandum does indicate how Hitler was moving towards implementing his longer-term programme.

TALKING POINT

What other sources might be available to a historian to analyse Hitler's aims in foreign policy?

ACTIVITY

1 How, in *Mein Kampf* and the *Zweite Buch* (Second Book), does Hitler justify German expansionism?
2 Which country is Hitler most hostile to? Why?
3 What change in his attitude to Britain occurs between *Mein Kampf* and the Hossbach Memorandum?
4 Why, in the Hossbach Memorandum, does Hitler argue that war for *Lebensraum* is required by the mid 1940s?
5 Which source do you consider most valuable in seeking to understand Hitler's foreign policy? Refer to background and content.

On pages 382–92 we will look at the key events in Hitler's foreign policy until 1939. In many ways, this proved to be a remarkably successful period for him. But first we are going to look at the context in which Hitler was able to pursue his aims.

B How did the situation in Europe in the 1930s help Hitler?

How some of Germany's potential opponents viewed each other

SOURCE 20.6 American Secretary of State Henry Morgenthau

The French are a bankrupt, fourth rate power.

SOURCE 20.7 French Prime Minister Edouard Daladier in 1939 told the American Ambassador

[He] fully expected to be betrayed by the British ... he considered Chamberlain a desiccated [dried-up] stick; the King a moron ... England had become so feeble and senile [old and decrepit] that the British would give away every possession of their friends rather than stand up to Germany and Italy.

SOURCE 20.8 British Prime Minister Neville Chamberlain

[France] never kept a secret for more than half an hour, nor a government for more than nine months.

ACTIVITY

1 Read Sources 20.6–8 and study Chart 20A. List the contemporary factors that might
   a) help Hitler
   b) prove to be a problem
   in his aim of revising the Versailles settlement.
2 You are going to assess how the international context favoured or hindered Hitler's plans for German expansion. First study the map of inter-war Europe in Chart 20A and the quotations from Hitler in Source 2 on page 371. Now work out which country a spokesperson for Hitler could be describing in the comments below.

> Contrary to what many consider, I believe it is our potential ally. We can dominate the continent; it can, for the moment, dominate the seas and keep its empire.
> 1

> This state defies nature. It's a mess of nationalities, and includes Germans ruled by Slavs. Intolerable. It's jutting into the heart of Germany, and is allied to our enemies. We must destroy it.
> 5

> It should be hostile to France, and should be our ally. Our ideological links with it reinforce it as our natural ally.
> 2

> This Slav state cuts Germany in two. We must liberate our Germans who live there, and then turn it into a client state.
> 6

> Our greatest enemy; it is an inferior nation, ruled by Jewish Marxists, and it holds land that Germany needs for our living space.
> 3

> It should never have been cut off from Germany in the first place. It is as German as Bavaria and must form part of the new Germany.
> 4

> We must get revenge for its victory in the last war. It is our major enemy in Europe, and will never accept our rightful dominant position in Europe until it is put in its place.
> 7

France

- Very concerned at possible German threat; had wanted harsh Versailles terms but did not get independent Rhineland nor US guarantee of its borders. Built Maginot Line (defensive fortifications)
- After 1919 treated Germany badly, but this just increased France's own insecurity. In 1923 had invaded the Ruhr, but this backfired; afterwards it was reluctant to intervene again
- Saw military preponderance and COLLECTIVE SECURITY as central to its defence
- Concerned to develop links with countries on Germany's eastern borders; alliances with Poland, Czechoslovakia, Romania and Yugoslavia
- Wary of Russia, its previous anti-German ally, since Russia was now the communist USSR
- Politically divided; a series of weak governments
- Major economic problems
- In 1935 made defensive alliance with Czechoslovakia, and later with the USSR

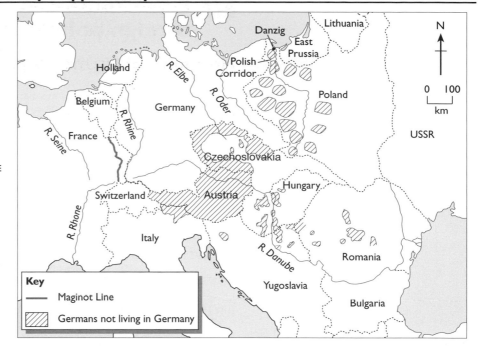

Key
— Maginot Line
▨ Germans not living in Germany

Britain

- British Empire at its largest, but resources overstretched; afraid of expansionist Japan in east, as well as Nazi Germany and Fascist Italy
- Strong determination to avoid another war; overall policy to Germany was more pragmatic than France's
- Politicians and public divided. Many considered Versailles unfair, and supported the 'redress of legitimate grievances'
- Some saw eastern Europe as proper German sphere, which would furthermore divert Germany's attention from British maritime and imperial concerns
- Many on the Right hostile to the communist dictator Stalin; sympathised with Hitler

Italy

- Fascist government, but initially Mussolini did not have good relations with Hitler
- Concerned to uphold BRENNER frontier and defend Austrian independence
- Looking to expand in Mediterranean
- In 1935 invaded Abyssinia, which led to a quarrel with Britain and France, and revealed the weakness of League of Nations

USSR

- Communist USSR aroused great suspicion in the West but its main concern was economic development
- Since 1922 Rapallo Pact, had economic (and secret military) links with Germany
- Made defensive alliances in 1935 with France and Czechoslovakia, but weakened by Stalin's purge of the military 1936–8

Austria

- A German state, but had not become part of a united Germany
- By 1919 no longer a great power
- *Anschluss* forbidden at Versailles, but many Austrians favoured it

Poland

- A newly recreated state surrounded by potential enemies, the USSR and Germany
- Contained large German minorities
- By 1933 had developed a strong army
- Ruled by dictatorial nationalist government

Danzig

- Population 95 per cent German but administered by League of Nations

Czechoslovakia

- New Slav state; formerly ruled by Germans as part of Austro-Hungarian Empire
- Contained ethnic minorities, including 300,000 Sudeten Germans
- Successful democratic government
- In 1935 signed mutual assistance pacts with France and the USSR

Belgium

- Since 1920 had had military co-operation pact with France
- In August 1936 withdrew from French pact, declaring its neutrality
- Weak link in French security system?

Maginot Line

- French defensive barrier along western border
- Variable level of fortifications depending on terrain
- Constructed 1929–38
- Stopped at Belgian border, but Franco-Belgian agreement for French troops to move to Belgian–German/Dutch border if need be

South-east Europe

- Host of quarrelling small states, with many national minorities
- Area ripe for German economic expansion; governments keen to sell surplus agricultural products and to buy industrial goods

Japan

- Expansionist military government; possible threat to the USSR and the empires of Britain and France
- Potential ally for Fascist regimes
- In 1931 invaded Manchuria in China; League of Nations took no effective action
- In 1937 invaded the rest of China

USA

- Isolationist; in 1920 Senate failed to ratify the Treaty of Versailles

League of Nations

- International body set up to preserve peace and prevent aggression. Power to call for economic sanctions and military action by member states
- Members should submit disputes to League before taking up arms
- USA, USSR (until 1934) not members. Germany joined in 1926

Disarmament

- Major conference eventually met December 1932 but little happened

Little Entente

- France built up a series of alliances with powers (Yugoslavia, Czechoslovakia, Romania) that had gained from the Versailles settlement to defend the status quo against revisionist powers

General situation

- World trade slump dissolved international solidarity and fostered attitude of national insularity (narrowmindedness)
- Memories of horrors of the First World War so strong that many people and statesmen determined to avoid another war

ACTIVITY

Divide into groups. Each group should research one of the periods/events below and report back.

a) 1933–5
b) The Rhineland, 1936
c) Austria, 1938
d) Czechoslovakia, 1938–9
e) The Nazi–Soviet Pact, 1939
f) Germany's relations with its allies

Offstage
Oct 1935 *Mussolini's attack on Abyssinia helps Hitler, since it diverts attention away from Germany; it moves Mussolini closer to Germany, and shows the feebleness of the League of Nations. It encourages Hitler to become more assertive*

C Key events and personnel in Hitler's foreign policy 1933–9

■ 20B Key steps in Hitler's foreign policy in 1933–9

Oct 1933 Withdraws Germany from the Disarmament Conference and the League of Nations: Hitler resents the discrimination against Germany over armaments and dislikes the MULTILATERAL nature of the League of Nations, created at Versailles; but also makes conciliatory noises

Jan 1934 Makes Non-Aggression Pact with Poland. A surprise move, given Germany's hostility to, and territorial claims on, Poland, but Hitler does not feel able yet to challenge Poland, and the agreement weakens the French security system

Jul 1934 Austrian Nazis assassinate Chancellor Dolfuss in an attempt to unite Austria with Germany (*Anschluss*). Mussolini sends troops to the Brenner frontier and the attempt fails. Hitler has great influence over Austrian Nazis but disclaims any responsibility

Jan 1935 As laid down at Versailles, plebiscite held in Saarland. Vote is overwhelmingly (90 per cent) in favour of rejoining Germany. Triumph for Hitler

Mar 1935 One weekend Hitler announces Germany has a military air force; the next weekend he announces Germany will introduce conscription to build up an army of 750,000. Britain, France and Italy do nothing except denounce Germany and threaten action over further changes to the status quo

Jun 1935 Germany makes Naval Agreement with Britain limiting its navy to 35 per cent of that of Britain. This bilateral agreement to modify the Versailles terms breaks the Stresa Front against Germany. Hitler hopes it will lead to a broader agreement with Britain

Mar 1936 A force of 20,000 German troops marches into the demilitarised Rhineland. Hitler has rejected the advice of his generals and gambles on no French military reaction. Prepared to withdraw if opposed, but troops enter without challenge. Key turning point, since it emboldens Hitler

July 1936 Hitler sends aid to General Franco's uprising in Spain

Nov 1936 Axis and Anti-Comintern Pact. Hitler makes alliances with Italy and Japan Hitler increases his military assistance to Franco in Spanish Civil War by sending the Condor Legion (including 5,000 men, 117 planes, 48 tanks). Germany gains military experience, economic concessions and closer links with Mussolini, who has also sent military aid

Nov 1937 'Hossbach Meeting': Hitler tells his generals of the need to increase rearmament to prepare for major war in mid 1940s

Mar 1938 Hitler encourages Nazis' pressure in Austria. Chancellor Schuschnigg goes to Berlin to try to sort out the crisis, but is bullied into accepting new Nazi ministers. Schuschnigg calls a plebiscite on *Anschluss*. Hitler pressurises the government to postpone this, and to call for German intervention. German army invades and is well received. Hitler annexes Austria

May 1938 Hitler encourages Sudeten Germans in Czechoslovakia to cause unrest. Czech government prepares for war

Sept 1938 Chamberlain meets Hitler and arranges for transfer of Sudetenland to Germany. At second meeting, Hitler insists on immediate transfer, and prepares for war. Then he agrees to attend a conference at Munich where Sudetenland given to Germany by 10 October. Great triumph for Germany, though Hitler is disappointed, as he had hoped to attack and fully dismember Czechoslovakia

Mar 1939 Hitler bullies Czechs into agreeing to German take-over of Bohemia–Moravia and German PROTECTORATE over Slovakia

May 1939 Pact of Steel with Italy. Military support to be provided if either power at war

Aug 1939 In response to Anglo-French guarantee of Poland and their attempt to make an agreement with the USSR, Ribbentrop signs the Nazi–Soviet Pact with USSR: ten years of non-aggression, and secret carve-up of Poland and Baltic states

Sept 1939 Tension over Danzig escalates. Germany invades Poland on 1 September. Britain and France declare war. The USSR invades Poland from the east and Poland is crushed

Count Konstantin von Neurath 1873–1956: Foreign Minister 1932–8

A conservative aristocrat and career diplomat, Neurath became Foreign Minister under Papen in June 1932. President Hindenburg insisted he remain in Hitler's government. On 31 January 1933 he joined the Nazi Party and the SS. As Foreign Minister, Neurath had to contend for influence with the committed Nazis Rosenberg and Ribbentrop. After the 'Hossbach' conference, he criticised Hitler's expansionist plans and was dismissed in February 1938.

He was given a series of token posts, including Minister without Portfolio. In March 1939 he became Reich Protector of Bohemia–Moravia. He was convicted at the Nuremberg trials, and sentenced to fifteen years' imprisonment.

FOCUS ROUTE

Explain the significance of the personnel changes in the army and foreign ministry in 1938.

Who was involved in Hitler's diplomatic and military machine?

Many elements of continuity with the foreign policy of the Weimar governments can be seen in the early years of Hitler's regime. At first, Hitler used most of the Foreign Office personnel he inherited and Neurath remained Foreign Minister. Typically, however, alongside the official machinery there were various Nazi bodies (for example the Dienststelle (Bureau) Ribbentrop and Rosenberg's Foreign Affairs Department of the Nazi Party) and individuals to whom Hitler gave special missions.

Once Hitler's regime had survived its period of vulnerability and his traditionally minded officials were becoming critical of his more ambitious plans, for example at the 'Hossbach' conference, Hitler made major changes in his military and diplomatic machines, increasing his own power and that of genuine Nazis. He set up a division of power at all levels below his own, as he had done in the political and economic spheres.

■ 20C Hitler's increasing control of the army

a) 1934–7

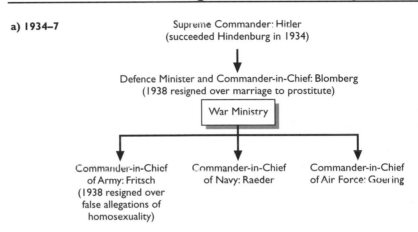

Supreme Commander: Hitler
(succeeded Hindenburg in 1934)

↓

Defence Minister and Commander-in-Chief: Blomberg
(1938 resigned over marriage to prostitute)

War Ministry

Commander-in-Chief of Army: Fritsch (1938 resigned over false allegations of homosexuality)

Commander-in-Chief of Navy: Raeder

Commander-in-Chief of Air Force: Goering

b) 1938 onwards

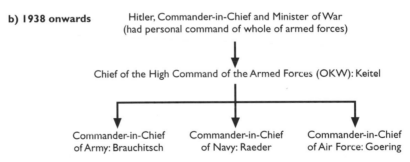

Hitler, Commander-in-Chief and Minister of War
(had personal command of whole of armed forces)

↓

Chief of the High Command of the Armed Forces (OKW): Keitel

Commander-in-Chief of Army: Brauchitsch

Commander-in-Chief of Navy: Raeder

Commander-in-Chief of Air Force: Goering

Note: War Ministry abolished and replaced by Oberkommando (OKW), the High Command of the Armed Forces, headed by Hitler with day-to-day management by Keitel

Joachim von Ribbentrop 1893–1946: Foreign Minister, 1938–45

Ribbentrop was won over to the Nazis by the force of Hitler's personality and his vision for Germany. He was vain and domineering and was resented as an ambitious upstart, hence his nickname 'von Ribbensnob'. He was of middle-class origins and bought his noble status. He socialised amongst the German elite, including many Jews. However, Hitler was impressed by him, partly because he told Hitler what he wanted to hear.

From 1933, Hitler used him as an adviser on foreign policy. He set up the Bureau Ribbentrop as a rival to the Foreign Office. In 1934 Ribbentrop was made plenipotentiary for disarmament and an extraordinary ambassador. He had special powers and could bypass Neurath (Foreign Minister at the time) and go straight to Hitler.

In 1935 Ribbentrop negotiated the German–British naval agreement, and in August 1936 he was appointed ambassador to Britain. He hoped to arrange an alliance but was not helped by his arrogant, blustering behaviour, which included giving King George VI a Nazi salute. He became increasingly hostile to Britain, arguing that it was weak and would not resist German expansion. He was a strong supporter of the Rome–Berlin–Tokyo Axis. In February 1938 he replaced Neurath as Foreign Minister, a post he kept till 1945. During the war he lost influence, but he was found guilty of war crimes at Nuremberg and hanged in 1946.

D Why was Hitler able to smash the Versailles settlement?

We now focus on the four most important events in Hitler's foreign policy 1933-9.

Remilitarisation of the Rhineland, March 1936

From 1933 to 1935 Hitler's approach was cautious, as Germany was in a weak position compared to its potential opponents. By 1935 Hitler felt secure enough to announce in public Germany's rearmament. He also sensed in parts of Europe a mood of reluctance to risk war in defence of a possibly unjust and outdated settlement. In 1936 Hitler raised the stakes higher by entering the Rhineland.

Why did the West not intervene?

In Britain, public opinion was hostile to military action. In January 1935 the British government decided that the Rhineland was not vital. It favoured negotiations, since Hitler offered a bulwark against Bolshevism. France was militarily too weak for offensive action. The French government had cut military expenditure by 17 per cent between 1930 and 1934 and had concentrated resources on building the defensive Maginot Line instead of modernising equipment. A general election was six weeks away and military action would be unpopular. In addition, Britain and France were quarrelling over their response to Mussolini's invasion of Abyssinia. On 3 March the French government asked Britain for assurances of support over the Rhineland. Britain refused to give them.

FOCUS ROUTE

1 Explain how Hitler was able to remilitarise the Rhineland without Allied military intervention.
2 Explain the significance of this move.

SOURCE 20.9 Hitler's interpreter, Paul Schmidt, writing in 1949

More than once, even during the war, I heard Hitler say: 'The 48 hours after the march into the Rhineland were the most nerve-wracking in my life.' He always added, 'If the French had then marched into the Rhineland we would have had to withdraw with our tails between our legs, for the military resources at our disposal would have been completely inadequate for even moderate resistance.'

■ 20D The Rhineland 1936

The Rhineland was German territory run by the German government, but Germany did not exercise full SOVEREIGNTY, since under the terms of the Treaty of Versailles it was unable to fortify it

Key

← German troop movements
I 7th March, 3 battalions cross the River Rhine
G Garrisons set up
L 4 squadrons of Luftwaffe sent to bases
〰 German frontier
▨ Occupied or demilitarised zone

Permanently demilitarised to 50 km east of the Rhine

15 million Germans in area

Saar returned from control of League of Nations 1935

Germany vulnerable to French invasion, as 1921 and 1923

Maginot Line

Germany could not be aggressive in the east whilst its western border was unprotected

Hitler's aims
- To regain full control of the Rhineland
- To secure Germany's border against France, thus allowing greater assertion in the east

Timing
- Hitler originally planned to REMILITARISE the area in 1937, but in 1936 the international situation seemed favourable
- Domestically, Hitler needed to distract attention from economic problems caused by his increased rearmament programme
- He overrode the worries of generals and diplomats who considered it too risky

Events
- Hitler sent 14,000 lightly armed troops plus 22,000 local police into the Rhineland
- Most stayed on the east bank; only 3,000 went as far as the border near Aachen, Trier and Saarbrücken
- German troops had orders to withdraw if they met opposition. The French took no military action

Hitler's justification
The Rhineland was his own territory; he cited the 1935 French–Soviet alliance which he claimed broke the terms of Locarno; he offered non-aggression pacts

TALKING POINT

Is it a clear 'lesson' from history that all dictators should be resisted before it is too late?

Effects

Hitler's prestige, at home and abroad, soared. He dissolved the Reichstag on 7 March and on 29 March held a plebiscite asking the German people to approve his remilitarisation of the Rhineland. Ninety-nine per cent of the electorate voted; and of them 98.8 per cent voted in favour of Hitler's action. Abroad, other threatened regimes now distrusted British and especially French resolve. Some felt they would have to be conciliatory towards Germany. Germany, secure on its western border, now felt it was safer to expand in the east. Hitler began to construct a fortification line, the West Wall, on the French border. Resistance might have persuaded Hitler to withdraw or led to a minor war that Germany would have lost, but would probably not have caused a major war.

SOURCE 20.10   Hitler justifies his actions in a special address to the Reichstag on Saturday 7 March 1936

The German Government has continually emphasised during the negotiations of the last years its readiness to observe and fulfil all the obligations arising from the Rhine Pact so long as the other contracting parties were ready on their side to maintain the pact. This obvious and essential condition can no longer be regarded as being fulfilled by France. France has replied to Germany's repeated friendly offers and assurances of peace by infringing the Rhine Pact through a military alliance with the Soviet Union directed exclusively against Germany. In this manner, however, the Locarno Rhine Pact has lost its inner meaning and ceased in practice to exist. Consequently, Germany regards herself for her part as no longer bound by this dissolved Treaty. The German Government is now constrained to face the new situation created by this alliance, a situation which is rendered more acute by the fact that the Franco-Soviet Treaty has been supplemented by a Treaty of Alliance between Czechoslovakia and the Soviet Union exactly parallel in form. In accordance with the fundamental right of a nation to secure its frontiers and ensure its possibilities of defence, the German Government has today restored the full and unrestricted sovereignty of Germany in the demilitarised zone of the Rhineland.

In order, however, to avoid any misinterpretation of its intentions and to establish beyond doubt the purely defensive character of these measures, as well as to express its unalterable longing for a real PACIFICATION of Europe between states equal in rights and equally respected, the German Government declares itself ready to conclude new agreements for the creation of a system of peaceful security for Europe . . . In this historic hour when German troops are presently occupying their future garrisons of peace in the Reich's western provinces, we may all join together to stand by two sacred, inner vows:

First, to the oath that we shall never yield to any power or any force in restoring the honour of our Volk *and would rather perish honourably from the gravest distress than ever capitulate. Secondly, to the vow that now more than ever we shall dedicate ourselves to achieving an understanding between the peoples of Europe . . . After three years, I believe that today the struggle for German equality of rights can be deemed concluded . . .*

We have no territorial claims to make in Europe. Above all, we are aware that all the tensions resulting either from erroneous territorial provisions or from the disproportion between the size of the population and its Lebensraum *can never be solved by wars in Europe. However, we do hope that human insight will help to alleviate the painfulness of this state of affairs and relieve tensions by means of a gradual evolutionary development marked by peaceful co-operation . . . I have come to the decision to dissolve the Reichstag so that the German* Volk *may pass its judgement on my leadership and that of my co-workers. In these three years, Germany has regained once more its honour, found once more a faith, overcome its greatest economic crisis, and ushered in a new cultural ascent. I believe I can say this as my conscience and God are my witnesses. I now ask the German* Volk *to strengthen me in my belief and to continue giving me, through the power of its will, power of my own to take a courageous stand at all times for its honour and freedom and to ensure its economic well-being; above all, to support me in my struggle for real peace.*

SOURCE ACTIVITY

(Marks are given in brackets.)
1 Explain the references in Source 20.10 to
   a) the Rhine Pact
   b) the 'Reich's western provinces'
   c) *Lebensraum.* [6]
2 Why do you think Hitler dissolved the Reichstag? [2]
3 How does Hitler seek to justify his actions? [2]
4 What view does Hitler take of territorial changes in Europe? [5]
5 With reference to the provenance, content and tone of this speech, explain what you consider might be Hitler's purpose in making it. [5]
6 What qualities of Hitler as a politician and statesman does this address show? [5]
(Total: 25 marks)

ACTIVITY

1 'A wild gamble.' Explain whether you agree with this view of Hitler's action over the Rhineland.
2 'The West could and should have stopped Hitler's remilitarisation of the Rhineland.' Argue the pros and cons of this view.

FOCUS ROUTE

Explain how and why Hitler was able to achieve *Anschluss* in March 1938.

Anschluss: the union of Austria with Germany

After his success in the Rhineland Hitler next turned his eyes to Austria. With his opponents far from united, Hitler saw opportunities to increase German influence in Austria. Versailles had banned *Anschluss,* although at the time the majority of Austrians probably favoured it. When the Nazis came to power, *Anschluss* seemed more possible but less attractive to many Austrians. An Austrian Nazi coup was suppressed in 1934 and Kurt von Schuschnigg established a right-wing government. In July 1936 an Austro-German Agreement saw Germany promising to respect Austrian independence, while Austria agreed to have a policy 'based always on the principle that Austria acknowledges herself to be a German state', and the National Opposition (Austrian pro-Nazis) would be given a role in government. By 1938 problems in the Austrian economy, still badly hit by the Depression, encouraged support for joining the more prosperous Germany. In 1937 Germany had sounded out opinion in Italy, Britain and France over closer German–Austrian links and had received indications that these countries would not resist German control of Austria.

■ 20E Austria and its neighbours

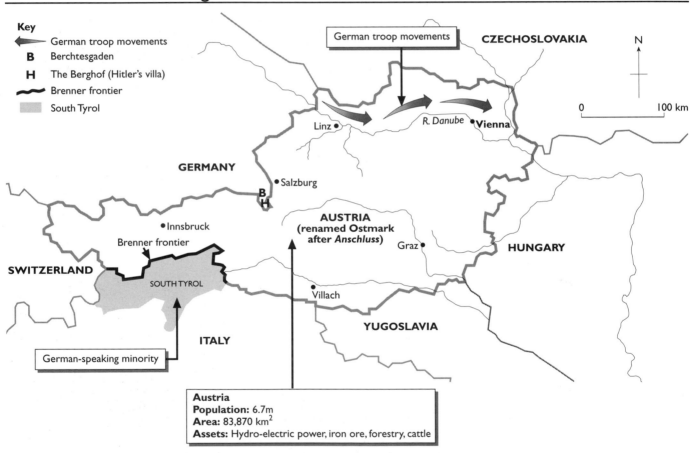

Key
- German troop movements
- **B** Berchtesgaden
- **H** The Berghof (Hitler's villa)
- Brenner frontier
- South Tyrol

German troop movements

CZECHOSLOVAKIA

N

Linz •   R. Danube • **Vienna**

GERMANY

• Salzburg

B
H

Innsbruck

**AUSTRIA
(renamed Ostmark
after *Anschluss*)**

Graz •

HUNGARY

Brenner frontier

SWITZERLAND

SOUTH TYROL

• Villach

German-speaking minority

ITALY

YUGOSLAVIA

0   100 km

**Austria
Population:** 6.7m
Area: 83,870 km²
Assets: Hydro-electric power, iron ore, forestry, cattle

Italy
In 1934 Italy had mobilised along the Brenner frontier to resist a possible German take-over of Austria. By November 1937 Mussolini, moving increasingly into Hitler's orbit, said he would not move against Germany over Austria

France
On 10 March 1938 Camille Chautemps' government fell, so there was no effective government during the crisis

Britain
The Foreign Minister Anthony Eden supported a strong line, but others thought the issue less important. The government gave no serious warning throughout the tension of winter–spring 1937–8

Key characters
Kurt von Schuschnigg – right-wing Austrian Chancellor
Artur Seyss-Inquart – adviser to Schuschnigg but pro-Nazi; passed information to Hitler; became Austrian Chancellor and invited Nazis in
Wilhelm Miklas – Austrian President
Franz von Papen – German Ambassador in Vienna
Hermann Goering – eager to gain Austria's economic resources; conveyed Hitler's demands to Austria via the telephone

Hitler favoured an evolutionary extension of German influence but encouraged Austrian Nazis to stir up trouble. This would provoke a reaction from the Austrian government to restore order, which could be used as an excuse for German intervention.

12 February 1938

Papen arranged for Schuschnigg to meet Hitler to discuss growing tension. Hitler bombarded him with a two-hour speech, insisting on German domination of Austria and demanding he immediately sign a document agreeing to this. Surrounded by German generals, the intimidated Schuschnigg signed a document appointing Seyss-Inquart as Interior Minister and agreeing to co-ordinate economic and military policy with Germany. Hitler was content with what he had achieved for the time being.

9 March 1938

Schuschnigg, alarmed at growing Nazi power, called a plebiscite on Austrian independence, hoping for popular support against *Anschluss* and to undermine Hitler's position. The plebiscite asked for approval of the statement: 'With Schuschnigg for Austria, we want a free and a German Austria, an independent and a social Austria, a Christian and a united Austria.'

11 March 1938

Hitler was furious but hesitant over what action to take. Goering argued for a tough line, and Hitler demanded the plebiscite be cancelled; otherwise, Germany would invade. Schuschnigg backed down. Goering pressed home the climb-down and demanded Schuschnigg's resignation as Chancellor. He agreed. President Miklas refused at first to appoint Seyss-Inquart to replace him, but eventually gave in. Goering then dictated by telephone the composition of a new Austrian government headed by Seyss-Inquart. Despite this, Hitler, wary of how much control he would have, decided to invade. Goering told Seyss-Inquart to request the entry of German troops. In a radio broadcast Schuschnigg told the Austrians not to resist.

12 March 1938

At dawn, German troops entered Austria. There was no resistance. In the afternoon, Hitler was well received by the Austrian crowds. Hitler decided to go further than just securing a SATELLITE GOVERNMENT and to absorb Austria into Germany. The new Austrian government issued a law on the Reunion of Austria with the German Reich, making Austria a province of Germany (*Ostmark*). Thousands were arrested. Jews were attacked. Hitler dissolved the Austrian Reichstag and held a plebiscite on 10 April, when 48.8 million (99 per cent of Germans and Austrians) voted 'yes' for union. In April, Britain recognised the enlarged Germany.

SOURCE 20.11 Austria welcomes the *Anschluss* in March 1938

Primary sources on the *Anschluss*

Sources 20.12–16, relating to a 24-hour period, reveal in fascinating detail Hitler's methods and suggest the general mood of the international community.

SOURCE 20.12 Schuschnigg's account of Hitler's remarks to him at their meeting, as described in his memoirs, *Austrian Requiem*, 1947

You have done everything to avoid a friendly policy . . . The whole history of Austria is just one uninterrupted act of high treason . . . I am absolutely determined to make an end of all this. The German Reich is one of the great powers, and nobody will raise his voice if it settles its border problems . . .

I have a historic mission, and this mission I will fulfil because Providence has destined me to do so . . . Who is not with me will be crushed . . . I have made the greatest achievement in the history of Germany, greater than any other German. And not by force, mind you. I am carried along by the love of my people . . . I am telling you that I am going to solve the so-called Austrian problem one way or the other . . . I have only to give the order and your ridiculous defence mechanism will be blown to bits . . .

Don't think for one moment that anybody on earth is going to thwart my decisions. Italy? I see eye to eye with Mussolini . . . England? England will not move one finger for Austria. And France? France could have stopped Germany in the Rhineland, and we would have had to retreat. But now it is too late for France . . . Think it over, Herr Schuschnigg, think it over well. I can only wait until this afternoon.

SOURCE 20.13 Britain's response on 11 March to Schuschnigg's request for advice, recorded in *British Documents on German Foreign Policy 1918–1945*

His Majesty's government cannot take responsibility for advising the Chancellor to take any course of action which might expose his country to dangers against which [it is] unable to guarantee protection.

SOURCE 20.14 Transcript (recorded in shorthand by Goering's Research Department) of the telephone call from Goering to his agent Wilhelm Keppler, the evening of 11 March 1938

Goering: 'The main thing is that Seyss-Inquart takes charge of all the functions of government now; that he secures the broadcasting facilities et cetera. And listen – Seyss is to send the following telegram to us. Take it down. "The provisional Austrian government, which after the resignation of the Schuschnigg cabinet sees its duty in the re-establishment of law and order in Austria, urgently asks the German Government to send German troops into Austria as quickly as possible."'

SOURCE 20.15 Schuschnigg's description in his memoirs of what happened in the Austrian Chancellery, 11 March

Suddenly I noticed a number of young people in the hall again with that close-cropped haircut. One young man brushed past me without an apology. He turned around and looked me up and down with a purposely offensive, superior smile. Then he went on and slammed the door as if he were at home. I stared after him, and suddenly I realised: Invasion! Not at the borders as yet, but here, in the Chancellery: the Gestapo.

SOURCE 20.16 An interview with Hitler on 12 March by the journalist Ward Price of the *Daily Mail*

What injustice have we done to any country, whose interests have we violated, when we concur with the desire of the overwhelming majority of the Austrian population to be Germans? These people here are Germans . . .

I assure you in all earnestness that, four days ago, I had no inkling of any of what was to happen today or that Austria was to become a German land, just as Bavaria or Saxony. I did this because I was deceived by Herr Schuschnigg, and deception is something I will not tolerate. When I shake hands and give my word on something, then I adhere to it.

SOURCE ACTIVITY

(Marks are given in brackets.)

1 With reference to its content and tone, explain what Source 20.12 shows about Hitler's views of Germany and his own role. [3]

2 To what extent does Source 20.13 justify Hitler's assessment of foreign reactions to *Anschluss*? [4]

3 What do Sources 20.14 and 20.15 reveal about the methods used by the Nazi government to achieve *Anschluss*? [4]

4 With reference to their origins, discuss the value of Sources 20.12 and 20.14 as evidence about Hitler's methods. [4]

5 'A useful insight into Hitler's approach to foreign policy.' How far do you agree with this comment on Source 20.16? [4]

6 How well do these sources explain why Hitler achieved *Anschluss* without using force? [6]

(Total: 25 marks)

Historians' assessment of Hitler and the *Anschluss*

SOURCE 20.17 Bullock, 'Hitler and the Origins of the Second World War', 1967; a lecture, reprinted in *Origins of the Second World War*, ed. M. Robertson, 1971, pp. 204–5

The Anschluss *seems to me to provide, almost in caricature, a striking example of that extraordinary combination of consistency in aim, calculation and patience in preparation with opportunism, impulse and improvisation in execution which I regard as characteristic of Hitler's policy.*

The aim in this case was never in doubt; the demand for the incorporation of Austria in the Reich appears on the first page of Mein Kampf . . .

No doubt the Anschluss *is an exceptional case. On later occasions the plans were ready: dates by which both the Czech and Polish crises must be brought to a solution were fixed well in advance, and nothing like the same degree of improvisation was necessary. But in all the major crises of Hitler's career there is the same impression of confusion at the top, springing directly (as his generals and aides complained) from his own hesitations and indecision.*

SOURCE 20.18 William Carr, *Arms, Autarky and Aggression*, 1972, p. 84

The invasion and annexation of Austria . . . was an unexpected development. When Schuschnigg . . . announced on 9th March the holding of a plebiscite to enable the Austrians to determine their own future, he precipitated a crisis which forced Hitler's hand . . . Because Anschluss *was an essential preliminary to eastward expansion, Schuschnigg's initiative threatened to sabotage Hitler's whole programme . . .*

When news arrived of the cancellation of the plebiscite Hitler was easily persuaded by Goering, the leading protagonist [advocate] of a violent solution, to exploit the advantage and oust Schuschnigg from power, Ribbentrop's confident assertion that Britain would not intervene played its part in the decision to force the pace of events . . .

. . . Only after receiving a tumultuous reception in Linz did he abandon the idea of a satellite government under Seyss-Inquart and decide on annexation.

SOURCE 20.19 I. Kershaw, *The Nazi Dictatorship*, third edition, 1993, p. 119

In the actual Anschluss *crisis which unfolded in March 1938 it was Goering rather than Hitler who pushed the pace along, probably because of his interest in seizing economic assets.*

SOURCE 20.20 C. Thorne, *The Approach of War 1938–39*, 1973, p. 35

It was . . . the most improvised in its execution, an apparent lesson of the easy triumphs to be obtained by ruthless pressure and swift action in the face of a critical but passive Europe.

ACTIVITY

1 Read Sources 20.17–20 and identify how the following contributed to the German take-over of Austria:

- Hitler's long-term aims
- Hitler's use of intimidation
- the influence of other individuals
- economic factors
- the international context
- other factors.

2 Why does Bullock consider *Anschluss* such an important event?

Czechoslovakia: September 1938–March 1939

Hitler's attention turned to Czechoslovakia after his *Anschluss* triumph. This democratic state created by Versailles was to be dismembered by whatever means necessary. Czechoslovakia was a member of the League of Nations and had been allied to France since 1924 and to the Soviet Union since 1935. However, these two countries had no borders with Czechoslovakia, and Poland and Romania would not allow Soviet troops through their territory to assist Czechoslovakia. Czechoslovakia's other weakness lay in the large minorities within its population. There were 2 million Slovaks, Poles and Hungarians who wanted autonomy and 3 million Germans in the area known as the Sudetenland.

■ 20G The destruction of Czechoslovakia

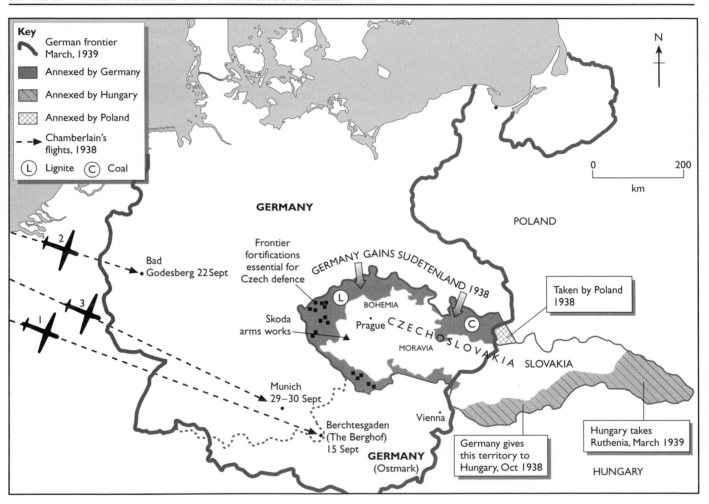

Key
- German frontier March, 1939
- Annexed by Germany
- Annexed by Hungary
- Annexed by Poland
- Chamberlain's flights, 1938
- (L) Lignite (C) Coal

GERMANY

POLAND

0 — 200 km

GERMANY GAINS SUDETENLAND 1938

Bad Godesberg 22 Sept

Frontier fortifications essential for Czech defence

(L)

BOHEMIA

Prague C Z E C H O S L O V A K I A

MORAVIA

Skoda arms works

(C)

Taken by Poland 1938

SLOVAKIA

Munich 29–30 Sept

Vienna

Berchtesgaden (The Berghof) 15 Sept

GERMANY (Ostmark)

Germany gives this territory to Hungary, Oct 1938

Hungary takes Ruthenia, March 1939

HUNGARY

Hitler's strategy
- Use the argument of the Sudeten Germans' right to SELF-DETERMINATION in order to undermine the Czech state, then conquer it
- Threaten war to persuade the weak West to let him dismember Czechoslovakia

Key characters
Eduard Benes, Czech Prime Minister
Emil Hacha, Czech President
Konrad Henlein, leader of the Sudeten German Party
Bela Tuka, leader of the Slovaks

European context
- France: generally followed lead taken by Britain
- Britain: Prime Minister Chamberlain determined to avoid war and viewed Czechoslovakia as unimportant; he considered the transferring of the Sudetenland to Germany reasonable, and that it was Hitler's last territorial demand

MOVE ONE: 1938

1938

Early in 1938, Henlein complains at mistreatment of the German minority by Czechs. On 28 March Hitler tells Henlein to make demands that the Czech government cannot accept

20–22 May 1938

War scare. Czechs mobilise against feared German invasion. Hitler denies he is planning to invade. The lack of a German attack looks like a victory for Czechoslovakia over Hitler

30 May 1938

Hitler orders plans to smash Czechoslovakia by 1 October. Throughout summer, German propaganda campaign against Czechoslovakia

12 September 1938

Hitler attacks Czechoslovakia in a speech at Nuremberg. He hopes for a Sudeten German rising, but it does not occur
The French government urges Chamberlain to try to negotiate a settlement. Hitler agrees to the idea of a meeting

15 September 1938

Chamberlain flies to see Hitler at the Berghof, his house on the Obersalzberg, near Berchtesgaden. He agrees that Czechoslovakia should cede all areas over 50 per cent German. The British and French pressurise the Czechs to agree. Hitler hopes the Czechs will refuse, so they will be isolated

22 September 1938

Chamberlain succeeds in pressurising Benes to accept Hitler's demands. Confident that the crisis is over, Chamberlain meets Hitler at Bad Godesberg. Hitler now raises his demands; he wants the Sudetenland by 1 October. Talks break down. Major fear of war in Europe
Chamberlain persuades Mussolini to arrange conference at Munich. The views of the German generals and Goering, the lack of German public enthusiasm for war and Mussolini's views all help persuade Hitler to agree to attend the proposed conference

29–30 September 1938

Four Power Conference at Munich: Britain, France, Germany, Italy. (Czechoslovakia and the USSR are not invited.) Agree to the German occupation of the Sudetenland between 1 and 10 October, followed by plebiscites in mixed areas, and international guarantees of Czechoslovakia
German troops occupy the Sudetenland. President Benes resigns and goes into exile. On 10 October Poles take Teschen district. The plebiscites agreement is ignored

Effects

- Czechoslovakia loses 41,000 sq km, including its richest industrial sites and its strongly fortified border; its communications system is disrupted. Czechoslovakia is no longer able to take on Germany militarily
- Germany gains major economic and military resources
- Hitler's domestic popularity increases and the plans of some generals to replace Hitler if he has a diplomatic setback are ruined. It boosts Hitler's confidence as the West appears feeble
- Generally, the USSR sees appeasement as evidence that the West will not stand up to Hitler, so it reinforces the Soviet idea of doing a separate deal with Germany. The French alliance system is broken and this classic example of appeasement, by encouraging further German expansion, contributes greatly to the Second World War

MOVE TWO: THE FINAL DESTRUCTION OF CZECHOSLOVAKIA: 1939

1 October 1938

The German army draws up fresh plans for attacking Czechoslovakia. Hitler encourages Poles, Romanians and Hungarians to demand pieces of Czechoslovakia, and Slovaks to demand autonomy

February 1939

Hitler meets Bela Tuka, the Slovak leader, and tells him to demand Slovakia's complete separation from Czechoslovakia. President Hacha declares MARTIAL LAW to try to stop the break-up of Czechoslovakia. He dismisses the Slovak government, and sends troops into Slovakia to crush unrest stirred up by the Nazis

13 March 1939

Hitler demands Slovakia declare its independence or it will be taken over by Hungary. Next day, the Slovak government complies

14 March 1939

President Hacha, in desperation, goes to Berlin to see Hitler. Hitler keeps him waiting till 1.15 a.m. whilst he finishes watching a film. Hitler demands Hacha agree to split Czechoslovakia otherwise German troops will enter Czechoslovakia within a few hours. At 4 a.m. Hacha gives in. Bohemia–Moravia to become a German protectorate, while Slovakia to remain nominally independent

15 March 1939

German troops march into Prague; Bohemia–Moravia is incorporated into the Reich

16 March 1939

Slovakia asks for German protection; German troops are sent to establish the satellite state of Slovakia. The Hungarians take over Ruthenia

Effects

- Germany makes major economic gains, especially Skoda armaments works
- Hitler has for the first time conquered non-German territory
- The West's belief in Hitler's moderation is weakened. Britain resolves to resist further German moves

Primary sources on the crisis over the Sudetenland, 1938

SOURCE 20.21 After a conference with his generals on 28 May, Hitler signed a new plan on 30 May

Political assumptions: It is my unalterable decision to smash Czechoslovakia by military action in the near future. It is the business of the political leadership to await or bring about the suitable moment from a political and military point of view.

An unavoidable development of events within Czechoslovakia, or other political events in Europe providing a suddenly favourable opportunity which may never recur, may cause me to take action.

The proper choice and determined exploitation of a favourable moment is the surest guarantee of success. To this end preparations are to be made immediately . . .

Most favourable from a military as well as a political point of view would be lightning action as the result of an incident, which would subject Germany to unbearable provocation and which, in the eyes of at least part of world opinion, affords the moral justification for military measures.

SOURCE 20.22 Hitler speaking at the Nuremberg Nazi Party rally, 12 September 1938

Czechoslovakia . . . is a democratic state, founded on democratic lines by forcing other nationalities without asking them into a structure manufactured at Versailles. As good democrats they began to oppress and mishandle the majority of the inhabitants . . . Among the nationalities being suppressed in this State are 3,500,000 Germans . . . These Germans are the creatures of God . . . That conditions in this nation are unbearable is generally known. Three and a half million were robbed in the name of a certain Mr Wilson [US President] of their right to self-determination. Economically these people were deliberately ruined and afterwards handed over to a slow process of extermination. The misery of the Sudeten Germans is without end.

SOURCE 20.23 German Foreign Office record of Hitler's meeting with the Hungarian Prime Minister and Foreign Minister on 21 September 1938

He, the Führer, was determined to settle the Czech question even at risk of a world war. Germany demanded the entire German area. He was convinced that neither England nor France would intervene. It was Hungary's last opportunity to join in . . .

In his opinion the best thing would be to destroy Czechoslovakia. In the long run it was quite impossible to tolerate the existence of this aircraft carrier in the heart of Europe. In [the Führer's] opinion action taken by the Army would provide the only satisfactory solution. There was, however, the danger of the Czechs submitting to every demand.

SOURCE 20.24 Weizsäcker, State Secretary in the German Foreign Ministry, wrote in his diary, 9 October 1938

. . . We appeared to have won the game when Chamberlain announced his visit to the Obersalzberg in order to preserve peace. This represented a rejection of Czechoslovakia's crisis politics. One could have reached an agreement without difficulty, on the basis of English mediation, about how the Sudetenland was to be split off and transferred to us in a peaceful manner.

However, we were dominated by the determination to have a war of revenge and destruction against Czechoslovakia. Thus, we conducted the second phase of discussions with Chamberlain in Bad Godesberg in such a way that, despite our basic agreement, what had been decided was bound to fail. The group who wanted war, namely Ribbentrop and the SS, had nearly succeeded in prompting the Führer to attack. Among numerous similar statements made by the Führer in my presence during the night of 27–28 September was one to the effect that he would now annihilate Czechoslovakia. Ribbentrop and I were the sole witnesses of these words: they were not designed to have an effect on a third party.

Thus, the assumption that the Führer was intending a huge bluff is incorrect. His resentment stemming from 22 May, when the English accused him of pulling back, led him on to the path of war. I have not quite managed to establish what influences then finally decided him to issue invitations to the four power meeting in Munich on 28 September and thereby to leave the path of war. Naturally one can find 100 different reasons for this change of course . . .

Two factors were probably decisive: (a) His observation that our people regarded the approach of war with a silent obstructiveness and were far from enthusiastic (Dr Goebbels said that loudly to the Führer at table in the Reich Chancellery over the heads of all those present), and (b) Mussolini's appeal at the last moment, i.e. on the morning of the 28th, when the mobilisation was planned for 2 p.m. The idea of a four power conference was first mentioned in my presence by the Führer and received general and warm approval with the exception of those referred to above. Herr von Ribbentrop was still working against the agreement on the evening of the 28th and on the 29th, since he obviously considered war to be the best solution.

SOURCE ACTIVITY

(Marks are given in brackets.)

1 What light does Source 20.21 shed on Hitler's foreign policy methods? [3]

2 Study Sources 20.22–24. What reasons does Hitler give for wanting war against Czechoslovakia? [3]

3 With reference to the origins and tone of Source 20.22, what can be inferred about Hitler's purpose in making this speech? [4]

4 What aspects of Hitler's strategy are revealed in Source 20.23? [3]

5 With reference to the provenance, content and style of Source 20.24, assess its value as evidence for the nature of German foreign policy in 1938. [7]

(Total: 20 marks)

Poland and the outbreak of war, September 1939

Poland was the next target for Hitler. He had negotiated a Non-Aggression Pact with Poland in 1934 but had no qualms about breaking it. In March 1939 Germany demanded that Lithuania return Memel (lost in 1919). On 23 March, Lithuania was forced to agree, and Germany annexed Memel. Hitler continued to pressurise Poland. He claimed Germans were being mistreated and demanded the return of Danzig, together with a rail-and-road route through the corridor to East Prussia. Negotiations were possible, but Poland took a hard line, especially after 31 March 1939 when Chamberlain, convinced now that Hitler could not be trusted, announced a British guarantee of Poland. This was intended to be the first part of a comprehensive security system in the east. (Britain later extended her guarantee to Greece and Romania.) Hitler was furious because the Anglo-French guarantee to Poland reduced his chances of bullying Poland into submission.

■ 20I   Poland 1939

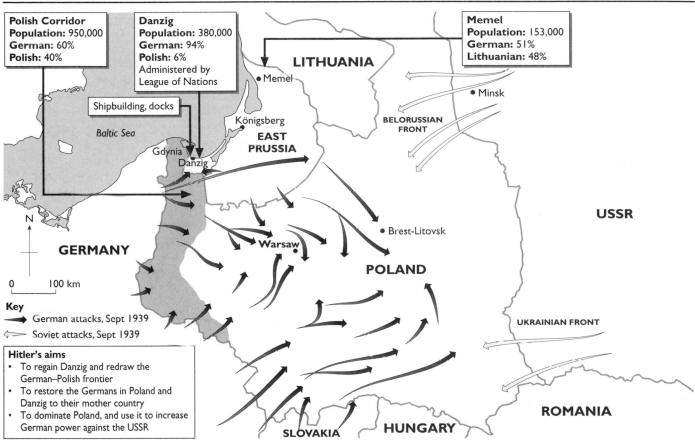

Polish Corridor
Population: 950,000
German: 60%
Polish: 40%

Danzig
Population: 380,000
German: 94%
Polish: 6%
Administered by League of Nations

Memel
Population: 153,000
German: 51%
Lithuanian: 48%

Shipbuilding, docks

Key
→ German attacks, Sept 1939
⇨ Soviet attacks, Sept 1939

Hitler's aims
• To regain Danzig and redraw the German–Polish frontier
• To restore the Germans in Poland and Danzig to their mother country
• To dominate Poland, and use it to increase German power against the USSR

■ 20J   Key events

3 Apr 1939   Hitler orders a plan to be drawn up to attack Poland

May   Hitler signs Pact of Steel with Italy to give mutual assistance if either side is at war

23 May   Hitler decides on war against Poland; he still considers Britain and France will not intervene. He develops contacts with the USSR over a possible alliance to counter Anglo-French–Soviet talks

22 Aug   Hitler addresses his generals; he says he has always been right; the international situation is favourable; it will be less so in two or three years; his only fear is last minute mediation plans, as at Munich in 1938

23 Aug   Ribbentrop goes to Moscow with full authority to negotiate an agreement. The Nazi–Soviet Pact publicly stipulates non-aggression for ten years and makes economic agreements. In secret PROTOCOLS, each agrees to help the other if there is war against Poland; they share out spheres of influence in eastern Europe. On the same day, Hitler orders the attack for 26 August, then postpones it until 1 September, since on

25 August   Britain RATIFIES its guarantee to Poland, and Mussolini says Italy is not ready to fight. There is possibly a chance of negotiations, but they ultimately fail. Hitler is probably set on invading

31 Aug   SS troops, dressed as Polish soldiers, 'attack' a German border radio post, leaving behind dead concentration camp prisoners in Polish uniforms. This 'Polish' provocation is used to justify war

1 Sept   Germany invades Poland

3 Sept   Britain and France declare war after the expiry of an ultimatum for Germany to withdraw. Hitler is caught by surprise; his intended local war is turning into a far broader war. But, despite declaring war, Britain and France are unable to take any real action to help Poland

17 Sept   The USSR invades Poland from the east: Poland is crushed. Hitler is dissuaded by his generals from immediately turning west to smash France; he launches the western war in May 1940

The Nazi–Soviet Pact

This agreement between Germany and the USSR was, on the face of it, an amazing about turn, since Hitler had always stressed that the Soviet Union was his main enemy, ruled by Jewish Bolsheviks and inferior Slavs and occupying Germany's *Lebensraum*. But in many ways it was a master stroke, as it left Poland isolated, ruined attempts by the West to bring the USSR into a formal alliance against Germany, and thus avoided the danger of a war on two major fronts. Germany gained vital raw materials from the Soviet Union that relieved her domestic economic problems and helped her rearmament drive. Hitler was prepared to break the agreement whenever he wanted.

SOURCE 20.25   Hitler's speech to his commanders, 22 August 1939. This version is based on notes taken by Admiral Canaris, since no official minutes were kept

It was clear to me that a conflict with Poland had to come sooner or later. I had already made this decision in the spring, but I thought that I would first turn against the West in a few years, and only after that against the East. But the sequence of these things cannot be fixed. Nor should one close one's eyes to threatening situations. I wanted first of all to establish a tolerable relationship with Poland in order to fight first against the West. But this plan, which appealed to me, could not be executed, as fundamental points had changed. It became clear to me that, in the event of a conflict with the West, Poland would attack us. Poland is striving for access to the sea. The further development appeared after the occupation of the Memel Territory and it became clear to me that in certain circumstances a conflict with Poland might come at an inopportune [unfavourable] moment. I give as reasons for this conclusion, first of all two personal factors: My own personality and that of Mussolini. Essentially all depends on me, on my existence, because of my political talents. Furthermore, the fact [is] that probably no one will ever again have the confidence of the whole German people as I have. There will probably never again in the future be a man with more authority than I have. My existence is therefore a factor of great value. But I can be eliminated at any time by a criminal or a lunatic. The second personal factor is the DUCE. His existence is also decisive. If anything happens to him, Italy's loyalty to the alliance will no longer be certain. It is easy for us to make decisions. We have nothing to lose; we have everything to gain. Because of our restrictions our economic situation is such that we can only hold out for a few more years. Goering can confirm this. We have no other choice, we must act. Our opponents will be risking a great deal and can gain only a little. Our enemies have leaders who are below the average. No personalities. No masters, no men of action.

Besides the personal factors, the political situation is favourable for us: in the Mediterranean, rivalry between Italy, France and England; in the Far East, tension between Japan and England; in the Middle East, tension which causes alarm in the Mohammedan world. All these favourable circumstances will no longer prevail in two or three years' time. No one knows how much longer I shall live. Therefore, better a conflict now.

The creation of Greater Germany was a great achievement politically, but militarily it was doubtful, since it was achieved by bluff on the part of the political leaders. It is necessary to test the military machine. If at all possible, not in a general reckoning, but by the accomplishment of individual tasks.

The relationship with Poland has become unbearable. My Polish policy hitherto was contrary to the views of the people. My proposals to Poland were frustrated by England's intervention. Poland changed her attitude towards us. A permanent state of tension is intolerable. The power of initiative cannot be allowed to pass to others. The present moment is more favourable than in two or three years' time. An attempt on my life or Mussolini's could change that situation to our disadvantage. One cannot for ever face one another with rifles cocked. The probability is still great that the West will not intervene. We must take the risk with ruthless determination.

The enemy had another hope, that Russia would become our enemy after the conquest of Poland. The enemy did not reckon with my great strength of purpose.

Our enemies are little worms; I came to know them in Munich. I brought about the change towards Russia gradually. The day after tomorrow von Ribbentrop will conclude the treaty. Now Poland is in the position in which I wanted her. We need not be afraid of a blockade. The East will supply us with grain, cattle, coal, lead and zinc. It is a mighty aim, which demands great efforts. I am only afraid that at the last moment some swine or other will yet submit to me a plan for mediation.

The political objective goes further. A start has been made on the destruction of England's hegemony [domination]. The way will be open for the soldiers after I have made the political preparations . . .

SOURCE 20.26   Hitler's second address later that day

No shrinking back from anything. Everyone must hold the view that we have been determined to fight the Western Powers right from the start. A life and death struggle. Germany has won every war when she was united. An inflexible, unflinching bearing, above all on the part of superiors, firm confidence, belief in victory overcoming the past by becoming accustomed to the heaviest burdens. A long period of peace would not do us any good. It is therefore necessary to be prepared for anything. A manly bearing. It is not machines that fight each other, but men. We have better men as regards quality. Spiritual factors are decisive.

On the opposite side they are weaker men. The nation collapsed in 1918 because the spiritual prerequisites [requirements] were insufficient . . . The destruction of Poland has priority. The aim is to eliminate active forces, not to reach a definite line. Even if war breaks out in the West, the destruction of Poland remains the priority. A quick decision in view of the season.

I shall give a propagandist reason for starting the war, no matter whether it is plausible or not. The victor will not be asked afterwards whether he told the truth or not. When starting and waging war it is not right that matters, but victory.

Close your hearts to pity. Act brutally. Eighty million people must obtain what is their right. Their existence must be made secure. The stronger man is right. The greatest harshness. Swiftness in making decisions is necessary. Firm faith in the German soldier. Crises are due solely to leaders having lost their nerve.

SOURCE 20.27   This cartoon was published in the *Daily Mail* on 6 September 1939. Hitler is speaking to Mars, the god of war

"THERE'S SOME MISTAKE, IT WAS YOUR SMALL BROTHER I SENT FOR".

ACTIVITY

1 Referring to the provenance and contents of Sources 20.25 and 20.26, comment on their value as evidence for the following areas:
   a) Hitler's planning of foreign policy
   b) his views of and policy towards Poland
   c) his views on peace and war
   d) his attitude to war with the West and to its timing
   e) the requirements for military success
   f) the importance of leadership.

2 A. J. P. Taylor described the Polish question as 'the most justified of German grievances'.
   a) Do you agree with this comment?
   b) Why, then, did the West declare war over this issue?

3 Study Source 20.27. Explain the point it is making.

E How did the major powers react to Hitler's foreign policy 1933–9?

Europe in the 1930s was divided into three broad ideological camps: liberal democracies, headed by Britain and France, a growing number of dictatorships of the Right, most notably Fascist Italy, and thirdly the communist regime in the Soviet Union, headquarters of the Comintern. However, although ideology was a considerable factor in diplomacy, it was by no means the sole determinant, as all states were prepared to be pragmatic to further their national interests. The 1930s saw a series of agreements based far more on self-interest than ideology. Here we examine sources that illustrate the changing attitudes of Hitler's potential opponents and suggest reasons why Hitler was able to smash the Versailles settlement without major opposition until September 1939.

Democratic Britain

SOURCE 20.28 Lord Lothian, British politician, March 1936

The Germans ... are only going into their own back garden.

SOURCE 20.29 Stanley Baldwin, British Prime Minister, 1936

We all know the German desire, as he has come out with it in his book, to move East; and if he moves East, I shall not break my heart ... If there is any fighting in Europe to be done, I should like to see the Bolsheviks and the Nazis doing it.

SOURCE 20.30 Lord Halifax, a member of the British Cabinet and Foreign Secretary 1938–40, to Hitler, November 1937

He [Halifax] must emphasise once more in the name of HM government that the possibility of change of the existing situation was not excluded, but that changes should only take place upon the basis of reasonable agreements reasonably reached.

SOURCE 20.31 A July 1938 cartoon by David Lowe: 'What's Czechoslovakia to me, anyway?'

SOURCE 20.32   The British Prime Minister Neville Chamberlain's diary, 20 March 1938

You have only to look at the map to see that nothing France or we could do could possibly save Czechoslovakia from being overrun by the Germans, if they wanted to do it. The Austrian frontier is practically open … Russia is 100 miles away. Therefore we could not help Czechoslovakia – she would simply be a pretext for going to war with Germany.

SOURCE 20.33   Chamberlain broadcasts to the nation, 27 September 1938

How horrible, fantastic, incredible it is that we should be digging trenches and trying on gas masks here because of a quarrel in a far away country between people of whom we know nothing …

After my visits to Germany I have realised vividly how Herr Hitler feels that he must champion the other Germans, and his indignation that grievances have not been met before this. He told me privately, and last night he repeated publicly, that after this Sudeten German question is settled, that is the end of Germany's territorial claims in Europe.

SOURCE 20.34   Earl de la Warr, member of the British Cabinet, March 1939, quoted in the *Daily Herald*, 17 March 1939

This action of the Nazi regime has torn to shreds the last semblance of an excuse for their policy. Hitherto there has always been some attempt to justify their actions in terms either of the reincorporation of those of German race or destroying some part of the Versailles Treaty they felt unjust. But today this veil … is no longer deemed necessary and aggression stands forth, naked and arrogant.

Fascist Italy

SOURCE 20.35   A *Punch* cartoon published 20 June 1934

CONSULTING THE ORACLE.
(*As recorded by Mr. Punch's magic microphone.*)

HERR HITLER. "WHAT IS YOUR MESSAGE FOR GERMANY!"
SIGNOR MUSSOLINI. "TELL HER SHE MUST BE CAREFUL TO KEEP ON THE RIGHT SIDE OF ITALY."
HERR HITLER. "AND HOW CAN SHE MAKE SURE OF DOING THAT!"
SIGNOR MUSSOLINI. "BY KEEPING ON THE OTHER SIDE OF AUSTRIA."

SOURCE 20.36   This *Punch* cartoon appeared on 23 February 1938

GOOD HUNTING

Mussolini. "All right, Adolf—I never heard a shot"

SOURCE 20.37 'Circus games': this French cartoon from *Marianne* appeared on 23 February 1938. Hitler the gladiator has caught Schuschnigg in his net. The spectators are giving the 'thumbs down' to indicate that the defeated gladiator should be killed

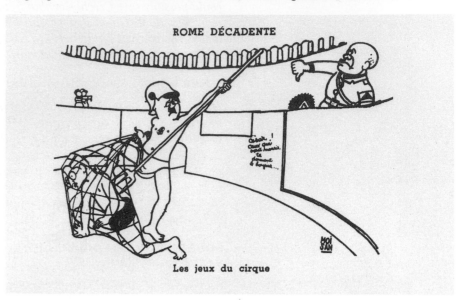

ROME DÉCADENTE

Les jeux du cirque

SOURCE 20.38 Extract from the diary of Count Galeazzo Ciano, the Italian Foreign Minister, on Hitler's seizure of Czechoslovakia, March 1939

The Axis functions only in favour of one of its parts, which tends to preponderate [be dominant], and acts entirely on its own initiative with little regard for us. I expressed my point of view to the Duce. He was cautious in his reaction and did not seem to attach great importance to the event.

The Soviet Union

SOURCE 20.39 'The peaceful snarl of Fascism': a Soviet cartoon comments on Hitler's reoccupation of the Rhineland, March 1936

„МИРНОЕ" РЫЧАНИЕ ФАШИЗМА

SOURCE 20.40 This 1936 Soviet cartoon shows Hitler surrounded by the 'fairy godfathers' of the Western powers

SOURCE 20.41
A 1939 Soviet
cartoon

SOURCE 20.42 Signing the Nazi–Soviet Pact in Moscow on 23 August 1939. Molotov, the Soviet Foreign Minister, is in the foreground, with Ribbentrop and Stalin behind him

ACTIVITY

1 You would expect Britain (and France) to be the most likely to take action to stop Hitler. Referring to Sources 20.28–33, explain what they show about why Britain did not intervene to stop Hitler until September 1939.

2 How does Source 20.34 help explain why the British government changed its approach?

3 What do Sources 20.35–38 illustrate about the Italian government's changing reaction to Hitler?

4 **a)** Explain the point of each of the cartoons in Sources 20.39–41.
   b) What does Source 20.42 show about the Soviet Union's changing reaction to Nazi Germany?

FOCUS ROUTE

Draw up two lists of points suggesting that Hitler was
a) a master planner
b) an opportunist.

■ **Learning trouble spot**

Hitler and Britain

Popular perceptions of the Second World War can be misleading. There is a patriotic assumption that Britain was the most heroic resister of Germany and did more than other countries, including the USSR, to defeat Hitler. The idea that Hitler wanted an alliance with Britain jars against this popular view, but nevertheless he did. Hitler, wrongly, believed that Britain would accept German domination of Europe in return for the maintenance of its empire. Hitler was quite prepared, at least until the mid 1940s, for Britain to retain its empire (he actually admired the British Empire and his favourite film was the imperialist tale *The Lives of the Bengal Lancers*). He anticipated that once Germany had achieved *Lebensraum* in Europe there would be a struggle against the United States for world supremacy, in which Britain might be an ally, though more likely an opponent.

The hostility felt amongst the British elite for the Soviet Union and the traditional Anglo-French rivalry reinforced Hitler in his belief in the possibility of an Anglo–German alliance. However, Hitler did not grasp Britain's determination to prevent any one power dominating Europe, which meant Britain would never accept the realisation of Hitler's full programme. On the other hand, the following factors suggest that Hitler's view of the possibility of co-operation with Britain was not totally unrealistic:

- Popular hostility in Britain to war and criticism of the Treaty of Versailles as untenable
- Britain's quarrel with France over Italy's actions in Abyssinia
- Britain's distrust of the Soviet Union as a possible ally against Nazi Germany
- Britain's acceptance of the bilateral Naval Agreement of 1935 with Germany.

F Was Hitler a master planner or an opportunist?

Since the 1960s a fierce historical debate has been waged over the nature of Hitler's foreign policy. Some historians, most notably Hugh Trevor-Roper, argue that Hitler had a clear vision that involved a master plan for war, and that he controlled the events that culminated in his desired war in 1939. Thus the ideas expressed in *Mein Kampf* and the *Zweite Buch (Hitler's Secret Book)* are the key to understanding German foreign policy after 1933. Others, such as A. J. P. Taylor, argue that he had no clear aims and was essentially a pragmatist (opportunist). His views in *Mein Kampf* and elsewhere were largely daydreams. Events took the course they did because of circumstances, not according to the clear intentions of Hitler. These two contrasting viewpoints have been seen as the intentionalist and structuralist schools (see pages 206–7). A similar debate, as we have seen, exists over the Holocaust.

Most historians now follow Bullock's compromise position: that Hitler did have a clear overall view, but within this he was prepared to be flexible. A fuller understanding of German foreign policy also requires a consideration of the influence of earlier German foreign policy traditions and a range of domestic factors, especially economic pressures.

Did Hitler plan for world war in 1939?

Right from the beginning Hitler prepared Germany for war, as he considered this inevitable. He believed that nations, like animals, competed for survival and that Germany was in a life-and-death struggle with Jewish Bolshevism. He originally intended this major conflict, which would decide the future of Europe, to begin in 1943–5. This date appeared frequently in his writings and speeches. Although the Four-Year Plan of 1936 was intended to get Germany ready for war in four years' time, policy was not dictated by this date. He was prepared for a minor war before 1940, and did not envisage the final war for world control against the United States would come before 1943. By this time Germany would be strengthened by its European conquests and its own rearmament would be at a peak, whereas its opponents, although they would eventually be militarily stronger, would not yet have completed their rearmament.

Hitler's views on the timing of war can be summarised as follows:

- 1933–6: make Germany strong enough to resist possible French/Polish attack
- 1937–40: be strong enough, if conditions were right, to conquer Czechoslovakia and absorb Austria, to adjust the border with Poland and intimidate other eastern countries to make concessions. War with France would be a possibility
- By 1943–5: be strong enough, having exploited eastern Europe, to seize *Lebensraum* from the USSR
- Later, with Germany at maximum strength, take on the USA (and possibly Britain) for world domination.

Of course, this summary is far too schematic (simplified): Hitler did not have a master plan, but he did have a clear view of his overall aims. His policy, both diplomatic and economic, was largely based on the above assumptions and then modified in the light of circumstances. Thus, whereas in *Mein Kampf* Hitler spoke of being allied with Britain to fight the USSR, in September 1939 he was allied with the USSR and fighting Britain! He was not planning a general war in 1939, but having decided war with Poland was necessary rather than the alternatives of war against the USSR or France, he embarked on what he considered would be a limited war against an isolated Poland. When Britain and France unexpectedly declared war, he switched to knocking out the West, before attacking the USSR.

ACTIVITY

Study Sources 20.43 and 20.44.
a) Pick out parts of these speeches that might be used to portray Hitler as a master planner.
b) Pick out parts that might be used to portray him as an opportunist.

SOURCE 20.43 Hitler gives an overview of his foreign policy 1933–9 in a secret speech to senior officers, 10 February 1939

All our actions during 1938 represent only the logical extension of the decisions which began to be realised in 1933. It is not the case that during this year of 1938 – let us say – a particular action occurred which was not previously envisaged. On the contrary, all the individual decisions which have been realised since 1933 are not the result of momentary considerations but represent the implementation of a previously existing plan, though perhaps not exactly according to the schedule which was envisaged. For example, in 1933 I was not exactly certain when the withdrawal from the League of Nations would occur. However, it was clear that this withdrawal had to be the first step towards Germany's revival. And it was further clear that we would have to choose the first appropriate moment. We could see from the start that the next step would have to be rearmament without the permission of foreign countries, but naturally we could not gauge the exact speed and extent of this rearmament right from the start. It was also further obvious that, after a certain period of rearmament, Germany would have to take the daring step of proclaiming to the world its freedom from restrictions on rearmament. At the beginning, naturally one could not foresee the right moment for this step. Finally, it was further clear that every further step must first involve the remilitarisation of the Rhineland. The date for this was in fact envisaged as being one year later: I did not think I would carry it out until 1937. The circumstances at the time made it seem appropriate to carry it out as early as 1936. It was also quite obvious that the Austrian and the Czech problems would have to be solved in order to further strengthen Germany's political and, in particular, her strategic position . . . to start with, I was not quite sure whether both problems ought to be or could be solved simultaneously or whether one should deal first with the question of Czechoslovakia or with the Austrian question. There was no doubt that these questions would have to be solved and so all these decisions were not ideas which were realised at the moment of their conception, but were long-made plans which I was determined to realise the moment I thought the circumstances at the time would be favourable.

SOURCE 20.44 Hitler addressing his generals in November 1939

The next step was Bohemia, Moravia, and Poland. It was clear to me from the first moment that I could not be satisfied with the Sudeten territory. That was only a partial solution. The decision to march into Bohemia was made. Then followed the establishment of the protectorate and with that the basis for the conquest of Poland was laid. I was not quite clear at that time whether I would start first against the east and then against the west or vice versa. By the pressure of events it came first to the fight against Poland. One might accuse me of wanting to fight and fight again. In struggle I see the fate of all beings. Nobody can avoid fighting if he does not want to go under.

ACTIVITY

Debate: 'Master Planner' or 'Improviser'? Which is the more accurate view of Hitler and his foreign policy? Key issues to consider:

- Views in *Mein Kampf*
- Hossbach Memorandum
- Hitler's views on Germany's needs
- Clear views on Germany's need for racial superiority
- His improvisations
- Planning
- Exploiting circumstances outside his control, e.g. Abyssinia, Spanish Civil War
- His actions in relation to the plans, with reference to various contingencies.

Other issues to consider might be:

- Did he have plans but no master plan?
- The extent to which one can improvise within an overall plan
- The extent to which in foreign policy in particular no one leader can be in full control, as Hitler realised.

G Review: Why was Hitler's foreign policy so successful 1933–9?

Before answering this question, you need to assess how successful Hitler's foreign policy actually was. You can then explain the success he had in the light of his aims and strategy, Germany's strength, the actions of other countries and the overall international context.

How successful was Hitler?

The following activity will help you address this question.

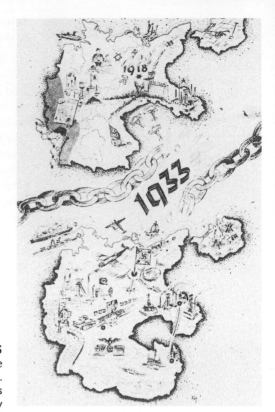

SOURCE 20.45
A cartoon published in the *Westfälische Landeszeitung*, a German newspaper, in 1939. It shows two maps of Germany: the top one is Weimar Germany, the bottom Nazi Germany

ACTIVITY

1 Study Source 20.45. List the changes between Germany in 1919 and in January 1939. Refer to as many of the marked features as possible.
2 Study the following table, which shows the statistics of Hitler's gains. How useful is this in assessing the success of Hitler's foreign policy?

Territorial gains	Area (sq km)	Population	Nationality	Assets
Saar	2,000	818,000	98% German	Coal
Austria	84,000	6,700,000	German	Hydro-electric power, iron ore, forestry, cattle, fruit
Sudetenland	29,000	3,561,000	74% German 26% Czech	Coal, copper, lignite, textiles, chemicals, steel works
Bohemia–Moravia	49,000	7,485,000	97% Czech 3% German	Steel works, coal, engineering, weapons factories
Polish corridor	18,000	950,000	60% German 40% Polish	Farming, forestry
Danzig	1,920	380,000	94% German 6% Polish	Shipbuilding, dockyards
Memel	2,660	153,000	51% German 48% Lithuanian	Farming, forestry, fishing, shipbuilding

3 Now copy and complete the following assessment chart on the extent to which Hitler achieved his foreign policy aims in 1933–9. You may consider that Hitler had not achieved some of these aims fully by 1939, but did he plan to by then? This might affect your final assessment of his success.

Aim	Extent fulfilled (0–5)	Evidence and assessment
Smash Versailles		
Unite all Germans in one Reich		
Lebensraum		
World conquest		

4 List any mistakes Hitler made or setbacks he suffered during 1933–9.

ACTIVITY

Use Sources 20.46–9 and Chart 20K to explain how the balance of power shifted towards Germany during the 1930s.

Why was Hitler successful?

SOURCE 20.46 Military expenditure as a percentage of Gross National Product, Germany and Britain

	Germany	Britain
1932	1	1
1933	3	3
1934	6	3
1935	8	2
1936	13	5
1937	13	7
1938	17	8

SOURCE 20.47 Size of the German army (in battalions)

	Infantry	Artillery	Panzer
1933	84	24	
1934	166	95	6
1935	287	116	12
1936	334	148	16
1937	352	187	24
1938	476	228	34

SOURCE 20.48 Military expenditure (billions of marks)

1932	0.8
1933	3.5
1934	4.1
1935	9.5
1936	10.8
1937	16.5
1938	17.2

SOURCE 20.49 Growth of the German military 1932–9

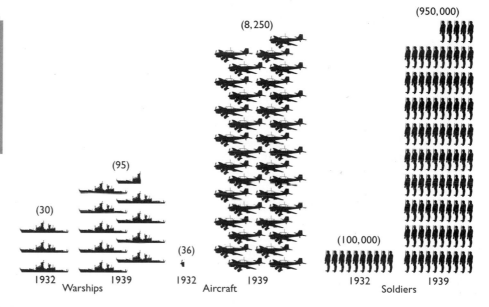

Warships: (30) 1932 — (95) 1939
Aircraft: (36) 1932 — (8,250) 1939
Soldiers: (100,000) 1932 — (950,000) 1939

■ 20K The changing balance of power in the 1930s

Germany's potential opponents	Diplomatic alliances	Events exploited by Germany	Growth of German power
Britain, France: some tension over how to react to Italy's invasion of Abyssinia	(Background: Versailles 1919, Locarno 1925) **1935** **Stresa Front:** Britain France } v. Germany Italy **Czech–Russian–French pacts** **1936** **Axis** Britain, France v. Germany, Italy and Japan (**Anti-Comintern Pact**)	Italian invasion of Abyssinia Spanish Civil War	Economic growth / Rearmament Rhineland remilitarised
Britain suspicious of USSR, fails to co-operate fully Pacifist feeling strong in Britain. France politically divided	**1938** Munich: Britain, France, Italy, Germany **1939** Britain France } v. Poland Germany and Italy (**Pact of Steel**) Germany and USSR (**Nazi-Soviet Pact**)		Austria annexed Sudetenland annexed Bohemia annexed

■ 20L Hitler's foreign policy: a summary

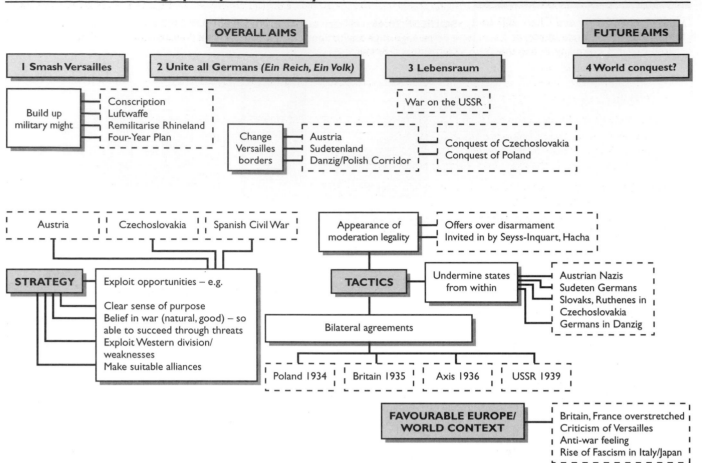

OVERALL AIMS

FUTURE AIMS

1 Smash Versailles   2 Unite all Germans (*Ein Reich, Ein Volk*)   3 Lebensraum   4 World conquest?

Build up military might
- Conscription
- Luftwaffe
- Remilitarise Rhineland
- Four-Year Plan

War on the USSR

Change Versailles borders
- Austria
- Sudetenland
- Danzig/Polish Corridor

Conquest of Czechoslovakia
Conquest of Poland

Austria   Czechoslovakia   Spanish Civil War

Appearance of moderation legality

Offers over disarmament
Invited in by Seyss-Inquart, Hacha

STRATEGY
Exploit opportunities – e.g.

Clear sense of purpose
Belief in war (natural, good) – so able to succeed through threats
Exploit Western division/weaknesses
Make suitable alliances

TACTICS

Undermine states from within
- Austrian Nazis
- Sudeten Germans
- Slovaks, Ruthenes in Czechoslovakia
- Germans in Danzig

Bilateral agreements

Poland 1934   Britain 1935   Axis 1936   USSR 1939

FAVOURABLE EUROPE/ WORLD CONTEXT
- Britain, France overstretched
- Criticism of Versailles
- Anti-war feeling
- Rise of Fascism in Italy/Japan

ACTIVITY

Copy and complete the following assessment chart with examples of the factors contributing to the success of Hitler's foreign policy. (You could either just put a tick in the relevant box or a cross if the opposite applies, or you could write a brief comment.)

	Reason for success	Rearmament 1935	Rhineland 1936	*Anschluss* 1938	Sudetenland 1938	Czechoslovakia 1939	Nazi–Soviet Pact 1939	Poland 1939
Hitler's approach	Appearing reasonable; right on his side							
	Stirring up, exploiting internal unrest							
	Improvising							
	Good timing							
	Using intimidation, threats							
	Other methods							
Context	Potential opponents divided							
	Opponents weak							
	Other factors							

Make notes to prepare for the essay: 'Why was Hitler's foreign policy so successful 1933–9?'

1 First, do not just take the question at face value. Challenge any assumptions in the question. Was his foreign policy so successful? How might you assess this? You need to establish the criteria:
- Did he achieve his aims?
- Did his policy strengthen the position of Germany – territorially, economically, militarily, diplomatically?
- Was his foreign policy popular at home?

2 Hitler might score highly on these grounds, but you might also want to consider:
- Did he increase external opposition to Germany?
- Did he lead Germany into world war?
- Were his policies in the long-term interest of Germany?

3 You might order your material around the following points:
a) Hitler's strategy and ability
- Appearance of reasonableness
- Exploitation of internal unrest in other countries
- Improvisation
- Sense of timing
- Gradual escalation of demands
- Ruthlessness stemming from his conviction of the rightness of his cause and from his ideological vision

b) Germany's inherent might
- Expanding economic resources
- Growing military might
- Developing political unity

c) Context in which he was operating
- Weak opponents
- Britain overstretched, desperate to avoid war
- France internally divided, with a series of weak governments

d) Broader international context
- Weak, newly established regimes in eastern Europe
- Growing assertiveness of Mussolini; Italy's closer links with Germany and move away from Britain and France
- Soviet Union's priority of building up its own strength and avoiding a risky war with Germany
- Western powers' distrust of the USSR
- Western powers' fear of expansionist Japan
- Weak League of Nations
- Versailles increasingly criticised
- Widespread determination to prevent another war and support for appeasement.

KEY POINTS FROM CHAPTER 20: Why was Hitler's foreign policy so successful 1933–9?

1 Foreign policy was a major preoccupation for Hitler.
2 Hitler wanted to make Germany great by smashing Versailles, uniting all Germans and expanding in the east for *Lebensraum*.
3 The changing international context of the 1930s gave Hitler considerable opportunities for expansion.
4 Hitler proved skilful initially in appearing more reasonable than he was and in exploiting the West's appeasement policies.
5 For four years he had a series of major foreign policy successes: remilitarising the Rhineland, gaining Austria and destroying Czechoslovakia, without military opposition.
6 Hitler showed his flexibility in 1939 by making an alliance with the Soviet Union, which he considered his greatest opponent.
7 It was only with his invasion of Poland that Hitler, to his surprise, provoked Britain and France into declaring war.
8 There has been considerable debate over Hitler's responsibility for the Second World War.
9 Some historians argue that domestic factors were a major influence in causing the war (see Chapter 12).
10 Some historians argue that Hitler planned the war in advance, others that he was essentially an opportunist, with no clear plan. Probably the most convincing view is that he combined flexibility in his strategy with consistency of aims.

21

Why did Germany's initial success in war turn to defeat?

CHAPTER OVERVIEW

In this chapter we look briefly at three aspects of the Second World War: Germany's changing military fortunes between 1939 and 1945, the nature of the Nazi empire and developments within Germany. We have already considered some of the latter in previous chapters on domestic policy, so here we concentrate on the overall response of the German people.

We are not treating this period as thoroughly as the years 1933–9. This reflects many examination boards' concentration on the first six years of the Third Reich. Some historians have also argued that the earlier period shows the true nature of Nazism, before it became submerged in the overriding demands of war. Most historians, however, argue that the Second World War must be seen as the fulfilment of, rather than a diversion from, Nazism. In the Nazi *Weltanschauung* a war for national supremacy was inevitable, and Hitler set out to make Germany militarily and psychologically ready for war.

A Why was Germany so successful 1939–41?

FOCUS ROUTE

1 Study pages 406–8 and Chart 21A. List the reasons for Germany's successes.
2 What ominous signs were there for the Nazis by the end of 1941?

Although Hitler had been preparing Germany for conquest, it was not properly prepared for the sort of war it initially experienced in 1939. The anticipated local war he launched against Poland in September 1939 led to a European and eventually a worldwide conflict by 1941, several years sooner than Hitler had intended. Despite this miscalculation, the string of victories from September 1939 to November 1941 bear witness to the formidable military power exerted by the Nazi war machine at the time. By June 1940 Hitler had conquered a greater area of Europe than any other leader in history.

On 1 September 1939 Germany invaded Poland. On 17 September the USSR invaded from the east, met the Germans at Brest-Litovsk and together partitioned defeated Poland. Hitler was successful in Poland against a numerically superior army because of his Blitzkrieg tactics, using armoured columns on a narrow front, covered by dive bombers and supported by motor-borne infantry. The Poles could offer little resistance after the early air assaults. Their fate was sealed when the USSR attacked from the east and destroyed their defences. Britain and France had declared war in support of Poland, but in practice were not able to do anything to help.

Hitler's plans to move west in November were delayed by disagreements with some of his senior generals, although it is clear that his immediate aim was to neutralise the western democracies by beating France and getting the compliance of Britain, before turning east. The focus of attention moved north in early 1940 because of the strategic importance of Norway for both sides. Hitler needed to safeguard iron ore supplies from neutral Sweden that passed through Norway. In April 1940, he first occupied Denmark, which, with few national defences, put up no resistance. Norway was conquered in two weeks. Hitler installed the collaborator Vidkun Quisling as leader. Germany now had crucial Atlantic bases as well as secure ore supplies. Britain and France could do little to protect Norway, because a wholesale commitment in the far north would have made it hard to supply their own forces and would weaken the defences in France itself.

Holland and Belgium were the next target. Both countries depended on small armies which had little artillery and air support. Their defensive systems, reliant on rivers and canals, proved ineffective. On 10 May 1940 Germany attacked in the west. Holland fell in five days; Belgium in eighteen. France then felt the full fury of the German onslaught. Years of inadequate military preparation, over-reliance on the circumvented (evaded) Maginot Line and a defeatist (pessimistic) attitude meant that France surrendered within a month on 14 June. Germany occupied the north and the west coast. A puppet VICHY government was set up in the unoccupied south, which retained the French colonies. However, Hitler made the mistake of delaying his advance on Dunkirk for two days which allowed over 300,000 Allied troops to be evacuated to Britain.

Britain was now alone in Europe. Having achieved his primary objectives, Hitler hesitantly offered Britain peace in a speech to the Reichstag on 19 July when he appealed to the 'reason and common sense of Britain'. No compromise was acceptable to Winston Churchill, Britain's Prime Minister, and Hitler then ordered Operation Sealion, the invasion of Britain. In August Goering tried to establish air supremacy over the Channel ports but the Luftwaffe suffered heavy losses and Hitler postponed Sealion. Hitler experienced his first setback when the Battle of Britain was lost. The British victory was won because of a technically superior aeroplane, the Spitfire, and by the increasing use of radar. Furthermore, Hitler switched his aerial attacks from Britain's airfields to her cities on 7 September to try to break civilian morale. Great damage was done but morale held up and the airfields gained from the reprieve.

The Germans' relentless string of victories had been stalled, although, between August 1940 and February 1941, Hungary, Romania and Bulgaria were forced to become Nazi allies. Hitler then made the personal decision to switch the attack to the east against the USSR. It had always been part of Hitler's plans to capture the south of the Soviet Union and to take its rich cornfields and extensive supplies of raw materials. After his great victories in Europe, the ill-equipped Soviet troops did not appear to be too big an obstacle. Hitler's advisers suggested, on the basis of intelligence reports and the poor performance of the Soviet army in Finland in 1939–40, that an eight-week campaign should be sufficient to reach Moscow and bring the Soviet government to its knees.

However, Hitler was forced to delay his attack. Mussolini had attacked the British in North Africa in September 1940 and invaded Greece the following month but suffered setbacks. In February 1941 Hitler sent troops under General Rommel to Africa, temporarily reversing the tide of the North African war. In March he had to respond to a coup that had installed an anti-Nazi government in Yugoslavia. Hitler was fearful these developments might leave his vital oil supplies in Romania vulnerable to the RAF. He postponed his planned attack on the USSR by one month to attack Yugoslavia and Greece. Although Yugoslavia fell in eleven days and Greece in fifteen, the delay turned out to be fatal.

The massive German invasion of the USSR was finally launched on 22 June 1941. One hundred and eighty-seven German divisions, together with Finns and Romanians, invaded the Soviet Union in Operation Barbarossa. The Germans made rapid advances on three fronts, heading for Leningrad, Moscow and the Ukraine. In many western areas of the Soviet Union German troops were initially greeted as liberators, but Stalin rallied the Russian people in what came to be known as the Great Patriotic War. The Russians adopted a SCORCHED EARTH policy so that the Germans were forced to transport their own equipment over enormous distances. Over 40,000 km of railway track had to be either rebuilt or converted to German gauge in the central region alone. The delay in the Nazi attack meant that German troops suffered badly during the winter of 1941–2. They had not been equipped for a winter campaign. Their boots were too small for extra socks to be worn, and vehicles could only be kept from freezing by burning fires under them, wasting valuable fuel.

The German army was halted at Moscow and Leningrad in December 1941. Hitler's gamble on a quick victory had failed. He compounded his problems by declaring war on the USA after the Japanese attack on Pearl Harbor. This decision was to prove a decisive factor in the outcome of the war.

■ 21A The progress of war 1939–41

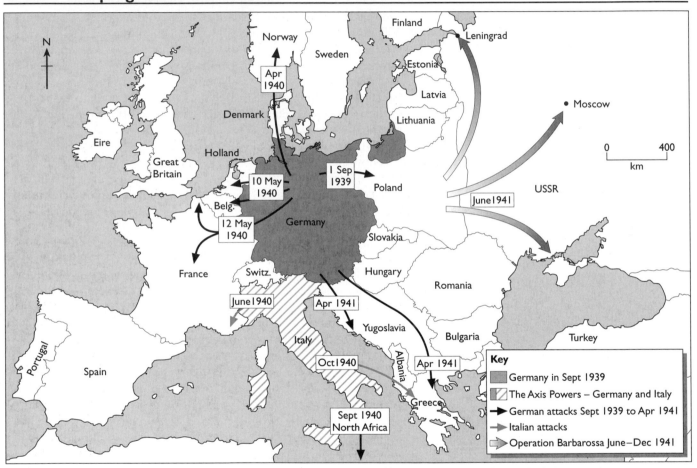

Germany's assets
- Speed and concentrated power of Blitzkrieg
- Attacked countries one by one
- Hitler's bold leadership
- Exploitation of foreign countries: e.g. Germany exacted 1.75 billion RM from France in 1940 and 5.6 billion in 1941, as well as raw materials
- In 1941 there were 3.3 million foreign workers in Germany

Opponents' weaknesses
- France demoralised
- USSR unprepared for sudden attack by its ally

FOCUS ROUTE

Read pages 408–9 and study Chart 21B. List the main reasons why Nazi Germany was eventually defeated.

B Why did Germany eventually fail?

After Hitler's great successes, 1942 was a year of mixed fortunes in both key war theatres, the Eastern Front and the Mediterranean. The more the war dragged on, the more the economic balance shifted against him, for Germany was fighting the two greatest powers in the world. Germany was overstretched, fighting not just in the USSR, but in North Africa and in the Atlantic. Germany's ruthless exploitation of its satellite and conquered territories could not match the potential resources of the Soviet Union and the United States.

In 1943 the tide moved against Germany after its massive defeat at Stalingrad. Already forced out of Africa, Germany had to fight in the USSR, in Italy and, from June 1944, in France. To virtually everyone bar Hitler, it was clear that defeat was only a matter of time. Hitler's last hopes failed to materialise. The use of his secret weapons, the V1 and V2 rockets, was stopped by the Allied invasion of Europe, and the USA–USSR alliance failed to break up. Defeat finally came with the Soviet occupation of Berlin in May 1945.

■ 21B The progress of the war in Europe 1942–5

(7) The tide turns in the Battle of the Atlantic. German U-boats have been having a serious effect on Britain's crucial Atlantic lifeline, but improved Allied technology and US air power leads to serious U-boat losses and diminishing Allied shipping losses.

(6) May 1943 First major Allied bombing of Germany, the British by night, Americans by day. Goering had boasted Germany would never be bombed, but now it has to face the full horror of aerial bombardment.

(14) 30 April 1945 Hitler commits suicide.
2 May Berlin captured by Soviet troops
7 May Germany accepts unconditional surrender.

(8) From 1943 onwards, Soviet troops continue to advance. In July 1943 they win the crucial battle of Kursk, the greatest tank battle ever.

(4) November 1942 Soviet counter-attack, but Hitler refuses to allow his Sixth Army to retreat. In January 1943, 300,000 Germans surrender at Stalingrad. Turning point in Russian campaign.

(11) June 1944 Allied troops land in Normandy on D-Day and steadily advance. In August Paris is liberated, but fuel problems and stiff German resistance delay the Allied advance.

(1) May 1942 New German offensive against Stalingrad and the Caucasus oil region. Germans advance 450 miles and capture much of the prestige city of Stalingrad.

(12) Dec 1944 German offensive in Ardennes eventually fails with great losses.

(10) By 1944 the Red Army has entered Poland, Romania and Bulgaria.

(5) November 1942 Anglo-American landing in Algeria. Make major advances. In May 1943, 250,000 Germans and Italians surrender.

(2) June 1942 General Rommel's combined Italian and German troops invade Egypt. Hitler sees the Mediterranean as a secondary consideration, and does not try to occupy the crucial British naval base of Malta.

(13) By the spring of 1945 Germany faces a major offensive from Soviet troops and from Anglo-American forces. Some German leaders try to make peace, but Hitler still believes in final victory. In March 1945 Hitler, finally accepting the inevitable, blames the Germans for their lack of spirit and issues a scorched earth order but this is undermined by Speer.

(9) July 1943 Anglo-American force lands in Sicily, then crosses to the southern mainland. Mussolini overthrown. The new Italian government signs an armistice, but Germany occupies most of Italy. The Germans stop the Allied advance south of Rome, but in 1944 are forced back.

(3) Germans in North Africa suffer fuel shortages. In September 1942 British counter-attack at El Alamein forces Axis retreat.

Key
✾ Main Allied bombing targets
→ Allied attacks

SOURCE 21.1 The bombing campaigns: bombs dropped

Date	On Germany	On Britain
1940	10,000	36,844
1941	30,000	21,858
1942	40,000	3,260
1943	120,000	2,298
1944	650,000	9,151
1945	500,000	761

Germany's weaknesses
• Hitler's self-delusion and disagreements with his generals
• War effort diverted by Mussolini's failings
• War on two fronts
• Mistake of war against the USA
• Economy not prepared for major conflict

FOCUS ROUTE

1 Study Chart 21D. List the main areas under the following categories:
   a) territories annexed to Germany
   b) allied states
   c) occupied states.
2 What does the account of Poland under Nazi control in Source 21.3 show about the way the Nazi regime operated?
3 What do the sources reveal about how the Nazis treated conquered peoples?
4 What does Source 21.6 suggest might be the consequences of such treatment?

C How did the Nazis treat their conquered territories?

The Nazi leadership saw the war as a 'racial war', in which the superior Aryans would triumph over the Slavs and other inferior groups, and the whole of Europe would become 'Jew free'. This racist view directly contributed to the brutality with which the Germans treated conquered territory. The Nazis' policy of naked exploitation, as opposed to fostering satellite states, alienated local populations, making it more difficult for the Germans to hold the territories. Thus the Nazis' racism contributed to their eventual defeat.

Mass murder began in 1939. Special *Einsatzgruppen* (see page 342) were created to kill Polish Communists, Jews and other 'undesirables', such as intellectuals. The campaign against the USSR in 1941 heralded even worse atrocities, with millions of 'undesirables' being shot by Wehrmacht units as well as by the *Einsatzgruppen*. Conquered peoples were brutally exploited for their labour and fed starvation rations.

Poland under Nazi rule

German policy towards Poland illustrates the semi-chaotic nature of the Nazi state that we have already encountered within Germany itself. When the Nazis invaded in 1939, they had not decided how to reorganise the Polish state. Their broad aim was to turn Poles into slaves to serve German needs. Hitler simply issued a general instruction to the *Gauleiter* that they had 'ten years to tell him that Germanisation of their provinces was complete and he would ask no questions about their methods'. The three main leaders were Artur Greiser in Warthegau, Albert Föster in West Prussia (the two areas fully incorporated into the Third Reich) and Hans Frank, in charge of the General Government (the name given by the Germans to the rest of the Polish territory they controlled and intended to use as a dumping ground for unwanted Poles).

The Nazis' priority was to use the Polish land incorporated into Germany to resettle ethnic Germans from the Baltic states and other territories now in the Soviet sphere, as agreed in the Nazi–Soviet Pact. Germans were told to treat Poles as inferiors, and to have minimum contact with them beyond using their labour. Local inhabitants were classified as to their suitability for the new German rule, according to their appearance, language and attitudes. Some were deemed worthy of becoming Germans; others were to be kept as workers for their new German masters; whilst Jews and other 'undesirables' were to be removed, initially into GHETTOS, and ultimately to the General Government.

In practice, what happened was somewhat chaotic, with improvisation and disagreements between top Nazis. Greiser was a hard-line Nazi and applied strict criteria for the Germanisation of Poles. Föster, however, declared whole groups Germanised without individual examination. His apparently greater success led Greiser to complain to Himmler about Föster's 'cheap successes by Germanising people who could not provide clear proof of their German origin'. Himmler agreed, warning, 'You know that one drop of false blood which comes into an individual's veins can never be removed.' Hitler refused to intervene, and the two *Gauleiter* continued their different approaches.

Greiser also came into conflict with Frank. Greiser wanted to rid his region of 'undesirables' as soon as possible, and like Himmler saw the General Government's main value as helping to Aryanise other German territories by being a dumping ground for unwanted people. Frank complained at the excessive number being dumped in his territory which he wanted to organise as the main source of grain for Germany.

Key
- ----- Polish boundary before 1 September 1939
- — — · Border between Germany and the USSR until 22 June 1941
- Annexed by Germany
- Annexed by the USSR
- Under German civil administration

0   100
km

In February 1940, top Nazis met to resolve the issue. Goering, economic overlord, supported Frank against Himmler and Greiser. Frank was told he had the final say over deportations. Himmler, however, got Hitler to agree to his broad vision of removing 'inferior people'. Madagascar was proposed as the final destination after the General Government, so deportations could continue. When military setbacks made this option unworkable, German policy shifted towards extermination. The overall effect of Nazi rule in Poland was the death of 6 million Poles (including nearly 3 million Jews), 18 per cent of the population.

Life under Nazi rule

■ 21D The Nazi empire at its peak in 1942

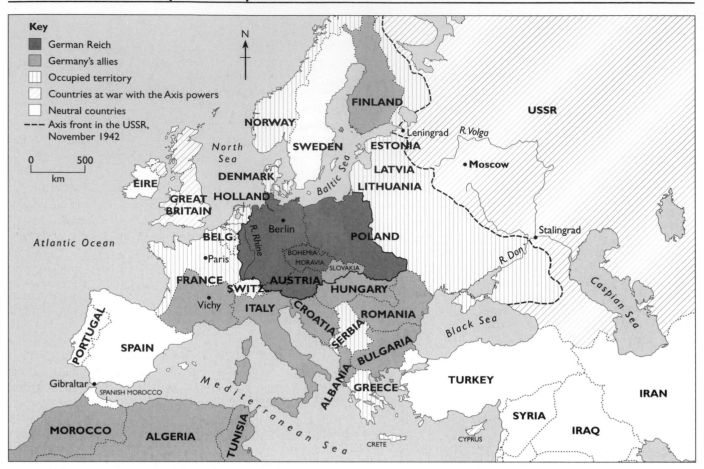

Key
- German Reich
- Germany's allies
- Occupied territory
- Countries at war with the Axis powers
- Neutral countries
- --- Axis front in the USSR, November 1942

0   500
km

The German master race

SOURCE 21.2   From *Hitler's Table Talk*, August 1941

What India is for England, the territories of Russia will be for us. If only I could make the German people understand what this space means for our future! . . . The German colonist ought to live on handsome, spacious farms. The Germans will be lodged in marvellous buildings, the Governors in palaces.

The conquered peoples

SOURCE 21.3   Hans Frank, Governor General of Poland (the General Government), in May 1940

The Führer told me that the implementation of German policy in Poland is a matter for the men who are in charge of the General Government to deal with themselves. He put it this way: We must liquidate those people whom we have discovered form the leadership of Poland; all those who follow in their footsteps must be arrested and then got rid of after an appropriate period. We do not need to burden the Reich [Government] . . . with that.

SOURCE 21.4   Letter from Martin Bormann, 1941

The Slavs are to work for us. In so far as we don't need them, they may die. Therefore compulsory vaccination and German health services are unnecessary. The fertility of the Slavs is undesirable. They may use contraceptives or practise abortion, the more the better. Education is dangerous. It is enough if they can count up to one hundred. Every educated person is a future enemy . . . As for food, they won't get any more than is absolutely necessary. We are the masters. We come first.

SOURCE 21.5   An order from Hitler, September 1941

The Führer has decided to have Leningrad wiped off the face of the earth ... In this war for existence we have no interest in keeping even part of this great city's population.

SOURCE 21.7   Otto Ohlendorf, a German soldier who had been in charge of *Einsatzgruppen* in the east, described events at his 1946 trial

The Einsatz unit would enter a village or town and order prominent Jewish citizens to call together all Jews for the purpose of resettlement. They were asked to hand over their valuables and shortly before execution to surrender their outer clothing. They were taken to the place of execution, usually an anti-tank ditch ... Then they were shot, kneeling or standing, by firing squads in a military manner and the corpses thrown into the ditch.

SOURCE 21.6   A German soldier on leave told his wife of conditions on the Eastern Front. From Else Wendel, *Hausfrau at War*

'At first it was fine,' Rudolf went on. 'We swept on, adding towns and villages by the score. Then the troops began to get stale. Do you know how we behaved to the civilians? ...

'We behaved like devils out of hell. We left those villagers to starve to death behind us, thousands and thousands of them. How can you win a war in this way? Do you think they won't revenge themselves somehow? Of course they will ...'

We sat in awful silence for a moment. Then Rudolf went on to tell us more details of the partisans behind the lines.

'We shoot the prisoners on the slightest excuse,' he said. 'Just stick them up against the wall and shoot the lot. We order the whole village to look while we do it, too ... It's a vicious circle. We hate them, they hate us. And on and on it goes, everything getting more and more inhuman.

'Another of our mistakes was in the Ukraine. I was one of those who marched in to be received, not as a conqueror but as a friend. The civilians were all ready to look on us as saviours. They had years of oppression from the Soviets. They thought we had come to free them. Does it sound absurd? Perhaps it does. What did we do? Turn them into slaves under Hitler.

'You can take my word for it, Else, if the Russians should ever knock at this door and only pay back one half of what we have done to them, you wouldn't ever smile or sing again.'

SOURCE 21.8   Himmler to SS officers at Posen in 1943

We must be honest, decent, loyal and comradely to members of our own blood, but to nobody else. What happens to a Russian or to a Czech does not interest me in the slightest. What the nations can offer in the way of good blood of our type, we will take, if necessary by kidnapping their children and raising them here with us. Whether nations live in prosperity or starve to death interests me only in so far as we need them for slaves for our Kultur; otherwise, it is of no interest to me. Whether 10,000 Russian females fall down from exhaustion digging an anti-tank ditch interests me only in so far as the anti-tank ditch for Germany is finished ... It is a crime against our blood to worry about them.

SOURCE 21.9
The destruction
of Lidice
(see page 341)

D How well did the Nazi state cope with the demands of war?

We now turn to look at developments on the domestic front. You may have already studied aspects of life in Germany during the war in earlier chapters. The table below summarises the key points and directs you back to where these issues have been addressed. In this chapter we will discuss issues that shed particular light on the nature of the regime.

Aspect	Summary of developments	Chapter
Popularity of Hitler	After initial increase, decline in power of Hitler myth	11
Repression	Increased power of SS	11
Economy	Inefficiencies of Blitzkrieg economy 1939–41; improved efficiency under Speer 1942–5	12
Propaganda	Increased government control of media; series of escapist films	13
Youth	Increasing militarisation of Hitler Youth creates some fanatical soldiers but also sees the growth of non/anti-Nazi groups, e.g. Swing	14
Women	Some increase in women's employment; reluctance to conscript women	15
Churches	Some relaxation of pressure, through concern not to alienate the population; growth in church attendance as war goes badly	16
Opposition	Series of plots in military, especially July 1944 Bomb Plot; White Rose movement	17
Outsiders	Escalation of measures against outsiders, starting with euthanasia in 1939; the beginning of the killing of Jews	18

How well initially did the regime organise the wartime economy?

When war started in 1939 there were many indications of inefficiency in the Nazi economy. One of the most surprising features of the early war economy was the fact that there was no coherent overall plan for the allocation of resources to meet a clear strategy. The Nazi economy was characterised by shortages, bottlenecks, duplication and waste. In 1940 Britain spent only half as much as Germany but produced 50 per cent more aircraft, eleven times more armoured cars and nearly as many tanks. There was fierce rivalry between the main branches of the armed forces (Wehrmacht, Luftwaffe, navy) and even within these branches. Furthermore, there was a lack of standardisation, with different branches of the armed forces using different equipment, a reflection of the lack of overall control. In theory, Hitler had the power to fulfil this role, but he failed to co-ordinate effectively and allowed different power centres to compete.

Throughout the war, Hitler's idiosyncratic (individual) style of government hindered the effective utilisation of resources. He put excessive faith in his so-called miracle weapons, the V1 and V2 rockets, and failed to exploit Germany's technical advantage in jet aircraft. The development of the potentially war-winning ME262 fighter suffered initially from Hitler's preoccupation with the rockets. When eventually persuaded of the ME262's potential, he insisted the plane be developed as a bomber not a fighter. The regime's anti-semitism also weakened Germany. The nuclear weapons development programme was fatally harmed by the exodus of several key Jewish scientists, and by Nazi scientists' rejection of particle physics as a Jewish theory. The use of railways for the transportation of Jews to camps hindered their utilisation for military purposes.

Furthermore, military requirements still had to compete with the regime's other plans, such as Hitler's grandiose (overlarge) public buildings schemes and the regime's concern to maintain civilian morale by keeping the production of consumer goods and food supplies close to pre-war levels. A classic example of the failure of the so-called totalitarian Nazi state to organise the country effectively can be seen over the crucial issue of the use of labour. Despite a severe shortage of labour, the Nazis initially failed to use what was available. Most women remained in their pre-war roles, because Nazi ideology took precedence over economic need. This reluctance to exploit women's labour was also due to concern that the mass movement of women into industrial production might lower the morale of troops. Even male labour was not effectively utilised. Most factories ran only one or two shifts, instead of a possible three.

Some of the problems began to be tackled when Fritz Todt was appointed Minister for Armaments and Munitions in 1940. He imposed a pragmatic compromise between military requirements and industrial capacity. The underlying principle was industrial self-responsibility (*Selbstverantwortung*), giving industrialists greater control over production and reducing military interference. After Todt's death, this approach was developed by Albert Speer.

Fritz Todt 1891–1942

Fritz Todt trained as an engineer and was wounded in the air corps in the First World War. He joined the Nazis in 1923 and became a colonel on Himmler's staff. He was a strong advocate of creating jobs by public works and in 1933 he was put in charge of the new autobahn programme, directing the building of over 3,000 kilometres of autobahn by 1939, with a further 1,600 under construction. In 1938 he became general plenipotentiary for all public construction works. His responsibility spread from roads to fortifications, docks, harbours and waterways. By 1941 the Todt organisation had 800,000 men in the USSR and 250,000 men at work on the West Wall, the Atlantic fortifications which used 800,000 tons of concrete a month. In 1940 he was appointed Minister for Armaments and Munitions and had begun to improve the efficiency of Germany's war economy.

Todt was a technician with great organisational ability rather than a politician. He was the first top Nazi to lose faith in Hitler's adventurism and thought Hitler's biggest mistake was to declare war on the USA, which Germany could never match for industrial potential. He did not like the maltreatment of Soviet prisoners of war and could not convince Hitler that Soviet tanks were better than German ones. He twice told Hitler that the war was unwinnable. On 8 February 1942 he was killed when his plane crashed after take-off from Hitler's headquarters at Rastenburg.

How did Speer improve Germany's war economy?

FOCUS ROUTE

Study Chart 21E and pages 416–17; then copy and complete the following table.

Problem (see Chart 21E)	Details of problem (from text)	How Speer tried to tackle it

Over the next three years, from 1942 to 1945, Speer revolutionised the economy's performance despite increasingly adverse circumstances. The armed forces had to submit their requirements to Speer's ministry, which possessed more accurate information on the current state of industrial production. Requirements and capacities were thus co-ordinated, and it was possible to tailor orders more closely to both.

At his first Führer conference, Speer managed to issue a decree punishing arms manufacturers who made false claims for labour, parts, equipment or raw materials. Typically, there were objections from people who felt their areas of responsibility were being infringed, such as Goering and Justice Minister Otto Thierack.

Speer was concerned to prioritise more effectively. He campaigned against the allocation of vital resources to non-military uses, and placed a ban on all plans for post-war construction. He had a rubber stamp made inscribed with the words 'Return to sender – irrelevant to the war effort', which he used on orders for non-essential products. On a train trip to Hitler's headquarters in 1942, Speer detached an array of unnecessary metal fittings, such as clothes hangers and reading lamps; he ordered that such items should be stripped from trains and sent for scrap metal. He also brought in greater standardisation in the use of ammunition, and rationalised transport production, for example concentrating production on only three types of lorry. He also reduced wasteful stockpiles.

Speer tried to tackle the disruptive autonomy of the *Gauleiter*, who were the biggest obstacles to a total war effort. His position as minister in itself cut little ice with these powerful local figures, but his close links to Hitler boosted his authority. He was also prepared to use blackmail, for instance threatening a *Gauleiter* with no coal supplies if he did not help with food supply.

Speer made considerable strides in the more effective utilisation of available labour. He pressed for the increased use of three shifts a day and for the

■ 21E Problems of the war economy

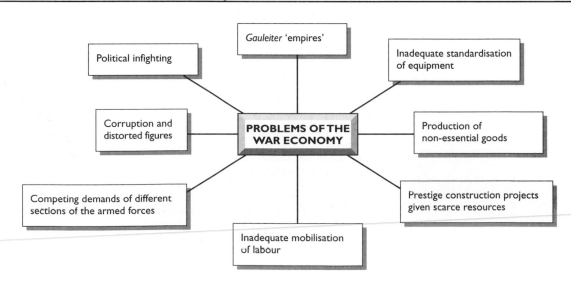

efficient use of foreign labour in the countries of origin rather than in Germany itself. Concentration camp labour was extended, but other Nazis still resisted his attempts to exploit female labour effectively. Speer showed how this compared unfavourably with the Allies' war effort, and eventually half a million women were taken out of domestic employment and put to more productive use.

In other areas, he had only partial success. He frequently complained that key production was being disrupted by the conscription of skilled workers. However, even when, in May 1943, he gained Hitler's promise to block military recruitment of skilled workers, this failed to have the desired effect. Speer's efforts were also hindered by perennial (constant) Nazi infighting. He had hoped his associate Hanke would be granted power as Labour Deployment Commissioner, but he was baulked by Bormann and Lammers who engineered their man into the position.

Speer's achievements in greatly increasing production were all the more remarkable considering the escalation of the Allied bombing campaign. He set up special task forces to repair bombed factories. Temporary accommodation for workers could go up in a day. To some extent, he was helped by Allied mistakes. British area bombing failed to break German morale, and the impact of American daytime bombing was reduced by their failure to follow up raids. Speer later commented that unrelenting attacks on the ball-bearing industry, especially the key factory at Schweinfurt, would have brought the Wehrmacht to a halt in four months.

SOURCE 21.10 Production of combat aircraft

	Germany	Britain
1941	1,030	20,100
1942	14,700	23,600
1943	25,520	26,200
1944	35,950	26,500 (but 110,752 in USA)

Effects
Within six months of Speer's appointment in 1942

- ammunition output rose by 97 per cent
- tank production rose by 25 per cent
- arms productivity went up 60 per cent.

Between 1941 and 1944

- production of tanks increased from 2,875 to 17,328
- ammunition production increased sixfold.

Did the Nazi regime become more efficient during the war?
Although Speer gradually improved the efficiency of the war economy during 1942–5, the same improvement cannot be seen in the way the state was run. The Nazi state continued its haphazard development, with the growth of new bodies, such as the Armaments Ministry, and ongoing personal struggles, both at the centre and between the *Gauleiter* and the centre. Recent historians have stressed a process of 'cumulative radicalisation' that continued during the war, driven by Hitler's vision of conquest and racial warfare, and by the competition between Nazi leaders to 'work towards the Führer'.

The German historian Dieter Rebentisch, in his masterly *Der Führerstaat im Zweiten Weltkrieg* (The Führer State in the Second World War), has analysed Hitler's total and arbitrary dominance of the regime, arguing that it was 'Hitler's regime, Hitler's policies, Hitler's victories and Hitler's defeat'. Formal state structures were increasingly bypassed. Meetings, such as Hitler's periodic meetings with the *Gauleiter*, were audiences for his speeches, not part of the decision-making process. The struggle between feudal chiefs, with victory going to the strongest, intensified.

The power of the SS continued to grow. Bormann, who replaced Hess as Hitler's secretary, developed his power base to become the second most powerful person in Germany, controlling as he did access to Hitler. Hitler himself became increasingly remote; he was rarely seen in public, and spent most of his time at his military headquarters, Wolfsschanze (Wolf's Lair), in Rastenburg, East Prussia.

E How did the German people view the war?

There is much evidence that initially the German people were wary of war. The lack of enthusiasm for war and rejoicing at the securing of peace were evident during the Munich crisis in 1938. However, the great and relatively painless successes of 1939–40 won most Germans over, and on his victorious return from France Hitler was greeted rapturously.

However, Hitler remained cautious about the German people's commitment to war, and he hoped to win the war without imposing too great a strain on the country. Limited rationing was introduced in 1939, along with increased taxes, but there was no major clampdown on public consumption. By 1942, however, there were far more controls and more sacrifices were necessary. Goebbels was given the job of persuading Germans to accept them. In a speech in February 1943 he inspired his audience to apparent enthusiasm for 'total war'.

SOURCE 21.11 From Goebbels' speech at the Berlin Sport Palace, February 1943

I ask you: do you believe with the Führer and with us in the final victory of the German people? I ask you: Are you determined to follow the Führer through thick and thin in the struggle for victory and to put up even with the heaviest personal burdens? ...

I ask you: Do you want total war? Do you want it, if necessary, more total and more radical than we can imagine it today?

[The crowd roared its approval.]

ACTIVITY

Study Sources 21.11 and 21.12. How does Goebbels try to gain support for the war? How might the location help achieve the desired effect?

SOURCE 21.12 Goebbels speaking at the Berlin Sport Palace in February 1943

The government, via the SD, continued to monitor popular feelings closely, and several of its reports reveal considerable nervousness over popular reactions, especially when it became increasingly clear that the war was going badly. The government was concerned about reaction to the brutal nature of the war in the east, and there was a mixed response to increased Allied bombing. Contrary to British hopes, there was little evidence of a collapse of morale undermining the Nazi war effort, but there was increased grumbling and more widespread expression of opposition. However, at no time was there a popular threat to the regime. The internal threat when it came was from the army elite (see pages 322 and 324).

SOURCE 21.13 In her autobiography, *The Past is Myself* (1968), Christabel Bielenberg, an English woman married to a German, wrote about the experience of the bombing in 1943

I learned when I was living in Berlin that those wanton, quite impersonal killings, that barrage from the air which mutilated, suffocated and destroyed, did not so much breed fear and a desire to bow before the storm, but rather a fatalistic cussedness [obstinacy], a dogged determination to survive and, if possible, help others to survive, whatever their politics, whatever their creed.

TALKING POINT

Can the bombing of cities, such as happened at Hamburg and Dresden, be justified?

SOURCE 21.14   A German witness of the Allied air raid on Hamburg, 28 July 1943

It is hard to imagine the panic and chaos ... Most people loaded some belongings on carts, bicycles, prams or carried things on their backs, and started on foot, just to get away, to escape. People who were wearing [Nazi] party badges had them torn off their coats and there were screams of 'let's get that murderer'. The police did nothing.

SOURCE 21.15   Government summary of *Gauleiter* reports, spring 1943

The rumour mongers are still with us, or more correctly they are busier than ever ... An especially dangerous aspect of this situation is the fact that some people are openly risking criticism of the Führer himself, attacking him in the most hateful, vulgar manner. Unfortunately, too many of our countrymen blabber and repeat everything they are told ... Again and again the sad observation has to be made that our party members often exhibit an unbelievable indolence and laxity; they witness subversive [destructive] enemy propaganda but seldom muster the courage to strike a blow.

SOURCE 21.16   SD report from Franconia, December 1942

One of the strongest causes of unease among those attached to the Church and in the rural population is at the present time formed by news from Russia in which shooting and extermination of the Jews is spoken about. The news frequently leaves great anxiety, care and worry in those sections of the population. According to widely held opinion in the rural population, it is not at all certain that we will win the war, and if the Jews come again to Germany, they will exact dreadful revenge upon us.

SOURCE 21.17
German wartime atrocities: from the underground newsletter *The Freedom Fighter*. Part of the text is below

Innocent Russian women, men and children were dragged by SS bandits to the place of execution.

A Russian family a few metres from the mass grave of innocent murdered people. The terror-stricken woman desperately protests her innocence.

**In the name of the German people!
In the name of every German!**

**How much longer are you prepared to tolerate this shame?
Bring down Hitler!
Fight the SS and the Gestapo!
Stop this tyranny!**

The family at the edge of the mass grave ...

This is where SS gangsters shot a young Russian mother ...

A Russian woman is shot ...

SOURCE 21.18   A Nazi poster: 'Adolf Hitler is victory!'

Adolf Hitler ist der Sieg!

SOURCE 21.19   Opposition poster: 'Homeland destroyed. Family dead. Overthrow Hitler. Fight for peace!'

DIE HEIMAT ZERSTÖRT DIE FAMILIE TOT STÜRZT HITLER KÄMPFT FÜR DEN FRIEDEN!

SOURCE 21.20   Extract from a leaflet distributed by the White Rose group, February 1942

Hitler is leading the German people into the abyss with calculable certainty. He cannot win the war, merely prolong it. His guilt, and that of his accomplices, extends beyond all known bounds. His just retribution [punishment] approaches.

But what does the German people do? Germans see and hear nothing. They blindly follow their leader to their ruin. 'Victory at any price' is the slogan on their flags. 'I shall fight to the last man,' says Hitler – when the war is, in fact, already lost.

Germans! Do you and your children wish to suffer the same fate as that which has already befallen the Jews? Do you want to be judged by the same standards as those leaders who have led you astray? No! Disassociate yourselves, therefore, from the depravity of National Socialism. Act to show that you reject it ... Do not succumb to National Socialist propaganda which has terrified you with its Bolshevik bogeymen. Stop believing that Germany's security is bound up inevitably with the victory of National Socialism. Disassociate yourselves with everything concerned with Nazism, while there is still time.

ACTIVITY

1   Explain the different views of Hitler in Sources 21.18 and 21.19.
2   How could Sources 21.17 and 21.20 be used both by historians who are highly critical of Germans during the Third Reich and by those with a more positive view of German history?
3   What do Sources 21.11–20 show about how the Germans reacted to the war?
4   What does this suggest about the extent to which Hitler succeeded in creating a true *Volksgemeinschaft*?

Why did the Germans fight to the end?

> **FOCUS ROUTE**
>
> 1 What do Sources 21.21–23 suggest as to why the Germans kept fighting to the end?
> 2 What other reasons were there?

In July 1943 the Italian Fascist Grand Council, knowing that the war was lost, voted to dismiss Mussolini. King Victor Emmanuel III dismissed him as Prime Minister and he was arrested. Nazi Germany, on the other hand, continued to fight when all was lost, and no one removed Hitler. The result of this was to bring great and unnecessary destruction upon Germany. As many Germans died in the last year of the war as in the previous four.

There are many reasons for this difference between the fate of the two dictators. Firstly, whereas Mussolini could be removed legally by the King, there was no legal way of removing Hitler. It was also hard to replace him by a revolt. Increasingly, only a few top Nazis and officers had access to him. A brave minority, realising the war was lost, tried and failed to remove him, but the July 1944 Bomb Plot may, in fact, have increased Hitler's popularity, as letters from the front seem to testify. Most officers still felt bound by their oaths to Hitler. Staff at the Führer's headquarters claimed that despite failing health he could still dominate people with his personality. Many Germans were still in the grip of a man whom they had viewed as a virtual messiah for ten years. The regime also survived through terror. Five thousand people were executed in the aftermath of the July Bomb Plot (see page 324), and any criticism could lead to fierce repression, especially from the Flying COURTS MARTIAL, formed to ensure discipline as defeat loomed.

Another reason for the continuation of the fighting was that most top Nazis were deeply involved in war crimes and could not expect leniency from the Allies, who offered no terms but unconditional surrender. Growing awareness of the horrors of the Eastern Front and fear of what the USSR would do if Germany were defeated was another major factor buttressing German resistance. As the Soviet troops advanced inexorably, thousands of German civilians committed suicide.

The Nazis' racial state also convinced many Germans to see themselves as a superior race and so made them determined to defend the regime against their inferior enemies. Many probably believed the propaganda that the fate of the German nation in its struggle against the Jews depended on winning the war. There was also a determination not to repeat the experience of 1918, when the collapse of morale had led to the hated Versailles settlement.

SOURCE 21.21 An ex-Eastern Front officer, Graf von Kielmansegg

All those who had been in Russia at least knew what Germany could expect if Bolshevism came to Germany ... If it had only been England and France, we would have stopped earlier in a simplified manner. Not against Russia.

SOURCE 21.22 An ex-Eastern Front soldier, Hermann Teshemacher

We told ourselves that there's a storm over Asia and it will come over Germany, and then brutal extermination, mistreatment and killings would follow, we knew that. So we defended ourselves to the end and remained loyal to the oath ... The worst would have been if Bolshevism stormed over Germany – then the whole of Europe would be lost. But first and foremost we thought about ourselves and our families and that is why we defended ourselves to the end.

SOURCE 21.23 Heino Vopel was a 19-year-old lance-corporal fighting a forlorn rearguard action in 1944

We had a driver from Munich in our team who was 32 and had two children. He was always saying 'This is madness – why don't they just give up? We haven't got a chance.' But we younger ones were still hopeful and we had been influenced by propaganda since our time in the Hitler Youth [so] that we thought we could never go under.

TALKING POINTS

1 If Hitler had been blown up in July 1944, how much difference do you think this would have made?
2 The British government drew up various plans to assassinate Hitler. Do you think it should have implemented them?

TALKING POINT

An estimated 1 million German soldiers deserted in the First World War. Very few did so in the Second World War. What explanation could you offer?

F   Death of a dictator

On 7 September 1944 the main party newspaper, the *Völkischer Beobachter*, carried an editorial personally instigated by Hitler. It called on Germans to ensure that the enemy found 'every footbridge destroyed, every road blocked – nothing but death, annihilation and hate will meet him'. This theme became increasingly dominant in his thoughts as the German army was pushed back on all fronts. Six months later, in March 1945, he told Speer: 'If the war is lost, the people will be lost also . . . For the nation has proved to be the weaker, and the future belongs to the stronger eastern nation. In any case only the inferior will survive this struggle since the good have already been killed.'

Hitler's last hours

SOURCE 21.24
The last known photograph of Hitler

SOURCE 21.25   Staff officer Captain Boldt was taken aback by the wretched physical state of the Führer in 1945

His head sways slightly. His left arm hangs down as if paralysed, the hand trembling all the time. His eyes shine in an indescribable way, suggesting almost inhuman anguish. His face and the pockets under his eyes show how tired he is, and how exhausted. He moves like an old man.

In late April 1945 Hitler was the only man left in Germany claiming that the war could end in victory. Clearly this was not the judgement of a sane man. On 20 April, on his fifty-sixth birthday, Hitler once more rejected several strategies to stop the fighting. Next day he ordered SS General Steiner to launch a counter-attack against the Soviet army outside Berlin. General Steiner said it was impossible. Hitler burst into one of his terrible rages: 'I have been betrayed by the SS. This is something I should never have expected! By the SS!'

On 29 April, just after midnight, Hitler married Eva Braun. In the next hours he dictated his final will. It contained not the slightest self-examination or conflict of conscience. When saying goodbye to his staff Hitler remarked, 'National Socialism is dead. We have lost the game. All that remains is for us to die worthily.'

SOURCE 21.26   Hitler's Political Testament, set down in Berlin, 29 April 1945

It is false that I wanted war in 1939. The war was sought and provoked exclusively by international Jewish politicians belonging to the Jewish race or working for the Jews. The numerous offers that I made to disarm are there to testify before posterity that the responsibilities for the war cannot be ascribed to me. I said often enough after the First World War that I had no desire at all to fight with Great Britain. Nor did I want war with the United States. In times to come the ruins of our cities will keep alive hatred for those who bear the real responsibility for our martyrdom; the agents of international Jewry . . .
I call upon the leadership of the nation and those who follow to observe the racial laws most carefully, to fight mercilessly against the poisons of the peoples of the world, international Jewry.

On 29 April, in the afternoon, Hitler heard the news of Mussolini's death the day before. He then made arrangements for his own death, as described below.

■ 21F   The events of 30 April 1945

- **2 a.m.** Hitler receives at his own request all the women who work in the bunker – secretaries, cooks and chambermaids. He wishes while still alive to hear their condolences on his approaching death.
- **10 a.m.** Hitler, dressed in a brand-new uniform and wearing his iron cross and gold party badge, asks Hans Linge, his valet, for the latest news. Linge reports: 'All resistance has ceased nearly everywhere. The Russian vice gripping Berlin is unbreakable. The Russians will be here tomorrow at the latest.'
- Artur Axmann, leader of the Hitler Youth, offers a tank for one last chance of escape. The offer is rebuffed.
- **Lunch** – Hitler lunches with Eva Braun.
- Hitler says his last goodbyes. Hearing that Goebbels and his wife are to kill their six children as well as themselves, Hitler unpins his gold party badge and fastens it on Frau Goebbels' dress, kissing her as he does so.
- Hitler goes to his quarters.
- **3.35 p.m.** A shot is heard.
- **3.40 p.m.** Linge goes to Hitler's room where he says he finds Hitler who has shot himself and Braun who has been poisoned. Later Soviet evidence seems to discount a gunshot wound and suggests poison for both of them.
- Linge and three others take the bodies out of the bunker and attempt to burn them, using 180 litres of petrol. (Hitler did not want his body kicked around as Mussolini's had been.) The partly burnt bodies are placed in a shell hole. Later on, Soviet forces find the bodies and take them away for identification.

SOURCE 21.27   Lawrence Rees, in *The Nazis. A Warning from History*, p. 236, summarises the end of the regime

The Nazis and their leader were motivated at the core by hatred and had created a structure within which the most evil ideas in modern history could grow and flourish. In the end Hitler's own hatred had turned on the Germans he ruled and, like a fire, had ended by consuming itself – a fitting and predictable end for Hitler and the Nazi Party. Born of crisis and hatred they had died in crisis and hatred.

ACTIVITY

1   How can you reconcile Hitler's comments about Germans in 1945 with the view of Hitler as a German nationalist?
2   What does Hitler's behaviour in his last few days suggest about him?

 G   Review: Why did Germany's initial success in war turn to defeat?

KEY POINTS FROM CHAPTER 21: Why did Germany's initial success in war turn to defeat?

1   Hitler had not planned on a world war starting in 1939.
2   The Nazis' Blitzkrieg tactics were initially very successful in 1939–40.
3   The Germans nearly succeeded in defeating the Soviet Union in 1941, but then became bogged down.
4   To declare war on the USA in 1941 when Germany was tied down in the USSR was a crucial mistake.
5   From 1943 the tide of war turned against Germany.
6   The Nazis' horrific mistreatment of conquered peoples contributed to their eventual defeat.
7   The German economy was not fully mobilised for the initial war effort.
8   Speer considerably improved production of war supplies after 1942.
9   Although there was increasing grumbling by Germans, they fought on doggedly until the end.
10   At the end Hitler wanted all Germany to be destroyed with him.

section

4

Conclusion

So where has the Third Reich left Germany and the world? It is arguable that no regime, with the possible exception of the Soviet Union, has made such an impact on history. Germans are still coming to terms with their past; eastern Europe is only now breaking free from the communism which was imposed by the Soviet Union in the wake of Hitler's defeat. On a broader basis, the knowledge that such horrors as the Holocaust could be committed has made us all aware of the fragile humanity of mankind. Here we examine various aspects of the legacy of Hitler's Germany.

The cost of the Second World War (estimated)			
	Casualties		
	Military	**Civilian**	**Total**
UK	326,000	62,000	388,000
USA	500,000	–	500,000
USSR	13,600,000	7,000,000	20,600,000
Germany	3,250,000	3,600,00	6,850,000
Italy	330,000	80,000	410,000

22

The legacy of the Third Reich

SOURCE 22.1 A cartoon published in the *St Louis Post*

WITNESSES FOR THE PROSECUTION

The Allied leaders were divided upon virtually everything apart from their determination to punish the leading Nazis. Their decision in August 1945 to put the Nazi ringleaders on trial was endorsed by the infant United Nations. The International Military Tribunal (with judges from the four main Allied nations) indicted (charged) 24 leading Nazis on four counts:

1 Crimes against peace
2 Crimes against humanity
3 War crimes
4 Conspiracy to commit the crimes alleged in the first three counts.

Of the 24 charged, Robert Ley committed suicide in prison on 25 October 1945 before the trial began; Gustav Krupp von Bohlen und Halback, the armaments manufacturer, was considered physically and mentally unfit to stand trial; Martin Bormann had escaped and was tried in his absence.

Hitler, Goebbels and Himmler had committed suicide in May 1945 and so escaped indictment and punishment.

■ 22A   The Nuremberg verdicts

The trial lasted from November 1945 until October 1946. The verdicts are given in the table below.

Accused	Verdict (on which counts)	Punishment
Martin Bormann* (in absentia)	Guilty 2, 3	Death
Karl Doenitz	Guilty 1	10 years' imprisonment
Hans Frank	Guilty 2	Death
Wilhelm Frick	Guilty 2	Death
Hans Fritzsche	Not guilty	Acquitted
Walther Funk	Guilty 1, 2	Life imprisonment
Hermann Goering*	Guilty all 4	Death†
Rudolph Hess*	Guilty 1, 4	Life imprisonment
Alfred Jodl	Guilty all 4	Death
Ernst Kaltenbrunner	Guilty 2	Death
Wilhelm Keitel	Guilty all 4	Death
Konstantin von Neurath*	Guilty all 4	15 years' imprisonment
Franz von Papen*	Not guilty	Acquitted
Erich Raeder	Guilty 1, 2	Life imprisonment
Joachim von Ribbentrop*	Guilty all 4	Death
Alfred Rosenberg*	Guilty all 4	Death
Fritz Sauckel	Guilty 1, 2	Death
Hjalmar Schacht*	Not guilty	Acquitted
Baldur von Schirach*	Guilty 2	20 years' imprisonment
Artur Seyss-Inquart	Guilty 1, 2	Death
Albert Speer*	Guilty 2, 3	20 years' imprisonment
Julius Streicher	Guilty 2	Death

* Biography earlier in this book.
† Committed suicide the night before his execution.

ACTIVITY

Choose two Nazis who were condemned to death and two who were acquitted; from what you have learnt about their roles, suggest reasons for the contrasting verdicts.

In a series of trials lasting for several years, thousands of other Nazis were tried. The Gestapo, SS and SD were condemned as criminal organisations.

There has been considerable debate whether the Nazis were the victims of 'victors' justice'; but it can be argued that the nature of the war they conducted was such as to fully justify their treatment. Similar trials took place in Japan but not in Italy. Trials of alleged Nazi war criminals have continued in other countries into the 1990s. The Nuremberg precedent was followed in Yugoslavia in the 1990s.

TALKING POINTS

1   'Victors' revenge' or 'upholding morality'? Do you think trials should be held after the end of wars if atrocities have been committed?
2   Some Germans argued that Soviet leaders and even British leaders ought to have been accused of war crimes. Can you see any logic in this?
3   Which other political leaders of the twentieth century do you think ought to have been tried for war crimes?

TALKING POINT

Can the Allied post-war indoctrination and propaganda exercise be justified?

B Denazification

The Western Allies embarked upon a programme of converting the Germans from Nazism to democracy. As part of this process Germans were shown the horrors of the camps virtually on their doorsteps. The Nazi Party was declared illegal. Millions of Germans had to fill in questionnaires as a part of a policy of trying to exclude committed Nazis from important positions in post-war Germany. Thousands of colleges were set up to re-educate adults. Unrepentant Nazi teachers were replaced, others were retrained, and new textbooks were written. The Allies controlled the press, radio and films.

SOURCE 22.3 German civilians being shown the extermination ovens at Belsen concentration camp as part of the post-war Allied re-education programme

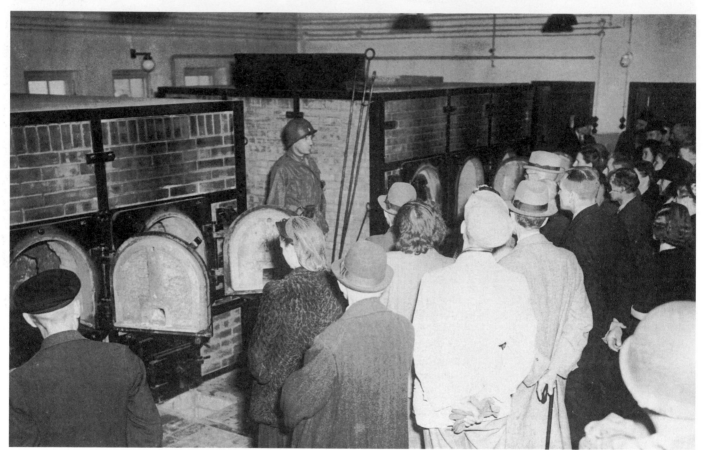

The circumstances of the Cold War, however, meant that many former Nazis were deemed valuable resources, especially by the USA, in the struggle against communism, and were quickly rehabilitated (reintegrated into society). Surveys of Germans' opinions suggest that eventual acceptance of the evil of Nazism was combined with continued acceptance of what was seen as its positive side. Some historians argue that the denazification programme was a failure, mainly on the grounds that it was not necessary. It could be argued that more Germans were committed to Hitler as a leader than to Nazi ideology, and that even this was weakening in the face of military defeat. The fostering of democracy in Germany was further helped by the economic success of the new Federal Republic.

SOURCE 22.4 M. Balfour, Chief of Information Services 1945–7, commented in 1985 on the impact of denazification in its first years

Thirty per cent of [Germans] retained their faith in Hitler till very near the end. The proportion of those progressing to think Nazism 'a good thing badly carried out' never dropped below 42 per cent between November 1945 and January 1948. There is good evidence that 10 per cent of the adult male population remained convinced Nazis – 4 million people.

ACTIVITY

1 What is your reaction, as a history student, to Source 22.5?
2 How do you think you would have reacted to the cartoon if you had been a student in Britain in 1943?

Neo-Nazism

For the overwhelming majority of Germans, full knowledge of the horrors of the Holocaust has permanently discredited Nazism. However, as late as the 1950s surveys of opinions still showed considerable nostalgia for the 'good' aspects of the Hitler regime before its excesses. Given the benefits the regime brought to many Germans in the 1930s, this is not surprising.

There has remained a hard core of committed supporters of Hitler and Nazism amongst a declining band of ex-soldiers and in fringe movements attracting alienated youth. This has manifested itself in occasional rallies, especially on the anniversary of the death of Rudolph Hess (in many ways an unlikely Nazi hero). Occasional racist violence, especially against immigrant workers such as Turks, has reminded the German majority of the ever-present dangers of racism. Politically, these groups have gained only marginal representation, as the Federal Republic has remained economically prosperous and politically secure.

The greater economic difficulties in eastern Europe, suppressed under communism, have resulted in a growth in neo-Nazism in the ex-communist areas of the unified Germany, but such groups remain on the fringe. The overwhelming majority of German youth, horrified by their grandparents' acquiescence in (silent acceptance of) the barbarities of the Third Reich, remain committed to democratic and liberal values.

ACTIVITY

1 Explain how the Allies tried to reduce the danger of a recurrence of Nazism.
2 How successful have they been?

C Post-war Germany: from division to reunification

The Allies, especially the Soviet Union which had suffered so massively from the Nazi invasion, were determined to prevent a resurgence of German military power. Initially Germany was occupied by the invading forces and divided into four occupation zones, intended to last until it could be trusted to rule itself (see Chart 22B). However, the developing Cold War between the USSR and the West meant that these divisions hardened into two states after 1949, with the three western zones becoming the Federal Republic of Germany (BRD), and the Soviet zone becoming the communist-controlled Democratic Republic of Germany (DDR). As part of the same process, the Soviet Union also established a series of satellite communist regimes on its borders. Thus, ironically, one of Hitler's most important legacies was the spread of the communism he so hated to much of Europe, including Germany.

Territorially, Germany once again suffered the imposition of new borders dictated by military considerations. To accommodate the USSR's insistence on regaining land lost to Poland during the 1920–1 war, Poland was shifted west at the expense of Germany, with the new border on the Oder–Neisse line. This resulted in vast population movements, as millions of German refugees fled back into the remaining German lands.

The DDR developed into a bleak communist state, dictated to by the Soviet Union, which also extracted reparations for war damage. It was notable for its sporting achievements, but otherwise it was an unattractive, economically inefficient and politically repressive regime, guarded by strong barriers. During the reforms of Mikhail Gorbachev in the USSR, Soviet control was relaxed and in 1989 the whole system collapsed, sparking off similar movements in the rest of eastern Europe.

In contrast to the USSR's exploitation of East Germany, the USA poured economic aid under the Marshall Plan into West Germany to help it recover economically and become a firm buttress against the feared communist advance. West Germany developed into a secure democratic regime, based in the new capital, Bonn. The Federal Republic revived the Weimar Republic's black, red and gold flag, and the Weimar regime's legacy was also evident in the new democratic constitution, with proportional representation. This time, assisted by economic success, the system succeeded in securing democratic government. After 1990 this was extended to the new reunified German state, and in 1999 the capital returned to Berlin.

This success of democracy in Germany since 1945 casts an interesting light on some historians' stress on the authoritarian bent in the German nation. Germany has used her growing economic muscle to foster European economic integration, and has been a major player in the development of the European Community. It is possible that within the next few years Germany may become a permanent member of the United Nations Security Council, thus confirming her rehabilitation.

TALKING POINT

Why do you think recent European history has been marked by considerable Franco-German co-operation?

ACTIVITY

Explain how Germany came to be divided in the 1940s and reunified in 1990.

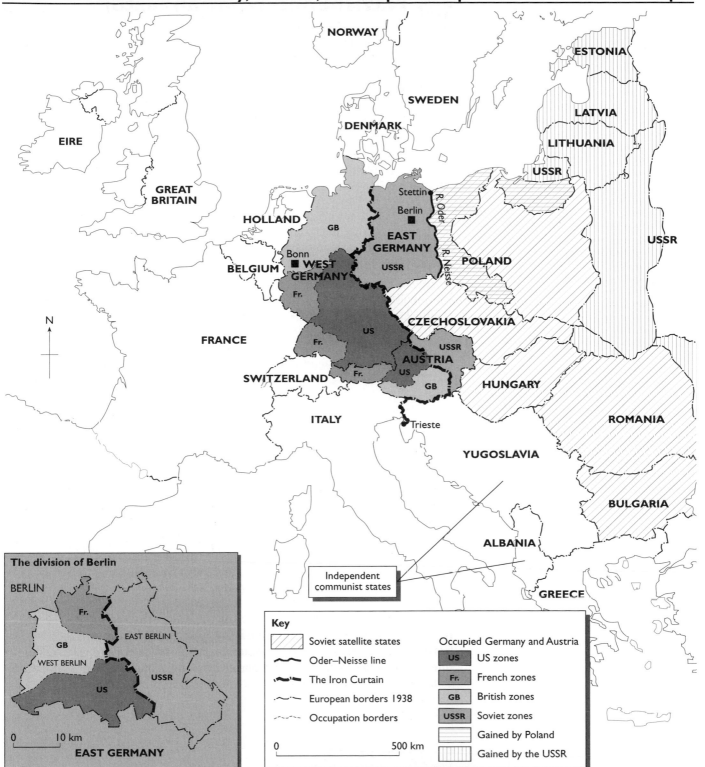

Independent
communist states

Key

▨	Soviet satellite states
〜	Oder–Neisse line
▬〜▬	The Iron Curtain
-·-·-	European borders 1938
-·-·-	Occupation borders

0   500 km

Occupied Germany and Austria

US	US zones
Fr.	French zones
GB	British zones
USSR	Soviet zones
	Gained by Poland
	Gained by the USSR

The division of Berlin

BERLIN

Fr.

GB   EAST BERLIN

WEST BERLIN

US   USSR

0   10 km

EAST GERMANY

The Iron Curtain
Winston Churchill, Prime Minister of Britain during the Second World War, first used the phrase 'an iron curtain' to describe the political, military and ideological barrier erected by the USSR to seal off itself and its satellites from contact with the West. In a speech in the US in 1946 he said: 'From Stettin in the Baltic to Trieste in the Adriatic, an iron curtain has descended across the continent.'

D Nazism and German history

Hitler and the Third Reich is one of the most controversial subjects in history, and we have tried to illustrate this throughout this book. We began (pages 2–3) by looking at two simplified views of German history. One view, stressing the aggressive elements in German traditions, saw the Weimar Republic as doomed to fail, with the Third Reich as the culmination of forces with deep roots in German history. The alternative view placed a more positive interpretation on German history and saw the Third Reich as a brief, atypical interlude. The debates over the inevitability of the Weimar Republic's failure were examined more fully in Chapter 9.

During your study of the domestic and foreign policies of the Third Reich you have encountered yet more debates. We try to summarise the main ones in Chart 22C. The Third Reich is now normally seen as a far more complex 'system' than the traditional view of it as a totalitarian state. The confused nature of the state and the way the Gestapo operated challenge to some extent stereotypes of German efficiency. Increasing evidence on nonconformist behaviour, especially amongst youth, and on the importance of the Hitler myth all suggest a more complex view of the Nazi period, as does recent stress on the attempt to create a *Volksgemeinschaft*, with both positive and horrific features. Neither the view of Germans as the terrified victims of an all-powerful state nor the image of them as committed Nazis and anti-semites reflects the complexity of the German people's experience of the Third Reich. The historians' debate over the role of Hitler within the system, and especially his role in the Holocaust and in planning the Second World War, is a further reflection of the continuing controversy over the nature of the Third Reich.

As new research is pursued and more records, especially from the former east German state, are made available, so the debate will continue, with analyses influenced, as ever, by the changing context in which historians operate. The ideological conflicts of the Cold War produced an atmosphere hostile to objective historical research, and the shadow of Auschwitz made Germans wary of formulating a balanced view of the Third Reich. It was perhaps only in the 1990s that it was possible for German historians to argue that Hitler brought some benefits to many Germans without being accused of pro-Nazi sympathies. This calmer atmosphere, the greater political self-confidence brought by the successes of the German Federal Republic and the ending of the Cold War have all assisted fuller understanding of the dramatic events in Germany between 1918 and 1945. All this should reinforce our suspicion of such simplified views as those presented in the Introduction.

Interpreting the Third Reich

In Chart 22C we identify some of the major debates over the Third Reich and consider the reasons for these, by identifying some of the factors that influence historical explanation.

DEBATES ON THE THIRD REICH

WEIMAR GERMANY AND THE ORIGINS OF THE THIRD REICH
(see Introduction and Chapter 9)
• Weimar's failure: inevitable or due to mistakes/bad luck?
• Third Reich: culmination of German history or aberration?
(These two debates are closely linked.)

THE ROLE OF HITLER
(see Chapter 11)
• All-powerful dictator or weak ruler?
• A popular leader: myth or reality?

NATURE OF THE NAZI STATE
(see Chapter 11)
• Efficient totalitarian state or polycratic chaos?
• Gestapo omnipotent or dependent on popular support?

FOREIGN POLICY (see Chapter 20)
• Hitler: master planner or improviser?
• Hitler's war?

ORIGINS OF THE HOLOCAUST
(see Chapter 18)
• Ordered by Hitler or developing structurally?
• The Germans: willing executioners or innocent bystanders?

ECONOMY
(see Chapter 12)
• Priority to guns or butter?
• 1939 crisis causing war?

IMPACT OF THE THIRD REICH
(see Chapters 15, 17 and 19)
• *Volksgemeinschaft*: deep commitment or mere conformity?
• Opposition: minimal or surprisingly widespread?
• Women: victims or beneficiaries?
• Reactionary or modernising?

APPROACHES TO HISTORY
Historians may have different overall perspectives on the most significant influences in history, and may specialise in particular areas.

ROLE OF THE INDIVIDUAL
• Importance of the ideas and aims of Hitler (intentionalist view): e.g. Hitler's *Weltanschauung*, with his determination to eliminate Jews from Germany and to embark on a war of conquest
• Importance of Hitler's personality (psycho-history): e.g. his troubled childhood, experiences as a failed artist, etc.

IMPORTANCE OF BROADER CONTEXT/STRUCTURES
• Stress on the way the Nazi state operated: e.g. cumulative radicalisation
• Stress on general diplomatic context in explaining outbreak of war in 1939

GENERIC APPROACH
• Stress on broad trends in history, applicable to several countries during a period: e.g. Third Reich as an example of the broad trend of Fascism and/or totalitarianism

HISTORY FROM BELOW
(*ALLTAGSGESCHICHTE* (literally, the history of everyday life))
• Concentration on the experiences of ordinary Germans: e.g. W. S. Allen's study of the Nazis' seizure of power in Northeim, Gellately's work on the Gestapo in Düsseldorf

INEVITABILITY V CONTINGENCY
• Some historians see the course of history as the result of major broad trends, and may stress the CONTINUITIES in history
• Others stress how particular decisions or events can change the course of history
• Both the failure of the Weimar Republic and the outbreak of war in 1939 have been explained from these differing perspectives

IMPORTANCE OF ECONOMIC FACTORS
• Some historians, especially Marxists, stress importance of economic structures and developments: e.g. in the collapse of Weimar, the outbreak of war in 1939
• Some Marxists see Weimar as brought down by the economic elite, who then continued to use Hitler as their tool to protect their business interests

INFLUENCES ON HISTORIANS
TIME WHEN WRITING
• 1950s: Cold War encouraged totalitarian view
• 1980s–1990s: success of German democracy and ending of Cold War encouraged more varied assessments
• Passage of time weakens burden of guilt

SOURCES
• More research has opened up new perspectives
• Greater access to sources, especially in the former East Germany
• Greater exploration of local sources, e.g. about youth movements and the Gestapo in Düsseldorf
• Greater use of oral history to study Germans' perceptions

E The creation of Israel

One of the most tangible legacies of the Third Reich has been the creation of Israel. The Zionist Movement (desiring to create a national home for the Jews), which was already growing during the inter-war period, received massive impetus from the Holocaust, as the need for greater protection for Jews and compensation for Hitler's attempted genocide seemed unanswerable. Thus in 1948 the United Nations voted overwhelmingly to create a new state of Israel in part of the former British mandate of Palestine. However, many Arabs, who found themselves in or surrounded by a new Jewish state, did not see why they should have to pay the penalty for the crimes of the Nazis. The Middle East remains an area in conflict.

TALKING POINT

Do you think the creation of a Jewish state in Palestine was justified?

F What lessons can be learnt?

The final legacy of the Third Reich must be the determination that such horrors will never be permitted again. The fact that thousands of educated Germans were prepared to commit mass murder, and that millions were prepared to support such an inhumane regime, sends a warning to humanity. Unless one accepts the racist argument that such a phenomenon is exclusively a product of the German mind, we must all be on guard lest circumstances arise in which similar events are possible. Growing awareness of the genocide of Armenians in the early twentieth century, the horrors of the Khmer Rouge in 1970s Cambodia, and recent genocidal massacres in Rwanda, Bosnia and Kosovo suggest that the civilised veneer of humanity can be fragile. Detailed examination of how the Holocaust was possible can help us avoid its repetition.

Let us conclude by quoting the German historian Peukert on what we can learn from studying Nazism:

TALKING POINTS

1 Should historians let current developments influence their views of the past?
2 Why has such a brief period in German history as the Third Reich taken on such prominence?

SOURCE 22.6 Peukert, *Inside Nazi Germany*, p. 244

The values we should assert in response to this historical experience are easily stated but hard to practise: reverence for life, pleasure in diversity and contrariety, respect for what is alien, tolerance for what is unpalatable, scepticism about the feasibility and desirability of CHILIASTIC schemes for a global new order, openness towards others and willingness to learn even from those who call into question one's own principles of social virtue.

Glossary

ABSOLUTIST   believing in an all-powerful ruler, usually a
   monarch
ABWEHR   German military intelligence organisation
AGRARIAN   landed, agricultural
ANNEXATIONIST   person or party wanting to take over other
   countries
ANNEXE   to take over another country
ANNIHILATIONIST   person who wants to destroy something
ANSCHLUSS   political union of Germany and Austria;
   specifically, the take-over of Austria by the Third Reich
ANTI-CAPITALIST   hatred of capitalism, an economic system
   based on private property and private profit, on the
   grounds that it exploits workers
ANTI-SEMITISM   hatred of Jews
APPEASEMENT   policy of making concessions, especially to
   buy off an aggressor by sacrificing one's principles
ARBITRARY   unrestrained; exercising power without
   justification or legal backing
ARBITRATION   accepting the decision of an agreed third
   party to settle a dispute
ARMISTICE   agreement to stop fighting
ARTISAN   skilled craftsman
ARYAN   Nazi term for a non-Jewish German; technically,
   someone who speaks an Indo-European language
ARYANISE   to remove non-Aryan elements from German
   society: to get rid of the Jews
ASOCIAL   undesirable person in society
AUTARKY   national economic self-sufficiency
AUTHORITARIAN   tyrannical; belief in government by a
   strong, non-democratic leader
AUTOCRATIC   all powerful
AUTONOMY   self-rule

BDM   Bund Deutscher Mädel (League of German Girls);
   a Nazi youth organisation
BELLIGERENT   warlike
BILATERAL   two sided; involving two parties or countries
BLITZKRIEG   lightning war
BOLSHEVISING   converting to Bolshevism (see below)
BOLSHEVISM   Russian Communism (see below);
   government by workers' councils or soviets
BOURGEOISIE   the middle class
BRD   Bundesrepublik Deutschland (the Federal Republic
   of Germany): West Germany; the western part of
   partitioned Germany from 1949 until unification in
   1990
BRENNER   mountain pass in the Alps: the frontier between
   Austria and Italy
BVP   Bayerische Volkspartei (Bavarian People's Party);
   Catholic political party

CALVINIST   member of a Protestant Church based on the
   teaching of John Calvin
CAPITALISM   economic system based on private enterprise
CAREERISTS   people mainly concerned with advancing
   their careers

CARTEL   group of businesses linked together to control the
   market
CARTELISATION   domination by cartels
CHANCELLOR   leader, prime minister, of Germany
CHARISMATIC   inspiring
CHAUVINISM   extreme nationalism, hostile to other
   countries
CHILIASTIC   believing in the coming of a messiah or new
   world
COALITION   combination; government formed from more
   than one party
COLD WAR   Post-1945 hostility between the democratic
   West and the Soviet Union
COLLECTIVE SECURITY   countries working together to
   protect everyone's security
COMINTERN   Communist International; international body
   trying to spread communism
COMMISSAR   government minister in the USSR; also name
   for a Communist Party official
COMMON LAW   law that has developed through custom; not
   based on statutes or legal code
COMMUNIST   believer in communism, in a society where
   all are equal and there is no private property
COMMUNIST INTERNATIONAL   see Comintern
CONSERVATIVE   in favour of maintaining society and political
   institutions as they are; opposed to revolutionary change
CONSTITUENT   having the power to draw up a constitution
CONSTITUTION   document laying down basic laws of how a
   country should be run
CONTINUITIES   things staying the same over time
CORPORATIST   economic system based on workers and
   employers working together as one body to increase
   production
CORPORATIVIST   see corporatist
COSMOPOLITAN   belonging to the whole world not a
   particular country
COUNCIL   body elected by ordinary people; see soviet
COUNTER-REVOLUTION   a revolution in reaction to an
   earlier revolution, to reverse its results
COUP (D'ÉTAT)   blow; sudden seizure of power by a small
   group; see putsch
COURT MARTIAL   trial by military court
DAF   Deutsche Arbeitsfront (German Labour Front); Nazi
   organisation that replaced trade unions in the Third
   Reich
DAP   Deutsche Arbeiterpartei (German Workers' Party);
   forerunner of the Nazi Party
DDP   Deutsche Demokratische Partei (German
   Democratic Party)
DDR   Deutsche Demokratische Republik (German
   Democratic Republic); East German Communist state
   1946-1990
DEFICIT FINANCING   spending money on credit; financing
   government expenditure by borrowing
DEFLATIONARY   economic policies to slow down the
   economy, leading to falling prices

DEMAGOGIC   appealing to the masses; see demagogue

DEMAGOGUE   leader who stirs up popular passions and exploits the prejudices of the mob

DEMILITARISED   containing no military personnel or fortifications

DEMOCRACY   government by the people

DEMOGRAPHIC   to do with population

DENAZIFICATION   attempt to remove Nazi influence

DESPOTIC   behaving like a despot or tyrant

DÉTENTE   relaxation of tension, of strained relations, between nations

DETERMINISM   belief that events are bound to happen, for fundamental reasons not just through chance or due to actions of individuals

DFW   Deutsches Frauenwerk (German Women's Work), a Nazi organisation for women

DICTATORSHIP   rule by one all-powerful person or group

DISSOLUTION   shutting down; dismissal, for example of an assembly or parliament

DIVINE RIGHT OF KINGS   belief that a king's right to rule comes from God

DNVP   Deutschnationale Volkspartei (German National People's Party); conservative

DUCE   leader; Mussolini's title as leader of the Italian Fascist party and dictator of Italy

DVP   Deutsche Volkspartei (German People's Party); moderate conservatives

ECONOMIC LIBERALISM   policy of government not intervening in the economy

EINSATZGRUPPEN   SS Special Action Groups; responsible for the brutal killing of thousands of civilians in territories occupied by Germany

ELITE   powerful groups at top of society, e.g. industrialists, landowners, Church leaders

EMANCIPATION   setting free

EMPIRICAL   based on experience, not on theory

ENCYCLICAL   letter from Pope to all his bishops

ENTENTE   international understanding between countries to follow a united course of action; specifically, the Anglo-French Entente

EUGENICS   the science of genetic improvement of a race

EUTHANASIA   mercy killing; the Nazis misused the term to describe their policy of killing mentally and physically disabled people

EVANGELICAL   member of a German Protestant church

EXPRESSIONISM   art form based on distorting reality to express an inner vision

FASCISM   extreme nationalist political movement

FEDERAL   central government of a state divided into smaller units with considerable power

FEUDAL   medieval social structure based on land holding

FINANCE CAPITAL   money for investment

FRANCHISE   the right to vote in elections

FREEMASON   secret society, with liberal leanings

FREIKORPS   right-wing group of ex-soldiers; a private army

FULFILMENT   complying with terms, especially of Versailles Treaty

GAU(E)   regional unit(s) of Nazi party

GAULEITER   leader of a *Gau*

GENOCIDE   killing of a whole race

GHETTO   special section of a city where Jews forced to live

GLEICHSCHALTUNG   co-ordination; under the Nazis a policy of bringing everything under state control

HARZBURG FRONT   in 1931 a right-wing Nationalist alliance against Brüning's government

HEGEMONY   dominance

HELOT   slave

HJ   Hitler Jugend (Hitler Youth); a Nazi youth organisation

HOHENZOLLERN   name of the Prussian royal family; emperors of Germany from 1871 to 1918

HOLOCAUST   mass slaughter; the Nazi murder of over 6 million Jews

HY   Hitler Youth; a Nazi youth organisation

HYPERINFLATION   massive rise in prices

IDEOLOGICAL   to do with a set of ideas or principles

IDEOLOGUE   someone committed to a set of ideas or principles

IMPERIALIST   taking over other countries

INDICT   charge with a crime

INFLATIONARY   causing prices to rises

INSTRUMENTAL   causing something to happen

INSURRECTION   rising

INTENTIONALIST   stressing intentions of people as a major cause of historical events

INTERNATIONALISM   countries and people from different countries working together

JEWRY   Jews as a whole

JUNKERS   Prussian landed aristocracy

JURISTS   legal experts

KdF   Kraft durch Freude (Strength through Joy); Nazi leisure organisation

KPD   Kommunistische Partei Deutschlands (Communist Party of Germany)

LAISSEZ-FAIRE   literally, to leave alone; policy of non-interference by government in economic affairs

LANDTAG   elected assembly of the *Länder*, the provinces/states of the German Republic

LEBENSRAUM   living space; aim of German expansion in east

LEGISLATIVE   to do with making laws

LIBERAL   concerned with representative government and individual liberty

LUFTWAFFE   German air force

MARTIAL LAW   emergency powers given to governments to use army to re-establish order

MARXIST   supporter of the ideas of Karl Marx; a communist

MERCENARY   hired soldier fighting for money in the service of another country

MESSIAH   great leader come to save or free his people

MESSIANIC   to do with a messiah

MILITANCY   aggressive, radical action

MILITARISM   admiration for the army and its values

MITTELSTAND   the lower middle class; petty bourgeoisie

MOBILISE   put armed forces on a war footing

MODERNIST   a modern style of art that rejects the past and seeks new forms of artistic expression

MORATORIUM   delay; a legal agreement to postpone the payment of a debt

MULTILATERAL   many sided; involving several countries

NAPOLAS   Nationalpolitische Erziehungsanstalten (National Political Institutes of Education); elite Nazi schools to train future government leaders

NATIONALISM   belief that a nation should rule itself

NEO-CLASSICAL   imitating ancient Greece and Rome

NEPOTISM   favouring one's family and friends (with appointment to a position or job)

NONCONFORMIST   not obeying the system; a Protestant in the Christian religion

NORDIC   Germanic (people)

NSBO   Nationalsozialistische Betriebszellenorganisation (National Socialist Factory Cell Organisation); Nazi factory organisation for workers

NSDAP   Nationalsozialistische Deutsche Arbeiterpartei (National Socialist German Workers' Party); the Nazi Party

NSF   Nationalsozialistische Frauenschaft (National Socialist Women's Organisation); Nazi organisation for women

NSLB   Nationalsozialistische Lehrerbund (National Socialist Teachers' League); Nazi organisation for teachers

NSV   Nationalsozialistische Volkswohlfahrt; Nazi welfare organisation

OCTOBER   Communist Revolution in Russia in October 1917

OKW   Oberkommando der Wehrmacht (High Command of the Armed Forces)

OPPORTUNIST   seizing opportunities when they occur (often without regard to principle or consequences)

ORDINANCE   regulation; order

ORTHODOXY   conforming to the established system; sound in doctrine

PACIFICATION   put down or subdue by force

PAN-CLASS   across all social classes

PAN-GERMANISM   belief in bringing together all Germans into one country

PARAMILITARY   organised unofficially on military lines; private army

PENAL CODE   laws laying down punishments

PETTY BOURGEOISIE   the lower middle class

PLEBISCITE   referendum

PLENIPOTENTIARY   person with full powers to take decisions and make agreements

POGROM   massacre of helpless people (normally of Jews)

POLITBURO   ruling body of the Communist Party in the Soviet Union

POLYCRACY   system of overlapping ministries or agencies

PORTFOLIO   government department

PRAGMATIC   realistic; not concerned with ideology

PROLETARIANISED   becoming like an industrial worker; losing status

PROLETARIAT   industrial working class

PROPAGANDA   means of spreading political ideas, often through distortion

PROTECTIONISM   economic measures designed to protect domestic production from imports

PROTECTORATE   a weak state dependent on a more powerful one

PROTOCOL   agreement, official record

PROVENANCE   where something comes from; origins of a historical source

PUBLIC WORKS   employment schemes financed by the state to provide jobs

PUPPET   person controlled by someone else

PURGE   cleanse; remove unwanted elements

PUTSCH   plot to overthrow the government; see coup

RAD   Reichsarbeitsdienst (Reich Labour Service); compulsory labour service for young German men; extended in 1939 to include women also

RADICAL   extremist

RAPPROCHEMENT   moving together; an improvement in relations between states

RATIFY   to confirm, approve (an agreement)

REACTIONARY   wanting to return to the old days; opposed to change

RED   socialist

RED GUARDS   armed socialist workers

REFLATION   boosting the economy

REICHSRAT   national assembly of German states

REICHSTAG   German parliament

REICHSWEHR   German army

REMILITARISE   allow troops to be stationed in an area again

RENTIER   person living off income from property or investments

REPARATIONS   payment as compensation, especially payments imposed on Germany by the Treaty of Versailles

REPUBLIC   country with government that has a president as head of state not a monarch

REVISIONIST   person who wants to revise or modify something; e.g. change the terms of a treaty

RMVP   Reichsministerium für Volksaufklärung und Propaganda (Ministry of Public Enlightenment and Propaganda)

ROMAN LAW   law originating from the Roman Empire; a written code of law

RRG   the Reich Radio Company

RUNIC   mysterious, magical; to do with the runes, the earliest form of German alphabet

RWHG   Reichswerke Hermann Goering: state steel works set up by Goering as director of the Four-Year Plan

RSHA   Reichssicherheitshauptamt (Reich Security Head Office): the security agency of the SS set up in 1939 under Heydrich

SA   Sturm-Abteilung (storm troopers); Nazi paramilitary organisation

SATELLITE GOVERNMENT   a government dependent on another state

SCHOOL   term used to describe scholars who follow the same teacher and share the same viewpoint

SCORCHED EARTH   destroying crops, buildings in advance of enemy

SD   Sicherheitsdienst (Security Service); the intelligence service of the SS (see below)

SECULAR   non-religious; to do with worldly things

SELF-DETERMINATION   principle of nation states ruling themselves

SEPARATISM   wanting to break away from existing larger state to create a new one

SHOW TRIAL   trial of political opponent, often on false charges; held to influence public opinion

SOCIAL DARWINISM   belief that countries, as do animals, compete to survive

SOCIALISATION   policy of the state taking control; e.g. of an industry

SOCIALIST   left-wing political movement stressing the good of society as a whole, with emphasis on collective rather than individual ownership of property

SONDERWEG   Special (or peculiar) path

SOPADE   the name of the Social Democratic Party (SPD) in exile; based in Prague and later in Paris and London, the exiled opponents of the Nazi regime received many reports from their agents within Germany

SOVEREIGN   ruler

SOVEREIGNTY   supreme political power

SOVIET   elected council; system of government in communist state

SPARTACIST   member of communist revolutionary group in Germany

SPD   Sozialdemokratische Partei Deutschlands (Social Democratic Party of Germany); the main socialist party

SS   Schutzstaffel (Protective Squads); beginning as Hitler's bodyguard, then the Nazi Party's police force

STAHLHELM   right-wing, nationalist ex-servicemen's organisation (literally, steel helmet)

STRUCTURALIST   view stressing importance of broader forces/structures in determining course of events

STURM-ABTEILUNG   see SA

SUFFRAGE   right to vote

SWISSIFICATION   turning into a minor state like Switzerland

SYNOD   meeting of church governing body for debate

TERTIARY   in economics, the term used for luxury goods and their production

TEUTONIC   ancient Germans

THEORETICAL   speculative or hypothetical

TOTALITARIAN   state in which all power is centralised in the hands of one man or a small group; the opposite of democratic

UNILATERAL   action by one person or state

USPD   Unabhängige Sozialdemokratische Partei Deutschlands (Independent Social Democratic Party of Germany)

USSR   Union of Soviet Socialist Republics

UTILITARIANISM   belief that things should be as useful, beneficial as possible

VASSAL   subordinate; a servant, slave

VATICAN   area ruled by Pope in Rome; the government of the Catholic Church

VICHY   the semi-independent French government after the German conquest of part of France; named after the town in central France where it was based

VÖLKISCH   nationalist, concerned with Germanic identity

VOLKSGEMEINSCHAFT   literally, people's community; the Nazi ideal community

WAR BONDS   money lent to government during war

WEHRMACHT   German army

WELTANSCHAUUNG   literally, world view; a philosophy of life

WELTPOLITIK   literally, world policy; playing a leading part in world politics: imperialism

XENOPHOBIC   hatred of foreigners

Z   Zentrum (Centre Party); a Catholic party

ZAG   Zentralarbeitsgemeinschaft (Central Labour Community); a joint worker-employer association during the Weimar Republic

Reading list

Few topics in history have had so many books written on them as Weimar Germany and especially the Third Reich. There are numerous books specifically written for A level students. Below are some academic books that you should find both accessible and stimulating.

General

Ian Kershaw *Hitler* (Longman 1991). A powerful, clear, concise analysis of Hitler's rise to power and the Nazi regime, by Britain's leading expert on the period.

Dick Geary *Hitler and Nazism* (Routledge 1993). An excellent rival to Kershaw's concise summary of all aspects of Nazism.

Ian Kershaw *Hitler 1889–1936. Hubris* (Allen Lane 1998). Volume 1 of very detailed two-volume biography that covers most aspects of the Nazi regime, incorporating recent research. Worth at least dipping into. Volume 2 covers 1937–45.

John Hiden *Republican and Fascist Germany* (Longman 1996). Examines the overall period thematically, covering some neglected areas. Comprehensive in its coverage, and clearly written.

Mary Fulbrook (ed.) *German History since 1800* (Arnold 1997). Contains some very clear chapters conveying recent analyses of key issues.

Weimar Germany

Conan Fischer *The Rise of the Nazis* (Manchester University Press 1995). The best, recent, detailed study of the nature of the Nazi movement and the reasons for its eventual success in the Weimar period.

Detlev Peukert *The Weimar Republic* (Penguin 1993). A brilliant, though quite challenging, analysis of the tensions within the Weimar Republic.

Simon Taylor *Germany 1918–1933* (Duckworth 1986). Combines clear analysis with a wealth of fascinating visual material.

Ian Kershaw (ed.) *Weimar: Why did German Democracy Fail?* (Weidenfeld 1990). A brilliant collection of contrasting articles on key areas of debate.

The Third Reich

Ian Kershaw *The 'Hitler Myth'. Image and Reality in the Third Reich* (OUP 1987). A fascinating examination of a crucial area of the regime; far more accessible than some of Kershaw's other specialist work.

Detlev Peukert *Inside Nazi Germany. Conformity, Opposition and Racism in Everyday Life* (Penguin 1982). A stimulating examination of the variety of ordinary people's reactions to Nazi policies.

Martin Burleigh and Walter Wippermann *The Racial State: Germany 1933–1945* (CUP 1991). Analyses Nazi domestic policies, concentrating on the regime's treatment of outsiders.

Richard Grunberger *A Social History of the Third Reich* (Penguin 1971). A pioneering history of Nazi policies that remains a clear and perceptive survey of key groups during the Third Reich.

To supplement the above academic studies, you might like to study some accounts by participants. Two of the most interesting from very different perspectives are:

Albert Speer *Inside the Third Reich* (Cardinal 1975)

Primo Levi *The Drowned and the Saved* (Abacus 1989). A concentration camp survivor, Levi gives a profound insight into the experience of the Holocaust.

Finally, there are three particularly useful reference books:

J. Noakes and G. Pridham *Nazism 1919–1945* (University of Exeter Press 1983). A vast collection of documents; an invaluable mine of information, including concise introductions to each area of study.

Tim Kirk *Longman Companion to Nazi Germany* (Longman 1995).

Richard Overy *The Penguin Historical Atlas of the Third Reich* (Penguin 1996).

Bibliography

Secondary sources quoted in the text are given below. The date in brackets is the date of first publication if different from that of the edition quoted.

Abel T., *Why Hitler Came into Power*, Harvard University Press 1986 (1938)

Adam P., *The Arts of the Third Reich*, Thames & Hudson 1992

Allen W. S., *The Nazi Seizure of Power. The Experience of a Single German Town 1922–45*, Franklin Watts 1965 (Penguin 1989)

Balfour M., *Withstanding Hitler*, Routledge 1988

Bankier D., *Germans and the Final Solution: Public Opinion Under Nazism*, Blackwell 1996 (1992)

Bessel R., *Weimar Germany. The Crisis of Industrial Society, 1918–1933*, Open University, 1987

Bessel R. (ed.), *Fascist Italy and Nazi Germany: Comparisons and Contrasts*, CUP 1996

Bessel R. (ed.), *Life in the Third Reich*, OUP 1987

Blackbourn D., T*he Peculiarities of German History: Bourgeois Society and Politics in Nineteenth Century Germany*, OUP 1984

Bookbinder P., *Weimar Germany: The Republic of the Reasonable*, Manchester University Press 1996

Browning C., *Path to Genocide: Essays on Launching the Final Solution*, CUP 1992

Brustein W., *Logic of Evil. Social Origins of the Nazi Party 1925–33*, Yale University Press 1996

Bullock A., *Hitler: a Study in Tyranny*, Penguin 1962 (rev. edition)

Bullock A., *Hitler and Stalin: Parallel Lives*, HarperCollins 1992

Burleigh M. (ed.), *Confronting the Nazi Past*, Collins & Brown 1995

Burleigh M., *Death and Deliverance: Euthanasia in Germany, c. 1900–45*, CUP 1994

Burleigh M. and Wippermann W., T*he Racial State: Germany 1933–1945*, CUP 1991

Carr W., *A History of Germany, 1815–1985*, Arnold 1987

Carr W., *Arms, Autarky and Aggression*, Arnold 1972

Cesarani D. (ed.), *Final Solution*, Routledge 1996 (1994)

Childers T. (ed.), *The Formation of the Nazi Constituency*, Croom Helm 1986

Childers T. and Caplan J. (ed.), *Re-evaluating the Third Reich: New Controversies, New Interpretations*, Holmes and Meier 1990

Cohen A. (ed.), *Comprehending the Holocaust*, Verlag Peter Lang 1988

Crew D. (ed.), *Nazism and German Society, 1933–45*, Routledge 1994

De Grand A., *Fascist Italy and Nazi Germany*, Routledge 1995

Douglas R., *Between the Wars, 1919–39: The Cartoonists' Vision*, Routledge 1992

Dülffer J., *Nazi Germany, 1933–45: Faith in the Führer and Pursuit of a War of Annihilation*, Arnold 1996 (1992)

Evans R. (ed.), *Rereading German History: From Unification to Reunification, 1800–1995*, Routledge 1997

Evans R. and Geary D. (ed.), *The German Unemployed*, Croom Helm 1987

Fest J., *The Face of the Third Reich*, Penguin 1979 (1963)

Feuchtwanger E., *From Weimar to Hitler: Germany, 1918–33*, Macmillan 1995 (1993)

Fischer C., *The Rise of the Nazis*, Manchester University Press 1995

Fischer C. (ed.), *Rise of National Socialism and the Working Classes in Weimar Germany*, Berghahn Books 1996

Fischer K., *Nazi Germany. A New History*, Constable 1995

Freeman M., *Atlas of Nazi Germany*, Longman 1987

Frei N., *National Socialist Rule in Germany: the Führer State 1933–1945*, Blackwell 1993 (1987)

Frevert U., *Women in German History*, Berg 1988

Friedländer S., *Nazi Germany and the Jews: the Years of Persecution, 1933–39*, Phoenix 1998

Fulbrook M., *The Fontana History of Germany, 1918–1990: The Divided Nation*, Fontana 1991

Fulbrook M. (ed.), *German History Since 1800*, Arnold 1997

Geary D., *Hitler and Nazism*, Routledge 1993

Gellately R., *Gestapo and German Society: Enforcing Racial Policy, 1933–45*, OUP 1990

Gilbert M., *The Holocaust*, Collins, 1987 (1986)

Goldhagen D., *Hitler's Willing Executioners*, Little, Brown 1996

Golomstock I., *Totalitarian Art*, Collins 1990

Gordon S., *Hitler, Germans, and the Jewish Question*, Princeton 1984

Grau G., *Hidden Holocaust. Lesbian and Gay Persecution in Germany 1933–1945*, Cassell 1995 (1993)

Grunberger R., *A Social History of the Third Reich*, Penguin 1974 (1971)

Hamilton R., *Who Voted for Hitler?*, Princeton 1982

Hayward Gallery, *Art and Power: Europe under the Dictators*, South Bank Centre 1995

Hayward Gallery, *Images of the 1930s*, South Bank Centre 1995

Heiber H., *The Weimar Republic: Germany 1918–33*, Blackwell 1993 (1966)

Heiden K., *Der Führer: Hitler's Rise to Power*, H. Pordes 1944

Henig, R., *The Weimar Republic 1919–1933*, Routledge 1998

Hiden J., *Weimar Republic*, Longman 1974

Hiden J., *Germany and Europe 1919–39*, Longman 1993 (1977)

Hiden J., *Republican and Fascist Germany*, Longman 1996

Hiden J. and Farquharson J., (ed.) *Explaining Hitler's Germany. Historians and the Third Reich*, Batsford 1983

Hillenbrand F., *Underground Humour in Nazi Germany 1933–45*, Routledge 1994

Housden M., *Resistance and Conformity in the Third Reich*, Routledge 1996

Hughes M., *Nationalism and Society. Germany 1800–1945*, Arnold 1988

Jonge A. de, *Weimar Chronicle*, Paddington 1978

Kershaw I., *The 'Hitler Myth'. Image and Reality in the Third Reich*, OUP 1989 (1987)

Kershaw I., *Hitler*, Longman 1991

Kershaw I., *Hitler 1889–1936. Hubris*, Allen Lane 1998

Kershaw I., *The Nazi Dictatorship. Problems and Perspectives of Interpretation*, Arnold 3rd Edition 1993

Kershaw I. (ed.), *Weimar: Why did German Democracy Fail?*, Weidenfeld 1990

Kershaw I. and Lewin M. (ed.), S*talinism and Nazism: Dictatorships in Comparison*, CUP 1997

Kirk T., *Longman Companion to Nazi Germany*, Longman 1995

Koch H. (ed.), *Aspects of the Third Reich*, Macmillan 1985

Kolb E., *Weimar Republic*, Unwin 1988

Koonz C., *Mothers in the Fatherland*, Methuen 1988

Laffen M. (ed.), *Burden of German History*, Methuen 1989 (1988)

Landau R., *Studying the Holocaust*, Routledge 1998

Leber A., *Conscience in Revolt*, Westview 1994 (1957)

Lee M. and Michalka W., *German Foreign Policy 1917–33*, Berg 1987

Lehmann-Haupt H., *Art under a Dictatorship*, 1954

Marks S., *Illusion of Peace*, Macmillan 1976

Marrus M., *The Holocaust in History*, Penguin 1989 (1987)

Martel G. (ed.), *Modern Germany Reconsidered: 1870–1945*, Routledge 1992

Mason T., *Nazism, Fascism and the Working Class*, CUP 1995

Mason T., *Social Policy in the Third Reich: the Working Class and the National 'Community' 1918–39*, Berg 1993 (1977)

McKenzie J., *Weimar Germany*, Blandford 1971

Mitchell A., *Nazi Revolution*, Heath 1990 (1973)

Mommsen H., *Weimar to Auschwitz*, Polity Press 1991

Mosse G., *Nazi Culture*, Schocken 1981

Neumann R., *Pictorial History of the Third Reich*, Bantam 1962

Nicholls A., *Weimar and the Rise of Hitler*, Macmillan 1979 (1968)

Noakes J. and Pridham G. (ed.), *Nazism, 1919–1945. A Documentary Reader*, University of Essex 1983

Overy R., *The Nazi Economic Recovery 1932–38*, Macmillan 1983 (1982)

Overy R., *The Penguin Historical Atlas of the Third Reich*, Penguin 1996

Overy R., *War and Economy in the Third Reich*, OUP 1995 (1994)

Owings A., *Frauen: German Women Recall the Third Reich*, Penguin 1995 (1993)

Payne S., *History of Fascism 1914–45*, UCL 1995

Peterson E., *The Limits of Hitler's Power*, Princeton 1969

Peukert D., *Inside Nazi Germany. Conformity, Opposition and Racism in Everyday Life*, Penguin 1989 (1982)

Peukert D., *The Weimar Republic*, Penguin 1993 (1987)

Pine L., *Nazi Family Policy 1933–45*, Berg 1997

Pulzer P., *Germany 1870–1945*, OUP 1997

Rees L., *The Nazis. A Warning from History*, BBC 1997

Ritter G., *The Third Reich*, Weidenfeld 1955

Robertson M. (ed.), *Origins of the Second World War*, Macmillan 1971

Rogasky B., *Smoke and Ashes. The Story of the Holocaust*, OUP 1988

Ryder A. J., *Twentieth Century Germany*, Macmillan 1973

Sax B. and Kuntz D. (ed.), *Inside Hitler's Germany. A Documentary History of Life in the Third Reich*, Heath 1992

Shirer W., *The Rise and Fall of the Third Reich (abridged edition)*, Bison 1987 (Secker & Warburg 1972)

Smelser R. and Zitelmann R., *The Nazi Elite. Twenty-two Biographical Sketches*, Macmillan 1993

Snell J. and Mitchell A. (ed.), *The Nazi Revolution: Germany's Guilt or Germany's Fate?*, D. C. Heath 1973 (1959)

Snyder L., *Encyclopaedia of the Third Reich*, Hale 1995

Speer A., *Inside the Third Reich*, Cardinal 1975 (1970)

Stachura P. (ed.), *Unemployment and the Great Depression in Weimar Germany*, Macmillan 1986

Stachura P. (ed.), *The Nazi Machtergreifung*, 1983

Supple C., *From Prejudice to Genocide: Learning about the Holocaust*, Trentham Books 1993

Taylor A. J. P., *The Course of Germany History*, Methuen 1961 (1945)

Taylor B. and Will W. van der (ed.), *The Nazification of Art*, Winchester Press 1990

Taylor J. and Shaw W., *Dictionary of the Third Reich*, Grafton 1987 (reissued as *Penguin Dictionary of the Third Reich*, Penguin 1997)

Taylor S., *Germany 1918–1933*, Duckworth 1986 (1983)

Thorne C., *The Approach of War 1938–39*, Macmillan 1973

Time Life editors, *The SS*, Time Life 1989

Waite R. (ed.), *Hitler and Nazi Germany*, Holt, Rinehart & Winston, 1965

Walther H. (ed.), *Der Führer*, Bison Books 1978

Welch D., *Third Reich. Politics and Propaganda*, Routledge 1994 (1993)

Wehler H-U, *The German Empire 1871–1918*, Bergh 1985

Wheeler-Bennett J., *Hindenburg, 'The Wooden Titan'*, Macmillan 1967 (1936)

Wilt A., *Nazi Germany*, Harlan Davidson 1994

Acknowledgements

Text acknowledgements

The authors would particularly like to thank Tom Holden and Dick Geary for their help in the preparation of this book.

The authors and publishers are grateful to the following for permission to reproduce copyright material:

p.23 source 1.13 M. Hughes, *Nationalism and Society: Germany 1800–1945*, *p.184*, Edward Arnold Publishers 1988; source 1.14 W. Carr, *A History of Germany 1815–1985*, *p.249*, Edward Arnold Publishers 1987; **p.30** source 1.24 A. Nicholls, *Weimar and the Rise of Hitler*, *p.128*, Macmillan 1979; source 1.25 K. Fischer, *Nazi Germany: A New History*, *pp.56–9*, Constable 1995; source 1.26 D. Peukert, *The Weimar Republic*, *p.50*, Penguin 1991; **p.39** source 2.7 A. Nicholls, *Weimar and the Rise of Hitler*, *p.44*, Macmillan 1979; source 2.8 J. Hiden, *The Weimar Republic*, *p.14*, Addison Wesley Longman 1974; **p.45** source 2.19 K. Heiden, *Der Führer: Hitler's Rise to Power*, *pp.106–7*, Caroll & Graf Publishers 1944; **p.50** source 2.27 M. Fulbrook, *Fontana History of Germany 1918–1990: The Divided Nation*, *p.34*, HarperCollins 1991; **p.54** source 2.31 A. Bullock, *Hitler and Stalin; Parallel Lives*, *p.100*, HarperCollins 1992; **pp.68, 69** P. Bookbinder, *Weimar Germany*, Manchester University Press 1996; **p.87** source 4.8 S. Marks, *Illusion of Peace*, *pp.64–5*, Macmillan 1976; **p.98** source 1, R. Bessel, from *German History since 1800*, ed. Mary Fulbrook, *pp.252–3*, Edward Arnold 1997; source 2, K. Fischer, *Nazi Germany: A New History*, *pp.179–87*, Constable 1995; source 3, M. Fulbrook, *Fontana History of Germany 1918–1990: The Divided Nation*, *pp. 7–8*, HarperCollins 1991; source 4, P. Pulzer, *Germany 1870–1945*, *p.3*, Oxford University Press 1997; **p.122** source 7.17 J. Noakes, *The Rise of the Nazis*, *p.11*, from *History Today*, January 1983; source 7.18 J. Falter, 'How Likely were Workers to vote for the NSDAP?' in *The Rise of Nationalism and Working Classes in Weimar Germany*, ed. C. Fischer, *pp. 34 and 40*, Berghahn 1996; source 7.20 C. Fischer, *The Rise of the Nazis*, *pp.63 and 99*, Manchester University Press 1995; **p.123** source 7.21 R. Geary, *Hitler and Nazism*, *p.27*, 1993, reproduced by kind permission of Dr Dick Geary, University of Nottingham; source 7.22 J. Falter, as before, *p.10*; **p.129** source 7.37 B. Brecht, *Song of the SA Man*, from *Poems*, ed. Willett and Manheim, Eyre Methuen; **p.145** source 8.19 I. Kershaw, *Hitler*, *p.55*, Addison Wesley Longman 1991; **p.156** source 9.2 W. Shirer, *The Rise and Fall of the Third Reich*, *p.29*, Secker and Warburg 1960; source 9.3 H. Wehler, *The German Empire 1871–1918*, Berg 1985; source 9.4 D. Blackbourn, *The Peculiarities of German History: Bourgeois Society and Politics in Nineteenth Century Germany*, *pp.290–2*, Oxford University Press 1984; **p.157** source 9.5 G. Ritter, *The Third Reich*, *pp.22–3*, Weidenfeld and Nicholson 1955; source 9.6 I. Kershaw, *Hitler*, *p.38*, Addison Wesley Longman 1991; **p.185** source 11.4 and 11.5 I. Kershaw, *The Hitler Myth: Image and Reality in the Third Reich*, *pp. 1 and 171*, Oxford University Press 1984; **p.192** source 11.11, I. Kershaw, *Hitler*, *p.198*, Addison Wesley Longman 1991; **p.206** source 11.22 I. Kershaw, *The Nazi Dictatorship*, *p.74*, Edward Arnold 1993; **p.207** source 11.23, S. Payne, *History of Fascism 1914–45*, *p.206*, UCL 1995; **p.238** source 12.47 R. Overy, *The Nazi Economic Recovery 1932–1938*, *pp.2–3 and 63*, Macmillan 1982; source 12.48 J. Noakes and G. Pridham, *Nazism 1918–45: A Documentary Reader*, *p.295*, University of Exeter 1984; **p.254** source 13.24 P. Adam *The Arts of the Third Reich*, *p.21*, Thames and Hudson 1992; **p.272** source 13.59 P. Adam, *as before*, *p.21*, Thames and Hudson 1992; **p.290** source 14.41 A. Wilt, *Nazi Germany*, *p.66*, Copyright 1994 by Harlan Davidson Inc.; source 14.42 D. Peukert, *Inside Nazi Germany: Conformity and Opposition in Everyday Life*, *pp.152 and 173*, B T Batsford 1987; source 14.43 K. Fischer, *Nazi Germany: A New History*, *p.353*, Constable 1995; **p.291** source 14.45 M. Housden, *Resistance and Conformity in the Third Reich*, *p.81*, Routledge 1997; **p.302** source 15.32 T. Mason, 'Women in Germany 1925–1940', in *Nazism, Fascism and the Working Class*, ed. T. Mason, *p.132*, Cambridge University Press 1995; source 15.34 U. Frevert, *Women in German History*, *pp.248 and 250*, Berg 1989; **p.314** source 16.20 J. Noakes and G. Pridham, *Nazism 1918–45: A Documentary Reader*, *p.582*, University of Exeter 1984; source 16.21 R. Geary, *Hitler and Nazism*, *p.55*, 1993, reproduced by kind permission of Dr Dick Geary, University of Nottingham; source 16.22 A. Wilt, *Nazi Germany*, *p.81*, Copyright 1994 by Harlan Davidson, Inc.; source 16.24 M. Housden, *Resistance and Conformity in the Third Reich*, *p.64*, Routledge 1997; **p.328** source 17.12 I. Kershaw, *The Hitler Myth: Image and Reality in the Third Reich*, *pp.6–8*, Oxford University Press; **pp.329–30** source 17.13 F. Hillenbrand, *Underground Humour in Nazi Germany 1933–45*, Routledge 1995; **p.332** source 17.16 J. Hiden, *Republican and Fascist Germany*, *p.189*, Addison Wesley Longman 1996; **p.350** source 18.41 R. Evans, *Rereading German History*, *p.150*, Routledge 1997; **p.352** source 18.46 M. Housden, *Resistance and Conformity in the Third Reich*, *p.160*, Routledge 1997; **p.353** source 18.48 I. Kershaw, 'German Popular Opinion during the Final Solution', in *Comprehending the Holocaust*, ed. Asher Cohen, *p.154*, Peter Lang Publishing Inc.1988; **p.361** source 19.3 I. Kershaw, *The Nazi Dictatorship*, *p.147*, Edward Arnold 1993; **p.366** source 19.24 M. Roseman, 'National Socialism and Modernisation' in *Fascist Italy and Nazi Germany*, ed. R. Bessel, *pp.216 and 223*, Cambridge University Press 1996; source 19.26 M. Hughes, *Nationalism and Society: Germany 1800–1945*, *p.214*, Edward Arnold 1988; **p.367** source 19.27 I. Kershaw, *The Nazi Dictatorship*, *pp.145–6*, Edward Arnold 1993; **p.389** source 20.17 A. Bullock, 'Hitler and the Origins of the Second World War', reprinted in *Origins of the Second World War*, ed. M. Robertson, *pp.204–5*, Macmillan 1971; source 20.19 I. Kershaw, *The Nazi Dictatorship*, *p.119*, Edward Arnold 1993; **p.434** source 22.6 D. Peukert, *Inside Nazi Germany*, *p.244*, B T Batsford 1987.

Photo credits

Cover: Bildarchiv Preussischer Kulturbesitz, Berlin/AKG photo, London; **p.1** *l* Scherl/Süddeutscher Verlag Bilderdienst, *c & r* AKG London; **p.5** *l & r* AKG London; **p.10** *t* AKG London, *b* Ullstein; **p.13** AKG London; **p.15** AKG London; **p.17** *l* Scherl/Süddeutscher Verlag Bilderdienst, *c* AKG London, *r* Ullstein; **p.20** *l* Süddeutscher Verlag Bilderdienst, *r* AKG London; **p.21** AKG London **p.22** Stiftung Archiv der Akademie der Künste, Berlin (photo: Ilona Ripke, Berlin). © DACS 2000; **p.29** AKG London; **p.35** Ullstein; **p.38** *tr* Wiener Library; **p.40** AKG London; **p.42** Süddeutscher Verlag Bilderdienst; **p.43** *t* Süddeutscher Verlag Bilderdienst, *b* AKG London; **p.45** AKG London; **p.46** *t & bl* Ullstein; **p.47** *tr & br* Weimar Archive, *bl* AKG London; **p.51** *l, tr & ctr* AKG London, *cr, cbr & br* Süddeutscher Verlag Bilderdienst; **p.55** *all* AKG London; **p.59** *tl* AKG London, *tr* Süddeutscher Verlag Bilderdienst, *c* Scherl/Süddeutscher Verlag Bilderdienst, *b* Weimar Archive; **p.64** *tl, tr & br* AKG London, *bl* Bildarchiv Preussischer Kulturbesitz; **p.65** *tl* Netherlands Institute for War Documentation, Amsterdam, *tr* Weimar Archive, *bl* F/Süddeutscher Verlag Bilderdienst, *br* AKG London; **p.78** AKG London; **p.86** *t* AKG London, *bl* Süddeutscher Verlag Bilderdienst; **p.88** AKG London; **p.89** Stiftung Archiv der Akademie der Künste, Berlin, DR 2974.XIII (photo: Roman März). © DACS 2000; **p.90** *t* AKG London. © DACS 2000, *b* AKG/Erich Lessing. © DACS 2000; **p.91** *t & bl* Ullstein, *br* Willy Saeger/Bildarchiv Preussischer Kulturbesitz; **p.92** *tl* AKG/Hilbich, *tr* AKG/Erik Bohr, *b* AKG London; **p.93** *t* AKG London, *b* Ullstein; **p.95** Ullstein; **p.99** AKG London; **p.106** AKG London; **p.107** Weimar Archive; **p.113** Süddeutscher Verlag Bilderdienst; **p.124** *t* Süddeutscher Verlag Bilderdienst, *bl* Weimar Archive, *br* AKG London; **p.125** *b* AKG London; **p.133** *tr & ct* AKG London, *cb* Ullstein, *l & b* Süddeutscher Verlag Bilderdienst; **p.141** *l* Ullstein, *r* Mary Evans Picture Library; **p.144** *tl* AKG London, *tr* Stiftung Archiv der Akademie der Künste, Berlin (photo: AdK). © DACS 2000, *b* Wiener Library; **p.149** *tl & tr* AKG London, *c & br* Ullstein, *bl* Süddeutscher Verlag Bilderdienst; **p.161** AKG London; **p.164** *both* AKG London; **p.165** *tl* Süddeutscher Verlag Bilderdienst, *tr* Bundesarchiv, Koblenz (Plak 3/2/46), *b* AKG London; **p.166** *all* AKG London; **p.167** By kind permission of the Evening Standard; **p.173** Stiftung Archiv der Akademie der Künste, Berlin (photo: AdK). © DACS 2000; **p.175** Süddeutscher Verlag Bilderdienst; **p.178** Stiftung Archiv der Akademie der Künste, Berlin (photo: AdK). © DACS 2000; **p.183** Bildarchiv Preussischer Kulturbesitz; **p.185** Courtesy Oxford University Press; **p.186** AKG London; **p.191** *t* AKG London, *b* Scherl/Süddeutscher Verlag Bilderdienst; **p.200** *t & c* AKG London, *b* Süddeutscher Verlag Bilderdienst; **p.202** *both* AKG London; **p.204** *t* Stadtbildstelle, Essen; **p.211** Institut fur Stadtgeschichte, Frankfurt; **p.217** AKG London; **p.221** *t* Stiftung Archiv der Akademie der Künste, Berlin (photo: AdK). © DACS 2000, *b* AKG London; **p.228** Ullstein; **p.231** Ullstein; **p.233** *t* Süddeutscher Verlag Bilderdienst, *c & b* Ruhrlandmuseum, Essen; **p.244** AKG London; **p.248** AKG London; **p.249** *t* Bundesarchiv, Koblenz (183/K VI Q), *b* Scherl/Süddeutscher Verlag Bilderdienst; **p.250** AKG London; **p.251** *tl, tr, cl & cr* AKG London, *bl* Bildarchiv Preussischer Kulturbesitz, *br* Ullstein; **p.252** *tl, tr & cl* AKG London, *bl* Bildarchiv Preussischer Kulturbesitz; **p.253** *tl, tr & bl* AKG London, *bc* Imperial War Museum, London, *br* Süddeutscher Verlag Bilderdienst; **p.256** *l* Ullstein, *r* Scherl/Süddeutscher Verlag Bilderdienst; **p.257** *l* AKG London, *c* Stiftung Archiv der Akademie der Künste, Berlin (photo: AdK). © DACS 2000, *b* Ullstein; **p.258** Bildarchiv Preussischer Kulturbesitz; **p.259** AKG London; **p.261** *tl cl & cr* AKG London; **p.262** *both* Bildarchiv Foto Marburg; **p.263** *tl & b* Scherl/Süddeutscher Verlag Bilderdienst, *tr* AKG London; **p.264** *t* Bildarchiv Preussischer Kulturbesitz, Berlin, *c & b* AKG London; **p.265** *tl* Bildarchiv Foto Marburg. *tr* AKG London. © DACS 2000, *c* AKG London. Copyright (for works by E.L. Kirchner) by Ingeborg & Dr. Wolfgang Henze-Ketterer, Wichtrach/Bern, *bl* Paul-Klee Stiftung, Kunstmuseum Bern, Inv. Nr. F 122. © DACS 2000, *bc* AKG London; **p.267** Ullstein; **p.268** *tl* Ullstein, *tr, cl, bl & br* AKG London; **p.269** *both* Süddeutscher Verlag Bilderdienst; **p.270** *both* AKG London; **p.271** *tl* AKG London; **p.275** AKG London; **p.276** *t* AKG London, *b* Bundesarchiv, Berlin (NSD 43/124); **p.278** Ullstein; **p.279** AKG London; **p.281** Scherl/Süddeutscher Verlag Bilderdienst; **p.282** AKG London; **p.284** Ruhrlandmuseum, Essen; **p.285** *t* Stadtbildstelle, Essen, *b* Scherl/Süddeutscher Verlag Bilderdienst; **p.286** Bundesarchiv, Berlin (NSD 43/124); **p.287** Süddeutscher Verlag Bilderdienst; **p.292** Bildarchiv Preussischer Kulturbesitz; **p.293** *l* Bildarchiv Preussischer Kulturbesitz, *r* AKG London; **p.296** AKG London; **p.298** AKG London; **p.299** *l* Bildarchiv Preussischer Kulturbesitz, *r* AKG London; **p.301** AKG London; **p.304** *l* Bundesarchiv, Koblenz (Plak 3103/1), *r* Stiftng Archiv der Akademie der Künste, Berlin (photo: AdK). © DACS 2000; **p.307** Spaarnestad Fotoarchief/NFGC; **p.310** *tl & tr* AKG London, *bl & br* Ullstein; **p.311** *t* Süddeutscher Verlag Bilderdienst, *bl & br* AKG London; **p.316** Süddeutscher Verlag Bilderdienst; **p.324** *t & cbl* Süddeutscher Verlag Bilderdienst, *ctl, cr & b* AKG London; **p.325** *tl & cr* Süddeutscher Verlag Bilderdienst, *bl* Scherl/Süddeutscher Verlag Bilderdienst, *tr & br* AKG London; **p.336** AKG London; **p.337** BFI Films: Stills, Posters and Designs; **p.339** *tr* Wiener Library; **p.340** AKG London; **p.341** *t* Bildarchiv Preussischer Kulturbesitz, *b* AKG London; **p.342** *t* AKG London, *c* Süddeutscher Verlag Bilderdienst, *b* Wiener Library; **p.343** *tl* Süddeutscher Verlag Bilderdienst, *tr* Wiener Library, *bl* Ullstein, *br* AKG London; **p.363** *t* Ullstein, *b* AKG London; **p.364** *tl* Ullstein, *tr* AP/Süddeutscher Verlag Bilderdienst, *cl & bl* Bildarchiv Preussischer Kulturbesitz, *cr* Süddeutscher Verlag Bilderdienst; **p.365** *tr* Wiener Library, *b* AKG London; **p.371** Süddeutscher Verlag Bilderdienst; **p.372** *both* AKG London; **p.373** AKG London; **p.375** *t* By kind permission of the Evening Standard, *b* AKG London; **p.376** Scherl/Süddeutscher Verlag Bilderdienst; **p.382** AKG London; **p.383** AKG London; **p.387** Süddeutscher Verlag Bilderdienst; **p.395** By kind permission of the Evening Standard; **p.396** By kind permission of the Evening Standard; **p.399** *b* Süddeutscher Verlag Bilderdienst; **p.413** Ullstein; **p.415** AKG London; **p.418** AKG London; **p.420** *l* Imperial War Museum, London, *r* Weimar Archive; **p.419** Ruhrlandmuseum, Essen; **p.422** Süddeutscher Verlag Bilderdienst; **p.425** Daniel Fitzpatrick in the St. Louis Post-Dispatch; **p.427** AKG London; **p.428** Popperfoto.